The Research Craft

An Introduction to Social Research Methods

John B. Williamson

Boston College

David A. Karp

Boston College

John R. Dalphin

Merrimack College

Paul S. Gray

Boston College

in collaboration with

Stephen T. Barry

Boston State College

Richard S. Dorr

Boston College

The Research Craft

An Introduction to Social Research Methods

SECOND EDITION

Scott, Foresman and Company

Glenview, Illinois   Boston   London

ISBN 0-673-39606-1

9 8 7 6

MV

The authors acknowledge permission to use material from the following source:

Quotation (pages 333–334 and 342) from *Evaluative Research: Principles and Practice in Public Service and Social Action Programs* by Edward A. Suchman © 1968 by Russell Sage Foundation. Reprinted by permission of the publisher, Russell Sage Foundation.

Preface

The second edition of *The Research Craft* represents a major revision of the first edition. One of our goals has been to make a book originally designed primarily for use in sociology courses into a book that would work equally well in a variety of other disciplines. To this end we have made extensive use of examples drawn from political science, criminology, education, social psychology, and social work.

The most distinctive feature of the book remains its comprehensiveness in the explanation of a variety of research strategies. Most methods texts focus on a few of the more common alternatives; by contrast, we have covered the full range of methods available to the social researcher.

This edition is divided into three parts. In Part I, Foundations of Social Research, we discuss the basic issues that must be confronted by all who engage in social investigation: problems of measurement, study design, sampling, reliability, validity, and ethical considerations. Here our goal is to acquaint the reader with the complexities of the research process. We seek to convey the idea that social research is both a craft and a science. For a first course in research methods this material is a must; for a more advanced course it provides a thorough review. In Part I we introduce a number of themes and dilemmas to which we refer again in connection with each of the specific methods subsequently described.

In Part II, Procedures of Social Research, we examine nine different research strategies. This section of the book provides a comprehensive treatment of a number of methods that we believe are not given adequate coverage in other texts. We devote a full chapter each to such important subjects as evaluation research, intensive interviewing, historical analysis, and procedures of comparative research. We seek to provide an even-handed treatment of both qualitative and quantitative techniques and perspectives. In these chapters our goals are to foster an understanding of each method's distinctive advantages and limitations, a familiarity with some of the mechanics of using each one, and an appreciation of the kinds of research problems for which each strategy has been found to be appropriate.

The instructor should keep in mind that the chapters in Part II can be studied in any order. Similarly, some chapters can be omitted without any loss of continuity. Those who seek a more qualitative emphasis in their methods course may select a different set of chapters from those who seek a more quantitative emphasis. Some instructors will want to cover one or more chapters in greater detail. In some cases students will want to carry out research projects using a particular method. In this connection the exercises at the end of each chapter will provide inspiration. The annotated readings section should also prove useful to both the student and the instructor. Note that we include one set of suggested readings *about* each method and a second set illustrating the *use* of that method. The readings about the method will be particularly helpful to those who plan to undertake their own research.

In Part III, Quantitative Analysis, we provide an overview of issues related to the use of quantitative data. We include a discussion of index and scale construction (Chapter 15). The chapter on basic statistical analysis (Chapter 16) is designed for students who have no prior background in the topic. More advanced readers will appreciate the discussions of multivariate analysis and statistical inference (Chapter 17).

Readers familiar with the first edition will be interested in the following summary of the substantive changes in the present edition. (1) As mentioned above, this text is now aimed at a broader social science audience. (2) We have added an entirely new Chapter 1 (The Research Process: Science and Craft), which incorporates a number of issues from the first two chapters of the previous edition. (3) We have added an entirely new Chapter 2 (Research Design). (4) Major revisions have been made in the chapters on measurement (Chapter 3), survey research (Chapter 6), intensive interviewing (Chapter 7), observational field research (Chapter 8), historical analysis (Chapter 10), and evaluation research (Chapter 14). Particularly noteworthy is the thorough reworking of the chapter on survey research. (5) We have added Part III (Quantitative Analysis), comprising three chapters; this markedly expands the treatment of this material in the previous edition. Here we have included an entirely new chapter on indexes and scales (Chapter 15). The chapter on quantitative analysis in the first edition has been used as the basis for the preparation of two new chapters, one dealing with basic statistics (Chapter 16) and the other covering multivariate analysis and statistical inference (Chapter 17).

John Williamson has had the primary responsibility for overseeing the preparation of the second edition. Paul Gray has had the primary responsibility for the actual preparation of most of the new material. Gray is author of Chapters 1, 2, and 15 and coauthor of Chapters 3, 8, 10, and 14. He has, in addition, made significant editorial revisions in the remaining chapters. John Williamson is author of Chapter 17 and coauthor of Chapters 3–7, 9, 12–14, and 16; David Karp is coauthor of Chapters 3 and 8–12; John Dalphin is coauthor of Chapters 4–6, 13, and 14; Stephen Barry is coauthor of Chapters 3, 6, 8, and 16; and Richard Dorr is coauthor of Chapters 5–7, 9, and 11.

Contents

PART I. FOUNDATIONS OF SOCIAL RESEARCH

1   The Research Process: Science and Craft   3

Introduction   3
The Scientific Method   6
Theory and Social Research   17
Intellectual Craftsmanship   29
Summary   32
Key Terms   32
Exercises   33
Suggested Readings   33
References   34

2   Research Design   36

Introduction   36
The Components of Research   40
Putting It All Together   54
Summary   60
Key Terms   61
Exercises   61
Suggested Readings   61
References   62

3   Measurement in Social Research   63

Introduction   63
Levels of Management   64
Operationalization   67
Evaluating Reliability and Validity   69
Sources of Measurement Error   73

The Situational Nature of Variables   79
Improving the Quality of Measurement   81
Summary   83
Key Terms   84
Exercises   84
Suggested Readings   85
References   86

4   Ethical and Political Considerations   87

Introduction   87
Objectivity   88
Formulation of the Research Question   90
Data Collection   92
Analysis, Interpretation, and Presentation of Results   96
Application of Research Results   98
Summary   99
Key Terms   100
Exercises   100
Suggested Readings   101
References   102

5   Sampling   103

Introduction   103
Sampling Plans   105
Problems and Issues in Sampling   113
Summary   119
Key Terms   120
Exercises   120
Suggested Readings   121
References   121

PART II. PROCEDURES OF SOCIAL RESEARCH

6   Survey Research   125

Introduction   125
Survey Design   127
Survey Execution   143
Secondary Analysis   155
The Strengths and Limitations of Survey Research   156
Summary   158
Key Terms   158
Exercises   158
Suggested Readings   159
References   161

7   Intensive Interviewing   163

Introduction   163
Applications of Intensive Interviewing   165
Distinctive Characteristics of Intensive Interviews   165
Conducting an Interview   172
Comparative Strengths and Limitations   182
Current Developments in the Technique   186
Summary   187
Key Terms   188
Exercises   188
Suggested Readings   189
References   191

8   Observational Field Research   192

Introduction   192
Doing Field Work   195
Limitations of Observational Field Research   206
Summary   209
Key Terms   210
Exercises   210
Suggested Readings   211
References   212

9   Experimental Research   214

Introduction   214
The Elements of True Experimentation   215
Threats to Validity in Experimental Research   219
Field Experimentation   225
A Final Word   233
Summary   234
Key Terms   235
Exercises   235
Suggested Readings   236
References   238

10   Historical Analysis   239

Introduction   239
History and Culture   240
History and the Growth of Knowledge   241
Sources of Historical Data   243
Uses of History: Some Examples   246
Historical Analysis in Perspective   254
Summary   255
Key Terms   255
Exercises   256
Suggested Readings   256
References   258

11   Content Analysis   260

Introduction   260
An Overview of the Method   261
Applications of Content Analysis   263
Performing Content Analysis   269
Computer-Assisted Content Analysis   275
The Technique in Perspective   277
Summary   278
Key Terms   278
Exercises   279
Suggested Readings   280
References   282

12   Aggregate Data Analysis   284

Introduction   284
Applications of Aggregate Data Analysis   286
Fallacies in the Interpretation of Aggregate Data   298
Summary   301
Key Terms   301
Exercises   302
Suggested Readings   302
References   305

13   Comparative Research Methods   306

Introduction   306
Why Do Comparative Research?   307
Specifying the Conditions Under Which Theory Applies   310
Obstacles to Reliable and Valid Comparison   312
Ethical Considerations   323
Summary   324
Key Terms   325
Exercises   325
Suggested Readings   326
References   328

14   Evaluation Research   330

Introduction   330
Evaluation Research Process   332
Summary   344
Key Terms   345
Exercises   345
Suggested Readings   346
References   348

PART III. QUANTITATIVE ANALYSIS

15   Indexes and Scales 353

Introduction 353
Index Construction 356
The Scaling of Responses 364
Standardization of Composite Measures 371
Summary 373
Key Terms 374
Exercises 374
Suggested Readings 375
References 376

16   Basic Statistical Analysis 377

Introduction 377
Univariate Analysis 377
Bivariate Analysis 386
Statistical Control 393
Summary 401
Key Terms 401
Exercises 402
Suggested Readings 402
References 403

17   Multivariate Analysis and Statistical Inference 404

Introduction 404
Multivariate Analysis 405
Statistical Inference 409
Summary 414
Key Terms 415
Exercises 415
Suggested Readings 416
References 417

Epilog: The Value and Limits of Social Science Knowledge 419

Name Index 425

Key Term and Subject Index 431

Part I

Foundations of
Social Research

1 / The Research Process: Science and Craft

CHAPTER OUTLINE

INTRODUCTION
What Is Social Research?
  Data Collection and Analysis
  Adding to Knowledge
  Sources of Data
  Social Significance
What Is Methodology?
THE SCIENTIFIC METHOD
The Research Cycle
  Theory
  Observation and Testing
  Conclusions and Findings
History of Social Science
Common Sense and Social Science
Why Common Sense Fails Us
  Distance
  Familiarity, Not Understanding
  Emotions

Principles of Scientific Investigation
  Objectivity
  Replication and Reliability
  Precision
  Validity
  The Critical Perspective
  Conclusion
THEORY AND SOCIAL RESEARCH
What Theory Looks Like
  Taxonomies
  Models
  Typologies
  Paradigms
  Axiomatic Theory
  Description and Explanation
The Discovery and Verification of
  Theory

Deduction
Induction
The Development of Research Ideas
  Curiosity
  Pure and Applied Research
  Already Existing Theory
  Training and Experience
INTELLECTUAL
  CRAFTSMANSHIP
The Idea of a Craft
Learning the Craft
  Research Imagination
SUMMARY
KEY TERMS
EXERCISES
SUGGESTED READINGS
REFERENCES

Introduction

WHAT IS SOCIAL RESEARCH?

Several years ago one of the authors of this book was attending a family reunion. His cousin, a business executive as well as a trained engineer, began to make conversation. "So, what are you doing these days?" he queried. "Social research," replied the author. "Really," came the rejoinder, "you mean they actually pay you to sit around and *think*?" This remark reflects a misunderstanding of the idea of social investigation. Researchers who work in universities, or in private and public agencies, whether they call themselves political scientists, psychologists, sociologists, or whatever, are of course paid to think. In order to find out about the world, however, they do much more than spin out ideas from the comfort of an easy chair. They are, in fact, engaged in a dynamic process that is more rigorous and complicated than many people realize.

DATA COLLECTION AND ANALYSIS. Systematic research in any field of inquiry involves two basic operations. The first is to observe, measure, and record information —in other words, DATA COLLECTION. The second is to arrange and organize these data so that we may find out what their significance is, generalize about them, or tell what they mean. This exercise is called DATA ANALYSIS. If you note down the weather in your home town each day for a period of one year, that would be data collection. If you then divide this information into three categories: "fair," "cloudy," and "stormy," you will have performed a simple data analysis.

If, say, 70 percent of the days were either cloudy or stormy, it would be justifiable to conclude that the weather is not very pleasant where you live. A less superficial finding, and a practical recommendation, would be that a solar-powered electrical system would not be feasible there. No matter what interpretation is made, however, it must be "grounded"; that is, it must be related to, and follow logically from, the evidence collected. The conclusions of a reputable study are not merely the first thoughts or ideas that occur to the researcher; they are the ones supported and sustained by the data at hand.

ADDING TO KNOWLEDGE. The goal of social research is to add to what is already known about individuals in society and about the behavior and composition of human groups. This may be accomplished in three major ways: exploration, description, and explanation. EXPLORATION is finding out about some previously unexamined phenomenon. Often its purpose is to discover what is most significant or useful about the research setting, first by gaining a general overview. DESCRIPTION is noting in meticulous detail how something or someone looks and acts, both as a separate entity and in combination with other things or people. Finally, EXPLANATION is telling why something or someone behaves as it does. We might imagine a study of religious cults that combines these three research functions. After doing some reading on the subject, and perhaps after spending some time in the company of cult members and leaders, we may decide that it would be important to know what sorts of people belong to the group, how they are recruited, and what they are taught to believe. We might then attend their rituals, observe the participants as they try to attract new members, and speak to people who were attracted to the group as well as to those who were repelled by it. We would be careful to note conversations, what people were wearing, how they reacted to one another, and so forth. If we gathered enough data, we might then be able to explain *why* people join religious cults and how it is possible for these groups to inspire so much loyalty from their members in a relatively short period of time.

SOURCES OF DATA. The data that are discovered and analyzed in social research may originate anywhere people interact. Some important sources of information about society are the family, schools, and the business corporations and other bureaucracies in which we work. Other observation and listening posts may be the voluntary associations—recreational and charitable groups—to which we belong. In addition, data are generated from the realm of politics: parties, states, nations, and international organizations.

Researchers want to discover how these groups change and the extent to which they get along with one another. Thus they might examine whether the increasing number of working women has influenced child-rearing practices in America. Or they might study the impact of the conservation movement on the enactment of laws to reduce air pollution. The area covered by an investigation may be relatively restricted, or it may be very broad. Thus the investigation may concentrate on trying to understand the interplay between two people at a cocktail party or the conflict between a rich country and a poor one.

SOCIAL SIGNIFICANCE. In recent years social researchers have become more visible to the public than ever before. It is not unusual to find sociologists, psychologists, or political analysts as guests on television and radio talk shows. This publicity reflects the growing importance of social science data for forming government policy, evaluating legislation, and even guiding judicial decisions. The data from social surveys helped to justify the War on Poverty of the 1960s and the plans for affirmative action in employment that were developed in the 1970s. The decision to continue programs such as Head Start and the Job Corps has often hinged on the recommendations of fact-finding research projects. The courts have relied on the conclusions of researchers in making rulings that affect us all as citizens—for example, in deciding what the punishment should be for crimes of violence. In fact, the social and psychological evidence contained in the plaintiffs' argument in the famous case of *Brown* v. *Board of Education,* in 1954, helped usher in an era of civil rights legislation and an awakening of social concern.

WHAT IS METHODOLOGY?

Our familiarity with the findings and recommendations of some social research has, indeed, increased. Knowledge about the research process itself, about how studies are actually conducted, is much less widely disseminated. Newspapers and magazines have popularized the work of Alfred Kinsey, who reported that 13 percent of men and 5 percent of women in the United States are homosexuals.[1] But the media usually ignore some critical questions, such as:

What kinds of people were interviewed or observed?

What questions were these people asked?

How many individuals provided the answers on which the researcher's conclusions were based?

What categories were used for data analysis?

These are questions of METHODOLOGY; they explore the principles, procedures, and strategies of research. They are often thought to be too boring or too technical to sustain the interest of the public. This is unfortunate, because the data that comprise any study, and the conclusions that are based on these data, are only as good as the methods of investigation that were used to obtain them.

One of our goals is to increase the general awareness of how research is done. After reading this book, you will have an understanding of the nature and complexities of the process. Even if you are not a future social worker, probation officer, educational specialist, or other professional-in-training, you will be able to critique research and to begin to recognize faulty conclusions that are based on poor evidence or that are unsupported by the data.

There are many different techniques for gathering information and a variety of

---

[1]See, for example, *Time,* April 23, 1979.

procedures for analyzing data. These alternatives are explored in Parts II and III of the book. Researchers may contact a handful of people, or thousands; they may do this in person, or by means of a list of questions sent through the mail. They may use the identical categories of analysis that have been used in previous studies, or they may develop an entirely new set of concepts to make sense of the data collected. Research strategy is influenced by the questions that must be asked, the time and resources available to the researcher, and the purpose of the work, that is, whether it is primarily exploratory, descriptive, or explanatory. In most cases several choices of technique are open to the researcher, regardless of the subject of the investigation. In her book *Worlds of Pain,* Rubin (1976) studied working-class life by conducting a series of intensive, highly personal interviews of seventy-five families. Instead she might have relied on census data showing the health, occupation, education, and spending habits of much larger numbers of people with low to moderate incomes. Her conclusions might have been less poignant and dramatic, but no less informative and original.

The principles of research methodology are flexible. There are relatively few specific do's and don'ts and many general guidelines and suggestions. Much investigation of human behavior today is self-consciously "scientific." But, as you read the following explanation of the scientific method, keep in mind that science has not eliminated choice making and intuition from social research. Rather, it has made us more aware of the necessity for choosing wisely our techniques of data collection and analysis.

The Scientific Method

The SCIENTIFIC METHOD is a general model for inquiry in the physical and natural sciences, such as chemistry and biology, and the social sciences, such as psychology and sociology. It is, of course, possible to study human behavior within the framework of history, philosophy, or theology, but these disciplines do not use the language and procedures of science. When researchers claim to be scientists, they subject themselves and their work to scrutiny and judgment according to the standards and canons of scientific investigation. In this section we will enumerate these criteria, explain how the scientific method came to be applied to social research, and examine the differences between scientific and nonscientific research, and modes of explanation.

THE RESEARCH CYCLE

Figure 1.1 shows the major elements in the process of scientific research: theory, observation, and conclusion.

THEORY. One of the central goals of social science research is to make generalizations about human behavior. A general explanation is called a THEORY. It is a set of principles that tells why people do what they do in a variety of contexts. Labeling theory, for example, addresses many kinds of deviant behavior, including both mental illness and criminality, by proposing that people act as society expects them to act (Becker, 1963). Once the label "mental incompetent" or "felon" has

FIGURE 1.1   The Scientific Method

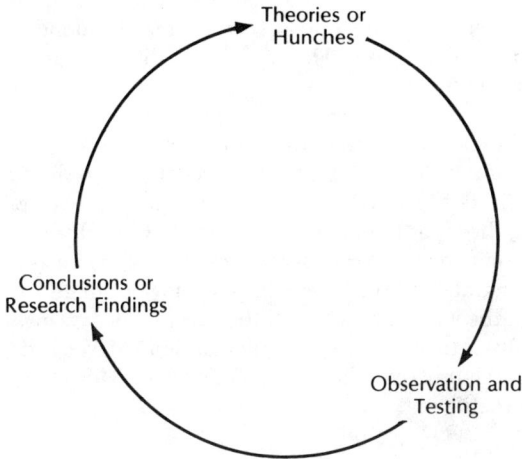

Theories or
Hunches

Conclusions or
Research Findings

Observation and
Testing

been applied to a person by the courts or the medical establishment, it is difficult to remove. Therefore, the individual accepts the label and behaves in such a way as to deserve it.

Fully elaborated theories are rarely created all at once. Often they begin as HUNCHES, less formalized ideas or guesses that may eventually be refined into a theory. One might suspect, for example, that the procedures for diagnosing and keeping records on mental patients hamper their reintegration into society after confinement. Or one might speculate that patients' knowledge of the diagnosis itself affects their self-concept. If these hunches are confirmed as data are collected, we might be encouraged to devise a more comprehensive theory dealing with more kinds of labeling and deviance.

A good reason for conducting a scientific study is to find out whether an already existing theory makes sense in light of new observation. Therefore, when scientists do research, they are not merely adding to the storehouse of descriptive information about the world; they may also be making additions and corrections to theory. One such modification is called VERIFICATION. A theory is verified when its generalizations are found to be accurate in several different settings. Thus labeling may be discovered outside the courts and mental hospitals, perhaps within the welfare system, or even on a Little League baseball team. Labeling theory may help us appreciate that welfare recipients and third-string, 8-year-old athletes can have something in common, namely, a relatively low level of self-confidence, as well as performance consistently below expectations. It is the theory that explains these commonalities. The welfare system labels its clientele as inferior by making them wait for benefits, subjecting them to personal investigations, not paying them very much, and doing little or nothing to help them improve their position in life. The coach may constantly berate marginal ballplayers, subjecting them to humiliation or invidious comparison with peers.

As labeling theory is verified in these and other examples, we move beyond the specific context of the welfare office or the baseball diamond to generalize about people everywhere. For the same purposes of generalization, scientific discoveries in atomic physics concerning the construction of matter per se are useful to the chemist, biologist, and astronomer. But a theory does not have to be verified in order for research to be useful. In fact, it may be DISCONFIRMED: it may be found to be inaccurate, at least within a particular setting. This is also valuable, because it may lead to the reformulation of the theory.

OBSERVATION AND TESTING. In science no theory may be either accepted or rejected without obtaining relevant information. This is accomplished during the field, or data collection, phase of research. The investigator uses data in order to (1) verify or disconfirm an already existing theory or hunch, or (2) establish, from observation, some new, general principle of behavior. The scientific method is shown as a circle in Figure 1.1 in order to illustrate that the research cycle may be entered at any point. One may begin with a theory or a hunch and then test it. Or one may begin with observation and construct theory bit by bit, much as a bricklayer adds to a wall.[2] In either case the research process is, in reality, continuous. One study merely lays the groundwork for the next.

CONCLUSIONS AND FINDINGS. As Figure 1.1 implies, theory is never static in science; it changes constantly. The conclusions or FINDINGS, what we have learned about the world as a result of the research, always carry implications for the endless process of theory creation and alteration. Theories are rarely completely proven or disproven. Often they are merely made more specific, in that the particular conditions under which they apply are stated explicitly. Therefore, findings influence theory by refining it, sharpening it, making it a more precise tool of explanation.

The scientific method is a system for keeping track of the accumulation of theoretical generalizations and data in the physical and social sciences. This model for research is designed to be efficient, in that through making us aware of theories that were disconfirmed, or of findings that were not fruitful for the creation of new theory, we should be able to avoid the mistakes of previous investigators. In fact, the scientific method does not guarantee success; the results of many studies are inconclusive. Despite this, it has brought about unprecedented advances in medicine, space travel, and agricultural and manufacturing productivity.

These technological triumphs have led some to believe that there are scientific solutions to many of our problems of social disorganization: crime, political apathy, the declining authority of school and church. Thus far, breakthroughs in the social sciences have been perhaps less dramatic than in the natural and physical sciences. Systematic research has, however, brought the world many fascinating and useful insights about human behavior.

HISTORY OF SOCIAL SCIENCE

As a basic model for asking questions about humankind and its environment, the scientific method is a relatively recent historic occurrence. The idea of the research cycle was first formalized in the seventeenth century, when the modern study of the natural sciences was initiated. There developed the search for laws, axioms, and principles of the physical world. To find these, the science laboratory

---

[2]See the discussion of induction and deduction later in this chapter.

was created. This work space, isolated from the outside world, served as a sanctuary where the scientist could test theories in a controlled setting. EX- PERIMENTATION then, as today, involved keeping records of everything that occurred and repeating procedures again and again, perhaps each time changing only one small aspect of the environment—temperature, space, light, or the amount of materials used in testing.

Early social thinkers were encouraged by the successes in physics, genetics, and medicine. They tried to develop laws and theories of human behavior. But the full significance of scientific methodology for social investigation was not to be realized immediately. The first pseudoscientific theorizers about society were really social philosophers, whose work held more in common with the specula- tions of classical Greek and Roman authors than with the experimenters of the new physical and natural sciences. The major reason for the comparative back- wardness of social investigation until well into the nineteenth century was the tendency to avoid systematic observation. The first psychology laboratory was not established until 1879, in Germany.

Few investigators actually engaged in FIELD WORK—the examination of what people say and do in their own, natural surroundings. A rare exception was Alexis de Tocqueville, a French researcher whose analysis of the United States, *Democ- racy in America,* written in 1835, is still considered a classic in both political science and sociology. Its scope and careful attention to detail, combined with sensitivity to theory, were unique. Auguste Comte (1798–1857), the originator of the term *sociology,* and other authors of the time set the tone for much of the pioneering social investigation. Comte's was an "armchair" treatise on how soci- ety *ought* to be organized, rather than a description of how it *was* structured, and why. Comte wanted social analysis to be scientific, and to separate itself from the theological and metaphysical explanations of an earlier era, but he did not sub- ject his theories to the test of data collection.

A major turning point in the application of scientific techniques to the study of society was the publication of Charles Darwin's *Origin of Species* (1859). Darwin, of course, became famous for his theory of evolution, but it is essential to realize that he was, first and foremost, an astute and thorough observer. The records he kept as naturalist aboard the *H.M.S. Beagle* as it made its voyage became both the inspiration and evidence for his theories. Darwin brought together and reconciled two major strands of nineteenth-century thought: the ideas of the natural sci- ences and those of human development and progress. Subsequently, such think- ers as Herbert Spencer (1820–1903) made the analogy between the growth of society and the evolution of the biological organisms that Darwin had described. This prepared the way for Emile Durkheim (1858–1917), Max Weber (1864– 1920), and other theoreticians who were highly skilled in techniques of observa- tion and cross-cultural comparison. Similar developments were occurring in psy- chology. The theories of Sigmund Freud (1856–1939) and his disciples were tested continually, in the context of psychiatric treatment. Other psychologists began to study learning and perception, following the studies of biology and physiology.

Social science entered the twentieth century with the traditions of laboratory and field research firmly established and with a degree of theoretical sophistica- tion. However, in an age in which the prestige of physical science has reached new heights because of its explanatory and predictive powers, social scientists have largely been preoccupied with trying to convince others that their disciplines are legitimate, and that they are truly engaged in building a cumulative body of knowledge. This preoccupation has been especially apparent in the United States, where today science possesses elements of the sacred.

These efforts of the social scientists have met with only partial success. There are still those who argue that despite their claims to scientific stature, disciplines such as political science, sociology, and social psychology cannot easily meet the standards of scientific investigation. Let us consider some of the technical demands of science, and how science is distinguished from common sense. Are social scientists unjustifiably trying to share the spotlight with their more "exact" and well-respected cousins?

COMMON SENSE AND SOCIAL SCIENCE

When we search out bargains in the supermarket, describe how our favorite football team won the big game, or speculate about the causes of inflation and high taxes, we are attempting the same intellectual tasks that social researchers set for themselves: exploration, description, and explanation. These activities are, in fact, as essential for human survival in society (for obtaining food, clothing, and shelter) as for leading a productive and satisfying existence. It is therefore not surprising that the public's reverence for physical science has exceeded its acceptance of social science. Biologists and physicists also describe and explain phenomena, but their subject matter has a mysterious quality. By contrast, many people believe themselves to be familiar with, and competent to perform, the same operations for which professional social researchers are paid a salary.

It is difficult for most of us to have our own ideas about the causes of cancer or the logistics of space travel, but it is relatively easy to feel expert about social life. If you doubt this, the next time you attend a gathering of friends or acquaintances, listen for "theories" about the causes of crime, poverty, prejudice, emotional problems, or political conflict. Many people believe that when it comes to social issues, one person's opinion is every bit as good as another's. To support this contention, some individuals, who may think they understand science but who really do not, may cite the disagreements among sociologists, psychologists, and educators regarding fundamental social processes. But genuine science is not merely opinion; it is opinion supported by data and connected to a body of theory.

The scientific method does not guarantee consensus in research findings, and this is no less true in the chemistry laboratory than in social analysis. But it does guide the attempt to transcend the relatively restricted world of our own personal experience. If two social researchers disagree about how ethical big business in America is, it will not be because one has been a worker and the other a factory owner. They will both have made observations according to the canons of scientific research—viewing the world from unfamiliar perspectives, talking with people with whom they would never otherwise associate, taking seriously and addressing directly many possible objections to their findings. These activities are rarely, if ever, done systematically in daily life. The result is that COMMON SENSE is really unsupported opinion, or attitudes inspired by insufficient and unreliable information. We are not saying that a trained social researcher never makes an error in observation or judgment. Rather, the scientific method decreases the *probability* of error.

WHY COMMON SENSE FAILS US

"There's more crime in rich neighborhoods than in poor neighborhoods," said Uncle Ed, puffing on his cigar. "How do you know?" I asked. " 'Cause crooks aren't stupid," said he. "They know there's nothing to steal in poor neighborhoods!" In fact, in contrast to Uncle Ed's commonsense view of the world, the poor are victims of crime more often than any other segment of our society. Lower-class individuals are less safe from crime than members of the middle class; losses from robbery and burglary in the ghetto are staggering (Schmid, 1960). How is it that these unambiguous research findings appear so different from the lay person's conventional wisdom?

DISTANCE. First, most people think they are more accurate observers than is the case. They are frequently deceived by the unfamiliar or the remote. Get far enough away, and skimmed milk looks like heavy cream; in baseball a scratch hit tonight will look like a line drive in tomorrow's box score. To the middle-class observer, poverty sometimes is seen as moral degeneracy, mental retardation as sickness, and lack of education as laziness. The roots of much prejudice and stereotyping may be found in overgeneralizations that people make from a distance. If Uncle Ed had lived in a poor neighborhood, he might have been better able to appreciate how dangerous it can be. His commonsense view of crime is neither an accurate description nor an accurate explanation; he is just too distant to see the problem clearly.

FAMILIARITY, NOT UNDERSTANDING. Second, we may in fact be quite familiar with a phenomenon, yet not understand how it works. We ride in an elevator or we watch television, but we are powerless to fix these machines if they break down. Most of us do not even know the principles of electricity by which they operate. Yet they are very much a part of our lives. We act as consumers without understanding the social economy, obey laws while ignorant of theories of social control, and try to learn from our teachers without necessarily appreciating the process of learning. And we may be the victims of crime without realizing what motivates the criminal. In sum we are never quite as knowledgeable about society as we may think we are.

Human behavior is so diverse and complex that systematic research is required in order to determine the norms and social regularities of society. Our personal experiences do not necessarily give us an accurate view of behavior in general because we rarely move beyond our own awareness. If the thief who is caught removing Uncle Ed's stereo turns out to be from a rundown neighborhood, it would be natural for Ed to see crime as a social problem through the prism of his personal involvement with it. It is easier for him to imagine millions of other victims who are also in his relatively comfortable position than to imagine victims who themselves are poor. His own experience may reinforce the idea that criminals are economically desperate individuals, a generalization that ignores so-called respectable, or white-collar, crime in business or government.

A related point is that we often make assumptions about our immediate environment that other people, equally experienced, would not make. The television industry appears differently to performers, producers, and technicians, depending in part on their function and status within the network hierarchy. The same family that is described by authoritarian parents as being free of conflict may be characterized by their outwardly compliant children as a prison. In short, our perception of society is usually limited and shaped by the various demographic categories into which we fall, including our age, sex, income, ethnicity, religion, occupation, and educational level. Our economic behavior, our political attitudes, and our sense of what is "normal" psychologically—all are dependent in large measure upon our membership in these kinds of social groupings.

The arena with which most of us are familiar is circumscribed and relatively simple, when compared to the multiple realities that social researchers must understand if they are to obtain a comprehensive view of social relations. Most of us lack the skill, or the inclination, to expand our horizons in a way that would let us appreciate the world as others see it.

EMOTIONS. Another reason that common sense fails us is that our everyday observations are colored by our emotions. Feelings are not bad in themselves, but their impact on our powers of judgment may go unrecognized. Some of us feel uncomfortable around handicapped people; they may act in unexpected ways or appear different, and this makes us feel embarrassed and self-conscious. If we have to decide whether handicapped students should attend classes with normal children, we may find ourselves saying that their disabilities will prevent them from profiting from the experience. But is it their own lack of skill or our own discomfort that prompts this assessment?

Many of us fail to recognize our own negative reactions to others. People may profess love for humanity in general although they may actually have great difficulty relating to specific individuals who deviate from their norms of behavior. In addition, most of us find it difficult to overcome negative feelings toward others. Prejudice against blacks, Jews, Italians, or any other racial or ethnic group will not necessarily be reduced by exposure to favorable evidence about them. Through a process of SELECTIVE OBSERVATION, the data that might disconfirm the negative stereotypes can be screened out. It may prove to be too much of a challenge to the observer whose favorable self-image is intimately connected with a poor view of others. How many times, in polite conversation, do we say, "Well, let's drop the subject"? The feeling of being bored or otherwise dissatisfied with an encounter may result from having heard an argument that is threatening to one's ego or world view.

Thus our commonsense notions of how society works are often not accurate or complete because we are either too distant from the data, or too close, or because our emotions act as a smokescreen. In spite of these barriers to understanding, we may still believe that we are astute observers because we are rarely forced to recognize our mistakes. Prejudice, ignorance, and fear may be perpetuated generation after generation. People in everyday life are usually not held responsible for their opinions and may not always appreciate the far-reaching consequences of the domestic and foreign policies that they favor. It is much easier to advocate "bombing the enemy into the Stone Age" than to drop the bomb oneself or to cope with the human suffering that results from it.

PRINCIPLES OF SCIENTIFIC INVESTIGATION

Although we may make many errors of omission and commission as we judge and observe, we may nonetheless function acceptably as private citizens in society. A scientist, however, is not allowed this luxury. Before research findings and procedures are scrutinized by outsiders, they are rigorously monitored by researchers themselves. A good scientist is really a self-critic who wants to eliminate, or at least to reduce as much as possible, biased, prejudiced, or incomplete observation.

OBJECTIVITY. Some scientists assert that their work is objective, meaning that their own private values never intrude in determining their findings. In other words the researcher's race, creed, color, or political beliefs are of absolutely no significance in determining the outcome of a study. The canon of OBJECTIVITY maintains that, ideally, any two researchers who study the same behaviors, processes, or phenomena should arrive at identical findings.

Objectivity, so-called, is perhaps approached more closely in the physical science laboratory than in most social research, because in the laboratory it is easier to control the environment for the collection of data. In all fields of systematic inquiry, however, objectivity remains an ideal. The fact that most research reports in the natural sciences ignore the personal motives of investigators does not mean that they really were completely objective. When a renowned biochemist lets us catch a glimpse of what goes on behind the scenes (Watson, 1968), we discover that the background, personality, financial needs, and career interest of scientists do influence their work. The orderly accumulation of knowledge may be upset by professional rivalry and jealousy, sexism or racism.

Recognizing that researchers in all fields, because they are human, cannot be wholly objective, many social scientists in recent years have given up chasing the ghost of objectivity. The investigator is not like a robot who works the same way in every case. Each person observing a social phenomenon will inevitably exercise some selective observation and memory. Even in choosing a topic for study, a researcher is indicating certain value biases; our perception of what constitutes a social problem may depend, to some degree, on our own position in society. Moreover, it is virtually impossible to keep from taking sides in studying some social phenomena (Becker, 1967). How would a study of the criminal justice system avoid adopting either the perspective of the courts and police, on the one hand, or the criminal, on the other? Can an analysis of the social welfare bureaucracy really be written from the point of view both of social workers and clients?

Because objectivity is so elusive a concept, some scholars, particularly those who practice what may be called FORENSIC SOCIAL SCIENCE, believe that all investigation should stem from a clearly enunciated value position. They claim that little or no effort need be made to present opposing points of view. A Marxist who personally supports the aims of the Cuban revolution may describe the ways in which that revolution has succeeded, deemphasizing its failures, on the assumption that more conservative writers will take on the responsibility of pointing them out. Based on a similar assumption, an advocate of free enterprise as a principle of economic organization may concentrate on the beneficial effects of competition and give less attention to the problems of unemployment that capitalism may create.

Most researchers, including the authors of this book, would not advocate a forensic approach. Objectivity is a worthy goal because we *do* have control over many sources of bias and error. In order to test our theories fully, we must actively seek out evidence that challenges them. One does not strengthen a theory by omitting, or dismissing as irrelevant, the data that do not support it.

To increase objectivity, researchers can solicit the views of all, not only those with whom they agree. By using a number of sources, they can verify the information they receive, in order to guard against deliberate or unintentional misrepresentation of the facts. We cannot eliminate our feelings, but instead of ignoring their potential impact on our work, we can be explicit about our own biases and assumptions. Such an explicit statement will be useful to those who evaluate our work. In addition, such INTROSPECTION, or self-examination, will help us to present as balanced and complete a view of society as we can.

Finally, communication among social scientists is not precluded by the differences in their subjective orientation. Regardless of the variation in their backgrounds, two researchers may agree upon a great deal of factual information. Our confidence in the report of a race riot is increased when we discover that both black and white observers describe the scene similarly; our faith in the diagnosis of mental illness is strengthened when psychiatrists, psychologists, and social workers can achieve consensus. Even in cases where two investigators differ regarding the significance of a given event, they may still "agree to disagree," in the sense that their argument is attributed to an honest difference of opinion, rather than to stupidity, bigotry, or mutual antipathy. This opens the way for scientists to learn from each other, although their research findings may sometimes be contradictory.

REPLICATION AND RELIABILITY. Another scientific ideal is REPLICATION. Research should be conducted in such a way that those who question its outcomes can repeat it and obtain the same results. A measurement instrument, such as a test of intelligence or personality, that yields the same results when repeated is said to have high RELIABILITY. Since scientific knowledge has to be cumulative, reliability is a cornerstone of science; one cannot build a coherent body of information without reliable measurement tools.

In the physical sciences, it is possible to replicate a study under conditions virtually identical to the original. The laboratory environment may be monitored and controlled so that, for example, every time the two substances sodium and chlorine are combined in the proper amounts, we get table salt. In social research, by contrast, it is often difficult to recreate the original setting. Herbert Gans (1962) studied Italian-American families in the West End of Boston. Today the streets he walked are gone; the people he talked to are displaced. The entire area is a giant complex of government buildings, hospitals, and high-rise apartments. Gans's study thus could never be replicated.

Even when the buildings remain, the research environment may be altered. Suppose you study a nursing home and discover that the elderly residents are quite satisfied with their treatment. You might convey a relatively benign picture of convalescent care. Six months later another researcher visits the same place and finds the facilities in disrepair, patients lying in squalor, many of them demoralized and dissatisfied. What has happened? Either you were an unusually poor observer or some events have occurred that changed the setting dramatically, events over which the investigator had no control—for example, the owners of the home went bankrupt, the custodial staff staged a work stoppage, supervisory personnel quit or were terminated. Any one of these happenings might affect the research conclusions in a major way.

In this example, and in any duplication of a study, the variation in results could be caused by differences in the conditions for observation rather than by a lack of objectivity in the original study. In many cases researchers have little choice but to contend with these difficulties. Nevertheless they are obligated to design their data collection procedures in such a way that replication is, at least, not precluded.

Studies that use highly reliable data collection tools are more easily replicated than those that depend on the questions that individual researchers devise "on the spot." For this reason pencil-and-paper tests and printed schedules of questions have been developed to measure the skills, opinions, and attitudes of large numbers of people, again and again. These instruments ensure that the identical questions are asked each time a study is repeated, but they are still not perfect measures because it is difficult to control the environment in which the answers are being provided. Peoples' opinions may be influenced by their health, life situation, or even the temperature or noise level in the room. Therefore, as with the goal of objectivity in social research, replication and reliability are scientific ideals worth trying to attain, but no instrument is perfectly reliable.

PRECISION. A fourth principle of science is PRECISION in measurement. In the laboratory, microscopes and scales have been developed to an extremely fine tolerance. We may know exactly how much of two chemical elements are present in the experimental environment. So precise are these measurement tools, in fact, that researchers may verify the existence of a compound by separating it into its component parts and recombining them at will.

Measurement is much more problematic in social science because in many ways the social world is more complex than the physical world. One can analyze a piece of paper blown about by the wind in terms of its velocity, weight, and gravity, but people cannot literally be placed under a microscope in order to determine how and why they are swept along by crowd emotion. In spite of this we do have means available for checking on the quality of our measures. So, while social science can no more make the claim to perfect measurement than to perfect objectivity, we must again consider the problem to be one of degree.

VALIDITY. Social researchers are frequently interested in measuring complicated and abstract phenomena, such as happiness, alienation, community solidarity, political conservatism, the popularity of a president, and various psychological conditions. There is a great deal of disagreement regarding how best to measure these concepts, since no unique, explicit, and comprehensive set of observable behaviors is indicative of each, to the exclusion of everything else. Moreover, the meaning of each of the concepts varies with its social context. The alienation suffered by white-collar workers is different from that experienced by ghetto residents. The situational nature of these abstractions makes them more difficult to manipulate than concepts such as height, density, distance, and pressure, in the physical sciences.

These problems of defining many of the concepts used in social research frequently create a dilemma: Are we really measuring what we claim to be measuring? Schizophrenia, a form of mental illness, is usually defined as disorientation in time, place, and person. A schizophrenic may suffer hallucinations or delusions, and is highly distractible, losing a sense of emphasis and subordination in conversation and action. If we observe someone with these symptoms, how confident can we be that we are measuring what we want to measure? Perhaps, instead of mental illness, we are merely seeing the temporary effects of LSD or some other mind-altering drug.

VALIDITY refers to the "fit" between the concept that a researcher wants to examine and the evidence for that concept. Increasing validity is another important goal of science. We want to make the fit between concept and evidence as exact as possible and to be aware of potential slippage between the two. In our last example, the longer we observe the various symptoms, the more valid representations of schizophrenia they become, in that the chances of the patient being in a temporary, drug-induced state diminish over time. As another example, a ballot cast for the incumbent president may not be the most valid measure of his popularity. Instead it may be indicating how *un*popular his opponent is!

We need to pay careful attention to the manner in which complex concepts like schizophrenia and political popularity are defined in social research. If some important component of a concept is omitted from its definition, the investigator will have difficulty assessing how much of that concept is really there. At the same time, if the definition is too broad, we may create a less precise measure than we need. If social researchers are as explicit as possible about the definitions of the concepts they use *and* the situations in which they apply, it is possible to construct a cumulative body of knowledge about social reality. Ingenuity in devising concepts is a challenge in all sciences, and particularly in the study of human behavior.

THE CRITICAL PERSPECTIVE. Thus far we have examined some canons of scientific inquiry: objectivity, replication, reliability, precision, and validity. These criteria are useful as a baseline for evaluating the scientific status of social research, but they do not fully capture its quality. There is, in addition, a particular attitude that social researchers share. In his book *The Sociologist as Detective*, William B. Sanders calls this attitude the CRITICAL PERSPECTIVE (1976:23). To be critical is not necessarily to be negative about society, but it entails looking "beyond the obvious into the many possible meanings to be found in the world about the world. . . . it is a perspective that requires the researcher to 'check it out,' to look at it from a different angle." The comparison to a police detective is an apt one. The social scientist is like the lieutenant knocking at the door of the witness to murder whom he has already questioned for an hour: "You know," he says earnestly, "you've been very helpful to me and I don't mean to trouble you again, but there's just one more thing that's been nagging me, and if I don't get an answer I won't be able to sleep tonight."

Scientists are bothered by the quality of the knowledge they produce. They adopt a skeptical attitude that forces them to question the truth of the data being collected. They ask continually, "Are my data reliable and valid? What are the potential errors that might be intruding into my findings? What kinds of data will cause me to reevaluate my theoretical ideas?" Scientific understanding and explanation are not predicated on faith alone. The scientist considers theoretical speculation to make sense only when it is accompanied by supporting data. Scientists should never become so committed to a set of theoretical ideas that they are unwilling to modify them in the face of conflicting evidence (Merton, 1949). Although they may be disappointed when their own promising theories are challenged or disconfirmed, the canons of science dictate that researchers press on with their work.

Science is, in some sense, subversive. It cannot accept, without testing, the explanation of the status quo offered by the powers that be. The "official" reasons for war, economic recession, the high rates of crime, or poor national reading scores are merely part of the evidence. The social researcher is "compelled by what he is doing to fly in the face of what those around him take for granted," notes sociologist Peter Berger (1963:38). This imperative to "unmask the pretensions and the propaganda" by which humans cloak their actions with each other is a logical outcome of research methodology. We do not stop once we learn peoples' explanations for their own behavior. On the contrary, we check out their explanations by talking to other people and by making our own observations. Utilizing this strategy, what we discover through scientific investigation becomes both less obvious and more comparable from one setting to another.

CONCLUSION. What may we say at this point about the scientific status of social research? Plainly, some attempts to understand the world, including theology on the one hand and common sense on the other, are wholly nonscientific. By contrast, the modern practices of physics, biology, and chemistry are highly scientific. When speaking of social research, however, it seems fruitless to look at the issue of science in either/or terms. There is general agreement among the social sciences that the principles and goals of scientific inquiry are worthy. But there is great variation in the extent to which the canons of science are met in practice. Some political science, psychology, and sociology studies are every bit as scientific as studies in the discipline of physics; others are no more scientific than most of what is today called philosophy. This diversity makes it foolish to classify the various social sciences in relation to one another, or to claim that social investigation as a whole lies somewhere between science and nonscience.

It is legitimate to conclude that the application of the scientific method to the study of human behavior is more than a sterile exercise of aping the physical sciences. The scientific method represents a mechanism for the systematic reduction of error in the description and analysis of society. Through social science we are held accountable for our theories and explanations, and we are compelled to consider their impact on the world. If our findings are incomplete or our recommendations unwise, it is we who are responsible.

Theory and Social Research

There are numerous options open to the investigator in choosing a theoretical perspective. Moreover, the many different kinds of social theory vary in terms of the specific concepts they contain, how complete or well articulated they are, and in the way they are expressed on paper, with words or diagrams. An exhaustive review of these formulations is beyond the scope of this book; however, in this section we offer some examples of theories that have been particularly influential in social research. Our aim is to illustrate three key points about the relationship between theory and the research process:

1. The scientific method is compatible with a variety of theoretical approaches to data.
2. Creating and expanding theory itself are prime motives for research.
3. The choice of theory is crucial, because it may influence one's topic for investigation, as well as one's conclusions.

WHAT THEORY LOOKS LIKE

What we have called hunches in our diagram of the scientific method (Figure 1.1) are really theories in embryo form; they are speculations that have a relatively short life span. They may never actually be written down. By contrast, social theories are more elaborate, general explanations of human behavior, and they usually take a concrete form. Some of the formats used to express theory in social research are called taxonomies, models, typologies, paradigms, and axioms. These will be examined below to show what theory actually look like in practice.

Taxonomies, models, and typologies are schemes for classifying data. Some of them are extremely lengthy and intricate. In practice they represent conceptual frameworks that guide the analysis of data as they are being collected. To understand how these schemes work, consider what happens when the morning mail arrives at a bustling business office. It has to be sorted; perhaps it is distributed in boxes or pigeonholes, each one with a person's name on it or with the name of a department. In this analogy the morning mail is the data. At first it is all jumbled up and undifferentiated, but we can make sense of it by placing each piece in the proper box.

Many theories approach the explanation of social reality in a similar way, by atomizing it, or breaking down observable phenomena in a systematic way. Data are organized according to a diagram or to a list of categories, corresponding to a row of mailboxes. Thus each bit of information gathered by the researcher, whether it be what someone says, how someone looks, or what someone has written, fits in somewhere in a well-articulated scheme.

If a taxonomy, model, or typology merely supplies labels for each of its conceptual "boxes," it is basically descriptive, rather than explanatory. It may be suggestive of theory, but it cannot stand as a complete presentation of theory. We can make only a few generalizations about the business office by looking at each pigeonhole separately. What makes these schemes more valuable theoretically is the explanation of how their various components relate to one another. Thus each datum not only belongs in a certain category; it also carries implications for the rest of the data. It is useful to know how many letters go in each mailbox; it is perhaps more important to know why some mailboxes are always much fuller than the rest.

The foregoing generalizations are illustrated in the following examples.

TAXONOMIES. Perhaps the easiest of the classificatory schemes to understand is a TAXONOMY, or list of categories. An example is the *Taxonomy of Educational Objectives* (Bloom et al., 1965), used in research on teaching and learning in schools. The authors created definitions of general concepts such as knowledge and intellectual ability and separated each into its component parts. They designed this to be an *exhaustive* list, in other words, to contain every type of knowledge and every kind of intellectual ability and skill.

The taxonomy is an aid in sorting data. The researcher may, for instance, observe the work of a particular teacher for several weeks, placing each class exercise and homework assignment somewhere in the scheme. It may be discovered that there are many occasions where students showed their "comprehension" of the lessons by making outlines of chapters, reciting what they had memorized, or putting the teacher's lectures into their own words. There might be fewer entries in other categories, that is, comparatively less opportunity for students to apply, analyze, or synthesize what they had learned.

These data might help the teacher understand why some students appear uninterested in class or are discipline problems, or why test scores are lower than expected. Because the taxonomy shows that there are many types of learning that the data indicated had been ignored, the researcher may suggest some specific changes in assignments and lectures, in order to involve students more actively in

TABLE 1.1   The Taxonomy of Educational Objectives

KNOWLEDGE	INTELLECTUAL ABILITIES AND SKILLS
Knowledge of specifics	Comprehension
Terminology	Translation
Specific facts	Interpretation
Knowledge of ways and means of dealing with specifics	Extrapolation
	Application
Conventions	Analysis
Trends and sequences	Analysis of elements
Classifications and categories	Analysis of relationships
Criteria	Analysis of organizational
Methodology	principles
Knowledge of the universals and abstractions in a field	Synthesis
	Production of a unique communication
Principles and generalizations	Production of a plan or proposed set of operations
Theories and structures	Derivation of a set of abstract relations
	Evaluation
	Judgments in terms of external criteria

Source: Adapted from *Taxonomy of Educational Objectives, Book 1: Cognitive Domain,* edited by Benjamin S. Bloom et al. (New York: David McKay Co., 1965). Copyright © 1956 by Longman Inc. Reprinted by permission of Longman Inc., New York.

learning. Thus taxonomies may point the way toward the explanation of human behavior and toward policy recommendations.

It is important to realize that aside from the exhaustive description of knowledge and abilities, there is no real theory of learning expressed in the list of categories in Table 1.1. Nowhere in the scheme is it stated that the curriculum in each school subject must contain all types of knowledge, or that tests must measure all kinds of intellectual ability. The taxonomy does not state that it is more difficult, or more desirable, to acquire one type of knowledge than another. It does not specify the degree of difficulty for each academic skill, nor that each must be acquired in a logical sequence or order. In fact, there is no particular relationship proposed between any of the elements in the taxonomy; they are merely labels. As the authors themselves note, the categories may be used by researchers "in very arbitrary fashion," out of sequence in the scheme, so long as their definitions remain intact (Bloom et al., 1965:10–11).

Thus the primary utility of taxonomies is for description. A complete list of objectives in any field, whether it be education, business, community organization, or medical treatment, is invaluable as a baseline against which to measure performance. Having commonly accepted definitions of concepts such as intellectual skill makes it easier to compare behavior in a variety of settings. This same list of categories could be used to evaluate the curriculum in English, chemistry, sociology, history, or any other school subject. Finally, the taxonomy is useful for devising strategies of data collection. It tells us what the possible types of behavior are in a given setting; thus we are encouraged to look for them and, if some behaviors are not present, to wonder why not.

MODELS. A MODEL is a visual depiction of how something works. It is a prototype to which the real world is compared as data are gathered.

Some models are almost entirely descriptive, in that they are really labels arranged spatially in a diagram. Figure 1.2 is an organizational chart of a mental health clinic. It tells us who the principal actors in the bureaucracy are, and it specifies the lines of communication and authority between them. It also details the responsibilities of the various parts of the clinic. Note that the administrative wing, on the right, relates to the departments that provide direct service, on the left, through the office of the executive director. It is apparent that the various clinical departments, for example, geriatric services and adult counseling, communicate with each other directly, although they all are the responsibility of the director of clinical services.

Like the taxonomy we have already examined, this model is suggestive of theory. We may, for instance, speculate that there could be friction between administrators and clinicians, because they rarely, if ever, interact on a daily basis. In analyzing the role of the executive director, we may look for evidence of tension between administrative and clinical duties. Finally, the chart may lead us to investigate the difficulties of coordinating the several, diverse departments on the left of the diagram.

These hunches and insights may help us determine how the organization works, but the chart itself does not contain a real theory of group functioning or structure. It could not explain why two clinics, set up with substantially the same official positions and lines of authority, may differ greatly in their effectiveness and efficiency. The diagram, informative as it is, does not indicate how many

FIGURE 1.2   An Organizational Model

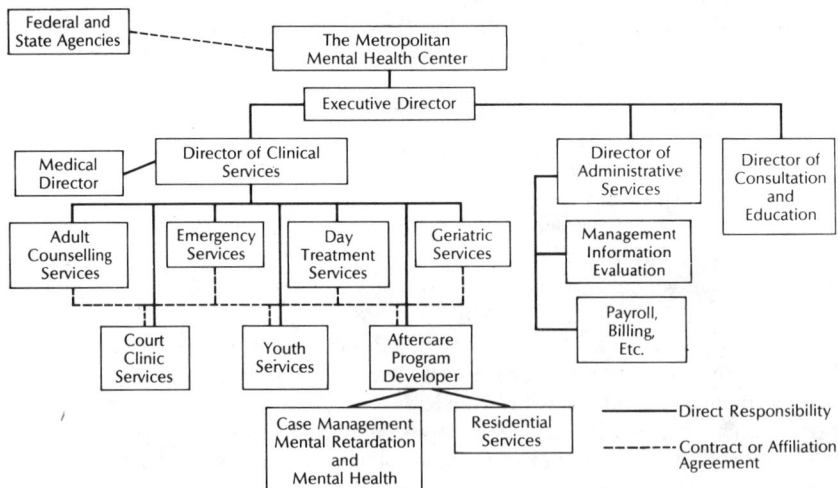

FIGURE 1.3   A Model of the Process of Socioeconomic Achievement

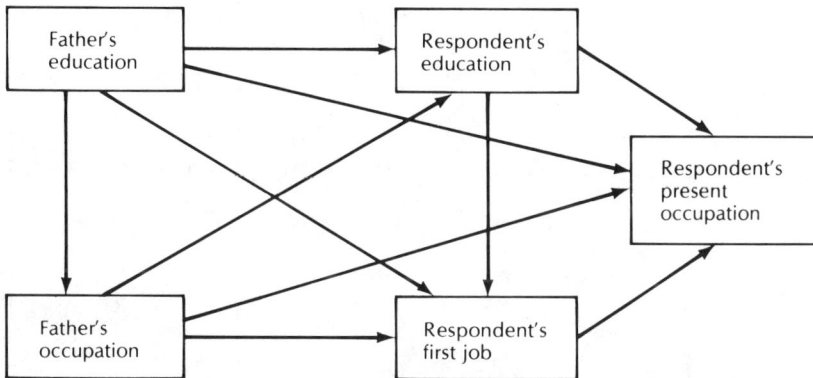

employees work for the clinic, what the caseload is, what sort of neighborhood it serves, nor other details that may be theoretically relevant to the study of mental health care delivery.

Figure 1.3 presents a model that is primarily explanatory. The components of Figure 1.3 are not parts of any single organization. Instead they are VARIABLES (characteristics, attitudes, or behaviors that can be measured and that take on differing values). These variables are used to explain part of the process of social-class formation, namely, what leads a RESPONDENT (person who is the subject of investigation) into a particular occupation.

According to the model in Figure 1.3, a respondent's choice of employment is influenced by the nature of the first position that person obtained on entering the job market. Equally important, in theory, is the amount of education that the respondent has received. Two other variables are thought to be significant, namely, the education and the occupation of the respondent's father. The model thus reflects the idea that a person's own educational history is greatly influenced by his or her parents. A father's occupation may influence his children's career patterns directly ("following in his footsteps") as well as indirectly, through the amount of education that they are given and the initial occupational goals that they are encouraged to set for themselves. There are many statistical procedures that may be used to verify the relationships among the variables in a model of this type.[3]

Figure 1.3 has much more explanatory power than Figure 1.2, the model of the mental health clinic. In order to create general explanations, however, we often must sacrifice rich, descriptive detail. Both DESCRIPTIVE and EXPLANATORY MODELS are thus useful in the social sciences, but the former are only aids to theory construction, whereas explanatory models are theory itself.

TYPOLOGIES. A TYPOLOGY is a device for analyzing all the logical combinations of at least two variables. Figure 1.4 shows a simple descriptive typology for examining a population of college students according to the variables grade-point average

---

[3]More on this point in Chapter 17.

FIGURE 1.4   Typology of College Students According to Grades and IQ Scores

Intelligence (IQ)

	High	Average	Low
High	1 "Straight arrows"	4 "Pluggers"	7 "Overachievers"
Medium	2 "Apathetics"	5 "Normals"	8 "Strivers"
Low	3 "Underachievers"	6 "Nonscholars"	9 "Marginals"

Grade-Point Average

and intelligence measured by an IQ test. Nine student "types" are conceptualized in the cells, or boxes, in this table. A person classified as a "straight arrow" (type 1) is someone with both high grades and a high IQ. A "striver" (type 8) has fair grades but a low IQ. Two other types are "marginals," whose poor grades are perhaps more consistent with their low intelligence test scores, and "apathetics," who, in spite of superior IQs, have only fair grades.

This scheme lets us compare all students on a given campus; everyone may be placed somewhere in the typology. But it has additional theoretical utility. We expect to find some people with average tested intelligence in each of the three grade-point average categories (types 4, 5, and 6). The individuals whom we have labeled "overachievers" and "underachievers" (types 7 and 3) are probably more unusual, in that there is a great disparity between their tested intelligence and their grades in college. These are precisely the sorts of people we should be examining closely if we want to understand fully the theoretical connection between natural talent and actual performance. Yet, without the typology, we might fail to isolate them, or we might concentrate exclusively on students whose IQ scores were more closely related to their grade-point averages.

PARADIGMS. Another sort of theorizing is of broader scope and not so easily diagramed as those we have looked at so far. It is the application of a PARADIGM, or coherent world view, to social life. In effect, when we follow a paradigm, we put on a pair of glasses that colors all behavior with a particular interpretation.

An example from social psychology is the work of Erving Goffman (1959), who has attempted to explain social interaction by uncovering its basic processes. The inspiration for Goffman's paradigm is Shakespeare's claim in *Hamlet* that "all the world's a stage and all the men and women merely players." He takes that notion seriously and offers evidence for it. In fact, Goffman's work is called DRAMATURGICAL because of the close analogy between social life and what occurs "on stage."

According to this paradigm human beings are all "actors" who, depending on the situation, must play a variety of roles for society, the "audience." People are constantly trying to convince their audiences that their performances are genuine. Thus Goffman forces us, as observers, to confront the manipulative, sometimes artificial quality of people's contacts with one another. If the "act" is successful, the audience gives people approval and confirms them in their roles. Only "backstage" in areas hidden from the public are people permitted a respite from their acting chores.

If we accept this paradigm, we see the basis of social reality continually shifting along the dimensions of managing impressions, putting our "best foot forward," and hiding imperfections. The categories Goffman develops to organize an enormous quantity of data provide striking insights into interpersonal relations. No one act is seen as being any more real or true than any other. Acting per se is part of the human condition.

Another paradigm, perhaps the most influential one in American social science, is the image of society associated with Talcott Parsons (1902–1979). It is known as STRUCTURAL FUNCTIONALISM in sociology and political science, and as SYSTEMS THEORY in social work and business management. According to this paradigm every element of a society that exists over a period of time serves a distinctive function, helps to maintain the social system, and is supported by public consensus or agreement. Society is much like any living organism, claims Parsons, so that if there is a change in any one social institution, there will be corresponding changes in other elements of the system. Any alteration in the economic structure of a society, for example, will cause complementary changes in the political, religious, and educational spheres. Functionalists argue that any social system is always moving toward a state of equilibrium. In this paradigm society is much like a rubber ball that may on occasion be squeezed out of shape but is always striving to return to its original form. The questions for functional analysis are therefore: What function is performed by each social element, and what would be the consequences for the social system as a whole if it were absent?

The explanations provided by functionalism are not very concrete. They seem abstract and general because they are meant to apply, at several levels of analysis, to families, business enterprises, ethnic groups, nations, and even the world system. Nonetheless, functionalism has been an attractive paradigm because it confirms the scientific notion of an orderly universe, in which there is a place and a reason for every element of society. It makes a very complicated world seem more intelligible by proposing that the relatively small social groups to which we belong operate according to the same principles as the larger society. Finally, although the paradigm of functionalism is relatively weak in providing specific explanations, it is extremely flexible. Like the dramaturgical perspective, there is scarcely a human action or attitude that cannot be fitted into the functionalist conceptual scheme and vocabulary.

AXIOMATIC THEORY. One important task of science is to order complex data, and the frameworks we have discussed help us do this. Yet there are critics who maintain that real theory must be AXIOMATIC: it must begin with a general proposition and, using the rules of logic, explain some phenomenon by elaborating on the original statement and making it more concrete.

Let us assume that we wish to explain the behavior of juvenile delinquents. Drawing heavily on the work of Cloward and Ohlin (1960), we might devise the following theoretical sequence:

Proposition 1: There is a high cultural value placed on individual achievement in American society.

Proposition 2: There are societally designated legitimate means for achievement that involve movement through the educational system and into the occupational world.

Proposition 3: These means of achievement are not equally open to all persons in American society.

Proposition 4: These means of achievement are closed off to a significant proportion of lower-class persons.

Proposition 5: Where the legitimate means for achievement are blocked and persons have internalized the value of achievement, alternative or illegitimate means for achievement will be used.

Proposition 6: Delinquent behavior may be seen as representing one easily accessible means in lower-class culture of acquiring the material goods that reflect achievement in American society.

This explanation is clearly of a different sort than that provided by Goffman or Parsons. Instead of supplying tools for the analysis of all human behavior, axiomatic theory deals only with a discrete portion of it, in this case, delinquency. Thus it seems to be doing what an explanatory model is designed to do, but without the diagram and arrows.

Actually, many of the assumptions that underlie both paradigms and explanatory models could be recast in the format of axiomatic theory. We would then specify, in propositions, all of the logical inferences that the researcher makes in order to construct a model or create a paradigm. Those who argue that we should be using more axiomatic theory in social research point out that some of our models and paradigms would not stand up well under such scrutiny. It is claimed that some of them rest on unprovable assumptions that cannot be easily verified. For example, two notions underpinning Goffman's dramaturgical view are that humans are rational and self-serving and that they are approval-seeking animals. We may not actually *test* these assumptions, but we proceed as if they were true!

DESCRIPTION AND EXPLANATION. These objections notwithstanding, most researchers today accept both axiomatic and classificatory analysis as valuable contributions to social science. Theory, as we have seen, takes many forms, but all help us to understand the world. To find out how something works, we must know its dimensions and the identity of its components, as well as the general principles of its operation. Therefore, in making use of theory, a balance must be struck between description and explanation.

We must have both, but here is a dilemma: As we become wrapped up in the vivid description of a single event or person, it becomes difficult to generalize about other similar or related phenomena. Conversely, if we place less emphasis on description than on general explanation, theory tends to become a series of disembodied, self-evident propositions.[4] Perhaps there is no foolproof solution to this dilemma, but the attempt to solve it is a constant challenge in social science.

---

[4]For example, the Parsonian idea that every society needs "integrative" mechanisms or ways to resolve opposing points of view and disagreement concerning social goals.

THE DISCOVERY AND VERIFICATION OF THEORY

Thus far we have shown some of the many ways that social theory may be expressed. However, the form that theory takes does not determine its place in the research cycle. We may begin with observation and gradually discover or create a model, a typology, or a general explanation for behavior. Or we may initiate research with the theory firmly in mind, and through testing attempt to verify it. In this section we discuss the implications of these two approaches for the ongoing practice of research.

DEDUCTION. In the physical sciences the typical research strategy is to begin with a theory and then to subject it to observation. This mode of inquiry is called DEDUCTION, and it has been most influential in the social sciences as well. We start with general principles and subsequently deduce whether or not they are sound. Deductive theory does not emerge immediately *from* the data; it is conceived beforehand and applied *to* the data.

To apply theory to data, the researcher formulates HYPOTHESES, specific predictions that follow from the general theory. Recall the explanation of delinquency from our earlier example of axiomatic theory, namely, that juvenile delinquents are individuals who seek to acquire the material goods that reflect success in American society. How could we develop hypotheses from this theory? It might be proposed that people in particular social situations are more likely to engage in delinquent behavior than others, or that obstacles to achievement will be greatest for those who possess particular social attributes. The hypotheses, then, could look like this:

> The larger the number of persons in an individual's family, the greater is the individual's potential for delinquency.

> Among those who are blocked from the legitimate avenues for achievement, the potential for becoming deviant will depend on how deeply the value of achievement has been internalized.

The researcher, in fact, might produce a whole series of additional hypotheses that would lend themselves to specific testing.

Because the prediction of behavior is central to the process of deduction, it is difficult to begin that process with only a descriptive model or a very general paradigm. Each of the separate variables in a deductive theory must be carefully defined in advance, so that the researcher will recognize them when they appear in the real world, and so that they may be measured. We have to be as rigorous as possible, because as we create measures and variables, we are in effect creating a yardstick against which everything we later observe will be compared. If our model suggests that a large organization will experience difficulty in communication among its parts, we had better be specific about what constitutes a large organization and what constitutes a barrier to communication. We need such reliable measures because we may have to examine as many as a hundred different groups in order to confirm or disconfirm our theory.

The more general, abstract, and purely descriptive the model or paradigm is, the greater are the problems of measurement and explanation, and the more difficult it is to use in deductive research. For this reason, axiomatic theories and models that specify the relationship between several well-defined variables are more easily adapted to the process of deduction.

INDUCTION. The major alternative mode of inquiry is INDUCTION; its hallmark is the discovery and building of new theory as research progresses. The research cycle is begun with observation. From the data collected, a generalized understanding of behavior is gradually *induced*. Measurement of variables is as important to inductive research as to deductive research, but neither hypotheses nor measuring tools are developed in advance. Instead the research problem emerges as a result of direct confrontation with a set of behaviors. The primary focus for study, the development of theory, and the production of an analysis may emerge at any point in inductive research, even toward the very end of the process.

Induction is initially exploratory and vividly descriptive. Investigators must take in a vast amount of information because they have to develop categories for classifying data, based not on already existing theory, but on the actual range and variety of data in the field.

No list of examples could do justice to the vast amount of inductive research that has been conducted in the United States in recent years. The variety of settings that have been explored include the fields of education, occupational sociology, gerontology, and politics.

We have detailed accounts of ghetto schools (Eddy, 1967; Levy, 1970), community colleges (Clark, 1960), and large state universities (Becker et al., 1968). There have been studies of truck drivers (Blake, 1974), welfare caseworkers (Blau, 1960), Wall Street lawyers (Smigel, 1968), and machine operators (Roy, 1952). Using inductive strategies, researchers have examined elderly street hustlers (English and Stephens, 1975), nursing homes (Gubrium, 1975), and middle-class retirement communities (Jacobs, 1974). They have also investigated congressional representatives (Fenno, 1978), convention delegates (Kirkpatrick, 1976), and Washington lobbyists (Milbrath, 1963). As you read further in this book, you will learn some of the methodological techniques that were employed in order to obtain data in these diverse contexts.

Although induction is usually identified only with the research goals of exploration and description, the explanation of social reality may also be created as research is being carried out (Glaser and Strauss, 1967). By generating hypotheses on a day-to-day basis, and discarding them when predictions are not verified by observation, we may create a theory. Becker (1953) began to study marijuana use by looking at the history of people's experience with the drug, and eventually formulated a theory of becoming deviant. Lofland and Stark (1965) produced an explanation of the process of religious conversion as they investigated a small millenarian cult in California. More recently Allon (1975) observed dieters in a weight-losing organization and formulated a theory of "latent social services," explaining that people often join voluntary associations to obtain benefits not identified with the official goals of the group.

These, and countless other inductive explanations, tend to be highly *valid*, particularly when they are based on lengthy field work. Over many months the process of induction gradually eliminates the weaker alternative explanations for the behavior of the particular individuals observed. The chances become less and less that important variables remain hidden from the investigator. On the other hand, inductive explanation tends to be less *reliable* than it is valid. The measuring tools used in this mode of inquiry are developed on an *ad hoc* basis, and they are influenced to a considerable degree by the unique experience of individual researchers. Thus if we use inductive, as opposed to deductive, research strategies, the chances are increased that another investigator may come to equally valid, yet different, conclusions. The theoretical explanations created by induction also may be less generalizable from one setting to another.

In spite of these difficulties, inductive research is no less scientific than the deductive approach. The tension over reliability and validity is felt by all researchers, no matter what their field of inquiry. We may have to sacrifice a little of one in order to improve the other. Indeed, the purely deductive strategy is often not followed to the letter, even in the physical and natural sciences. In all disciplines the development of theory is necessarily both inductive and deductive. Scientists may begin with a deductive theory, try to test it with actual data, and find that it does not predict well. At that point they may choose to modify the theory to make it more consistent with the data. When they do this, they are beginning to engage in an inductive process of inquiry.

THE DEVELOPMENT OF RESEARCH IDEAS

We have explained what research is, and we have also begun to clarify the relationship between theory and research. Yet, an important question remains to be asked: Where do research ideas come from?

CURIOSITY. Social researchers are generally intensely curious people. They want to know about those different from themselves, for example, a tribe in Africa, mental patients in a back ward, the very poor, or the very rich. Often they begin to investigate some setting or group for little reason other than that they are intrigued by, or perplexed by, a set of behaviors. What is it like in a nudist colony? Why can't "Johnny" do math at the appropriate grade level? Why didn't any states west of the Rockies vote for Jimmy Carter in the 1976 elections? What happens to people's mental health after an accident at a nuclear power plant? These are all questions that have inspired social research. All scientists grapple with mystery. Social scientists, in particular, are attracted to those whose actions and motives are, at least at first glance, unclear or puzzling. Once they are attracted to a subject, the logic of science fuels their curiosity. The scientific method disciplines the raw enthusiasm of the researcher, but does not dampen it.

PURE AND APPLIED RESEARCH. The investigator's curiosity is not confined to bizarre settings and to social problems of an immediate nature. Some science involves basic, or PURE RESEARCH—finding the solution to questions that are intellectually challenging but that may not have practical applications in the short run. Pure research in social science is primarily devoted to expanding theoretical horizons; thus the actual setting for data collection may be of secondary importance. If, for example, we are keenly interested in how people learn the grammatical structure of language, we might choose to gather data in an elementary school. There we would find out a great deal about how schools function, how teachers organize their time, and how young children dress and play. Any and all of this information might be of use to school administrators, teachers, and parents, but our concentration in this setting would be on data about language acquisition. In fact, we could probably discover similar processes of learning in another setting entirely, say, on a streetcorner, or in a home.

APPLIED RESEARCH, on the other hand, is inspired by the needs of social action. Its findings and conclusions are applied immediately to solve a problem or to improve the effectiveness of an existing or proposed social program. Are the agencies set up to help poor people serving their intended clientele? How many parking meters should be put on Main Street? How can hospital emergency rooms be made more efficient? These are examples of questions that inspire applied research. It may turn out that the answers to these questions have theoretical significance, but the investigations were manifestly intended to help people. The results of basic research may offer practical assistance to the public sooner than expected, but its primary purpose is the accumulation of knowledge for its own sake.

ALREADY EXISTING THEORY. A major source of research ideas is the storehouse of theory that has been built and expanded by social science. These ideas channel the development of research. It is easy to see why this is so when we consider that deductive strategies for the collection of data have dominated the study of human behavior for the past forty years. Even when we use the inductive approach to data, however, it is extremely difficult to enter the field with a clean slate. Ideally, induction begins with no theoretical preconceptions, but although researchers may not write down hypotheses or sketch models in advance, they still cannot fully erase the memory of a lecture, a book they have read, or the example of conceptual skill provided by another investigator whom they respect or admire.

In a widely read and discussed book, Alvin Gouldner (1970) argues that there is now a reluctance to work at testing new ideas in the investigation of social life and a tendency to deal with the same old assumptions about society, merely applying them to new settings. While we might agree with him concerning the limitations of the theories bequeathed to us by previous generations of researchers, we must also recognize that science develops through the continual testing of already existing theoretical ideas (Kuhn, 1967).

Often the setting or subject for research is chosen because it appears to be ideal for testing a theory, or a part of a theory. In one of an extraordinary number of studies that have stemmed from the work of Parsons and Shils (1959), Kingsley Davis (1961) applied the paradigm of structural functionalism to prostitution. He argued that prostitution serves a distinctively useful function in any society by operating a kind of "safety valve." It lets people act out some kinds of sexual behavior that might create tension or be considered illegitimate within the context of the family. He then makes the point that prostitution actually works to preserve the family system.

Other investigators, starting off with functionalist theories, have analyzed large-scale organizations, schools, and the military, as well as the general phenomenon of social stratification. Davis and Moore (1945) concluded that our system of distinct social classes was of great value to society, in part because we need to reward people of talent and skill at a higher rate than those with less ability and ambition. The great disparity between rich and poor in America is desirable, according to this view, in order to motivate people to perform the important tasks of leadership in business and government.

As you may appreciate from this last example, studies based on Parsons's paradigm have been challenged by those who see functionalism as inherently conservative and overly supportive of the status quo and the interests of the "establishment." Therefore, much research has been generated out of what social scientists see as the limitations of systems analysis. Marxists and other CONFLICT THEORISTS argue that structural functionalism does not deal effectively with issues of social change and deviance (Wallerstein, 1976; Quinney, 1974). Their paradigm contrasts sharply with Parsons's because they see change and conflict as continuous and natural, not disruptive of social order. Whereas functionalists maintain that every society rests on the consensus of its members, their critics believe that every society exhibits constraint of some of its members (Dahrendorf, 1958).

A change in theoretical position encourages changes in the kind of data that need to be acquired. Thus, as some researchers have moved away from the paradigm of functionalism, there has been increased emphasis on the investigation of groups that contribute to the disruption of the social system (for example, radical students and Vietnam veterans). In addition, more attention has been devoted to power relations of dominance and subordination in the economy, law enforcement, among racial and ethnic groups, and between the sexes.

TRAINING AND EXPERIENCE. Finally, in reviewing the sources of research ideas, we must consider the training and experience of the investigator. The nature of one's employment is important, because a certain type of research may be expected in a particular department or agency. The priorities of the government bureaus that provide much of the funding for the social sciences also influence the goals of the research and the settings chosen. Often the selection of a specific model or paradigm is influenced by one's colleagues and teachers at work or in the university.

These pressures can never be entirely eliminated, nor should they be. Science is a cooperative enterprise, and researchers often require some assistance in formulating research ideas. It is important to realize, however, how crucial the choice of theories, models, and paradigms is. It may, as we have seen, help determine the subject of an investigation. Even more significant is the impact of theory selection on research findings and conclusions. Whether a criminal is portrayed as a victim of society or as one who victimizes society may depend less on the crime committed than on whether the investigator was influenced by labeling theory or by functionalist theory.

To the lay person this may not sound very scientific, but the scientific method does not specify which theory is most appropriate, or the form in which it should be presented. Because these choices are to be made by researchers, they need to be aware of the ways in which their prior training, and the expectations of others, influence the decisions they make. Data do not "speak for themselves." It is up to the researcher, using social theory, to say what the significance of data is. It is an awesome responsibility.

Intellectual Craftmanship

If by now you suspect that there are some dilemmas in research methods that cannot be resolved once and for all, you are right. To learn methodology, and to do research itself, requires a tolerance for ambiguity and living with some uncertainty. It is always possible that the data we collect may continually support our hypotheses, but that our theory itself may be wrong. Or our stated hypotheses may be supported by the data, but for reasons simply unknown to us.

The canons of science are a basic blueprint, but to do good research we must do more than follow their direction. The scientific method does not tell us whether to maximize description or explanation in data analysis, nor does it tell us how much validity may be sacrificed in order to improve the reliability of a study. It does not guide us automatically to the theory that fits our data best or to the most effective technique of data collection. Weighing such decisions skillfully is only partly a science; it is also a craft. The researcher is both a scientist and the practitioner of a craft.

THE IDEA OF A CRAFT

What is craftsmanship? So few people actually practice any craft today in our society that we may be out of touch with the phenomenon. We seem not to have craftsmen and craftswomen, but people who know how to put together parts that someone else, or a machine, has made.[5] Noted sociologist C. Wright Mills (1951:215–223) explains that a true craftsman is someone who maintains the image of a completed product from start to finish, someone who knows everything that goes into it, even if some of the tasks are performed by others. It is in this sense that the skilled researcher practices a craft.

Craftsmanship follows a plan devised by the worker. This plan, whether it is the pattern for carving a rocking chair or the design for examining a social problem, is of course shaped by the worker's prior experience. A researcher may use a theory that has been used before, in the same manner as the carpenter decides to make another chair like the one in his parlor. But the plans of both are also highly individualistic, and subject to modification as the work progresses. The result, therefore, reveals the personality and interests of the worker. The scientific canon of objectivity does not mean that research has to be uniform and colorless. The difference between ordinarily and finely crafted studies is comparable to the distinction between mass-produced and one-of-a-kind items. In spite of the freedom to create which craftsmanship affords, there is, inevitably, some mechanical drudgery in some phases of the work. However, says Mills, the craftsman is "carried over these junctures by keen anticipation" of what the finished product will look like, and by pride at its completion.

LEARNING THE CRAFT

In generations past, young apprentices received instruction in the workshop of a master. They first acquired some basic skills from books and perfected the essential "hands on" techniques by practicing continually. In teaching research methods the authors of this book can perform some of the same functions. We

---

[5]One of the authors is reminded of the quaint sandal shop he visited in Maine, where "custom-made" footwear was assembled from precut patterns pulled from a box labeled "made in Taiwan."

will clarify the criteria that social scientists use in evaluating their work, and the work of others. We will show you techniques for improving reliability and validity, and we will offer you helpful suggestions as you go, step by step, through the research process. When you finish, you will be acquainted with most of the tools in the researcher's "workshop."

Your ability to use these tools is indispensable for the collection of data about the world, but it will not, in itself, make you a craftsman or craftswoman. No rules or set of procedures will ever replace a keen imagination in producing a good study. Technique is important, but showing off methodological expertise for its own sake is pointless. The purpose of research is to produce findings that add to our knowledge. Sociologist Peter Berger (1963:13) has aptly noted that in the social sciences, as in love, an overemphasis on technique can lead to impotence.

RESEARCH IMAGINATION. How, then, does one go about cultivating an "imagination"? Contrary, perhaps, to popular conception, creativity is not something that one either possesses or does not. One can acquire the knack of being an imaginative researcher by continually structuring one's thoughts and ideas. It takes work to develop this talent; how perceptive an observer you are will depend more on your own energy than on anything we can tell you.

In his essay on intellectual craftsmanship, Mills (1959) suggested ways of channeling mental energy. He said that ideas and problems for research gradually take shape as social scientists "play around" with concepts. It is not uncommon to begin toying with an idea and wait, sometimes several years, before actually beginning to work on it. During the intervening period, the problem remains in the back of the mind, and each time one reads something, or has a relevant personal experience, a mental note is made. Part of intellectual craftsmanship is this continual reflection on ideas over time.

Mills, in fact, advocated that researchers keep a file, or journal, to serve as a reservoir for ideas. Entries in this file should continually reflect one's own life experiences. In this sense, to be a scientist does not mean separating our personal intellectual life from our career. Our private troubles, as workers, parents, consumers, and voters, are in reality public issues. We must appreciate this point and try to get others to understand it as well.

In our journal we may keep memos to ourselves, excerpts from books, half-baked theories, snatches of conversations heard on the street, even our dreams. As the file begins to grow, it is useful to go through the entries, trying to see which pieces of information seem to have things in common. This periodic rearranging of data itself constitutes an exercise of the research imagination and frequently generates new ideas. We may find through such a continual reorganization that certain key concepts emerge and that many of our entries, previously seen as wholly independent and discrete, begin to fit into a larger mosaic.

One of the features of such a process is that we will eventually reach a point where we have generated more ideas than we could likely investigate in a lifetime. We find ourselves necessarily setting priorities among our several ideas. In Mills's own words, "Any working social scientist who is well on his way ought at times to have so many plans, which is to say ideas, that the question is always, which of them am I, ought I, to work on next?" (1958:198). A true craftsman or craftswoman, whether working in wood, clay, paint, or ideas, is never without something to do.

Summary

Social research is a dynamic process that involves the collection and analysis of data and the formation of conclusions based on those data. Its goal is to add to knowledge through the exploration, description, and explanation of social reality. The sources of data are diverse, from the interaction between two people to the behavior of states and nations. The recommendations of social researchers have in recent years become important in the formation of government policy, the evaluation of legislation, and the determination of judicial decisions.

Methodology is the study of the research process itself—the principles, procedures, and strategies for gathering information, analyzing it, and interpreting it. The conclusions of a study are only as good as the methods of investigation that were used to obtain them. Therefore, in order to be able to judge research critically, as well as to conduct it, we need a thorough knowledge of methodology.

The scientific method is a general model of inquiry in education research, political science, psychology, sociology, and other disciplines. Theories, general explanations for behavior, are continually being modified in light of new findings. This model was initiated in the physical and natural sciences. It has been adopted by the behavioral sciences with profitable results, because it requires the systematic elimination or control of biased and inaccurate observation based on emotion or inadequate measuring tools. Principles of scientific investigation include the ideals of objectivity, reliability, precision, and validity. One must be able to replicate a scientific study, and to assess whether it measures, in fact, what it was designed to measure, in theory. Scientists are self-critical and skeptical about the procedures they use and the data they obtain. They try to find as many explanations as possible for each phenomenon observed.

The selection of an existing theory, or the construction of new theory, is as important to social research as the perfection of techniques for the collection of data. Theory may be classificatory, as in many taxonomies, models, typologies, and paradigms, or axiomatic. A variety of theoretical forms are compatible with the scientific method. Creating and expanding theory are prime motives for research. The choice of theory is crucial because it may influence not only the topic of an investigation, but the research findings as well.

Existing theoretical models and paradigms exercise great influence over the research enterprise, but neither these formulations, nor any guidelines for gathering social data, can substitute for a creative imagination. The individual investigator as practitioner of a craft remains at the heart of the process.

Key Terms

applied research
axiomatic theory
common sense
conflict theory
critical perspective
data analysis
data collection
deduction
description
descriptive model
disconfirmation

dramaturgical paradigm
exhaustive
experimentation
explanation
explanatory model
exploration
field work
findings
forensic social science
hunch
hypothesis

induction
intellectual craftsmanship
introspection
methodology
model
objectivity
paradigm
precision
pure research
reliability
replication

respondent
scientific method
selective observation
structural functionalism

systems theory
taxonomy
theory
typology

validity
variable
verification

Exercises

1. Select one or more books or articles in which social research findings are presented and analyze each study from the standpoint of exploration, description, and explanation. Can you give examples of each research function? Did the researcher(s) emphasize one function more than the others? How do you know?

2. We have suggested that the same form of social life might be investigated in a number of diverse empirical contexts. Try to list as many different settings or contexts as possible where you could conceivably do a case study of alienation.

3. Attend a social gathering and note down five commonsense conclusions about social life from ordinary conversation. How would a scientific researcher attempt to verify each conclusion?

4. Imagine that you are about to embark on a study of the behavior of college students in their dormitories. Without specifying in great detail what you would study, write a short essay on the difficulties you might expect to face in meeting the three canons of the scientific method—objectivity, precision, and replication.

5. Choose any three pieces of research in the social sciences that attempt to offer theoretical explanation of some phenomena. For each, indicate whether the theoretical explanation is arrived at through an induc-

tive or a deductive process. Indicate whether you feel the theories have been adequately verified by the data collected.

6. Using the same pieces of research as for exercise 5, try to do the following:
   a. Indicate as many as possible of the unstated assumptions that you feel underlie the respective theories.
   b. If the theory is stated only in verbal terms, try to create a model similar to Figure 1.3 to illustrate the proposed causal connections between the variables in the theory.

7. Using Richard Cloward and Lloyd Ohlin's book *Delinquency and Opportunity* as a basic reference, find at least two competing theories of delinquency. Indicate which theory you find most reasonable and why. Also try to indicate the type of data that might be necessary to test each of the chosen theories.

8. On the basis of your personal observation, try to construct a classificatory scheme for describing the types of students on your campus.

9. In this chapter we have referred to sociological investigation as both a science and a craft. Do you see any contradiction in the use of these two descriptions of sociological work? Justify your position.

Suggested Readings

Ary, D., L. C. Jacobs, and A. Razavich
1979 *Introduction to Research in Education.* New York: Holt, Rinehart and Winston.
    A useful, general treatment of methods in educational research.

Blalock, Hubert
1969 *Theory Construction.* Englewood Cliffs, N.J.: Prentice-Hall.
    An especially helpful book for students with some mathematical sophistication. Blalock's purpose here is to describe the process of moving from verbal theories to more rigorous formulations in terms of mathematical models.

Cole, Stephen
1972 *The Sociological Method.* Chicago: Rand McNally.
    An easy-to-understand introduction to social research, with an emphasis on quantitative methods.

Denzin, Norman K.
1970 *The Research Act.* Chicago: Aldine.
    An introduction to social research methods written from a symbolic interactionist perspective.

Gouldner, Alvin
1962 "Anti-Minotaur: The Myth of a Value-Free Sociology." *Social Problems* 9 (Winter):199–213.

A sharp, literate critique of sociological attempts at objectivity.

Hammond, Phillip
1964   *Sociologists at Work.* New York: Basic Books.

A compilation of articles by famous sociologists on how they did their work. One of the few attempts to give a real picture of the research process.

Homans, George
1950   *The Human Group.* New York: Harcourt, Brace & World.

Homans is one of the leading proponents of deductive theory in the social sciences. In this book he demonstrates the utility of deductive theory in explaining a number of empirical events.

Lazarsfeld, Paul F.
1969   "The American Soldier—An Expository Review." *Public Opinion Quarterly* 33:377–404.

A perspective analysis of the research on the military conducted by Samuel Stouffer et al., in which Lazarsfeld shows how common-sense conclusions were contradicted by the evidence.

Lundberg, George
1955   "The Natural Science Trend in Sociology." *American Journal of Sociology* 61 (November):191–202.

Lundberg is one of the most outspoken advocates for a highly quantitative, scientific sociology. This article reflects his bias for continuing scientific development in the social sciences.

Parsons, Talcott
1950   "The Prospects of Sociological Theory." *American Sociological Re-view* 15 (February):3–16.

A statement on the status of sociological theory by a leading systems theorist.

Robinson, W. S.
1951   "The Logical Structure of Analytic Induction." *American Sociological Review* 16 (December):812–818.

A clear presentation of the strengths of analytic induction as a model for research.

Sanders, William B., ed.
1976   *The Sociologist as Detective.* New York: Praeger.

An introductory anthology that attempts to draw a parallel between social research and the research of a detective.

Spradley, James P.
1979   *The Ethnographic Interview.* New York: Holt, Rinehart and Winston.

Numerous examples of different taxonomies and how they are constructed can be found on pages 132–154 of this book.

Wrong, Dennis
1961   "The Oversocialized Conception of Man in Modern Sociology." *American Sociological Review* 26 (April): 183–193.

A critical statement of contemporary sociological theory, with special emphasis on the assumptions underlying functional theory.

Zetterberg, Hans
1965   *On Theory and Verification in Sociology.* Totowa, N.J.: Bedminster Press.

A useful text concerning the nature and production of axiomatic theory in the social sciences.

References

Allon, Natalie
1975   "Latent Social Services in Group Dieting." *Social Problems* 23, 1 (October):57–69.

Becker, Howard S.
1953   "Becoming a Marijuana User." *American Journal of Sociology* 59 (November).
1963   *Outsiders: Studies in the Sociology of Deviance.* New York: Free Press.
1967   "Whose Side Are We On?" *Social Problems* 14 (Winter):239–248.

Becker, Howard, et al.
1968   *Making the Grade.* New York: Wiley.

Berger, Peter
1963   *Invitation to Sociology.* New York: Doubleday.

Blake, Joseph
1974   "Occupational Thrill: Mystique and the Truck Driver." *Urban Life and Culture* 3, 2 (July).

Blau, Peter
1960   "Orientation Toward Clients in a Public Welfare Agency," *Administrative Science Quarterly* 5:341–361.

Bloom, Benjamin S., et al.
1965   *Taxonomy of Educational Objectives.* New York: David McKay.

Clark, Burton
1960   *The Open Door College.* New York: McGraw-Hill.

Cloward, Richard, and Lloyd Ohlin
1960   *Delinquency and Opportunity.* New York: Free Press.

Dahrendorf, Ralf
1958   "Toward a Theory of Social Conflict." *Journal of Conflict Resolution* 2:170–183.

Davis, Kingsley
1961   "Prostitution." In *Contemporary Social Problems,* ed. Robert Merton and Robert Nisbet. New York: Harcourt, Brace & World.

Davis, Kingsley, and Wilbert Moore
1945   "Some Principles of Stratification." *American Sociological Review* 10 (April):242–249.

Eddy, Elizabeth
1967   *Walk the White Line: A Profile of Urban Education.* Garden City, N.Y.: Anchor.

English, Clifford, and J. Stephens
1975   "On Being Excluded: An Analysis of Elderly and Adolescent Street Hustlers." *Urban Life* 4, 2 (July).

Fenno, Richard F.
1978   *Home Style.* Boston: Little, Brown.

Gans, Herbert
1962   *The Urban Villagers.* New York: Free Press.
1968   "The Participant Observer as a Human Being: Observations on the Personal Aspects of Field Work." In *Institutions and the Person,* ed. Howard Becker. Chicago: Aldine.

Glaser, Barney, and Anselm Strauss
1967   *The Discovery of Grounded Theory.* Chicago: Aldine.

Goffman, Erving
1959   *The Presentation of Self in Everyday Life.* New York: Doubleday.

Gouldner, Alvin W.
1970   *The Coming Crisis of Western Sociology.* New York: Basic Books.

Gubrium, John
1975   *Living and Dying at Murray Manor.* New York: St. Martin's Press.

Jacobs, Jerry
1974   *Fun City.* New York: Holt, Rinehart and Winston.

Kirkpatrick, Jeane
1976   *The New Presidential Elite.* New York: Russell Sage Foundation and The 20th Century Fund.

Kuhn, Thomas
1967   *The Structure of Scientific Revolutions.* Chicago: University of Chicago Press.

Levy, Gerald
1970   *Ghetto School: Class Warfare in an Elementary School.* New York: Pegasus Press.

Lofland, John, and R. Stark
1965   "Becoming a World Saver: A Theory of Conversion to a Deviant Perspective." *American Sociological Review* 30, 6 (December):862–875.

Merton, Robert
1949   *Social Theory and Social Structure.* Glencoe, Ill.: Free Press.

Milbrath, Lester W.
1963   *The Washington Lobbyists.* Chicago: Rand McNally.

Mills, C. Wright
1951   *White Collar: The American Middle Class.* New York: Oxford University Press.
1959   *The Sociological Imagination.* New York: Grove Press.

Parsons, Talcott, and Edward Shils
1959   *Toward a General Theory of Action.* Cambridge, Mass.: Harvard University Press.

Quinney, Richard
1974   *Critique of Legal Order: Crime Control in Capitalist Society.* Boston: Little, Brown.

Roy, Donald
1952   "Quota Restriction and Goldbricking in a Machine Shop." *American Journal of Sociology* 57 (March).

Rubin, Lillian Breslow
1976   *Worlds of Pain.* New York: Basic Books.

Sanders, William B., ed.
1976   *The Sociologist as Detective.* New York: Praeger.

Schmid, Calvin F.
1960   "Urban Crime Areas." *American Sociological Review* 25 (August and October).

Smigel, Edwin
1968   "Recruitment of Wall Street Lawyers." In *Organizational Careers,* ed. Barney Glaser. Chicago: Aldine. Aldine.

Wallerstein, Immanuel
1976   "Modernization: Requiescat in Pace." In *The Uses of Controversy in Sociology,* ed. Lewis A. Coser and Otto H. Larsen. New York: Free Press.

Watson, James D.
1968   *The Double Helix.* New York: Atheneum.

2 / Research Design

CHAPTER OUTLINE

INTRODUCTION
The Research Cookbook
  Menus and Recipes
  Budgeting
  From Kitchen to Table
THE COMPONENTS OF
  RESEARCH
Selecting a Topic
Conceptualizing a Topic
  Concepts and Variables
  The Role of the Literature in
    Research Design
  Choosing Sources of Data
Strategies of Data Collection

Theory and Data Collection
Types of Information and Research
  Strategies
Spending Time and Resources
  Wisely
The Other Components of Research:
  Data Collection and Beyond
  Collecting Data
  Analyzing and Processing Data
  Making Inferences and
    Recommendations
PUTTING IT ALL TOGETHER
The Final Report
The Ups and Downs of Research

An Example: A Study of
  Undergraduate Life
  How Was the Topic Selected?
  How Was the Topic
    Conceptualized?
  How Was a Strategy for Data
    Collection Selected?
  Issues of Data Collection
SUMMARY
KEY TERMS
EXERCISES
SUGGESTED READINGS
REFERENCES

Introduction

A question frequently asked by students is, "What is a proper problem to write about in my term paper?" No one should be embarrassed to ask this question. Finding an appropriate topic is the most crucial issue to be addressed in social research. It is also the first element in RESEARCH DESIGN, the overall process of choosing the strategy and tactics to guide the collection and analysis of data.

The dilemmas of research design are sometimes difficult to resolve. Professional social scientists with years of experience sometimes wonder if investigating a problem that happens to interest them personally constitutes a worthy addition to knowledge in their field of inquiry. A related, and equally thorny issue that we will explore in this chapter is whether it is legitimate, or desirable, to be wholly descriptive in one's work, rather than explanatory. In other words, should all research make some theoretical contribution? In addition, we will examine the question of how much information is needed to substantiate an argument. The old axiom that "the more we know, the more we realize our own ignorance" certainly applies in social research. Are there guidelines to help us determine when we should stop collecting data and begin to analyze it? Finally, we will outline the difficulties that may occur when a research topic demands more time, attention, and money than the social scientist can possibly give it. How does one match the available resources to one's research interests?

To answer such questions, we need to know more than the general canons and logic of the scientific method. This chapter explains the specific components of the research process in order to aid you in conducting your own investigations, and also to convey what happens as professional social scientists actually begin to design a study.

THE RESEARCH COOKBOOK

As a craft, social investigation may be compared to the fine art of cooking. In the kitchen, creativity and skill each play a part in the preparation of a tasty meal, and things do not always turn out as expected. The first time you try to duplicate Grandma's prize recipe for homemade clam chowder, it may look (and taste) like low tide at Coney Island. The more you practice, the better your results will be. The more relaxed you are, the more you feel like experimenting with new combinations of ingredients. Grandma herself may seem like a magician, adding a "pinch of this" and a "dash of that." She may claim that intuition tells her when the oven is hot enough or when the baked apples are soft enough. Actually, however, most excellent cooks keep an extensive library of others' recipes, for information and inspiration. In the following section we present the "ingredients" of the research enterprise, and show how they interact with each other. Knowing what goes into the mixture will not make you an instant success, but it is a good place to begin to learn. You will become more confident, and research will seem less a mystery, as you discover what others have done, and as you spend time in the field yourself.

MENUS AND RECIPES. Continuing the analogy, Table 2.1 compares and contrasts the various tasks of research design with the process of putting a meal on the table. If in planning our meal, we decide to serve chocolate cake for dessert, we have made a decision similar to the selection of a topic for research, a choice that focuses our energy and calls for some specific skills. In addition, as you can see from Table 2.1, the initial choice of dish (or topic) sets in motion a sequence of necessary and related activities.

Having decided on chocolate cake, we are immediately faced with a problem. Will the outside be milk chocolate or dark; will the inside be devil's food or yellow? Will the icing be smooth and creamy, thick and fudgy, or hard and sugary? Are we going to bake a cake with two large layers, several small layers, or a "sheet cake" with only one layer? To answer these questions, we may turn to a recipe that, in effect, refines the general concept *chocolate cake*. This same process occurs in social research after we choose to study a general concept, for example, *alienation*. We must then select a "recipe," that is, we must make the concept more specific. In this case one of the things we must do is decide whether the phenomenon we want to explain is alienation from work, alienation from loved ones, or alienation from the political system.

A recipe gives the cook a list of ingredients to use and tells what amounts of each are called for. In social research a similar function is performed by OPER-ATIONAL DEFINITIONS. These are lists of the specific components of each concept, or the actual evidence for each variable. We may denote a politically alienated per-

TABLE 2.1   The Researcher as "Cook"

Preparing a meal...	Doing social investigation...
Deciding on the menu	Selecting a topic
Picking recipes	Conceptualizing a topic
Budgeting time, space, and money	Choosing a strategy for data collection
Shopping	Collecting data
Cooking	Processing and analyzing data
Inspecting	Interpreting and making inferences
Serving	about data
	Writing the final report

son as an adult who has never voted or supported a candidate of the two major parties.

There are many possible, valid operational definitions of a given variable, in the same sense that hundreds of different combinations of ingredients may still produce delicious chocolate cake. In fact, there are no absolute, one-and-for-all definitions of concepts or lists of evidence for variables in social research. Conceptualization and operationalization are dependent, to a certain extent, on the purpose of the research. To return to our analogy, a large single-layer cake might be appropriate for a child's birthday party; a small, elegant, multilayered cake may be the perfect ending for a gourmet meal. If it is our concern about declining labor productivity in the United States that inspires our study of the topic alienation, we are likely to examine the specific concept *alienation from work*. We might define it by looking at three variables: evidence of employees' lack of pride in their work, absenteeism, and industrial sabotage. Each of these three dimensions of alienation from work also must be operationalized—for example, does absence from work because of illness count as alienation?

BUDGETING. In the realm of cooking, the recipe we select carries implications for the allocation of time, space, and money. We must set aside an hour or more if we have to follow a complex series of steps in the preparation of our dessert. If we must cook an entree (say, a roast) in the oven, beginning at four o'clock, then we must arrange to bake the cake ahead of time. If we are planning a gala feast, we had better check to see whether we have exceeded our household budget for the month. If we are pressed for time, space, and money, we may elect to use a packaged mix in which the major ingredients have already been combined.

The comparison with social research strategy is an apt one, because we may have only a few months to complete a study, a limited research staff, or a restricted budget. These considerations influence research design, and may even preclude the selection of a topic that, though interesting, is too complex for an individual researcher. If we are planning to use a questionnaire as part of a social survey, we may save time and money by selecting an already completed instrument that has been used in a similar context by other researchers. We may even decide to avoid the collection of information ourselves, and rely on data collected by others.

The choice of recipe and allocation of our resources affect the exercise of shopping for the ingredients for our cake. Shall we patronize an exclusive little store that sells delicious (but expensive) imported chocolate? Or if we have more time than money, perhaps we can travel several miles to the supermarket in a neighboring community where a sale is in progress. Maybe it would be a good idea to obtain our ingredients at a wholesale outlet where we can get a substantial discount by buying in large quantities. Of course, we'd need plenty of room to store cases of chocolate and 50 pound sacks of flour.

The principle of shopping in the most desirable place for our ingredients applies as well to the research process. The setting for the collection of data is influenced by the concepts that interest us and the very real limits that restricted resources may impose. A single factory could be the ideal place to study alienation from work, but we also could investigate the same phenomenon in a large number of work places. Alienation from loved ones might be analyzed either in the context of therapeutic interviews or through using data from counseling agencies. Political alienation could be uncovered via public opinion polls or through in-depth examination of radical political movements. In each case the choice of location may be affected by the nature of the topic, the purposes of the investigation, and by what is possible, given the size of the research staff and available funding.

FROM KITCHEN TO TABLE. RAW DATA are bits of information in the original form in which they were gathered, for example, answers to questionnaires, field notes, or tape recordings. Just as the ingredients for a cake must be cooked, data need to be processed and refined before they are usable. Sometimes a computer is programed to place raw data into predetermined categories, or to perform statistical operations. It is often assumed, in error, that this phase requires little creativity on the part of the researcher. Many professionals will tell you that their excitement or enthusiasm does not diminish during the data processing portion. There is the anticipation of results (perhaps similar to the family peeking through the oven door and imagining how delicious the cake will be when it's done). And there is also the possibility that emergencies may require immediate attention. Sometimes these unexpected events are the results of unwitting errors such as giving the computer incomplete instructions. Often, however, strategy itself changes as the data are being processed. A cook may conclude that his two-layer cake would really be more impressive as a triple-decker, and as we have noted, a researcher may decide to expand her analysis of data beyond what was originally planned.

When the cake is baked and frosted, the cook may give it a critical eye. Did it turn out as it was supposed to? Would it be better if the ingredients were modified slightly? At what other occasions would it be appropriate to serve? This inspection and critique is similar to what social scientists do when they interpret data and draw inferences from it. They ask what theories have been confirmed, disconfirmed, or created? What modifications in already existing theory are suggested? In what other contexts would a similar study be useful? These are questions that must be posed if scientific inquiry is to take place.

Once the cook has examined his own work, perhaps even made a note to revise the recipe the next time he bakes the cake, it is time to serve it. The cook's judgment will, it is hoped, be confirmed by the diners at the table. It may happen that a guest or family member offers a suggestion that, if followed, would make future cakes tastier. It should be clear that serving the cake is analogous to preparing a final report of research, so that it may be evaluated by the scientist's peers and by the public.

Remember these parallels between cooking and research as we discuss each of the elements of research design in the sections that follow. Use the "cookbook" as a device to help you to recall the various components of social investigation and to appreciate how they are interrelated.

The Components of Research

Let us suppose that as one requirement of the course in which this book is assigned, a student must conduct original research, that is, choose a topic and engage in scientific inquiry to answer questions that follow from it. How would you go about completing this exercise successfully? You would indeed have to perform each of the tasks mentioned in the "research cookbook" (although not necessarily in the exact order presented).

SELECTING A TOPIC

The TOPIC is the subject about which you wish to generalize. We have already explained that there are several sources of inspiration for good research ideas, but as a beginning exercise it is perhaps most helpful to select a group, or an individual, or a set of behaviors and attitudes in which you have some personal interest. Perhaps you are concerned about the possibilities for employment after graduation, the changing and sometimes conflicting values of marriage and career, or the increase in crime in major urban areas. Whichever topic you choose, your own curiosity will supply much of the energy needed to overcome research difficulties.

To initiate *exploratory* research, all you need to know is the subject for investigation. To move beyond exploration, to *description* and/or *explanation,* you will need to begin specifying the RESEARCH PROBLEM—the question or questions concerning your topic that you believe are most important to answer. Let us assume that you have decided to investigate the increase in crime. To begin to convert this general interest into a design for research, you might ask: "What intrigues me most about this topic?" Is it the loss of property, the threat to human life and personal safety, or, more specifically, the experience of women, the aged, or the handicapped as victims? You might be more curious about the perpetrators of crime, perhaps the phenomenon of juvenile delinquency. In this case an appropriate research problem would be to investigate the connection between the occurrence of crime and drop-out rates from schools in certain urban areas. This, in turn, may lead to a corollary issue: What, if anything, can schools do to deter or discourage juvenile crime?

Note that the formulation of a research problem narrows the topic to manageable proportions and suggests strategies for research design, particularly the possible variables to be used and settings for the collection of data. But the fact that some succinct questions have been asked does not, in itself, determine how the abstractions *crime, juvenile,* and *school drop-out* will be defined. This choice is still up to the researcher.

Sometimes the *purpose* of a study is as important as the topic in determining research design. We may discover the purpose of a piece of research by asking why and to whom it is useful to have the answers to the questions being asked.

Sometimes there is no special motive for research other than to explore some phenomenon or to add to human knowledge in a particular area. In this situation the investigator enjoys a great deal of latitude in the defining of concepts and operationalizing of variables. But on other occasions, particularly in deductive inquiry or in applied social science, the purpose of the investigation is much more focused, in that a specific hypothesis is being tested, or human behavior is being evaluated according to a predetermined set of standards. In these instances the purpose of the study has a profound impact on research design. Indeed we often cannot begin to choose the most appropriate measuring tools for the variables we are manipulating until we know why the data are being collected in the first place.

CONCEPTUALIZING A TOPIC

Once your topic has been chosen and a more specific research problem has been formulated, some CONCEPTUALIZATION is necessary. You will need to discover:

1. which concepts are most appropriate to your topic
2. which variables follow from these concepts and how they are defined
3. how your variables relate to one another
4. what the specific sources of your data will be

Ideally, in inductive scientific inquiry, each of these tasks is accomplished gradually, after research is initiated. The answers emerge as the investigator proceeds. By contrast, the more deductive the strategy for inquiry, the more likely that all four questions will be tackled at an early stage in research design, before the investigator goes into the field.

CONCEPTS AND VARIABLES. A CONCEPT is a general idea applicable to particular instances or examples of behavior. More than one conceptual label may be applied to the same human behavior. When we see a police officer pushing someone against a wall and applying handcuffs, is that an instance of effective law enforcement or harassment? As we have noted, observers may legitimately disagree regarding the definition of complex concepts. It is relatively easy to spell out the meaning of the concept *chair,* because we can point to several types of chairs, explain their use, and distinguish them from other types of furniture. What about a more complicated idea, such as *trust in government*? We know that this abstraction exists, in some measure, but it has no obvious, observable referents. The researcher must isolate its component variables.

Let us say that your topic is citizen-government relations in the United States and that your research problem is to determine whether Americans' trust in government has increased or decreased over the past twenty years. How would you define *trust* in such a way that the components of the definition could be measured? Figure 2.1 shows how an investigator at the Institute for Social Research did it. The heavy black line in the graph represents the general concept trust in government; each of the remaining lines reflects four separate variables that comprise trust, namely, public opinion concerning the honesty and competence of leaders, and the extent to which government is perceived as benefiting all the people and spending tax dollars wisely. Notice that overall trust in government has declined steadily for two decades, and that the public appears to be most

FIGURE 2.1   Public Trust in Government

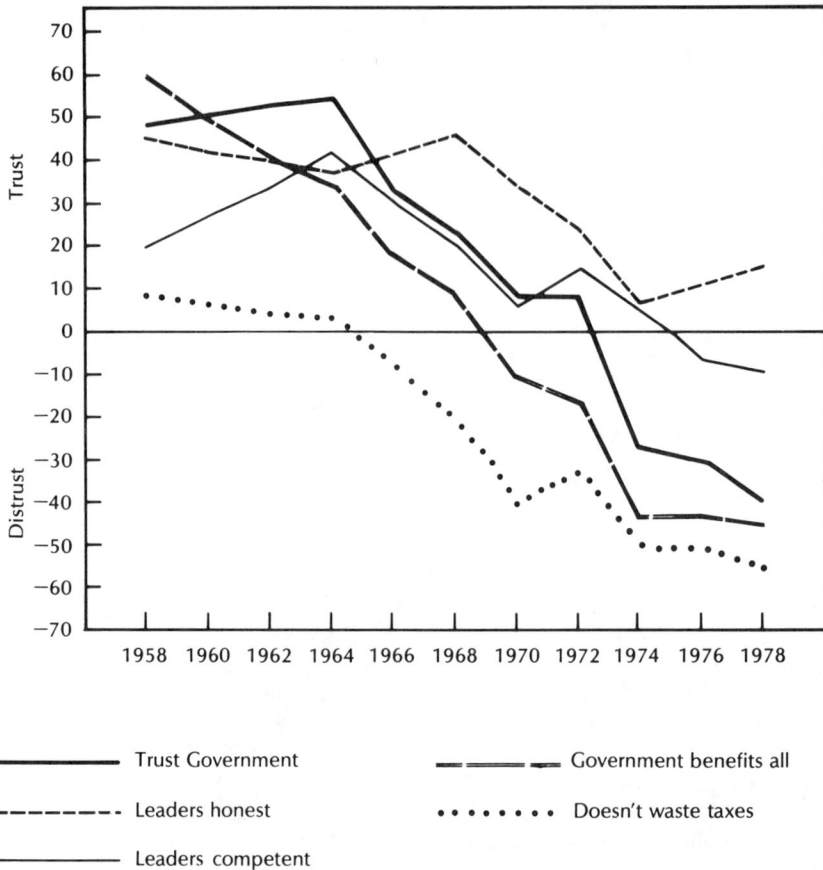

Source: Adapted from Miller, 1979.

upset over the issue of waste. It is also significant that trust in the institutions of government has continued its tailspin since 1974, in spite of the fact that belief in leaders' personal honesty has grown.

The investigator could have included additional variables in his definition of the concept trust. He might have asked people to evaluate the impartiality and fairness of the judicial system, or the speed with which government responds to public needs. The indicators he *did* select, however, are so central to the idea of trust, that the addition of more components would be unlikely to influence the research findings. In addition, the four variables depicted in Figure 2.1, taken together, present a *valid* approximation of trust. We know this because it is most unlikely that a person rating government highly on each of these four dimensions would, in fact, distrust it.

Therefore, a wise procedure, as you conceptualize any topic, is to choose or create definitions that are relatively simple and straightforward. These definitions should contain only a few variables, those that are most important. Each variable should be conceived in a way that allows it to be readily and precisely measured. The same principles apply in the selection or construction of theory (that is, the overall blueprint for relating each variable to the others). We may seek to explain the declining level of public trust in government depicted in Figure 2.1 by hypothesizing that trust is a function of negative publicity given to political leaders by the media. That is, when reports of scandals and dishonesty dominate the news, perceived trust declines. To test this hypothesis, we would need to define *negative publicity* as a concept, just as carefully as trust was defined. Appropriate and readily measurable variables in this case might be the content of editorials exposing fraudulent practices by elected officials, the proportion of air time on national network news devoted to malfeasance in office, or the number of indictments of politicians in local, state, or national government.[1]

THE ROLE OF THE LITERATURE IN RESEARCH DESIGN. In Chapter 1 we mentioned that the motivation for research may in fact be theoretical, for example, to resolve arguments between competing theories or to add to theory. Even if your work is largely descriptive, or only incidentally theoretical, you will need to immerse yourself as deeply as possible in the existing literature relating to the topic you have selected. In the deductive model for research, conceptualizing any topic will be greatly influenced, even determined absolutely, by the existing literature. On the other hand, if you are following a model of inquiry that is primarily inductive, you will not begin data collection with concepts, definitions, or theories that are identical to those found in the literature. In either case a review of previous efforts to understand similar or related phenomena is essential, even for the beginning researcher. To ignore the existing literature may lead to wasted effort on your part. Why spend time merely repeating what other investigators have already done? If you are aware of earlier studies of your topic, or related topics, you will be in a much better position to assess the significance of your own work and to convince others that it is important.

A glance through professional journals in social work or sociology, political science or psychology, may be somewhat intimidating to the apprentice researcher. You may be unfamiliar with many of the references cited, or the techniques used to analyze data. Each academic and professional body of literature has its characteristic jargon, and this may serve as a barrier to understanding for the uninitiated. It is important to work up the courage to "take the plunge" into the literature. You may be timid at first, but with practice, you will find that you can "wade through" it efficiently and with increasing confidence.

Remember that you do not have to know everything about the complexities of theory in order to see contradictions in the literature. Ask yourself some basic questions about what you are reading, for example:

Is the author trying to prove something to you, as a reader? If so, what is it?

Are there any gaps or inconsistencies in the author's argument?

Are there any other studies that analyze the same or related phenomena in a different way?

Which of the different ways of looking at your topic appeals to you most? Why?

---

[1]The process of generating operational definitions for research variables is examined in more detail in Chapter 3.

Later on, when you become more expert at reading the reports of others' work, you will be able to be more critical in your questioning of the authors' methodology, the choice of data, and the quality of the inferences drawn from the data.

CHOOSING SOURCES OF DATA. We have shown how a research topic might be selected and provided an illustration of the process of concept formation. Only one important step lies between conceptualization and the planning of strategies for the actual collection of data. That step is to figure out where to look for the information that is needed. If you have already chosen your topic, you know what you want to generalize *about*. But what will you be generalizing *from*? For any given research topic, there are numerous possible answers to this question.

Let us say that we wish to generalize about the topic *growing old*. We might collect information from the elderly occupants of several retirement communities concerning their age, state of health, income, relations with children, and so forth. Or we could look at the communities themselves, perhaps noting their population density, economic structure, politics, medical facilities, and the leisure-time activities available for residents. No matter which of these options is selected, we shall nonetheless be able to generalize about growing old. We may examine the topic *divorce* by speaking with individuals who have separated, by attending self-help support group meetings, or by researching the history and functioning of voluntary organizations created to help single-parent families.

Deciding where the data will come from is, in part, a practical issue. It may be more expensive and time-consuming to select one type of data, rather than another. To conduct personal, in-depth interviews of 200 people requires a different set of resources than does the continuous observation of a group as it goes about its business, or the processing of answers from a multiple-choice questionnaire. If we are indeed to study growing old, the location of our data may depend on these practical considerations, since we could probably obtain data about the retirement communities as a whole by doing some reading in a library and by examining census data or publicity materials. On the other hand, we may have to undertake a more lengthy project if we are to observe the behaviors of the residents themselves or to discover their attitudes. If divorce is the topic under investigation, it will probably take longer to attend several weekly meetings of a singles group than would be needed to interview each member of the same group for 30 minutes.

Having made this point, however, it must also be said that deciding on the source of data may be as much a conceptual issue as a practical one. The decision is often influenced, even determined, by the theoretical concerns of researchers, or the level of human interaction that they feel most comfortable explaining. In ascending order of complexity, the major types of interaction examined in social science research occur between two individuals, between an individual and a group, and between groups. Note that the same topic may be studied at each of these levels of interaction. A social psychologist looking at the phenomenon of divorce is likely to be intrigued by the conflict between individuals that leads to the dissolution of marriage. Personal interviews may be useful in obtaining such data. Another feature of the social reality surrounding this issue might be provided by a case study of a divorced person in the community. Alternatively, one might examine divorce at the group/group level, perhaps by examining the lobbying process to trace the impact of groups composed of separated men and women on changing divorce and child custody laws.

These examples all illustrate the point that sources of data are not necessarily the same as research topics. We may study big business in America by using data about corporate executives as well as data about corporations; we may approach politics as a profession by examining politicians as personalities and/or by looking at their politicking; juvenile delinquency may be understood by collecting biographical information about youngsters with police records, or by obtaining data about the quality of life in the neighborhoods in which they grew up. In short, people, the things they create, and the environment in which this activity occurs all may be legitimate sources of data. "Recipes" for social research do indeed differ. As we end this summary of the important issues researchers face in conceptualizing a topic, you should have a clearer idea of *what* to look for as you begin your own research, and *where* to begin looking for it. Now for the next question: *How* shall the data be gathered?

STRATEGIES OF DATA COLLECTION

There are several major modes of data collection in social research, including participant observation, surveys, content analysis, and experimentation. Each of these involves a distinct series or combination of activities, and each requires the mastery of certain techniques, from one-on-one interviewing skills to complex statistical analysis. Subsequent chapters explain the full variety of strategies and techniques for gathering data. For now, let us define some of them and note the general criteria for selecting one strategy over another.

In PARTICIPANT OBSERVATION, social phenomena are observed firsthand in their natural setting. The researcher, or field worker, establishes continuing social relations with the individuals being studied. The extent of actual participation may vary greatly, in that the researcher may or may not play an active part in events (Zelditch, 1962). However, interviewing of respondents, when it does occur, is always part of the process of observation.

By contrast, in the SOCIAL SURVEY, durable personal relations between researcher and subject are seldom necessary or possible. Contact between the two parties, when it occurs, is relatively brief. Interviewing is done with the aim of obtaining reports of social phenomena, attitudes, or attitudes apart from the natural setting in which they actually occur (Backstrom and Hursh, 1963). Whatever observation takes place entails minimum participation; in fact, it is possible to use a questionnaire sent through the mail. In this case the investigator may never actually meet respondents face to face.

A third mode of data collection, CONTENT ANALYSIS, avoids the issue of personal involvement with research subjects and the problems of reliability associated with interviewing. It concentrates on one aspect of human behavior, "the manifest content of communication" between individuals or groups (Berelson, 1952). To measure and describe the words and pictures that comprise human communication, content analysis does not rely on interviews, but on ENUMERATION, or the counting of the number of times that specific types of communication occur in a variety of settings. This enumeration does not necessarily involve firsthand observation of interaction (for example, in the screening of newspaper editorials). Observations may be carried out in a natural setting (as in the content analysis of leader/member relations in a small group). Either way, the categories used in the enumeration of data are determined in advance, and the counting exercise itself has minimal impact on what takes place.

Finally, EXPERIMENTATION in social research may involve face-to-face interaction between subjects and researchers, for the purpose of observation, interviewing, enumeration of behaviors, or all three. The hallmark of the experimental method is that the duration and nature of such contact are determined in advance and rigorously controlled by the researcher. The individuals participating in an experiment may be asked to report how they feel, or to say why they have acted in a particular manner, and what they do may be photographed or recorded with words or numbers. Social behavior is not, however, explained merely by citing peoples' subjective responses or the researcher's descriptions. For an experimenter the source of social explanation is the relationship between modifications made in the subjects' environment and subsequent changes in their behavior or reports of their behavior (Wuebben et al., 1974). It is apparent, therefore, that the experimental environment must be one that can be manipulated by the researcher. For this reason (although a few ingenious designs have been created in natural settings) most experiments take place in the laboratory, an artificial setting in which no encounters take place except those desired by the investigator.

There is, of course, no one best technique for gathering data, any more than there is one best theory for analyzing and drawing inferences from data. How would you go about selecting a strategy for collecting information about society? Your choice will depend on these four criteria, among others:

1. how well formulated your theory is before you begin observation
2. the level of social interaction you need or wish to observe
3. the type of information you want to know
4. the resources you have available for research

THEORY AND DATA COLLECTION. It is wise not to select experimentation as a strategy unless you have a theory in mind and have developed, on your own or from the literature, some specific hypotheses that follow from that theory. Experimental research is wholly deductive in nature. Each alteration in the laboratory environment is made for a reason, namely, to help you prove or disprove some theory or to test a hypothesis. Therefore, the meanings of concepts and the operational definition of the variables used in experimental research are determined in advance, not discovered as the research progresses.

In a famous study Zimbardo (1972) wanted to test the theory that the behavior of prison guards and inmates is determined by the structure of the prison as an institution rather than by the personalities of the prisoners or their keepers. He simulated lock-up conditions in the laboratory and carefully divided a homogeneous group of student subjects into "inmates" and "guards." He purposively altered the environment by allowing rumors of a prison rebellion to spread. The student guards reacted with surprising brutality, providing data in support of the theory. Note that you could study the same topic, prisons, more inductively using either survey or participant observation techniques. In both cases you would have less control over the research environment than Zimbardo did; your work would take you outside the laboratory, perhaps for firsthand interviews with prison officials or inmates. Even if you did not confirm or disconfirm a particular theory, or create a new theory of your own, you might nonetheless produce a valuable description of actual prison conditions.

Content analysis depends on some prior conceptual homework. You cannot begin to enumerate types of television commercials, for example, until you have developed a list of "types" or categories into which each advertisement might be placed. Once this sort of preliminary scheme is devised, content analysis may be used as part of either inductive or deductive investigation. We might want to discover the number of unfavorable stereotypes of women and girls found in a particular collection of children's books (Weitzman and Eifler, 1972). We can do this successfully, even without having formulated a theory of learning that connects the content of the books with the process of opinion formation in young people. On the other hand, we might begin with a relatively well developed theory, such as the Marxist notion that the news media in a capitalist society attempt to influence the public to accept the leadership of the business elite. Then we might test this theory using content analysis of network television news broadcasts, looking for favorable images of big business and its representatives.

There is no necessary, logical relationship between survey research as a mode of investigation and either induction or deduction. Social surveys may be more or less descriptive or explanatory, and there is no way to determine in advance just how much theoretical analysis must be done prior to, during, or following data collection. In the world of research practice, however, social survey procedures and deductive inquiry are often paired.

Because contact between researcher and respondent is typically of short duration, survey work must rely on reaching large numbers of respondents to produce data. This exercise can be time-consuming and may also require many interviewers. The nature of the contact with research subjects in survey work is, therefore, often standardized by determining in advance the specific questions to be asked. This has the advantage of reducing wasted time, both during the interview and later in data analysis. It ensures that all subjects will be responding to the same issues. It also helps to eliminate the effects of the interviewer's personal interests upon the research results, since all subjects are being asked the same questions. Because the questions are formulated in advance, survey research may more easily employ less expert, yet fully competent, interviewers. This is especially important because it would be quite expensive for highly qualified investigators to personally interview hundreds or thousands of respondents.

It is useful to devise questionnaires in advance, but it is also difficult to do so without some theoretical guide. For this reason most social surveys, particularly large-scale ones, are initiated deductively. Since a questionnaire limits the nature and type of data that will be collected, a major function of surveys is to verify or test existing theories and hypotheses, rather than to discover theory. But because they generate such a large quantity of information, some of it unexpected, social surveys may also inspire later inductive theory building. A certain degree of theoretical sensitivity in the researcher is required in order to begin a survey project involving more than a few dozen respondents. It is often helpful to obtain copies of the questionnaires used by other researchers, which you may alter slightly to suit your own needs. If this is not practical, try to create questions that use definitions of concepts, or variables, that are similar to those used in previous studies. In this way you will increase the probability that your survey will be more than a descriptive exercise, and that it will actually *explain* social behavior scientifically.

There is no logical reason why participant observation cannot be used to verify existing social theory. Yet it is used less frequently for this purpose than is survey research. Typically, field workers contact only a small number of respondents, and this makes it difficult to generalize their findings to a much larger population. To increase the number of people observed or interviewed using participant observation might be prohibitively expensive. Moreover, because this technique relies to a great extent on the personal involvement between researcher and subjects, it is difficult to repeat the investigative procedure exactly. Thus social surveys are often utilized to verify existing theory because they can be replicated more easily and may, on that account, be more reliable than participant observation.

The major strengths of observational techniques are that (1) they permit vivid description, based on intimate personal involvement of the researcher in the everyday life of respondents, and (2) they provide explanations for human behavior that evolve gradually as theory is created inductively. Such theories are often verified using other techniques. Participant observation is, in some respects, ideal for the beginning researcher. Its small-scale, intensive approach is intrinsically interesting; it does not require mastery of complex statistical procedures. On the other hand, this data gathering strategy does place a premium on interpersonal skills (e.g., being a good listener) and the intellectual capacity to make sense out of complex phenomena. Because questions are not usually developed in advance, many beginning researchers assume, erroneously, that little or no knowledge of theory is necessary to do an observational study. Actually, although inductive inquiry may require less sophistication to begin with, it places more of a burden on the individual researcher-in-training to develop theory than does the typical deductive survey.

No mode of inquiry is really easier than any other, but each does tap different strengths of the researcher. Your personal research and theoretical interests may influence your choice of method. A researcher setting out to investigate patterns of interaction in a relatively small social system, such as a bar or a service club, may find direct observation of behavior a wholly appropriate way to acquire data. It would certainly be more difficult to use participant observation when investigating the interrelations between the major institutions in a society. As the level of research shifts, so the problems faced by the researcher change. To the extent that a theory is more or less abstract, and more or less verifiable by investigating small social groups or larger institutions, the theory you select will itself help to determine which techniques are appropriate for you to use in gathering data.

TYPES OF INFORMATION AND RESEARCH STRATEGIES. The nature of the information that researchers need may itself help to determine the most appropriate methodology. If you were a sports reporter assigned to cover an important football game, you might go about it in any of several ways. You could record each play in sequence, telling the results of each one. You might compile lists of statistics from the game, including first downs, completed passes, yards gained, and scores for each team. Or you might ask the players what it felt like to be in the game, in order to determine the meaning of victory or defeat for the participants themselves. This example illustrates three of the most important types of information in the social sciences:

> moment-to-moment description of the incidents in which people participate
> the number of the characteristics of persons or events
> people's subjective impressions of social interaction

Let us examine the differences between them, so that we can see how the nature of the data we need affects the selection of specific methods for gathering them.

Incidents are discrete events; describing them from moment to moment gives us histories, or chains of events. Social scientists use this kind of information not only to find out what happened in the distant past, but also to recreate a wide variety of present-day phenomena. These include performances, such as athletic contests; social rituals, such as weddings and funerals; and work activity, such as the mass production of automobiles. Historical data often take the form of a journal or log that provides a record of conversations or other interactions between people, or rich accounts of what they were wearing, what they ate, how active they were, and so forth.

If we count up the characteristics of persons or events, a different sort of picture is created. We might obtain data on numbers of civil and religious ceremonies or on how much food was consumed at each, rather than a moment-to-moment description of any single wedding or group of weddings. We may learn about auto production by, for example, tallying the number of cars completed each hour, rather than by following a single car on the assembly line from start to finish.

Counting gives us two important descriptive statistics, frequency and distribution. A FREQUENCY expresses how often a particular characteristic occurs; a DISTRIBUTION is the range and variation of its occurrence within a population. Last year, for example, there might have been 3,000 weddings in your town (frequency) but many more in some neighborhoods, or among some ethnic groups, than others (distribution). Often these kinds of data are generated when the researcher is more distant from the subjects of investigation than would be the case in obtaining histories firsthand. If we were researching the interaction of workers on the shop floor of a factory, we could record the actual content of conversations as they occurred, if we could get close enough. But even if we could not, we would learn a great deal about the work routine in the factory by simply counting the number of times people conversed (frequency) and noting who talked to whom (distribution).

This last example illustrates the need for another major type of information in some settings: the subjective perceptions of participants in social interaction. Counting up the attributes of persons and things, or writing a moment-to-moment description of events, will not necessarily tell us what it is like to work on the assembly line, from the point of view of the worker. In the factory there are formal and informal codes of conduct to which most people adhere. But even careful observation and recording of dialogue may not reveal whether a worker is complying eagerly and willingly or out of the fear of losing his job. This is one reason why we may need to uncover the subjective meaning of the prevailing rules and norms for the workers themselves. Similarly, the behavior of a bride and groom at a wedding occurs within a cultural setting of which the participants are aware. Relationships between families, between the judge or clergy and the wedding party, or between children and adults, are difficult to separate from the context of existing patterns of power and deference and standards of etiquette. The source of these standards of behavior is the larger society, and the researcher may need to know what the participants think of these standards before the participants' behavior can be fully explained.

These three types of information may be obtained using a variety of methodologies. But a good rule of thumb is that social surveys and content analyses, as we have described them in this chapter, are usually the most effective methodologies for isolating the frequencies and distributions of characteristics within a population. Data about a large number of individuals and groups may be summarized in an efficient manner using these strategies. Although researcher and respondent may interact for only a few minutes in a survey, this is often quite enough time to enumerate just those characteristics that are important for the investigator to know. Generally, more lengthy and sustained contact with individuals or groups, or the use of written, historical materials, is required in order to obtain data about sequences of events. Prolonged observation and interviewing may be necessary to discover the subjective meaning of events for the people who participate in social interaction.

Whatever the topic of your own research, ask yourself which of these broad types of data will help you to understand it most effectively. The answer to this question depends, in part, on the level at which you are using or constructing theory. In many cases you will have a number of options. A single critical event, such as the stock market crash of 1929, may profoundly affect a family, as well as a nation. In this example, as in many others, you would have a choice as a researcher. Would you prefer to spend your time examining the declining employment and income figures for the entire United States during the 1930s in order to determine the impact of the stock market crash? Or would you rather conduct a series of in-depth personal interviews in which you would observe and interact with individuals who lived through the Great Depression? The nature of the data you need might well determine whether yours is to be survey research, content analysis, participant observation, or some other mode of data collection.

SPENDING TIME AND RESOURCES WISELY. There is a story told in jest about a New England state in which the legislature, desperate for revenue and having already taxed every available resource, imposed a tax on air. One frugal Yankee, intent on saving everything possible, suffocated to death! This story has a message for us all as researchers. It is important to use time and money efficiently as we go about our work, but an underfunded study, or one that fails to take the time to contact as many respondents as it should, may be useless and even dangerous.

SAMPLING is one procedure that makes research manageable. When investigators take a sample, they select a relatively small number of cases from the social whole, for enumeration or observation. The television viewing habits of the entire nation may be discovered by sampling the behavior of several hundred families. Sampling saves time and money, and if it is done correctly, it does not prevent us from making accurate generalizations about the population from which the sample is taken. If it is done poorly, sampling may have serious negative consequences. If a political survey does not sample the full variety of voter opinion, it may not accurately predict the outcome of an election. If the true number of low-income households in a community is underestimated by a sample, federal or state aid may be restricted or reduced, causing hardship to the families concerned. As a beginning researcher, your own work may not have this sort of direct impact immediately, but it is still important to understand that your attempts to conserve resources may indeed affect the accuracy of your conclusions.

If investigators have only the time, funds, and staff to perform certain types of methodological procedures, they will be able to acquire only certain types of data. If you are doing a participant observation study of a single organization, you may indeed have enough time to personally call the respondents within the group who have relevant information to give you. If you are doing a social survey, which asks comparatively fewer questions of more people, or if you are performing a content analysis, you will need a sample of sufficient size to permit you to make generalizations about a much larger population or range of data.[2] To sample correctly, you may require the services of several co-workers, or of sophisticated computers and other expensive hardware. You can overcome some of these financial obstacles by performing a secondary analysis of another researcher's data. This procedure is generally less costly than working with PRIMARY DATA, information that you have collected using your own resources. In secondary analysis, data may be manipulated in a manner different from the original research or used for another purpose. These SECONDARY DATA may not, however, contain all of the variables you need, or they may not enable you to measure them in a manner appropriate to your own work.

Some data collection strategies will commit you to spending time and money over a period of months, or even years. This is LONGITUDINAL RESEARCH, which involves the gathering of information at different points in time. The purpose of longitudinal research may be to monitor and predict social change, to compare equivalent populations during different years, or to follow a particular group of people through time to see whether their behavior or attitudes have altered from the time when the research began. To understand changes in consumer spending habits, for example, it is necessary to discover how families budget their income over several years. Surveys of middle-class families are taken periodically. Such TREND STUDIES note the amount of increase in disposable income, major purchases made, and plans for future purchases. We cannot predict trends with confidence unless we gather information over a sufficient period of time. Thus this type of research can be quite costly.

A COHORT STUDY looks at a more specific group of people as it changes over time. One "cohort" whose progress we might wish to follow is women who first obtained employment as a result of the affirmative action legislation of the 1970s. We might sample females in selected occupations every five years to determine their income, promotions, job satisfaction, and so forth. In a cohort study, the specific individuals in each sample differ, although they are all survivors of the original group being investigated.

In a PANEL STUDY, one of the most elaborate longitudinal research designs, the same respondents are followed through time and contacted again and again. An example of a panel study is the examination of the careers of gifted individuals initiated by the psychologist Lewis B. Terman (Goleman, 1980). In 1922 a sample of males and females, aged 3 to 19, with very high IQs was selected and interviewed. Careful track was kept of their whereabouts, so that they could be reinterviewed. Results have been obtained for seven points in time, so that the researchers have compared data from periods when the panel members were completing their education, when they embarked on careers or became parents, and when they were nearing retirement. Subjects were polled to determine their goals in life, whether these aspirations were met, and what careers these very intelligent people found to be most rewarding. The Terman study, which began with a panel of 1470 people, has proven to be a major undertaking. The project has maintained an office and staff on the campus of Stanford University, in California, for nearly sixty years.

Cost is only one factor in the selection of a strategy for data collection, but if it

---

[2]The procedures for determining sample size and selecting samples are explained in Chapter 5.

is your major stumbling block, remember that the cost of doing individual case studies, including in-depth interviewing or participant observation, is likely to be lower than for large-scale survey work. This is particularly significant for apprentice researchers, who typically spend a good deal of time working for little or no pay while they are learning the craft, and who in any event usually have more time than money to spend.

THE OTHER COMPONENTS OF RESEARCH: DATA COLLECTION AND BEYOND

If you are using this chapter as a guide to doing your own research, you will have selected a topic and decided how to go about studying it by now. Consider all the mental and physical energy you have expended, and you have yet to collect even the first bit of information. Experienced researchers spend much of their time thinking about what they are going to do before they actually do it. There is a natural eagerness to go out into the field, but you were wise to prepare, to plan, to review the literature and your own resources. Now you are ready to collect data, and to interpret them.

COLLECTING DATA. In Chapters 6, 7, and 8, we will describe formats for acquiring raw data, using predetermined lists of questions, making tape recordings, or taking detailed notes on behavior that you observe in the field. Sometimes you need do no more than make a series of check marks, or write a series of numbers, on the printed page. On other occasions you may take brief notes that can later be expanded to a rich description of events. In any case the format for data collection should be tailored to the needs of the research. The theory you are testing or constructing, the variables you are examining, and your sources of information all will influence the specific form that your raw data take. As a general rule, the more inductive the research, the less elaborate is the advance preparation of instruments for data collection.

In experimental research the investigator knows when to stop collecting data, since the nature and amount of information required are specified in the research design. In social surveys that utilize only questionnaires to obtain information, the duration of the information-gathering phase of the project will be determined by the length of time required to contact all of the respondents in the sample. The more inductive the investigation, or the more observational techniques employed in data collection, the more ambiguous are the guidelines for bringing data collection to a halt.

Aside from the limitations imposed by our own resources, the data themselves may help us to decide when to wind down the process of accumulating evidence. Observational research is, after all, an adventure (Glazer, 1972), especially in the early stages of data collection. After a time, however, it becomes more routine. The investigator becomes used to the research setting and notices more and more social behavior that, although interesting, is not particularly novel or puzzling. As more data are collected, more questions are answered, and eventually a "saturation" point is reached, at which more data simply do not take the investigator any closer to the solution of the research problem. This is a sure sign that data collection is nearing an end.

ANALYZING AND PROCESSING DATA. At this juncture it may be useful to recall the analogy between researcher and cook. The processing and analysis of data may be compared to cooking because even if two cooks use identical recipes, the results may differ depending on the cooking method, time, and temperature used. Similarly, raw data do not arrange themselves. The researcher groups them together and processes them in a variety of ways, in order to show what they mean and to facilitate their interpretation. Raw data gathered about individuals and institutions may be lumped into categories and the results compared for each group. If we have asked a hundred people how they like their jobs, we may separate the findings for men and women if sex is a relevant variable; or we may divide the answers according to the social class of the respondents, their place of residence, their religion, and so forth. The categories for analysis are largely determined in advance in studies that are primarily deductive; they are allowed to emerge from the data themselves in studies that are basically inductive. Both in participant observation and social survey, however, surprising results are often obtained through imaginative data analysis.

DATA PROCESSING often consists of translating raw information, which may appear in the form of words or descriptions, into letters or numbers that can be manipulated by computer at high speed. This procedure is especially useful with large samples of respondents. Statistical tests may be employed to compare or contrast two or more groupings of data. These tests may tell us whether men's job satisfaction is significantly different from women's, or just how dissatisfied each group is. These procedures may indicate what happens to job satisfaction as socioeconomic status rises, or whether the results for respondents in various parts of the country correlate well with the results for respondents who belong to different religious denominations. Most statistical tests will not yield reliable results when only a small number of respondents have been contacted. Therefore, data analysis with small samples may employ simpler summary measures: percentages, fractions, and ratios. Even with samples of only ten to twenty people, it is still useful to know that 80 percent of those polled prefer one candidate to another, that 60 percent of the members of a certain church committee are women, or that in a particular month divorces in your town outnumbered marriages by a margin of three to one. Note that data analysis may be presented in several different forms, including tables, charts, graphs, recorded dialogue with accompanying comments from the investigator, or a critical essay.

MAKING INFERENCES AND RECOMMENDATIONS. After data have been processed, they are used to draw inferences from behavior. This exercise is called INTERPRETATION. Suppose we find that divorces substantially outnumber marriages. What does this mean for the individuals directly involved, for the community, or for a society as a whole? These are the questions you should begin to think about after data have been collected and processed. Research conclusions or findings are not merely a rehash of the raw data; they should include an assessment of the significance of the data, in terms of the development of theory, the adoption of social policy, or both.

In a study in which deductive procedures have been followed, the results of hypothesis testing should be noted after the data have been processed. Do the data support existing theory, and if so, under what circumstances? How might other studies be designed in order to test the hypotheses still further? What new hypotheses are suggested by the results?

If the investigation has been inductive, this is the place to summarize the process of theory construction. What underlying principles of behavior might explain the data that were collected? In both cases it is appropriate to spell out the policy implications of the findings and conclusions. If, for example, our findings indicate that divorces outnumber marriages, we might predict increases in the number of single-parent families, in the demand for housing space, and in the need for places where single adults may meet each other. These implications follow directly from the data, and may themselves suggest future research.

Putting It All Together

THE FINAL REPORT

Once research is completed, there remains the task of producing a FINAL REPORT, to show the world what has been done. This report cannot tell everything; it summarizes how the investigator has crafted each of the components of research. Often the final report takes the form of a journal article, a paper read at a professional conference, or a fact-finding memorandum to be presented to the agency or organization sponsoring the research. For the student researcher it may be a term paper! Whether done professionally, or as part of a learning exercise, the final report should be an honest recapitulation of your own thoughts, activities, conclusions, recommendations, and suggestions for additional work by other investigators in the area of your interest.

At a minimum the final report should contain the following:

1. a statement of the research problem
2. a review of the literature relating to the problem
3. a theoretical framework for explaining phenomena associated with the problem (developed either deductively from the literature and prior research, or inductively from the present investigation)
4. identification of the major relevant variables (and in a deductive study, specification of the major relevant hypotheses)
5. explanation of the criteria used for measuring these variables, including a summary of the methodology used in the research, specific questions asked of respondents, and so forth
6. an indication of the sampling procedures used, if any, the setting for data collection, and the length of time required to complete the investigation
7. an outline of the manner in which data were processed and analyzed, including statistical tests that were employed, if any
8. the findings or conclusions, emphasizing those that contribute the most to knowledge, theoretically or descriptively; those that have potential for solving social problems; and those that are surprising or that violate conventional wisdom

This outline represents a workable guide for your term paper, as well as a summary of the key elements in most scholarly writing. Let us emphasize that it is a *minimum*; do not be afraid to add elements to your own final report.

As an apprentice researcher you may find it useful to record the process of learning that you experienced as the research progressed. Examples of such self-analysis include answers to the following questions:

1. How did I come upon this particular research problem, and why is it important to me?
2. Which prior research have I accepted, and which have I rejected, entirely or in part, and why?
3. What problems did I encounter in theory construction, or in making additions to existing theory?
4. What anticipated, or unanticipated, difficulties occurred during the data collection phase of the research?
5. What were the limits to my ability to analyze data or to draw inferences from them? How might I proceed differently if I were to begin the same project again?

All social scientists, whether neophytes or veterans, confront each of these questions as they go about their work. Unfortunately, reports of the "natural history" of the actual conduct of social investigation rarely accompany summaries of the research findings. What one typically sees as a finished product is a document that presents only the hypotheses, data, and conclusions in a manner that conceals, rather than reveals, the difficulties and unexpected problems that arise during all social investigations. Many journal articles convey the impression that once we have defined a problem for study and chosen an appropriate data gathering technique, research proceeds trouble-free. Do not be deceived by research reports that fail to relate how projects actually take shape! There are always problems, and although personal experience is a good teacher, we may also learn much from the failures of other investigators—as well as from their successes.

THE UPS AND DOWNS OF RESEARCH

Mistakes, as well as sudden inspirations, are part of the research process (Hammond, 1964; Horowitz, 1969; Jacobs, 1974). Like police detectives, social scientists often have to contend with false leads and dead ends. It is quite common for research design to undergo a number of unanticipated turns and twists, pushing the investigator in new directions. In fact, even the original questions that a particular study was designed to answer may change in subtle ways, or it may become apparent, after a project is well underway, that there are additional questions that need answering.

As research progresses, the investigator may realize that new theoretical insights are called for, or that it is desirable to use data collection strategies quite different from those with which the study began. One may begin by looking at phenomena at one societal level (say, behavior between individuals) and soon realize that certain issues cannot be analyzed only at that level. Thinking about the conditions under which people misinterpret each other's communications, a researcher may find it necessary to examine the respondents' social values. This may lead to an examination of the group affiliations of those being studied. One might, therefore, shift from one level of analysis to another, with the result that new types of data will be needed. A researcher operating from a deductive model of investigation may discover that the questionnaire so painstakingly devised to test a particular hypothesis is not eliciting the information desired; perhaps some in-depth interviews with a selected sample of respondents would solve the problem.

Given the complex scheduling that is often necessary to coordinate a research project, it is no wonder that some social scientists have nightmares about natural disasters (snowstorms, earthquakes) that force delays in data collection. In fact, many disasters can, and do, occur. Anticipated resources, in money or staff, may not materialize, necessitating a redesign of a project after it has begun. It may be impossible to gain access to the individuals from whom data are needed, whether they be inmates in a prison, business executives, or politicians. Or we may obtain access, only to discover that our presence has upset the status quo among respondents to the point where we cannot obtain reliable information about their usual behavior.[3]

The lesson to be learned here is that you should not become discouraged if things do not go just as you planned them. Whether your work is primarily deductive or inductive, there is still plenty of room for surprises, as well as the potential for "spinning your wheels" in frustration. Remember, however, that the same flexibility that allows for the possibility of error, and for the occurrence of the unexpected, also allows for creativity. Your individual effort and inspiration *can* make a difference in the outcome of research.

AN EXAMPLE: A STUDY OF UNDERGRADUATE LIFE

The goal of this chapter has been to help you to grapple with the issues in research design. Your personal experiences will, of course, depend on your own resources, talents, and interests. It may be instructive, however, to describe the natural history of an ongoing project conducted by one of the authors and his colleagues—a project that took shape even as this chapter was being written. What follows is an illustration of how professional investigators deal with the issues we have been discussing in this chapter.

HOW WAS THE TOPIC SELECTED? The examination of undergraduate student life outlined here actually was inspired by a very ordinary event: lunchtime conversation among a group of professors. The discussion centered around the topic of university students, but it was not at all systematic or academic. Obviously, students are frequently the subject of faculty's interest and speculation. On this particular day, and given the curiosity of the particular group of professors who participated, certain puzzling themes emerged from the conversation. Based on gossip from secondhand sources, and on occasional, brief conversations with students outside the classroom, a disturbing vision of undergraduate student life was expressed. A number of students reported that they had cheated on examinations and term papers; an anti-intellectual attitude was said to exist in some students. Their social life was described as centering not around regular or occasional dating in couples, but around rituals of partying that sometimes occupied three or four nights a week. There was concern expressed about alcoholism, and about general student alienation from peers, from the faculty, and from the university. Most of those present left the table with a feeling of unease. They did not know how much of what they had heard, or spoken, was actually true. It was apparent that very little was known about how undergraduate university students

---

[3]Ethical issues of social research are discussed in Chapter 4.

in the 1980s view themselves, their schools, and their prospects for the future. Is college the place for learning and intellectual growth that so many university catalogs describe? Or is it experienced primarily as a ritual of necessary steps toward future employment, as a passage from late adolescence into adulthood, or simply as a place to "hang out"?

Later that day, and for the next few days, some of the professors met again to explore the idea of doing a systematic study in order to answer these questions. As a potential topic for research, undergraduate life had several attractions for these researchers. First, it was intrinsically interesting to them; because they share much of the university setting with students and interact with them constantly, it would be of concrete help to the professors to understand student behavior better. Moreover, the topic had wider social significance. Whatever was discovered might be useful to students and their parents, teachers, and administrators at many institutions of higher learning. As a result of these initial meetings, three of the professors decided to put something on paper, a proposal for research, mostly to get clear in their own minds just what they would be investigating, and why. At this point they still had not specified the variables they would be using to assess student behavior and attitudes.

HOW WAS THE TOPIC CONCEPTUALIZED? The first step in isolating the variables for investigation was a brainstorming exercise, in which the researchers, individually and together, wrote down all of the possible, logical components of the concept *student life*. They produced a document in which the following eleven major variables were defined:

1. *the classroom experience* and its impact on activities and attitudes outside the classroom
2. *student aspirations and values,* and in particular the extent of conformity or rebellion in relation to the larger society
3. *students' use of time*: How, with whom, and where do undergraduates spend time?
4. *students use of space*: Where are students found; where do they like to be; how do they use the facilities of the university?
5. *social differentiation* in the student population: the subworlds of residence, race and ethnicity, income, sex and age
6. *interpersonal relationships*: including friendships, dating, and shared sexuality
7. *the use of student services* (counseling, health care, advisement, etc.): Who uses which services, and why?
8. *religion*: changes in spirituality, belief, and practice
9. *social control*: enacting and enforcing the formal and informal rules that restrict behavior
10. *extracurricular activities*: student government and organizations, as well as athletics
11. *leisure*: partying, playing, and recreation

There is some overlapping of categories in this list (e.g., several of the variables are related to students' use of time). Moreover, although it covers much conceptual territory, the list is not exhaustive. One may imagine other variables, including students' relations with their families, or with the community bordering on the university, which were not directly specified. It should be remembered, however, that the list is a preliminary one. There is a strong element of induction in the way these researchers are proceeding. The list of variables may be changed or whittled down and the definitions made specific, as the research progresses.

Conceptualization of the topic was influenced primarily by the investigators' own interests and their prior training and experience. In fact, a basic, deductive model of inquiry was rejected early on because little research has been done on this topic in recent years and because there is no well-developed theory of student behavior and attitude formation. A number of studies conducted by sociologists and educators have appeared, but the vast proportion of social science research on college life precedes the major upheavals of the 1960s and 1970s in American society. The topic was indeed broadly defined initially, in order not to miss relevant information about the influence upon student life of changes in morality, sex roles, norms of student political activity, and career opportunities.

How Was a Strategy for Data Collection Selected? Although previous studies suggested some effective strategies for obtaining specific kinds of information in the college setting, the researchers decided to employ a variety of methods in this instance, in order to cast as wide a net as possible for the collection of data, and to capture the total college experience. The researchers planned to obtain information about individual students via several techniques: participant observation of their daily routine, survey interviewing, and examination of records and documents.

The planning of this study of undergraduate life illustrates the point made earlier in this chapter that theory helps to determine the type of information required by investigators, and that this, in turn, has an impact on the scope and costs of research. Initially, all levels of theory were explored in the attempt to explain student behavior and to suggest data collection strategies. If major social trends were thought to have affected student life within the university, then data would be needed about the larger society, for example, the availability of jobs and the income of families sending their children to college. If students' actions and attitudes were to be seen as a function of the structure and priorities of the college in which they enroll, then detailed data about the college would be called for, such as admissions practices, grading policies, disciplinary procedures, and the history of the college. The frequency and distribution of particular behaviors among the student population would have to be measured. Finally, if student behavior were conceptualized primarily in social psychological terms, that is, as exchange and communication among individuals, then detailed information about interpersonal episodes and encounters would comprise the data. The researchers would have to be near students when they felt pressure, pain, and anxiety; wondered about their futures; and experienced their pleasures. In fact, because of the wide range of theory that could potentially explain student behavior, there were no restrictions placed on data sources during the early planning of the project. Dormitories, student discos, cafeterias, classrooms, the libraries and administrative offices of the university—all were potential valuable settings for the collection of data.

It is significant to note that up to this point there had been little or no discussion among the researchers regarding financial support for the project. They estimated that such a wide-ranging study would take from three to five years to conduct. Such longitudinal research is expensive. Even if the professors involved donated their time and recruited graduate students to help out, the costs would be substantial. As these words are being written, the project is under review. If its scope can be scaled down to the point where the research is manageable in practical terms, it will likely proceed with vigor and high hopes. At the same time it is well to recognize that the extent of available research resources helps to determine what sorts of data may be collected, and that this, in turn, has an impact on the theoretical significance of the project. We can say a great deal more about students, and society as a whole, after having conducted a five-year study employing several techniques of data collection than we can after having spent, say, one year only digging in university records, or only talking to students or to administrators.

ISSUES OF DATA COLLECTION. Even as the project takes shape conceptually and financially, some concrete proposals for collecting data from students and from the university are being laid on the table. These are particularly interesting because of the ethical issues they raise. It has been suggested, for instance, that graduate students in social science departments be appointed as resident assistants in undergraduate dormitories. From this vantage point they could note those aspects of student life that revolve around residence halls, leisure time, friendships, and so forth. This seems like a good idea, if students do not feel that they are being spied on. Suppose the graduate students discover some prohibited activity occurring in the dormitories. Are they obligated to report it to university authorities? This issue is especially vexing if the researchers are accepting financial aid from the university.

Another proposal involves a course that undergraduates could take for credit, entitled "Student Life." Its manifest purposes would be to acquaint the class with the full range of student behavior and opportunities on campus and for students to study their own behavior and that of their peers in a systematic way. In addition, those enrolled in the course would be required to write papers about their own experiences. This seems to be an effective way to generate data about student aims and attitudes, and to open up many of the themes of the research project for discussion among groups of undergraduates. Ethically, it raises the dilemma of students being "paid" (in course credits) for information. How reliable would these data be? Clearly, to be part of a scientific investigation, the information produced in the "Student Life" course would have to be cross-checked via other data sources, either observational or secondary.

A third proposal would use data obtained from university files. A sample of undergraduates might be selected at admission, and followed through their four years at college. In this manner their behavior and values could be matched with demographic factors such as their place of residence, ethnicity, and parents' income. A college may be willing to supply this sort of information for a bona fide research project, particularly if student records are kept confidential. Should students be given the opportunity of refusing to participate?

These ethical issues have to be added to the equation, along with any financial limitations or conceptual problems, to determine whether or not to proceed with the project. The preliminary work described above has been intriguing, and even enlightening, for the participants, but they need to answer a number of important questions of research design before substantial resources are expended or commitments made. We cannot say just how the proposed study of undergraduate life will turn out. If we could tell you, there would be no need to conduct the research in the first place! What we can predict with some certainty is that in order to be successful, the project will undergo changes in focus, in methodology, and/or in theory, as the research situation demands.

This example illustrates the complexity and diversity, as well as the promise, of social research. It also shows that there are countless conceptual recipes, and that the ingredients of each may be combined in many ways and still adhere to the principles of the scientific method. The "research cookbook" is, alas, not foolproof. Do not become discouraged if your own work comes out "underdone" or "overdone" at first. It takes practice to draw all the possible valid inferences from a set of data, or to avoid belaboring the obvious. With a little imagination, persistence, curiosity, and the wise use of time, many a study that seems hopelessly bogged down can be transformed into something useful.

Summary

This chapter outlines the specific components of research, from selecting and conceptualizing a topic, to writing a final report in which the data collected on that topic have been processed, analyzed, and interpreted. Initially, social scientists specify a research problem—the questions concerning the topic that they believe are most important to answer. This problem is further refined by identifying the most appropriate variables and by defining them operationally so that they may be measured. Then, a theory showing how each of the variables relates to the others may be constructed inductively or be adapted from prior studies or from the literature. Practice is required to be able to evaluate the theoretical explanations in many professional journals, but if one's work is to become part of the accumulation of scientific knowledge, the effort is worth it.

Four major strategies of data collection are survey research, participant observation, content analysis, and experimentation. Selecting a particular strategy depends in part on how much inductive inquiry one is prepared to conduct, and on the level of social interaction one wishes to observe. The sources of available data and the type of information sought also affect selection of method, since certain kinds of data are more easily obtained with surveys, for example, than with observational techniques.

No mode of inquiry is inherently easier than another; each taps different talents of the investigator and is compatible with different research interests. Resources (in money and staff) also play a part in the planning of any project, because some research designs are inherently less expensive, or typically take less time, than others. It is wise to weigh the possible conceptual and methodological problems of studying a chosen topic carefully before actually going out into the field, in order to minimize the unexpected, but inevitable, difficulties that can arise. Even in deductive social surveys, where the size of the sample to be contacted is known, and the questions to be asked are determined in advance, there are often difficulties in obtaining access to respondents, or ethical dilemmas for the researcher to ponder.

Data, once collected, are in their "raw" state and must be processed in order to show what their significance is and to make interpretation easier. The conclusion of social science research ought to be more than a mere summary of the data gathered. It should include an assessment of the new information as it relates to theory, social policy, or both. The final written report of social investigation cannot restate everything that has occurred, but it should show how each of the components of research was crafted. It should be an honest recapitulation of the investigator's thoughts, activities, conclusions, and recommendations and suggestions for additional work by others.

Key Terms

cohort study	final report	raw data
concept	frequency	research design
conceptualization	interpretation	research problem
content analysis	longitudinal research	sampling
data processing	operational definition	secondary data
distribution	panel study	social survey
enumeration	participant observation	topic
experimentation	primary data	trend study

Exercises

1. Review some of the professional journals in your field and select two articles for analysis according to the research cookbook. How did the authors of the articles craft each of the seven essential components of social investigation listed in Table 2.1? In your opinion, which article reflects more research skill and insight, and why?

2. Using the same two articles as in question 1, indicate whether the primary motivation for each study was to add to theory or to solve some problem of social policy. How do you know?

3. Select one of the following three topics and describe how you would conceptualize it:
  "Political Apathy in America"
  "Is There an Energy Crisis?"
  "Are Men and Women Equal?"
Hint: Begin by identifying the variables that might represent the concepts *apathy*, *crisis*, or *equality*.

4. Let us assume that you are planning to use this chapter as a guide to conducting your own research. Answer the following:

What is your topic?
How would you conceptualize it?
Which of the four major strategies of data collection do you feel is most appropriate for you and why?

5. Look through a newspaper or magazine and select five pictures that represent particular concepts. What concept do you think each picture represents? Give two *different* conceptual interpretations of each picture.

6. Locate three different sources of data for each of the following variables:
  personal influence
  success in school
  racial discrimination

7. Briefly write down how you would resolve the ethical dilemmas raised by the study of undergraduate life. Now read Chapter 4 and answer the question again. What have you learned?

8. By yourself or with others, plan and carry out a study of faculty life at your college or university.

Suggested Readings

Backstrom, Charles H., and Gerald D. Hursh
1963 *Survey Research*. Evanston, Ill.: Northwestern University Press.
    One of the best short guides to the logic and planning of social surveys.
Bynner, John, and Keith M. Stribley, eds.
1979 *Social Research: Principles and Procedures*. New York: Longman.
    A thought-provoking collection of classic essays on methodological topics. See especially Chapters 6 to 11.
Hammond, Philip E., ed.
1964 *Sociologists at Work*. New York: Basic Books.
    Lively and informative natural his-

tories describing how several professional researchers actually went about their work.

Horowitz, Irving Louis, ed.
1969   *Sociological Self-Images: A Collective Portrait.* Beverly Hills, Calif.: Sage.
       Similar to Hammond, but devotes more attention to the intellectual development of researchers as their careers have evolved.

Jacobs, Jerry, ed.
1974   *Deviance: Field Studies and Self-Disclosures.* Palo Alto, Calif.: National Press Books.
       Natural histories of participant observations of deviant behavior. These are exercises in self-analysis.

Stern, Paul C.
1979   *Evaluating Social Science Research.* New York: Oxford University Press.

The goal of this book is to enable students to critically review the research literature in areas of their interest. The evaluation of social science is presented as a series of skills that can be mastered in sequence.

Wuebben, Paul L., et al., eds.
1974   *The Experiment as a Social Occasion.* Berkeley, Calif.: Glendessary Press.
       Comprehensive collection of writings about experimentation, its promise and limitations.

Zelditch, Morris, Jr.
1962   "Some Methodological Problems of Field Studies." *American Journal of Sociology* 67:566–576.
       A brief guide to the various types of information in the social sciences.

References

Backstrom, Charles H., and Gerald D. Hursh
1963   *Survey Research.* Evanston, Ill.: Northwestern University Press.

Berelson, Bernard
1952   *Content Analysis in Communication Research.* Glencoe, Ill.: Free Press.

Glazer, Myron
1972   *The Research Adventure: Promise and Problems of Field Work.* New York: Random House.

Goleman, Daniel
1980   "1,528 Little Geniuses and How They Grew." *Psychology Today* (February).

Hammond, Philip E., ed.
1964   *Sociologists at Work.* New York: Basic Books.

Horowitz, Irving Louis, ed.
1969   *Sociological Self-Images: A Collective Portrait.* Beverly Hills, Calif.: Sage.

Jacobs, Jerry, ed.
1974   *Deviance: Field Studies and Self-Disclosures.* Palo Alto, Calif.: National Press Books.

Miller, Arthur H.
1979   "The Institutional Focus of Political Distrust." Paper presented at the annual meeting of the American Political Science Association.

Weitzman, Leonore J., and Deborah Eifler
1972   "Sex Role Socialization in Picture Books for Pre-School Children." *American Journal of Sociology* 77 (May):1125–1144.

Wuebben, Paul L., et al., eds.
1974   *The Experiment as a Social Occasion.* Berkeley, Calif.: Glendessary Press.

Zelditch, Morris, Jr.
1962   "Some Methodological Problems of Field Studies." *American Journal of Sociology* 67:566–576.

Zimbardo, Philip G.
1972   "Pathology of Imprisonment." *Society* 9 (April):4–8.

3 / Measurement in Social Research

CHAPTER OUTLINE

INTRODUCTION
LEVELS OF MEASUREMENT
Nominal Measures
Ordinal Measures
Interval Measures
Ratio Measures
Precision and Accuracy
OPERATIONALIZATION
Example: Assessing Excellence in
Education
Example: Assessing Happiness
Behavioral Indicators
EVALUATING RELIABILITY AND
VALIDITY
The Criterion of Reliability
The Criterion of Validity

SOURCES OF MEASUREMENT
ERROR
Random Error
Systematic Error
Situational Error
Measurement Error and the Research
Process
Problems of Face Validity
Problems of Reliability in the
Research Instrument
Researcher Bias
Respondent Bias
Lying as a Source of Error
Error Arising from Special
Circumstances
Errors in Data Processing

THE SITUATIONAL NATURE OF
VARIABLES
Measurement in the Physical and
Social Sciences
Lack of Consensus in Measurement
IMPROVING THE QUALITY OF
MEASUREMENT
Triangulation
Using a Variety of Methods
SUMMARY
KEY TERMS
EXERCISES
SUGGESTED READINGS
REFERENCES

Introduction

MEASUREMENT is the process of determining dimension, value, or degree. To find the height of a man, the price of a piece of property, or the temperature outside on a winter day, we need measuring devices—yardsticks, calculators thermometers—as well as units of measurement—inches, dollars, and degrees. Social scientists may encounter many problems in selecting both the tools and the units of measurement. It is usually more difficult for us to agree about the dimensions, value, and degree of human behavior, attitudes, and ideas than about the physical description of people, the size of things, or the characteristics of the physical environment. It is, however, essential that an attempt be made to perfect the tools and categories of measurement in social science. If theories of social action are to be accepted as reasonable explanations, and if we are to test these theories systematically, we must use measurement procedures that are adequate to the task.

As noted earlier, there are many ways of gauging complex variables such as *violent crime, freedom, mental illness,* or *political popularity.* A craftsperson in the tool and die industry must often be accurate to one ten-thousandth of an inch in making the parts for a complex machine. By contrast, in the social sciences there is no absolute standard. The manner in which behavior and attitudes are measured will vary depending on the purpose of the investigation. However, craftsmen and women in social research do share one skill with their counterparts in industry: they often have to design their own measurement tools and to adapt them to specialized situations. Thus in discussing problems of measurement, this chapter deals with the creation of new measures, as well as with the selection of those that are "tried and true."

Another problem faced in all science is information loss during the process of measurement itself. As a child, you may have played the game "Telephone," in which an originally clear message was whispered from person to person until, by the end of the line, it had become unrecognizable. This is a danger we face continually in social research. Each time we process words, opinions, or pictures, we may be destroying some of the original evidence on which our findings must be based. Some loss is perhaps inevitable, but we need to guard against the disappearance of vital information caused by errors in recording, transmitting, conceptualizing, and storing data.

Keep these central issues—the choice of measuring device, standards for measurement, and the potential for information loss—in mind as we consider the following topics in this chapter: (1) *the various levels of measurement,* and what sort of data is appropriate to each; (2) *operationalization*—saying exactly how each variable we are using will be measured; (3) problems of *reliability,* or consistency, in our measures, and of *validity,* making sure that we are measuring the variables that we wish to measure; (4) sources of measurement *error,* particularly errors that may occur again and again unless their sources are found and eliminated; (5) difficulties in defining variables in research; and (6) suggestions for improving the quality of measurement in the social sciences.

Levels of Measurement

There are four general levels of measurement—nominal, ordinal, interval, and ratio—each level providing us with a different kind of information. We need to be aware of the advantages and limitations of each.

NOMINAL MEASURES

At the simplest level, categories are generated so that we may determine whether the objects of investigation are the same or not. These are called NOMINAL measures. "Male" and "female" are nominal categories, as are one's birthplace, religion, race, position on a team, eye color, and political affiliation. Indeed, the variety of nominal categories is immense. One criterion for nominal measures is that they must be MUTUALLY EXCLUSIVE; a person is either a man *or* a woman, has blue eyes *or* brown eyes, plays first base *or* shortstop, and so on. The other criterion for nominal categories is that they be EXHAUSTIVE, in that every person or thing observed may be classified. Suppose our variable is *state of birth* and it has fifty categories corresponding to the fifty states. As long as our sample includes only people who were born in the United States, who know the state they were born in, and who report it accurately, the criterion for a nominal level of measurement is met. If we add a fifty-first category designated as "other," our revised variable achieves the nominal level even if some of the respondents were born outside the country.

The best nominal measures isolate similarities and differences and are designed to minimize the number of ambiguous cases. Denoting "male" and "female" is quite adequate for almost all individuals, although it does not clearly separate out hermaphrodites and transsexuals from the rest of the population.

ORDINAL MEASURES

In addition to distinguishing units as being the same or different from one another, we often wish to make statements as to whether they possess "more" or "less" of a particular attribute. This level of measurement is called ORDINAL because it allows us to place people or things along a continuum from the greatest amount to the smallest amount of the characteristic we are measuring. We may say that people are young, middle-aged, or old; thin, of average weight, or fat; and so on. It is possible to measure even more complex concepts ordinally. If we were interested in describing citizens of a town in terms of their prestige in the community, we could include an item on a questionnaire that asked a group of judges to rank individuals accordingly. Based on these data, citizens might then be placed in the ordinal categories of "high," "medium," or "low" prestige. Other concepts that may be ranked in terms of their degree or intensity are athletic skill, intelligence, leadership, political liberalism, the tendency to conform, tolerance for pain, and sense of humor. It is easy to see why most variables dealt with by the social scientist are of the ordinal type.

INTERVAL MEASURES

We can do more than categorize responses (at the nominal level) or rank order them (at the ordinal level). It is also often possible to measure the distance between the rankings, so that we can know not only that one response is lower or higher than another, but *how much* lower or higher it is. This is the INTERVAL level of measurement. In contrast with ordinal designations, the difference in interval rankings is expressed in units that have some absolute value and that remain constant from the bottom of the rankings to the top. Thus the variable *temperature* may be expressed intervally in degrees Fahrenheit, and a degree's difference is the same between 40° and 41° as between 80° and 81°. Obviously, if we are dealing with more complex variables, such as prejudice or conformity or intelligence level, it becomes more difficult to specify the value of the units that separate one rank from another. The IQ (intelligence quotient) score is an attempt to measure aptitude at the interval level. Each IQ point has the same value.

RATIO MEASURES

The highest and most precise level of measurement is the RATIO. It allows us to distinguish among persons or objects not only by adding and subtracting units of rank, as in the case of degrees or IQ points, but by using multiplication and division as well. We may say that Mrs. A weighs *twice* as much as Mrs. B, or that Mrs. X is *half* as old as Mrs. Y, because ratio scales have a "true zero" point. Variables such as age, weight, and income do not have an arbitrary zero. A baby about to be born has no age; a penniless person may be completely without income; using a centrifuge, we may produce a state of "weightlessness." By contrast, we may measure prejudice with interval-level precision, using a questionnaire, but we would be hard pressed to state that a respondent had no prejudice at all (the zero point on the scale). Similarly, we cannot say that a person with an IQ of 80 is half as intelligent as a person with an IQ of 160.

PRECISION AND ACCURACY

Regardless of the level of measurement employed, measures should always be accurate. They should also be as precise as possible, given the limitations of time and resources available for research. Let us examine these two interrelated ideas. In everyday language, to be accurate is also to be precise. We ask, "Precisely how tall are you?" and we expect an accurate answer, say, "Five feet four inches tall." But, in fact, precision and accuracy, as they are considered in science, are not the same.

When measures are PRECISE, they are expressed in fine degrees. Consider these two responses to the question, "What time is it?"

"A little after ten o'clock."

"Fourteen minutes and twenty seconds after ten."

The second answer is the more precise one. A building may be described as being 737 feet high, instead of simply as being tall; a crowd may be reported as containing 10,875 people, rather than being called a multitude; a person may be noted as being born in Provo, Utah, rather than just west of the Rockies.

The highest possible degree of precision is not absolutely essential in all social research. Sometimes it will be sufficient to use ordinal categories, for example, to note that families in a particular neighborhood are "poor," rather than specifying their income, or that certain foodstuffs are "unaffordable," without stating their prices. Usually, however, it is important to reach as high a level of measurement as our data permit, in order to reduce information loss and to legitimately apply the more powerful statistical techniques in data analysis. We may construct ordinal measures from interval or ratio scales, but we may not be able to reverse the process. Knowing the exact vote tally for candidates in an election, we might decide to label them "high," "medium," or "low" in popularity. But unless we are careful in preserving the original data and in recording the guidelines for the assignment of each candidate to the ordinal categories, the exact election figures may be lost forever.

Although it is generally important to be precise, the decision to use one level of measurement instead of another often depends on practical considerations, such as how precise we really need to be and whether appropriate measuring tools are available. This decision is one of the many that have to be made in the planning of research. Perhaps the energy and money required to increase precision would be better spent in broadening the scope of a study or in increasing the number of variables being considered.

ACCURACY differs from precision in that it is simply the correspondence between our measure of some phenomenon and the actual thing, person, or event. A totally accurate measure is a mirror image of the original. If my sleeve length is, in fact, 35 inches, and two tailors measure it, the more accurate result will be the one most closely approaching 35 inches. Precision and accuracy are logically related, because the more precise a measuring tool is, the easier it may be to achieve absolute accuracy. But do not confuse these two ideas. It is possible for measures expressed in extremely precise terms to be grossly inaccurate. If a building described as being 726.5 feet tall is actually 710 feet high, we have an example of a precise, yet inaccurate, measure. It is important to recognize this distinction, since in evaluating reports issued by government or business, or in watching television advertisements, we are often persuaded of the accuracy of numbers merely by the degree of precision with which they are expressed.

Operationalization

In Chapter 2 we noted that each variable in social investigation has to be defined in order for us to recognize and understand it when we see it in the data collection phase of research. The process of arriving at a measure for a variable is referred to as OPERATIONALIZATION. Let us examine this process in greater detail.

EXAMPLE: ASSESSING EXCELLENCE IN EDUCATION

Suppose we are doing a study of excellence in American college education. How could we define the variable *excellence* in such a way that it could actually be used as a measuring tool to separate out the excellent schools from those which are merely good, average, or poor? These are nominal measurement categories that have no intrinsic meaning until we specify the INDICATORS, or criteria, used to assess excellence. To formulate a list of such indicators, we might say that the "excellent college" is one that:

1. is highly selective
    a. requires that 80 percent of the entering freshman class have combined mathematics and verbal Scholastic Aptitude test scores of at least 1200 in order to be admitted.
    b. requires that 80 percent of students in each entering class were in the top 10 percent of their graduating high school classes
2. has a well-qualified faculty
    a. 90 percent of full-time instructors possess a Ph.D. or its equivalent in their field of expertise
    b. books and articles written by the faculty are regularly reviewed in recognized journals
3. has substantial academic and financial resources
    a. a library of at least one million volumes
    b. laboratories and research facilities in the top 20 percent of all universities surveyed
    c. scholarship aid offered to at least 40 percent of each entering class

4. has a superior reputation
   a. recommended as excellent by a panel of one hundred university presidents
   b. graduates' starting salaries in their fields of interest are in the top 20 percent for graduates of all American universities

To some degree the selection of appropriate indicators calls for guessing on the part of the researcher, particularly in the absence of prior studies or of a well-articulated theory that is being tested. A problem we always face in our efforts to operationalize a complex variable is that we can never be sure that the indicators named adequately reflect the presence or absence of the characteristic we wish to measure. Obviously, the number of potential indicators of a variable are many. In our example we did not mention living accommodations, athletic facilities and programs, and advisement and counseling services, all of which may be legitimately construed as being part of excellence in education.

The point is that when we operationalize any variable, we cannot be all-inclusive; we have to limit our definition according to our theory or to the purposes of the research. Given the fine reputation of schools such as Cal Tech, MIT, and the University of Chicago, it might be argued that Division I varsity athletic programs in football and basketball are not part of excellence. If, on the other hand, we do include the availability of some kind of sports activity as an indicator, then even the absence of an intramural sports program may be enough to disqualify a particular institution from the overall category of excellence.

A second point is that operational definitions must be unambiguous: they must state *exactly* the criteria for inclusion or exclusion. Note that in each part of our definition of excellence, these criteria are spelled out. "Highly selective" relates to actual test scores and properties of each entering class; a "well-qualified faculty" is one that has obtained a specific proportion of advanced degrees. It is not enough to describe the academic or financial resources of a school as "substantial"; these too are expressed concretely. Similarly, the "reputation" of the excellent college is not verified by asking just anyone, but by eliciting the opinions of a particular group of people. Of course, you or any other observer are free to disagree with these measures and to substitute ones you feel are more valid. But the operational definitions of all new variables must be at least as specific and explicit as those they replace. In this manner the researcher's choice of measurement tools may be evaluated.

EXAMPLE: ASSESSING HAPPINESS

If we wish to examine the complex and sensitive variable *human happiness,* the same principles apply. We may decide, for instance, that the ability to function successfully during the day, or a strong sense of self-esteem, or a feeling of general well-being are all reasonable indicators of happiness. How do we determine whether the individuals we observe manifest these capacities and attitudes, and to what degree? Our choice of measures is not restricted to nominal categories. We may, in fact, use ordinal measures to compare attitudes among individuals.

The sources of data that become the indicators for variables in social research are many. They may be actual behaviors, written records, or attitudes expressed

TABLE 3.1

We have listed below two statements. Please circle the number that best describes how you feel about each of these statements. For each of these statements you may *strongly agree* (SA = 1), *agree* (A = 2), *be neutral* (N = 3), *disagree* (D = 4), or *strongly disagree* (SD = 5).

	SA	A	N	D	SD
I often feel depressed during the day.	1	2	3	4	5
Sometimes I wish that I were someone else.	1	2	3	4	5

in interviews or on questionnaires. We may administer an attitude survey to a selected sample of people and use their responses to operationalize the variable *happiness*. Then we may assign numbers to the responses that reflect the strength of the presence of the attitude under investigation. The form and content of such questions may vary, but anyone who has ever answered an attitude survey has probably seen questions like those in Table 3.1. After these have been answered, we have a score for each question for each respondent that runs from 1 (for those we classify as least happy) to 5 (for those we classify as most happy). For certain purposes we may want to total the scores to get an overall index score of happiness.[1]

BEHAVIORAL INDICATORS

Because people sometimes say one thing and do another, it is important to corroborate self-reported indicators of attitudes with some other measure. Perhaps people are not as happy as they report. Generally, what people *do* is a more convincing indicator than what they *say* they do, and it is highly desirable to use such BEHAVIORAL INDICATORS when possible. In their studies of the American soldier, Samuel Stouffer and others wanted to know the extent to which men inducted into the armed forces maintained an attachment to civilian life. The researchers could have asked the men directly, but they perceived that the subjects might be reluctant to reveal their true attitudes. Instead, the investigators measured the soldiers' preference for wearing military uniforms while on furlough. The researchers felt that those who were more tied to civilian life would choose not to remain in uniform when on leave. This is an eloquent behavioral indicator of the attitude of attachment (Merton and Lazarsfeld, 1950).

Evaluating Reliability and Validity

When we set out to measure a particular attribute, any differences among the people we study should reflect "true" differences on that attribute. If we were measuring mental health status, all the differences among individuals' scores on

---

[1]See the discussion of indexing in Chapter 15.

our mental health inventory (or on whatever measure we were using) would, ideally, reflect actual differences in their mental health. Or if we were measuring peoples' intelligence, any measured differences in the results of an IQ test would represent true differences in their intelligence. If this could be accomplished, we would have achieved a perfect state of measurement, maximum validity and reliability. In a perfect state of measurement, differences among people would be entirely the result of the variable in which we were interested; they would not reflect "chance" variation (variation due to the effects of factors unknown to the investigator) or the process of investigation itself. From Chapter 1 recall that RELIABILITY and VALIDITY are among the canons of scientific investigation. They are criteria used by social researchers in evaluating the quality of their measures. A good measure is one that is consistent, that can be used over and over again with comparable results (reliability). A good measure reflects accurately what exists in the observable world, and only that part of the world that we have decided is important to measure (validity). Scientific theories stand or fall in terms of our ability to make reliable and valid measurements.

THE CRITERION OF RELIABILITY

We have already mentioned that the use of survey questionnaires has become increasingly popular over the past generation, in part because of their positive effect on reliability. With a properly administered questionnaire, one is assured that the identical questions are asked of each respondent, a necessity for consistency in social research. Asking the same questions, however, although necessary to maximize reliability, is no guarantee of it.

One factor known to affect reliability is the personal state of the subject when the data are collected. If one were to take college board examinations twice and receive somewhat different scores, part of the difference would probably reflect changes in one's mood, alertness, physical and emotional well-being, and anxiety. This would mean that the test had less than perfect reliability because of its sensitivity to extraneous factors. Variations in the environment and in data gathering procedures themselves may also affect reliability adversely. The weather, time of year, environment, appearance or approach of an interviewer, can all vary from one administration of an instrument to the next. Although we cannot completely control these factors, if we know how they influence the data, we can measure them and correct for their influence as we analyze the data.

Because part of the change in results from one test to the next may reflect a true change in the subject, rather than just less than perfect reliability of the measure, it is extremely difficult to gauge reliability precisely by the so-called TEST-RETEST method of comparing scores. This is a constant problem in measuring either change or reliability, and there is no simple solution to it. Sometimes the confusion resolves itself, as when the test and the retest are close enough together in time that imputing significant change to the subject makes little or no sense. Sometimes the direction of change in scores unmistakably indicates a reliability problem, as when a person's IQ appears to drop twenty points within a week.

A second method of testing reliability is available when a survey instrument is fashioned from a number of subparts, all of which are expected to measure essentially the same thing. Such is the case with most test batteries, in which a number of questions are designed to get at the same phenomenon. Reliability is tested by computing how closely the items tend to resemble one another in the results they produce. This is done in a variety of ways. Each item can be correlated[2] with every other item and an average inter-item correlation can be reported as a RELIABILITY COEFFICIENT.

THE CRITERION OF VALIDITY

In practice, social scientists have concentrated much attention on problems of reliability and too little attention on matters of validity. The reason for this is quite simple. We know how to conceptualize and deal with reliability, but we feel at a loss to pin down validity with testing operations.

Part of the problem with judgments about validity stems from a proliferation of terminology. Since validity cannot be tested directly, there have sprung up a variety of ways to test it indirectly. To add to the confusion, different authors sometimes use a variety of terms to describe the same criterion. We may reduce the assortment of terms to three basic approaches—content, pragmatic, and construct validation.

CONTENT VALIDITY, sometimes referred to as FACE VALIDITY, refers to whether a question or type of measure appears to be valid "on the face of it." In other words, content validity depends on the plausibility of a measuring strategy in the eyes of researchers or their critics. The more complicated and disputable the concept, the more any judgment about the content validity of a measure is likely to reflect the predispositions, status, and role of the researcher.

Consider the problem of measuring the quality of academic performance. If six different professors were to construct comprehensive examinations for introductory psychology students, there would be a great deal of divergence as to what was deemed important and worthy of emphasis on each of the exams. The exams might say more about the individuals who made them up than they do about students' knowledge of psychology per se. Each instructor would probably judge his or her own test to be most valid and would doubtless offer solid logic to back up this claim. Hence content validation is often less a real testing procedure than a method of justification and legitimation.

The essential problem with face validity is that it assumes, rather than proves, that the content of a measure is obvious. Can we ever be sure of the obvious? A good example of the dangers of such an assumption is afforded by the comprehension tests given to people at the conclusion of some commercial "speed reading" programs. Such tests are designed to prove that the course has increased reading speed several times without any loss of comprehension. A standard ploy over the years has been to give comprehension tests by having participants read passages about subjects of which they can be expected to have some prior knowledge (such as a basic point from American history or a biographical sketch of Abraham Lincoln). Another ploy is that the comprehension questions asked are often framed in a way so that common sense comes close to suggesting the answer. It has thus been shown that people reading fast and people reading at a slow, normal pace score about the same on these tests. In fact, people who have

---

[2]See Chapter 16 for a discussion of correlation.

never seen or read the passages also get about the same comprehension scores as the other two groups.

On the face of it such a test clearly deals with the topic at hand, and it would appear to be a valid measure of comprehension even though it has virtually no discriminatory power. It is only when we create and apply a scientific test (using a third group of persons who have not taken the course as a comparison or "control" group) that the "self-evident" logic behind the instrument falls apart.

PRAGMATIC VALIDATION judges a measure strictly according to its ability to predict. A good intelligence test, for example, is one that predicts future success in school reasonably well. In a sense, so-called PREDICTIVE VALIDITY sidesteps the whole issue of measurement. Instead of worrying about the meaning of measures, a researcher can rest content with demonstrating that "it predicts, so it must mean something." Avoiding the more difficult validity questions can have serious, unanticipated ideological consequences. Some would argue that intelligence testing, for example, proceeds from and tends to reinforce the Social Darwinist theory—that ability varies widely from person to person and from group to group, and that success depends on the survival of the most able. But let us consider this: perhaps intelligence test scores do predict, but only because knowledge of their results constitutes a self-fulfilling prophecy.

The evolution of intelligence tests suggests that they have been somewhat tainted from the start. Some of the earliest instruments were validated by means of a pragmatic method called CONCURRENT VALIDATION, by which a measure is judged according to its ability to distinguish between groups of people already considered to be different. A test of psychosis should thus distinguish between people who have been institutionalized and labeled "psychotic," and those who are "normal." Such a method automatically reinforces the status quo, be it wisdom or folly. In the case of intelligence test validation, one of the procedures used compared test results against teacher ratings of pupils. If a teacher believed a certain pupil to be dull-witted, a good test was defined as one that came to the same conclusion. To the extent that teachers' feelings about students affect the distribution of rewards (the "Pygmalion effect"), IQ tests based partly on the feelings of the teacher will necessarily correlate with grades, perseverance, and other teacher-influenced measures of performance. The fact is that there are simply too many reasons why a measure might predict behavior for us to consider predictive potency, by itself, to be a valid indicator.

Probably the most popular roundabout approach to the assessment of validity is CONSTRUCT VALIDATION. Here, measures of concepts are judged to be valid if they relate to other concepts as anticipated in theory. A complex analytical construct such as *authoritarianism* may be defined, initially, by its relationship to other variables. Construct validation asks, in effect, whether or not these expected relations hold. We might expect that there will be a relationship between authoritarianism and voting behavior. We hypothesize that the more authoritarian individuals are likely to support political candidates who advocate a vigorous law-and-order position. If we were interested in validating a measure of authoritarianism, we might go to some community in the midst of a political campaign. We might choose a place in which the candidates for office clearly vary in their positions on law and order, take a random sample of residents, score them on authoritarianism, and finally ask them their preference with respect to the candidates running for office. If there is a high correspondence in the predicted direction between residents' scores on the authoritarianism scale and their choice of candidates, we might conclude that our technique does validly measure authoritarianism.

This is a valuable and increasingly accepted way of approaching the validation of indirect measures of phenomena. But if relations do not hold as expected, does one blame the theory or the measures? Construct validation is a good deal more sophisticated than previous approaches, but it is still biased in favor of the assumptions of the researcher. A measure's failure to predict does not necessarily mean that the theory must be discarded. Typically, the researcher renews the search for a measure that does predict. But should such a measure be found, it is likely to be accepted as valid even though the chance still exists that the original theorizing was faulty.

Ironically, the most direct method of validation is one of the least often used. Much of the information essential to researchers is available from sources other than the subject. For this reason, much interview material can be CROSS-VALIDATED against independent but parallel sources of information. Official records can be consulted to determine a person's age, marital status, ethnic background, political party affiliation, income, academic performance, consumption habits, and so forth. Unfortunately, to do so usually involves much more time and energy than are available. The fact that this is so seldom done, even though the results are startingly relevant and sometimes eye-opening, shows the low priority researchers and funding agencies have attached to studying validity. Some prominent social scientists have recently expressed the opinion that social research cannot progress much farther until it attends more seriously to questions of measurement, especially to the question of validity.

Finally, it is often useful to distinguish between internal validity and external validity (Campbell, 1969). Let us return to our earlier example of the researcher who has prepared a questionnaire to measure happiness. If we question the ability of the questionnaire to accurately assess happiness for the sample of respondents the researcher has interviewed, we are calling into question the INTERNAL VALIDITY of the measure. If we question the extent to which the results based on this sample can be generalized to other segments of the population, we are calling into question the EXTERNAL VALIDITY of the measure. External validity will be low if, perhaps because of poor sampling, we have no idea of how generalizable our results are.

Sources of Measurement Error

Measurement is part of research, from the way in which we conceptualize and operationalize variables to data processing. There is the possibility of error creeping into the measurement at each point along the way. There are three major sources of inaccurate measurement: random error, systematic error, and situational error.

RANDOM ERROR

Manipulating social science variables is a multistage process, and unknown, random factors may deceive us into believing that we have really measured what we set out to measure. To understand RANDOM ERROR, we might think of data as a combination of information and noise. The researcher's task is to collect data that are as rich in information as possible, and somehow to separate the information from the noise, so that the message can come through clearly.

Mathematically, random error appears as unexplained variation. Social science deals with variation among individuals, groups, institutions, nations, and so forth. The data we collect consist of systematic variation (information) and random variation (noise). Systematic variation is that portion of the total that represents true differences; random variation is that portion attributable to measurement error. In practice, it is very difficult to separate these two types of variation. We often have little or no idea how much of the variation in our observations is the result of true differences and how much derives from error in our measurement procedures. At the end of any statistical analysis, we are left with what is called unexplained variation. This is produced both by relevant variables that have not been considered in our analysis and by measurement error, but we generally have no indication of the relative contribution of each to the unexplained variation.

Given the uncertainty of random error, how is research possible? The answer is that if errors are truly random, they will cancel each other out, especially if our sample of subjects or number of observations is large enough. We may estimate the effect of the variable as greater or lesser than it actually is, but our overall research findings should not be influenced, so long as there is no systematic inaccuracy.

TABLE 3.2   Measurement Errors at Various Stages of the Research Process

Phase of research	Typical error
Conceptualization	Problems of face validity
Choosing a strategy for data collection	Problems of reliability in the research instrument
Sampling	Problems of external validity
Data collection	Problems of reliability and validity as a result of:
	bias of researcher or respondent
	poor rapport between researcher and subject(s)
	faulty observation or recording of information
	personal characteristics of the respondent (e.g., dishonesty, fatigue)
	special circumstances making the research encounter untypical (e.g., distractions, crises)
Data processing	Validity problems caused by analysis of imprecise or inaccurate data, missing data, or placing raw data into improper conceptual categories

SYSTEMATIC ERROR

Inaccuracy of measurement that occurs repeatedly, and for the same reasons, is called SYSTEMATIC ERROR. Sometimes it is the result of improper research procedures, such as faulty conceptualization of a research problem, a poorly designed questionnaire, or the researcher's own BIASES. These and other sources of systematic error are summarized in Table 3.2. Note that the respondent may also systematically generate inaccurate data. If, for example, an interviewer and a subject are of different races and the subject is highly prejudiced against the interviewer's race, this bias could affect the reliability of all of the subject's responses. Researchers must be ever vigilant for sources of systematic error. It is these that will compromise the results of an investigation.

SITUATIONAL ERROR

SITUATIONAL ERRORS are ones that occur not at random but as the result of particular personal characteristics of the subject(s) or other special circumstances that can influence the research encounter, such as fatigue of respondents or unusual environmental distractions. It is, by definition, difficult to predict situational errors of measurement. If we could predict them, they would be, in some sense, systematic! Often we realize, after the fact, that situational errors have occurred and try to correct for them. Thus we may prolong the data collection phase of research in order to augment or replace unreliable data.

MEASUREMENT ERROR AND THE RESEARCH PROCESS

From Figure 3.1 we can see that certain kinds of systematic and situational errors are associated with particular phases of the research process. Let us explore this idea further as we examine several examples of errors.

PROBLEMS OF FACE VALIDITY. If we have conceptualized variables in such a way that we are measuring them incompletely or are measuring phenomena other than those we think we are measuring, then all subsequent work will be subject to systematic error. Suppose that your objective is to assess the skill of baseball managers, and that you select teams' won-lost records as an indicator of the variable *skill*. Plainly, managers of teams with losing records will be systematically viewed as lacking in skill. Yet there are many possible reasons for losing (such as not enough player talent or injuries to key players) that are unrelated to managerial skill. There are also explanations for winning (easiness of schedule or abundance of skilled players, for example) that are unrelated to the variable we are examining, but the managers of winning teams will be systematically favored in the assessment. This is a problem of *face validity*. No matter how carefully the data collection and data processing phases of the research are executed, the result will probably be inaccurate because of an initial conceptual mistake.

PROBLEMS OF RELIABILITY IN THE RESEARCH INSTRUMENT. No matter how deliberately a strategy for data collection is chosen, it is worthless if the exact information desired cannot be determined by respondents. Suppose a researcher is interested in the concept *alienation* and, in particular, whether workers experience this primarily as a feeling of powerlessness or of meaninglessness, a legitimate theoretical issue that has inspired much debate (Seeman, 1959). The following item might be proposed for inclusion in a survey questionnaire[3]:

> When you experience *anomie* on the job, is it due to powerlessness or meaninglessness? (circle one)

This question can only be reliable if the respondent understands what anomie is and has some idea of the meaning and connotation of the words *powerlessness* and *meaninglessness*. In the absence of such understanding, answers are likely to be no more than guesses. A questionnaire containing several items like this one will be systematically inaccurate in assessing both types of alienation, and the extent of alienation in general. A more effective (and reliable) survey might ask subjects to respond to a series of statements by selecting answers from among the following:

strongly agree   agree   neutral   disagree   strongly disagree

Plausible statements might include:

1. In this job I usually tell people what to do, rather than people telling me.
2. Sometimes I don't know why I even bother coming to work in the morning.

RESEARCHER BIAS. The canons of the scientific method help to reduce bias by encouraging researchers to look for all relevant information, including that which runs counter to their own, preexisting beliefs. Experience has shown, however, that interviewer bias during data collection itself may lead to systematic error, even in studies which are conceptually even-handed. In one opinion survey, when Christian interviewers did the questioning, half of the respondents agreed with the assertion that Jews in America had too much influence in the business community. However, when Jewish interviewers were used, only 22 percent of the respondents agreed with this assertion (Hyman, 1954). Different results in other studies have been obtained depending upon whether interviewers were male or female, religious or nonreligious, liberal or conservative. Note that such errors have occurred not only in informal, oral interviews, but also when identical questions were written down in advance but administered by different categories of researchers. Often the manner in which the question is read to the respondent, or the facial expression and body posture of the interviewer, can betray bias that leads to systematic error.

RESPONDENT BIAS. Commonly held beliefs or ideologies may influence the answers that research subjects give. Derek Phillips (1971) presented an example from his own work illustrating how respondent bias may be built into a mental health survey. Puerto Ricans in New York scored consistently lower on measures of mental health than did white, middle-class individuals. Not willing to accept this relationship at face value, Phillips did some further probing. He found that middle-class subjects attached stigma or social undesirability to the very characteristic of psychosomatic disturbances for which they were being tested. His middle-class subjects tended to avoid any admission of psychosomatic distur-

---

[3]The construction of survey questions is covered in Chapter 6.

bance. They had reason to avoid telling the truth when that truth appeared damaging to them. In contrast, the Puerto Ricans in the sample felt neutral in revealing the information about themselves. Phillips discovered that Puerto Ricans did not suffer disproportionately from mental health problems as had originally appeared to be the case. He concluded that his apparently scientific data served only to reflect differences of *attitude* toward psychosomatic symptoms — a far cry from the superficial finding about the relative incidence of mental health problems among different races and social classes. Less industrious investigators might simply have asserted the face validity of their measure and presented conclusions with potentially racist implications.

Suppose a study showed that less educated persons in our society tend to have harsher racial prejudices than their more educated counterparts? If we looked no further at our data and our research instruments, we could be subject to the same sort of error Phillips found in his and others' investigations. And we might be moved to suggest social action policies designed to reeducate the "racist" lower classes, while simultaneously printing encouraging articles in liberal media to reinforce the smug self-righteousness of much of the suburban middle class.

LYING AS A SOURCE OF ERROR. When official birth records were compared with the age subjects reported for the 1960 U.S. Census, disagreement between the two sources was found among 27 percent of the white males, 35 percent of the white females, 57 percent of the black males, and 66 percent of the black females (Phillips, 1971). Some of these discrepancies were probably the result of inaccurate records, and some might have been caused by peoples' ignorance of their own true age. If we consider only these sources of error, the discrepancies appear to be a simple nuisance factor keeping us from analyzing the relationship between age and some other socially relevant variable. But what if the subjects were actually lying about their age, or trying to forget their true age?

People do not always respond truthfully to even the simplest questions, and there may be an important pattern to what types of people lie and on which types of issues. It may be relevant to investigate how subjects define the situation and consequently how they respond when a stranger interviewing them asks what appears to be a routine question. Even the most innocuous questions mean different things to different people. Though interviewers are probably accustomed to asking people their age, which kinds of people have gotten used to being asked and to answering such a question? Here, at least, there is reason to believe that we can validly measure a variable such as age in a questionnaire because we have the means to verify responses, thereby separating truth from untruth. But what if we are dealing with more complex issues?

We may find that welfare mothers respond differently from upper-income mothers to a series of questions about child care. How certain could we be that the variation in responses tells us something reliable and valid about differences either in the subjects' true feelings or in their true child-rearing practices? This is more than a statistical question. We have to know whether it is a difference in the true feelings of the two groups or only a difference in the way they approach being interviewed. The welfare mothers may have in common the experience that people who ask them questions are a threat to their well-being. Upper-income mothers probably have had quite different experiences in this regard. This could have a bearing on how the two groups respond to questionnaire items. Further, if the interviewers are middle class (or tend to be drawn from any one class), one group will feel more comfortable with them than the other group. This is one of the most consistent findings in social research.

In a famous study done many years ago, LaPiere (1934) presented some very compelling evidence that what people say on matters of race relations cannot necessarily be taken as a predictor of how they will behave. From 1930 to 1932 he and two Chinese associates traveled twice across the country seeking services or accommodations or both at hotels, motels, and restaurants. In 250 out of 251 cases they received service ranging from extremely warm to cordial to reserved. In some instances LaPiere accompanied his Chinese friends; in others he did not. After a lapse of six months, he sent a questionnaire to each of the establishments, asking whether or not it accommodated members of the Chinese race. The answer he received from 92 percent of the same people from whom he and his Chinese friends had recently received service was a flat "No." Instead of concluding that his subjects were liars, LaPiere judged that people typically respond to symbolic situations differently from the way they respond to real ones.

LaPiere's and others' studies provide us with concrete evidence that calls into question the simple, common assumption that attitudes are handy predictors of future behavior. The discrepancy between people's words and deeds has in fact been documented in a number of different contexts (Deutscher, 1973). If some attitudes of respondents are stable enough to be used for purposes of prediction, many others are mainly rationalizations or are stated by respondents to test the feelings of other persons, including perhaps the interviewer. Thus the measurement of attitudes is subject to systematic error.

ERROR ARISING FROM SPECIAL CIRCUMSTANCES. Expressed attitudes are sometimes situational, generated out of the dynamics of group pressure, conversation, or the interaction in a particular interview. It is unwise to generalize from such data; the encounter with the researcher may be so untypical of a normal life situation that it acts as a barrier to explaining human behavior, rather than as a window on behavior. A subject who has just gone without sleep or nourishment for an extended period, in violation of normal routine, might appear to the investigator to be more irritable or muddle-headed than is really the case. If a woman receives a forty-item questionnaire in the mail and decides to answer it during her daughter's disco party, her responses may differ considerably from those she might give in silence and solitude. Some environmental factors that may affect reliability are purely situational, for instance, an unusually cold or hot day. Others are systematic, in the sense that winter days are typically colder than fall days. We would expect some random error in a survey of consumer buying habits if some people had recently made unusually and unexpectedly large purchases. Unless we were looking for seasonal trends, we would wait until the end of the Christmas holiday season to sample consumers, since December buying habits are systematically untypical.

ERRORS IN DATA PROCESSING. Data processing is never subject to perfect quality control and, as Table 3.2 indicates, errors of omission and commission may occur after data have been collected. Experienced survey researchers have developed an assortment of techniques to minimize these faults and, properly applied, they can be quite effective.[4] However, at least one critic has suggested that so long as

---

[4]See Chapter 6 for a discussion of some of these techniques.

portions of the research effort are carried out by hired hands, who have less of a stake in keeping the data as uncontaminated as possible, large errors will be introduced at this stage, and they will quite often go undetected (Roth, 1966).

The Situational Nature of Variables

Precise, reliable, and valid measurement lies at the very heart of any science. Precision is fundamental to scientific advancement because good measuring devices extend our ability to see, hear, feel, and generally get close to the people and objects we are studying. The better our measurement, the more critically we can test our ideas about the world. Our ability to resolve disputes over ideas or competing sets of ideas is in large part contingent on the accuracy of our measurements. Theological idea systems, for example, can compete with each other endlessly without any clear resolution because no one has figured out a way to observe (let alone measure) the divine.

If the "correctness" of any theory is to be properly evaluated, it is necessary for the researcher to obtain measures of all the variables contained in the theory. If, for example, a critical proposition in a particular theory is that the higher the level of anxiety among a group's members, the greater will be the cohesion in the group, we must have precise ways of measuring both *anxiety* and *cohesion* if we are to have any hope of accepting or rejecting the proposition. To discover the relationships between social class and rates of mental illness, teacher expectations and student performance, and ethnicity and child-rearing practices, we must be able to measure the variables involved with a sufficient degree of precision.

A problem in social science is that the meaning of variables may change, depending on the situation being observed. Most social phenomena are more like liquids than solids; that is, their shape depends on the circumstances in which they occur. In our discussion of measurement error, we noted how difficult it may be to measure attitudes. One reason for this is that attitudes may change according to the context in which they are expressed. People may not have the same feelings about race when they are among blacks as they do when they are among whites. Adolescents' attitudes toward sex expressed in a discussion among their peers may differ from those they express in front of their parents. The differences do not necessarily indicate lying or concealment of the truth. These attitudes really do vary as peoples' definition of their social situation changes. Normally, we drink water as we need it and don't think twice about it. Were we suffering from dehydration after a week in the desert, however, even a sip of water could take on special significance.

MEASUREMENT IN THE PHYSICAL AND SOCIAL SCIENCES

The variability of social phenomena goes beyond the issue of attitude measurement and has profound implications for the development of scientific explanation in sociology, psychology, political science, and related fields. Can we generate social laws analogous to the kinds of laws that can be generated about the physical world? It is worth considering the realtionships between scientific theorizing and the variability of social phenomena. We can begin by examining the nature and structure of a scientific explanation of the physical world.

How would we explain the phenomenon of water boiling at lower temperatures on a mountaintop than at the seashore? We might construct the following explanation:

1. The air surrounding the earth exerts atmospheric pressure on the surface of the earth.
2. There is an inverse relationship between altitude and pressure; the higher the altitude, the less the atmospheric pressure.
3. Water will boil at different temperatures depending on the magnitude of pressure applied to it; the lower the pressure, the lower the temperature at which water will boil.

Hence

4. Water boils at a lower temperature on a mountaintop than at the seashore.

The form of the explanation here is deductive. This is the model of explanation in the natural sciences. Let us consider the measurement conditions necessary to produce this type of explanation.

The logic of deductive explanation demands that each assertion, each element, each concept, each variable entering into the argument, have a stable, universal meaning. In our example, the meaning of such variables as *altitude, pressure,* and *temperature* will be understood and measured in the same way by all scientists. The meaning of the variables will not change each time the scientist goes to a different mountain or seashore to test the theory. But is this stability true of the variables in the realm of the social sciences?

Suppose we are interested in explaining why suicide rates are higher in Sweden than in the United States. We might explain it by saying that the welfare state robs a person of initiative; that when persons are robbed of initiative, they are likely to get depressed; and that there is a much higher incidence of suicide among depressed persons. We might conclude logically that suicides will be higher in Sweden (a welfare state) than in the United States. This explanation certainly has the *structure* of a deductive explanation. What makes this explanation quite different is the nature of the variables.

The major concepts in the suicide explanation—*initiative, depression,* and even *suicide*—do not have constant meanings. The meaning of *initiative* is going to vary in different situations. Does initiative mean the same thing for a poverty-stricken person as for a millionaire? Will initiative have the same meaning in the United States as in other countries? The answer is no. Most concepts in social science allow for a variety of interpretations and meanings.

LACK OF CONSENSUS IN MEASUREMENT

Because most of the concepts we deal with in social research are not real, in the sense of having obvious, single definitions or referents in the physical world, we need to be meticulous in saying how concepts are defined and measured. Consider the example of two reporters for a college newspaper who were asked to assess political opinion among undergraduates. One said that about 5 percent of the students were "conservatives"; the other, about 45 percent. It is possible that one reporter is simply more skilled than the other, but the results differ so markedly that a problem of measurement is the more likely explanation for the discrepancy. The reporter with the lower figure may have used an extremely strict measure of conservatism, perhaps membership in a right-wing political organization. The higher percentage may have resulted from use of a less exclusive measure of conservatism, perhaps those students who favored a Republican in the last presidential election. The only way to resolve the dilemma of these divergent findings is through knowing the measures that were used in each case. In this example, and in countless others that could be drawn from the professional social science literature, there is little or no consensus in measurement.

Three sociologists (Bonjean, Hill, and McLemore, 1967) inventoried the measurement scales and indexes that appeared in four major social science journals over a period of twelve years. They found 2,080 separate measures, which they could reduce to 78 conceptual categories. This means that each of these concepts was measured an average of twenty-six different ways. Further, the concepts were used in nearly as many different ways as they were measured. Over all, only 28 percent of the measures were used more than once, and only 2 percent were used more than five times. There were some concepts that seemed to have generated a degree of consensus—status, racial and ethnic stereotypes, segregation, and authoritarianism. There is, nevertheless, an inescapable conclusion to be drawn from this study: there is wide disagreement regarding the measurement of key concepts in social science.

Part of the reason for the failure to achieve consensus is the difficulty of establishing face validity for measures of abstract variables. The further removed are concepts from direct observation, the less unanimity may be expected in devising measures. The differing theoretical positions of researchers, as well as the variety of uses to which data may be put, also account for the lack of consensus in social science measurement. A Marxist economist intent on showing flaws in the capitalist system may measure *profits* in such a way that they appear larger than when a conservative researcher measures them. The official government definition of *unemployment* has excluded those not looking for work and those not expecting to work in the future (Jaffe and Stewart, 1951). If the government included all individuals who were simply not employed at the time the data were collected, the official unemployment rate would be much higher.

Improving the Quality of Measurement

The many problems entailed in producing quality measures of our concepts have caused quite a stir among social researchers. Long-overdue discussion and debate about the validity of our measures have begun. One of the effects of criticism leveled at social research techniques has been a growing effort to develop strategies to better cope with some of the problems outlined in this chapter. The most general outgrowth of this concern and intellectual exchange has been a renewed emphasis on the use of multiple measurement techniques.

TRIANGULATION

The logic behind the use of multiple measurement techniques is elegantly simple. It is referred to as TRIANGULATION. Just as in trigonometry one can indirectly but precisely measure the location of a point by appropriate sightings from two other points, so also can one apply the method of triangulation to social measurement. All indirect measures have their own peculiar weaknesses. But by concentrating on the point at which a series of independent, indirect, and perhaps weak indicators converge, we can effectively minimize their separate errors and maximize their overall validity.

As an example of triangulation, let us look at the variable *teaching skill.* How can we discover whether a particular teacher is "skilled" or not? We could ask his students, but they might be overly influenced by his friendly personality or lenient grading standards. We can increase the likelihood of measuring skill, instead of these other factors, if we look for alternative sources of data about the same teacher. We might compare achievement test scores of students enrolled in his classes with the scores of students enrolled in other teachers' classes, or we might interview parents or school administrators. By itself, each individual source of data may be suspect; taken together, assuming results are consistent among them, they present a powerful argument that we have measured skill in a valid manner.

An important warning is necessary in discussing the logic of triangulation. We must continually bear in mind that the reason for using a number of measures is to better affirm their validity. The logic of triangulation gets short-circuited if the measures used are based on very similar types of data; that is, unless the data are diverse in nature, we will be doing nothing more than testing the reliability of our measures. That is far from the validity assertion we would like to make—that the techniques used are all measuring the dimensions of a particular variable.

Consider tests of the proposition that all bodies falling in a vacuum accelerate at an equal rate. If we dropped a one-pound steel ball and a two-pound steel ball and arrived at measures of acceleration very close to what we expect theoretically, there might still be those who would criticize the test by saying that the two objects had too much in common in the first place. If we drop a steel ball, a piece of wood, and a feather and find that the rates of acceleration are identical for each, there would be less reason to question the validity of our original proposition.

The key to triangulation, then, is independence among our various estimates. If a series of measurement estimates are all collected by the same method (say, a series of questionnaires), they may not be sufficiently independent to meet the logic required by triangulation. Each of these separate questionnaires could conceivably suffer from similar flaws, biases, or errors.

USING A VARIETY OF METHODS

Imagine that we are concerned with assessing worker attitudes in a company town. Suppose that we choose to assess workers' satisfaction with living and working conditions by using a questionnaire with twenty-five separate "satisfaction" questions. If 75 to 80 percent of the workers respond to each of the twenty-five questions by saying that they are quite satisfied, might we still have reason to doubt the validity of our data? In terms of the logic of triangulation, would we be twenty-five times as confident of the validity of our satisfaction measure as we would have been if we had used only one satisfaction question? If we add another twenty-five questions to our questionnaire and the results remain constant, will we double our faith in the validity of our findings on satisfaction? The answer is no. There are several reasons why we may fail to assess accurately the percentage of satisfied workers in the town; one is the possibility that workers fear reprisal by their superiors if they show discontent. Given this type of potential respondent bias toward showing satisfaction, we could multiply our questions *ad infinitum* and still be uncertain about our results.

Since it is possible to increase the validity of our satisfaction measure by collecting diverse types of data, we may decide to employ a number of independent data gathering techniques. Along with our use of a questionnaire, we could also send a participant observer into the town and the factory. Suppose that over a period of time the observer hears little talk of dissatisfaction and sees few instances of conflict. Suppose, further, that we check migration patterns into and out of the town and find that few persons leave the town while many enter it. Beyond that, we carefully read the town newspaper and find few expressions of discontent. The larger the number of methodologically independent measures we utilize, the fewer doubts we will have about our assertions.

Unfortunately, it seems to be the case in social science that researchers adopt a particular methodological approach, and do virtually all of their work using that technique. This is to some degree the effect of graduate training in the various disciplines. Some schools or departments stress the development of quantitative, statistical skills. Others emphasize qualitative field work. We have already pointed out that this patterning of training has implications for the selection of research problems and topics. In addition, the methodological provincialism we have been describing presents an obstacle to better measurement. If we are to treat the idea of triangulation seriously, it demands the simultaneous use of a number of methodological procedures, including survey research techniques, participant observation, content analysis, experimentation, and historical research.

Summary

Measurement is at the heart of any scientific discipline. The creditability and testability of any theory depends upon adequate measurement tools. In social science, the major obstacles to be reckoned with in obtaining such tools are the abstract and situational nature of many of the variables with which we deal.

There are four levels of measurement: nominal, ordinal, interval, and ratio. They vary in complexity and in the degree of precision that they express. It is important to reach as high a level of measurement as our data permit; however, the choice of measure also depends on the purpose of the investigation and the nature of the phenomena being measured. We need to be as accurate as possible, that is, as close to the true value of what we are measuring as we can be.

The selection of appropriate indicators for our variables is called operationalization. Our operational definitions will be limited by theory and by the goals of the particular study, but they must in any case be *exact*: we must present clearly the criteria for evidence that each variable exists and to what extent it exists. It is possible to quantify a wide variety of abstract variables so that they may be studied using ordinal measures.

Reliability may be assessed by the test-retest method of comparing results from different administrations of the same instrument, but it is often difficult to gauge the impact of the environment on score changes. Another technique for establishing reliability involves comparing results from various subparts of the same instrument. The validity of a given measure may be assessed by examining the extent to which it predicts behavior (pragmatic validation) or enables us to discriminate between individuals and groups already considered different (concurrent validation) or thought to differ according to theory (construct validation). When an instrument is checked against some outside source, this is called external validity.

The criteria for judging reliability and validity help us to measure how much error has crept into our investigative procedures. There are three main types of error: random, systematic, and situational. Random error is practically unavoidable, but it is generally correctable. In studies using large samples, random errors tend to cancel each other out. Situational and systematic errors tend to occur at specific stages of the research process. Some systematic errors result from faulty study design or researcher bias; others result from respondent bias. Situational error is caused by research encounters that are untypical of normal interaction among respondents. Some error takes the form of subjects' lying to the investigator. Lying is usually systematic and often is elicited by the subject's perception of the researcher's purpose or role. Some systematic error results from the complex nature of attitudinal variables; people do not always do as they say they do. For this reason the use of behavioral indicators is desirable.

There is little consensus regarding the choice of measures in social science or how to use them. This is in part the result of the abstract nature of the variables, but it is also traceable to the differences in social science disciplines and in traditions of training. To improve our measures, we need to cooperate more across disciplinary lines and to employ a variety of independent corroborating measures of the same phenomena.

Key Terms

accuracy	indicator	predictive validity
behavioral indicator	internal validity	random error
bias	interval	ratio
concurrent validation	measurement	reliability
construct validity	mutually exclusive	reliability coefficient
content validity	nominal	situational error
cross validation	operationalization	systematic error
error	ordinal	test-retest reliability
exhaustive measure	pragmatic validation	triangulation
external validity	precision	validity
face validity		

Exercises

1. Create lists of indicators for the following: *death*; *studiousness*; *attractiveness* in a man or a woman.

2. Choose a variable or concept of particular interest to you and *triangulate,* i.e., suggest as many concrete measurement strategies as you can. Try to explain how the different strategies affect or compensate for each other's weaknesses.

3. Recall the problem of face validity associated with measuring the skill of baseball managers according to their teams' won-lost records. Design a more valid set of measures for *managerial skill.*

4. Choose any research article of interest to you from a social science journal. How much attention does the author devote to assessing and evaluating the quality of the

measures used in the research? Summarize the relevant discussion. If there is little or no attention given to the issue, criticize this absence.

5. How is class standing (your rank in class) computed at your school? What level of measurement is used: ordinal, interval, or ratio? What, if any, theoretical implications does the choice of measure carry?

6. How would you measure *poverty*? Would income and other objectively measurable sources be enough, or would you take into account how people *feel* about their material status? After developing your own operational definition, read Stephen Campbell's discussion of the difficulties and inconsistencies in official definitions of poverty (1974:16ff).

7. Christopher Jencks offers a thorough appraisal of the measurement reliability and validity in the Coleman (1966) study of equality and educational opportunity, a document that justified widespread school busing to achieve racial balance in America. Read Jencks's critique in Mosteller and Moynihan (1972), and then read Jencks's reanalysis of the same data in Jencks et al. (1972, Chaps. 3, 5). Is Jencks's reanalysis of the Coleman study consistent with his own criticism of the quality of the data?

Suggested Readings

Blalock, H. M., Jr.
1979 "Measurement and Conceptualization Problems: The Major Obstacle to Integrating Theory and Research." *American Sociological Review* 44 (December).

An important, advanced-level summary of the current problems of measurement in social science and a plea for us not to sidestep the difficult questions.

Campbell, Donald, and J. Stanley
1966 *Experimental and Quasi-Experimental Designs for Research.* Chicago: Rand McNally.

An assessment of the validity of a number of experimental designs frequently used in the social sciences.

Deutscher, Irwin
1966 "Words and Deeds: Social Science and Social Policy." *Social Problems* 13:226–254.

A clear statement of the relationship between attitude and behavior. Also spells out the policy implications of the contradiction between the two.

Douglas, Jack
1967 *The Social Meanings of Suicide.* Princeton, N.J.: Princeton University Press.

In the course of generating his analysis, Douglas engages in a lively critique of the measurement procedures that have typically been used in evaluating suicide rates.

Miller, Delbert C.
1977 *Handbook of Research Design and Social Measurement.* 2nd ed. New York: David McKay.

A single-volume encyclopedia of measures. Well worth looking at for information and inspiration.

Osgood, C., et al.
1957 *The Measurement of Meaning.* Urbana, Ill.: University of Illinois Press.

Osgood's pioneering use of a device called the *semantic differential* for measuring complex individual attitudes is detailed in this book.

Osmond, Marie Withers, and Mary Durkin
1979 "Measuring Family Poverty." *Social Science Quarterly* 60, 1 (June).

Illustration of the difficulty of gauging the economic welfare of families and a call for the use of multiple criteria.

Robinson, John P., and Philip R. Shaver
1979 *Measures of Social Psychological Attitudes.* Ann Arbor, Mich.: Institute for Social Research, University of Michigan.

Reviews and evaluates the major measures of variables such as *life, satisfaction, happiness,* and *self-esteem.*

Rosenthal, Robert, and Lenore Jacobson
1968 *Pygmalion in the Classroom.* New York: Holt, Rinehart and Winston.

Illustrates the frailty of many of our measures of student skill.

Schaeffer, Nora Cate
1980 "Evaluating Race of Interviewer Effects in a National Survey." *Sociological Methods and Research* 8, 4 (May).

A recent treatment of the problem of systematic error. Also contains a useful bibliography.

Seeman, Melvin
1959   "On the Meaning of Alienation." *American Sociological Review* 24 (December).

Reviews the five major conceptualizations of the variable *alienation*.

References

Bonjean, Charles M., Richard J. Hill, and S. Dale McLemore
1967   *Sociological Measurement: An Inventory of Scales and Indices.* San Francisco: Chandler.
Campbell, Donald T.
1969   "Reforms as Experiments." *American Psychologist* 24 (April):409–429.
Campbell, Stephen K.
1974   *Flaws and Fallacies in Statistical Thinking.* Englewood Cliffs, N.J.: Prentice Hall.
Coleman, James S., et al.
1966   *Equality of Educational Opportunity.* Washington, D.C.: U.S. Office of Education.
Deutscher, Irwin
1966   "Words and Deeds: Social Science and Social Policy." *Social Problems* 13:226–254.
Hyman, Herbert H.
1954   *Interviewing in Social Research.* Chicago: University of Chicago Press.
Jaffe, A. J., and Charles D. Stewart
1951   *Manpower Resources and Utilization.* New York: Wiley.

Jencks, Christopher, et al.
1972   *Inequality.* New York: Harper & Row.
LaPiere, Richard T.
1934   "Attitudes vs. Actions." *Social Forces* 13 (March):230–237.
Merton, Robert K., and Paul F. Lazarsfeld, eds.
1950   *Studies in the Scope and Method of "The American Soldier."* New York: Free Press.
Mosteller, Frederick, and Daniel P. Moynihan, eds.
1972   *On Equality and Educational Opportunity.* New York: Random House.
Phillips, Derek
1971   *Knowledge from What?* Chicago: Rand McNally.
Roth, Julius
1966   "Hired Hand Research." *American Sociologist* 1 (August):190–196.
Seeman, Melvin
1959   "On the Meaning of Alienation." *American Sociological Review* 24 (December).

4 / Ethical and Political Issues

CHAPTER OUTLINE

INTRODUCTION
OBJECTIVITY
The Strict Position
Contemporary Criticism
FORMULATION OF THE
    RESEARCH QUESTION
Topic Selection
Choice of Theory
Funding

DATA COLLECTION
Impartiality
Confidentiality
Disguised Observation
Ethics and Experimentation
Informed Consent
ANALYSIS, INTERPRETATION,
    AND PRESENTATION OF
    RESULTS
The Fudging Effect
Appraisals and Characterizations

APPLICATION OF RESEARCH
    RESULTS
Co-optation or Potency?
Misuse of Information
SUMMARY
KEY TERMS
EXERCISES
SUGGESTED READINGS
REFERENCES

Introduction

Suppose that a team of politically moderate social scientists has received a research grant from the federal government to investigate political extremism on both the left and the right in America. The researchers will interview members of the Communist party and the John Birch Society to find out what their attitudes are on a wide variety of political and social issues. Because they know that their respondents may not give completely honest answers, the research team will use an alternative means of data collection as a check on the validity of the interview results. They will also hire and train research assistants to become members of the Communist party and the John Birch Society, in order to observe the two groups from the inside without the groups knowing that they are being studied. These secret or disguised observational data will be compared with the interview data.

This hypothetical research example shows that ethical and political considerations enter into the process of conducting social research. Some of these considerations relate directly to the standard of objectivity, which guides scientific research. How can social researchers minimize the effect of personal prejudices and biases on what they observe and on how they interpret what they observe? How can a group of politically moderate social scientists examine political extremism without having their values color the conclusions of their study? The researchers should also consider the ultimate social use of their research findings.

87

What role should the researchers play in determining this use? Research findings can be used either constructively or destructively. In our hypothetical situation they could conceivably be used by the government to undermine politically extreme groups. Does the research team have any ethical or political responsibility with regard to this possibility?

Other ethical and political considerations for researchers are less directly related to the question of objectivity. Are there ethical limits on the relationship between researchers and the individuals studied? In our hypothetical example the second means of data collection involves the disguised entrance of research assistants into the political groups to be observed. The groups will not be asked for their permission to be studied. Does such a research tactic violate the ethics of social science research? In this chapter we will consider a variety of ethical and political issues that confront the social researcher. But, before discussing these issues, let us turn again to the issue of objectivity.

Objectivity

Most social scientists have immediate intellectual and emotional reactions to the word OBJECTIVITY. To some it is a straightforward term that refers to the scientific method and the belief that researchers should remove the effect of their personal biases on their research so that social reality may be uncovered. To others the term refers to the disguise that social scientists often use in order to escape moral responsibility.

THE STRICT POSITION

A good starting point for unraveling this diversity of opinion is to examine the position taken by Max Weber. Weber is generally considered to have strongly supported the traditional position that social scientists should rule out biases or VALUE JUDGMENTS in doing research. Value judgments are our personal evaluations of the goodness or badness, rightness or wrongness, of what we are investigating. In other words value judgments depend on our personal belief and biases. According to Weber (1968), it is impossible to establish the ultimate validity or invalidity of such judgments on the basis of scientific investigation alone. Related to this point is Weber's argument that the goal of the social sciences is to understand "what is" and not "what ought to be." The latter, or normative, type of knowledge lies within the domain of social philosophy. Consider the researcher who studies homosexuality. Weber would consider it appropriate to describe the life styles and socialization of homosexuals, to report on their experience with discrimination at work, and the like, but not to conclude that homosexuality is either superior or inferior to heterosexuality.

The strict position on the issue of objectivity is that the value judgments of researchers should not enter into the collection, analysis, and interpretation of data. Even in the writings of Max Weber, one can find the admission that it is very difficult for social scientists to remove the effect of their own values on analysis and interpretation. Despite these difficulties, however, Weber seems to be arguing that objectivity is a goal or ideal that should be aimed for in the research process.

Those who agree would make the point that although the ultimate validity of value judgments or goals cannot be substantiated by scientific investigation, the means for achieving them *can* be determined. If, for example, the goal is racial integration, the social sciences can explore what the best ways are for achieving it. The effect of researchers' values on the problems selected for investigation may not create any difficulty. An American immigrant might choose to study the assimilation process, or a person who is experiencing marital difficulties may want to study the dynamics of the American family system. The crucial consideration is for such researchers to strive for objectivity in the collection, analysis, and interpretation of data. Weber (1958) encouraged social researchers to distinguish between their role as scientists and their role as private citizens. Such a segregation of roles would, in his view, increase the likelihood of objectivity in social science.

CONTEMPORARY CRITICISM

Many objections to the plea for objectivity and a VALUE-FREE SOCIAL SCIENCE have been raised by contemporary writers. According to Gouldner (1962), many strict interpreters of Weber's ideas are "narrow technicians who reject the cultural and moral consequences of their work." Behind Gouldner's attack is his belief that the value-free notion once allowed for the growth and independence of the social sciences. Today, however, he believes that the dogma of objectivity is used too often as a rationalization. It allows us to sell our goods to the highest bidder while ignoring the possible social consequences of our work. This dogmatic approach also excludes the possibility of any social criticism developing from social science research.

Becker (1967) has also criticized the demand for rigorous objectivity. He maintains that we cannot separate our personal values from the research process. Becker argues that researchers' biases influence which societal perspectives are accentuated in research. He sees society as based on hierarchical relationships of *superordination* and *subordination*. The superordinates possess authority in a given situation; the subordinates are the "have-nots" in terms of authority. Wardens and prison guards are the superordinates in a penitentiary; the prisoners are the subordinates. Becker maintains that research generally does not include both perspectives. In fact, researchers encounter difficulty when they try to avoid this situation.

> A student of medical sociology may decide that he will take neither the perspective of the patient nor the perspective of the physician, but he will necessarily take a perspective that impinges on the many questions that arise between physicians and patients; no matter what perspective he takes, his work either will take into account the attitudes of subordinates, or it will not. If he fails to consider the questions they raise, he will be working on the side of the officials. If he does raise those questions seriously and does find, as he may, that there is some merit in them, he will then expose himself to the outrage of the officials. (Becker, 1967:244)

According to Becker, the perspective that becomes emphasized is related to the researcher's biases.

There is clearly a great difference of opinion over the role of objectivity. One school of thought maintains that objectivity is achieved by removing the lenses of personal bias to view what really is going on in society. This is the traditional

Weberian position. The other view is that objectivity is virtually impossible; it is being used as a shield for escaping moral responsibility. The solution to this seeming dilemma is to develop a balanced position, emphasizing both our desire to make scientific observations of society with a minimum of bias and the need for social responsibility. In this chapter we will try to develop such an approach while looking at various ethical and political considerations relating to objectivity in each major step of the research process. The major research junctures to be considered are: (1) formulation of the research question; (2) data collection; (3) analysis, interpretation, and presentation of research results; and (4) application of research results.

Formulation of the Research Question

Ethical and political issues relating to objectivity appear at three stages in the formulation of the research question: (1) in choosing the research topic and precisely posing the question to be pursued, (2) in choosing a theoretical model, and (3) in obtaining funds.

TOPIC SELECTION

Out of all social reality, which slice is to be cut out for examination? Some researchers would suggest that the topic be important in one's field of study and personally interesting. Others would add that it should be relevant to the improvement of society. Such topics are not always easy to come by, but let us assume that the researcher at least picks a topic of personal interest. Suppose that the general topic is crime. We imagine that the researcher has personal opinions and values related to the topic. As we have seen, some would argue that this situation does not, by any means, automatically rule out objective social research. But such an appraisal becomes more difficult to accept when the precise research question is articulated. Will the general topic of crime be pursued from the perspective of the superordinates or the subordinates? What kind of crime will be studied: lower-class crime or upper-class crime? theft in the inner city by poor people? tax evasion by the rich? illegal political contributions by the large corporations? And, once again, from whose perspective will these more specific questions be pursued? Although the precise questions examined in research cannot always be categorized as being from the perspective of either the superordinates or the subordinates, some of them can. Even when they cannot, social researchers should see that their personal biases and values can affect how they conceptualize a research topic. The effect of bias can become apparent when one thinks about which questions and aspects of a topic are ignored and why. Perhaps the investigator should write down such thoughts about the conceptualization of the research topic and refer to them when interpreting and presenting the results.

CHOICE OF THEORY

Closely related to the choice of topic is the choice of a theoretical model that will help us to organize and interpret the data. There are many theories in the social sciences, but none has been proved beyond doubt. Many of the theories compete;

for example, the functional and conflict theories. In Chapter 1 we saw that functionalists like Talcott Parsons see society as a system made up of different parts. Each part is viewed from the standpoint of what it contributes to the functioning of the system. Some functionalists believe that social classes in America, which differ widely in terms of economic well-being and political power, are functional. Stratification, they say, operates as a reward system, encouraging people to work hard. In brief, the functionalists tend to view most realities in society as having some positive function. Otherwise, they say, these conditions would not exist in the first place. Researchers who adopt such a perspective are encouraged to predict that social change will be in the direction of maintaining the status quo.

The conflict model, on the other hand, views society from the standpoint of internal strains and conflict rather than consensus. Researchers who favor this theoretical perspective are much more likely to predict revolutionary developments. A conflict theoretician might expect the existence of relatively widespread poverty in our affluent society to lead to upheavals that would transform the very nature of our social system. The choice of models is not confined to the functional and conflict theories. Recently, social scientists have also tried to develop synthetic theories that achieve balance between the two.

The theoretical model chosen to back up a research question is of tremendous importance in determining what will be observed and how the observations will be interpreted. Do the personal biases of researchers affect their choice of theoretical model? Will conservatives choose the functional theory and radicals opt for the conflict theory? Or will researchers objectively choose the theory that seems to explain the most? Quite often the answer may be the first suggested possibility. The second alternative encourages skepticism. Indeed, how can anyone be sure that personal values have not played a role in the choice of a theoretical model? The solution here is similar to the one we suggested for the first problem area. Once again, researchers should try to become sensitized to the role played by their own values and be ready to discuss this issue during the interpretation and presentation of research results. They should also aspire to the goal of collecting data that are not contaminated by personal biases. How to accomplish this will be discussed later in this chapter.

FUNDING

Martin Nicolaus (1969) has argued that most social research has served the interests of those in positions of power in society. He describes sociologists as having "their hands up and their eyes down," meaning that they have typically obtained grant money from people in higher positions and have then studied those at the bottom of the social class ladder. The information gathered, Nicolaus says, has been used to keep those at the bottom in their place. Is there merit in this argument?

It is true that many social scientists have to depend on allocations from the government, private corporations, and private foundations in order to support their research. Obviously, such sources will support the research in which they are interested. Some social scientists point out that this bias is not always bad; the federal government, for example, supports research that is related to reducing poverty and crime. Others note that the influence of the funding source explains why research that is likely to support the status quo is more often funded than research that might eventually lead to different societal arrangements. A large corporation is more likely to fund research to find out how laborers can work more efficiently than it is to fund research aimed at discovering how workers might better organize themselves politically.

An excellent example of the funding issue can be seen in the case of Project Camelot, research sponsored by the Department of Defense that involved a $6 million budget and the services of many social scientists (Horowitz, 1967). The broad goal of the project was to examine social change in underdeveloped countries. But there was considerable ambiguity about the more specific goals of the project. It has been suggested that the lure of all that government research money may have kept the participating social scientists from caring very deeply about what the exact aims were. Eventually, it became apparent that the real interest of the Defense Department was to develop knowledge regarding the possibility of containing political unrest in the Third World countries. The social scientists were not encouraged to deviate from the Defense Department's counterinsurgency perspective. Revolutionary developments as a positive force in the underdeveloped world would have been given little, if any, attention. This has caused social scientists to describe Project Camelot as an example of "hired-hand" research. Many were relieved that the project was canceled before it really got off the ground.

What is the solution to the funding dilemma? Are all sources of funding suspect? Should they all be rejected? Clearly, this is a rather extreme and self-defeating position. Caution, however, should be taken in negotiating with any prospective sponsor of research. As Kelman (1968:78) has pointed out, "The crucial issue, it should be noted, is not the sponsorship of the research or the source of the funds, but the nature of the explicit and implicit contract under which the funds are obtained." In brief, no matter who might be supporting a given research project, researchers should know what strings will be attached.

There are broad issues connected to the funding question. Who is going to use the knowledge developed by the research? How will the knowledge be used? Will the knowledge be used constructively or destructively? We will discuss these issues further when we examine the application of research results. As in all research, decisions at each step of the process affect decisions at later steps. One should not begin to worry about the application of research results only after the research is completed; rather, one should begin to worry right from the outset.

Data Collection

IMPARTIALITY

Although it is apparent from the preceding discussion that the personal values of researchers can color the choice of research topics and theoretical perspectives employed, the quest for objectivity in data collection still remains as an ideal. Social scientists have devised a number of techniques that increase the likelihood that valid and reliable data, minimally contaminated by personal bias, will be obtained. Modern sampling techniques enable researchers to include diverse segments of a population in a predictable manner so that their research is truly representative of the people being investigated. Advances have been made in questionnaire construction so that "loaded" questions are less likely to appear in surveys conducted today. The point to be emphasized is that our data collection techniques should be used impartially.

> By using our theories and techniques impartially, we ought to be able to study all the things that need to be studied in such a way as to get all the facts we require, even though some of the questions that will be raised and some of the facts that will be produced run counter to our biases. . . . Whatever side we are on, we must use our techniques impartially enough that a belief to which we are especially sympathetic could be proved untrue. (Becker, 1967:246)

A crucial issue in collecting objective data is the relationship between researchers and the people who are observed.

> Social research is caught in a highly magnified version of what physicists have termed the "Heisenberg principle": the very process of observation changes, to a greater or lesser extent in the shorter or longer run, the action it seeks to register. (Friedrichs, 1968:9)

Many examples of observation that changes the nature of what is observed can be cited. An interesting case is described by a white social scientist who investigated race relations in South Africa. When he asked black workers about their attitudes toward whites, he received cautiously indifferent replies. When his black research assistant made the same inquiries, however, the responses revealed attitudes bordering on hatred toward the white ruling elite (van den Berghe, 1967).

The effect of observation on what is observed can be diminished. One strategy is to compare what different observers find when they examine the same social phenomena. In the hypothetical study of political extremism mentioned at the beginning of the chapter, it would make sense to have researchers of both radical and conservative political persuasions observe both groups. Another guideline is to make sure that data gatherers are carefully trained to carry out precisely defined observational tasks. They should have no question about what is to be observed and how it is to be observed. A final recommendation is that observations be recorded as soon as possible in order to lessen the possibility that the biases of observers will alter their memory of what has been observed.

CONFIDENTIALITY

The reluctance of respondents is at least partially explained by the fact that some people place a high premium on privacy and do not want their personal lives exposed via the research of social scientists. A very general guideline for overcoming this problem is for social researchers to develop a good rapport with potential respondents. One inducement commonly offered is the promise of CONFIDENTIALITY or ANONYMITY. If data are confidential, the identities of respondents are known to the researcher, but they are kept secret; if data are anonymous, it is impossible for anyone, including the researcher, to match particular responses with individual subjects.

The question of ethics is relevant here. Obviously, if such promises are made, they should be kept. Confidentiality can be achieved in large-sample surveys by removing the identifying information about individual respondents from the questionnaires. When a research project involves a small sample, it may not be possible to ensure confidentiality. In the community study *Small Town in Mass*

Society (Vidich and Bensman, 1958), the promise of confidentiality was made to the community members. When the research findings were published, the identities of some respondents became apparent even though code names were used instead of the respondents' real names. Needless to say, this unfortunate result caused an uproar in the community.

The lesson to be learned from this example is that it is ethically desirable not to offer confidentiality or anonymity when they cannot be delivered. Our inability to guarantee confidentiality does not necessarily reduce the possibility of cooperation of potential respondents. If we can demonstrate the social usefulness and significance of a research project, we may be able to gain cooperation without the guarantee of confidentiality. In fact, showing the social usefulness of a research project to respondents may be just as great an inducement as the promise of confidentiality.

DISGUISED OBSERVATION

Faced with the possibility of rejection by potential respondents, social researchers have sometimes used deception and manipulation in their work. One example of such deception is DISGUISED OBSERVATION, in which the people who are being observed are unaware of it. The group might be the army, Alcoholics Anonymous, a street gang, or any other group of interest. The example at the beginning of the chapter included disguised observers of the Communist party and the John Birch Society. Some social scientists argue that this method of observing is unethical because it invades the privacy of people who have not given their permission to be observed. They maintain that using such research approaches may alienate the larger society and threaten the acceptability of more straightforward research by the broader social science community (Erikson, 1967). Others contend that such tactics should not be rejected automatically, because they may be useful for advancing scientific knowledge in areas where other means of data collection are not feasible (Denzin, 1970).

A famous study, *Tearoom Trade* (Humphreys, 1970), raised the fundamental dilemma of the scientist's need to know versus the respondent's right to privacy. Humphreys was interested in the phenomenon of impersonal sex between male homosexuals. He observed numerous encounters among men in public restrooms (or "tearooms"), with the consent of the subjects but without their knowing that he was a researcher. His role was to act as "watch queen," to warn of possible interruptions during the encounters. Subsequently, in order to find out more about the backgrounds of the men, he noted their automobile license numbers and traced some of their addresses. He then presented himself at their homes, suitably disguised, and introduced himself as a researcher, asking what appeared to be innocuous questions regarding the men's family life, socioeconomic status, physical health, and friendship networks. This study stirred up a major controversy. In his own defense, Humphreys argued that the behavior he had observed was important to know about, although the great majority of respondents would have wished it kept secret. He also kept all data strictly confidential. Disguised observation was justified in this case, Humphreys maintained, in order to obtain valid background data and also to minimize embarrassment to his research subjects. "Clearly," he writes, "I could not knock on the door of a suburban residence and say, 'Excuse me, I saw you engaging in a homosexual act in a tearoom last year, and I wonder if I might ask you a few questions.'"

ETHICS AND EXPERIMENTATION

Disguised observation is not the only research strategy that raises ethical questions concerning the relationship between social researchers and their subjects. Other strategies of deception and manipulation have been used in both psychology and sociology experiments. If a social worker who wants to test the effectiveness of a particular form of therapy decides without informing the subjects, to treat only a selected group of mentally ill patients and to give the other patients no treatment, is this fair to those who need help? Should all patients be informed of the purposes of the research—as well as of the methods to be used in conducting it? Sometimes it is not being excluded from treatment, but being selected to participate in experiments, which will actually threaten the well-being of research subjects. A classic example is Stanley Milgram's (1973) experiment that had the apparent purpose of studying the effect of punishment on learning but that had the concealed purpose of investigating obedience to authority. Subject *A* enters a laboratory and meets subject *B* and the experimenter in charge of the research. Subject *B* is actually a member of the experimental team. The experimenter tells subject *A* to be the "teacher" in an experiment for studying the effect of punishment on learning. When subject *B* gives wrong answers, subject *A* is to give what he thinks are real electric shocks to subject *B*. They are not real shocks. The experiment begins. Subject *B* gives wrong answers and supposedly receives shocks of increasing voltage. Subject *B* screams and pleads that the experiment be stopped. When subject *A* asks the experimenter if he should stop, the experimenter replies in the negative. Subject *A* continues with the experiment. The real purpose of this experiment is to see whether or not subject *A* will follow the directions of the experimenter even though he thinks he is causing pain to subject *B*. Although the subject *A*s were later debriefed, and the reason for the study explained to them, several reported feeling acute anguish over what they had done, and subsequent mental depression.

This experiment, and others like it, have been criticized for their unethical treatment of human subjects. Once again, some argue that such research strategies can add to scientific knowledge and therefore can be used in certain situations. The question is whether the ethical treatment of subjects should ever be sacrificed. Some suggest that if more conscientious attention were addressed to this question at the outset of research, fewer studies employing deception and manipulation would be done (Kelman, 1968). The question, however, is a relative one. The practices of deception and manipulation range from the fairly innocent to the outlandish. Some practices should obviously be avoided. When deception is employed, precautions should be taken. If the true purpose of an experiment is concealed, an explanation emphasizing the scientific merit of the research should be given afterward. When researchers decide that disguised observation is ethically tolerable in a particular research situation, special efforts should be made to ensure that the identities of the subjects will be protected. Perhaps the overall ethical guideline is that the people who are being studied should not be hurt by the research process.

INFORMED CONSENT

Reacting in part to the furor created by the Milgram experiments and by other studies that have used disguised observation, the federal government has recently issued guidelines requiring the INFORMED CONSENT of all subjects in all research projects receiving government funding. It has, however, been extremely difficult to achieve this goal (Thorne, 1980). The guidelines do not really resolve the ethical dilemma because of the inherent and frequently apparent differences in status between researcher and subject. It is difficult to eliminate the possible effects of intimidation, which can induce a respondent to sign a consent form. Moreover, there is no real proof that a research subject actually understands the complicated theoretical rationale that may justify a particular study. In fact, people sometimes give their "consent" because they are embarrassed that they do not understand the explanation provided them. Plainly, the guidelines, while perhaps ethically desirable, are not a substitute for the researcher's own soul-searching and personal sense of fairness in the conduct of research.

It should be underscored that the issues of confidentiality, deception, and manipulation are relevant not only because of ethical considerations but also because of their effect on the possibility of objectivity. If respondents fear that their confidences will be broken or that they will be manipulated and deceived by social scientists, how can we expect to gain their trust and find out what is really going on in the segment of society with which we are concerned? In other words, how can we expect to collect objective evidence?

Analysis, Interpretation, and Presentation of Results

THE FUDGING EFFECT

Although outright deception of the public by manufacturing or "fudging" all or most of the data is probably rare in the social sciences, "trimming" or conveniently ignoring certain parts of the data to make them fit the preconceived notions of the investigator occurs, according to some observers, with some frequency. Barber (1976) has listed numerous examples of the "FUDGING EFFECT" from the realms of physics, medicine, psychology, and physical anthropology. We may explain this phenomenon by noting that scientists often have a vested interest in the successful outcome of their own research. Moreover, there is a strong desire for recognition and fame, as well as for financial security (Merton, 1957). The implications of the isolated instances of the "fudging effect" are important:

> We are naive to believe that dishonesty in research is unique and aberrant. The rewards are just too tempting: prestige, ego enhancement, promotion. . . . Not only are the rewards tempting but, while the process of socialization in graduate school may give credence to veracity, it nonetheless emphasizes success. (Faber, 1974:734)

Of course, the vast majority of researchers do not consciously conceive of their personal ambition as being inconsistent with the goals and norms of science. Constraints, however, do arise which impinge on the ability of researchers to conform to these norms. These constraints range from the biases of researchers, which may direct the analysis and interpretation of data in predictable directions, to outside forces such as one's relationship to the sponsor of the research. A researcher employed by a large business corporation noted that there were

> distortions and unanalyzed data caused by the pressure for results and restrictions on time. Because our relationship to the organization was both an emergent and continuing

one, the results of any study directly affected the possibility of further studies by the involved researcher as well as by the rest of us. This led us to examine the data in order to uncover problems that management had not been aware of. The more difficult it was to secure permission for a study or to include sensitive questions in a questionnaire, the more we felt we had to justify ourselves by providing results that had a payoff. (Goldner, 1967:261)

This assessment reveals a submission to the demands of the sponsor of the research, which should be avoided. It also shows the difficulties in maintaining a completely dispassionate view.

APPRAISALS AND CHARACTERIZATIONS

Determining the facts and assessing the weight of the evidence are crucial to the goal of objectivity in our research. Regarding the determination of facts, Nagel (1961) has discussed the role of value judgments. He makes a subtle distinction between judgments that characterize and those that appraise. APPRAISING JUDGMENTS express approval or disapproval of what is under investigation and should be ruled out. CHARACTERIZING JUDGMENTS involve an evaluation of the degree to which some state or condition exists in the phenomena under investigation and are important for analysis to proceed at all. An investigator who is studying power relationships in the family must make a technical judgment about what kind of behavior is dominant and shows power and about what kind of behavior is submissive and shows a lack of power. This would be an appropriate characterizing value judgment. If the researcher proceeded to argue that either dominant or submissive behavior is good or bad, an improper appraising value judgment would be made. This distinction seems to clarify the desired role of value judgments in analyzing and interpreting data.

Assessing the weight of the evidence is also important. The process of reaching conclusions from the data can be affected by the values of the researcher in either the natural or the social sciences. To combat this difficulty, the researcher should state his or her values clearly. We should remember, however, that we are not always fully aware of our precise values with respect to a particular research topic. In this situation the worth of any claim we make to objectivity will be measured by the critical evaluation of others in the social science community. This fact, however, should not deter us from striving for openness in the interpretation of data nor from including evidence that contradicts what we might like to find out.

The written presentation of research results should discuss methods in enough detail so that others can replicate the work if they so desire. If a complete report of the research is given, the claim to objectivity can be tested by those with different values, who may reach the same or different conclusions. Another aspect of the complete presentation of research results is discussion of both the positive and negative findings. Sometimes we are reluctant to discuss findings that do not confirm our hypotheses because we feel that they represent failure. What this attitude overlooks is that in the long run, such findings may be even more significant from the standpoint of truly understanding social phenomena than the ones we are pleased with. Many of the great breakthroughs in knowledge developed from evidence that contradicted accepted explanations.

Application of Research Results

CO-OPTATION OR POTENCY?

The findings of social science quite often have implications for action in the realm of politics. Sometimes research data have a minimal effect on changing national and local policy; they are merely CO-OPTED, or used to legitimate a policy position already decided upon by government officials. Alternatively, if research findings are contrary to the ideological position of the decision makers, the research may be dismissed as invalid or of little consequence. The Report of the President's Commission on Pornography (Lockhart, 1970) seemed to provide evidence that pornography was not only harmless, but potentially beneficial. Such findings implicitly suggested that pornography ought to be legalized. The failure to act on the report was largely a function of the political undesirability of its findings.

On the other hand, social research may be potent and directly applicable to human problems. A survey on attitudes toward contraception in a particular country can reveal whether or not the implementation of a birth control program is likely to achieve a reduction in population. Studies on black-white relations in America can tell us how to accomplish integration with a minimum of racial conflict. Research can help us to ascertain the dynamics of poverty and thus to take steps to reduce the extent of the problem. Michael Harrington's book *The Other America* had a profound effect on President Kennedy, who then initiated a war on poverty. Such examples point to the potential relevance of social science research for society.

MISUSE OF INFORMATION

All new knowledge can be manipulated for either constructive or destructive ends. We are all familiar with the example of nuclear energy, which can be used for bombs or as a diagnostic tool in medicine. On a somewhat less grandiose scale, the same can be said about social science knowledge. The analysis of black-white relations in America could be used by powerful racists to create backlash conditions that would wipe out what little progress has been made in improving race relations. There is no question that the advertising industry has used social science knowledge to manipulate consumer behavior. The subtle use of opinion poll information by our highest political leaders is often noted. An example from our involvement in Vietnam is that

> if 80 percent think it is a "mistake" that we ever "went into" Vietnam, but 51 percent think that we would "lose prestige" if we "pulled out now," then the "people" have been "consulted" and the war goes on with their "approval." (Roszak, 1969:16)

As mentioned earlier, the time to worry about the use of research findings is not at the end of the research process but at the outset, during the stage of problem formulation. Regarding the potentially destructive utilization of some research, two social scientists have made this observation:

> This is a knotty issue, and one which perhaps can only be resolved by an act of faith. If you believe that in the long run truth makes men freer and more autonomous, then you are willing to run the risk that some people will use the facts you turn up and the interpretations you make to fight a rear guard action. If you don't believe this, if you

believe instead that truth may or may not free men depending on the situation, even in the long run, then perhaps it is better to avoid these kinds of research subjects. (Rainwater and Pittman, 1967:361)

The message seems clear. If we feel that the knowledge gained from our research will be put to destructive purposes in the long run, we should not do the research in the first place. Many times, however, the situation is not so apparent, and we feel drawn to the act of faith noted above.

In the more ambiguous cases, how can we guard against the destructive use of social science knowledge? Two courses of action appear. The first involves trying to form a standard for evaluating a proposed research project. Perhaps social researchers can commit themselves to doing research aimed at discovering the best means for achieving humane, as opposed to inhumane, goals. Such research can be described in the following way:

> The research is based on the assumption that social change is desirable. It is designed to contribute to the understanding of ways to facilitate constructive change in the direction of meeting human needs and of expanding the participation of people all over the world in the political, economic, and social processes of their respective societies. (Kelman, 1968:65)

It seems less likely that the findings from such research would be used for destructive purposes.

A second safeguard against the destructive use of social science knowledge is for researchers to press for the constructive use of their findings after the research is completed, thus blending their roles as scientists and as private citizens. The possible social uses of new knowledge could be communicated to the public at large, and researchers could comment upon them, particularly to groups that are in a position to implement decisions related to the knowledge.

Value judgments are indeed involved in such communication and comment, but as Gouldner (1962) has argued, perhaps the technical competence possessed by social scientists provides a warrant for making such judgments within the area of their expertise. Even if one disagrees with Gouldner's assertion, it must be admitted that social researchers are as free to make value judgments as is anyone else. Moreover, if their technical competence does not give them a special mandate to say what *ought* to be, it does give them a unique responsibility to spell out the alternatives of what *can* be, so that the public may know and decide.

Summary

Ethical and political considerations may affect the objectivity of social research. The traditional position regarding objectivity, exemplified by Max Weber, is that investigators should rule out their own value judgments and maintain a separation between their roles as researchers and as private citizens. Those who object to the traditional view argue that so-called value-free social science is too often a rationalization for uncritical research that supports the status quo and that ignores the possible social consequences of the findings. In discussing the various stages of the research process, this chapter attempts to find some middle ground between these differing conceptions of ethics and objectivity.

The choice of both topic and theory for one's work may be influenced by power relationships in society or by the lower-level "politics" of universities or other funding organizations. It is possible for the sources of funding to subvert the process of scientific inquiry altogether. The critical issue may not be the actual source of money but the explicit or implicit contract between the researcher and the funder. Sometimes the investigation is co-opted by government, business, or a private foundation, and research findings are used merely to justify policies already decided upon. Nevertheless, social research frequently has had potent and lasting effects on public policy.

During data collection the researcher should take steps to ensure impartiality and should protect the identity of research subjects who wish their privacy preserved. In no case should promises of anonymity or confidentiality be made if they cannot be kept. Debates have flourished over the ethical implications of disguised observation and human experimentation. It has been suggested that there is rarely an unresolvable conflict between the scientist's "need to know" and the privacy and dignity of respondents. If attention is addressed to ethical dilemmas before research actually begins, many of the potential problems may be anticipated and their impact mitigated. The issues of confidentiality and exploitation of research subjects need to be addressed, not only because of ethical considerations but also because of their effect upon the validity of data. Recently, federal guidelines have been issued in an attempt to eliminate abuses. A nagging difficulty is that we can never know whether the consent for observation or experimentation that has been given to researchers by respondents is really voluntary and fully informed.

The fabrication of research results during data analysis and presentation occurs perhaps more frequently than we realize. The temptation to make the data fit desired outcomes is ever-present. But researchers rarely confront any conflict between their personal ambition and truthfulness on a conscious level. Rather, in many research contexts, the peculiar conditions of funding or the pressures of time exert continuous constraints on the researcher not to adhere fully to scientific norms. This pressure must be recognized and counteracted.

To prevent the misuse of information and to inject higher ethical standards into our work, we may have to deviate from the traditional Weberian view of value-free social science. We may, for example, commit ourselves to doing research that carries humane, as opposed to inhumane, goals. And we can inform the public of the wider social implications of our research findings.

Key Terms

anonymity	co-optation	objectivity
appraising judgments	disguised observation	value-free social science
characterizing judgments	fudging effect	value judgments
confidentiality	informed consent	

Exercises

1. Briefly describe three research situations in which the personal biases of the investigators may be a problem. What can be done to increase the likelihood of objectivity in each of these cases?

2. Briefly describe three research situations in which deception may have to be used. Why is this the case? What kind of deception would you use? In each situation how would you defend your use of deception on ethical grounds?

3. In what ways could the Milgram ex-

periment described in this chapter be improved upon from the standpoint of treating human subjects in a humane way?

4. You are approached by a large industrial firm and asked to conduct research on how to increase worker productivity in its factories. What ethical considerations occur to you, and how would you deal with them?

5. You are engaged in participant observation of a student political group. Other members suggest that the group participate in: (a) a peaceful, though illegal, demonstration; (b) the theft of some documents from a university building; (c) sabotage of college facilities. How would you, as a researcher, react to each of these suggestions?

6. How much cheating occurs at your college or university? Design a study to assess the incidence of cheating and its impact on student life.

7. Can you think of any exceptions to the general rule that the researcher has an obligation not to harm those studied? How about a study of illegal political campaign contributions by officers of large corporations? Any other possible exceptions?

Suggested Readings

Appell, G. N.
1978   *Ethical Dilemmas in Anthropological Inquiry: A Case Book*. Waltham, Mass.: Crossroads Press.
    A summary of the most important ethical issues in anthropology, in the context of individual cases.

Becker, Howard S.
1967   "Whose Side Are We On?" *Social Problems* 14 (Winter):239–247.
    A concise argument for social scientists to take sides in their research while still seeking to collect valid and reliable data.

Cassell, Joan, and Murray L. Wax, eds.
1980   "Ethical Problems of Fieldwork." *Social Problems* 27, 3 (February).
    An entire issue devoted to the topic.

Denzin, Norman K.
1970   *The Research Act*. Chicago: Aldine.
    A symbolic interactionist perspective on doing research is presented. There is a very thorough treatment of the ethical and political problems in doing social research. Denzin argues for the use of deception as a research strategy in certain situations.

Diener, Edward, and Rick Crandall
1978   *Ethics in Social and Behavioral Research*. Chicago: University of Chicago Press.
    Drawing on examples from psychology, sociology, and anthropology, the authors focus on the treatment of respondents, codes of professional ethics, and the relationship between science, values, and society.

Erikson, Kai T.
1967   "A Comment on Disguised Observa-

tion in Sociology." *Social Problems* 14 (Spring):366–373.
    A good statement of the problems in the use of deception in social research.

Gouldner, Alvin W.
1962   "Anti-Minotaur: The Myth of a Value-Free Sociology." *Social Problems* 9 (Winter):199–213.
    An excellent presentation of some of the problems in maintaining a strict interpretation of the Weberian plea for a value-free social science.

Kelman, Herbert C.
1968   *A Time to Speak: On Human Values and Social Research*. San Francisco: Jossey-Bass.
    A discussion of the ethical and political considerations at the major points in the research process. Kelman is especially perceptive in discussing foreign research.

Nagel, Ernest
1961   *The Structure of Science*. New York: Harcourt, Brace & World.
    One of the best books on the philosophy of science. It deals with the difficulties in obtaining objectivity in both the social and physical sciences.

Sjoberg, Gideon, ed.
1967   *Ethics, Politics, and Social Research*. Cambridge, Mass.: Schenkman.
    An excellent collection of essays by social scientists about the ethical and political dilemmas that have entered into their own work.

Weber, Max
1968   *The Methodology of the Social Sci-*

ences, ed. and trans. Edward A. Shils and Henry A. Finch. New York: Free Press.
The classic statement of the tra-

ditional position concerning the role of values in social science research. Originally published in 1949.

References

Barber, Theodore X.
1976 *Pitfalls in Human Research.* New York: Pergamon Press.
Becker, Howard S.
1967 "Whose Side Are We On?" *Social Problems* 14 (Winter):239–247.
Denzin, Norman K.
1970 *The Research Act.* Chicago: Aldine.
Erikson, Kai T.
1967 "A Comment on Disguised Observation in Sociology." *Social Problems* 14 (Spring):366–373.
Faber, B. L.
1974 "The Sloan-Kettering Affair." *Science* 185:734.
Friedrichs, Robert W.
1968 "Choice and Commitment in Social Research." *American Sociologist* 3 (February):8–11.
Goldner, Fred. H.
1967 "Role Emergence and the Ethics of Ambiguity." In *Ethics, Politics, and Social Research,* ed. Gideon Sjoberg. Cambridge, Mass.: Schenkman.
Gouldner, Alvin W.
1962 "Anti-Minotaur: The Myth of a Value-Free Sociology." *Social Problems* 9 (Winter):199–213.
Horowitz, Irving L., ed.
1967 *The Rise and Fall of Project Camelot.* Cambridge, Mass.: MIT Press.
Humphreys, Laud
1970 *Tearoom Trade.* Chicago: Aldine.
Kelman, Herbert C.
1968 *A Time to Speak: On Human Values and Social Research.* San Francisco: Jossey-Bass.
Lockhart, William B., Chm.
1970 *Report of the Commission on Obscenity and Pornography.* New York: Random House.
Merton, Robert K.
1957 "Priorities in Scientific Discovery: A Chapter in the Sociology of Sci-

ence." *American Sociological Review* 22:635–659.
Milgram, Stanley
1973 *Obedience to Authority.* New York: Harper & Row.
Nagel, Ernest
1961 *The Structure of Science.* New York: Harcourt, Brace & World.
Nicolaus, Martin
1969 "Remarks at ASA Convention." *American Sociologist* (May):154–156.
Rainwater, Lee, and David J. Pittman
1967 "Ethical Problems in Studying a Politically Sensitive and Deviant Community." *Social Problems* 14 (Spring):357–366.
Roszak, Theodore
1969 *The Making of a Counter Culture.* Garden City, N.Y.: Doubleday.
Thorne, Barrie
1980 "'You Still Takin' Notes?' Fieldwork and Problems of Informed Consent." *Social Problems* 27, 3 (February): 284–297.
van den Berghe, Pierre L.
1967 "Research in South Africa: The Story of My Experiences with Tyranny." In *Ethics, Politics, and Social Research,* ed. Gideon Sjoberg. Cambridge, Mass.: Schenkman.
Vidich, Arthur J., and Joseph Bensman
1958 *Small Town in Mass Society.* Princeton, N.J.: Princeton University Press.
Weber, Max
1958 *From Max Weber: Essays in Sociology,* ed. and trans. Hans H. Gerth and C. Wright Mills. New York: Oxford University Press.
1968 *The Methodology of the Social Sciences,* ed. and trans. Edward A. Shils and Henry A. Finch. New York: Free Press. Originally published in 1949.

5 / Sampling

CHAPTER OUTLINE

INTRODUCTION
Populations
SAMPLING PLANS
Nonprobability Sampling
  Accidental Sampling
  Quota Sampling
  Purposive Samples
Probability Sampling
  Random Sampling
  Probability Theory
  Systematic Sampling
  Stratified Sampling

Cluster Sampling
  Multistage Cluster Sampling
  Combining Sampling Plans
PROBLEMS AND ISSUES IN
  SAMPLING
Sample Size
Nonsampling Error
  Poor Sampling Frame
  Nonresponse
  Bias in Panels
  Bias in Respondent Selection
Sampling in Qualitative Research

Time Sampling
Place Sampling
Event Sampling
Status, Role, and Relationship
  Sampling
Sampling and the Creation of
  Theory
SUMMARY
KEY TERMS
EXERCISES
SUGGESTED READINGS
REFERENCES

Introduction

In social research, as in everyday life, when we *sample* we gather information about a few cases and seek to make judgments about a much larger number of cases. Most people are much more expert at sampling methodology than they probably realize. We all engage in various forms of sampling. When we take a sip of milk from that carton that has been in the refrigerator for the last two weeks to determine whether it is sour, or when we select a few plums at the market for close scrutiny prior to a 2 pound purchase, we are carrying out a sampling procedure. When we pick up a book of poems in a bookstore and leaf through it, reading one poem at the beginning, another in the middle, and a third at the end, we are again sampling. In everyday life we adapt our sampling procedure to the situation. We find that for some purposes a sample of one (for example, the one sip of milk) is more than adequate as evidence for the generalization we are interested in making; for other purposes a more sophisticated sampling procedure is called for.

Sometimes our objective is to sample in such a way as to get an UNBIASED or REPRESENTATIVE SAMPLE, as in our three-poem example. At other times our objective is to draw a biased sample in an effort to find the best. This procedure can be seen in mate selection for marriage. Young men and women usually go through a phase of their lives where they date many people with the intention of finding the best possible husband or wife. Obviously, we cannot date all possible candidates for the position of marriage partner. Some people would like to try, but the exigencies of time and money rule out this alternative. In other words, in this crucial part of our lives we are forced to sample from among the possibilities. Our final selection is hopefully one of the best among the possibilities. The sampling process is in evidence to some extent when we choose a school to attend, look for a job, or pick a place to live. To the degree that we are free to choose in these areas of our lives, we want the best as defined by our personal likes and dislikes. The emphasis in these situations is not on finding the average or typical mate, school, job, or home, but, rather, on finding the best. We want a sample that will be disproportionately weighted in favor of our biased objective of finding the best.

Social scientists use sampling in their research because typically they do not have the time and money to study all the cases in the population of interest to them. Usually their aim is not to find the best case but to find a representative distribution of cases that will allow for generalizations about the average or typical. In other words social researchers often want an unbiased sample so that on the basis of the cases considered they can GENERALIZE ACCURATELY to all the cases in the population.

It is generally assumed that results based on a total count are more reliable than results based on a sample. In fact, a well-designed sampling plan contributes to both the *reliability* and the *validity* of our research findings. If we do our sampling carefully and in accordance with one of the standard sampling plans, it should be possible for another researcher to replicate our findings; this is an important aspect of reliability. Careful sampling ensures we have drawn our cases so that our sample accurately reflects the composition of the population of cases about which we wish to generalize; this contributes to the validity of the generalizations we make on the basis of our sample.

It is as important to the consumers of social research as to the producers of the research to know the logic behind sampling, the alternative sampling methods available, and the relative precision that can be expected from each of these alternatives. A major objective of this chapter is to present a nontechnical introduction to each of these issues. It is a common misconception that sampling is relevant only to quantitative survey research. Although sampling procedures for use in quantitative research are more highly developed, sampling can play a very important role in field work. We shall therefore consider sampling as it is employed in both major types of social investigation. Let us begin by examining a few basic sampling terms.

POPULATIONS

As we know, a sample is made up of some but not all instances or cases of some general category of people, things, or events. It is the specific group selected from all possible cases of interest in a particular research project. The term used to describe all the possible cases of interest is the POPULATION. The population for a particular study might be all adult women in the United States, all Jews living in Cairo, or all students at State University. The population of interest varies, depending on the purpose of the research. A particular subgroup within the population is referred to as a STRATUM. All the male students at a college would make up one stratum, and all the female students would make up another stratum. Different strata within a particular population are usually formed on the basis of such characteristics as age, race, and sex. The characteristics of relevance for determining strata depend, of course, on the purpose of the study.

Any individual case in the population is called an ELEMENT of the population. For example, in a study of State University, Fred Fraternity and Suzie Sorority are two different elements of the population. Usually the elements are individual people, but they can also be poems, newspaper articles, families, plums, or even nations. Another key concept is that of SAMPLING FRAME. Once a population has been defined for a particular study, it is necessary to list all the elements so that a sample can be drawn from the population. The sampling frame is such a list. The sampling frame at a college would probably be all the students registered at the school during the semester when the study was being conducted.

Sampling Plans

There are two basic kinds of samples: *probability* and *nonprobability*. In a PROBABILITY SAMPLE, every element of the population has a known, though not necessarily equal, chance of being selected for inclusion. Furthermore, every element has at least some chance (a nonzero chance) of being part of the sample. Neither of these conditions generally holds for NONPROBABILITY SAMPLES. Probability sampling plans allow us to estimate how closely our sample results approximate what we would have found out if we had considered the total population. The reason for this is that there are certain statistical regularities associated with probability sampling that are related to our knowing the chance that each element has of being included in a given sample. In contrast, such estimates of precision generally cannot be made with nonprobability samples because we do not know the chances that each element has of being selected for a particular sample. Nonprobability sampling is actually quite similar to the kind of sampling that we do in our daily lives.

NONPROBABILITY SAMPLING

Nonprobability sampling is particularly well suited for exploratory studies, where the focus is on the generation of theory and research ideas. It is also useful in observational and qualitative research. In this section we will consider the three most important types of nonprobability sampling: accidental, quota, and purposive.

ACCIDENTAL SAMPLING. ACCIDENTAL SAMPLING comes closest to the familiar "eyewitness interview" we have heard on radio and seen on television. An important event has occurred, such as the landing of men on the moon. The media coverage of the event switches to various reporters who stand on busy streetcorners and interview people as they pass by. The same kind of sampling is sometimes (but not frequently) done in social research. A survey of student attitudes at your school might be carried out by having interviewers stand at the main entrance door to the student union and ask those who enter and leave how they feel about a number of issues. The assumption behind such a strategy is that by simply interviewing whoever happens to stroll by we should get a reasonably representative cross section of the population of interest. The obvious problem is that there is no assurance that this is going to be the case. Indeed, just as the people who congregate in Times Square may not represent a cross section of the American people, the group of students who frequent the student union may not represent a cross section of students at your school. There is no reliable basis for checking how representative an accidental sample is. In view of this we must be particularly cautious about generalizing from the data acquired through accidental sampling.

QUOTA SAMPLING. A QUOTA SAMPLE is one in which interviewers are told to screen potential respondents in terms of desired characteristics. A quota is sometimes established in accordance with the percentage of the population that a particular stratum makes up and sometimes in accordance with the theoretical focus of the study. For a survey on attitudes toward the women's movement, the quota sampling plan might call for 50 percent of the interviews with women and 50 percent with men, or the plan might call for 50 percent of the interviews with white women and 50 percent with black women. The first example illustrates quotas based on the proportion of the population that the stratum represents; and the second sample illustrates quotas based on a study's theoretical focus—assuming that there were theoretical reasons for expecting the attitudes of black women to differ from those of white women. The main advantage of quota sampling over accidental sampling is the assurance that certain strata of the population will be included in the sample. The fact remains, however, that the sampling done from the different strata in quota sampling is essentially accidental. The "eyewitness interview" is still being conducted, but interviewers are told to make sure to stop certain kinds of people. Interviewers are afforded a large degree of latitude in the quota sampling procedure, which can lead to biased sampling.

The tendency for interviewers to search for respondents in congested areas has already been mentioned. Another bias is that if interviewers are sent out into a neighborhood to interview householders, they are likely to skip houses that are not as physically appealing or houses that have a "Beware of Dog" sign in the yard. Possibilities such as these reduce the precision of estimates based on quota samples.

PURPOSIVE SAMPLES. PURPOSIVE SAMPLING is a general term for judgmental sampling in which the researcher purposely selects certain groups or individuals for their relevance to the issue being studied. This sampling method is often used in studies of deviance or other social phenomena that are too rare to be dealt with effectively using a representative cross section of the population. If, for example, we were interested in assessing whether or not there is an impact of pornography on sex crimes, one thing we might decide to study is the pornography consumption habits of those who are or have been in prison for sex crimes. If we were interested in monopolistic practices among large corporations, we might select a specific industry such as the computer industry and attempt to get interviews with top management at several of the major firms. While management at IBM might have very little to say about their own practices, the management of their competitors might have a good deal to say about actions taken by IBM. In such situations the researcher must often make do with whoever will grant an interview. Elaborate sampling procedures are out of the question. A major advantage of purposive sampling is that it is a way to assure that we get at least some information from respondents who are hard to locate and crucial to the study. A major drawback with such samples is that there is little or no control over who is selected within the category. There is no assurance that those selected are in any way representative of some clearly specified population of more general interest.

PROBABILITY SAMPLING

A *probability sample* is one in which every element of the population has a known, nonzero chance of being selected for the sample. The probability of selection does not have to be equal for each element of the population. Since we know the chance each element has of being included in the sample, we are in a position to estimate how accurately results for the sample estimate the characteristics of the total population. We will consider the four most basic probability sampling plans: simple random sampling, systematic sampling, stratified random sampling, and cluster sampling.

RANDOM SAMPLING. Simple RANDOM SAMPLING is the most basic of the probability sampling plans, and the others involve some form of it. A simple random sample is one in which each element of the population has an *equal* chance of being included. Let us assume that the library at State University has one hundred books on the subject of marine biology. Fred has to write a term paper on this subject, and he decides that he needs five sources for his bibliography. It is late in the semester and Fred does not have time to do a purposive sample of the library's best books on marine biology. As a compromise he decides to write down the names of all the books dealing with the topic on individual slips of paper. He places the slips of paper in a box and then shakes the box vigorously. After the slips of paper are well mixed, Fred picks five of them from the box and copies the book titles for his bibliography. The bibliography represents a simple random sample of all the library books on marine biology because each book has been given an equal chance of being included in Fred's sample.

The requirement that every element of the population has an equal chance of being selected has an important implication: a complete listing of all population elements must be available. In other words, an adequate *sampling frame* must be located. (Notice that this requirement was not mentioned with respect to any of the nonprobability sampling plans.) Sometimes this requirement presents no major problem. In studies of college students, for example, a list of registered men and women often serves the purpose. In other research situations, however, a good sampling frame may be difficult to find.

When complete listings of a given population are not available, some researchers may be tempted to use incomplete sources that are readily at hand. This must be done with caution because use of an incomplete sampling frame can lead to biased results. Some survey research is conducted by telephone, and the telephone directory is used as the sampling frame. It should be noted that a substantial number of homes either have no telephone or have an unlisted number. In some areas fewer than 80 percent of the households have listed telephone numbers. Unlisted telephones may be located in upper-income households (which try to avoid being besieged with solicitations or checked out by would-be robbers) and in low-income households (which use the device to escape the pressure of creditors). Also, all the families that have moved into new homes in the past year are unlikely to be listed; in our mobile society, that can be a good-sized percentage of the population of a town. The findings of a study that has employed the telephone directory as its sampling frame may be biased if the sample underrepresents the very high income, the very low income, and the newly relocated households.

For a simple random sample the choice of elements from the sampling frame must proceed in a manner that gives every element an equal chance of being chosen. The method used by Fred for his bibliography can be described as the "picking a name from the hat" approach. This method is feasible when small samples are being selected. The process becomes awkward, however, when larger samples are chosen.

Let us assume that State University has 16,000 students and that we want to select a simple random sample of 400. The list of those currently registered has been obtained and will be used as our sampling frame. Tables of random numbers are commonly used for the process of selecting elements from a sample of this size.[1] These tables are composed of random numbers that range from one to as high a number as the total size of any sampling frame is likely to be. Such tables are found in the Appendix of most statistics textbooks. In order to use a table of random numbers for the purpose of selecting elements, one must first number all the elements in the sampling frame. In our case each of the 16,000 students would be assigned a number, beginning with the number 1. If the first number picked from the table of random numbers is 379, the student who has been assigned the same number in the sampling frame would be selected for inclusion in our simple random sample. We would continue picking random numbers until we had selected 400 students for the sample.[2]

PROBABILITY THEORY. How do we know the extent to which our simple random sample reflects the larger population from which it has been drawn? To answer this question, we need to distinguish between the PARAMETERS of a population and the STATISTICS produced from a sample. A parameter is a characteristic of the total population. The percentage of all 16,000 students at State University who feel that undergraduates should have a responsibility in the hiring and firing of faculty members is a population parameter. A statistic is a characteristic of a sample. The corresponding percentage of students in our sample of 400 who hold this opinion is a sample statistic. The issue of accuracy may now be rephrased. How exactly do sample statistics reflect population parameters?

Probability theory tells us that for a simple random sample such statistics as

---

[1]Suppose we were to put the number 1 on 100 gum balls, the number 2 on 100 gum balls, and so on up to the number 1,000, which we would also put on 100 gum balls. Then suppose we were to very thoroughly mix all these balls and put them into a large fish bowl. If we now select a very small fraction of these balls one at a time, recording the numbers as the balls are selected (e.g., 243, 71, 528, etc.), the resulting list of numbers could be used to construct a table of random numbers. This table would allow us to select numbers between 1 and 1,000 at random; with appropriate modifications in the procedures used we could construct a table that would allow us to select numbers between one and a million or one and a billion at random. It is possible that some of the numbers in the specified range will be selected several times and that others will never be selected. In actual practice computers are used to construct such tables.

[2]Alternatively, we might first select the 400 random numbers between 1 and 16,000, put them in ascending order, and then count down an alphabetical list of all students selecting student numbers 7, 29, 36, 53, and so on, until the 400 students had been selected.

the sample mean fluctuate around population parameters in a known manner.[3] If many samples are drawn from the same population, the resulting sample estimates cluster around the population parameter. The measure of this variation is called the STANDARD ERROR. In general, the larger the sample size, the smaller the standard error of our estimate. That is, the larger our sample, the closer our sample estimate is likely to be to the true population value. Moreover, the logic of probability tells us that the more HOMOGENEOUS (similar) the elements in a population are, the more likely is the sample to reflect the true values within that population. This is the case since if all the elements in a population were identical, there would be no need for these random sampling strategies at all. Individuals picked by even the most accidental procedures would still be representative.

Probability theory allows us to estimate standard error (using a formula that is beyond the scope of the present discussion) so long as we know the size of a given population and sample and can estimate how homogeneous the responses to our questions are. If, as in our previous illustration, 80 percent of the students agreed with the proposition that undergraduates should be given responsibility in the hiring and firing of faculty, we could then estimate the standard error to be 2 percent. The true population parameter (that is, the result we would get were we to do a complete count of the attitudes of all the students) will generally be within two standard errors of our sample estimate.[4]

SYSTEMATIC SAMPLING. A SYSTEMATIC SAMPLE is very similar to a simple random sample. It also initially requires an adequate sampling frame. A random starting point is selected on this list and every nth name or unit is selected from that point on.

If we decided to select a systematic sample of 400 students from the list of those currently registered at State University, we would first obtain a SELECTION INTERVAL by dividing the population size (16,000) by the desired sample size (400). In this case, the selection interval is forty, which means that every 40th student would be selected from the sampling frame for the systematic sample. In order to ensure that each student has an equal chance of being selected, the starting point for the selection process must be randomly chosen. In other words, the first student would be selected from somewhere in the first interval of 40 on the list and the "somewhere" is determined randomly. Let us assume that the numbers 1 through 40 are thrown into a hat and the number 5 is selected. The initial student selected for our systematic sample would be the fifth student on the list of those currently registered at State University. The selection interval would then be applied by adding 40 to 5, so that the 45th student on the list would be selected next. This process would continue until we had chosen 400 students for the sample.

The principal advantage of systematic sampling over simple random sampling is the relative ease in executing the selection process. Only one act of randomization is required (selecting a random starting point) with systematic sampling, whereas simple random sampling requires the random selection of *every* element to be included in the sample. We do not have to refer back and forth constantly between the sampling frame and a table of random numbers. One disadvantage of

---

[3]For a more complete discussion of this issue, consult any introductory statistics textbook.

[4]You will note that we have selected a range of plus or minus two standard errors. For an explanation of why we have done this and a discussion of the formula used to compute the standard error, see an introductory statistics book.

systematic sampling is that it may be subject to bias if the sampling frame that is used has a regular, recurring pattern or cycle. Consider a research situation where the sampling frame is a list of street addresses for housing units (the population elements are housing units rather than individual people). Imagine that the selection interval is ten and that the randomly chosen starting point for the selection of elements is also ten. If city blocks containing ten housing units apiece are being studied, this might mean that one of the corner housing units on every block would be selected for the systematic sample. It is possible that corner housing units tend to be inhabited by people with higher incomes because they may have larger lots or better views and consequently command higher rentals. The same problem could occur if we did a systematic sample of newspapers with a selection interval of seven. This could result in a sample that contained only Sunday newspapers. It should be clear from these examples that if systematic sampling is used, the sampling frame should be checked beforehand for the possibility of such cyclical bias.

STRATIFIED SAMPLING. STRATIFIED RANDOM SAMPLING is another form of probability sampling. It involves dividing the population into two or more strata and then taking either a simple random sample or a systematic sample from each stratum. (Notice that quota sampling is very similar to this. The difference is that accidental samples are taken from different strata in quota sampling.)

The hypothetical behavior of Suzie offers an illustration of stratified random sampling. She has just met Fred outside the library, and he has related to her how he handled the problem of researching the literature for his paper on marine biology. We recall that Fred in his inventive way has done a simple random sample of five books from the one hundred that are in the library. Suzie is in the same class and is faced with a similar time pressure, but she knows intuitively that there is something shaky about Fred's procedure. She is certain that some of the books on marine biology are more important than others. Her suspicion is that the hardbound books are more scholarly than the paperbacks, and therefore she wants to make sure that at least some are included in her bibliography. There are sixty hardbound books and forty paperback books on marine biology in the library. Suzie writes down the names of all sixty hardbound books on individual slips of paper and places them in one box. She does the same for all forty paperback books, and she places these slips in a different box. She shakes up both boxes thoroughly and then picks out three slips of paper from the first box and two slips of paper from the second box. Suzie copies the selected book titles for her bibliography, which represents a stratified random sample of all the library books on marine biology.

Social scientists often use stratified random sampling in their research. It is necessary, of course, to have an adequate sampling frame in order to implement a stratified random sample. The sampling frame must be divided into separate lists for each stratum. The next step is to take a simple random or systematic sample from each of the lists. As with quota sampling, the strata are selected on the basis of variables relevant in the context of a particular research project.

A very important reason for selecting a stratified random sample is that if it is chosen correctly, it should yield more precise results than a simple random sample. The trick is to form strata that are internally homogeneous yet different from one another. In a survey on attitudes toward United States foreign policy in the Middle East, it would be appropriate to consider stratified sampling by religion or ethnicity so as to assure that there would be a specified proportion of Jews in the sample. If strata are formed that are internally homogeneous yet different from one another, the amount of sampling error is less than with a simple random sample of the same size. In brief, the sampling error (as estimated using the standard error) is smaller for a stratified random sample than for a simple random sample. This means that the precision of a stratified random sample can be greater than that of a simple random sample.

The general procedure in stratified random sampling is to sample from each stratum according to its percentage in the total population. If a particular stratum makes up 20 percent of a given population and the designated sampling size is 500, a selection of 100 elements from that stratum should be made. This is called PROPORTIONATE SAMPLING. There are, however, research situations where it becomes apparent that a proportionate sample will result in very small numbers of elements for particular strata. In such cases DISPROPORTIONATE SAMPLING, in which the strata are not sampled according to their percentages in the population is more appropriate. The goal in disproportionate sampling is to select enough elements from each stratum so that a fairly detailed statistical analysis of each stratum can be carried out.

In a study of the student body at State University, the population might be stratified by subject major. Some majors have very few students (e.g., physics), and for some purposes it would make sense to sample from them in larger numbers than their proportion of the entire student body warrants. When a disproportionate sample is selected, all of the elements of the population no longer have an equal chance of being included in the sample. Remember that the crucial aspect to probability sampling is that we have to know what the chance is of each element being selected. In this case we might decide to give physics majors twice the chance they would have of being selected for a simple random sample. When our goal is to estimate a population characteristic (e.g., mean income) based on a disproportionate sample, the results for each stratum must be weighted according to the percentage of the total population that the stratum represents. Since physics majors have been given twice the chance of being included as have students with other majors, their responses must be weighted by a CORRECTION FACTOR of one-half when information about the total student body is calculated. If physics majors had been given four times the normal chance of being included in the sample, the correction factor would have been one-fourth.

CLUSTER SAMPLING. One potential difficulty with all the probability sampling plans discussed so far is the requirement of ascertaining an adequate sampling frame. In some cases an actual list of the elements of the population is not readily available. It is not too difficult to find a sampling frame for the student population of a university. It would be difficult, however, to find a good sampling frame for all students who are currently enrolled in all of the colleges and universities throughout the United States.

CLUSTER SAMPLING can sometimes be used in situations where it would be impractical or impossible to obtain a complete list of all the elements in the population. Cluster sampling involves an initial stage wherein sampling is done from groups of elements that are called clusters. A simple, systematic, or stratified random sample of clusters is selected from a total list of such groups. Once a sample of clusters has been picked, a simple, systematic, or stratified random sample of individual elements is obtained from the chosen clusters. In the case at hand, one might first sample from a list of colleges (clusters of students) in the United States that could be derived from a publication such as the *Comparative Guide to American Colleges*. A stratified sample by size of institution might be very appropriate. The final stage of sampling would entail the selection of a simple, systematic, or stratified random sample of individual students from the chosen colleges. We might, for example, decide to carry out a stratified random sample of students at each college according to their subject major.

A key advantage of cluster sampling is that initially a complete listing of all the elements in the population is not necessary. Only a listing of the relevant clusters is required. One disadvantage of cluster sampling is that the accuracy of estimates based on such samples is less than that for other probability samples of the same size. One way to deal with this problem is to use a larger sample size. In cluster sampling, interviewers are sent to a few randomly chosen areas and they interview a substantial number of people in each. In contrast, a simple random sample might result in a situation where interviewers are dispatched to many more locations and they might interview only one person in each. The obvious advantage of cluster sampling is a savings of time and money.

MULTISTAGE CLUSTER SAMPLING. Let us look at another example that involves more stages of sampling from clusters than the previous illustration and that also shows the advantage of cluster sampling in saving time and money when interviewers are used. Imagine that we are interested in conducting a survey of the entire adult population in the United States. A list of the entire adult population would be impossible to obtain. Therefore, we decide to use MULTISTAGE CLUSTER SAMPLING on an area basis.

In our first stage of sampling, we might define counties as our initial sampling clusters. A list of every county in the nation is not difficult to obtain. Suppose we begin by selecting a simple random sample of seventy-five counties. This is the first stage of our cluster sampling procedure, and it yields county-sized clusters. (Incidentally, when selecting the seventy-five counties, we should take account of the varying population sizes through a weighting process that makes the probability of selection for any given county proportionate to the relative population size of that county compared with the other counties.[5])

The second stage of sampling would be designed to produce even more manageable cluster sizes. We would select three census tracts (for which listings are readily available) from each of the seventy-five counties by using the same probability sampling procedure described above. Even census tracts are quite large and are not easy to work with for the purpose of assigning neighborhoods to interviewers. Therefore, we could proceed to a third stage where we would select city blocks or census enumeration districts. This would depend on the relative urbanization of each area. (In rural areas it is sometimes necessary to designate physical boundaries such as streams because there is an absence of regular artificial boundaries such as city blocks.) If we select 3 blocks (or block equivalents) from each census tract by using probability sampling methods, we would have a total of 675 blocks in our sample. We would then proceed to take a probability sample of dwelling units from each block equivalent. If we select two dwelling units from each block and interview one adult in each unit, our total

---

[5]To actually do this would get us into more sophisticated sampling designs than would be appropriate to consider here.

sample size will be 1,350. It should be apparent from this example that the cost of interviewing would be considerably lower for a national cluster sample than it would be for any other probability sampling plan at the national level (if, indeed, other probability sampling plans could be carried out at that level). In any event, when a cluster sampling procedure is used, a relatively small number of interviewers is needed to cover the entire sample.

COMBINING SAMPLING PLANS. To this point we have discussed probability and nonprobability sampling as if the choice were to use one or the other. In actual practice the two are often combined. When we employ both probability and nonprobability stages in our sampling design, the final sample is always a nonprobability sample. Despite this it is very common for such well-known public opinion organizations as Harris and Gallup to combine sampling plans. The design for a national sample typically combines probability cluster sampling at the initial stages (e.g., county, census tract) with quota sampling at the final stage. When probability sampling is combined with quota sampling in such a way that the interviewer has relatively little freedom of choice with respect to where to obtain respondents, the resulting sample can be a very close approximation to a probability sample. The success of such organizations as Gallup and Harris in forecasting national elections is evidence of the accuracy that is possible with a sampling design that combines probability and nonprobability procedures.

Problems and Issues in Sampling

In this section three key issues in sampling that need further attention will be discussed. These are: (1) selection of sample size, (2) nonsampling error, and (3) sampling in qualitative research.

SAMPLE SIZE

One of the questions most frequently asked of the sampling expert is: "How large must my sample be?" This question is crucial because sample size has a major impact on the amount of time and money that must go into the data collection phase of the research. Under very special circumstances it is possible to give an explicit answer to this question. But far more common are situations where the researcher does not have all the information that must be available for there to be a precise statement of the necessary sample size. We do know, however, that simple random samples need to contain between thirty-five and forty elements to fall within the scope of probability theory. This is a bare minimum! Generally, it is wise to select a sample of at least one hundred elements of a population. The implication is that if the population under investigation is small (say, under 150), elaborate sampling procedures are probably inappropriate.

We can state the exact sample size required by a particular study if the following three conditions are met:

1. We must be able to identify a specific population parameter that is the primary focus of the study (for example, the answer to a question asking how the respondent intends to vote in November).

2. We must be able to make a reasonable estimate of the split on the question (for example, 50/50 or 90/10 on a question with two choices).
3. We must be able to specify how precise a result is desired (for example, will an error of 1, 2, or 5 percent be tolerable?).

If these conditions have been satisfied and simple random sampling has been used, then a table such as 5.1 will specify the sample size that will be needed. You will note that a larger sample is required for 99 percent CONFIDENCE LIMITS than for 95 percent. (If we use the 95 percent confidence limits, we can be sure that ninety-five out of one hundred samples of the specified size will be within the specified percent error of the population parameter.) These estimates are given for a question with a 50/50 split, but they can be used with other splits because the error is greatest for the 50/50 split; that is, the sample sizes specified are large enough for items with more extreme splits.

In most studies the investigator is interested in not one but many questions. If each of these questions has a different split among the response categories, a case can be made for a different sample size for each question. The way this problem is usually handled is to select a sample size appropriate for a 50/50 split; this provides a conservative estimate of the sample size needed for all others. It is also quite possible that different levels of error are acceptable from one question to the next. If the question is how the respondent intends to vote, we would not want to accept more than a 2 percent error if the expected split were 52/48. On the other hand, if the split were 90/10, we could predict the election outcome with a much smaller sample and we would be willing to tolerate a much greater error in our estimate. One way to deal with this problem is to select the question that is of greatest importance and use the sample size that corresponds to the acceptable level of error for this question. Another alternative is to select the question for which the acceptable level of error is lowest and choose the sample size that corresponds to this question. For most studies, however, neither of these alternatives is possible because the investigator does not have a clear idea of what level of error is acceptable. The acceptable level will in large measure depend on aspects of the statistical analysis that are difficult to anticipate prior to the data collection.

In general, the larger the sample, the smaller the sampling error, and the more

TABLE 5.1   Simple Random Sample Size for Several Degrees of Precision

	Confidence limits	
Tolerated error	95 samples in 100	99 samples in 100
1%	9,604	16,587
2%	2,401	4,147
3%	1,067	1,843
4%	600	1,037
5%	384	663
6%	267	461
7%	196	339

Source: Charles H. Backstrom and Gerald D. Hursh, *Survey Research* (Evanston, Ill.: Northwestern University Press, 1963), p. 33.

accurate will be estimates based on the sample. As can be seen in Table 5.1, the increase in accuracy with increased sample size does reach a point of diminishing returns. We need much more of an increase in sample size to reduce the level of error from 2 to 1 percent than from 7 to 6 percent. With a stratified random sample, smaller sample sizes are needed for a specified level of precision. For such samples the estimates presented in Table 5.1 can be used because they are conservative. For cluster sampling a larger sample size is needed for a specified level of error than is the case for a simple random sample. Thus Table 5.1 would not be appropriate for use with a cluster sample. One estimate is that a national cluster sample of 1,500 cases is roughly equivalent in terms of accuracy to a simple random sample of 1,000 cases (Davis, 1973:72). Typically, Harris and Gallup use cluster samples of between 1,200 and 1,500 respondents to reflect the opinions of the adult population of the United States. It turns out that approximately the same size sample would be needed to estimate the opinions of the adult population of one state (or even one large city) with the same degree of precision.[6]

As we mentioned at the outset, it is usually not possible to meet the conditions necessary for making a precise estimate of the needed sample size. In such situations the researcher is forced to fall back on the experience of others. If the topic of the research or the population being sampled is of great interest and if it has not been studied before, it is quite possible that even a study based on a small sample (and consequently of relatively low accuracy) will be of general interest. On the other hand, if the topic is one that has been repeatedly studied using large national samples, it is quite possible that there will be little interest in the proposed study unless it too is based on a large national sample.

Often the funds available set an upper limit on the possible sample size for a study. When this is the case, a judgment must be made as to whether the precision that is possible with a sample of this size is adequate to justify carrying out the study.

NONSAMPLING ERROR

Sampling error is a general term referring to those differences between sample statistics and the corresponding population parameters that are unavoidable but measurable and that arise as the result of probability sampling methods. In most social research, however, there are many other factors that tend to reduce the accuracy of estimates based on sample results. These are called nonsampling errors. The term bias is also used to refer to the distortion caused by the various sources of nonsampling error.

Poor Sampling Frame. One source of bias is the failure to choose an adequate sampling frame. A classic illustration of this error was the 1936 presidential poll conducted by *Literary Digest* to see whether Landon or Roosevelt would win. Telephone directories and lists of automobile owners were used as the sampling frame. Questionnaires were sent to 10 million adults in the United States who

---

[6]For smaller populations (e.g., 10,000 and under) it is appropriate to take into consideration the size of the population when deciding on a sample size. For a table to use in doing this, see Slonim (1960:78).

owned a phone or an automobile; more than 2 million responded. The prediction made on the basis of the poll was that Landon would win by a landslide. Unfortunately, the *Literary Digest* sample was severely biased. Only 40 percent of the homes in the United States had telephones at the time. Only a slim majority of families owned a car. This meant that the sample was biased in the direction of higher socioeconomic groupings, which traditionally vote Republican. More sophisticated researchers were well aware of the flaws in the *Literary Digest* poll considerably before history proved it to be wrong (Gallup, 1948:73–75).

NONRESPONSE. Another potential source of bias that may lead to inaccurate sample findings is nonresponse. In sample surveys of many types (door-to-door, mail, or telephone), there may be a difference between those persons who respond and those who do not. The potential differences are greatest in mail surveys (such as the *Literary Digest* poll) where the opportunity to refuse cooperation with the survey is almost completely unrestricted. Nonresponse, however, is a problem with all methodologies. When door-to-door interviewing is used, people who are very active are less likely to be at home than nonactive people. Consequently, a good survey will allow for several return visits to the not-at-homes. The return visits will be more successful if they are staggered over various times of day and different days of the week. One technique that has been proposed for dealing with the nonresponse problem is to ask those people who *are* at home during the initial call how many nights of the previous week they had been at home. Those who were not usually at home but happened to be there when the interviewer called are weighted more heavily in the data analysis stage of research than the people who were always at home (Politz and Simmons, 1949).

BIAS IN PANELS. A special biasing factor occurs in panel studies wherein the same respondents are interviewed repeatedly over time on the same topic or different topics. The original composition of the panel may be representative of the population of interest, but over a period of time, people leave the panel (because of moving, death, or lack of interest). Unless some provision is made to assess the change in makeup of the panel and to compensate for this change, the results will be biased. Another potential problem is that some panel members may become "expert respondents" during the course of their association with the panel. They may thoroughly research the various topics covered in the questionnaires (which are frequently self-administered) and then try to give the "right" answers. Thus membership on a panel may encourage some respondents to become less than representative of their counterparts in the population of interest. In order to circumvent this possibility, panel studies are sometimes supplemented by concurrent studies of "fresh" respondents to determine whether there is serious bias caused by membership on a panel.

BIAS IN RESPONDENT SELECTION. Even when a probability sample has been selected scientifically in order to maximize similarities between those interviewed and the entire population of interest, there are a variety of sources of bias that the interviewer may introduce into the sampling procedure. One is the possibility that interviewers will cut corners on sampling and either not do all of the work assigned or fabricate responses. This is particularly likely when they are being paid by the interview rather than by the hour. Another danger is that interviews will attempt to save time or money on return visits or calls by substituting respondents. Suppose a cluster sample calls for contacting every seventh house, but the interviewer finds that people are not at home. Is it legitimate to use the sixth or eighth house instead? Absolutely not! Similarly, if you are using a table of random numbers to generate a telephone sample, you must make every possible attempt to contact the exact people or households to whom you are directed by the table. If a researcher fails to adhere to the proper procedures for administering a probability sample, be it a simple random, stratified, or cluster sample, the accuracy of the results will be highly questionable. The laws of statistical probability work only when they are followed to the letter.

Unfortunately, while chance error due to sampling fluctuation can be estimated, there is no simple formula for estimating the magnitude of the various sources of nonsampling error and bias. The best the researcher can do is be aware of these sources of error and attempt to keep them to a minimum.

SAMPLING IN QUALITATIVE RESEARCH

We have seen that a major reason for sampling in survey research studies is to ensure that the people from whom we gather our data are representative of the larger population about whom we seek to generalize. One might suppose that sampling procedures are unnecessary in QUALITATIVE RESEARCH, or field work. Those doing field research typically observe only one case—one organization, one community, a single area of a city, or a discrete set of events. Since participant observers rarely seek systematic information from a large number of people, they do not ordinarily randomly select people to interview nor do they typically devise quota or purposive samples before entering the field. Nevertheless, sampling procedures are used in qualitative investigations. Participant observers must fashion sampling procedures to be certain that observations made in some setting are representative of what generally goes on in the setting. To see how and why field researchers might sample "times," "places," "roles," or "statuses," we will imagine an investigation of a large city hospital.

TIME SAMPLING. After a few weeks of preliminary observation, the researcher recognizes that activities in the hospital vary at different *times* during the day. Perhaps more automobile accident cases show up in the emergency room in the early hours of the morning, or certain types of operations are scheduled in the afternoon. The researcher begins to sense that there are times when doctors are not easily accessible and that this might alter the functioning of the organization. In short, as in virtually all contexts, there is an ebb and flow to activity. To get a total picture of a setting, one must avoid doing all the observational work at the same time each day. Field researchers will often sample times for doing their observation so as to ensure that their image of the organization is not based solely on the kinds of activities occurring during a particular time interval. It would be possible for the researcher to break the 24 hour day into discrete time units and let the times of observation be dictated by a random sampling of these time units.

PLACE SAMPLING. Activities and events also vary in different *places* within an organization. Imagine the biased picture of the hospital obtained if a field researcher restricted all observation to the emergency room. The activities of doctors, nurses, patients, and administrators observed in this particular area of the hospital are likely to be quite different from those in other areas. Our researcher correctly decides, therefore, that it is necessary to witness activities in different places within the hospital. One strategy might simply be to make a list of various strategic locations (e.g., the emergency room, the nurses' station, the admitting office, the cafeteria, the waiting rooms) and to systematically do observations in each. It might be reasonable in some studies to combine time sampling and place sampling. Researchers must, of course, use good judgment with regard to place sampling. They might discover after a short period of observation in a particular place that they have likely seen all the essential activities that go on there. Our researcher would be foolish to spend hours observing clothes drying in the hospital laundry room simply because a regimented sampling plan demanded it.

EVENT SAMPLING. Related to time and place sampling is *event* sampling. Schatzman and Strauss (1973) note that in any organization there are typically routine, special, and unexpected events. In organizations like hospitals, the vast majority of happenings are routine—meetings at specific times, meal serving, visiting hours, doctors' rounds, and so on. And although special events occur infrequently, they may still be anticipated. If one learns, for example, that an examining board responsible for continuing the hospital's accreditation will be visiting, one surely would want to observe how this special event alters the routine operation of the organization. Once researchers have gained the trust of people in the setting, they may even ask to be called if unexpected events are in the process of occurring. It is possible to make a list of routine events and selectively sample each. Although it is more difficult to plan observations of special and unexpected events, researchers will want to make a determined effort to observe them. Past research experience suggests that a great deal is learned about the functioning of any social system by observing its responses to special events.

STATUS, ROLE AND RELATIONSHIP SAMPLING. Finally, there will be occasions when a participant observer wants to discover the behavior of, or to interview, specific types of people in an organization. People in unique positions within an organization or setting will have quite different perspectives on it. Field researchers rarely try to interview a large number of people systematically in a particular setting. They might determine, as the research progresses and theoretical ideas begin to take shape, that people occupying certain statuses in the organization can supply them with important information. They may choose, therefore, to sample *statuses and roles*. In the hospital setting the researcher might want to observe the behavior of, or talk to, individuals who serve specific functions. David Sudnow (1967), who studied death and dying in one hospital, made it a special point to observe the activities of the hospital morgue attendant. If the researcher wanted to find out the kinds of changes that have occurred over time in the hospital, it might be reasonable to sample some of the "old-timers" there. As an extension of status and role sampling, a field researcher might even be interested in sampling social relationships. The researcher might decide that it is theoretically important to observe a sampling of interactions between doctors new to the job and nurses who have long service on the staff.

SAMPLING AND THE CREATION OF THEORY. An important point emerges from our examination of the sampling procedures frequently employed in qualitative research: the basis for sampling in many qualitative studies is not to make statistical estimates of population parameters based on sample data, but to make theoretical generalizations. Certainly, any social scientist wants to ensure that observations made of people, events, and places are typical. At the same time the qualitative researcher would rarely be concerned with having observed every type of event, situation, status, or role. The task in field work is more usually to sample from among the universe of events, statuses, and the like, only those that are most integrally related to emerging theoretical ideas. It is not a criterion of such sampling that the elements of the sample closely approximate the characteristics of some known universe.

In survey research, sampling procedures are chosen only once, at the beginning of the investigation. By contrast, in qualitative research, sampling is an ongoing practice. As theoretical ideas develop during the researcher's observations, it may become necessary to sample features of the situation that were not anticipated earlier. It is then that a quota or purposive sample may be decided upon, primarily to help the field worker understand a particular setting.

Summary

In social research as in daily life, we sample, that is, we must make generalizations about the world on the basis of examining relatively few cases. The major difference is that a researcher consciously takes precautions to ensure that the sample is as representative and unbiased as possible. This chapter is a nontechnical introduction to the logic and rules of sampling for both quantitative survey research and qualitative field work.

There are two basic kinds of sampling techniques. One is nonprobability sampling (for example, accidental, quota, and purposive). Nonprobability sampling plans require substantial judgment on the part of the researcher. The other type is probability sampling, which reduces the chances of bias by limiting the role of the researcher in the process of selecting the elements for the sample. In simple random, stratified, and cluster sampling, each element in the population of interest has a known, nonzero chance of being selected. The accuracy of probability samples is measured by the standard error, which, generally speaking, decreases as sample size increases. The more homogeneous the original population, the smaller the error is likely to be. Stratified sampling procedures utilize this principle, in that the sample is separated into different segments, which are internally homogeneous. The result is more accuracy than would be obtained with a simple random sample. Cluster sampling is also a modification and expansion of the logic of random sampling and is especially useful where it would be difficult or impossible to obtain an adequate sampling frame. As a general rule, one should use the most precise sampling plan that time and resources permit. Probability and quota sampling procedures may be combined and produce good results, so long as the interviewer's freedom to select individual respondents is limited.

Three major issues in sampling are size, nonsampling error, and sampling in qualitative research. It is usually difficult to determine exactly how large a sample ought to be, and it is impossible unless specific population parameters are identifiable and unless the distribution of responses to given questions may be estimated with reasonable accuracy. If these conditions are met, we may project the sample sizes necessary for obtaining varying degrees of precision and confidence in our findings. For some purposes a tolerated error of 3 or 4 percent is all that is necessary. In other cases (as in forecasting election results) a tolerated error as high as 3 percent would be useless. The sample size needs to be increased in order to raise confidence limits and lower tolerated error, but there is a point of diminishing returns, above which it may not be helpful to contact more respondents.

Probability sampling plans make use of mathematical principles to reduce bias and increase representativeness. But nonsampling errors may still occur as the result of using a poor sampling frame, the nonresponse of subjects, or bias in the administration of the sample after it has been selected. The researcher should be aware of these and other sources of error and attempt to minimize them.

Because there are many research situations where the use of probability samples is impossible or impractical, sampling in field work is receiving renewed attention. Often some form of judgment sampling is utilized that is open to modification as the research progresses. The sampling of places, events, and peoples' roles and statuses at different points in time achieves greater representativeness. It also aids in the construction through induction of social, political, and psychological theory, by demonstrating principles of behavior based on carefully selected individual cases.

Key Terms

accidental sampling	multistage cluster	random sampling
bias	sampling	representative sample
cluster sampling	nonprobability sample	sampling error
confidence limits	nonsampling error	sampling frame
correction factor	parameter	selection interval
disproportionate sampling	population	standard error
distribution	probability sample	statistic
element	proportionate sampling	stratified random sampling
generalization	purposive sampling	stratum
homogeneous	qualitative research	systematic sample
	quota sample	unbiased sample

Exercises

1. Describe the sampling you do in your everyday life with respect to dating and marriage, selecting a school to attend, or buying a car. What kind of sampling do you do? How good a sample do you choose? Is the issue of accuracy relevant to your sampling? Why?

2. Suppose you were sampling the households in a metropolitan area and you wanted a sample of 600. The area is covered by four telephone directories, one of which contains 300 pages of central city listings. Each of the other three directories covers a portion of the suburbs and contains 100 pages. Since the four directories have a total of 600 pages, and you desire 600 interviews, what problems of bias, if any, would be involved if you randomly selected one name

from each of the 600 pages for your sample?

3. Qualitative research is sometimes criticized for its lack of attention to sampling design. Select one observational study from the literature and critique its sampling procedure. Does the author of the study you chose deal with issues of sampling reliability and validity? If so, how?

4. Describe a research situation in which a nonprobability sample would be most appropriate. Which nonprobability sampling plan would you select? How large a sample would you choose? How would you attempt to minimize bias in the execution of your sample?

5. Suggest appropriate items, locations, events, roles and statuses to sample when doing participant observation of:

a.   an airport
b.   a factory
c.   a city park
d.   a doctor's waiting room
e.   a bar

6.   The national media ratings, which influence advertising as well as the production and cancellation of television series, are usually based on samples of less than 1,200 households. Investigate this procedure. Does it give us a reliable and valid picture of America's taste in television programing? Is it fair that 1,200 families carry so much weight in determining what programs we all can see?

7.   A survey is being conducted to determine the favorite popular music performer among college students, and you are asked to select a sample of one hundred undergraduates at your school. Compare sampling plans for accidental, quota, and simple random samples. After you have described the differences between them, speculate on the likely differences in results of the survey depending on which sampling plan is used.

Suggested Readings

Backstrom, Charles H., and Gerald D. Hursh
1963   *Survey Research.* Evanston, Ill.: Northwestern University Press.
Chapter 2 is a treatment of sampling at the nuts-and-bolts level that will be of use to those actually planning to draw a sample for a survey research study.

Blalock, Hubert M.
1972   *Social Statistics.* 2nd ed. New York: McGraw-Hill.
Chapter 21 on sampling will be of interest to the reader with some background in statistics. It goes into more depth on the issues that we have treated in a nontechnical way.

Cochran, William G.
1963   *Sampling Techniques.* New York: Wiley.
A thorough but highly technical treatment of sampling procedures.

Denzin, Norman K.
1970   *The Research Act.* Chicago: Aldine.
Chapters 4 to 6 discuss the relationship between theory and sampling procedure. Denzin raises a number of issues of interest to those who do qualitative research.

Kish, Leslie
1965   *Survey Sampling.* New York: Wiley.
This book is considered by many to be the most thorough available on the subject. It requires extensive mathematical background for full comprehension.

Schatzman, Leonard, and Anselm L. Strauss
1973   *Field Research.* Englewood Cliffs, N.J.: Prentice-Hall.
Chapter 3 contains a useful discussion of sampling in field work.

Slonim, Morris J.
1960   *Sampling.* New York: Simon and Schuster.
An excellent nontechnical introduction to sampling, this book is written in a humorous vein and contains a number of illustrations.

Williams, Bill
1978   *A Sampler on Sampling.* New York: Wiley.
A thorough yet highly readable discussion of the major issues in sampling, written in an engaging and entertaining style, with helpful exercises to test comprehension.

References

Backstrom, Charles H., and Gerald D. Hursh
1963   *Survey Research.* Evanston, Ill.: Northwestern University Press.

Davis, James A.
1973   *General Social Survey: 1973 Codebook.* Chicago: National Opinion Research Center.

Gallup, George
1948   *A Guide to Public Opinion Polls.* Princeton, N.J.: Princeton University Press.

Politz, Alfred, and Willard Simmons
1949   "An Attempt to Get the 'Not-at-Homes' into the Sample Without Call-Backs." *Journal of the Ameri-*

can Statistical Association 44 (March):9–31.

Schatzman, Leonard, and Anselm L. Strauss

1973   *Field Research.* Englewood Cliffs, N.J.: Prentice-Hall.

Slonim, Morris J.

1960   *Sampling.* New York: Simon and Schuster.

Sudnow, David

1967   *Passing On: The Social Organization of Dying.* Englewood Cliffs, N.J.: Prentice-Hall.

PART II

Procedures of
Social Research

6 / Survey Research

CHAPTER OUTLINE

INTRODUCTION
SURVEY DESIGN
Formulating Objectives and
    Hypotheses
Choosing a Time Frame
    Cross-Sectional Design
    Longitudinal Design
    Panel Studies
Planning a Sampling Strategy
Choosing a Data Gathering Technique
    Self-Administered Questionnaires
    Face-to-Face Interviews
    Telephone Surveys
Formulating Questionnaire Items
    Question Content
    Multiple Indicators
    Structured Versus Unstructured
        Questions

Question Wording
Constructing the Questionnaire
    Introduction
    Instructions
    Sequence of Questions
    Layout and Response Format
    Pretesting
SURVEY EXECUTION
The Self-Administered Survey
The Interview Survey
    Preparation
    Developing Rapport
    Providing a Uniform Stimulus
    Probing
    Recording Responses
Preparing the Data for Processing
    Precoding
    The Data Matrix

Coding
    Preparing a Codebook
    Keypunching
    Code Checking and Cleaning
    A Hypothetical Survey
SECONDARY ANALYSIS
    Data Banks
THE STRENGTHS AND
    LIMITATIONS OF SURVEY
    RESEARCH
SUMMARY
KEY TERMS
EXERCISES
SUGGESTED READINGS
REFERENCES

Introduction

Surveys are the most common form of research in the social sciences, and we are all regularly exposed to them in one form or another. We may be stopped on the street or in a shopping mall by interviewers who ask our opinions on current issues or our preferences for consumer items. We are telephoned by surveyors who ask how we intend to vote in an upcoming election or why we chose one airline over another. We receive a variety of questionnaires in the mail—from government agencies, business corporations, and community organizations. Newspapers report the latest public opinion polls; the major television networks employ their own pollsters. All these are forms of *survey research*: systematic attempts to collect information to describe and explain the beliefs, attitudes, values, and behavior of selected groups of people. Virtually every topic of interest in the social sciences has been studied through surveys, and the broad adaptability of this research method is one of its greatest strengths.

The characteristic of surveys that best illustrates their value and explains their extensive use is their ability to produce a representative distribution or *cross section* of the "target" population, whether that population be the entire American voting public or the people who stayed at a certain hotel during a given month. Because the value of a survey depends on the representativeness of the group surveyed, the sampling plan and its execution are almost as crucial to final success as are the planning and execution of the overall survey itself.[1] Hence anyone conducting a survey would be well advised to begin by thoroughly reviewing all issues and options related to sampling.

A major difference between the survey and other research methods lies in the number of persons from whom data are usually collected. Surveys generally use much larger samples of subjects than are used in research involving intensive interviews, experiments, or observational studies. Stouffer (1966) conducted a survey of beliefs about the threat of communism and about the extent to which civil liberties ought to be curtailed in order to deal with the perceived threat. The study was based on two national samples, a total of approximately 5,000 people, drawn to represent a cross section of the national population. In order to permit systematic comparison of the views of an influential elite with those of the general public, the study also included interviews with 1,500 community leaders. Stouffer's sample was larger than that required for most surveys, but minute compared with that of James Coleman et al.'s study entitled *Equality of Educational Opportunity* (1966), which surveyed 570,000 students and 60,000 teachers. The U.S. Bureau of the Census conducts a monthly mail survey of approximately 50,000 households in order to arrive at an accurate description of current labor force characteristics, such as the unemployment rate. Despite these examples of massive studies, the standard, accepted sample size for contemporary national surveys is about 1,500 cases, and in carefully designed and well-executed surveys, much smaller samples can and do regularly produce surprisingly accurate results.

After the size and type of sample have been determined, several other decisions must be made before a survey can be conducted. How much personal contact will be necessary in order to gather the data? Must each of the subjects be contacted in person? And if so, how much time and expense are involved? Would it suffice to contact the subjects by mail or telephone? The savings in time and expense can be enormous, but the data will not be as accurate or as detailed, and the tendency of subjects to refuse to provide data will be higher. Can the objectives of the research be met with a single survey? Or must several surveys be conducted at different times in order for changes and trends to be measured and analyzed? These overriding design issues must be resolved before a researcher can construct a questionnaire or establish specific tactics for data collection.

A survey research project may be thought of as a sequence of major steps to be carried out. These steps include: formulating research objectives, deciding how to collect the data, constructing the questionnaire, choosing a sampling method, preparing the collected data for processing and analysis, and processing and analyzing the data. Since sampling techniques and methods of data analysis have been treated in detail in other chapters, the discussion that follows will concen-

---

[1]Some surveys, instead of sampling, study all members of their target populations. The U.S. Census is an example.

trate on the other major considerations and issues involved in survey design and execution.

Survey Design

As has been emphasized in earlier chapters, no research method flows from one discrete step to the next by a totally rational and trouble-free process, because no researcher can anticipate all possible contingencies. But research methods do differ in their degree of rigor; in one method the stages of planning, data collection, and data analysis may be more distinct than in another. Compared with other research techniques, surveys are fairly rigid and structured; each step builds on what has gone before and necessarily inherits all the limitations of preceding plans and procedures. If a researcher has a brilliant insight in the middle of an interview, it is probably too late at that point to formulate and test a new hypothesis. Hence in survey research the planning stages are crucial, for upon those stages will depend the worth and relevance of the survey's results.

FORMULATING OBJECTIVES AND HYPOTHESES

Although the survey method has wide applicability, one can never assume that a survey will be an appropriate research strategy until the aims of the inquiry have been fully articulated. Thus the formulation of objectives must precede the choice of research method. Begin, therefore, by asking yourself, "What do I need to know, and why do I need to know it?" Most research projects start with very general answers to this question, but those answers must then be narrowed, focused, and justified.

Motivated simply by curiosity, a political scientist might begin a study about the degree of public support for certain local and national politicians, both incumbents and challengers. The researcher may then anticipate possible results and try to imagine what related popular sentiments might produce one or another election outcome. Does the project aim simply to describe the current popularity levels of a group of politicians, or does it also aim to discover the reasons behind the differing fates of public figures? What are the general issues that concern people and that affect their attitudes toward public figures? Are politicians being judged on style or performance, on local or national issues, on action or rhetoric, on work or visibility, on their own records or the general tide of events during their tenure in office? These research questions could be studied in a number of different ways.

A survey could be conducted in which a researcher first asked a sample of people to name some politicians they like and some whom they dislike and then probed for detailed reasons behind the stated preferences. The data thus collected might reveal a great deal about what people *believe* to be true about political figures and might help to explain the figures' relative levels of popularity. Another researcher might approach the same set of questions by means of a different method, relying on other kinds of data, such as politicians' legislative voting records, campaign speeches, and literature, measured against the length of their political careers and the percentage of votes they have polled in each election.

Whether the result of these procedures proved more or less useful or illuminating than the findings produced by a survey would depend largely on the priorities of the individual researcher and on the nature of the specific questions asked.

Before you decide that the survey method is necessary and suitable for your research project, thoroughly review all the existing literature (books and articles) written by other researchers on the same general topic. Many of the points of interest to you may have been resolved by previous studies. Or relevant data may exist in "underanalyzed" form, which you could obtain and turn to your own purposes. Only after you have reviewed and exhausted these possibilities should you embark on a fresh survey of your own. Although a review of past research might occasionally produce satisfactory answers to your queries, it is far more probable that reading the results of others' work will help you to clarify exactly what questions, out of the many that will probably occur to you, are most worth pursuing.

Another procedure helpful in the formulation of survey objectives is the PILOT STUDY: a tentative examination, using relatively unstructured interviews, of a handful of subjects who are similar to those who will be the target of the later survey. Pilot studies, like rehearsals, are intended to allow the researcher to try out various possibilities before deciding which ones to adopt. Such studies can often stimulate new lines of inquiry, prompted by the reactions or unsolicited responses of the subjects. They can also suggest new types of data that should be collected, point up and resolve ambiguities in the way that questions are being asked, indicate modifications needed in the order of topics covered, and help to eliminate fruitless lines of inquiry. If a study of migration to cities were planned, the pilot phase might involve in-depth, intensive interviews with migrants in several different areas. It might serve as a guide to the sampling of those who have moved and to uncovering reasons for migrating that had not occurred to the researcher. Any investigator who contemplates an extensive survey should consider the pilot study as an opportunity to discover and correct mistakes before they become serious or irremediable.

CHOOSING A TIME FRAME

After you have formulated a research question, and if you have decided that a survey is the most appropriate method for collecting data, you must determine whether all necessary data can be collected at once or whether it must be collected by means of surveys conducted at different times.

CROSS-SECTIONAL DESIGN. A single, unrepeated survey, referred to as a CROSS-SECTIONAL DESIGN, has the virtue of producing prompt results; such a study can often be completed within a few months or weeks, or even within a few hours.[2] The cross-sectional design is most appropriate for drawing inferences about the characteristics of the population from which you drew your sample and about the degree of association between those characteristics.

---

[2]Television news services sometimes sponsor "instant surveys" immediately after a presidential speech or a major controversial event. Usually, such a survey is conducted by telephone, and the results are available within twenty-four hours.

Suppose a team of researchers interested in exploring the fear of crime in American cities chooses six cities of different sizes, carefully selects samples of households within each city, hires interviewers, and conducts a survey in each city. When the data have been collected and analyzed, the researchers may generalize about the extent and distribution of fear of crime in each city and about the variations in levels of fear within the population of each, and they may make comparisons among the cities. Using a cross-sectional survey design, they may draw an elaborate picture of fears of violence and victimization at one moment in the history of six American cities. Through detailed examination of variations in fear levels within and among cities, they may even be able to suggest the sources or causes of those fears. Other questions, however, will remain largely unanswered. The cross-sectional survey design is sometimes referred to as the "snapshot approach," because although the single survey can provide a momentary, representative portrait of a population, it cannot trace the processes of change.

LONGITUDINAL DESIGN. The more suitable procedure for studying the processes of change is the LONGITUDINAL SURVEY DESIGN in which a survey is repeated several times in order to measure the rate and degree of change occurring in patterns of response. As noted in Chapter 2, one type of longitudinal design, the TREND STUDY, consists of several successive surveys, each based on a different sample of subjects. Each sample is independently drawn, at regular intervals, from the same general population. Gallup polls are conducted in this way, and comparisons of the results of several different polls can be quite useful for analyzing trends. A single poll indicating that 62 percent of American people expect the economy to get worse before it gets better would probably be interpreted pessimistically. But if a trend analysis indicated that only three months earlier 82 percent of those polled felt the economy was going to turn downward, the later finding might be interpreted more optimistically.

Although our ability to study processes of change is greatly enhanced by the trend study, one major limitation of this design seriously reduces the reliability of measured differences that appear between surveys based on separate samples. In such studies changes in patterns of response from one survey to the next arise in part from real shifts in behavior or sentiments and in part from sampling variations. Neither the amount of sampling error in a survey nor its effects on the figures that the survey produces can be assumed to be equal or constant from one survey to the next. Suppose a trend study of attitudes toward work requirements for mothers on welfare showed a decline from 50 percent supporting work as a requirement in 1970 to only 25 percent supporting the same policy in 1980. How reliably can we conclude from these figures that support for "workfare" has been cut in half in a decade? The answer to this question depends on the amount of sampling error that occurred in each survey. It is entirely conceivable that sampling fluctuations inflated the 1970 figure, deflated the 1980 figure, and produced an apparent difference much larger than any shift that may have actually occurred. Indeed, there is a tendency in trend studies for the analyst's attention to be drawn to shifts that are abnormally large or small. Unfortunately, these deviations, which may be the most interesting results, are often heavily influenced by sampling error.

PANEL STUDIES. The PANEL STUDY is a longitudinal design devised specifically to minimize the effects of sampling error. A sample, or panel, is chosen, and that same group of respondents is resurveyed at selected intervals. Thus the later responses of any subject or category of subjects, or of the sample as a whole, can be directly compared to responses given at an earlier time. The measures of change that are produced by such a design are highly reliable.

A classic example of a panel study is found in *The People's Choice,* by Lazarsfeld, Berelson, and Gaudet (1944). Six hundred residents of Erie County, Ohio, were interviewed once a month between May and November of 1940 about how they intended to vote in the upcoming presidential election. The investigators were particularly interested in charting the factors that voters weighed before making their eventual choice.

Besides eliminating the problem of variations between successive surveys due to sampling error, the panel study has another distinct advantage over other longitudinal survey designs: the sheer volume of information that can be collected from each respondent. The time during which a volunteer subject can be expected to remain cooperative and attentive is limited, and a great deal of that time is usually devoted by the researcher to collecting necessary background information (age, race, gender, income, education, etc.). Thus the limits of comprehensive coverage of relevant topics are fixed by the average respondent's tolerance and attention span. In panel studies, however, there is no need to repeat background questions after the initial interview, so subsequent contacts with subjects can focus progressively more attention on issues at the heart of the inquiry. Moreover, the data accumulated in the successive interviews, when considered as the overall record of an extended investigation, are more detailed and comprehensive than could ever be produced from a single contact. Since Lazarsfeld introduced the technique, the panel—because of its usefulness for predicting outcomes and because of the relative detail and accuracy with which it recreates patterns of persuasion and decision making—has become a standard tool in the study of voting behavior.

Panel studies are not without their disadvantages and limitations. The sheer cost of repeatedly conducting the same survey creates pressure upon the researcher to restrict the size of the initial sample, and as a consequence, the sample's representativeness is restricted as well. This problem is magnified by the inevitable loss of some subjects before the study has been completed. Remember that the longer the study design, the more probable it is that some respondents will lose interest, move without leaving a forwarding address, or die. Some of the problems typical of panel studies are found in the Survey Research Center's *Panel Study of Income Dynamics* (1972), which involved personal interviews in 5,000 households during the spring of each year from 1968 to 1972.[3] The study yielded detailed information about various sources of income, and that information has been applied to many research questions, including studies of the characteristics of those moving into and out of poverty. But although a great effort was made to avoid sample loss, only 62 percent of those in the original sample remained at the end of five years.

---

[3]Most reports on the *Income Dynamics* data that have been published thus far have been based on data collected up to 1972. The study continues, however, and as is characteristic of longitudinal surveys, there is no need to terminate ongoing data collection as long as the results justify expenditures.

PLANNING A SAMPLING STRATEGY

The strengths and weaknesses of alternative sampling methods have already been discussed in detail in Chapter 5. These are of central importance to survey research. In general, probability sampling is desirable. But quota sampling is widely used by commercial pollsters because it is less expensive than other options. The choice of a sampling strategy is most often determined by: (1) available funds, (2) the numerical and geographical scope of the survey, (3) the availability of an adequate sampling frame, and (4) the method chosen for collecting the data.

When data are being collected by mail or by telephone, it is often possible to do simple random sampling, or even stratified sampling, for no more than the cost of a less complex sampling method. If data are to be collected through personal interviews, however, methods that involve individually selecting and contacting each subject can consume large amounts of time and money. Funds thus devoted to locating subjects are no longer available for other aspects of the research, and the increased cost per interview may seriously restrict the size of the final sample. These concerns become more and more critical as the geographical dispersion of the target population increases. If the Social Security Administration were to draw a simple random sample of Social Security recipients for personal interviewing, the travel costs involved in locating subjects would far exceed all other expenses. It is for this reason that national surveys rely on complex, multistage combinations of stratified, quota, and cluster sampling techniques.

The type of probability sample most widely used in survey research is cluster sampling, in which a sample of groups (clusters) is drawn before individuals within them are identified and selected. If, in a given survey, clusters are represented by neighborhoods, travel time and expense may be minimized, for interviews could be conducted in concentrated areas, not in households scattered throughout the city. As the area to be covered increases, so also does the potential savings to be derived from the use of a multistage cluster design.

Whatever type of sampling strategy you choose, it must involve vigorous and successful efforts to contact and gain the cooperation of as many members of the sample as possible. Nonresponse is a plague that can ruin any sample, and it must be minimized. Individuals not at home during a door-to-door survey should be followed up by telephone, by mail, or in person. More than one call-back is often necessary for that small percentage of subjects who are most difficult to reach, until arrangements are finally made to complete the interview. Similar and equally persistent efforts are necessary in phone or mail surveys.

Despite the researcher's best efforts, surveys nearly always fall short of the ideal of 100 percent cooperation, although some do achieve response rates of 80 percent or better. Hence the question inevitably arises, "At what point can a rate of response be considered adequate?" Unfortunately, there is no simple or direct answer to this question. A low response rate can occur for a variety of reasons, and does not necessarily render the sample unrepresentative. It does, however, cast a shadow over the results of the research, and it transfers the burden of proof to the researcher to demonstrate that the sample remains representative and unbiased despite the low rate of response. For this reason whenever adequate data are available, it is wise to compare the characteristics of respondents to those of nonrespondents. If the two groups from the sample can be shown to be similar in important respects, confidence in the representativeness of the respondents is greatly enhanced.

CHOOSING A DATA GATHERING TECHNIQUE

Researchers may collect data from subjects through face-to-face interviews, through telephone contacts, or through self-administered questionnaires. All three approaches allow the same options for the kinds of information that can be gathered. What varies is the degree of personal contact used to elicit the data.

SELF-ADMINISTERED QUESTIONNAIRES. SELF-ADMINISTERED QUESTION-NAIRES, whether distributed to a captive audience (as in a classroom) or distributed through the mails, are the least costly data gathering technique, for no interviewers are needed. This technique has the added advantage of allowing respondents as much time as they require to consider each question carefully before answering. There is no pressure to produce an immediate reply, as there often is perceived to be in an interview, and there is not likely to be any embarrassment regarding sensitive questions. Some respondents feel more comfortable about expressing their honest reactions to questions on sensitive topics (such as sex, politics, or religion) on a questionnaire than they do in an interview. These advantages, particularly the relatively low cost involved, make the self-administered questionnaire one of the most popular methods of social research.

The major disadvantage of self-administered questionnaires is their tendency to inspire only a low degree of enthusiasm and involvement in potential respondents. Unstructured questions that require serious consideration (for example, "What do you think the government ought to be doing about the energy crisis?") seldom elicit more than perfunctory replies. Hence self-administered questionnaires rely heavily on items that offer predetermined response alternatives and thus can seldom probe issues in any real depth. Worse yet, the most typical reaction to a mail survey is to throw it away! The rate of response to mail questionnaires is considerably lower than that for either face-to-face or telephone interviews. Although homogeneous populations tend to be fairly responsive, when a cross section of the population is surveyed by mail, return rates of 10 percent or less are common.

The prevailing low rates of return for self-administered questionnaires may stem from subjects' unwillingness to reply and also from their inability to reply. A skilled interviewer can help almost any subject through a set of questions, but "for purposes of filling out even simple written questionnaires," it has been estimated that "at least 10 percent of the adult population of the United States is illiterate. For complex questionnaires, the percentage would undoubtedly be considerably higher" (Selltiz et al., 1976). The most carefully selected sample is unlikely to remain cross-sectionally representative if only a small fraction of those sampled choose to reply.

The self-administered questionnaire also transfers a great deal of control from the researcher to the subject. If some subjects fill out their questionnaires hastily or without reflection, or if some subjects seek the aid of friends or family members, the researcher has no way of detecting or controlling these disturbing influences—no way even of estimating their effects.

FACE-TO-FACE INTERVIEWS. The best data gathering technique for survey research, if the interviewers are well trained and the substantial expense involved can be met, is the FACE-TO-FACE INTERVIEW. Face-to-face interviews allow the researcher to collect data from a much larger percentage of those sampled than is usually possible with self-administered questionnaires. Subjects tend to be more impressed with the seriousness of a study when the researcher contacts them personally than when they receive a form letter and questionnaire through the mail. Personal contact may make an interview seem far less routine and standardized than it actually is. It is also far more difficult for a subject to refuse an interviewer in person than it is to relegate a questionnaire to the wastebasket.

The presence of an interviewer can also improve the quality, as well as the quantity, of responses from each subject. If a subject does not understand a question, the interviewer can clarify its meaning. If a respondent's answer seems not to fit the intent of the question, the alert interviewer will seek clarification through the use of a PROBE—asking, for example, "Could you explain exactly what you mean by that?" Such probes can both clarify and add depth to the information the respondent is providing. A trained interviewer also heightens the validity of the data by detecting and weeding out insincere respondents and obviously false replies.

TELEPHONE SURVEYS. Less expensive than face-to-face interviews, TELEPHONE SURVEYS avoid most of the problems that can arise when mailed questionnaires are used and, within certain limits, can meet a wide variety of research needs quite effectively. Telephone interviews generally cost less than half as much as the same number of face-to-face interviews, and the increasing availability of toll-free telephone service is further reducing costs while extending the useful range of the telephone survey. Researchers with very limited resources often find it within their means to conduct regional, statewide, or even national surveys by telephone. Because in a telephone survey all contacts can be made from a single location, the researcher is better able to monitor the quality of work done by hired interviewers.

Early telephone surveys developed an unfortunate reputation for sampling bias because some categories of respondents tended not to have telephones, while others tended to have unlisted numbers. The potential for such bias, however, has greatly diminished in recent years. The telephone has become so standard an item that the poor are no longer necessarily underrepresented (except, perhaps, in rural areas). In fact, in some inner city neighborhoods plagued with high crime rates, potential subjects of face-to-face interviews may pretend that they are not home or refuse to let the interviewer in because of their fear of strangers. The biases incurred by this refusal to cooperate may often be far greater than the bias created by missing those individuals who have no phone. As a result phone surveys can sometimes better represent the poor than door-to-door surveys. People who have unlisted telephone numbers can be reached through the technique known as RANDOM-DIGIT DIALING. If the researcher knows the exchanges (the first three numbers) in the areas under study, the last four digits can be chosen by a random method, and all telephone numbers, listed or unlisted, will have an equal chance of being dialed.

The major limitation of telephone surveys is the length of time involved in a telephone interview. A contact that will run more than fifteen or twenty minutes may be refused or prematurely terminated by the subject. This reduces the amount of information that can be gathered to between one-third and one-half of the data usually collected in a face-to-face interview. Questions must also be kept fairly simple, since no written lists or illustrations can be displayed as aids to the subject's understanding. On balance, however, if the topic of your research is relatively brief and straightforward, the telephone survey may prove an accurate, representative, and cost-effective option.

FORMULATING QUESTIONNAIRE ITEMS

All three data gathering techniques (through the mail, face-to-face, and by telephone) are based on a set of questions to which subjects are asked to reply. The generation of measures for concepts—specifically, the transformation of research objectives into carefully chosen questions—is one of the most important steps in the survey research process. In this section the types of questions most often used in surveys and the general rules for determining the form in which these questions are to be presented to the subject will be considered.

QUESTION CONTENT. In general, the content of specific questionnaire items should be determined by the goals of the research project. Questions should be as direct and as relevant to research objectives as possible. There are four types of data that are most often sought in surveys: (1) information about the respondents' *backgrounds,* (2) information about their *activities* (past and present behavior and experiences), (3) information about their *knowledge,* and (4) information about their *sentiments* (opinions, values, attitudes, and feelings).

Background questions are designed to elicit respondents' personal history and current situation (sex, race, income, religion, marital status, age, education, ethnic group, and so on). Usually, these data are gathered in order to check the representativeness of the sample and in order to enable the researcher to make statistical comparisons of DEMOGRAPHIC CATEGORIES (men/women, old/young, and so forth) with regard to variations in their patterns of response to other questionnaire items. Though these questions are both necessary and basic, some subjects may feel that they are embarrassing or too personal. This reaction can be minimized if the researcher words the questions carefully and waits to ask them until a degree of understanding and rapport has been established with the respondent. It is often helpful for the interviewer to explain why the questions need to be asked and to remind the subject that all responses will be kept in confidence.

By the same token, questions about a person's activities and experiences can seem too personal unless the respondent sees them as justified. Instead of apologizing for questions, or unduly calling attention to their somewhat personal nature, you may find it most effective to simply phrase and organize them in ways that make their relevance to the stated purposes of your research apparent. A subject should never have to wonder, let alone ask, what bearing a question has on the objectives of the research.

Along with being manifestly relevant, questions should always be as *specific* as possible. The following item is designed to elicit information about respondents' voting behavior:

How often do you vote in national elections?
1. Always
2. Often
3. Seldom
4. Never

The question is worded clearly, but it is very general. A more specific question would ask:

Did you vote in last month's national election?
1. Yes
2. No

The more specific question could then be followed by another:

In how many of the last five national elections have you voted? (Indicate the number, from 1 to 5, in which you cast a ballot.)

What are the advantages of the second scheme? First, since it is a general precept of American civics that every responsible adult citizen ought to vote, many more people feel they *should* vote than actually *do* vote. The first question almost invites the occasional voter to magnify his or her civic image by liberally interpreting the word *often*. The second scheme, on the other hand, first ties honest respondents (as most are) to the memory of their most recent vote or nonvote, and then poses a more general question in a way that elicits from the respondent a very definite answer. Also, asking about the last five national elections, instead of asking about national elections in general, reflects a more reasonable view of the limits of the respondent's memory. Moreover, the responses that will result from the second scheme will convey a great deal more information: the percentage of people who say they voted in three or more of the last five national elections is a much more meaningful, definite, and interpretable finding than the percentage of people who say that they vote "often" in such elections.

Questions about a person's sentiments are probably the most common items found on questionnaires. Views about the future of the nation's economy, attitudes toward abortion, beliefs about the poor, opinions regarding law enforcement and the court system, evaluations of the president's performance, and similar public and private sentiments are the staples of survey research. But such questions can be misused or overused if the objectives of the research are not kept in mind constantly while the individual questions are being framed. Before you decide to ask an attitude question, be certain that you are really most interested in what the subject feels. Beginning researchers sometimes mistakenly ask a person's opinion when the research design would be better served by asking what a person knows or how a person acts. As a rule, questions should be framed so that data do not become more subjective than they need to be. Remember also that subjects are less likely to consciously or unconsciously misrepresent facts about their behavior than they are to idealize their inner and unverifiable attitudes and preferences. Questions concerning attitudes are most effective when they are related to concrete realities by being combined with questions concerning behavior.

Questions concerning knowledge are asked sometimes for their own sake and sometimes for use as FILTERS to determine which respondents have sufficient information on an issue to provide meaningful opinions. Consider the following question (Davis, 1977:128):

Have you heard or read about the recent U.S. Supreme Court decision concerning abortion?
1. Yes
2. No

This question, aside from its intrinsic content, could be used to screen people before deciding to ask them whether they agree or disagree with the position of the U.S. Supreme Court regarding abortion. Surprisingly, many respondents will automatically agree or disagree with things they know nothing about rather than admit ignorance on an issue. Questions should be carefully worded to avoid the implicit assumption that "everyone knows and should have an opinion," thus making it easier for respondents to gracefully withhold uninformed comment.

Sometimes, rather than merely testing knowledge, a question can convey information to provide the respondent with a context for expressing an opinion. Consider the following example (Davis, 1977:90):

> The U.S. Supreme Court has ruled that no state or local government can re-quire the reading of the Lord's Prayer or Bible verses in the public schools. What are your views on this—do you approve or disapprove of the Court's ruling?
> 1. Strongly approve
> 2. Approve
> 3. No opinion/neutral
> 4. Disapprove
> 5. Strongly disapprove

This question has the advantage of assuring that all respondents will share a minimum factual background, which improves their competency to answer.

The content of questions should never be treated as obvious or predetermined. Content is as much a function of what the subject perceives as it is of what the researcher intends. Hence, in deciding exactly what to ask respondents, always keep in mind: (1) your own intentions, (2) the impression a question is likely to make on subjects, and (3) the response motivations (particularly the desire to appear knowledgeable and to express the "right" opinions) your questions are likely to arouse.

MULTIPLE INDICATORS. Questionnaire items should be thought of as indicators of the concepts that underlie the research design. As such they can at best only roughly reproduce the ideas the researcher has in mind. This is especially true of items that deal with matters of subjective disposition and of items that measure complex and abstract concepts. Because of this, questionnaires frequently contain several closely related items that are all intended to measure a complex or subtle concept from different angles and in slightly different ways.

Let us look again at *anomie,* a sense of isolation in a world without guiding values. Though the concept of anomie may be clear, ways of measuring it are not so clear. As a composite measure of anomie, survey researchers usually devise a series of related questions (multiple indicators) such as those in Table 6.1.

It is unlikely that any one of these questions alone could serve as a valid and reliable indicator of anomie, because several factors probably affect each person's response to each question. The overall pattern of responses to the group of related questions may be substantially more accurate and dependable as an indicator of anomie. Thus the use of a series of related questions to produce multiple mea-sures of a single concept has become a regular and important part of effective questionnaire construction.

TABLE 6.1   Multiple Indicators

Please indicate whether you agree or disagree with each of the following statements:
1. You sometimes can't help wondering whether anything is worthwhile anymore.
   a. Agree
   b. Disagree
2. To make money, there are no right and wrong ways anymore, only easy ways and hard ways.
   a. Agree
   b. Disagree
3. Nowadays a person has to live pretty much for today and let tomorrow take care of itself.
   a. Agree
   b. Disagree
4. It's hardly fair to bring a child into the world with the way things look for the future.
   a. Agree
   b. Disagree
5. Most people don't really care what happens to the next fellow.
   a. Agree
   b. Disagree

Source: Adapted from James A. Davis, Cumulative Codebook for the 1972–1977 General Social Survey (Chicago: National Opinion Research Center, 1977), pp. 115–117.

STRUCTURED VERSUS UNSTRUCTURED QUESTIONS. There are two kinds of questions used in questionnaires: STRUCTURED (CLOSED-END) QUESTIONS and UNSTRUCTURED (OPEN-END) QUESTIONS. Structured questions provide a set of fixed alternatives from which the respondent must choose a reply. The following example is adapted from Davis (1977:78):

Would you favor or oppose a law that would require a person to obtain a police permit before he or she could buy a gun?
1. I would favor such a law.
2. I would oppose such a law.
3. I have no opinion on the issue.

Structured questions are relatively easy to answer, and the responses are easy to code and record as data. If the researchers know what they want from the question and can anticipate most or all of the ways in which respondents will be inclined to answer, structured questions are both efficient and appropriate.

Unstructured questions permit respondents to answer as they see fit, and encourage free and lengthy discussion:

What, in your view, would be the major advantages or disadvantages of a strict gun-control law?

Substantial space must be left for the respondent to write an answer to the questions or for the interviewer to record as much of what the respondent says as possible.

Unstructured questions are most useful when researchers expect an issue to provoke a wide range of responses or when responses are likely to be quite detailed. But such questions should not be mistaken for, or substituted for, the kind of involved exploration and probing that characterizes intensive interviews — a wholly different research method. Nor should they be expected to produce revealing or provocative, in-depth responses. In fact, heavy use of unstructured questions can lead to great disappointment, for respondents will frequently either neglect to respond to such items or provide only brief, superficial answers.

In interviews, when open-end questions fit more naturally into the conversational atmosphere, they can be quite useful as general introductions to subjects that the interviewer will later probe with more specific, structured queries. In this situation the unstructured question helps to create a proper context for a line of inquiry that is to follow by encouraging the respondent to sort out ideas and feelings and to establish a clear frame of reference.

QUESTION WORDING. Questions should be worded in the most concise and direct way possible, avoiding both technical jargon and patronizing overelaboration. The meaning of every question must be clear to all respondents. Never assume that vocabulary common among social scientists will have meaning for any other group, let alone for all the individuals represented in a cross section.

Let us examine the following questionnaire item:

Do you favor or oppose the current effort to reduce taxes by making government more accountable and less wasteful?
1. Favor
2. Oppose
3. No opinion

The wording of this question violates several important standards of research practice. First, it is LOADED: it is so biased that a respondent would find it difficult to oppose a "tax revolt" in these terms. Questions are loaded or slanted whenever their wording even subtly suggests that one response is preferable to another. The question is also not ONE-DIMENSIONAL: it presents the subject with more than a single issue to respond to. In this case people who favor making government "more accountable and less wasteful" (laudable goals that no responsible citizen could oppose!) but who do not favor tax cuts are placed in a dilemma by the wording. Complex questions, often requiring involved responses do not fit well within the limits of survey techniques, especially the limits of the self-administered questionnaire. If complex issues are to be studied by means of a survey, they must first be broken down into a series of one-dimensional questions.

Slanting can also occur, despite neutral wording of the question itself, if the fixed responses presented to the subject do not cover the entire range of potential replies. Here is an example:

How many politicians do you think are a little bit corrupt?
1. All
2. Most
3. A few
4. None

Although the range of possible reactions seems to be covered, how should someone reply who believes that the great majority of politicians are much more than "a little bit" corrupt? The researcher has put the respondent into the strange position where the reply "none" is most logical and truthful but least likely to convey what the subject intends.

As mentioned in Chapter 3, the responses to any closed-end question must be mutually exclusive and exhaustive. In addition, a respondent should not be able to skim through a questionnaire, blissfully agreeing or disagreeing with everything in sight. Instead, "agree-disagree," "yes-no," or "favor-oppose" choices should be interspersed with other sets of response options that restate the substance of the question.

Look at the following item:

What connection, if any, exists between your present job and your college education?
1. I work at the specific career for which I was trained.
2. The work I do is related to my major field.
3. Though not directly related to my major field, the work I do draws on my college education.
4. My work is unrelated to my college education.

Now compare the wording of that question with the wording of the one that follows:

How related is your present work to the education you received in college?
1. Closely related
2. Somewhat related
3. Unrelated

Although both questions are of similar intent, the first version repeats the substance of the question in the responses. This helps to elicit more specific and informative data by directing the respondent to consider the question more carefully. The "contentful" response format also counteracts the tendency of some subjects to respond agreeably or disagreeably (according to their general dispositions, irrespective of the issues being addressed) in a patterned and unreflective way.

Another strategy that counters yea-saying (a pattern of agreement) and naysaying (a pattern of disagreement) is the use of contradictory questionnaire items. As Table 6.2 illustrates, the respondent cannot simply agree or disagree with all statements without demonstrating gross inconsistency.

CONSTRUCTING THE QUESTIONNAIRE

The principles of questionnaire construction remain fairly constant, whether it is being prepared for self-administration or as a "schedule" to guide the interaction between interviewer and subject. Both form and content must be considered, especially when subjects have only the printed questionnaire as a guide. Seemingly minor details regarding the organization, phrasing, and order of the questionnaire items, and the recording of responses, can make the difference between a successful research effort and a quagmire of confusion and frustration.

TABLE 6.2   Balancing Agree-Disagree Items

---

1. Since our society still expects a husband to be the breadwinner for his family, married men ought to be given hiring preference when seeking a job.
   a. Strongly agree b. Agree c. No opinion d. Disagree e. Strongly disagree

2. Men and women should receive equal pay for equal work.
   a. Strongly agree b. Agree c. No opinion d. Disagree e. Strongly disagree

3. Women should take care of running their homes and leave the world of work to men.
   a. Strongly agree b. Agree c. No opinion d. Disagree e. Strongly disagree

4. No employer should be allowed to discriminate against women by hiring less-qualified men.
   a. Strongly agree b. Agree c. No opinion d. Disagree e. Strongly disagree

---

INTRODUCTION. Every questionnaire should have an introduction that explains what the study is about in a way that captures the attention of potential respondents, impresses them with the importance of the study and their participation in it, and assures them that all data will be handled in a way that protects their identity. If the study can be linked to a sponsor known and trusted by members of the target population, identification of the sponsor in the introduction can have dramatic results on the rate of response. Presenting a survey as a "class project," for example, is generally less effective than identifying it with the college or university in which that class project is being conducted.

The tone of the introduction should be serious, in order to encourage potential subjects to treat the questionnaire seriously and to respond to the items conscientiously. The tone of the introduction must also be neutral. If controversial issues are to be covered in the questionnaire, nothing in the introduction should give the respondent the impression that the researcher advocates a particular attitude or is interested in eliciting a particular set of opinions. On the contrary, subjects must be impressed with the researcher's sincere desire that they express *their own ideas,* lest they instead express views intended to be agreeable to the researcher.

INSTRUCTIONS. Instructions prepared by the researcher for an interviewer may be quite elaborate, with several pages of general guidelines separate from the interview schedule and with many specific guidelines and reminders interspersed throughout the schedule. The guidelines for a self-administered questionnaire should be much simpler. It should include a very clear explanation of how responses are to be indicated: by checking, by circling, or by other means. The respondent's attention should be drawn to any questions that require or allow more than one response. Also, if the questionnaire contains some items that pertain only to a subset of the respondents, the rest should be explicitly directed to omit the items to which they are not expected to respond. In the absence of explicit instructions, subjects will often improvise, but improvisation does not promote uniform, interpretable data.

SEQUENCE OF QUESTIONS. Since questionnaires are of no use unless subjects are willing to fill them out, the researcher's initial aim must be to capture the potential respondent's attention. In an interview situation, where there is the additional necessity of developing rapport between interviewer and respondent, opening questions should also be general, nonthreatening, and easy to respond to.

The body of the questionnaire should consist of questions on a progression of topics, following some logical pattern that the respondent is likely to recognize and that will facilitate an orderly interchange between interviewer and subject. Sometimes the very nature of the material to be covered by the questionnaire suggests the best method of organization; at other times only trial and error can determine what pattern will most facilitate rapport and easy interchange. If necessary, alternate schemes can be evaluated when pretesting (see page 143) the questionnaire to iron out any minor problems it may contain.

When dealing with questions on the same subtopic, most researchers prefer to organize their queries from the more general items to the more specific. A series of questions on "issues of the day" might begin with a general item:

> What, in your view, are the most important issues facing the American people today?

This might then be followed by a more specific "issues inventory":

> Here is a list of ten issues and concerns currently facing the United States. We would like to know which of these you consider the most important and which seem to you the least important.
>   (list of issues follows)

The respondent might then be guided by the interviewer to rank all issues from 1 (most important) to 10 (least important). If the general question is intended to encourage the respondent to identify important issues other than those listed in the inventory, it must precede the more specific one. Otherwise, the answer to the general question will tend to mirror the issues identified on the researcher's list and will be likely to generate redundant data.

Finally, sensitive questions should be reserved for the end of the questionnaire. By this time the subject is used to replying and probably feels at ease with the interviewer. Careful wording, which makes personal questions seem less obtrusive and offensive, can greatly increase the rate of response. Let us compare these two items:

> Unemployment has been steadily increasing in the United States for the past two years. During this time have you yourself been affected by this growing problem?

> At any time during the past two years have you lost a job or been laid off?

The second question would probably stimulate a less open and frank exchange than the first. Surveys, unlike cross-examinations, do not seek a confession. They must respect, appreciate, and foster the good will of those respondents kind enough to give their time and share their experiences.

LAYOUT AND RESPONSE FORMAT. When a questionnaire is to be self-administered, the layout of questions and response alternatives on the printed page can seriously affect the ease, accuracy, and completeness with which subjects respond. Questions should be spread out evenly on the page, with sufficient blank space between them for subjects to note easily where one item ends and another begins, and to enable subjects to comment fully on all questions. This is especially important for items with subparts, for items with special instructions, and for filter items that are to be answered by only some of the respondents. Careful layout helps to minimize two problems: (1) subjects' failure to respond to questions intended for them, and (2) subjects' tendency to respond inappropriately to questions because they have misunderstood them or because they did not realize that the questions were not intended for them.

The mode for indicating responses should be consistent throughout the questionnaire, and should be made clear to respondents at the outset. It is helpful to include a sample question with the appropriate response clearly and properly marked. The absence of explicit instructions will lead subjects to improvise often in strange and undecipherable ways.

Respondents can be directed to record their answers in a variety of ways:

Please indicate your gender.

| _____Male | ☐Male | 1. Male |
| __x__Female | ☑Female | ②. Female |

The third alternative, that of circling a number that stands for the correct response, has the advantage of indicating simultaneously what the subject's response is and how that response is to be coded for data processing. This eliminates an error-prone intermediate step in the transfer of responses to punched data cards.

When a filter or CONTINGENCY QUESTION is used to identify a subgroup of respondents for further questioning, explicit instructions should direct subjects to the next item they are supposed to answer. The use of a page of a different color can help to isolate a series of questions intended for a specific category of respondents. Table 6.3 shows the use of arrows and special indentation and verbal instructions in the layout of a page.

Schemes in which one set of questions applies to one group of subjects and a different set applies to the remainder are very common in interview surveys, but they are considerably more difficult to build into self-administered questionnaires. As the contingency scheme becomes more complex, the chances increase for confusion on the part of the respondent. But the difference between a successful contingency questioning scheme and an unsuccessful one can often be a matter of proper physical layout.

When you design a questionnaire, it is wise to assume the worst—that many respondents will rush through it with much more motivation simply to be finished than to be thorough and accurate. If you word the questions and design the layout so as to politely but effectively focus the respondent's attention, the resultant data will be much more useful and informative.

Response formats on interview schedules are usually similar to those on self-administered questionnaires, although issues of style are not as crucial when the answers are being recorded by a trained interviewer. Sensitive or personal questions, however, do pose a special problem for the interviewer. To minimize uneasiness or embarrassment in subjects, the response choices to questions such as "Could you indicate which of the following income ranges your earnings for last year fell into?" are often printed on a card that the interviewer hands to the

TABLE 6.3   Layout of Contingency Items

25. Did you happen to vote in the 1976 presidential election?
    a. No (*Skip to Question 28.*)
    b. Yes

    26. Did you vote for Carter, Ford, or some other candidate?
        a. Carter
        b. Ford
        c. Other (please specify for whom you voted):

    27. How strongly did you prefer the candidate for whom you
        voted over other candidates?
        a. Very strongly   c. Weakly
        b. Strongly   d. Very weakly
        Please skip to Question 29.

28. If you had cast a ballot in 1976, who would have been your choice?
    a. Carter
    b. Ford
    c. Other (please specify): _____
    d. No preference

subject when asking the question. The respondent can simply indicate to the interviewer the appropriate category (by its code number) without actually talking about the sensitive topic.

PRETESTING. No amount of care and planning can ensure that the questionnaire will have the intended effect in all respects. For this reason the assumptions and judgments that go into questionnaire design should be tested before the actual survey begins. A PRETEST involves drawing a very small sample of subjects, conducting interviews or administering a questionnaire, and noting all the problems that arise for the interviewers and for the subjects. The subjects should be encouraged to comment freely about the questions themselves, as well as about the issues they address. In effect, an interview takes place within and about that interview. The pretest often suggests necessary or desirable changes in wording, format, or layout; identifies ineffective questions that should be deleted; and sometimes uncovers new issues to which additional questions should be addressed. If hired interviewers are being used, the researcher should also solicit their reactions during the pretesting phase.

Survey Execution

After the plans have been formulated and the pretest has been conducted, a number of problems may arise in carrying out your survey. In this section we shall concentrate on the major difficulties associated with implementing research using either self-administered questionnaires or interviews.

THE SELF-ADMINISTERED SURVEY

The main problem associated with self-administered surveys is their characteristically low rate of return. Questionnaires received by post are often mistaken for "junk mail" and ignored or discarded. Several techniques can be used to make mail surveys more appealing, thereby increasing the rate of response.

The introductory letter that accompanies the questionnaire should emphasize the importance of the research and appeal to the altruism of potential respondents. Such an appeal is realistic and, as many researchers have discovered, proves more effective than the suggestion that the subject has something to gain by participating. The inclusion of a "reward"—a pen or a small amount of money—also improves the rate of response, probably more because it is a token of the researcher's sincere appreciation than because of its intrinsic value.

The longer the questionnaire, the lower the response rate tends to be. Hence mail surveys must be restricted to essential questions. Perhaps because they seem less impersonal, prestamped, individually typed return envelopes produce higher return rates than do business-reply envelopes. Surveys that involve some personal contact, either at the outset or in later follow-ups of nonrespondents, show markedly better returns than those that rely exclusively on the mails.

Finally, and most important, mail surveys require aggressive and unrelenting follow-up. Second and third mailings can often prod listless subjects into responding to and returning the questionnaire. Telephoning can be an effective way of reminding people that they have not yet filled out their questionnaire. If reminders have been sent and have received no response, a personal call can sometimes result in a successful telephone interview. Thorough follow-up campaigns can often increase the rate of response to a mail survey by as much as 50 percent.

Even if all these techniques for increasing the rate of response in a mail survey are employed, it is unlikely that more than 70 percent of the questionnaires will be returned. When between a third and two-thirds of the subjects in a sample do not respond, the researcher should attempt to evaluate the possibility that sample biases have been introduced by this process of "self-selection." Suppose a mail survey is sent to a random sample of students at your college and that 60 percent of the subjects return completed questionnaires. Information from the survey about the respondents' age, race, sex, and major can be compared to similar data about the composition of the entire student body. If this comparison shows no startling differences between the 60 percent of the sample who replied and the student body as a whole, weight will be lent to the contention that the respondents are representative of the entire group (although other important differences between respondents and nonrespondents may lie undiscovered).

THE INTERVIEW SURVEY

Most interview surveys, depending on the size of the sample, require a team of interviewers so that no one person is burdened with an unwieldy or unduly protracted task. Whether the interviews are conducted by hired assistants or by a team of cooperating researchers (as in a class project), it is essential that the interviewers be consistent in their understanding of the schedule and in their manner of approaching and dealing with respondents. To ensure consistency and similarity among interviewers requires not only extensive discussion, common training, and practice, but also coordination and control by the chief investigator, who supervises the entire operation. The following discussion explores some of the major considerations and techniques that a chief investigator should emphasize and that interviewers should bear in mind and follow.

PREPARATION. All interviewers must thoroughly acquaint themselves with both the objectives of the study and the item-by-item content of the interview schedule. The interviewer should use the exact wording that has been set down for every question; however, he or she should not seem to be reading! A good interview is ideally a conversation between interviewer and subject, during which both feel at ease. For the interviewer, as for an actor, this means appearing spontaneous and at ease while rigidly adhering to a script. No one achieves this balance of ease and control without being thoroughly immersed in the intent of the research and in the execution of that intent.

Hired interviewers must be thoroughly prepared for their tasks; otherwise, their limited involvement in the overall project may lead to errors and misunderstandings that could undermine the quality of the data. Interviewers who are aware of the overall sampling strategy, for example, are less likely to succumb to the temptation to avoid approaching valid but inconvenient potential subjects (such as those who live on dark streets, who work at odd hours, or who live three flights up). Interviewers need to be impressed with the importance of procedural consistency and adherence to instructions. Group training of interviewers helps to ensure this consistency. Finally, interviewers, even more than respondents, must be convinced of the significance of the research project.

A manual of interviewer specifications, gleaned from past experience and from the results of the pretest, should accompany the questionnaire. The manual should include item-by-item instructions about what to do when faced with any conceivable contingency. Typical specifications include suggestions of ways to clarify the meaning of a question by explaining the meaning of its wording if a subject does not seem to understand it or asks for an explanation, and helpful probes that the interviewer can use to encourage the respondent who initially expresses no opinion on a question or who responds with "I don't know." In order to accommodate the variable statuses of respondents (for example, widows, single parents, the unemployed, members of minority groups), some slight rewording of questions may be necessary; in such cases the manual should specify exactly how the wording is to be modified.

DEVELOPING RAPPORT. Rapport between subject and interviewer depends upon a number of factors, including familiarity with the role being enacted. Since subjects are seldom experienced in the role of survey respondent, the interviewer must orient them and place them at ease. First, dress in a manner appropriate to the neighborhood in which you are conducting the interview, yet one that reflects the professional nature of your work. Establish your own identity. Show whatever credentials you have, so as to avoid being mistaken for a salesperson, a bill collector, or a potential burglar. If possible, interviewers should be matched with the average traits of their subjects so as to facilitate recognition and communication.

Once the interview is under way, it is important to convey a nonjudgmental attitude toward the subject and toward the subject's responses. With a series of nods or brief verbal expressions of encouragement ("yes," "uh-huh"), you can let the subject know that you are eager to hear and record whatever opinions are offered. In doing this, however, you must be careful not to inadvertently encourage the respondent to offer "pleasing" replies; offer the same level of encouragement whether you like or dislike what you hear.

PROVIDING A UNIFORM STIMULUS. In order for statistical comparisons between the responses of different groups of subjects to have any meaning whatsoever, the researcher must be able to assume that they all were asked the same questions in the same way. This requirement dictates that all interviewers adhere to the exact order and wording of questions as they appear in the interview schedule. It also demands a degree of control over the tone of voice in which an interviewer asks a question, since changes in inflection can substantially alter the subject's interpretation of a question even though the wording is followed exactly. The question "Do you sometimes drink more than you should?" would produce more admissions if the word *sometimes* were emphasized than it would if the word *drink* were emphasized. Practice and discipline help an interviewer to establish an appropriate tone and to maintain it from one interview to the next.

PROBING. In most instances questionnaires that have been carefully designed and pretested will pose little problem for subjects. Questions should be asked slowly and clearly; any misunderstanding can usually be dealt with by repeating the item.

Since surveys may solicit a wide range of opinions and feelings from subjects, it is not always sufficient for a question to be clear; it must also stimulate and encourage respondents to express their personal views freely and fully. One of the major advantages of the personal interview is the opportunity it affords the interviewer to immediately evaluate the completeness of the responses. When confronted with reticent subjects who, out of shyness or lack of confidence in the worth or accuracy of their own views, claim to have no opinion or offer only short, perfunctory, and unrevealing replies to open-ended questions, the skillful interviewer will use a variety of neutral probes to encourage fuller and more relevant replies. Often a momentary pause can convey your expectation that the respondent ought to have more to say. Simply repeating the subject's reply may bring forth a good deal of elaboration. Brief, nonloaded questions, such as "Could you explain that a bit more?" "Could you elaborate?" "Any other reasons?" "Why do you say that?" "Any other ideas on that?" can be very productive. Although some subjects occasionally have no opinion to offer, many others simply need a little time to work out their ideas on an issue, or a little encouragement to overcome their hesitation about offering their opinions. Lack of assertiveness on the part of a subject should never be taken for lack of a point of view, and the artful use of probes may help to compensate for the subject's reticence.

RECORDING RESPONSES. Most interviews involve a mix of closed-end and open-end questions. Recording the replies to closed-end questions is usually a simple and straightforward matter. But recording the replies to open-end questions can be quite a challenging task. You should make every attempt to record responses verbatim, writing key words instead of whole sentences if necessary, but returning to complete the record after the interview has been completed. Start to record as soon as the subject begins to reply, looking up occasionally to maintain some eye contact. Try to avoid distracting the subject or holding up the interview with your notetaking, lest the conversational atmosphere be lost. When you use probes, put them in parentheses in the record in order to distinguish your remarks from those of the subject. Finally, when the interview is complete, conduct a careful, item-by-item review to make sure you have recorded everything that was said and to aid you in preparing a written summary of your overall impressions of the interview. In the summary you should comment on the subject's general attitude and cooperativeness, describe the setting of and circumstances surrounding the interview, and express your personal feelings about its quality and tone.

PREPARING THE DATA FOR PROCESSING

Even modest surveys generate enormous amounts of data. A 50-item questionnaire, completed by a sample of 500 people, will result in 25,000 separate pieces of information that must be checked, recorded, and made relatively easy to handle. The data must be represented in a form that will permit them to undergo statistical manipulation and analysis. It is virtually imperative that the data be made MACHINE-READABLE; the processing of such a large volume of data can be carried out efficiently and accurately only with the aid of a computer (or other electronic data processing equipment). Both of these requirements are satisfied by quantifying the data—transforming them into a series of numerical codes that can be read, stored, manipulated and summarized statistically by machine. This process of coding typically proceeds through several stages, from the precoding of the questionnaire through the "cleaning" of the machine-coded information.

PRECODING. Whenever possible, the best way to organize the processing of data is to begin before the survey is actually carried out. PRECODING, a procedure that applies only to closed-end questions, involves two things: (1) attaching a numerical code to each response alternative and (2) designating a location for every questionnaire item, where the coded response to that item will eventually be stored in a data matrix. Codes are printed next to each possible response on the questionnaire, and the appropriate code is circled when the respondent answers the question. Usually, the location of the column(s) where each coded response will later be punched into a data card is also printed unobtrusively on the questionnaire.

THE DATA MATRIX. Understanding the concept of a data matrix is the key to the entire process of coding and recording data. A DATA MATRIX is an array of rows and columns. The intersection of a row with a column forms a CELL, or a location, in which a single digit can be stored. Each cell has a unique ADDRESS in the matrix that can be identified by the number of the row and the number of the column that intersect to form the cell. A data matrix is usually organized by assigning each row to a different respondent and each question to a different column. When the data matrix is organized in this manner, and all responses by all subjects have been coded and entered, the matrix will consist of as many rows as there are respondents and as many columns as there are questions on the questionnaire.[4]

---

[4]In actuality there are usually more columns than there are questions, since responses to some questions need several columns in which to be properly recorded. Recording a

If you were to read *across* any row in the matrix, you would see (in coded form) all the responses given by one respondent to all the items on the questionnaire. If you were to read *down* any column of the matrix, you would see the responses given by the entire sample of subjects to a single question. Once data have been stored in this matrix form, it is relatively easy to describe the shape and contents of the matrix to a machine and, simply by referring to the appropriate row(s) or column(s), to instruct the machine to locate and analyze specific parts of the data. Note that the first few columns of a data matrix are usually reserved for an IDENTIFICATION NUMBER. This number, which is also recorded on the original questionnaire, can subsequently be used to match any row of data to its source.

CODING. As soon as the interview is finished or the completed questionnaire returns by mail, it should be reviewed for completeness and edited to make sure that all questions have been answered properly. Sometimes spaces left blank on the questionnaire can be filled in on the basis of information provided on other questions. A person who fails to indicate his or her employment status but who lists an income of $0 can safely be categorized as having no paid job. If a person has skipped or refused to answer certain questions, the editor should enter a "missing data code," a number that signifies the absence of valid data and that the computer will later be instructed to treat separately from other codes. When the editing is finished, there should be some code to be entered into every address in the data matrix.

Open-ended items cannot be precoded; coding can occur only after the data have been collected. The categories into which responses are to be coded must be established by closely examining what the respondents actually had to say. This procedure is almost identical to the one described in Chapter 11 on content analysis (to which the reader may refer for more detail). In brief, the researcher reviews a sample of the verbal responses to an open-ended question and decides how many different kinds (categories) of responses exist. Each category must then be defined and illustrated with a concrete example, and a numerical code attached to it. Once this coding scheme has been settled, the full set of verbal responses can be reviewed one at a time and recorded as a compact series of numbers. Since a great deal of judgment is often involved in this translation of words into numbers, accepted practice dictates that at least two people independently code the entire set of responses and their judgments be compared so that differences can be resolved and consistency of coding can be achieved.

PREPARING A CODEBOOK. As soon as all decisions about coding have been made, a CODEBOOK should be prepared to serve as both a guide to and a record of the coding process. The codebook contains instructions for the transfer of all data from the questionnaires to some other medium (codesheets, punch cards, magnetic tape). For every questionnaire item, the codebook contains the number of the column(s) in the data matrix assigned to that item, the exact wording of the question, each legitimate response, the numerical code for each legitimate response, and the code used to signify missing data. It may be sufficient to state only once the

---

six-figure income requires six columns. A series of columns reserved for the recording of one large piece of information is called a field, and each question must be allotted a field wide enough to accommodate the largest code number you plan to use to record any response to the question.

FIGURE 6.1   A Punched Data Card

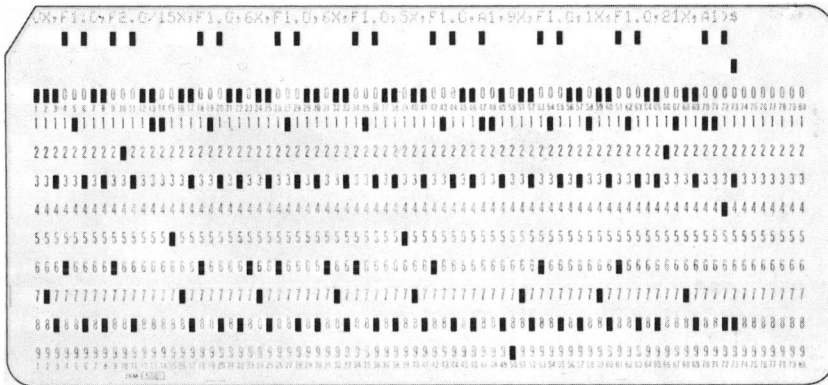

general rule for coding missing data, to be followed consistently throughout the transfer of data from the questionnaire to the data card. A common practice is to indicate missing data with the largest number that will fit in the cell(s) corresponding to that item (i.e., the number 9 or a series of 9s).

KEYPUNCHING. Once the codebook has been prepared and the questionnaires have been edited, data are usually transferred to codesheets, lined sheets resembling graph paper that have been designed to accommodate a data matrix. Since errors can occur in the transfer, it is essential that every line of code entered on a codesheet be checked at least once against the original record (the questionnaire). Sometimes an interview schedule can be laid out in such a way that all codes appear conveniently in the right-hand margin; when this is done, it is possible to dispense with codesheets altogether and go right to the next step: making the data machine-readable by transferring it to punch cards (Figure 6.1), using a KEYPUNCH machine.[5]

Punch cards contain eighty columns. A single digit can be punched into any column. Numbers of more than one digit must be punched into adjacent, consecutive columns (forming a multiple-column field). Columns may be left blank between separate items of information, although this practice is not necessary. The most important thing to remember when keypunching is to verify constantly that you are punching the data into the correct columns.

The complete set of responses made by a single subject is referred to as a record, and the representation of those responses as a single row of codes is called a LOGICAL RECORD. Logical records will very often exceed the maximum eighty columns that are available on a blank data card. Hence punching must continue on subsequent cards, and several cards may be needed to represent a single logical record. When this happens, each card must repeat the identification number in its first few columns and must also bear a CARD NUMBER indicating which portion of the logical record is contained on that card. These two identifiers are usually the first two items punched into each card.

---

[5]In some research settings an alternative data processing technique is used in which data are recorded on magnetic tape for reading by the computer.

TABLE 6.4   A Precoded Questionnaire

SOCIAL AND POLITICAL PRIORITIES: A SURVEY

Identification Number ____ ____ ____ ____   (1–4)
Please answer *all* questions in this survey to the best of your
ability. Remember, there are no right or wrong answers or
opinions; in all cases *we just want to hear your own, personal
opinion!*

In most cases you can answer the question simply by circling
the response that is true for you or that comes closest to your
own opinion. Feel free to write in comments or explanations
whenever you feel it is necessary.

Card 1
Column

1. There are a number of problems facing this country, none of
   which can be solved easily or inexpensively. The following is
   a list of some of those problems. Please consider each problem carefully, and then indicate whether, in your opinion,
   the government is *presently* spending too much, too little,
   or about the right amount to deal with the problem:
   a. To protect and improve the environment, the government
      is spending:
      (i) Too much
      (ii) About the right amount
      (iii) Too little   (7) ____
   b. To protect and improve the nation's health, the govern-
      ment is spending:
      (i) Too much
      (ii) About the right amount
      (iii) Too little   (8) ____
   c. To solve the problems of big cities, the government is
      spending:
      (i) Too much
      (ii) About the right amount
      (iii) Too little   (9) ____
   d. To halt the rising crime rate, the government is spending:
      (i) Too much
      (ii) About the right amount
      (iii) Too little   (10) ____
   e. To deal with problems caused by drug addiction, the
      government is spending:
      (i) Too much
      (ii) About the right amount
      (iii) Too little   (11) ____

Source: Adapted from James A. Davis, *Cumulative Codebook for the 1972–1977 General
Social Survey* (Chicago: National Opinion Research Center, 1977), pp. 70–73.

When all the data have been keypunched, a verifying machine is used to check the accuracy of each punch against the source. Every time data are transferred from one medium to another, the transfer must be verified. Happily, once the data have been read by machine, verification of every subsequent transfer is automatic.

CODE CHECKING AND CLEANING. Quality control is a very important part of the survey research process. Questionnaires are carefully edited; all coding of unstructured material is checked for reliability; and verification, item by item and digit by digit, is conducted each time the data are transferred. With proper verification procedures, error rates can be kept below 1 percent; without them, errors can occur and accumulate at every stage. Since these random errors (sometimes exceeding 10 or even 20 percent) tend to destroy data patterns and make the results of statistical tests inconclusive, the difference between the success and failure of a well-designed study can often depend on the adequacy of procedures for quality control.

The last step in verification involves checking for "bad punches." If, for example, the proper codes for the variable *gender* are 1 (for males), 2 (for females), and 9 (for missing data), the appearance of any other number, a 7 for instance, indicates a mistake that must be traced and corrected. Logical checks can also be conducted; all those subjects coded on one variable as not being employed should be coded as "not appropriate" on another variable that purports to measure job satisfaction. Many computer installations include programs that are designed to facilitate this type of data checking. Data should immediately be CLEANED by tracking down and eliminating all such errors; if the data are not cleaned, the errors will inevitably appear at later stages in the analysis when it is much more difficult and costly to correct them. Once cleaning is completed, the data are ready to be statistically analyzed.

A HYPOTHETICAL SURVEY. In the following illustration, portions of a precoded questionnaire, a codebook, a data matrix recorded on a codesheet, and a set of punched data cards have been prepared to record and transmit the data collected in a hypothetical survey. The purpose of the survey is to discover the social and political priorities of a cross section of American adults.

Table 6.4 presents the first page of the precoded questionnaire. When the questionnaire is edited, the proper code for each response selected by the subject is to be entered in the space provided in the right-hand margin. To the left of each space and enclosed in parentheses is the number of the column into which the particular response code is to be punched on the data card (No. 1 in this case); this notation facilitates accurate transfer of data onto a codesheet. Precoding also permits keypunching of edited questionnaire data directly onto data cards, eliminating the intermediate use of codesheets.

Table 6.5 includes the beginning and the end of a codebook that contains all relevant information about the numerical codes in which the data will now appear. Note that the questionnaire was quite lengthy, requiring four separate data cards (deck No. 1 to deck No. 4) for each logical record. Identification numbers and card numbers are repeated on each card, always punched into the same columns for ease of machine handling and sorting of complete card decks. Note too that the code 8 has been added in all parts of question 1, because some

TABLE 6.5   Excerpts from a Codebook

CONTENTS OF CARD DECK NO. 1

Question Number	Column Location	Question Wording and Response Codes
—	1–4	IDENTIFICATION NUMBER
—	5	CARD NUMBER: 1
1		There are a number of problems facing this country, none of which can be solved easily or inexpensively. The following is a list of some of those problems. Please consider each problem carefully, and then indicate whether, in your opinion, the government is *presently* spending too much, too little, or about the right amount to deal with the problem.
1a	7	Improving and protecting the environment 1 Too much 2 About the right amount 3 Too little 8 Not informed enough to answer (volunteered) 9 Missing data
1b	8	Improving and protecting the nation's health (same response codes as in 1a)
1c	9	Solving the problems of big cities (same response codes as in 1a)
1d	10	Halting the rising crime rate (same response codes as in 1a)
1e	11	Dealing with problems caused by drug addiction (same response codes as in 1a)
1f	12	Improving the nation's educational system (same response codes as in 1a)
1g	13	Providing adequate assistance to the poor (same response codes as in 1a)
1h	14	Reducing unemployment and improving working conditions (same response codes as in 1a)
1i	15	Meeting the needs of the nation's elderly citizens (same response codes as in 1a)

CONTENTS OF CARD DECK NO. 4

Question Number	Column Location	Question Wording and Response Codes
—	1–4	IDENTIFICATION NUMBER
—	5	CARD NUMBER: 4

88	7	Is there any area within a mile of your home where you would be afraid to walk alone at night? 1 Yes 2 No 9 Missing data
89	8	In general, do you think the courts in this area deal too harshly or not harshly enough with criminals? 1 The courts are too harsh with criminals 2 The courts' treatment of criminals is about right 3 The courts are not harsh enough with criminals 9 Missing data
90	9	Would you favor or oppose a law that would require a person to obtain a police permit before he or she could buy a gun? 1 I would favor a law requiring police permits for guns 2 I would oppose a law requiring police permits for guns 9 Missing data
91	10	Have you ever, as an adult, been punched or beaten by another person? 1 Yes 2 No 9 Missing data
92	11	Have you ever, as an adult, been threatened with a gun or shot at? 1 Yes 2 No 9 Missing data
93	12	Has anyone broken into your home or apartment within the last five years? 1 Yes 2 No 9 Missing data
		The following items of personal information are needed and will be used only for statistical purposes. We would appreciate it if you would tell us the following about yourself:
94	13–16	Year of birth (code the four-digit year exactly)
94	17	Gender 1 Male 2 Female 9 Missing data
94	18–19	The highest year of school that you completed (code number of years as a two-digit number: 01, 02, 03, etc.) 99 Missing data

FIGURE 6.2   Codesheet with Part of a Data Matrix

1 2 3 4 5	7 8 9 10 11 12 13 14 15 16 17 18 19 20
0 0 0 1 4	1 3 1 1 2 9 1 9 2 6 2 0 8
0 0 0 2 4	2 3 2 2 2 2 1 9 3 3 1 1 2
0 0 0 3 4	2 1 1 2 1 2 1 9 1 4 2 1 5
0 0 0 4 4	1 9 2 2 9 1 1 9 5 8 1 1 2
0 0 0 5 4	9 3 1 2 2 2 1 9 4 4 1 1 0
0 0 0 6 4	1 1 1 1 2 1 1 8 9 9 2 0 7
0 0 0 7 4	1 3 1 9 1 2 1 9 3 9 1 1 2
0 0 0 8 4	1 2 2 2 2 1 1 9 4 7 1 1 6
0 0 0 9 4	2 1 2 2 2 2 1 9 5 1 2 1 1
0 0 1 0 4	1 3 1 1 2 1 1 9 2 2 2 1 8

FIGURE 6.3   Punched Data Cards

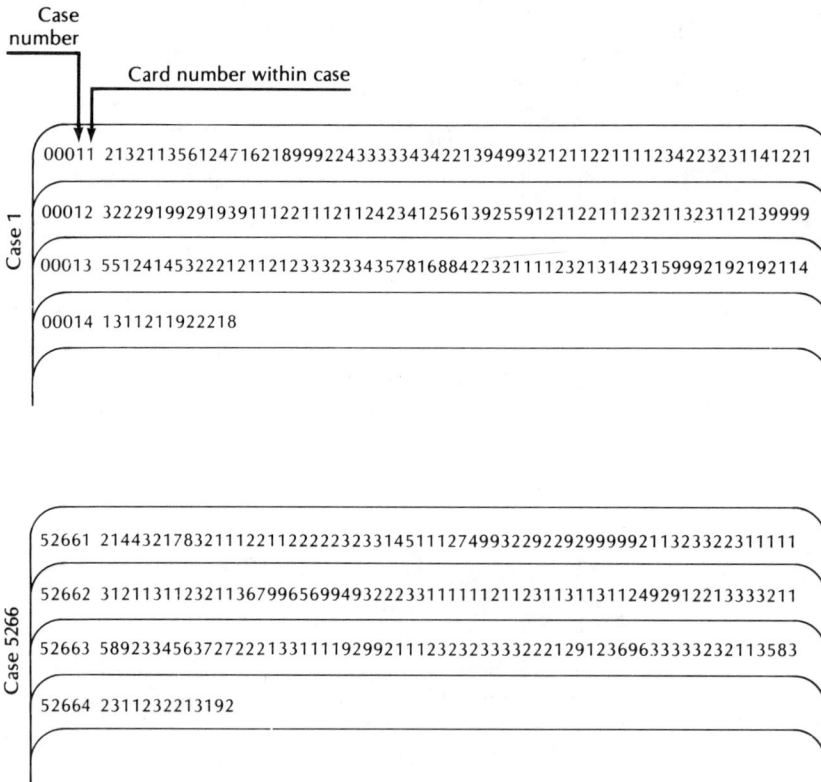

Case number

Card number within case

Case 1

00011 21321135612471621899922433333434221394993212112211112342232311141221

00012 32229199291939111221112112423412561392559121122111232112311321112139999

00013 55124145322212112123333233435781688422321111232131423159992192192114

00014 1311211922218

Case 5266

52661 21443217832111221122222323314511127499322922929299999211323322311111

52662 31211311232113679965699493222331111112112311311311249291221333211

52663 58923345637272221331111929921112323233333222129123696333332321135 83

52664 2311232213192

respondents wrote on their questionnaires that they had too little knowledge on which to base a meaningful reply.

Figure 6.2 presents a codesheet on which the data for deck No. 4 have been recorded for the first ten subjects. Note that column 6 has been left blank. Although not necessary, this blank column serves as a separator between the identifying information for each subject and the data for that subject. Blank columns can be useful as visual checks that help to ensure that all data are being properly transferred into the appropriate columns of both the codesheet and the punch card. The series of 4s punched into column 5 identifies the accompanying data as part of deck No. 4.

Finally, Figure 6.3 presents the finished data cards for the first and the last respondents in our sample. Note the correspondence between the punch cards and the rows in the data matrix (Figure 6.2) from which they were punched.

Secondary Analysis

Electronic data processing is only about 30 years old, and the large-scale collection and analysis of social science data are not much older. In recent years the cost of data processing has declined remarkably while the availability of facilities has greatly increased. Consequently, the costs of data collection now stand as the major barrier limiting the number of students and professionals who can afford to conduct major surveys without the support of government or other funding agencies. More and more researchers, however, are overcoming this final cost obstacle by engaging in SECONDARY ANALYSIS —building research projects around reanalysis of data originally collected by someone else for another purpose.

Suppose you want to isolate factors that predispose people toward racial prejudice and you find an already existing study of factors affecting voting behavior, in which a scale of racial prejudice was developed as one of the many variables under investigation. You can obtain the existing data and conduct a reanalysis in which prejudice becomes the most important variable. In this way you entirely avoid the cost of data collection by producing a new set of findings out of old data.

Secondary analysis may involve survey data, as in the example just discussed, but it may also involve information from sources other than surveys. Emile Durkheim's famous nineteenth-century study entitled *Suicide* involved a secondary analysis of approximately 26,000 suicide records from various countries in Europe, records collected long before survey research was a recognized methodology.

Today survey data are increasingly likely candidates for secondary analysis because of the quantity of such data and because of their availability in an inexpensive and well-organized form. Data collected by the U.S. Bureau of the Census, for example, are distributed for secondary analysis, and social scientists from a variety of disciplines take advantage of this abundant source. Secondary analysis has several other advantages, in addition to its low cost, that make it a useful research tool. Analysis of available records may often be the only way to obtain quantitative data about the past. As more and more survey data accumulate, trend studies comparing responses to similar survey questions asked over the course of many years become more practical and valuable for testing or creating theory. Secondary analysis can often be the basis for an important pilot study. Before embarking on an extensive and costly project, researchers may use secondary analyses of past research to assess the soundness of their research design, to pretest the plausibility of their hypotheses, and to determine the strengths and weaknesses of formerly used indicators and question wordings. To accomplish any of these purposes, it may be necessary to reanalyze a single survey or a combination of surveys, to treat several surveys as replications of each other and compare their results, or to compare several different indicators used within the same survey. Other designs for secondary analysis are described by Hyman (1972).

Despite these virtues secondary analysis is not without its problems. There can be serious risks involved in comparing studies in which either the sampling procedures were different or the questions were worded differently. Furthermore, the older the research you wish to reanalyze, the less likely it is that the original researcher will have provided thorough documentation of procedures used, in anticipation of later interest in the data. There may be no codebook or no account of how the sampling was done. Also, older data may not be in a form that can easily be processed with modern equipment. Secondary analysts must restrict their designs to those elements of data that an earlier researcher found relevant for a totally different purpose. This means that some important hypotheses will almost always be excluded and that others will be tested using indicators that are less than ideal. These limitations, the inevitable drawbacks that accompany the use of someone else's data, mean that researchers must be cautious in interpreting results and should not try to extend limited data to cover a broad, but only partially tested, set of research questions.

DATA BANKS. A number of DATA BANKS have arisen as repositories of survey data. Usually, data banks make their holdings available at cost in a machine-readable form (data cards or magnetic tape). Sometimes specific tables of data can be requested, and the data bank will process the data for a minimal fee. Hyman (1972) provides an extensive list of data banks, including many that specialize in collecting particular kinds of data. The following are some of the largest:

> Louis Harris Political Data Center, University of North Carolina, Chapel Hill (surveys conducted by the Harris pollsters)
>
> National Opinion Research Center, University of Chicago (general collection of NORC national surveys)
>
> Roper Public Opinion Research Center, Yale University (very large, international collection of surveys)

The Strengths and Limitations of Survey Research

We have already referred briefly to some of the strengths of the survey method. First, it is a method uniquely capable of generating a broad range of data about the characteristics of large populations. Since this coverage is usually accomplished by using carefully designed methods of scientific sampling, and since the data being sought are usually provided, without charge, by the good will of voluntary subjects, the method is also a very cost-efficient approach to large-scale research.

Surveys are also flexible and adaptable in terms of the wide variety of subjects and research problems that can be studied in this way. Only a limited range of either individual or group behavior is sufficiently public for a researcher to study it directly. And of the types of behavior that could be considered public and accessible, many are episodic, sporadic, and unpredictable, thus making it very inconvenient and costly to search them out, wait for them to occur, and record them. In contrast to these serious difficulties of observation, there is almost no type of behavior—public or private, regular or intermittent—that cannot be *talked about*. In a very real sense surveys substitute talk for action, and this thereby greatly extends their range of applicability. Unfortunately, in so doing, they also substitute reports of behavior for direct, empirical observation of it.

The problem of accepting self-reports as true has already been discussed in detail in Chapter 3. Briefly, the motives behind what people report (and what they fail to report) about themselves are a great deal more complex than any pure desire to provide the researcher with an accurate account. The motives of avoiding painful or embarrassing self-revelation and of highlighting personal qualities that may lead to respect or prestige make it difficult to assume that survey respondents' reports about either their actions or their attitudes are, in all cases, accurate.

Self-reports are also limited to those topics about which the average respondent can be assumed to have enough knowledge or insight to speak. Surveys conducted during the 1979 Senate debate of the SALT II arms limitation agreement, for example, showed that almost two-thirds of American adults did not even know that the Soviet Union and the United States were the two parties to the treaty. Equally limited are questions that ask the respondent to provide a self-diagnosis. It cannot be assumed that subjects are sufficiently aware of their own personalities, beliefs, or dispositions to accurately describe themselves on a questionnaire. Introspectiveness and self-awareness are themselves highly variable human traits that greatly affect respondents' abilities to analyze themselves. For these reasons the self-reporting method should not be relied upon exclusively in situations in which other, more direct methods of observation and measurement are available.

A simultaneous limitation and strength of the survey method is that it is typically deductive, theoretically, and that it relies upon adherence to a pre-planned research design. On the one hand, designing and finalizing a questionnaire before contacting subjects in the field means that the researcher must anticipate all that will be relevant and that flaws that might appear in the research design during the data collection stage cannot easily be altered. On the other hand, this rigid consistency about procedure can produce remarkably uniform and reliable results. A properly executed survey strives to maximize the comparability of data collected, and this strategy in turn increases the chances for clear and fruitful analysis.

An awareness of the breadth of the applications of the survey method should encourage you to experiment with many different ways of asking questions and with a wide variety of subjects. At the same time, keeping in mind the limitations of self-reports should lead you to design your questionnaire carefully and to consider whether available, supplementary methods of data collection might be combined with the survey to enhance the overall effectiveness of the research.[6]

---

[6]See Chapter 8 for further discussion of the limits of survey research methodology.

Summary

Survey research is a procedure for systematically collecting information about the attitudes, beliefs, background, experiences, and behavior of a sample of people by using interviews and questionnaires. This chapter has concentrated on six critical aspects of the survey research process: (1) planning the survey, (2) formulating questions, (3) constructing a questionnaire, (4) executing the self-administered survey, (5) interviewing, and (6) preparing the data for processing.

The survey is the most frequently used research technique in social science; most topics of any interest to social researchers have been studied in this way. The survey method is not only flexible and adaptable to a number of research purposes; it is also capable of producing, from a relatively small sample, results that can be generalized to a much larger population of interest.

Careful and thoughtful planning are crucial to successful survey research; the likelihood that any survey will produce data of interest and value to the social researcher is largely determined before any data are collected. A well-planned design, nonetheless, requires skillful execution and careful attention to every detail if the aims of the project are to be realized.

Survey research, like other methods, has its limitations and is not a solution for every research problem. Perhaps the greatest weakness of the method is its total dependence on the respondents—on their memory, their interest, their clarity of self-perception, their frankness, and their honesty. Although deliberate deception is rare, many factors determine how and what people report about their attitudes, beliefs, and behavior, and these factors affect the quality of the data generated in surveys. Consequently, every element, however minor, that goes into the construction of a questionnaire must be carefully designed to serve the aims of the project while minimizing the opportunities for error. The content, wording, sequence, and structure of questions as well as the overall layout of the questionnaire are crucial to the success of any survey.

Key Terms

address
card number
cell
closed-end question
codebook
coding
contingency question
cross-sectional design
data banks
data cleaning
data matrix
demographic categories

face-to-face interview
filter question
identification number
keypunch
loaded question
logical record
longitudinal survey design
machine-readable data
one-dimensional question
open-end question
panel study
pilot study

precoding
pretest
probe
random-digit dialing
secondary analysis
self-administered questionnaire
structured question
telephone survey
trend study
unstructured questions

Exercises

1. Design a brief questionnaire that might be used in a study of the type conducted by Garland F. White (1975, in Suggested Readings). What sources of bias do you think are inherent in this kind of study? If the occupations of the criminals and victims are reversed in half the cases and the sample is thus split into two halves for analysis, how do you know that the two halves are similar in terms of socioeconomic

characteristics? How can you ensure this similarity in conducting the study?

2. Two students should work separately on this exercise. Design a very brief questionnaire asking what people consider to be the main problems facing the leaders of the United States. One questionnaire should ask the question without suggesting any answers; the other should contain a list of possible answers to be shown to the respondents. Administer each questionnaire to ten classmates. Compare the answers received. What implications are there for questionnaire design? Which question format is preferable? Why? In what situations might each format be more effective than the other?

3. One concern of *The People's Choice* (Lazarsfeld, Berelson, and Gaudet, 1944) was to determine why people vote the way they do. Consider an upcoming election or one that has recently taken place. Conduct a survey to attempt to find out the reasons that people intend to vote for (or actually voted for) the candidate of their choice.

4. Two students should work on this exercise together. Work up a brief list of questions on a topic of interest to both of you. Each student should select five people to interview by means of these questions. One will conduct face-to-face interviews and the other will carry out telephone interviews. (Determine who will use which data collection technique by the flip of a coin.) After the interviews are completed, compare notes on your interviewing experiences.

5. Think of a topic about which you want to find out information through a questionnaire. Construct three structured and three unstructured questions for the topic. Ask another student in the class to respond to these questions. Then ask the student to offer constructive criticism of the questions.

6. Think of survey research situations in which it would be most appropriate to use each of the following data collection techniques: a self-administered questionnaire, a face-to-face interview, and a telephone interview. Compare your answers with others in class.

7. Choose a topic of special interest to you. Compare how you would carry out research on the topic by a survey and by another method. What ethical problems might occur in each instance? Does the survey method appear to have more or fewer ethical problems than the other method?

8. Suppose you wish to obtain data on the ethnic backgrounds of wealthy people. You must represent the entire United States with your research. How will you go about the study if:

a. you have an extremely limited budget?

b. you have an unlimited budget?

9. Considering the substantial costs attached to survey research, why is it the most widely used social science methodology? In your answer consider such factors as acceptability of results, availability of preexisting data, convenience to the researcher, reliability and validity, and quality of measurement.

Suggested Readings

READINGS ABOUT THE METHOD

Backstrom, Charles, and Gerald Hursh
1963 *Survey Research.* Evanston, Ill.: Northwestern University Press.

A good description of various phases of survey research. The heaviest concentration is on questionnaire construction and sampling. A series of fifteen useful checklists for the actual execution of survey research is also presented. This remains one of the best available sources for specific and explicit instructions about designing a survey and constructing a questionnaire.

Converse, Jean M., and Howard Schuman
1978 *Conversations at Random: Survey Research as Interviewers See It.* Ann Arbor, Mich.: Institute for Social Research, University of Michigan.

Survey interviewers relate their own experiences in the field and their attitudes toward the data they collect.

Glock, Charles Y., ed.
1967 *Survey Research in the Social Sciences.* New York: Russell Sage.

An analysis of the role and nature of survey research in several fields, including sociology, political science, psychology, education, and social work.

Groves, Robert M., and Robert L. Kahn
1979   *Surveys by Telephone*. New York: Academic Press.

Sample design, administration, and various types of error associated with telephone surveying are analyzed. A systematic comparison of telephone and face-to-face interviewing is presented.

Hy, Renn J.
1977   *Using the Computer in the Social Sciences*. New York: Elsevier.

A concise, nontechnical introduction to the basic components and operational logic of computers.

Hyman, Herbert
1972   *Secondary Analysis of Sample Surveys: Principles, Procedures and Potentialities*. New York: Wiley.

Advantages and pitfalls of secondary analysis are discussed in depth. Various approaches to this technique are examined in relation to their underlying theoretical perspectives. Numerous case studies and examples of empirical work are employed to illustrate various categories of

secondary analysis. Also included are references to many collections of secondary data.

Miller, Delbert C.
1977   *Handbook of Research Design and Social Measurement*. 3rd ed. New York: David McKay.

Miller's handbook is a popular and useful reference for students seriously interested in social research. It includes a number of practical discussions on how to write a grant proposal, what factors to consider when estimating the costs of projected studies, where to obtain data for secondary analysis, and where to submit results for possible publication.

Staff of the Survey Research Center
1976   *Interviewer's Manual*. Revised ed. Ann Arbor, Mich.: Institute for Social Research, University of Michigan.

The general guidelines given to researchers at the Survey Research Center, this work is applicable to any type of survey interviewing.

READINGS ILLUSTRATING THE METHOD

Blau, Peter M., and Otis Dudley Duncan
1967   *The American Occupational Structure*. New York: Wiley.

This study of the American occupational structure involves analysis of secondary data from the U.S. Census. Data on more than 20,000 American males aged 20 to 64 are examined to isolate trends and phenomena in American occupations. The volume contains an excellent discussion of the quality of the data, notably bias due to missing data.

Campbell, Angus
1975   "The American Way of Mating: Marriage, Sí, Children Only Maybe." *Psychology Today* 8 (May):37–43.

This article is based on the findings of a survey of over 2,000 American adults. A number of interesting questions are explored. Are married couples happier than single people? Does the presence of children lessen the happiness of married couples? What happens to the level of happiness for a married couple when their children grow up and leave home? Do men need relationships with

women more than women need relationships with men?

Coleman, James S., et al.
1966   *Equality of Educational Opportunity*. Washington, D.C.: U.S. Department of Health, Education and Welfare, Office of Education.

This is an epic study dealing with segregation in public schools and its implications. Massive numbers of teachers and students provided information about themselves. The fact that the questionnaires were controlled or administered by the teachers themselves rather than by trained professional interviewers may represent a methodological problem. Supplementary studies investigated black college students and school enrollments based on 1960 U.S. Census figures. Several case studies were also employed. This work is an excellent example of what happens when several methodologies and sources of data are included in a single investigation.

Lizotte, Alan J., and David J. Bordua
1980   "Firearms Ownership for Sport and

Protection: Two Divergent Models."
American Sociological Review 45
(April):229–334.

The data for this survey were collected via 764 telephone interviews. Heads of households were selected using the random-digit dialing method. Models explaining the ownership of guns are developed from these data.

Reed, John S.
1972 *The Enduring South.* Lexington, Mass.: Lexington Books.

Reed employs secondary analysis in a study of the Southern United States. His objective is to determine whether, as the South and other parts of the country become more similar demographically and economically, they are also becoming less distinguishable culturally. He utilizes survey data from public opinion polls conducted by someone else. Surveys covering three decades are involved in the study. Reed discusses the advantages and limitations of secondary analysis and the related effects on the study.

Stouffer, Samuel
1966 *Communism, Conformity, and Civil Liberties.* New York: Wiley.

This work is a classic example of research conducted via the survey method.

White, Garland F.
1975 "Public Responses to Hypothetical Crimes: Effect of Offender and Victim Status and Seriousness of the Offense on Punitive Reactions." *Social Forces* 53 (March):411–419.

A door-to-door interview survey in a large Midwestern city is the source of data for this study. The objective of the research is to determine how the occupational status of criminals and the seriousness of their crimes affect people's conceptions of "fair

punishment." The rigidly structured sample of 523 persons was exposed to each of several hypothetical crime episodes, which mentioned the criminals' and victims' occupations as well as the nature of the crime. In roughly half the cases, the occupations of the criminal and victim were reversed. Respondents were asked how severe the punishment should be. The seriousness of the crimes described in the episodes varied substantially. Thus the researcher was able to compare the suggested punishments for various degrees of crime severity and for differing occupations of the criminal for the same crime.

Williamson, John B.
1976 "Beliefs About the Rich, the Poor, and the Taxes They Pay." *American Journal of Economics and Sociology* 35, 1 (January):9–29.

This study of 375 respondents in the Boston metropolitan area appraises the public's perception of the relative tax burden of rich and poor Americans. Individuals at various income levels were interviewed. The author concluded that there was a general tendency to underestimate the total tax burden of the poor.

Wingrove, C. R., and Jon P. Alston
1974 "Cohort Analysis of Church Attendance, 1939–69." *Social Forces* 53 (December):324–331.

Secondary analysis of pre-existing survey data obtained by the American Institute of Public Opinion (the Gallup Poll) six times from 1939 to 1969 forms the basis of this study. Various age cohorts (or groupings) were analyzed to determine whether church attendance varies significantly by age. The study illustrates the use of cohort analysis and secondary analysis.

References

Coleman, James S., et al.
1966 *Equality of Educational Opportunity.* Washington, D. C.: U.S. Department of Health, Education and Welfare, Office of Education.

Davis, James A.
1977 *Cumulative Codebook for the 1972–1977 General Social Survey.* Chicago: National Opinion Research

Center. (Distributed by the Roper Public Opinion Research Center, P.O. Box 1732, Yale Station, New Haven, Conn.).

Hyman, Herbert
1972 *Secondary Analysis of Sample Surveys: Principles, Procedures and Potentialities.* New York: Wiley.

Lazarsfeld, Paul, Bernard Berelson, and Hazel Gaudet
1944   *The People's Choice*. New York: Columbia University Press.
Selltiz, Claire, et al.
1976   *Research Methods in Social Relations*. New York: Holt, Rinehart and Winston.

Stouffer, Samuel
1966   *Communism, Conformity and Civil Liberties*. New York: Wiley.
Survey Research Center
1972   *A Panel Study of Income Dynamics*. Ann Arbor, Mich.: Institute for Social Research.

7 / Intensive Interviewing

CHAPTER OUTLINE

INTRODUCTION
APPLICATIONS OF INTENSIVE
  INTERVIEWING
DISTINCTIVE CHARACTERISTICS
  OF INTENSIVE INTERVIEWS
Commitment and Reciprocity
Shared Meanings
Flexibility
Assimilation
Interviewing and Induction
Interviewing and Reliability

CONDUCTING AN INTERVIEW
Degrees of Structure
Access to Respondents
Preparation
Execution
Guidelines for Questioning
Recording Information
Remaining in Control
Rapport
Nonverbal Signs
Setting

COMPARATIVE STRENGTHS AND
  LIMITATIONS
Strengths
Limitations
CURRENT DEVELOPMENTS IN
  THE TECHNIQUE
SUMMARY
KEY TERMS
EXERCISES
SUGGESTED READINGS
REFERENCES

Introduction

Let us suppose we are studying the processes by which individuals seek acceptance into so-called deviant groups. We have decided to investigate occupations generally regarded as deviant and wish to begin by studying male go-go dancers. What method of data collection shall we employ?

We know relatively little about male go-go dancers, except that they are widely considered a deviant occupational segment. Will they agree to be interviewed? If so, will they be cooperative or will they be evasive or deliberately misleading in their responses? In what setting should we interview them? What types of questions should we ask?

We quickly dismiss the possibility of sending a task force armed with questionnaires to interview a random sample of male go-go dancers. The logistical problems alone could be overwhelming; imagine arranging for a number of interviewers to obtain access to this group. Of even greater consequence could be the difficulty of anticipating what the most productive lines of questioning would be. The very fact of engaging in an unusual occupation could mean that the respondents would be unpredictable and would vary greatly in their reactions to specific questions; so how do we devise a standard set of questions that would be productive in each interview and easy for hired-hand interviewers to administer?

Is there a data gathering method that might meet our needs better than traditional survey research? We know that participant observation has been useful in studies of deviant groups (see Chapter 8). But no one on our research team has the inclination to become a participant in the male go-go dancer occupation. Observation alone seems of minimal value. We suspect that when not on stage, male go-go dancers do not congregate in places where they can be easily and unobtrusively observed. We are so poorly informed about this occupation and its practitioners that we are likely to misinterpret at least some of the actions we would observe. It becomes apparent that information will have to be obtained from the go-go dancers themselves.

Some sort of direct interview seems a necessity, but the traditional form of survey research interviewing will not suffice. Faced with a similar dilemma in their study of stripteasers, Skipper and McCaghy (1972) settled on a method of data collection known as INTENSIVE, or IN-DEPTH, INTERVIEWING. They talked to a number of strippers individually, but the interviews were conducted differently from those used in most survey research.

The researchers prepared a list of question areas that they thought might be appropriate. But during the course of an actual interview, the use of a specific question was guided by the progress of that interview. If a respondent was especially responsive to a particular question, the topic was probed extensively via supplementary questions (some prepared in advance, others devised on the spot). Questions evoking minimal response were sometimes rephrased, if they still bore little fruit, they were usually put aside for another meeting. In short, these interviews were *customized* to each respondent and interviewing situation.

The interviews were lengthy, involving more than one meeting in some cases. The researchers saw some strippers in more than one setting, as they found certain environments (notably backstage) distracting and disruptive to the interviews.

More than most face-to-face interviews, these contacts were dependent on the rapport, mutuality of trust, and sense of reciprocity that developed between researchers and respondents during their transition from strangers to confidants of sorts. The quality of the INCIPIENT RELATIONSHIP between interviewer and interviewee is the cornerstone of the intensive interviewing method.

The preparation of the interviewers was also intensive. They attempted to gird themselves for any contingency by compiling a list of alternative reactions to possible developments during the conversations with subjects. The objective was to encourage spontaneity in the stripteasers' comments while minimizing the possibility that the interviewers would be so surprised by a remark or turn of events that they would retard the interview's momentum.

The intensive interviewing technique offers an opportunity to probe extensively for sensitive information from potentially evasive individuals, tailoring each interview so the interviewee feels as comfortable as possible and is encouraged to provide candid self-reports. The format is usually flexible, with the types and order of questions, the setting, and even the manner of the interviewer being governed not only by the study objectives and the cumulative information flow, but also by a continuing assessment of what it will take to make or keep the interviewee most responsive. While some standardized questions may be asked of every respondent, the interviewer takes account of each respondent's individuality in deciding what to ask, as well as when and how to ask it.

Intensive interviewing places a premium on the interviewer's ability to make quick judgments concerning what to say or do next at any given point in the interview. This factor, more than anything else, determines the ultimate productivity of the interview.

Most intensive interviews are lengthy, with three hours not an uncommon duration. This provides an opportunity for the good intensive interviewer to nurture the incipient relationship with the respondent, enhancing the development of a conversational, give-and-take rapport, and the likelihood of frank revelations.

Applications of Intensive Interviewing

The use of intensive interviewing to obtain information from stripteasers is just one example of how this method may be employed in studies of "deviance." Becker (1955) conducted intensive interviews with marijuana users, eliciting information on their experience with and attitudes toward the drug. Lindesmith (1947) interviewed opiate addicts, in his attempt to identify the processes involved in becoming addicted, remaining addicted, and breaking the habit.

Denzin and Spitzer (Denzin, 1970) conducted a study of mental patients, examining changes in their attitudes as they moved in and out of hospitals. One respondent, when asked if she "would be against a daughter of hers marrying a man who had been to see a psychiatrist about a mental problem," answered initially, "I know I shouldn't say this but I don't want any daughter of mine marrying a man who has been through what I have been." When the question was repeated, the woman replied, "No, I guess I wouldn't be against this!" (Denzin, 1970:129). The persistence of the interviewing revealed what appeared to be the difference between a hasty judgment and a more considered opinion.

The field of deviance represents only one of many possible applications for intensive interviewing. When Zuckerman (1972) was faced with the requirement of obtaining information on a highly prestigious group—Nobel laureates in science—she chose intensive interviewing as her data gathering method and eventually talked to forty-one of the fifty-five laureates who were living in the United States at the time. Lipset, Trow, and Coleman (1956) utilized four methods—participant observation, intensive interviewing, examination of records and documents, and survey research—to study the organization and internal party politics of a trade union. Although Trow has said that the review of documents and voting records, survey research, and participant observation were all useful in dealing with various objectives in the research, he pointed up the importance of intensive interviewing in evaluating the amount of legitimacy imputed to the party system by various groups and social categories within the union:

> The workings of the party system inhibited direct expressions of hostility to the system. In the ordinary give and take of conversation in the shop, party meeting, club meeting, informal gatherings after hours, such expressions were not likely to be expressed; they violated strongly held norms, and called down various kinds of punishments. It was only when we interviewed leaders individually and intensively that we could get some sense of the reservations that they held about the party system, how widely and strongly those reservations were held, and thus could make some assessment of those sentiments as a potentially disruptive force in the party system. (Trow, 1957:34)

Holmstrom (1972) engaged respondents in "flexible" or "free-style" interviews in her study of the two-career family; later she collaborated with Burgess (Burgess and Holmstrom, 1974) in applying the same type of interviews to the study of rape victims. Kubler-Ross (1969) produced a wealth of data from perhaps the most difficult group to interview—dying people—via intensive interviews in her study on death and dying. Lane (1967) employed the method to supplement other data collection techniques in a study of the public's political ideology.

In short, intensive interviewing is applicable to a wide variety of investigations. Whether it is employed as the sole data gathering mode or used in combination with other methods depends on a number of considerations to be discussed later. For the moment let us turn from the applied aspects to the more theoretical implications of this methodological tool.

Distinctive Characteristics of Intensive Interviews

Interviews involve direct interaction between two parties—the interviewer seeking information from the interviewee. As in any interaction the ultimate value of the interview depends on a number of considerations, notably:

1. *commitment:* the degree of interest in both parties in making the interaction mutually beneficial.
2. *meaning:* the ability of each party to recognize the true intent of the other's actions and statements.
3. *flexibility:* the extent to which the course or content of the interaction may be adapted to meet the needs of both parties.
4. *assimilation:* the ways in which the two parties digest and interpret the ongoing interaction.

Using these four criteria, we may contrast intensive interviews with STRUCTURED INTERVIEWS. Structured interviews utilize a questionnaire with precisely worded questions, appearing in a certain sequence, and administered by an interviewer who has no authority to change or amend either the wording or the order of these questions (except in clearly prescribed ways, as discussed in Chapter 6). Most survey research studies employ structured questionnaires.

COMMITMENT AND RECIPROCITY

Throughout any interaction each party consciously or unconsciously makes a series of decisions concerning the presentation of self to the other. Each is constantly deciding how much to reveal and what impression to make. The benefits each party feels as the interaction progresses will govern the extent and nature of continued personal commitment to the interaction.[1]

Theoretically, as the interaction proceeds, each party derives sufficient rewards from the relationship for it to continue; if the relationship fails to provide these rewards, it will be terminated either mutually or unilaterally. The burgeoning rapport between the two parties may be one source of satisfaction. Receipt of

---

[1] For an application of "exchange" theories of mutual trust and reciprocity to the interviewing process, see Gray (1980).

valued information (sometimes as formalized as a promised copy of the study report) may be another. Gratification at being the object of another's interest is sometimes sufficient reward.

We are not referring merely to inducing participation. This is not usually a severe problem, and cash payments are frequently useful incentives in difficult cases. It is the *quality* of participation that is crucial—the motivation and ability of interviewees to provide introspective and candid responses throughout the interview.

An intensive interviewer may frequently praise the effort of the respondent, contributing to the latter's self-esteem. Interviewers may reveal facts about themselves—facts that will not influence the respondent's opinions but that will make the interaction an exchange of information rather than a one-way flow:

> INTERVIEWEE: It's important to get out of the house once in a while. I have my kids, but they really get on your nerves.
>
> INTERVIEWER: I can understand. I have kids of my own.

Reinforcement of self-worth and a sense of RECIPROCITY are but two of several techniques for enhancing respondent commitment through the interview.

Most interviews are forced interactions on the part of at least one participant. The initial contact between interviewer and interviewee is usually an arbitrary meeting of two strangers. Intensive interviews are normally conducted in ways that encourage and nurture the development of this incipient relationship. In other words, the interviewer is relatively free to guide the emerging relationship into directions that offer the best chance for mutual reward. By contrast, a structured interview is less likely to progress much beyond its initial abruptness, arbitrariness, and remoteness.

SHARED MEANINGS

Even if interviewees are highly motivated to provide detailed and accurate responses, their ability to do so is at least partly dependent on their interpretation of the questions. Will a given question mean to the respondent exactly what it meant to the person who prepared it? This problem increases with the level of abstraction in the question. If a question refers to "success in life," will a given respondent interpret "success" as being measured by level of affluence, esteem from one's peers, occupational status, or some other indicator? To provide a detailed definition of success for respondents' edification might be helpful, but a questionnaire filled with definitions usually proves boring and fatiguing to interviewees.

A related consideration is whether respondents' answers will mean to researchers what the respondents intended. Most structured interviews include a few open-end questions that ask respondents to answer in their own words (for example, "What do you think are the most important pros and cons of capital punishment?") The people who analyze the answers to these questions are generally not the ones who conducted the interviews. Considering the various possible meanings or nuances of each comment, how likely are these analysts to interpret correctly the intended meaning of people they have never met?

Becker and Geer (1957:29) have recounted a situation in their study of medical students in which the word *crock* was used to describe a patient. One student explained that the term referred to any patient with psychosomatic complaints. Only after observing medical students for some time and hearing the word used frequently did the researchers realize that *crock* meant a patient in whom the students had invested substantial diagnostic time without finding a real malady. It was the perception of "wasted" time, rather than simply the patients' fantasies, that prompted the use of the derogatory term. If the researchers had accepted the initial definition reported by the medical student, they would have overlooked an important factor in the research. This example, although drawn from an observational study, illustrates the pitfalls of accepting interviewees' comments at face value.

Many survey research questions appear to get at the heart of a concept (sometimes termed face validity) without really doing so. What could be more concise or direct than the question "Are you prejudiced against minority individuals or groups?" The wording of the question, however, is so loaded as to almost demand a "no" response. Leaving terms such as "prejudiced" and "minority" open to respondent definition invites a different interpretation of the question from interviewee to interviewee. Forcing a "yes" or "no" response prevents an interviewee from indicating a degree of prejudice that is something less than total. If this question had been pretested among several respondents under mock survey research conditions, it would indeed have yielded answers; interviewees would have forced themselves in one direction or another (more likely the less damning one). But we should not always interpret the answering of a question as evidence that it has been clearly stated in the questionnaire or understood by the respondent.

Intensive interviewing, if conducted properly, can go much farther in ensuring against misinterpretation of meaning by either interviewer or interviewee. If the interviewee asks for clarification, the researcher can give it, unlike the survey interviewer who is generally warned not to change or amend a question in any way. If the intensive interviewer suspects even the opportunity for misinterpretation, it is a simple matter to ask subjects to repeat a question in their own words. Some intensive interviewers deliberately phrase the same question in different ways from respondent to respondent, either to make certain that the nature of the answer is not being biased by the way in which the question is asked or to customize the wording to the characteristics of the interviewee. (A question on occupational aspirations, for example, would probably be asked differently of a middle-aged physicist than of a junior high school student.)

Intensive interviewing emphasizes the direct interchange between a single respondent (or sometimes a pair or small group of respondents) and an individual researcher who is often the director of the study. The interviewer, in addition to gathering information, is actually conducting an analysis during the course of the interaction and should be particularly capable of knowing when and how to clarify meaning. The following hypothetical exchange would not be unusual:

INTERVIEWER: Do you consider this neighborhood a good place in which to live?

RESPONDENT: Do you mean generally or for me in particular?

INTERVIEWER: Well, why don't you discuss it generally at first and then for you in particular?

RESPONDENT: Generally speaking, it's a dump. It used to be nice but then it started going downhill.

INTERVIEWER: What do you mean by "downhill"?

RESPONDENT: Well, it started with parlors. And then we have lots of drug pushers in town. They hooked our kids on dope.

INTERVIEWER: Parlors?

RESPONDENT: Betting parlors. Bookie joints. Aren't you from around here?

INTERVIEWER: No, but I'm enjoying getting the inside story from you.

RESPONDENT: Well, these are places where you can go make a bet, like on the horses. They're illegal, and they operate in the backs of stores. Everyone has been in there at one time or another. I've lost a lot of money there lately. The police know about them, but they look the other way. I think it's the money from the parlors that financed the dope peddlers in the first place.

This brief example illustrates how both interviewee and interviewer obtained clarifications, which might not have been possible in a structured interview.

While each interviewee in an intensive interview study is likely to be asked a variety of questions tailored to his or her own knowledge or experience, there may be some questions that must be asked of all respondents. In these instances the emphasis is on *equivalence of meaning*. The objective is for a question to have the same meaning to each interviewee, even though it may have to be phrased differently from interview to interview in order to achieve this goal. Suppose we were interested in this question:

If some people in your community suggested that a book written by a socialist and advocating socialist policies be taken out of your public library, would you favor removing the book or not?

For some respondents, we might be able to ask the question in its present form; but for others it would not be safe to assume that they understood what we meant by the term *socialist*. Some might even interpret the word *removing* as meaning "borrowing." Faced with these dilemmas, the intensive interviewer would not hesitate to reword the question. Here is a possible rewording:

Suppose a person who favored government ownership of all the railroads and all major industries such as the steel industry, the auto industry, and so on had written a book that was in your public library, advocating government ownership of the railroads and major industries. If some people in your community suggested that the library get rid of the book, would you agree that it would be a good idea to make the library get rid of the book, or wouldn't you agree?

This revision might seem overly simplified, redundant, and even patronizing to some respondents; but it would be used only in those cases where it promised to communicate a meaning equivalent to the original question and to do it more easily than the original question would have.

FLEXIBILITY

In an intensive interview, as in any conversation, the participants may sometimes be unaware of exactly what direction the exchange will take until they are in the middle of it. They each have certain objectives, but the way they pursue them hinges on the flow of conversation. In a sense it is like a chess game, where a given move depends on what the other player has just done and affects what the other player will do next.

The researchers who studied stripteasers prepared a list of discussion areas but also were equipped with a number of alternative questions for use if various contingencies occurred. They could not foresee all possible eventualities, but they prepared as best they could. Most important, they were not restricted in the actual interviewing by either the wording or the sequence of the initial list of questions.

The flexible format of intensive interviews is important for a number of reasons. Whenever the interviewee mentions anything of particular note, the interviewer has the opportunity to probe immediately for additional information. This display of interest on the part of the interviewer also helps to solidify the relationship with the interviewee. In some intensive interviews the respondent will introduce a topic that the interviewer intended to discuss later. The interviewer may switch topics immediately, to capitalize on the momentum provided by the interviewee. This tactic also reaffirms the interviewer's interest in the respondent's comments. When switching topics, the good interviewer will take care not to interrupt an important train of thought of the interviewee. Sometimes instead of risking such an interruption, the interviewer will say, "That's interesting. I'd like to pursue that in greater depth soon," and will then proceed with the original topic.

Intensive interviews may be useful in probing into sensitive areas. If a respondent appears to evade a question because it is too personal, the interviewer may wait until rapport has grown and may then ask the question in a different way. If a question about the interviewee's family relationships elicits no response, the interviewer may later pose a more general question about family ties in today's society and then ask how the respondent's family contrasts with other families in this respect. Note that only the most highly trained and perceptive researchers can succeed in employing this technique without arousing the suspicion and/or ire of the interviewee. In fact, there are some sensitive subjects for which the anonymity provided by mail questionnaires may encourage more candid responses than many intensive interviewers can generate.

Intensive interviewing offers many options for investigators, in terms of what to say as well as when and how to say it. These options make it possible for the interview to approach the continuity and momentum characteristic of a productive conversation. One way in which intensive interviewing generally differs from normal conversation is the way in which both interviewer and interviewee assimilate the results.

ASSIMILATION

Typically, the interviewee's assimilation of what transpires in an intensive interview revolves largely around trust and gratification. It is natural for a respondent to have initial reservations or fears concerning the "real" intentions or objectives of the interviewer. As the interview progresses, if the researcher is performing well, the evolving conversation reassures the respondent that the interviewer's intent is to learn and share, not to exploit.

At the outset the respondent may regard the interview as an imposition or a chore, particularly if the interviewer has not been careful in explaining the significance of the study and of participating in it. The many potential sources of gratification from an intensive interview should become apparent to the respondent as the ongoing give-and-take is digested. The amount of genuine interest shown by the interviewer is probably the greatest determinant of how much benefit the interviewee perceives. For the interviewee assimilation is one key to producing useful results. Such assimilation takes place both within and between interviews.

For the researcher assimilation *is* the result. What the interviewer gleans represents the essence of the findings (sometimes supplemented by a few structured questions). The interviewer must constantly be aware of the implications of an interviewee's comments. While taking notes on the interviewee's replies, the interviewer has to be simultaneously alert for any inconsistencies in the respondent's "story," mindful of how this respondent differs from others, cognizant of whether the objectives of the study are being met by the cumulative flow of information, ready to formulate and/or test hypotheses, and, finally, prepared with what to say next.

INTERVIEWING AND INDUCTION

Between interviews the researcher may take advantage of a key benefit of intensive interviewing: the sequential nature of the contacts with respondents and the opportunity to use the process of induction (discussed in Chapter 1). The following steps reiterate the main elements of induction as research progresses:

1. Formulate a rough definition of the phenomenon you want to explain.
2. Devise a preliminary explanation of that phenomenon.
3. At this point examine only one case in light of our proposed explanation. Try to determine whether the facts of that one case can be accounted for by the preliminary analysis.
4. If the explanation fits the facts of that one case, turn to other cases to see if it still fits. If the explanation does not fit the one case, either reformulate the original theoretical explanation or redefine the phenomenon that you want to explain.
5. Keep examining a number of cases in sequence, reformulating the theory each time that a new case cannot be explained by the existing theory.
6. Continue this process of examining cases, redefining phenomena, and reformulating hypotheses until you are satisfied that you have formulated an explanation that will not be contradicted by additional data.

Sequential interviewing has other advantages. The researcher does not have to formulate arbitrary answer categories prior to the interviewing but can derive the answer categories from the cumulative responses given. By further refining these categories as the interviewing progresses, the researcher better describes the full range of respondent opinion.

INTERVIEWING AND RELIABILITY

Sequential interviewing allows the researcher to make it progressively more difficult for respondents to give answers that appear to be contrived to win the approval of the interviewer. Suppose we were conducting a study of attitudes toward gay rights among the students at a major college, using intensive interviewing. If the question "Do you think there should be laws against marriage between members of the same sex?" elicited negative responses from the first six students interviewed, we might begin to suspect that they were giving answers contrived to demonstrate their supposedly liberal attitudes. We might revise the question to minimize the possibility that one response could appear more socially attractive than another: "Some people feel there should be laws against marriage between members of the same sex; others feel there should *not* be laws against marriage between members of the same sex. Which way do you feel?" If sentiment continues to run in the same direction as before, we might try an even stronger inducement to "shake" ensuing respondents from this answer: "Many people suggest that there are good reasons for maintaining laws against marriage between members of the same sex. Would you agree with these people?

We do not advocate the wholesale slanting of research questions, but this measure may sometimes be judiciously employed for the special purpose of determining whether respondents are indulging in the sort of answer "shading" described above. This must be done with the greatest of care in order to prevent the deliberately slanted question from compromising the objectivity of the overall interview. Even when there is a strong suspicion that responses are not completely candid, intentional slanting of questions is a last resort, to be used only after other measures have been exhausted (for example, presenting two possible opinions, stating that each opinion may be widely held, and asking which comes closer to the respondent's view).

The sequential nature of intensive interviewing partially offsets one of the strongest criticisms of this method. In studies of large populations, users of research generally feel that large samples produce highly reliable results, which come close to reflecting the beliefs of the entire population. Intensive interviewing, which normally uses relatively small samples, is seldom mentioned in the same breath with the word *reliability* unless the total population is not much larger than the sample. But because intensive interviewing combines data gathering with a continuing analysis as the study progresses, this method can subject a hypothesis to many more tests than can survey research. Intensive interviewers believe that by varying many elements of the study (the order in which the questions are asked, the way in which a given question may be posed, the safeguards against biased questions or less than candid responses, etc.), they usually come up with results in which a high degree of confidence may be placed. The word *stability* is sometimes used to describe the cumulative results of sequential intensive interviewing that incorporates test after test to challenge the emerging results.

In short, when the cumulative results of an intensive interview study continue to fall within a given range with interview after interview, despite attempts by the researcher to identify deviations from this range, the researcher senses the sort of stability that can inspire a high degree of confidence. In studies involving matters other than easily observable phenomena, this kind of confidence may be more important than the statistical reliability attributed to survey research.

Conducting an Interview

We turn now to a more concrete examination of intensive interviewing procedures. Up to this point we have emphasized differences between intensive and structured interviews. There are, however, elements that fall along the continuum between these two.

DEGREES OF STRUCTURE

Interviews are usually characterized as being one of three types:

1. *Structured* or STANDARDIZED: All questions are asked exactly the same way and usually in the same order for all respondents.
2. NONSCHEDULE STANDARDIZED: All questions are asked of each respondent, but they may be asked in different ways and in different sequences.
3. UNSTRUCTURED or NONSTANDARDIZED: No standardized schedule of questions is used.

There are variations involving combinations of these types. SEMISTRUCTURED INTERVIEWS include questions that are asked of all respondents (either in structured or nonschedule form) as well as other, unstructured questions. Semistructured interviewing was used in the stripteaser study cited earlier. This is a popular form of intensive interviewing, since it provides some data that are comparable for all respondents (for example, age, marital status, and level of affluence) and other data derived from questions tailored to the unique experiences and perspectives of each individual.

ACCESS TO RESPONDENTS

In discussing the procedures of intensive interviewing, we shall employ a hypothetical case. Suppose we are about to begin a study of upper-middle-class suburbanites' attitudes toward active involvement in political campaigns, whether as candidates themselves or on behalf of others.

Our first problem is to entice upper-middle-class suburbanites to submit to intensive interviews. We wish to interview them at length in their rooms—half adult female household heads and half adult male household heads—and we cannot afford to pay them for their trouble. Why should they have the slightest inclination to participate in the study?

Ordinarily, we might seek the endorsement of a respected and well-known local organization as a means toward establishing our credibility, but in this case we cannot risk any respondent's thinking we represent a specific organization, so we abandon the endorsement idea. We write a letter to the chief of police, with details of the manner in which we intend to go about our study. We state that our objective is to determine what motivates an individual to become politically active and what some of the implications of the research may be, both for the person and for the community. We guarantee that no participant will be identified with specific responses in the report. The ultimate beneficiaries, we state, will be people and organizations wishing to nurture a healthy political system within the community. We formally request permission to conduct the study as outlined in the letter, verify that interviewers will have appropriate identification, and follow up the letter with a personal visit to the police station. We are granted permission to conduct the study.

We now send letters to a sample of homes (selected randomly if the study is a large one, or perhaps selected to reflect widely disparate neighborhood conditions if we will be conducting only a few interviews). In the letters we explain the broad purpose of our research, with no reference whatsoever to sponsorship of the study.

Now comes the tricky part—actually obtaining respondent cooperation. We visit a few homes that have received our letter and ask for an appointment to conduct an interview, stating that it may last as long as two or three hours. Most of the people we approach perceive themselves as being very busy. Some are suspicious of us and our motives. We emphasize that their participation is extremely important to us because we have selected only a few households to represent the entire community. We also stress that the information they provide will not be linked to them personally. We offer to make a synopsis of the results available to them. We assure them that our intent is not to inconvenience or exploit them but simply to collect information, at their convenience, that will be of benefit to a great many people in working toward a healthy and viable political system in the community. When they express concern over the length of the interview, we explain that it can be divided into more than one session and suggest that they start the interview to see if they find it as interesting as most people do.

In other words, we attempt to induce participation (1) by capitalizing on the fact that an intensive interview approaches the sort of sociable conversation enjoyed by most people. It is not, strictly speaking, a social occasion, but it tends in that direction and can be a positive experience for people who take pleasure in being asked their opinion. (2) In presenting ourselves as interviewers, we hope to be viewed by the people we approach as what Goffman (1963: 129) has called OPENING PERSONS—individuals such as newspaper reporters who, because of their roles, are implicitly granted the license to approach strangers without causing the suspicion and rejection that often accompanies such confrontations. Thus intensive interviewers may be accommodated because of their uniquely perceived role as people whose job is to talk to strangers.

We do *not* advocate that an interviewer plead with potential interviewees to "help me do my job." This borders on the unethical and is also a sign of weakness that could influence interviewees' later comments.

PREPARATION

Preparation for the actual interviews consists of two key elements. First, we obtain all available background information on local political organizations, residents' voting behavior and party affiliations, elective positions in the area, and other pertinent factors. Sources might include published material (for example, newspaper articles or editorials, voting records, voting registration lists, and books on the history of the community), and brochures or material made available by local political or other organizations. We speak with a few community and/or civic leaders. We also speak with leaders of specific political organizations.

This first type of preparation leads directly to the second type—formulation of a tentative guide for conducting the interviews. This guide will include hypotheses already formulated for testing, specific questions or topics that promise to be fruitful, contingency questions or topics, and a rough outline for the ordered placement of topics. Most researchers follow the rule of thumb that interviews should commence with some general questions that are relatively easy to answer;

with these as background, the topics and questions become progressively more specific and probing.[2]

Through this intensive preparation we obtain a "feel" for the community in general and for its political activity patterns in particular. It reduces the chances that we will appear completely shocked or unknowledgeable in the face of an interviewee's responses. Our investigation emerges from abstraction to reality. Our sense of personal involvement and commitment is heightened, and we gain confidence in our ability to cope with any exigencies that may arise during the interviews.

EXECUTION

We arrive at the home of the first respondent and introduce ourselves. We restate the purpose of the study and mention any pertinent ethical considerations. We might say something like:

> Hello, I'm _____. We spoke the other day about the study I'm conducting on political involvement. Thank you for giving me the opportunity to ask you some questions. I'm particularly interested in people's views on what political life and organizations are like, how political organizations function, what purposes they serve, why people participate in them, and anything else you can tell me about your impressions of political activity and political organizations. As I said the other day, I can promise that your name will never be linked with anything you say; you will remain completely anonymous. I'd like to tape-record our conversation, although I don't want your name to appear on the tape. Taping our discussion means that I don't have to take a lot of notes, which speeds up the process and ensures that I have an accurate record of what we say. No one except myself will hear the tape.

This introduction has suggested the range of topics to be discussed. The word *impressions* is important, since interviewees often leap to the assumption that they are inappropriate respondents if they do not participate frequently in the phenomenon under study. Tape-recording the interview, in addition to providing a permanent record of the exchange, will enable us to evaluate our interviewing technique after the interview is completed.

Note that nowhere in the introduction did we refer to the interview as an "interview." Since some people equate "interview" with "interrogation," it is important, at the outset, to present the exchange as a conversation or discussion between two *participants*.

Once the interview begins, we follow the predetermined topic outline until it seems natural to deviate from it. Let's say we have decided to conduct semistructured interviews, in which we will ask each person about involvement in political activities, parties, and organizations. These questions are relatively easy to answer, so we ask them at the beginning. The interviewee is reassured that partici-

---

[2]An exception to this rule involves research that places a premium on the memory of the interviewee. If we were interviewing older people to discover whether they were more satisfied now than during the period of their youth, it might be difficult for them to speak in generalities about their youth until they had reminisced for a while about specific aspects of that period.

pation in the discussion will not be a difficult task, and we now have knowledge about the respondent that later may be used as a frame of reference.

From this point the course of the interview and the questions that are asked will depend largely on input from the respondent. As in every conversation many devices may be used by the participants in manipulating the interchange to achieve a given purpose. It is the task of the interviewer to facilitate the accomplishment of both parties' objectives. As an example of the various intents that may motivate interviewer and interviewee input, a hypothetical dialogue is presented. Beside each comment is a statement of the underlying intent:

Conversation*	Intent
IR: Let's talk for a moment about the reasons why someone might become active in campaigning for a political candidate.	*Definition of purpose.*
IE: (Silence)	*Encouragement to proceed.*
IR: What are some of the reasons why someone might join this kind of activity?	*Restatement of purpose into question.*
IE: Well, you want to be of service to the community.	*Indication of opinion in response to direct question.*
IR: Uh-huh.	*Encouragement to proceed.*
IE: I mean you become politically active because you think your candidate will help other people.	*Restatement and expansion of earlier response.*
IR: I understand.	*Indication that no further restatement is needed; encouragement to proceed in another direction.*
IE: And of course you enjoy belonging to a club too.	*Additional opinion response to earlier question.*
IR: Club?	*Echo statement to elicit more information.*
IE: Well, I'd never be a candidate, so I think of political activity as being a member of an organization that is sort of like a club and having a common goal—at least the ones I'd want to join.	*Expanded definition in response to echo request.*
IR: So, there are some you'd want to join and others you wouldn't want to join.	*Restatement of IE's comment to elicit more information.*
IE: Sure. I'd rather work for a school committee member than for a mayoral candidate, because I feel	*Clarification of former statement in response to IR's restatement.*

Conversation*	Intent
a school committee member can make more of a difference.	
IR: What are some of the ways in which a school committee member can make more of a difference than a mayor?	*Probe for additional related information.*
IE: Well, there are many ways to make a difference.	*Evasion of question, perhaps because earlier response is difficult to substantiate or because the topic is too sensitive, or because IE is tired of discussing topic.*
IR: That's interesting. What are some of the ways in which you think the school committee members themselves might feel they make an important difference?	*Initial support, so as not to alienate IE. Refocus on previous topic, approaching question from different perspective.*
IE: Well, that's what I meant by a common goal. They have the ultimate goal of helping kids—or at least they *should* have.	*Partial amplification of previous response and indication of possible skepticism, which may provide yet another avenue for questioning.*

*IR = interviewer; IE = interviewee.

In addition to the many conversational devices that may be employed by either party, this example shows how the interviewer may seize on just one word ("club") to propel the interview in a related and useful but slightly different direction. The perceived importance of having a common goal, which might or might not be covered later in the interview, emerged at this point and provided important insights into the respondent's real outlook on political involvement.

Some of the conversational techniques that may be used by an intensive interviewer in the execution of the interview include:

repetition or restatement (exemplified above)

expressing ignorance to elicit information

expressing interest or support as a reward (exemplified above)

encouraging expanded response (exemplified above; also simple nodding)

legitimizing alternative responses—stating that some people feel one way while others feel another way, to reduce interviewee's fears of sanctions on a given opinion

introducing transitions—announcing a change in topic to avoid catching interviewee by surprise or making interviewee feel like "outsider"

summarizing—giving frequent summaries of the conversational highlights up to the time of the summary, in order to keep interviewee involved in the total conversation and to ensure that interviewer and interviewee are on the same "wave length" as to the results *challenging answers*—tactfully bringing up apparent inconsistencies in responses and seeking clarification

purging irrelevant responses—allowing respondent to become "talked out" concerning an irrelevant tack with which respondent seems preoccupied

granting vacation—allowing respondent to indulge in irrelevancies for a short period, in order to build up interviewee energy for next conversational tasks

revealing self-information—interviewer's mentioning of certain facts about self—facts that flow naturally into the conversation that will not change interviewee's responses or train of thought

GUIDELINES FOR QUESTIONING

Despite the generally open-ended nature of intensive interviews, they do involve an equivalent to a questionnaire, called a TOPIC OUTLINE, which lists specific issues to be brought to an interviewee's attention. The outline contains items that might be appropriate for a given interview, including some contingency questions that presuppose a certain comment or answer on the respondent's part. How many and which topics are covered with each person depend on several factors, including the respondent's nature and experience as well as time constraints.

The list of topics in the outline is usually quite extensive and is typically organized into general categories. A study of people's political behavior might have as a general category "Inducements to Political Involvement." This category, in turn, might be broken down into many topics, such as personal relationships with politicians, past family involvement in politics, political activities of friends or associates, desire to associate with powerful people.

As usual, the interview should begin with some questions that are easy to answer, reassuring the respondent that the discussion will not be too imposing. Personal questions that are not particularly sensitive (for example, whether or not the respondent is a long-time resident of the area) may suffice. These questions fortify the respondent's confidence in self and trust in the interviewer as a professional with a legitimate research mission. The shape of the remainder of the interview depends on the results of each ensuing question or topic covered.

Throughout the interview the interviewer should be on the lookout for any indications of fatigue or disinterest on the part of the interviewee. It may be necessary to halt the interview and resume it at a later point. Sometimes it is important to allow the respondent to ramble on about a seemingly irrelevant point, in order to provide a "vacation" from the topic at hand. The good intensive interviewer will develop several techniques for recognizing and dealing with respondent restlessness or boredom.

RECORDING INFORMATION

The recording of information may strongly influence the pace of the interview, the nature of the responses, and the quality of the analysis. Consequently, the interviewer must weigh several factors before deciding on the recording method to be used in a given study.

The recording method should enable the interviewer to record all *substantive communication* from the interviewee. Some interviewers simply write as much as they can, believing that exhaustive recording of the interviewee's comments is the best path. Others prefer to record only the main points of the respondent, sacrificing some recording in favor of being more heavily involved in the interaction. Only a few interviewers rely completely on a tape recorder, mainly in cases where precise quotations will be crucial. In fact, inarticulate respondents and/or noisy background conditions may require interviewers to go back over a tape, in order to hear each word slowly and distinctly, before attempting an analysis. The interviewer must decide (sometimes in advance, but often after the first few meetings) how much notetaking will be necessary and whether to supplement notes with tape recordings. Some intensive interviewers compromise by taking written notes in every interview but taping only a portion, in order to obtain verbatim quotes that may add "flavor" to findings based on the handwritten notes. Some balance between notetaking and taping usually is best.

The smooth flow of the interview should be facilitated by the recording method. Some intensive interviewers take notes on a series of cards, each of which deals with one of the general categories from the topic outline. This technique allows quick referral to previous comments on a given topic, thus ensuring that the respondent is being consistent and preventing interviewee boredom that might arise if the same topic were inadvertently covered twice. Other interviewers do the same sort of organizing on sheets of paper, on which they include several categories to minimize paper shuffling, which they feel can disrupt the interview flow.

The method of recording information should facilitate ongoing analysis of the responses. During the interview, the interviewer should identify implications, develop hypotheses, and formulate directions for the remainder of the particular interview and for future meetings. Tapes are of use only after the interview—one of the principal limitations of relying on a tape recorder instead of taking detailed notes. Some intensive interviewers employ symbols, forms of shorthand, or other special notations to indicate a variety of factors, including: a potential hypothesis, a question that should be asked immediately or later in the interview, whether a given respondent comment was the result of an interviewer probe, at what point in the interview particular communications occurred (if recording is being done by category rather than in simple sequential form), and even the footage point on a recorded tape at which a given comment occurred.

The relatively unstructured nature of intensive interviews may suggest that the recording of information from them should also be done in an unstructured way, but this is not necessarily so. The form shown in Figure 7.1 provides for some standardization of recording, without compromising the necessary freedom of the interviewer. On such a form, which might or might not be supplemented by tape recordings, the general categories would be listed at the left. Under a given category would be noted pertinent respondent communication. To the right of each category, the interviewer can jot down any analytical or procedural thoughts stimulated by that communication. An interviewer might even change the color of a pen or pencil at several junctures in the interview, to identify the approximate points at which certain communication occurred.

REMAINING IN CONTROL

Without being abrasive or overly authoritative, the interviewer in our hypothetical interview maintained control and guided the respondent into productive conversation. When the interviewee gave evasive or superficial answers, the interviewer

FIGURE 7.1   A Recording Form for Intensive Interviews

Communications from the Interviewee	Analytical Considerations	Procedural Considerations

judiciously pursued the line of questioning in order to obtain more meaningful responses. The interviewer maintained a steady PACE, not allowing the conversation to get bogged down with repetitions and not skipping over important points.

The matter of pacing is important: it is highly detrimental for an interview to gain momentum and then to deteriorate because the tempo has suddenly become too slow or too fast. The desired momentum is one that permits a steady and productive flow of conversation. If either of the participants speaks for a long time without some input from the other, the interview is suffering from a lack of control.

On the other hand, if the interview consists of a series of rapid-fire inputs between interviewer and interviewee, this is a sign that the researcher is failing to elicit responses of sufficient length to obtain relevant information. Banaka (1971) has stated that a sixty-minute in-depth interview should average between two and four inputs per minute (including inputs of both parties). This is just a rule of thumb, but it is a pretty good one.

Appropriate use of PREEMPTIVE TECHNIQUES—measures taken to prevent the respondent from taking certain conversational directions—can greatly enhance the efficiency and control of interviews. Many interviewees want to avoid revealing anything about themselves, so they speak about "people in general." The interviewer can preempt this tendency by saying to the interviewee at the outset that, "It is important that you answer only for yourself; we'll be asking other people how they feel." Respondents sometimes like to feel they are exceptions to norms—exceptions that make them unsuitable to answer a given question. The interviewer can preempt this avoidance technique by explaining that opinions or impressions are needed from all respondents and that the analysis can take note of the exceptional circumstance.

RAPPORT

We have already stated that the quality of the incipient or emerging relationship between researcher and respondent is the key to how productive the intensive interview will be. This does not mean that the two will become close friends, and in fact there is a danger of *overrapport,* which could compromise the researcher's detached perspective. It is important for the intensive interviewer to nurture rapport with the other party within the framework of an appropriate degree of objectivity. The best avenue for creating and perpetuating rapport with respondents is to ensure that they receive sufficient rewards from the relationship without their feeling that these gratifications are artificial. It is beneficial, for example, to praise the interviewee's contributions occasionally, but not to the point where such praise is overdone. Sometimes it is the timing, rather than the amount, of praise that is most important.

One of the attractions intensive interviewing has for respondents is that it gives them an opportunity to reveal in a nonjudgmental environment the multiple identities they perceive themselves as having. A woman who may know she is criticized by neighbors for "going off and leaving her child" with a babysitter while she pursues a career need fear no recriminations in this respect from the skilled intensive interviewer. In this sense, the interaction of an intensive interview may offer benefits not available in most day-to-day encounters. The intensive interviewer who accepts without judgment the various self-identities indicated by the interviewee is facilitating development of strong rapport with the other party, as well, perhaps, as greater self-acceptance on the part of the interviewee.

NONVERBAL SIGNS

At one point in the hypothetical dialogue (page 176), the interviewee remained silent at a time when it might have been appropriate to say something. This was a nonverbal message for the researcher. The interviewer interpreted the silence as a signal to proceed because the respondent needed more inputs. When in doubt about the meaning of such signals, it is best to take the positive approach and to proceed.

Nonverbal communication is an important part of any conversation and, therefore, of any intensive interview. Many signals may be given by either party, involving tone of voice, eye contact, body position, gestures, facial expressions, and pauses. (Even the point at which one person interrupts another can be meaningful.) Nonverbal signs offer interviewers many ways in which to manipulate an encounter while not appearing to do so. Since the same devices are available to interviewees, it behooves researchers to be aware constantly of any nonverbal communication in which the other party engages. Burgess and Holmstrom (1974:144–145) illustrate how a rape victim used nonverbal means to indicate her feelings of distress during an intensive interview:

> Laura, age 13, wouldn't say anything. She sat holding a little pink coin purse. Then she bent over and picked up a short screw from the floor that her mother had dropped. She took the screw and kept hitting,with some force,the purse with the screw. First she drew lines across the purse; then she really stabbed it, making holes in the purse.

Researchers should be acutely aware of the nonverbal messages they are giving off. One of the easiest ways to undermine rapport between interviewer and interviewee is for the former to look or act in a manner outside the bounds of acceptability. In most suburban communities, for example, a stranger entering a private home is implicitly expected to present a neat appearance and not to be dressed too informally. Although someone interviewing on a Saturday might find the respondent clothed in faded, torn jeans while doing household chores, the interviewer should not attempt to duplicate this appearance, as it may be interpreted as a lack of respect for the person whose home is being entered. Neither should the interviewer be so well dressed that the respondent will feel uncomfortable by comparison. Interviewers should maintain their own identities without overemphasizing differences between themselves and interviewees.

The mood of the intensive interviewer goes a long way toward encouraging rapport with the respondent. The interviewer must appear enthusiastic about the interview and about the prospect of being allowed to converse with the subject. Patience is an important attribute, as is the confidence afforded by advance preparation. Interviewees may expect interviewers to know certain facts, and failure to "do one's homework" may result in a loss of interviewer credibility.

SETTING

In our hypothetical example we initially decided to hold the interviews in people's homes. But there was no assurance that this would be the best setting. In fact, there was every likelihood that the respondents would have been distracted by events around them (including telephone calls or the needs of family members) or by the very presence of onlookers in the form of other residents of the home. The intensive interviewer should be prepared to change the setting of the interviews, as the researchers in the stripteaser study did. If our suburbanites are distracted by the home environment, we should be prepared to request that interviews be held elsewhere, such as an anteroom in the Town Hall or library.

In a sense the interviewer is part of the setting of an intensive interview. It is a fact that respondents generally relate better to interviewers of the same sex. Thus it may be necessary to change the "setting" by changing interviewers if this seems to be a problem in a given study.

Comparative Strengths and Limitations

The advantages and disadvantages of intensive interviewing should be taken into consideration when deciding whether or not it is the most appropriate method for a particular study. Many of the method's greatest strengths are also the sources of its most significant limitations. Much of what is said in this section to point up these strengths and limitations is based on comparisons with other approaches, particularly survey research and observational methods. We will first review the major strengths of the method.

STRENGTHS

There is a smaller chance that the interviewer and the interviewee will misunderstand one another in an intensive interview than in the structured interaction used in survey research. The intensive interviewer has the opportunity to cast questions in terms that are clear to a specific respondent and to ask the same question in a variety of different ways if there is any doubt as to the respondent's comprehension. If a person's responses seem to be inconsistent, the interviewer can confront him or her with the apparent inconsistency. In so doing, it is often possible to resolve the contradiction.

Intensive interviewing has the potential for providing more accurate answers on certain sensitive issues than survey research. There is a greater opportunity to develop rapport. It is also possible to approach a sensitive issue from a variety of directions. If the interviewer believes that the respondent is shading the truth, it is possible to ask another question to test the previous answer. Interviewees who claim to have a high degree of racial tolerance may be asked how they would feel about their children getting married to a person of a different race, or how they feel about a busing policy that would bring about a substantial shift in the racial composition of the local schools.

In intensive interviewing, questions and response categories can be tailored to fit the respondent's way of looking at things. Compared to survey research, there is less danger of imposing a set of irrelevant categories on the interviewee or of casting the question in a form that does not correspond to the respondent's view of how the world works. Typically, the intensive interviewer is also the principal investigator; in many survey research studies the researcher in charge of the project does not do any of the actual interviewing. Thus the intensive interviewer is directly confronted with the difficulty respondents are having in understanding the questions and the tendency of respondents to interpret the questions in ways other than those originally intended; in contrast, the survey researcher may be quite insulated from such problems.

A more complete picture of the individual respondent is provided by in-depth interviewing than is the case with survey research. In this respect the method is similar to participant observation. In survey research we get a flat view of the respondent, reduced to an atomized set of background characteristics and specific attitudes. In intensive interviewing there is an attempt to round out the image of the respondent by exploring underlying motives and personal experiences that can be linked to specific attitudes and beliefs.

As the researcher conducts interviews, there is a continual assimilation and evaluation of information. When appropriate, such information can be used to shift the line of questioning in a more fruitful direction. Depending on where the interview is held, observation of the environment may provide an important perspective on what the interviewee is saying. If a respondent describes himself as being extremely thrifty, but the interviewer notices lavish furnishings in the home, the credibility of the respondent's remarks may be called into question. The interviewer might interject a comment to challenge the interviewee such as:

> You're very fortunate to have such a beautifully furnished home while being able to save a lot of money at the same time [or while operating on a limited budget].

The respondent might reply that the furnishings were inherited, that he dislikes them, and that he intends to change homes in the near future; or he might say:

> What I meant before was that I think it's important to save systematically, but I don't believe in living like a monk.

In survey research, interviewing efficiency is often a major consideration and cost per interview is often an important measure of an interviewer's performance. In some studies interviewers are paid a fixed amount of money per interview, an unfortunate practice that implicitly encourages them to conduct as many interviews as possible in order to maximize their earnings. In such cases, when interviewers find a person who meets their sampling criteria, they will often attempt to complete even a very long interview on the spot. If the respondent is about to go shopping, the researcher may try to administer the interview in half the usual time, with obvious implications for the quality of the data that are obtained. In contrast, the intensive interviewer must take the time to develop the best possible rapport with respondents and to be sensitive to their needs. If the hour chosen for a contact proves to be inconvenient, another meeting is arranged. Since most intensive interviews are planned by appointment, this rarely occurs. If the interview becomes drawn out and the interviewee shows signs of fatigue, the meeting is continued at a later time.

Some types of respondents can be studied through intensive interviews while other data gathering methods would probably fail. United States senators, prominent judges, and presidents of major corporations may be too geographically dispersed to facilitate carrying out observational studies. They may perceive themselves as too busy and/or important to participate in a standardized survey research interview with a hired-hand interviewer. The ability of the intensive interviewer to accommodate their schedules and to converse knowledgeably about the study and its ramifications usually are highly persuasive aids in obtaining cooperation. The elite are not the only population segment that is particularly appropriate for intensive interviewing. This methodology should be strongly considered for any category of respondent that is highly likely to be unwilling or unable to participate in other forms of research investigation: convicted criminals, the elderly, welfare "cheaters," victims of rape, and invalids, to name a few.

Generally, a study using intensive interviewing can be carried out more rapidly than one using observation but less quickly than one using survey research. One reason that survey projects tend to take less time is that the interviews are usually shorter. Another is that the interviewing is generally divided among several investigators. Observational work may take from several months to several years, more time than is needed for most intensive interviewing studies. Perhaps the greatest advantage of intensive interviewing, compared to participant observation, is the speed with which in-depth data may be collected. Note that since some survey research projects call for data collection over a period of years, and since some observational studies are based on data collected in one afternoon, any generalization about the time involved in using the alternative approaches must be interpreted with caution.

A study using intensive interviewing will generally cost less than one using survey research. If we do not figure in a salary for the investigators, the cost of intensive interviewing can be quite modest. If the researcher is salaried, then the cost per intensive interview is greater. However, the total expenditure may still be less because the typical intensive interview study is based on fewer than fifty respondents, whereas the typical survey is based on several hundred.

LIMITATIONS

We turn now to a review of the most significant limitations of the intensive interviewing method. Although it is possible to minimize some of these problems, many are the unavoidable consequences of characteristics that represent the greatest strengths of the method.

First, it is very difficult to generalize about entire populations from studies based on intensive interviewing. This is not to say that generalizations cannot be made; the problem is that we usually have no way to assess the accuracy of these generalizations.

One source of difficulty is the sampling procedure. Intensive interviewing studies are generally based on small, nonprobability samples. Typically, no effort is made to obtain a random sample of some clearly definable population. Use of a sample of as many as fifty respondents is rare. Even if probability selection procedures are used, with such small samples the error involved in making any statistical generalizations from the sample to the relevant population would be too large to be useful. It would not help us much to know that 50 percent plus or minus 30 percent (that is, between 20 percent and 80 percent) of those in the population of interest oppose gun control legislation. One reason for the small sample is that the interviewing is usually done by one or two people on a limited budget. Another is that the data are not easily adapted to quantitative statistical analysis. Thus even if the number of respondents approaches the several hundred that are common in survey research studies, it becomes very difficult to analyze the data qualitatively.

Another threat to generalizability is the lack of standardization in the interviewing procedure. The way in which a question is asked differs from one interview to the next. The goal is to ask each respondent the question in such a way as to get the most complete and accurate information possible on the issues of interest, but we have no way of knowing that the alternative ways in which the question was asked are really comparable in meaning.

The amount of emphasis placed on a question is not standardized from one interview to the next. Typically, there will be a whole series of questions asked of a specific respondent and not asked of any other. Even for questions asked of all or most respondents, the length of the responses will vary considerably. This inconsistency is due partly to differences among subjects with respect to how much they would volunteer in response to the same question asked in exactly the same way. The same general question may elicit eight-word answers from some respondents and 800-word replies from others.

The lack of standardization in the data collection process makes it difficult to replicate an intensive interview study. Suppose we try to repeat such a study and come up with different conclusions. It will be difficult to pinpoint the reason for the discrepancy. Problems in replicating the sampling and interviewing procedures of the original study mean that the reliability of the method is low, relative to the reliability of survey research. There is generally no way to make statistical estimates of the reliability of the results of an intensive interview study.

Intensive interviewing is highly vulnerable to interviewer bias. Bias may occur in any form of data gathering based on interviewing, but it poses a much greater threat to the validity of in-depth interview data than to the questionnaire data used in survey research. Although interviewers are always instructed to avoid communicating their own views on the issues, they always give off some cues that can be used by the respondent as a basis for at least guessing where they stand on a variety of questions being considered. This is particularly true in intensive interviewing, which is informal and conversational. Even if interviewers are successful in avoiding verbal cues, there are many ways of communicating nonverbally of which they may not be fully aware and over which they do not have full control. In a long encounter it is likely that interviewers will unintentionally communicate a great deal about themselves, their values, and their attitudes. This has an impact on the opinions expressed by interviewees. The wish to give socially desirable answers and/or to please the interviewers is a problem in any kind of interviewing, but especially in intensive interviewing.

The flexibility the researcher has in casting questions and probing issues is another potential source of bias. In the simplest case the interviewer can ask leading or loaded questions, which make it more likely that the respondent will choose one answer over others. Taped interviews can be checked for evidence of this kind of responding, but since usually only the researcher (who is also the interviewer) reviews these tapes, it is not very likely that any bias present will be detected. By the time the results are prepared for publication, any such bias will be all but impossible to determine. And even if some bias is discovered from listening to the tape, the nonverbal cues, which can have a substantial impact on the interviewee's responses, will go undetected.

The quality of the data collected using the intensive interviewing approach depends very heavily on the skills of the interviewer. In this sense it is similar to participant observation research, which relies to a great extent on the acumen of the observer. In survey work it is also important to have competent interviewers, but the skills required are much narrower and are easier to teach. One reason that intensive interviewing studies are typically based on small samples is the difficulty of finding good intensive interviewers or of adequately training new ones.

One of the supposed advantages of in-depth interviews is that they provide more accurate responses on sensitive issues than do survey questionnaires, but we cannot always rely on this to happen. In fact, with some respondents the more formal survey encounter (or the anonymous mail questionnaire) may yield the most honest responses. Unfortunately, there are no clear guidelines available to tell us which substantive issues, or which conditions, make intensive interviewing most effective.

Finally, there is a lack of standardization in the data analysis procedures. In contrast to the typical research study, it is quite possible for two data analysts to come up with very different interpretations of a single body of data generated from intensive interviews. Because of the lack of any systematic procedures for analyzing such data, it would be very difficult to decide which interpretation was more valid; however, the situation does not arise very often because usually the interviewer and the data analyst are the same person. This dependence on the judgments of one investigator (or perhaps two) in data interpretation leaves the door wide open for the researcher's theoretical perspective and personal ideology to influence substantially the reported findings of the study.

Current Developments in the Technique

Intensive interviewing is becoming increasingly well established as a viable methodological alternative in research with objectives centered around answers to questions of why, what, and how. In virtually all social science research, intensive interviewing can help us explore what to ask and how to ask it, even if such information will be used only to formulate structured questionnaires for surveys. Its value remains limited, at best, in dealing with matters of who, where, when, and how many.

Intensive interviewing has typically involved face-to-face encounters and the associated expense of this form of data gathering. Experimentation has suggested, however, that abbreviated, special-purpose intensive interviews may be conducted successfully by telephone. The quality of these telephone contacts is highly dependent on the complexity of the research objectives; their scope must be somewhat limited for relatively brief telephone intensive interviews to work well. One advantage of the telephone intensive interview, in addition to financial savings, is that some people who perceive themselves as too busy to grant a personal audience will agree to a telephone contact lasting the same amount of time. Telephone intensive interviews generally last no longer than twenty minutes to half an hour.

Summary

Intensive interviews differ from other interviews in that they are less structured. They allow the interviewer flexibility in questioning the respondent—flexibility that enables the interviewer to ask for or give immediate clarification in cases of misunderstandings, to probe for additional detail on interesting comments volunteered by the interviewee, to defer or rephrase sensitive questions, and to achieve many other benefits.

Effectiveness is predicated on the interviewer's ability to know what to ask, when and how to ask it, and how to conduct a continuing and cumulative analysis of the entire process. One advantage of the sequential nature of intensive interviews is that the investigator is usually equipped to conduct analysis while asking questions; this ability enables the researcher to challenge and adjust or refute hypotheses as the study progresses and more interviews are conducted.

Intensive interviewing emphasizes the incipient relationship between interviewer and interviewee. The quality of this relationship is what determines how productive the interview will be. If both parties obtain sufficient rewards from the relationship as time passes, the interview will proceed; otherwise, it will terminate. Thus the intensive interview should be more of an information exchange than a one-way flow of data and of rewards or benefits.

In a sense the interviewer is the data gathering tool in an intensive interview study (as is the field worker in an observational study), in contrast to the questionnaire, which is the data gathering tool in a structured interview study. Intensive interviewers usually employ no questionnaires, although they may use topic guides, which may include a few structured questions to be asked of every respondent (a semistructured interview). Intensive interviewing is sometimes employed in exploratory studies, in which the researcher wants to obtain a "feel" for what to ask and how to ask it in a large survey research study. In other studies it may be the only method of data collection.

Like all research techniques, intensive interviewing has its limitations. The data generated do not lend themselves to quantitative analysis and do not permit statistical inferences to be made about the population from which the respondents were drawn. The method is highly dependent on the capabilities of the interviewer. The lack of standardization in sampling, interviewing, and data analysis makes it difficult to determine how generalizable the results are. This lack of standardization also increases the chance that the researcher's theoretical perspective and personal ideology will have a substantial impact on the outcome of the study.

Intensive interviewing is a technique that is highly useful in obtaining information in a relatively short period of time from potentially elusive or inaccessible respondents. The method permits direct solicitation and collection of information from subjects, rather than only the development of inferences based on observation. Those studied may be located in a relatively confined area or spread throughout the world. A currently experimental direction involves the use of the telephone for relatively brief, special-purpose intensive interviews.

Key Terms

in-depth interview	nonstandardized interview	semistructured interview
incipient relationship	opening persons	standardized interview
intensive interview	pace	structured interview
nonschedule standardized interview	preemptive techniques reciprocity	topic outline unstructured interview

Exercises

1. Organize the class into pairs, and have one member of each pair interview the other intensively about the most outlandish thing the interviewee has ever done. When the interview is completed, the interviewer should interpret the findings for the respondent, and the respondent should comment on these interpretations. Banaka (1971, in Suggested Readings) will help you in determining how to conduct and interpret the interview.

2. Using the same pairs of students as in exercise 1, have the interviewer and interviewee switch roles, with the *new* interviewer asking the other's opinion of people who do outlandish things such as those described in the first interview.

3. Discuss the differences that might arise between the intensive interviews you have just conducted and similar contacts among factory workers you have not previously known, made during their lunch breaks. What problems might arise in the factory-worker interviews that were not present during your classroom interviews? In what ways might the factory interviews be easier?

4. Discuss the ethical considerations and potential methodological pitfalls of conducting intensive interviews among dying patients in a hospital. Reference to *On Death and Dying*, by Kubler-Ross (1969), will be helpful. Consider the possibility that the hospital staff may become jealous of relationships between interviewers and patients. Think about the likelihood that respondents will be so grateful at receiving attention that they will simply try to find the "right" answers to please the interviewer.

5. In *On Death and Dying* Kubler-Ross (1969:22) says:

> We had no other preconceived ideas (other than who would be the interviewer and who would observe) nor did we read any papers or publications on this topic so that we might have an open mind and record only what we ourselves were able to notice, both in the patient and in ourselves. We also purposely did not study the patient's chart since this too might dilute or alter our own observations. We did not want to have any preconceived notion as to how the patients might react. We were quite prepared, however, to study all available data after we had recorded our own impressions. This, we thought, would enhance our perceptiveness and, we hoped, desensitize the rather frightened students through an increasing number of confrontations with terminally ill patients of different ages and backgrounds.

Discuss this viewpoint on preparation in light of the fact that most intensive interviewers obtain as much information as possible before starting the interviews so as not to be unduly shocked by a respondent's comments and so as to be able to interpret each statement *immediately* within the context of known data on the interviewee's frame of reference, background, and so on. The Stebbins article (1972, in Suggested

Readings) may help you in deliberating about the proper balance of subjectivity and objectivity in conducting intensive interviews.

6.   The next time you hold a substantive conversation with someone, take note of the various conversational gambits used by both parties. Try to determine what you and the other person were trying to achieve by each gambit. After completing the conversation, construct a highly structured questionnaire designed to elicit the same information that you discovered through the conversation. What problems did you have in devising such a questionnaire, and what are the implications of these problems for intensive interviewing?

7.   Devise a list of topics you might consider including in an intensive interview of "two-career" families, with the objective of determining what compromises the members of such families are forced to make. Conduct an intensive interview with one such family. What additional topics surfaced during the interview? Compare your findings with the results obtained by Holmstrom (1972, in Suggested Readings) and discuss the differences. To what extent might such differences be a function of interviewing technique or the idiosyncrasies of the one household in which you interviewed?

Suggested Readings

READINGS ABOUT THE METHOD

Banaka, William H.
1971   *Training in Depth Interviewing.* New York: Harper & Row.
This book contains detailed procedures for training oneself or others to become depth (or intensive) interviewers. There is an extensive listing and discussion of the pitfalls and procedural details involved in the technique. The author stresses the interactive process between interviewer and interviewee, including means of manipulating the conversation to the interviewer's best advantage. A lengthy section on methods of evaluating intensive interviews emphasizes the competency of the interviewer.

Gorden, Raymond L.
1975   *Interviewing: Strategy, Techniques, and Tactics.* Rev. ed. Homewood, Ill.: Dorsey Press.
A good, general work on interviewing, this volume is particularly strong on ethical issues and on how to deal with uncooperative respondents.

Richardson, Stephen A., et al.
1965   *Interviewing, Its Forms and Functions.* New York: Basic Books.
The interview as a data gathering device is compared with other methods of data collection. The authors discuss the interviewer's role, characteristics of interviewers, and relationships between interviewer and interviewee. Although valuable in providing an excellent philosophical overview, the volume is not strongly oriented toward applications.

Sanders, William B.
1976   *The Sociologist as Detective.* New York: Praeger.
Drawing parallels between detectives and sociologists in their quest for various forms of "evidence," the author's emphasis is on choosing the most appropriate investigation method or methods for the objective at hand. One chapter utilizes a study of convicted "white-collar" criminals to illustrate how intensive interviewing may be used to formulate and reformulate hypotheses.

Stebbins, Robert A.
1972   "The Unstructured Research Interview as Incipient Interpersonal Relationship." *Sociology and Social Research* 56 (January):164–179.
Stebbins discusses in depth the respondent-researcher relationship in an intensive interview. His focus is on the incipient (or emerging) connection between the two parties. Drawing from various theoretical perspectives in sociology and social psychology, the author suggests many ways in which the nature of the incipient relationship influences the acquisition of valid data. This is a strictly theoretical exposition but an important one for the practitioner of intensive interviewing.

READINGS ILLUSTRATING THE METHOD

Fallaci, Oriana
1976 *Interview with History.* New York: Liveright.

As a correspondent for the newspaper *L'Europeo,* the author intensively interviewed fourteen political figures in contemporary history, including Henry Kissinger, Nguyen Van Thieu, Golda Meir, Yasir Arafat, and Indira Gandhi. She dwells extensively on the problem involved in obtaining cooperation and in retaining the attention of respondents during the interview.

Goodman, Ellen
1979 *Turning Points.* Garden City, N.Y.: Doubleday.

Through conversations with more than 150 women and men over a four-year period, the author analyzes the impact of change on members of contemporary society. She presents numerous case studies of people in various "stages" of life. This is a good example of the use of intensive interviewing and the case study method in conducting research on "life processes." Methodological issues with which the author deals include respondents' rights to privacy.

Holmstrom, Lynda Lytle
1972 *The Two-Career Family.* Cambridge, Mass.: Schenkman.

The author uses intensive interviews to study the two-career family. Investigating a number of factors, including life cycle of the family, division of labor, and compromises, she develops conclusions about the nature of such families—their problems and their viability. An interesting feature of the book is an extensive section on methodological considerations, notably the advantages of intensive interviewing versus other data gathering techniques.

Pfuhl, Edwin H., Jr.
1978 "The Unwed Father—A 'Non-Deviant' Rule-Breaker." *The Sociological Quarterly* 19 (Winter 1978): 113–128.

Intensive interviews with 140 self-proclaimed unmarried fathers are the basis for an analysis of this phenomenon and its social implications. The author discusses the possible "atypicality" of the volunteer sample and blends questionnaire investigation with less-structured interviewing techniques.

Kubler-Ross, Elisabeth
1969 *On Death and Dying.* New York: Macmillan.

This study of dying patients in a hospital used intensive interviewing as the sole data gathering technique. On the basis of these interviews, Kubler-Ross developed a theory that people who are terminally ill go through a process of dying that has five identifiable stages. She found nonverbal communication between the interviewer and interviewee to be very important. The incipient relationship and its importance in eliciting information are well illustrated in this study.

Strub, Peter J., and T. B. Priest
1976 "Two Patterns of Establishing Trust: The Marijuana User." *Sociological Focus* 9:399–411.

The matter of trust is investigated through intensive interviews with marijuana users. Of particular interest is a discussion about "breaking down the walls of suspicion that surround the 'stranger.'" Among the forty-four respondents, only one refused to have the conversation taped. The encounters began as structured interviews but evolved into "interview-conversations."

Westoff, Leslie Aldridge
1978 *The Second Time Around: Remarriage in America.* New York: Penguin.

Conducting a number of intensive interviews because "in something as complex as remarriage, there are no simple yes-and-no answers," the author examines the social processes and complications of people who have remarried. Among other findings was the fact that these people are particularly anxious to discuss their remarriages and to obtain comparisons of their own and others' situations.

References

Banaka, William H.
1971 *Training in Depth Interviewing.* New York: Harper & Row.

Becker, Howard S.
1955 "Marihuana Use and Social Control." *Social Problems* 3 (July):35–44.

Becker, Howard S., and Blanche Geer
1957 "Participant Observation and Interviewing: A Comparison." *Human Organization* 16 (Fall):28–32.

Burgess, Ann Wolbert, and Lynda Lytle Holmstrom
1974 *Rape: Victims of Crisis.* Bowie, Md.: Brady.

Denzin, Norman K.
1970 *The Research Act.* Chicago: Aldine.

Goffman, Erving
1963 *Behavior in Public Places.* New York: Free Press.

Gray, Paul S.
1980 "Exchange and Access in Field Work." *Urban Life* (October):309–331.

Holmstrom, Lynda Lytle
1972 *The Two-Career Family.* Cambridge, Mass.: Schenkman.

Kubler-Ross, Elisabeth
1969 *On Death and Dying.* New York: Macmillan.

Lane, Robert
1967 *Political Ideology: Why the Common Man Believes What He Does.* New York: Free Press.

Lindesmith, Alfred R.
1947 *Opiate Addiction.* Bloomington, Ind.: Principia Press.

Lipset, S. M., Martin A. Trow, and James C. Coleman
1956 *Union Democracy.* Glencoe, Ill.: Free Press.

Skipper, James K., Jr., and Charles H. McCaghy
1972 "Respondents' Intrusion upon the Situation: The Problem of Interviewing Subjects with Special Qualities." *The Sociological Quarterly* 13 (Spring):237–243.

Trow, Martin
1957 "Comment on 'Participant Observation and Interviewing: A Comparison.'" *Human Organization* 16 (Fall):33–35.

Zuckerman, Harriet
1972 "Interviewing an Ultra-Elite." *Public Opinion Quarterly* 36 (Summer): 159–175.

8 / Observational Field Research

CHAPTER OUTLINE

INTRODUCTION
Applications
Promise and Problems
DOING FIELD WORK
Beginning the Research: A Question
  and a Research Site
Gaining Access
Taking a Role

Some Practical Suggestions
Data Collection and Notetaking
  Descriptions
  Explanations
Formulating an Analysis
  Conceptual Categories
  Data Coding
  From Analysis to Theory

LIMITATIONS OF
  OBSERVATIONAL FIELD
  RESEARCH
SUMMARY
KEY TERMS
EXERCISES
SUGGESTED READINGS
REFERENCES

Introduction

The famous researcher Robert Park is quoted as having issued the following methodological directive to his students:

> You have been told to go grubbing in the library, thereby accumulating a mass of notes and a liberal coating of grime. You have been told to choose problems wherever you can find musty stacks of routine records based on trivial schedules prepared by tired bureaucrats and filled out by reluctant applicants for aid or fussy do-gooders or indifferent clerks. This is called "getting your hands dirty in real research." Those who counsel you are wise and honorable; the reasons they offer are of great value. But one more thing is needful; first-hand observation. Go and sit in the lounges of the luxury hotels and on the doorsteps of the flophouses; sit on the Gold Coast settees and on the slum shakedowns; sit in Orchestra Hall and in the Star and Garter Burlesk. In short, gentlemen, go get the seats of your pants dirty in real research. (McKinney, 1966:71)

Park's statement implicitly contains the central point of this chapter on PARTICIPANT OBSERVATION: one important way to gain an understanding of human action and social process is for researchers to enter, as far as possible, the worlds of those whose behaviors they are trying to fathom. Researchers use participant observation in order to better see the world as their subjects see it, in order to capture those whom they study "in their own terms" and thereby learn how they achieve a coherent, ordered existence. Participant observation is, therefore, based on the presumption that by studying people in the "natural, ongoing environments where they live and work" (Schatzman and Strauss, 1973:9), social scientists will maximize their ability to grasp the motives, values, beliefs, concerns, troubles, and interests that underlie the actions of their subjects.

APPLICATIONS

Observational research has long been used in anthropology[1]; thus there is justification if the term conjures up the image of a social scientist living with some preliterate tribe, perhaps for several years. The investigator who becomes a member of a relatively unfamiliar American subculture is, in a real sense, doing anthropology. There are many studies in which researchers have become part of cultures otherwise unfamiliar to them. For his now-classic work William F. Whyte (1943) spent more than two years living in Boston's North End. Herbert Gans (1969) moved into Levittown, a new suburban community, in order to understand the quality of life in such a context. Eliot Liebow (1967), in his book *Tally's Corner,* describes his observations of the Negro streetcorner men with whom he spent more than a year.

The community studies mentioned constitute only one area in which observational field work has been done.[2] The range of contexts includes schools (Jackson, 1968), hospitals (Sudnow, 1967), industrial organizations (Gouldner, 1954), and asylums (Goffman, 1961). Nor have marginal institutions such as the taxi-dance hall (Cressey, 1932) or the pornographic bookstore (Karp, 1973) escaped qualitative researchers' attention. Deviant groups or subcultures have made up another major area of inquiry for observational work: prostitutes (Greenwald, 1958), alcoholics (Lofland and Lejeune, 1970), professional thieves (Sutherland, 1949), hippies (Davis, 1970), draft resistors (Thorne, 1971), drug users (Pope, 1971), homosexuals (Sagarin, 1969), have all come under investigation. Researchers have also gathered observational data from a number of diverse settings in order to better understand processes of social interaction. Edward Hall (1969) and Robert Sommer (1969) have studied spatial patternings among human beings in a number of different contexts. Hall, particularly, has put his observational powers to use in conducting cross-cultural studies.

PROMISE AND PROBLEMS

Field work, concentrating as it does on subjective experience, is inherently person-oriented. Typically, relatively small groups or well-defined social settings are studied through observation, so that the researcher can establish and maintain firsthand contact with subjects and their actions. Field workers assume that

---

[1]For a more complete description of the uses of anthropological field research, see Chapter 13.

[2]The terms *field research* and *field work* are sometimes used in a comprehensive, generic fashion to include any methodology requiring researchers to collect data from individuals in nonlaboratory settings. Given this definition, survey research and field experimentation could, for example, be labeled field research techniques. To avoid confusion, the authors wish to indicate that the terms *field research* and *field work* are being used in a more limited way here. They will use these terms interchangeably with observational research throughout this chapter.

the nature of social, political, and psychological reality is enormously problematic. For them the way people assign meaning to the objects, events, or situations that they confront daily must be the major concern of scientific investigation. Usually, those who engage in participant observation do not produce studies whose data are presented in quantitative form. Rather, the data consist of qualitative descriptions of events and statements from the individuals involved. These descriptions are called *ethnographies*.

It is difficult not to sympathize with the goal of providing rich, ETHNOGRAPHIC analyses of one or another culture. Unfortunately, however, advocates of participant observation have been much more diligent in making claims for the benefits of their methodology than they have in explaining just how field research gets done. Although it is certainly useful to read accounts of those who have done observational studies, we are nevertheless left with an uncomfortable feeling. If we want to do this type of research ourselves, we are going to have to resolve a number of questions: How exactly ought one to proceed? What must be done to gain access to those being studied? What exactly should be observed? How should one behave in the field? Just how much participation is allowed? Which data are important and which unimportant? What kind of identity should a researcher adopt in the field and how long must be spent there?

The standard response to such questions is that they cannot be answered definitively. Observation is indeed the primary and indispensable tactic distinguishing the technique, but field researchers must proceed by way of a kind of methodological eclecticism, choosing the research strategy that best suits their purpose and circumstances at any given point in the study. Hence unobtrusive measurement, life histories, documentary and historical analyses, statistical enumeration, in-depth interviews, imaginative role taking, and personal introspection are all important complements of direct observation in the field worker's repertoire. We are told that any method of inquiry that can enrich researchers' insight into the social processes they are observing, and in which they may be participating, is ipso facto appropriate.

Perhaps the most comprehensive statement we hear is that observational field work aims at a thorough and systematic collection, classification, and reporting of events as well as the specification of the relations between those events. Thus, while field workers set out to narrate and describe a "slice of social life," they must make their description more than a journalistic account of these events. By employing (or fashioning) concepts and propositions to order collected data, researchers try to illuminate the underlying structure of social and political organization. If successful, they do a good deal more than simply use abstract categories to describe the events observed; they add a new dimension to our understanding of a social setting or set of events. They break through the facade of faulty formulas that earlier observers have constructed to account for social labels, stereotypes, cultural taboos, fear, ignorance, indifference, or avoidance. And in so doing, observational researchers give us a fresh perspective on our own social positions. All these related aims of observational field research provide us the criteria according to which such research ought to be evaluated.

Impressionistic statements like those above are helpful. They give one a feeling for the nature of field work. But it is one thing to be told that the aim of participant observation is discovery of substantive theory and quite another to know when this has been adequately accomplished. The rhetoric demanding that field researchers "take the role" of those whom they are studying and thereby "see the world from their standpoint" is sensible in the abstract, but it certainly fails as a clear guideline for researchers in the field. It is, further, undoubtedly disconcerting for the novice field researcher to be given advice such as: "Don't worry about clearly delineating your problem too early. The focus of your research should emerge as you become involved in the context of your observation. Try to be sensitive to the underlying dimensions of the behaviors you are studying. Be flexible and responsive to changes in the setting investigated. Try to be complete in noting your observations and descriptions of persons, places, and events."

Our discussion to this point makes it quite apparent that one of the most striking aspects of observational field research is the absence of standardized operating procedures.[3] Since all cultures have their own distinctive characteristics, different demands are placed on researchers in observing them. A set of rules for doing good field research would be rather like a sex manual: though we are surely better off with a discussion of techniques that have worked for other people than with nothing at all, we can never carry out the actual practice with manual in hand. Both sex and field research are instances of intimate and sensitive human interaction, and neither can be reduced to a simple set of techniques. The object sought by the field worker, a deep understanding of the meaning of social action, cannot be realized by mechanically and unfeelingly using a simple set of instructions.

Although the field research process cannot be rationalized or mechanized, there are benchmarks along the path that observational field work "typically" follows. As we proceed through this chapter, we will examine these and also offer some practical suggestions based on the accumulated successes and failures of many field research projects.

Doing Field Work

Beginning with some general notions and perhaps some tentative hypotheses, field researchers observe a set of behaviors in detail. They then begin to formulate a series of questions, guesses, and hunches about the meaning of those observations. As more data accumulate, some hunches are supported, others eliminated. Hopefully, some general analytical structure begins to suggest itself. Hunches become more formal hypotheses; inquiry begins to center around these hypotheses; and tentative conclusions begin to solidify. Truly skilled field workers begin to refine their propositions through a vigorous search for NEGATIVE CASES— phenomena that do not seem to fit into their developing structure of explanation. In other words, theoretical propositions are not only generated in the field but, insofar as possible, *tested* in the field as well.

In sum, field workers do not begin with all their propositions formulated. They follow a long, arduous path that begins with a sense of something problematic to be investigated, and they try gradually and inductively to formulate a more sharply defined theoretical model for explaining the events at hand. Within this general process there are a number of stages through which the research passes.

---

[3]The general description of the research process offered here does not extend to those cases in which researchers do quite *structured* observation. In some instances researchers decide in an a priori fashion the data necessary to test their ideas and then construct standard coding categories for their collection. See Chapter 11 for a discussion of structured observation.

BEGINNING THE RESEARCH:
A QUESTION AND A RESEARCH SITE

Field research begins with these rudimentary elements: a general area of inquiry, a problem that calls for explanation, and a potential site where a phenomenon of interest may be observed. When we speak of an area of interest, we mean that in the broadest sense. A researcher might initially be curious about the culture of college students, the way that power is exercised in a community, or the possible alienation of workers in large organizations. Whatever area of interest is chosen, researchers do well to begin by asking themselves what they know and don't know about the area. If you have a general interest in social movements, ask yourself where it comes from. Have you had firsthand experience in such movements? Or have they been a prominent part of the recent social scenery? Have you read books or heard lectures or discussions that deal either directly or peripherally with social movements? What unanswered questions have been raised for you through these intellectual experiences? Is yours a general interest in social movements, or are you intrigued by a specific group?

These preliminary ruminations are important for three reasons. First, they should help you to pinpoint a manageable area for further inquiry. Second, they may help you to specify what you know already about the area of inquiry and therefore suggest the issues needing further investigation to round out your personal knowledge of the subject. Finally, some serious reflection on what motivates the choice of one sociological topic instead of another will be an invaluable base from which you may continually assess and reassess potential sources of bias as you collect and analyze data. This introspective questioning will also help in making explicit to an audience your personal sentiments—and so better allow them to assess for themselves the validity of the findings.

Most methodologists would argue that the choice of a research site should follow this general problem-formation process. But although some formulation must precede the choice of a setting, the very logic of naturalistic inquiry demands that these preliminary conceptualizations not become so elaborate and compelling that they become self-fulfilling prophecies. There is the danger of leaping from the choice of a generic problem area to the assumption that a particular research setting is indeed a species of that genus. Suppose that a researcher is interested in studying expressions of Black Power in the United States. The researcher should not set out with the absolutely rigid idea that Black Power is *in fact* a social movement with all the characteristics that have come to be associated with such phenomena. This is a matter to be investigated.

It is a sound principle of qualitative research (though perhaps not a widely practiced one) that one's initial interest should be with situations and settings more than with concepts and theories. If we start with the idea that Black Power is a social movement, it is likely that we will uncover a good deal of evidence that it is one. If we stick to the more open-ended guiding question "How can Black Power best be understood sociologically?" the self-fulfilling prophecy risk is reduced. Put simply, researchers must consciously avoid switching from inquiry to rhetorical demonstration.

The choice of a context for investigation is rarely made without some kind of rationale; somehow we expect the context chosen to inform us about some feature of social life. We must have some set of questions, explicit or not, that leads us to a particular setting for observation. Even researchers who claim to be merely curious about behavior in one place or another must have some prior idea about that place. They know enough about it to be curious. Rather than pretending, therefore, that we have absolutely no a priori assumptions in such cases, we ought to make our assumptions explicit and put them to work. If we make our assumptions clear, we can submit them to testing. If we allow our assumptions to remain hidden to us, they are potential obstacles to a full understanding of the situation under investigation.

We begin to perceive a complex relationship between our initial questions about a phenomenon, the choice of a research setting to answer these questions, and the data collected in the setting. Later, collected data may cause us to ask some questions more insistently, reject other questions as unimportant, and create the need for answers to previously unformed questions. As a research strategy, then, field work ideally allows us to create a balance between theory and data. We must not develop such an investment in one set of questions or theoretical ideas that we become blind to events in a setting unrelated to these questions or ideas. We must be prepared to accept the possibility that our original questions or ideas about a setting are irrelevant to an understanding of it.

GAINING ACCESS

Once you choose a site for study, you must face the GATEKEEPERS, or guardians, of that social arena to obtain entry. Some settings provide virtually free access while others are nearly impenetrable. In some places the field workers may be freely admitted with the full understanding of their hosts that they are researchers. Access to other settings may require the researcher to conceal both motives and profession. In still other instances observation may be done so unobtrusively that the issue of motives never arises.

The degree of difficulty faced by researchers in gaining access to settings and to people in those settings seems to be a function of two dimensions. First, just how public is the setting? Are involvement and membership in the setting clearly restricted, or is the setting open to anyone who chooses to be there? Fully public settings—such as bars, museums, and department stores—pose few problems of access. In other cases membership and participation are clearly restricted or, at least, monitored, as in private country clubs or labor union organizations. We could, of course, envision any setting as lying somewhere along this public/private continuum.

Second, and perhaps of greater importance, do the participants in the setting perceive the need to keep part or all of their activity (perhaps even their very membership) secret? To choose an example at the extreme end of the continuum, it would be virtually impossible for an outsider to study, firsthand, certain features of organized crime.

Given these two dimensions, we could conceive of situations in which access to the setting itself would pose no problem but in which it would be difficult to talk to participants directly. This might be the case for the researcher trying to study behavior in pornographic movie theaters. As a general rule, we can expect to have the fewest problems of access to those settings that are most public and in which people do not engage in secretive activities.

Few settings of interest to the observational researcher pose such difficult problems as those experienced by Laud Humphreys (1970) in his study of impersonal homosexual encounters in public restrooms (see Chapter 4). In fact, there have been many community studies done without raising the suspicions of the "locals" so much that they felt the need to question the researcher's motives extensively. In many observational studies it is not even necessary for researchers to identify themselves. Studies of bars, waiting rooms, subways, and the like pose few dramatic problems. Sometimes investigators take advantage of a role they normally occupy or adopt a specialized role for the sake of research. Howard Becker (1963) put his musical talents to work in order to study the professional musician. Joan Emerson (1970), a nurse, studied problems of maintaining reality definitions in gynecological examinations. Others have taken on roles as tame as pedestrian in a large city (Wolff, 1973) or as racy as member of a nudist camp (Weinberg, 1968) when the exigencies of research have so dictated.

TAKING A ROLE

Raymond Gold (1969) has summarized the array of possibilities into four basic roles that the field worker can assume: COMPLETE OBSERVER, OBSERVER-AS-PARTICIPANT, PARTICIPANT-AS-OBSERVER, and COMPLETE PARTICIPANT. The specification of these four conceptual roles results from Gold's response to two basic questions: How involved should researchers become in the ongoing activity? To what extent, if any, should researchers conceal their intentions?

The complete participant and the complete observer both remain totally disguised. The complete observer remains relatively or completely detached from the situation studied, perhaps operating from behind a one-way mirror, at the listening end of a tape recorder, or from some concealed observational vantage point. The complete participant, as in Humphreys's case, becomes almost fully involved both behaviorally and emotionally. The two remaining roles differ according to the amount of emphasis placed on detached observation as opposed to active participation. The participant-as-observer tends to get quite involved affectively and to downplay or conceal the role as researcher. The observer-as-participant, on the other hand, is completely open about research objectives and approaches people on that basis. The choice of any one of these roles depends on both the situation and the nature of the information sought.

Roles tending toward the covert, participatory end of the spectrum are generally chosen by researchers when respondents or informants consider the sharing of their knowledge potentially dangerous to themselves, or when the information is highly ego involved (buried under a protective layer of rationalization such that direct methods of information seeking could well elicit faulty data). The choice of a covert role always raises serious ethical questions. Is the information sought in any sense public? If it is strictly private, then what justification can the researcher give for "stealing" it? Whose interests must researchers protect? Do they owe anything to the subjects who have made the research possible? In general, are there any limits to the sociologist's right of inquiry?

These are, if not unanswerable, at least moot questions that continue to spark lively professional debate. Humphreys justifed his work by articulating the high sense of ethical duty he maintained toward his subjects throughout the study. But others have argued that laudable personal morality is no substitute for codified professional ethics that can be employed to evaluate systematically and uniformly any research effort in the social sciences. After all, good intentions are no assurance that the researchers can anticipate all the effects of their research. If subjects are harmed unwittingly, the researchers can in no way reverse these negative effects.

The more that naturalistic observation involves interaction between researcher and subjects, the more the role taken by the researcher has to be tempered to the individual personalities involved and the situations in which they mutually find themselves. Hence the only general rule that can be laid down is that each researcher must find his or her own best role and then adapt it according to the problem at hand. Some researchers will find that the individuals studied allow them to raise questions aggressively and vigorously. But others may see the need, at least at the outset, to remain unobtrusive. Finally, it should be noted once more that a researcher's role does not necessarily remain static. At different points during the research project, and in the company of different respondents, different roles may be demanded.

One thing is clear. Whenever research involves interaction between subjects and investigators, there is no such thing as total, bland unobtrusiveness. In effect, the ideal of "naturalistic" inquiry can never be fully realized. Subjects always place researchers in some meaningful frame or context and relate to them accordingly. Researchers who maintain a mechanically objective detachment may create an uncomfortable ambiguity that forces subjects to interpret their actions as best they can, possibly resulting in behavior toward the researcher that is atypical of them and detrimental to the research goals.

Participant observers should try to understand and take into account the identity that their subjects attribute to them. How do a researcher's race, sex, ethnicity, physical appearance, known affiliations, and the like affect respondents' behavior? Does the researcher pose any kind of threat to the group or to any particular individuals or factions? Is he or she being manipulated to serve the overt or hidden interests of anyone? How do subjects interpret the researcher's intentions? What kinds of rewards might especially cooperative subjects be anticipating? Serious consideration of these and related questions can help social scientists to see their already collected data in proper perspective and may also suggest useful strategies for future data collection.

Virtually all organizations are characterized by an elaborate stratification system such that certain individuals or groups of individuals have more power and authority than others. Researchers whose roles are too closely identified with one or another of these strata (subgroups) are likely to lose access to other groups in the setting. Robert Kahn and Floyd Mann (1969) have focused their attention on the problem of access to organizations where there may be intraorganizational disputes or competing hierarchies of authority. Their solution is for investigators to seek "dual or multiple entry." They advocate that researchers seek the acceptance of representative leaders from each faction before beginning to solicit any information. Hopefully, field workers can thus sidestep the sometimes fatal problem of exclusive identification with one or another faction. Myron Glazer (1972) has documented how harmful partisan identification can be. While studying student life in Chile in a highly politicized and suspicious atmosphere, he sought the approval of student leaders. Unfortunately, members of the Christian Democrats noticed him being introduced to and having coffee with the Socialists. Consequently, they greeted him only with coldness and a lack of cooperation.

Generally speaking, groups pursued, persecuted, or stigmatized by public authorities or private moralizers are least likely to accept an inquisitive outsider seeking their friendship and admission to their worlds of private knowledge. Researchers who encounter difficulties in foreign countries holding a poor image of the "Yanqui" are likely to find similar sentiments among many groups in the United States. Many New Left and minority groups have become increasingly suspicious of, if not openly hostile to, sociological "snoopers." We can no longer assume that social research will be unquestioningly accepted as a legitimate enterprise.

SOME PRACTICAL SUGGESTIONS

What all these tales of failures and mistrust signify is that researchers' conduct during the first few days and weeks in the field may be an enormously significant factor in determining the eventual success or failure of their study. If observers are initially viewed with distrust and suspicion by those whom they seek to study and they do not handle the situation well, this may spell the end of their work before it really begins. The most appropriate way, therefore, to summarize the issues we have been considering is in the form of some tactical guidance. Needless to say, if any recommendation offered below seems inappropriate for the situation being studied, it should be discarded. But here in the abstract both common sense and previous research experience lead us to make the following suggestions:

1. Whenever possible, level with people about what you are up to. This does not mean that you must engage in a detailed exposition of any developing theoretical ideas you might have. It might be useful for you, though, to develop some standard explanation that you can give of your work if asked. Generally, we agree with the maxim that "honesty is the best policy." If you feel that it is impossible to tell the truth or, even further, that you must actually disguise your research identity, you should take a particularly careful look at the ethical implications of your research.

2. For the first few weeks in the field it is best to adopt, if possible, a fairly passive research role. After all, your first task as a field researcher is to get a feeling for the context you are studying. If you begin active research before you know the "rules" of a particular setting or culture, you run the risk of unwittingly engaging in behaviors that members of the setting may find objectionable.

3. As a corollary to our second suggestion, it is probably not a good idea to conduct any in-depth interviews with informants at the beginning of your work. You simply do not know as yet what to ask. This does not, of course, mean that you should discourage people from talking to you if they seem eager to do so.

4. At least initially, it is unwise to get into the position of offering advice. Many people have the conception of social scientists as therapeutic agents who can solve personal or organizational problems. You are primarily an investigator, not a therapist. If people insist on telling you their problems, listen sympathetically, for what you are being told may constitute valuable data.

5. Don't be afraid to answer questions if the situation calls for it, but don't assume the role of the expert on anything. Make it plain to people that they are the experts and that you are there to learn from them.

6. Don't let people force you into one or another particular role. Your subjects should not be able to decide for you what you should and should not be observing. If you do not make plain that your job as a researcher is to investigate all features of the situation, you may find yourself observing only a limited number of events.

7. Don't become closely aligned with one or another group in the setting you are studying, at least not until you are confident that your decision to do so will not keep you from making valuable contacts with other groups. If you become viewed as a partisan during internal political battles, it will likely become impossible for you to observe certain segments of the organization.

DATA COLLECTION AND NOTETAKING

At this point we shall make the happy assumption that you have successfully gained access to a setting. Of course, you have been collecting data all along—preliminary thoughts about the broad area of concern, considerations of the best context in which to do observation, and experiences in making initial contacts with people in the chosen setting all constitute relevant data. But once you have gained access to a particular setting, the collection and continual interpretation of data become your most preoccupying research tasks. Since the essential advantage of participant observation is that it allows you constantly to integrate the processes of data collection and analysis, you will need some guidelines concerning the nature of the data that ought to be collected and the content of the notes you should keep.

The secret of successful systematic, objective, and analytical participant observation lies in keeping accurate and detailed field notes. The first and perhaps only unequivocal rule about the content of field notes is that they must be *complete*. We say that because researchers do not go into the field with a well-formulated problem or an explicit set of hypotheses to be tested; they simply cannot know which data will ultimately be important and which not. For that reason researchers who fail to be complete in their notetaking may very well miss a good deal of information that later on turns out to be important. Let us assume that you have begun to observe behavior in some reasonably well defined organizational setting. Especially during the first few weeks of field work, the following kinds of descriptions and explanations of data ought to find their way into your field notes.

DESCRIPTIONS. First, you ought to strive to produce a complete *description of the setting* under investigation. The description of the setting offered in the field notes should provide enough information so that anyone reading it will have a clear picture of, and a "feeling" for, what that setting is like. In order to accomplish this, you must develop an eye for detail. Let us suppose you have begun to investigate a small religious group, such as the devotees of Krishna. You would likely begin the research by visiting their temple. In the description of that setting you will want to note a number of details — the colors of the walls, the general condition of the place, the kinds of objects to be found there. If you see that there is a bulletin board in the setting, do not simply note its existence. Make some assessment of the kinds of things that are important enough to find their way onto the bulletin board. If there are magazines lying around on a table, note the titles. After all, the things that people read are often good unobtrusive indicators of their interests, beliefs, or ideological outlook. In short, your description of the setting should include anything that informs a reader about the nature of the setting or the people who use it. One useful strategy in this regard is to draw maps of the setting itself. What might the spatial arrangement of furniture, for instance, say about the quality of interactions occurring in that setting?

Second, you should include complete *descriptions of individuals*. These descriptions should accurately portray to any reader what your subjects are like. Again, such a task necessitates developing an eye for detail. Note the distribution of males and females, individuals' racial groups, their ages, and so forth. Try to be aware, as well, of less visible but important indicators of status. How are people dressed? What proportion of people wear wedding rings? Do people have noticeable accents? Do they have tattoos or other body markings, such as scars? It might be useful in some settings to get an indication of people's physical health: Are their teeth in good condition? Is their skin condition good? Are they as a group disproportionately underweight or overweight?

The task of complete description may sound a bit overwhelming. It would, of course, be impossible to note down every possible piece of description about the setting and the people in it. You have to be selective to some degree. Full descriptions of people and places need not be accomplished during the first visit or two to the setting. You can keep adding to your description on subsequent visits. Beyond that, it should become clear after a time that some people are more "important" than others in the group studied. When you discover who the influential members of the group are, you may want to give a more detailed description of them. In this sense, descriptions will be cumulative.

Along with descriptions of people and places, notes should be filled with quotations. It is important to include both conversations you have and those you overhear. Once more, the task is not to record every exchange that occurs, but to convey to the reader a good sense of the general content and tone of the conversations in the context studied. It is not absolutely necessary to remember the exact words of a conversation. But it is essential to retain the integrity of its substance. You should also work to recreate phonetically the dialects that individuals may use. If individuals have a distinctive way of speaking, try to capture it. If someone says, "Duya wanna gow-out?" record it that way instead of "Do you want to go out?" If a group has its own argot, it is your job to learn to understand it and ultimately to present it to others. Keep in mind that a good deal of communication is nonverbal. Part of your descriptive task is, therefore, to note nonverbal gestures, postures, facial expressions, and the like.

Go out of your way to record *anything* that you find inexplicable or unusual. The data that you simply cannot understand may turn out to be among the most significant. If you cannot make sense out of a conversation or an event, perhaps an important aspect of the meaning fabric of the setting is eluding you. The essential task of field researchers is to arrive at some understanding of the meaning structures of the individuals being studied. You should, therefore, note down these inexplicable conversations and events and keep them in mind as you continue to collect data. Try to orient your data gathering to lead you to ultimately understand these inscrutable phenomena.

EXPLANATIONS. Along with providing accurate description, it is the continual task of field researchers to be formulating tentative explanations of the things they are seeing. An absolutely critical element of the notetaking process is statements of your own personal feelings, hunches, and hypotheses. Include in your notes any guesses you have about why individuals are acting as they are. Try continuously to weave observations into some kind of theoretical or explanatory structure. If at any point during the observations you feel that you are seeing a theme that may emerge as the focus of your work, you must get it down in the notes. Force yourself to be speculative. Don't worry about the quality or correctness of the explanation offered. Remember that the notes do not constitute a finished product.

Include even brief theoretical ideas, such as the following:

There may be some kind of link in this organization between the status of persons and the conflict and hostility I am seeing.

You may want to expand some theoretical ideas into a larger memo. In THEORETICAL MEMOS, use some of the data already collected to show how they support the theoretical ideas. You may also want to include some discussion of already published research that bears on the theoretical issues you are raising. Aside from the actual collection of data, the continual attempt at theorizing is the most important activity in which you can engage. As you go along, continue to refine these ideas. As they develop, they will help you to narrow the range of data collected. Indeed, as you amend, expand, assess, and reassess these theoretical ideas in the notes, you are actually writing substantial portions of the final research report.

Keep METHODOLOGICAL NOTES. These are a recording of, and commentary on, the success or failure of the data gathering approaches you have used. Your own feelings and the reactions of your subjects as you attempt to explore various features of their lives can be used as an index of the quality of the data obtained. Resistance can be a valuable clue that more is going on than meets the eye. When subjects suddenly become recalcitrant, is it because you have touched on a particularly sensitive area that they would sooner bury than uncover? Or does it have something to do with the way they were approached? Might you have broken an informal norm by asking someone in a group to comment on the activities or character of another group member? If so, what might this imply about the maintenance of group solidarity? Much can be learned about a group by analyzing how and why the members expose or conceal knowledge about themselves.

A final word about recording field notes. It will often be impossible for you to take notes as action occurs before you. In such cases it is important that you look for opportunities to jot down key phrases so that you may later recapture the proceedings in full. Further, it is essential that you sit down to record complete notes as soon as possible after the actual observations are made. Memory tends to flag quickly unless stimulated by the active attempt to reconstruct events.

FORMULATING AN ANALYSIS

Our discussion of field notes should have been sufficiently clear to indicate that a number of activities are carried out simultaneously in field work. Methodological problems are dealt with as data are being collected, and data analysis accompanies both of these operations. If, however, for purposes of creating guidelines, we were to divide the field work process in terms of time and energy expended by the researcher, we would name three phases. We have already dealt with two of them: first, gaining access to the setting and beginning one's observations, and second, reconstructing past events and seriously collecting data. The third and last phase of field research is the actual analysis of the data.

At this point we will assume that you have left the field altogether. Analysis has already begun in that you have accumulated a substantial number of theoretical notes and memos. That being so, you have by now a pretty good idea of the various theoretical directions that the final research report might take. The time has come, however, to decide on the theoretical framework that will best allow you to make sense of the data. Given this task, what procedures might be most helpful in producing a comprehensive analysis?

We hesitate to offer a definitive set of criteria. Two researchers independently entering the same social situation might emerge with two quite different, equally cogent analyses of data collected. It may simply be that the two researchers saw quite different features of social life illuminated in the context studied. Any one context may display a number of generic forms of human behavior. The heart of an analysis, therefore, involves the researcher's application of a small number of well-selected concepts to show his or her reader the dimensions of social life reflected in the data. If successful, an analysis will cause us to see relations between pieces of data that might at first seem wholly discrete. In addition, what is uncovered through an analysis of the collected data may challenge or confirm some already existing theory or specify a new one.

CONCEPTUAL CATEGORIES. The beginnings of an analysis must be generated by means of a search for descriptive categories that will order good portions of the collected data. Standard concepts such as social class, ideology, identity, status, role, deviance, stigma, pathology, socialization, informal organization, and the like may provide a core for initial data classification. Sometimes these categories alone are sufficient to an analysis because they are flexible enough to be molded around the events at hand. And the unique linking of such concepts can itself be a creative and theoretically informative expression of the researcher's imagination.

In other instances the nature of the setting and the data collected necessitates the development of new conceptual categories. David Sudnow (1967) created the concept of *social loss* to explain observed variations in the attitudes of medical personnel toward dying patients with different social statuses. His data allow us to see how, in the minds of the hospital personnel, some deaths constitute a greater social loss than other deaths. Researchers led by Leon Festinger (1953) studied through participant observation a small group of zealots who were vociferously claiming that the end of the world was at hand. As the researchers began to learn about the group, they found that one question kept reasserting itself: How did the members of this group maintain their faith in the dicta of the group leaders in the face of the failed prophecy? As a result of this study the investigators developed a major theoretical notion in social psychology, known as *cognitive dissonance,* to explain what seemed to be irrational behavior from the perspective of an outsider.[4] Consistent with the general aims of participant observation research, the major focus or problem for investigation emerged only after much information had been collected.

---

[4]According to the theory of cognitive dissonance, people strive for consistency in their beliefs (cognitions). The existence of dissonance (inconsistency) among beliefs produces psychological discomfort that motivates people to change some of these beliefs in a direction that reduces the dissonance.

Before you can create new ideas, as these researchers did, or synthesize standard concepts in a novel way, you will need to divide your data into their logical components. John Lofland (1971) suggests six classes for the initial ordering of observational data: *acts, activities, meanings, participation, relationships,* and *settings.* Each class further suggests a series of questions to be asked of the data: What are the basic types of acts and activities that go on? What is the typical frequency of each activity, and what is its duration? How do actors define the situation? What does their action mean to them, and what kinds of collective norms dictate their choice of action? How deeply does each participant get involved? Are some participating more than others? Who relates to whom, and how? Who avoids whom, and why? Is there a chain of communication or command? Which individuals appear to be central? Finally, what are the distinctive characteristics of the setting and to what extent do they affect or limit what takes place, how it takes place, and who gets involved? How might the participants and their actions be different in another setting?

DATA CODING. The organizing categories suggested by Lofland are helpful, but they will not solve the problems of the researcher who has collected a large volume of field notes. Beyond raising the questions suggested by Lofland's categories, researchers must somehow take into account the specific kinds of data they have gathered. A usual procedure engaged in by field workers in order to get a closer picture is to somehow *code* their data. Although there are many ways to code qualitative data, all represent variations of an essentially similar process. We will look briefly at one coding procedure that may serve as a basis for any specific variation demanded by a researcher's own data.

The first step in coding qualitative data is to generate as many descriptive categories as possible. To accomplish this, researchers should carefully read through their data and write down on separate sheets of paper each new category that is suggested. We could imagine the data collected from observation of a religious community yielding the following categories: description of setting, description of individuals, eating habits, treatment of outsiders, internal conflict, proselytizing activities, value expressions, economic considerations, street behavior, conversion process, and patterns of leadership. Production of a hundred or more categories through this first close inspection of the data would not be unlikely.

After such initial categories have been produced, we begin to work with them more carefully. We may decide that some of the categories need to be broken down into even more subcategories and that a number of others really reflect one broader category. We arrange and rearrange the categories until we are satisfied that they are reasonably discrete and comprehensive. Then we simply assign each of the developed categories a number. Next, we again examine the data in the field notes, indicating by number the category(ies) into which each piece of data fits. We will find, of course, that one verbal statement, one story, or one event might properly be coded into a number of different categories.

In order to make the data more manageable, we might at this point turn to a pair of scissors and a pile of index cards. If possible, we should first make several copies of the field notes. We keep one copy intact and use the other copies to cut out specific pieces of data, placing each piece on a separate index card. If a specific piece of data fits in more than one category, make as many copies of that data specimen as there are categories to which it applies. As we go through this process, we record on the back of each card the category number to which each piece of data refers. We may now put together the cards of each category. After reading all the data referring to each category, we may choose to refine the categories even further. At the very least, this coding procedure will give us a clear idea of the areas in which we have the most data. It would certainly say something if we were able to uncover fifty pieces of data on, say, the conversion process, and only a couple on eating habits. The sheer volume of data on one or another feature of the situation studied will almost necessarily influence the organization and content of the final report.

FROM ANALYSIS TO THEORY. We have described the process of formulating an analysis largely in technical, procedural terms. Everything suggested to this point is preliminary to the actual writing of the analysis. Frequently, the work of writing the data analysis in a coherent fashion causes a reevaluation of old ideas and leads to the formulation of new ideas. The process of writing allows the researcher to see more clearly the possible solutions to theoretical problems. New ideas reflect back upon the organization and statement of initial ideas and so on. Ideas that may at first have been terribly jumbled and inarticulately framed assume new vigor and demand expansion. An analysis is not produced in a predictable, linear fashion. There is a reciprocal relationship between ideas, such that one idea suggests others, which in turn reflect upon and change the original idea, and so on.

Categorization alone will not produce a striking, convincing, compelling analysis. An analysis will be successful if the researcher can, through the use of the procedures described, and complemented by personal insight, uncover in the data what Schatzman and Strauss (1973) refer to as a "key linkage" — an overriding pattern or story line that provides new insight into the situation investigated. This pattern may be expressed as a typology or as a principle of behavior that has relevance in a variety of settings.

Such key linkages are at the heart of a developing theoretical perspective. Of course, different observers can look at the same set of events and come up with very different typologies. A psychiatrist and a city planner could analyze the same problem and produce quite different interpretations and suggestions. This is inherent in the nature of analysis because the description of a phenomenon is dependent on the choice of conceptual categories, and any system of categories is somewhat arbitrary and artificial. Just as wave theory and particle theory produce different interpretations of the nature of light, a functionalist and a Marxist analysis of any phenomenon will differ. It is not, therefore, important to produce a final, definitive interpretation. It is important to add something to the ongoing practical and intellectual discussion surrounding a phenomenon.

Limitations of Observational Field Research

In this chapter we have discussed the theoretical basis for field work, the areas in which it has traditionally been done, and the nature of the field work process. We have also considered, where appropriate, some practical guidelines for those who may eventually do field research. Now, let us look at some of the limitations of the observational method.

It should be apparent that qualitative techniques cannot be used as a substitute for quantitative research. Rather, as we have so often emphasized, structured and unstructured methods ought to be used in conjunction with one another. The in-depth understanding provided via field research constitutes an important contribution to our knowledge. At the same time we must recognize that qualitative research does not easily allow a researcher to produce reliable measurements of phenomena and consequently is of limited utility in definitively testing quantitative propositions. In addition to this general limitation we might list the following frequently mentioned and related weaknesses of field research:

1. The method is not applicable to the investigation of large social settings. The context studied must be small enough to be dealt with exhaustively by one or a few investigators.
2. The participant observer is most likely to be involved in a single case analysis, or CASE STUDY. As a result making generalizations about a great variety of phenomena on the basis of isolated field studies is always problematic.
3. There are few safeguards against the interference of the particular biases, attitudes, and assumptions of the researcher who does field research.
4. The likelihood of the researcher's selective perception and memory biasing the results of the study is very great.
5. There is the related problem of selectivity in data collection. In any social situation there are literally thousands of possible pieces of data. No one researcher can account for every aspect of a situation. The field researcher inevitably pulls out only a segment of the data that exist and the question inevitably arises as to whether the selected data are really representative of the situation.
6. The mere presence of the researcher may change that system or group being studied into something different from what it would be were he or she not present. It is often argued that it is impossible to observe human beings without both influencing their behavior and being influenced by them.
7. Because there is no set procedure defining the field research process, it is difficult for one researcher to explain to another exactly how the work was done. It is, therefore, virtually impossible to replicate the findings of a particular field work study.

Taken together, these problems add up to a major, severe criticism of field research. Aside from our own private feelings and experiences, there is no way to easily assess the reliability and validity of the interpretations made by the researcher. We are forced to presume that investigators have been careful in their data collection and interpretation. But as long as data are collected and presented by one or a few researchers with their own distinctive talents, faults, and foibles, there will remain suspicion concerning the validity of their rendering of the phenomena studied. Qualitative field researchers often respond to these criticisms by suggesting that the cost of imprecision is more than compensated for by the in-depth quality of the data produced.

Herbert Blumer (1954) has argued that we have not reached the point in our understanding of social processes (if, indeed, we ever can or will) where we can formulate our explanations using "definitive concepts" whose terms are unambiguous and whose empirical referents are precise. Blumer has argued for the necessity of using "sensitizing concepts" whose exact meaning can be adapted to our further unfolding of the mysteries underlying the "stubborn empirical world."

Such a position has a certain plausibility, but it can easily become an umbrella protecting shoddy research practices. In reviewing the substantive contributions of field workers, one is immediately struck by the failure of most to conscientiously review the validity and reliability of their data and the inferences made from that data. There have been many discussions of the relative merits of field work and of the special problems in evaluating qualitative data (Becker, 1969; Becker and Geer, 1969; Schwartz and Schwartz, 1969), but one finds few research reports in which the authors self-consciously consider these questions. We could, of course, raise the same questions about the effectiveness of quantitative researchers' checks against invalidity and bias. Those using structured techniques might not fully and satisfactorily resolve the questions raised here, but a review of quantitative research reports does reveal the need for a greater effort to assess the reliability and validity of findings.

We would ask field researchers to work harder at explicating the procedural and analytical processes through which they produce their data and interpretations. In order to better evaluate the quality of data presented to us, we need to know more than we are normally told about the researcher's sampling procedures.[5] We need to know more about the basis for data selectivity. We need to have a fuller sense of the researcher's biases and assumptions. We need to know more about the procedures used in developing the analysis produced. Field researchers must, in short, be more responsible for specifying the methods used in seeing what they have seen. We do not see these requests as an unnecessary imposition on field researchers because methodological judgments lie at the root of the analyses produced. The requests made, then, are not antithetical to the goals of field research. On the contrary, closer attention to the quality of data produced via field work techniques seems a necessary step in evaluating how well we have "respected the nature of the empirical world" (Blumer, 1969:60).

For a period of time in American social science, especially throughout the 1940s and 1950s, there was a considerable decline in the use of observational field research techniques. This decline was related to the simultaneous and rapid growth of quantitative methods. Survey research in particular grew in popularity as it allowed investigators to reach large numbers of people, increase the accuracy of generalizations made from collected data, replicate the findings of earlier studies, and test theoretical ideas with more precision.

Quantitative techniques such as survey research correctly remain central methodological tools today. There has been, however, a reemergence, a rebirth, of the use of qualitative field work. We make this judgment based on the large number of studies within the last fifteen years relying on qualitative methods, as well as on the growing volume of books describing the underlying logic of observational work and the strategies found useful in its execution. This change has been brought about in part by the recognition that other techniques alone cannot provide the rich insight and information that come when scientists involve themselves directly in the worlds of those they study.

---

[5]For a discussion of sampling procedures in qualitative research, see Chapter 5.

Summary

Observational field research is based on the assumption that we may understand peoples' motives, values, beliefs, and interests by studying them in their natural environment. Participant observation techniques have been applied in a wide variety of settings, from schools and hospitals to deviant subcultures. An important characteristic of this method is the absence of standard operating procedures. Data collection and the formulation of research questions and analysis are highly variable in practice. This chapter has attempted to provide some general guidelines.

Ideally, field work is an inductive, emerging enterprise; however, even in the choice of setting, the effects of the researcher's previous thinking and training may be apparent. The trick is to remain uncommitted to a given set of ideas or group of informants long enough to *discover* the full range of behavior in a particular setting, its significance for the participants, and its potential relevance to other settings.

To gain access to field work settings, the researcher must take on a role somewhere along the continuum from complete observer to complete participant. The role eventually selected may depend on the response of the subjects and on how public or private the setting is. Researchers also have to decide whether any of their activities are to be concealed, a controversial ethical issue raised by naturalistic inquiry. The more interaction that occurs between researcher and subjects, the more the role taken by the researcher has to be adapted to the individual personalities and situations involved. There is, however, no such thing as total unobtrusiveness. Adopting a research role satisfactory to one group of respondents may necessitate cutting oneself off from contact with others in the same setting. Generally speaking, field workers should be as honest as possible about what they are doing. They should let their research role evolve gradually and remain essentially data collectors, not agents of change. Moreover, they should avoid being used by respondents for their own purposes.

The secret of successful systematic, objective, and analytical participant observation lies in keeping accurate and complete field notes. These are essential not only for validity but also for maximizing theoretical flexibility. Notes should contain both description and explanation. They should be filled with dialogue, personal feelings, hunches, and speculative hypotheses.

Data analysis ideally is initiated as notes are being drafted and expanded during field work. But the real analytical homework may not come until the researcher has left the field. Analysis may consist of ordering one's data using standard concepts or of creating new ideas or combinations of ideas. A complete analysis requires an exhaustive inventory of data so that they may be coded into relevant categories. Coding itself is not analysis. We need to explain and assess the significance of coding categories before we can construct theories of human behavior.

In spite of its acknowledged strengths, particularly in the production of rich, descriptive data, field work is not a substitute for survey research. It has a variety of limitations in the areas of reliability and generalizability, in its vulnerability to researcher bias, and in the risk that participant observers will, by their presence, contaminate the research setting. Nevertheless, there has been a resurgence of interest in field work as a data gathering technique in recent years. This renewed attention has coincided with calls for social scientists who do observational research to be more thorough in their reporting of methodological procedures.

Key Terms

case study
complete observer
complete participant
ethnography

gatekeeper
methodological notes
negative cases
observer-as-participant

participant-as-observer
participant observation
theoretical memo

Exercises

1. Choose some relatively familiar context such as your dormitory room or a classroom and spend two hours doing careful observation. Consider some of the elements of good observation mentioned in the chapter. Write a brief essay indicating the things, events, or processes observed that you had previously taken for granted during your normal involvement in the setting.

2. Along with two or three other people in your class, visit and observe some public setting such as a bar, a park, a bus station, or a gathering such as a rock concert or a sporting event. Imagine that your collective goal is to understand how strangers either interact or fail to interact with each other in public places. Each of the people with whom you are working should independently make his or her own observations and record his or her own field notes. At the end of the observation period, meet as a group and compare notes. What similarities exist? What differences are there? After discussing your separate observations, each of you should write a brief report analyzing some feature of the situation studied. (You might, for example, focus on how individuals avoid one another, on spatial rules governing interaction, or on how persons begin conversations.) To aid you in producing your own analysis, you may want to look at research on the conduct of people in public places, such as Lyn Lofland's (1971a, 1971b) articles on self management in public settings and Erving Goffman's (1963) *Behavior in Public Places*.

3. Assume that you are about to embark on an observational study of a weight watchers group. Briefly indicate some of the methodological problems you might have. Do you speculate that there might be problems of access? Will there be difficulties in talking to group members? Might your own values intrude in your findings?

4. Kai Erikson (1970) has established two rules concerning the ethicality of observational work. First, researchers must never deliberately misrepresent their identities to enter a private domain where they would otherwise have no legitimate access. Second, investigators must never misrepresent their research intentions. Write an essay indicating whether you think these rules are too restrictive. Will it be possible to follow these two rules and still study most social groups?

5. Read an article presenting data acquired through participant observation. As a source you might want to look at the journal, *Urban Life*. After reading the article, answer the following questions:

a. How fully did the author describe his or her methodology?

b. What additional discussion could have been included to give you a clearer idea of the procedures used?

c. Did the analysis conform well to the data presented?

d. What questions do you have about the reliability and validity of the findings?

e. Could the subject studied be investigated using methods other then participant observation? If so, indicate the methods that could have been used.

Suggested Readings

READINGS ABOUT THE METHOD

Bogdan, Robert
1972 *Participant Observation in Organizational Settings.* Syracuse, N.Y.: Syracuse University Press.

Bogdan's short book is useful on two counts. First, his discussion of the stages in participant observation should complement our own treatment in this chapter. Second, the book focuses explicitly on observational research in organizational settings. It is one of the few books to do so. The reader should also appreciate the Appendix of the book, in which the author includes some examples of field notes.

Bruyn, Severyn
1966 *The Human Perspective in Sociology: The Methodology of Participant Observation.* Englewood Cliffs, N.J.: Prentice-Hall.

Bruyn's book is one of the more sophisticated treatments of field work techniques. It is particularly useful because of its careful attention to the philosophical roots of that methodology.

Filstead, William J., ed.
1970 *Qualitative Methodology: Firsthand Involvement with the Social World.* Chicago: Markham.

Filstead has compiled a number of important essays on nearly all features of observational field research. Among the general topics discussed are field work roles, processes of data collection, data analysis, and ethical problems in field studies. Several of the articles to which we made reference in this chapter are included among Filstead's selections.

Glaser, Barney, and Anselm Strauss
1967 *The Discovery of Grounded Theory.* Chicago: Aldine.

This book is among the most important on qualitative methodology. In it the authors provide a theoretical rationale for observational work and describe the logic of inductive inquiry. Concerned primarily with the question of how researchers generate theory, the authors present one of the most articulate descriptions available on the development of analysis from qualitative data.

Gray, Paul S.
1980 "Exchange and Access in Field Work." *Urban Life* (October):309–331.

This article describes the barriers to access encountered by the author as he studied a labor organization. It is a natural history of participant observation that explains how the investigator's announced role changed over time and that describes techniques for inspiring the trust of respondents as participation increases.

Lofland, John
1971 *Analyzing Social Settings.* Belmont, Calif.: Wadsworth.

The author first offers a broad description of the purposes and goals of qualitative analysis. He then establishes guidelines for collecting and analyzing observational data. Lofland's discussion should serve as a useful introduction to observational techniques for the student entering the field for the first time.

Shaffir, William B., et al.
1980 *Fieldwork Experience.* New York: St. Martin's Press.

A highly readable collection of researchers' actual experiences in obtaining access, maintaining rapport, and leaving the field in a variety of settings including corporate board rooms, pornographic bookstores, police patrols, and television newsrooms.

Spradley, James P.
1979 *The Ethnographic Interview.* New York: Holt, Rinehart and Winston.

Chapters 5 through 12 are among the best on analysis of field data. The author offers concrete suggestions for making sense out of a vast array of information.

Webb, Eugene J., et al.
1981 *Unobtrusive Measures: Nonreactive Research in the Social Sciences.* Chicago: Rand McNally.

As indicated by their title, the authors of this book describe a number of different types of measures that may be performed without the direct intervention of a researcher. Some of them can profitably be used by researchers doing qualitative field work. The reader should take special note of Chapter 5.

Whyte, William Foote
1943   *Street Corner Society*. Chicago: University of Chicago Press.

Whyte's book stands as a classic example of observational field research. It is also one of the few qualitative studies in which the researcher gives an in-depth description of how the study proceeded. To get a feeling for some of the typical problems any researcher doing participant observation is likely to experience, read the Appendix. It is an honest, sensitive statement on the practical, intellectual, and ethical issues Whyte had to face as he did his research. It is fascinating and informative reading.

READINGS ILLUSTRATING THE METHOD[6]

Becker, Howard S.
1963   *Outsiders: Studies in the Sociology of Deviance*. New York: Free Press.

Through his research on two separate subcultures—marijuana smokers and jazz musicians—Becker develops the theoretical idea of labeling to explain how and why certain persons embark on a "deviant career."

Cavan, Sherri
1966   *Liquor License: An Ethnography of Bar Behavior*. Chicago: Aldine.

In this study Cavan develops a typology of bars that organizes an enormous volume of qualitative data on various features of bar behavior. Readers will want to consider, possibly on the basis of their own experiences, whether bars familiar to them fit neatly into one or another of Cavan's categories.

Liebow, Eliot
1967   *Tally's Corner*. Boston: Little, Brown.

In this lively, well-written, and popular study, Liebow analyzes the lives of black streetcorner men in Washington, D.C. His data are used to construct a convincing argument that their behavior is explicable in terms of the obstacles they face in trying to realize the "middle-class" values of achievement and success. From a methodological point of view the reader will want to consider the threats to validity in a study in which a white researcher interacts with black persons. This is one of the several dilemmas Liebow discusses in his Appendix.

References

Becker, Howard S.
1963   *Outsiders: Studies in the Sociology of Deviance*. New York: Free Press.
1969   "Problems of Inference and Proof in Participant Observation." In *Issues in Participant Observation*, ed. George J. McCall and J. L. Simmons. Reading, Mass.: Addison-Wesley.

Becker, Howard S., and Blanche Geer
1969   "Participant Observation and Interviewing: A Comparison." In *Issues in Participant Observation*, ed. George J. McCall and J. L. Simmons. Reading, Mass.: Addison-Wesley.

Blumer, Herbert
1954   "What Is Wrong with Social Theory." *American Sociological Review* 19 (February):3–10.
1969   *Symbolic Interaction*. Englewood Cliffs, N.J.: Prentice-Hall.

Cressey, Paul
1932   *The Taxi-Dance Hall*. Chicago: University of Chicago Press.

Davis, Fred
1970   "Focus on the Flower Children: Why All of Us May Be Hippies Someday." In *Observations of Deviance*, ed. Jack Douglas. New York: Random House.

Emerson, Joan
1970   "Behavior in Private Places: Sustaining Definitions of Reality in Gynecological Examinations." In *Recent Sociology*, no. 2, ed. Hans Peter Dreitzel. New York: Macmillan.

[6]See also the references for this chapter and for Chapter 1, which contain numerous examples of observational research.

Erikson, Kai
1970 "A Comment on Disguised Observation in Sociology." In *Qualitative Methodology,* ed. William J. Filstead. Chicago: Markham.

Festinger, Leon, et al.
1953 *When Prophecy Fails.* New York: Harper & Row.

Gans, Herbert
1969 *The Levittowners.* New York: Random House.

Glazer, Myron
1972 *The Research Adventure.* New York: Random House.

Goffman, Erving
1961 *Asylums.* New York: Doubleday.
1963 *Behavior in Public Places.* New York: Free Press.

Gold, Raymond
1969 "Roles in Sociological Field Observations." In *Issues in Participant Observation,* ed. George J. McCall and J. L. Simmons. Reading, Mass.: Addison-Wesley.

Gouldner, Alvin
1954 *Patterns of Industrial Bureaucracy.* New York: Free Press.

Greenwald, Harold
1958 *The Call Girl.* New York: Ballantine Books.

Hall, Edward
1969 *The Hidden Dimension.* New York: Doubleday.

Humphreys, Laud
1970 *Tearoom Trade.* Chicago, Aldine.

Jackson, P.
1968 *Life in the Classroom.* New York: Holt, Rinehart and Winston.

Kahn, Robert, and Floyd Mann
1969 "Developing Research Partnerships." In *Issues in Participant Observation,* ed. George J. McCall and J. L. Simmons. Reading, Mass.: Addison-Wesley.

Karp, David A.
1973 "Hiding in Pornographic Bookstores: A Reevaluation of the Nature of Urban Anonymity." *Urban Life and Culture* 1 (January):427–451.

Liebow, Eliot
1967 *Tally's Corner.* Boston: Little, Brown.

Lofland, John
1971 *Analyzing Social Settings.* Belmont, Calif.: Wadsworth.

Lofland, John, and Robert A. Lejeune
1970 "Initial Interaction of Newcomers in Alcoholics Anonymous." In *Qualitative Methodology,* ed. William J. Filstead. Chicago: Markham.

Lofland, Lyn
1971a "Self Management in Public Settings, Part I." *Urban Life and Culture* 1 (April):93–117.
1971b "Self Management in Public Settings, Part II." *Urban Life and Culture* 2 (July):217–231.

McKinney, John C.
1966 *Constructive Typology and Social Theory.* New York: Appleton-Century-Crofts.

Pope, Harrison
1971 *Voices from the Drug Culture.* Boston: Beacon Press.

Sagarin, Edward
1969 *Odd Man In.* Chicago: Quadrangle Books.

Schatzman, Leonard, and Anselm Strauss
1973 *Field Research: Strategies for a Natural Sociology.* Englewood Cliffs, N.J.: Prentice-Hall.

Schwartz, Morris S., and Charlotte G. Schwartz
1969 "Problems in Participant Observation." In *Issues in Participant Observation,* ed. George J. McCall and J. L. Simmons. Reading, Mass.: Addison-Wesley.

Sommer, Robert
1969 *Personal Space.* Englewood Cliffs, N.J.: Prentice-Hall.

Sudnow, David
1967 *Passing On: The Social Organization of Dying.* Englewood Cliffs, N.J.: Prentice-Hall.

Sutherland, Edwin
1949 *White Collar Crime.* New York: Holt, Rinehart and Winston.

Thorne, Barrie
1971 "Resisting the Draft: An Ethnography of the Draft Resistance Movement." Unpublished Ph.D. dissertation: Brandeis University.

Weinberg, Martin
1968 "Sexual Modesty, Social Meanings and the Nudist Camp." In *Sociology and Everyday Life,* ed. Marcello Truzzi. Englewood Cliffs, N.J.: Prentice-Hall.

Whyte, William Foote
1943 *Street Corner Society.* Chicago: University of Chicago Press.

Wolff, Michael
1973 "Notes on the Behavior of Pedestrians." In *People in Places: The Sociology of the Familiar,* ed. Arnold Birenbaum and Edward Sagarin. New York: Praeger.

9 / Experimental Research

CHAPTER OUTLINE

INTRODUCTION
THE ELEMENTS OF TRUE
  EXPERIMENTATION
Independent and Dependent Variables
Experimental and Control Groups
Experimental Procedure
Establishing Causality
THREATS TO VALIDITY IN
  EXPERIMENTAL RESEARCH

Internal Validity
  The Solomon Four-Group Design
External Validity
  Modeling Effects
  Sampling and Generalizability
FIELD EXPERIMENTATION
The Negative Income Tax Experiment
The Invasion of Personal Space
Quasi-Field Experiments

A Study of Group Culture
  The Study of Organizations
Demonstration Experiments
A FINAL WORD
SUMMARY
KEY TERMS
EXERCISES
SUGGESTED READINGS
REFERENCES

Introduction

The idea of an experiment should not be foreign to most of us. We all use loose or incomplete forms of experimentation in our daily lives. Husbands and wives "experiment" with different ways of preparing food, noting their spouse's reaction to each modification of the prepared dish. Salespersons intent on finding the most persuasive "line" to use in selling a product may systematically test out a number of approaches until they find the one that works best. Teachers experiment with a variety of teaching formats, selecting one that allows students to learn the most. Vacationers in Las Vegas try out a number of different systems at roulette or blackjack, hoping to find the one that will make them winners.

Any time that we systematically "manipulate" our surroundings and try to assess the effects of these manipulations, we are engaging in an experiment. In all the cases mentioned, actors looked for changes in one or another phenomenon (expressions of pleasure in eating, number of sales made, and so on) after systematically altering some feature of the environment. The presumed purpose of our everyday experimentation is to assert the existence of a CAUSAL CONNECTION between two or more variables.

What, then, distinguishes incomplete experimentation from scientific experimentation? The most basic answer is that most of us typically do not go to the trouble of creating rigorous safeguards to ensure the correctness of the causal relationship suggested by our everyday experiments. Consider the teacher who has been testing a number of teaching methods. Suppose that in one class small-group discussion seems to produce the greatest amount of learning, as measured

214

by a quiz on the material. Should the teacher conclude that the best teaching technique has been uncovered and that small-group discussions should be used in all classes? Are there any kinds of procedural considerations that might cause us to be skeptical about the validity of these "findings"?

Here are some of the questions we might ask: Isn't it possible that the class responding well to the small-group discussions had better students in the first place and would have learned more regardless of the method used? Might the size of the class have had an effect on the amount learned—independent of the method employed? Might it have made a difference that the teacher's classes met at different times during the day and that, again, independent of the method used, students are more or less attentive during certain school hours? What about the distribution of males and females in the class? Is there any possibility that the sex composition of the class alters the willingness of students to participate in small-group discussions?

It seems plain that in order to make "safe" causal inferences we must somehow ensure that factors wholly unrelated to what we presume to be the cause of some phenomenon can be excluded or discounted. In the ideal experimental situation the only thing that will vary from group to group or situation to situation is the experimental treatment. Unless the situations studied are similar in *all* respects other than the presence or absence of an experimental treatment, we cannot be certain that it is indeed the treatment, and not some other difference existing between the groups, that causes certain changes to occur. If we hope to isolate the effects of one or another experimental treatment we must somehow *control for,* or rule out, all those factors other than the experimental treatment that could affect the behaviors of those studied. In the case at hand, if we want to demonstrate that the variable *small-group discussion* makes a difference in student learning, we must be careful to rule out the effects of class size, gender composition, the time of day the class is taught, and other such factors.

Both scientists and nonscientists are concerned with demonstrating causal connections between various features of the social world. Scientists, however, make every effort to set up their experimental procedures in such a way as to show clearly that any changes in behavior following an experimental treatment are not contaminated by factors extraneous to that treatment. Experimental research, therefore, may be defined as an investigation in which one or more variables are manipulated by the experimenter under carefully controlled conditions. The task of scientists is to assess the effects of their experimental manipulation by measuring changes in a specified variable. The key phrase in this definition is that experimental research is conducted under *carefully controlled conditions.* In this chapter we shall consider some of the difficulties involved in achieving such control. We shall see that some research problems do not easily submit to pure experimental procedures. The degree of control possible must be taken as the major criterion in assessing how surely we can claim the existence of a causal connection between two or more variables.

The Elements of True Experimentation

Perhaps we can achieve a better picture of how control is exercised and how causality between variables is established by looking at a hypothetical example— an experiment that might be conducted in a social psychologist's laboratory. We shall follow the researcher through the process of testing ideas experimentally, and we shall offer a rationale for each step in that process. Let us begin our discussion by assuming that a researcher has a theoretical reason for believing there is a relationship between the *degree of anxiety* in a group and the *cohesiveness* of that group. The hypothesis to be tested may be stated as follows:

> The greater the anxiety among the members of a group, the greater will be the cohesion of that group.

INDEPENDENT AND DEPENDENT VARIABLES

In order to determine the experimental procedures needed to test this hypothesis, the researcher must look carefully at its elements. Clearly, the two variables being related in the hypothesis are anxiety and cohesiveness. The convention in scientific research is to label the proposed causal variable in a relationship the INDEPENDENT VARIABLE and the proposed effect of the independent variable the DEPENDENT VARIABLE. In the hypothesis the researcher has proposed that anxiety causes cohesiveness. Hence, given our definitions, anxiety is the independent (or TEST) variable and cohesiveness is the dependent variable.

Logic demands that in order to test this hypothesis the researcher must compare at least two groups. The simplest test of the hypothesis would be to compare a low-anxiety group and a high-anxiety group, with the expectation that cohesiveness would be greater in the latter. One of the great strengths of experimental procedure is that the experimenter is in a position to create just the groups needed in order to test the hypothesis. More explicit, the experimental researcher may manipulate the independent variable and cause it to vary.

EXPERIMENTAL AND CONTROL GROUPS

The experimenter must think of some way to introduce or produce anxiety in one of the groups to be assembled and compared. In this simplest form of experimentation, where the investigator works with only two groups, the one in which the independent or test variable (anxiety) is introduced is called the EXPERIMENTAL GROUP; the other, in which it is not introduced, is called the CONTROL GROUP.

How does the experimenter create the two groups, and how exactly is the independent variable manipulated? It is not uncommon for university-associated researchers to advertise in their school newspaper for student volunteers to participate in an experiment. Usually, students who volunteer are paid a nominal sum for their participation.

Later we shall discuss the possible weaknesses of experimental procedures on human subjects. For now, let us note two possible difficulties raised by the recruitment procedure we are outlining here. First, students represent only one sector of the whole population. They are likely younger and better read, and possibly more intelligent, than the average person in society. If we use only students because of their accessibility, we must recognize that there will be limits to any generalizations made from our experimental findings. It may be that groups more heterogeneous in terms of age, ethnicity, and intelligence would behave quite differently from the relatively homogeneous groups of students. Second, our subjects would be SELF-SELECTED, individuals who choose to participate in an experiment. This raises another problem of selectivity. Might there be some systematic difference between the types of people willing to participate and those not willing? Researchers must be cognizant of these factors when they attempt to make generalizations about group process from their data.

Bearing these problems in mind, let us assume that volunteers have been instructed to sign up some time in advance of the date when the experiment will actually be carried out. Suppose that thirty students have indicated their willingness to participate. Since group size might affect people's behavior, the researcher makes the reasonable decision to have fifteen students in both the experimental and the control groups. The next decision must be to determine which fifteen will be in each group. This decision is an absolutely crucial one; if improperly made, it could void the results of the experiment. Let's consider the logic of the assignment of the students to the two groups.

What would be wrong with simply assigning the first fifteen names on the list to the experimental group and the last fifteen to the control group? Recall the purpose of the experiment: it is to assess the effects of anxiety on group cohesion. *All other variables must be ruled out.* This being so, we may begin to see why simply splitting the list in half to create the two comparison groups would be an unwise decision. It might be that women, or poor students, or psychology majors have a tendency to sign up for participation in experiments before others. The first fifteen students who sign up might, therefore, differ in important respects from the last fifteen. Since the researcher wants to rule out or control for any such systematic differences, a different procedure must be adopted for assigning subjects to experimental and control groups.

The researcher correctly chooses to make a RANDOM ASSIGNMENT of students to the groups. The laws of statistical probability dictate that the two groups would be neither overrepresented nor underrepresented by individuals with one or another distinctive characteristic. Random selection is, therefore, a key feature of experimental procedure, allowing the researcher to effectively control for all possible factors extraneous to the specific relationship under investigation.

EXPERIMENTAL PROCEDURE

Now the day has arrived when the volunteers will show up to participate in the experiment. Having solved the problem of group assignment, the researcher must be prepared to manipulate the independent variable in the experimental group (somehow create anxiety in that group) and to measure any changes that occur in group cohesiveness. At this point there are a number of variations that might be pursued. The following procedure would not be unusual:

1. After assignment of individuals to the two groups, the researcher asks the members of each to work together on some reasonably simple problem. The researcher is not interested in their ability to do the assigned problem. The goal is to get people interacting as a group so that certain features of that group interaction can be measured.

2. Prior to the arrival of the subjects the investigator has determined how to *measure* cohesiveness, the dependent variable. Although the difficulties of measurement are great and the researcher must be concerned with the reliability and validity of the measures, let us say for simplicity's sake that cohesiveness is

operationalized in terms of the number of times members refer to the group as a whole by using the collective "we." The researcher might listen to and observe the groups from behind a one-way mirror.

3. After observing each group for a time, the researcher will have arrived at a quantitative measure of cohesiveness for each group prior to the introduction of the test variable. Measurement of the dependent variable prior to the manipulation of the independent variable is often referred to as a *pretest*.

4. The experimenter is now prepared to provide a STIMULUS to the experimental group by somehow introducing or raising the level of anxiety in that group. Perhaps the members of the experimental group might be told that they are not performing as well as they should be on their assigned task and that unless their performances improve, they can expect a reasonably unpleasant punishment. Through such a communication the researcher has presumably increased the level of anxiety in the experimental group and is now in a position to observe any changes in group cohesiveness.

5. The experimenter returns behind the one-way mirror and again assesses the degree of cohesiveness in each group as measured by the frequency of collective group references by the members. The measure of the dependent variable following the experimental treatment is often referred to as the POSTTEST. Any change in subjects' behaviors or attitudes is established by comparing pretest and posttest measures.

ESTABLISHING CAUSALITY

If, when the researcher compares the pretest and posttest measures of cohesiveness for both the experimental and the control groups, a substantial increase in cohesiveness appears after manipulation of the independent variable in only the experimental group, this may be taken as evidence that the initial hypothesis relating anxiety and cohesiveness is correct. More than that, however, the experimental procedure used allows the researcher to make the even more powerful statement that anxiety is a *cause* of cohesiveness. Properly executed experimental research allows for collection of the evidence necessary for making causal statements. A review of the hypothetical research we have described will reveal that the investigator has met the following three criteria for establishing causality between variables:

1. First, the researcher must be able to show that the *independent and dependent variables are associated*. In other words, any measured change in the independent variable will be accompanied by a measured change in the dependent variable, and vice versa.

2. The idea of causality implies more than simple association, however. It involves, in addition, the *direction of the relationship* between two variables. It is one thing to say that variables X and Y are related and quite another to say that X caused Y. In order to establish the more precise direction of causality between two variables, the researcher must show that there is a time sequencing to any measured change in both independent and dependent variables. That is, showing the direction of causality is contingent on the demonstration that a change in Y clearly *follows* a change in X, and not the other way around. The experimental procedure involving the manipulation of an independent variable allows the re-

searcher to illustrate the time sequencing of events. One of the strengths of the experiment resides in the fact that the researcher frequently controls the timing of events. It may be demonstrated that any measured change in the dependent variable occurs *only after* the independent variable has been introduced.

3. Finally, in order to establish a causal relationship between two variables, the researcher must be able to give evidence that it is indeed the proposed independent variable, and not some other unknown factor, that is responsible for any measured change in the dependent variable. The experiment that allows for random assignment of subjects to both experimental and control groups ensures that the two groups are not substantially different in important respects. The control over extraneous variables exerted through random assignment allows the researcher to make a very important assertion; namely, that the only difference between the groups studied is that one has not been exposed to the experimental treatment, or stimulus, and the other has.

We have set the stage for further discussion by presenting in some detail, through example, the basic logic and structure of experimental research. We cannot assume, however, that once the minimal conditions for a true experiment are met, researchers can unequivocally establish just how the variables examined in their studies are causally related. As in all the methodologies employed by social scientists, there are sources of distortion, bias, or error that may render invalid the findings produced in a study. We turn, therefore, to a discussion of some of the threats to validity when the classic experimental design is employed.

Threats to Validity in Experimental Research

Methodologists typically distinguish between threats to internal validity and threats to external validity as they consider sources of distortion in experimental research.[1] When we speak of INTERNAL VALIDITY, we are referring to the ways in which the conduct or process of experimentation itself may affect the results obtained. Is there anything about the procedures used in conducting an experiment that may distort the "truth value" of the data collected? It is important to remember that the researcher wants to isolate the effects of specific independent variables. Threats to internal validity exist when our ability to see the effect of some independent variable is blurred because the experimental procedure has itself affected subjects' behaviors.

Suppose that we have conducted an experiment similar to the one outlined in the preceding section, to test the hypothesis that group anxiety produces cohesiveness. If the study takes several hours to complete, and the people in the experimental group spend a great deal of time together waiting for the researcher to perform the measurements, they might get to know each other quite well and become more cohesive as a result. The researcher might indeed find that their cohesiveness increased and attribute this to greater anxiety. The conclusion might be incorrect because the design of the experiment allowed another variable

---

[1]In our discussion of internal and external validity we drew heavily upon the work of Campbell and Stanley (1963).

affecting cohesiveness (*length of time spent together*) to intrude. This is a problem of internal validity.

When researchers speak of EXTERNAL VALIDITY, they refer to difficulties in *generalizing* the findings of experimental research. A frequent criticism of laboratory experiments is that they are artificially constructed situations and that people do not act in the real world as they do in the laboratory. For this reason there are limits to the generalizations we can make from experimental research. The external validity question asks whether groups created for purposes of experimentation are sufficiently different from naturally occurring groups that generalization beyond the experimental situation is unwarranted. Before we address ourselves to this so-called reality problem, let us consider some of the specific obstacles to internal validity in studies using the classic experimental design.

INTERNAL VALIDITY

Internal validity is the *sine qua non* of experimental research. We must be able to ascertain whether the experimental treatment is, in fact, responsible for any measured changes in a dependent variable. We saw earlier that random assignment of subjects to experimental and control groups ensures, according to the laws of probability, that the groups compared do not differ significantly from one another in their composition. Through random assignment we achieve a degree of control over the range of variables, other than the chosen independent variable, that could be causally related to the dependent variable in our study. We must now examine those factors associated with the experimental procedure itself that cannot be controlled through random assignment.

In all cases the concern of the researcher is to measure *change* in some dependent variable after the introduction of a test variable. In order to assess the change precisely, the researcher must measure the dependent variable at least twice—once before the introduction of the test variable and once after. There are, however, some complications that enter into the researcher's assessment of change.

First, the subjects of an experiment may become sensitized to the measurement procedures used. Any initial measurement (pretest) of subjects may reveal to them the interests of the experimenter and affect their responses to the second measurement (the posttest). Suppose researchers want to determine whether a movie showing natural childbirth makes people more or less favorably disposed toward delivery without medication. If the experimenters decide to use the control group/experimental group design and to show the movie (the independent variable) in the experimental group, they would undoubtedly want some initial measure of subjects' attitudes about natural childbirth. But if they ask subjects to fill out an attitude questionnaire on childbirth, the very activity of answering the questions might affect their attitudes. If this occurred, the experimenters would not easily be able to assess the effects of the movie itself (their independent variable) in changing subjects' attitudes.

Along with the danger of pretest sensitization there may be *maturational processes* that members of either or both groups experience. The subjects of an experiment may be exposed to an event or input from the general experimental environment that is unrelated to the experimental treatment per se but that may nevertheless influence their behaviors and attitudes. We could envision influential leaders becoming established in a group that has been meeting for even a short time. These leaders could modify the behaviors of other subjects in the study. Another example of maturational effects creating changes in behavior apart from the experimental manipulation is the possibility of subjects becoming bored or fatigued or hungry during the procedure. There are, in other words, a number of factors associated simply with the passage of time that might cause people to change their behavior.

Closely related to the effects of maturation are the potentially confounding effects of *history*. It could happen, especially in experiments in which there is a reasonable span of time between pretest and posttest measures of the dependent variable, that subjects will learn about an event that has occurred in the society that will influence their attitudes. Campbell and Stanley (1963) cite the example of a study done in 1940 in which the researcher wanted to assess the effects of Nazi propaganda on students. During the days in which the subjects were reading the propaganda materials, France fell to the Nazis. It is very likely that any changes in student attitudes were more directly a result of this historical event than of the materials they were reading.

In addition to the factors already named, there are occasions when the dependent variable is not measured in exactly the same way in the posttest as in the pretest. There are many experimental studies where observers, scorers, or raters evaluate changes in the dependent variable after some experimental treatment. It could happen that these people themselves go through a maturational process—become fatigued or bored—and do not, therefore, use exactly the same measurement criteria for the posttest as they did for the pretest. This problem of MEASUREMENT DECAY is further exacerbated if pretest and posttest measurements are done by altogether different sets of people. It could happen, in other words, that any measured change in the dependent variable is due to inconsistencies in measurement rather than to the experimental treatment.

Finally, we must mention the possibility that subjects will drop out of the experiment before it is completed. EXPERIMENT or SUBJECT MORTALITY will, of course, influence the comparability of the control and experimental groups and will cause researchers to question whether any measured changes in a dependent variable following the experimental treatment might be a function of the changed composition.

THE SOLOMON FOUR-GROUP DESIGN. In order to combat some of the threats to internal validity that we have been considering, investigators have developed elaborations on the classic experiment. To illustrate the ingenuity of researchers who are intent on maximizing internal validity, we shall examine a frequently used variation that employs four comparison groups. This procedure has come to be called the Solomon Four-Group Design and takes the form illustrated in Table 9.1. Note that up to experimental group 2 this design is identical to the classic experiment. Two additional groups have been added, however, in which no pretest measure of the independent variable is made. What is the rationale for adding experimental group 2 and control group 2?

We begin with the assumption that because individuals have been randomly assigned to all four groups they do not systematically vary from each other in any important respect. Although no pretest measures are taken in experimental group 2 and control group 2, we can assume, because individuals have been randomly assigned to all four groups, that if a pretest had been given in these groups, the

TABLE 9.1   The Soloman Four-Group Design

	Experimental Group 1	Control Group 1	Experimental Group 2	Control Group 2
Pretest Conducted	Yes	Yes	No	No
Exposure to Test Variable	Yes	No	Yes	No
Posttest Conducted	Yes	Yes	Yes	Yes

results would not differ substantially from the pretest measures of experimental group 1 and control group 1. We can also assume that the effects of any maturational processes would be the same in all four groups.

Now, let us suppose that the researchers were concerned with the possible sensitizing effects of a pretest measure. Consider the comparison they could make between experimental group 1 and experimental group 2. The only difference between these two groups is that a pretest measure has been conducted in one and not in the other. Therefore, if the pretest has had no effect in changing the individuals' attitudes or behaviors, we would expect that there will be no substantial difference in the posttest measures for these two groups. If there is a substantial posttest measure difference between experimental groups 1 and 2, the researchers can estimate how much influence the pretest has had in producing that change, since the only thing distinguishing those two groups is the absence of the pretest in one of them. Moreover, by comparing these experimental groups with control group 1 (pretest done, no experimental treatment), they can assess the effects of their experimental treatment.

What about maturation and history as confounding factors? How can the effects of these two related factors be evaluated? These possible biasing factors can be gauged by means of control group 2. Subjects in control group 2 have experienced neither a pretest nor the experimental treatment. Only a posttest has been done. Any change in control group 2 must, then, be due entirely to maturational processes and not to the effect of the experimental treatment. The pure effect of the experimental treatment can be determined by subtracting the posttest score of control group 2 (effects of maturation) from the posttest score of experimental group 2 (effects of maturation and experimental treatment).

In conclusion, we can see that the elaboration of the classic experimental design to include a larger number of comparison groups allows researchers to determine with much greater accuracy the effects of their stated independent variables. Several design variations are possible. By using a number of groups, researchers can administer several pretests; they can control in a number of ways the timing of events (that is, the timing of the introduction of the test variable); they can sometimes vary the *intensity* of the test variable in different groups (a researcher interested in the effects of anxiety could, for example, control the degree of anxiety created in groups studied); and they can administer a number of different posttests. While it goes beyond the scope of our discussion to study all these design variations, we must at the least understand their purpose. All elaborations on the classical experimental design allow researchers to evaluate more precisely the causal effects of their chosen independent variables.

EXTERNAL VALIDITY

Even when researchers conduct experiments in which they minimize the threats to internal validity, they must still worry about whether they can generalize from their experimental findings. After all, people may not behave in their "natural life situations" as they do when they know that their behaviors are being watched, measured, and evaluated by a scientist. Can we be certain that they conform, react to anxiety, learn how to perform tasks, respond to group leaders, develop group norms, and the like just as they would in situations in which they are not being studied? When we inquire into the correspondence between individuals' behaviors in experimental situations and their "natural world" behaviors, we are raising the question of external validity. If there is no correspondence between the two, it becomes logically dangerous to generalize beyond the experimental situation itself.

That individuals' behaviors may be altered because they know they are being studied was clearly demonstrated in a famous 1929 study of workers. The biasing effect of subjects' knowledge that they are part of a study has come to be called the HAWTHORNE EFFECT, after the name of the factory where the research took place. In the Hawthorne study a number of researchers set out to investigate factors affecting worker productivity. They manipulated patterns of lighting, monetary incentives for production, patterns of managerial leadership, and so on. The major finding of the study was that regardless of the experimental manipulations employed, the production of workers seemed to improve. One reasonable conclusion from this research is that the workers were pleased to be part of an experiment—they were pleased to receive attention from researchers who expressed an interest in them—and this was the most influential factor affecting productivity. We can, however, be somewhat more specific regarding how subjects' knowledge of their participation in an experiment might cause them to modify their "normal" behaviors.

MODELING EFFECTS. One danger in an experiment is that subjects may try to behave as they believe the experimenter expects them to behave. When this occurs, we say an EXPECTANCY or MODELING EFFECT is operating. All of us have a need to order and to make intelligible the situations in which we act, and the experimental situation is no exception. We ought to expect that subjects in an experiment will try to figure out what the experiment is about and what the researchers wish to know. Subjects no doubt have some conception of how people participating in an experiment ought to act; they realize their behaviors are being evaluated and, in most instances, will want to "look good." The problem is compounded by the demonstrated possibility that experimental researchers sometimes unwittingly convey their attitudes and expectations to their subjects, with the result that the subjects conform to those expectations.

The operation of expectancy effects was pointedly shown by Rosenthal and Fode (1963) in an experiment of their own. One group of researchers was given a number of laboratory rats and told that they had been specially bred genetically and could be expected to be fast learners. Another group of researchers was told that their rats were dull and consequently would not easily learn to run a maze. Despite the fact that there was in reality absolutely no difference between the two groups of rats, the "superior" rats performed much better than their "dull" counterparts. Rosenthal and Fode (1963:165) offer the following tentative account for these surprising findings:

> Rats are sensitive to visual, auditory, olfactory, and tactual cues. These last, the tactual, were perhaps the major cues mediating the experimenter's expectancy to the animal. . . . Experimenters expecting and obtaining better performances handled their rats more and also more gently than did the experimenters expecting and obtaining poorer performances.

Rosenthal and Fode's experiment is particularly striking in that these unwitting "communications" occurred between experimenters and non-symbol-using animals. When we think of the utterly enormous capacity of the human animal to symbolize, to pick up subtle cues, and to engage in elaborate processes of interpretation, we must recognize the heightened likelihood that expectancy effects are operative in determining the outcomes of experiments with people. In part to combat the influence of expectancy, some experimental designs are double-blind. In a DOUBLE-BLIND EXPERIMENT the researcher conducting the experiment does not know whether subjects are part of the experimental group or the control group. Thus medical experimenters, for instance, would not be inclined to expect improvement in certain patients since they would not know which patients had been given a particular drug and which had been given a sugar pill.

SAMPLING AND GENERALIZABILITY. We mentioned earlier that there are frequently special *sampling* problems in the conduct of experiments that may also flaw the representativeness of findings. More specifically, the subjects of laboratory experiments are often drawn from readily accessible populations. Very often, the subjects are students and then only those students who express a willingness to participate. The generalizability of our findings might therefore be compromised by selection processes that favor the inclusion of certain types of subjects and the exclusion of others. Consider the implication of the fact that experimental subjects are often volunteers. Substantial evidence has been accumulated to show that volunteers differ from nonvolunteers in the following ways (Jung, 1971:28):

> Volunteers are higher in the need for social approval.
>
> Volunteers tend to have more unconventional personalities.
>
> Volunteers more often tend to be first born.
>
> Volunteers for certain experiments are less well adjusted.
>
> Volunteers tend to have higher need for achievement.

It is important to know that the problem of generalizability does not belong to the experimental researcher alone. Systematic sample selectivity and expectancy biases must be considered as obstacles to generalization in participant observation and survey research studies as well. In the case of experiments, the problems of internal validity, we have seen, can be dealt with through the use of ingenious experimental designs. There is no such similar logical response to the question of external validity. Satisfaction that the results of our research allow for generalization always demands a leap of faith to some degree. Although we should refrain from claiming a one-to-one relationship between the laboratory situation and the "real world," we should not dismiss the power of the experiment in sensitizing us to important processes of social life. The words of social psychologist Leon Festinger (1971:6) are worth quoting:

It should be stressed ... that the problem of application of the results of laboratory experiments to the real-life situation is not solved by a simple extension of the result. Such application requires additional experimentation and study. It is undoubtedly important that the results of laboratory experiments be tested out in real-life situations. Unless this is done the danger of "running dry" or "hitting a dead end" is always present. A continuous interplay between laboratory experiments and studies of real life situations should provide proper perspective, for the results obtained should continually supply new hypotheses for building the theoretical structure and should represent progress in the solution of the problems of application and generalization.

The plea for a continuous interplay between experimental procedures and studies of real-life situations provides a useful transition to the next section of this chapter. We have noted that laboratory experiments have the great virtue of letting researchers exercise control over variables extraneous to their research interests. We may suggest that as research is done in the real world—that is, as we try to study people in their natural environments—it becomes more and more difficult to isolate a few variables for investigation. At the same time we wish to emphasize that it *is* possible to conduct experiments outside the laboratory situation; it is sometimes possible to have, as the saying goes, the best of both worlds. Researchers who are legitimately concerned with the artificiality of the laboratory situation often have the opportunity to conduct their experimental inquiries in natural settings. In the next section we examine some examples of field experiments.

Field Experimentation

Very often the phenomena or processes of interest to social scientists are not easily investigated in an artificial environment. It is difficult to study the development of group culture, consumer behavior, and the effects of mass communication, in experimental laboratories. At the same time sociologists, psychologists, and educators, aware of the multitude of factors that may inhibit their attempts to establish causal relationships between variables, want to utilize experimental models whenever possible. This is the primary rationale behind FIELD EXPERIMENTATION. More specifically, we mentioned in earlier chapters that one goal of social research is to use the knowledge acquired to formulate sound public policy. American society is beset by many problems that demand solutions. What is the best way to deal with poverty, racial segregation, delinquency, and the like? Very often we read about different programs suggested by citizens, social scientists, and legislators to ameliorate these ills. We must have some intelligent basis for choosing between alternative policies. There are situations in which social scientists may employ experimental procedures for gathering evidence about the likely success or failure of alternative proposals.

THE NEGATIVE INCOME TAX EXPERIMENT

As an example of a field experiment, we shall consider the case of the New Jersey negative income tax. The idea was first suggested in 1962 by economist Milton Friedman. Under the negative income tax proposal the federal government would pay out cash to families on the low end of the income scale so as to ensure a minimum to all in the country. The amount of money paid to a family would decrease as its income level increased. A family without any income might, hypothetically, receive $3,000. The negative income tax would subsidize a family while still providing some incentive to work. It has been suggested, therefore, that there might be a tax rate of 50 percent that would be applied to persons who are working but whose income still makes them eligible for government support. It would work this way: a family of four had an income level of $1,000, the 50 percent tax rate would demand that half of the $1,000 ($500) be subtracted from the guaranteed $3,000 baseline, reducing the government payment to $2,500; the total family income would then be $3,500. This hypothetical formula allows us to compute the total income for a family earning $2,000 as $4,000. Such a system would continue until the family's earnings reached $6,000, at which point no further subsidy would be paid.

There were a number of questions raised by opponents as well as proponents of the negative income tax. There was disagreement on what ought to be the baseline guaranteed income for a family of four. There was also a debate concerning what ought to be the tax on earned income for the same family of four. Disagreement existed around these technical features of the negative income tax plan because it was argued that these figures were crucial in determining whether the tax plan would kill any incentive for people to work. It was feared that if the subsidy were too high, people would be disinclined to seek employment. It was also felt that the different versions of the plan would have differential effects on family patterns of consumption, attitudes toward education, and so on.

Here, then, is a social policy plan with potentially great implications for the welfare and labor force participation of the poorest segment of our society. But there is confusion about which version of the plan would have what kinds of effects. Without any empirical data we would find ourselves accepting or rejecting a proposal without much sense of its potential effects. It is in the context of this ignorance that researchers endeavored to set up an experiment to find out the likely outcomes of the various plans. It seemed reasonable that one way to resolve some of the arguments was to let the different proposals themselves constitute experimental treatments.

The researchers designed their study to meet the criteria of a true experiment.

> Twelve hundred low income families [were selected] from four metropolitan areas in the state. These families have a number of characteristics in common in addition to the obvious characteristic that they are urban: each has a non-aged male head, an employable (although not necessarily employed) member, and a total family income below 150 percent of the poverty line.... Following a process of random selection, families are assigned to one of eight negative income tax plans in addition to a control group which does not receive payments.... Each of these families receives a regular cash payment for three years, the amount being based on the size of the family, the plan to which the family is assigned, and the current income of the family. In addition to these payments, each family will be interviewed quarterly for the three-year period. (Kershaw, 1969:17)

The purpose of the sequence of planned interviews was, of course, to measure various dependent variables of interest to the researchers, including family life style, the effort expended by people in looking for a job, and patterns of economic consumption. There are a total of nine groups involved, and it should be clear that it is a true experimental design. Families were randomly assigned to each of the nine groups, the different plans constituted variations of the experimental treatment, there was a clear control group that did not receive any experimental treatment, and there were a succession of measures designed to evaluate the effects of each test.

We should be quick to note that the experimental procedure outlined has its difficulties. There are several potential sources of bias. First, the families involved knew that they were participating in an experiment and this knowledge might affect their behaviors. Second, the study was designed to run for only three years and the subjects' knowledge of this fact may also have affected their behaviors. After all, no one could be complacent about a guaranteed income for life, because the experiment's termination date was known in advance. The employable members of these families were probably more motivated to seek jobs than they would have been if they had thought they would never again have to make any greater efforts at income production than they had been making when selected for the experiment. Related to these two points, the subjects were to be measured on various dependent variables a number of times during the course of the three years, and this frequent series of posttest measures might have some biasing effect. Even with these limitations, it seems clear that the experiment described should provide the most valid data possible on this complex problem—short of fully instituting a negative income tax plan.

The possibility of conducting naturalistic field experiments of the sort just described should be important to both social scientists and government officials concerned with social policy. Armed with powerful experimental procedures, we should not have to embark on social programs in ignorance of their possible effects or outcomes. If the government is about to institute a scheme that will entail the expenditure of billions of dollars, it does not seem unreasonable to invest a much smaller sum to determine the effects and viability of the proposed policy.

THE INVASION OF PERSONAL SPACE

Not all true field experiments involve the large expenditure of money necessitated by the negative income tax experiment. Filipe and Sommer (1966) have conducted a number of simple field experiments on people's use of space. In one of these studies, conducted at a state mental hospital, the investigators wanted to document people's behaviors when their personal space had been invaded. The violation of personal space was the experimental treatment. The experimenter would sit within 6 inches of randomly selected male patients who had been sitting alone on benches scattered throughout the hospital grounds. A comparable control group consisted of patients sitting by themselves who were left alone by the researchers. In both instances the experimenters quantified the rates at which subjects vacated their seats. Rates of vacancy in both experimental and control groups could be easily compared. The results of their elegantly simple experiment are expressed graphically in Figure 9.1.

If you have understood the techniques used in the two quite different field experiments just described, you should be able to guess without much difficulty the kinds of experimental procedures that have been devised in natural settings to study such diverse social phenomena as the effects of leafleting on political behavior (Hartmann, 1972), the effect of teacher expectations on student learning behavior (Rosenthal, 1963), and the effects of physician demands on the behavior

FIGURE 9.1   Cumulative Percentage of Patients Having Departed at Each One-Minute Interval

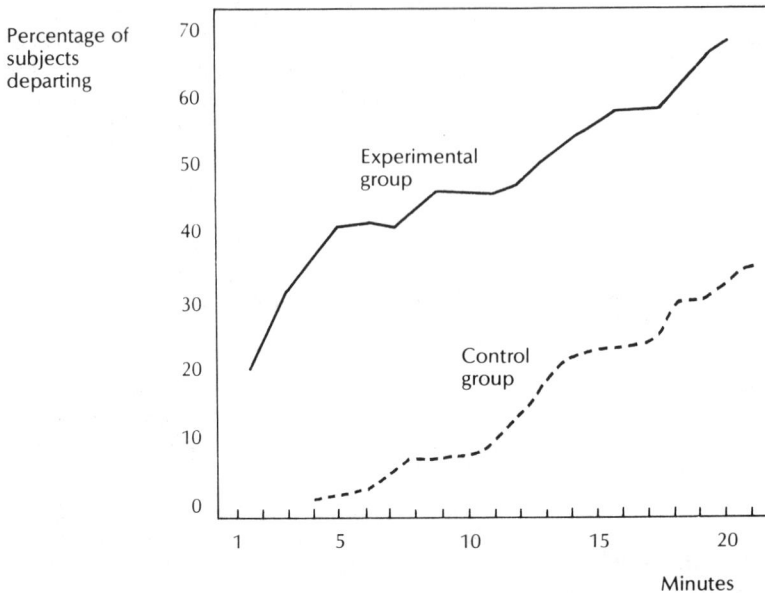

Source: Nancy J. Felipe and Robert Sommer, "Invasions of Personal Space," in *Social Problems* (Buffalo, New York: State University College, 1966) Vol. 14, no. 2, p. 210.

of nurses (Hofling et al., 1972). We have particularly meant to demonstrate through our examples that we need not think of the true experiment as possible only in the laboratory situation. There are instances in which we can create a kind of natural laboratory. There are situations in the natural world in which it is possible to randomize subjects and to make clear group comparisons. The investigator whose goal is to establish causal relations between variables ought to seek out these situations for natural experimentation whenever possible.

QUASI-FIELD EXPERIMENTS

Although the two studies we have described to this point meet the criteria of the true experiment, the problems that social scientists wish to investigate frequently do not lend themselves to this technique. Another strategy, therefore, is to perform QUASI-EXPERIMENTS, which stand in contrast to the true experiment in terms of the degree of control exercised by the researcher over possibly confounding extraneous variables. We have defined the true experiment in terms of three structural elements or conditions. When these three elements operate simultaneously in research design they afford researchers maximum control and give them justification for maximum faith in any causal assertions they make. In order to qualify as a *true experiment*, the project must meet the following criteria:

1. It must achieve its results through comparison of at least two groups.
2. It must assign people or subjects to groups randomly.
3. It must be constructed so the researcher has control over, or is able to evaluate, the timing of the experimental treatment.

Quasi-experiments are those in which all the elements of the true experiment are present *except for* the random assignment of people to groups.

A STUDY OF GROUP CULTURE. As researchers conduct their inquiries in natural field settings, they often find it either unfeasible or impossible to assign people randomly. Here is an example that will illustrate how and why this is so. Suppose researchers are interested in the formation of *group culture*.[2] Let us imagine that they have theoretical reason for believing that the development of group culture is enhanced or retarded by the relative success experienced by a group in realizing its collective goals. More explicitly, they believe that the more successful the group is in realizing collective goals, the more rapid and complete will be the development of a distinctive group culture. Conversely, the failure of a group to realize collective group goals will retard the development of group culture.

It would be possible for the researchers to set up their own groups through random assignment of individuals and then somehow to create a situation where these groups would be more or less successful in realizing artificially established goals. It would be possible, in other words, to create the conditions for a true experiment. In this case, however, the researchers have reason to believe that this kind of manipulation might have some distinct drawbacks. They recognize that the theoretical problem they have posed does not easily submit to solution through pure experimental techniques; the researchers see the difficulty of detailing the development of group culture in the short time they would be able to observe artificially created laboratory groups. Elaborated cultures simply do not develop in an hour or two, a day or two, or even a week or two.

At the same time the researchers realize the strength of experimental procedures in establishing causal relationships. They wish at least to approximate a true experimental procedure in testing their hypothesis. They decide, therefore, to look for some naturally occurring situation where they might be able to test their ideas. They are willing to give up some of the rigorous control afforded by true experimental procedure in order to study the phenomenon of interest in a more natural situation. They engage, in other words, in a trade-off. They know that it is virtually impossible to assess fully all the contemporaneous inputs from a natural environment that could affect behavior. They also know that by choosing to investigate already existent groups in some natural setting they will be unable to assign people to groups randomly; they will have no control over the composition of the groups studied.

To allow them to approximate the conditions of true experimentation, the researchers look for a naturally occurring context with the following characteristics:

1. a situation where they will be able to observe a number of groups from their inception over a long enough time period to see and somehow measure the development of group culture
2. a situation where, although people have not been strictly assigned to groups randomly, they might expect that the members of the various groups will not vary in any substantial respect
3. a situation where some groups are successful and others unsuccessful in realizing their collective group goals

---

[2]We are indebted to Gary Alan Fine for this example.

After giving considerable thought to whether there are natural situations where these three theoretically dictated conditions might hold, one of the researchers hits on an idea. Why not study the formation and operation of Little League baseball teams! Here, after all, one can observe a number of groups (teams) over time from the point of their very formation. The groups will all be of the same size. The age composition of the groups will be the same. Although the researchers will want to check out the procedure through which individuals are assigned to teams, they have no reason immediately to assume that there will be any gross or systematic variation in the background characteristics of the players from team to team. Finally, the researchers will not have to artificially manipulate the test variable—the relative success the groups experience in realizing their goals—since they can assume that the dominant goal for each group will be to win ball games, and it will naturally occur that some teams will be winners and others losers. As a matter of fact, they will be able to observe teams at a number of points along the continuum of goal realization because the better win/loss record of one team ensures that another team has a worse win/loss record.

THE STUDY OF ORGANIZATIONS. As a second example let us consider the kind of field experiment that can be conducted in large-scale organizations. Social scientist Max Weber (1947) noted that the trend of Western history is toward the ever-increasing bureaucratization of society. Virtually all of us find that a large portion of our daily lives is conducted within large-scale bureaucratic organizations. As students we are shaped in important ways by the educational establishment. Later on many of us take jobs and have careers that are carried out within the context of large-scale institutions. And as we move through our life cycle, we unavoidably come into contact with a variety of complex organizations: churches, hospitals, various government agencies, and so on. Since these entities so thoroughly dominate modern life, much effort has been expended in analyzing how they operate, how they influence us, and how we respond and adapt to them. In their studies of life in contemporary organizations, researchers have most commonly employed such methodological tools as participant observation of a single case, in-depth interviewing, the analysis of documentary materials, and sample surveys. More and more frequently, however, investigators (e.g., Evan, 1971) are seeing the value of adding the field experiment to their repertoire of methodological tools for analyzing organizations.

In institutional settings researchers must normally conduct their experiments on already existing groups. It would cause too much disruption if experimenters randomly assigned students to classes, employees to work groups, and so forth. In such cases researchers often use strategies alternative to random sampling. One such strategy designed to increase confidence in the initial comparability of groups is to be certain that the ones chosen match each other in obviously important respects. If researchers want to study the effects of a new teaching technique in grade schools, they will, at the very least, want to make sure that the classes chosen do not differ widely in such important characteristics as the racial, sex, age, and social class attributes of the students. To illustrate the type of organizational experimentation where a matching procedure was used, we will briefly describe a classic study on workers' resistance to organizational change.

In their early and influential work, Lester Coch and John French (1948) wanted to answer two related questions: (1) Why do people resist change so strongly? (2) What can be done to overcome this resistance? The study was carried out in a manufacturing plant employing approximately 500 women and 100 men. The workers, who were producing pajamas, were paid on an individual incentive system; that is, they were paid in terms of the number of "pieces" or units they produced. Because their pay reflected the efficiency of their individual production, the workers were very hesitant to change from one type of work to another, since the number of units they produced would decline while they were learning the new job. The policy of the company had been to give workers a "transfer bonus" when they were asked to change from one type of work to another. Presumably with this transfer bonus the factory operators would not suffer any loss of earnings while learning their new job. Nevertheless, workers were quite resistant to job changes and many preferred to quit rather than change. Believing that resistance to change stemmed from a combination of individual motivation and strong workgroup norms, Coch and French designed an experimental procedure to test whether *greater worker participation in change decisions* (the test variable) would lessen resistance to change.

The researchers decided to compare four already existing work groups—three experimental groups and a control group. In experimental group 1, a small number of employee representatives participated with management in designing their group's work changes. In experimental groups 2 and 3 all the workers participated in designing work changes. Changes in the work routines of the control group were made according to the traditional company policy. The researchers could not use random procedures in assigning workers to the four comparison groups and were, therefore, careful to choose four work groups matched with respect to:

1. the efficiency rating of the groups before job transfer
2. the degree of change involved in the job transfer
3. the amount of "we-feeling" (cohesiveness) observed in the groups

The results of this experiment demonstrated very clearly that the more participation the workers had in determining the nature of work changes, the less resistant they were to the change itself. In this study the dependent variable was a measure of how quickly the separate groups learned their new jobs and were able to produce pieces at an efficiency rate comparable to their rate prior to the transfer. Experimental group 1 (representative participation) showed a good relearning rate. During the period following their job change, they cooperated well with their supervisors. Also, none of the workers in this group quit their jobs during the first forty days following the work change. Experimental groups 2 and 3 (full democratic participation) learned their new jobs even more quickly than those in experimental group 1 and eventually produced at a level 14 percent higher than the prechange level. The control group, however, fell in its efficiency ratings and never improved during the forty days after the job change. Seventeen percent of the workers in this group quit within forty days of the job change. Moreover, "Resistance [in the control group] developed almost immediately after the change occurred. Marked expressions of aggression against management occurred, such as conflict with the methods engineer, expressions of hostility against the supervisor, deliberate restriction of production, and lack of cooperation with the supervisor" (Coch and French, 1948:522).

DEMONSTRATION EXPERIMENTS

We have been looking at how experimental procedures can be employed in real world situations. As part of our discussion of field experimentation we distinguished between true experiments and quasi-experiments. In quasi-experiments researchers are unable to use random assignment procedures in creating experimental and control groups. True and quasi-experiments do not, however, exhaust all the types of research that have been termed experimental. We should like to add to our discussion one other variation. In what we shall term DEMONSTRATION EXPERIMENTS, two of the criteria for a true experiment are not met. Demonstration experiments involve neither group comparison nor random assignment of subjects. Demonstrations, which may be conducted both in the laboratory and in the field, involve only the introduction of an experimental treatment in some group.

Despite the relative lack of control exercised by the researcher in conducting a demonstration, this variation of the experiment has produced some of the most compelling findings in the social sciences. Stanley Milgram's (1963) study of obedience and authority represents an outstanding example of the power of the demonstration to produce dramatic findings.

Recall that Milgram was interested in finding out the effects of authority on the willingness of people to administer punishments to others (see Chapter 4). Subjects who participated in Milgram's demonstration were told that the object of the research was to better understand how people learn. At the outset the subjects were each individually introduced to another person, who, they were told, was simply another volunteer like themselves. In fact, this second person was a confederate of Milgram's.

The real subject was assigned the role of teacher, and Milgram's confederate took the role of student. They were to occupy separate rooms, communicating by use of microphones. The subject taught his student, then tested him. For each wrong answer the student was to be punished by his teacher. The teacher punished by administering electric shocks, each one stronger than the preceding one. The teacher could only press the shock button, not control the voltage. Milgram stayed in the control room with the teacher.

The procedure was a deception. Milgram's confederate, the student, did not receive any shocks. As the voltage levels began to increase, however, Milgram did turn on a tape recording of a man indicating various degrees of pain—from slight involuntary pained sounds at the beginning to rather lengthy moans as the voltage increased with a succession of "planned" incorrect answers. As the moans became louder and more frequent, and the voltage indicator showed the shocks to be increasingly close to the "extremely dangerous" point, the naive subject would turn to Milgram and show concern, often indicating that he no longer wished to go on with the experiment. Each time, Milgram, who was dressed in an authoritative white lab coat, would simply express his wish for the subject to continue. In each replication of the procedure well over 50 percent of the subjects carried the experiment through to the end, administering what they believed to be extremely dangerous shocks to the learner.

One of the things suggested by Milgram's demonstration experiment is that in some situations people are capable of rather extraordinary behavior. Although most of us, if questioned, would say that *we* would never inflict that kind of pain on another human being, Milgram shows the power of authority in dictating our acts. Despite the nature and possible importance of findings such as those provided by Milgram for understanding, say, the behavior of soldiers at war, many have expressed concern about the ethical implications of the kind of demonstration described.

On the methodological side the Milgram example can be contrasted with true and quasi-experiments. In the latter two we find at least two clear comparison groups that differentially experience the experimental treatment. Such group comparisons are important because they help the researcher to pinpoint more precisely the extent of the subjects' change in some behavior or attitude following an experimental treatment. In the case of Milgram's demonstration, people certainly experience an experimental treatment. It is clear, however, that there are no discernible group comparisons to be made in terms of the intensity of treatment given. If there are any differences in the intensity of treatment received, they are controlled by the subject rather than the researcher. The treatment continues, in effect, as long as the subject is willing to continue in the experiment. The demonstration, and therefore the experimental treatment, ends when the subject decides that he or she will no longer administer shocks to another. The type of experimental research done by Milgram clearly "demonstrates," highlights, or illustrates certain features or aspects of human behavior (the willingness of persons to obey authority) and is highly informative on that level. The demonstration is, however, to be particularly distinguished from the true experiment in the following ways:

1. There are not clear comparison groups that experience different amounts or intensities of the same experimental treatment.
2. By definition, therefore, there is no random assignment of people to comparison groups. There is no control group.
3. There is no clear timing to the experimental treatment since it continues as long as the experiment itself continues.

These procedural or structural characteristics of the demonstration tell us something very important: it cannot be the goal of the demonstration to show causal relations between variables. Causality between variables may be strongly implied by the outcome of demonstrations like Milgram's, but given the structural conditions just outlined, causality cannot be as firmly established as is possible in a true experiment.

A Final Word

Norman Denzin (1970:147) has written: "In a fundamental sense the experiment is the point of departure for all other methods." It is fair to make this claim to the extent that a basic criterion used by social scientists in evaluating their methodologies is whether they can assert causal relations between variables. The certainty of social scientists' claims to causality rests in turn on how successfully they have been able to *control* those features of the world that could render their stated causal relations specious. We have meant to show that the experiment is the most powerful procedure available to us in achieving this control. This being so, we may use the true experiment as a baseline against which our other methods may be evaluated. It is not inconceivable that we could rank order our various methods in terms of the amount of control given up in their use.

The matter will not be resolved with such a simple ranking of techniques, however. Social scientists will inevitably have to attach to any of their findings, produced through whatever method, the silent caveat that these findings are true "all other things being equal." In short, they must learn to adopt a certain modesty about their research since they must live with the fact that in their investigation of the social world all other things will never be equal.

Indeed, this chapter on experimentation should help you to appreciate the enormous complexity of the social world. We have seen that the power of the experiment lies in the fact that it goes furthest in making all other things equal. At the same time we are forced to acknowledge that even in the most carefully controlled laboratory experiment, we cannot keep potentially contaminating factors out of our findings. We stress again the fact that no matter how elegantly we achieve an internal consistency in our methods, any methodology is, *by its very existence,* potentially reactive or biasing.

We should also note again the delicate tension existing between control over extraneous factors in our work and naturalism. As we achieve greater levels of control, as we reduce the possibility of variables unknown to us intruding into our findings, we simultaneously thereby create situations that resemble less and less the kinds of social situations in which people normally act. As we strive for naturalism, on the other hand, "all other things" become more and more unequal. We are caught in a kind of double bind. On the one hand, we want to strengthen our faith in any causal assertions we make. At the same time we must be concerned that the variables operating causally in contrived experimental situations may not operate causally as actors carry out their normal daily lives.

Summary

Scientific experimentation is distinguished from everyday manipulation and testing of the environment in that researchers create rigorous safeguards to ensure the correctness of the causal relationships suggested by their findings. The most important of these safeguards is to control for, or to rule out, all those factors other than the experimental treatment (independent variable) as influences on the outcome (dependent variable). To accomplish this, experimenters require carefully controlled conditions that are usually present only in the laboratory. In a true experiment, results are achieved through comparison of at least two groups to which subjects have been assigned randomly. The researcher alters the environment for one group (the experimental group) and does not expose the other (the control group) to the test variable. Subsequently, any differences in test scores, behavior, or other measures of the dependent variable, may be attributed to the experimental treatment itself.

The true experiment, if properly conducted, satisfies the minimum criteria for causality, in that independent and dependent variables are shown to be associated, the former precedes the latter in time, and this relationship cannot be explained away by the introduction of other, extraneous variables. There are, however, threats to the validity of experimental research that also threaten its ability to establish causal connections among variables. The problem is that subjects may react to uncontrolled internal and external stimuli or the experience of being studied. Moreover, unless they are careful, researchers may reveal enough of the rationale behind the experiment, or their own expectations for its outcome, to bias the results. Double-blind experimentation and variations on the classic experimental procedure such as the Solomon Four-Group Design are attempts to improve validity and control.

For some research problems and populations, laboratory experimentation is not feasible, and experiments in the field are possible. Some of these satisfy all the prerequisites for true experiments and many have valuable applications in the selection of appropriate social policies. But just as in the laboratory, there are dangers of bias. Quasi-field experiments meet the same requirements, except that people are not randomly assigned to groups. These experiments are useful for the researcher because it is often disruptive to enter a natural setting and create new groups artificially. Hence the investigator looks for groups and situations already existing in the real world that satisfy experimental conditions. Demonstration experiments are contrasted with true and quasi-experiments in that demonstrations do not contain two clear groups for purposes of comparison. Thus they cannot establish causality. Nonetheless, they may serve to highlight or illustrate significant patterns of human behavior.

The major limitation of laboratory experiments is that the conditions so carefully controlled for the purpose of establishing causality may in fact be so atypical or artificial that it becomes difficult to generalize from them to the outside world. Field experiments of various kinds have become increasingly popular precisely because of their greater potential for generalizability. In all kinds of experimentation, however, manipulation of subjects' behavior is a necessity, and in most it is an important part of the research design *not* to reveal critical details about the study. We must carefully consider the ethics of such deception. Experimentation has aided researchers in pursuit of a human science, but it must also be a *humane* science.

Key Terms

causal connection	external validity	pretest
control group	field experimentation	quasi-experiment
demonstration experiment	Hawthorne effect	random assignment
dependent variable	independent variable	self-selected subject
double-blind experiment	internal validity	stimulus
expectancy effect	measurement decay	subject mortality
experiment mortality	modeling effect	test variable
experimental group	posttest	true experiment

Exercises

1. In this chapter we briefly described the simple study conducted by Nancy Jo Filipe and Robert Sommer (1972) on people's reactions to violations of their personal space. Using some convenient context such as a public park or waiting room, try to replicate their study. You may find it helpful to read it in full before you try to set up your own experiment. Indicate in your findings just how well your own study supports the earlier findings of Filipe and Sommer. If your own findings differ significantly from theirs, try to explain the discrepancies.

2. Several years ago a woman named Kitty Genovese was murdered on a New York street while some thirty-eight people looked on without doing anything to help. No one even telephoned the police. This led many journalists to conclude that city living made people callous, indifferent, and uncar-

ing. Social scientists, however, were unwilling to accept this simple answer and began to do studies to discover the conditions under which people would either help or not help others. One interesting hypothesis tested was that the *more* people there are to witness someone in need of help, the less likely, or at least less quickly, will anyone help. The simple explanation offered was that each onlooker believes that someone else will help, and the result is that no one helps. There develops, in other words, a "diffusion of responsibility."

Suppose you wanted to test the diffusion of responsibility hypothesis. With a small group of people in your class, construct a field demonstration to test the hypothesis, carry out the experiment, and report your findings.

3. A longstanding theoretical idea in social psychology is that frustration leads to aggression. Describe the elements of a true laboratory experiment that could be employed to test this relationship. What would be the experimental treatment in your study? How would you measure the independent and dependent variables? How many groups would you study, and why?

4. In many studies experimenters deceive their subjects. In the case of Milgram's experiment on obedience, for example, subjects were led to believe that they were administering painful shocks to others. With regard to this and similar studies, people have raised strong ethical objections. What is your position on the ethicality of experiments like Milgram's? Do social scientists have the right to mislead "naive" subjects? What do you think are the limits of experimentation on human subjects?

5. An argument in this chapter has been that in the use of any social science methodology there is a continual tension between control on the one hand and naturalism on the other. Briefly answer the following in terms of this tension:
   a. Describe how maximum control is achieved through the use of experimental procedures.
   b. Make plain the relationship between control and establishing causality between variables.
   c. Indicate why experimental control is achieved at the expense of external validity.
   d. Discuss briefly the value of the field experiment in terms of your answers to a, b, and c.

6. Outline some of the major threats to internal validity in experiments, and then explain how elaborations on the classic control group/experimental group research design help researchers to evaluate the effects of these factors.

Suggested Readings

READINGS ABOUT THE METHOD

Campbell, Donald T., and Julian C. Stanley
1971 *Experimental and Quasi-experimental Designs for Research*. Chicago: Rand McNally.

In their much cited book, Campbell and Stanley exhaustively describe the various designs typically used in experimental research and the strengths and limitations of each research design. Although some of the discussion is highly sophisticated, the beginning student should have no trouble following their description of threats to internal and external validity in experimentation.

Jung, John, ed.
1971 *The Experimenter's Dilemma*. New York: Harper & Row.

The author explains some of the central threats to experimental validity. Separate chapters discuss such issues as the way people's behaviors are affected because they know they are participating in an experiment, the problem of sample selectivity in experiments, and the operation of modeling and expectancy effects. The reader will also find a series of essays written by prominent experimental researchers.

Plutchik, Robert
1968 *Foundations of Experimental Research*. New York: Harper & Row.

This clearly written text draws on examples from many areas of social science inquiry where experimental procedures have been used. The author illustrates the typical dilemmas faced by experimental researchers and then suggests rational procedures for solving them.

Wenglinsky, Martin
1975 "Feature Essay: Milgram's 'Obedience to Authority: An Experimental View.'" *Contemporary Sociology: A Journal of Reviews* 4 (November): 613–617.

Stanley Milgram's research on obedience has been highly controversial because of its ethical implications and its findings. In this review of Milgram's latest book, the author strongly takes issue with the idea that the willingness of the subjects in Milgram's experiment to follow his instructions to "shock" others can be taken as evidence of people's "evilness." The author suggests that experimental subjects simply play by what they see as the rules of the experimental game. This lively review is important because its implications go beyond an immediate critique of Milgram's research. The ideas contained in this essay cast some doubt on the external validity of any experiment.

Wuebben, Paul L., et al.
1974 *The Experiment as a Social Occasion.* Berkeley, Calif.: Glendessary Press.

A thought-provoking selection of articles and commentary with examples of experimental social psychology studies on attitude change and conformity. Major issues of both internal and external validity, and the ethics of the relationship between researcher and subject, are discussed.

READINGS ILLUSTRATING THE METHOD

Bickman, Leonard, and Thomas Henchy, eds.
1972 *Beyond the Laboratory: Field Research in Social Psychology.* New York: McGraw-Hill.

The authors have compiled a number of interesting experiments conducted in the field. Apart from their intrinsic interest, the studies included demonstrate the ingenuity of researchers who wish to combine experimental procedures with naturalistic observation. Many of the studies described could be easily replicated by students because they do not necessitate elaborate arrangements or expensive props.

Deutsch, Morton, and Mary Evans Collins
1951 *Interracial Housing: A Psychological Evaluation of a Social Experiment.* Minneapolis, Minn.: University of Minnesota Press.

In this well-known study, the value of using experimental procedures for planning and social policy is shown. The researchers examined how segregated and integrated housing patterns affected the attitudes of whites toward blacks. The study was conducted in two large-scale housing projects, one in New York and one in New Jersey.

Evan, William M., ed.
1971 *Organizational Experiments: Laboratory and Field Research.* New York: Harper & Row.

Evan has provided outstanding examples of both laboratory and field experiments. The reader ought to consider why most of the studies conducted in actual institutional settings fail to qualify as true experiments.

Replications in Social Psychology
1979 Volume 1, Issue 1 (Fall) and subsequent issues of this quarterly journal summarize experiments for purposes of replication. Each summary contains a useful bibliography of previous research. This journal may serve as a manual for beginning experimenters, as well as a resource for more experienced researchers who wish to confirm the results of earlier work.

Roethlisberger, F. J., and William J. Dickson
1939 *Management and the Worker.* Cambridge, Mass.: Harvard University Press.

This is the original report of the Hawthorne experiments on worker productivity. In recent years a renewed and lively debate has surfaced concerning the validity of the authors' findings. See H. M. Parsons, "What Happened at Hawthorne?" *Science* 183 (1974):922–932, and *American Sociological Review* 43, 5 (1978); 44, 5 (1979).

Werner, Carol, and Pat Parmelee
1979 "Similarity of Activity Preferences Among Friends: Those Who Play Together Stay Together." *Social*

Psychology Quarterly 42, 1:62–66.
An experiment that seeks to determine whether common attitudes or common activities are more instrumental in maintaining friendships. The results suggest that the opportunity to engage in mutually enjoyable activities may be a stronger motive in friendship choice and maintenance than the satisfaction of knowing the friend agrees with you.

References

Campbell, Donald T., and Julian C. Stanley
1963 *Experimental and Quasi-experimental Designs for Research.* Chicago: Rand McNally.

Coch, Lester, and John R. P. French, Jr.
1948 "Overcoming Resistance to Change." *Human Relations* 1:512–532.

Denzin, Norman K.
1970 *The Research Act.* Chicago: Aldine.

Evan, William M., ed.
1971 *Organizational Experiments: Laboratory and Field Research.* New York: Harper & Row.

Festinger, Leon
1971 "Laboratory Experiments." In *Research Methods: Issues and Insights,* ed. Billy J. Franklin and Harold W. Osborne, Belmont, Calif.: Wadsworth.

Filipe, Nancy J., and Robert Sommer
1966 "Invasions of Personal Space." *Social Problems* 14:206–214.

Hartmann, George W.
1972 "A Field Experiment on the Comparative Effectiveness of 'Emotional' and 'Rational' Political Leaflets in Determining Election Results." In *Beyond the Laboratory: Field Research in Social Psychology,* ed. Leonard Bickman and Thomas Henchy. New York: McGraw-Hill.

Hofling, Charles K., et al.
1972 "An Experimental Study in Nurse-Physician Relationships." In *Beyond the Laboratory: Field Research in Social Psychology,* ed. Leonard Bickman and Thomas Henchy. New York: McGraw-Hill.

Jung, John
1971 *The Experimenter's Dilemma.* New York: Harper & Row.

Kershaw, David N.
1969 *The Negative Income Tax Experiment in New Jersey.* Princeton, N.J.: Mathematica.

Milgram, Stanley
1963 "Behavioral Study of Obedience." *Journal of Abnormal and Social Psychology* 67:371–378.

Rosenthal, Robert
1963 "The Effects of Physician Demands on the Behavior of Nurses." In *Beyond the Laboratory: Field Research in Social Psychology,* ed. Leonard Bickman and Thomas Henchy. New York: McGraw-Hill.

Rosenthal, Robert, and K. Fode
1963 "Psychology of the Scientist: Three Experiments in Experimenter Bias." *Psychological Reports* 12:491–511.

Weber, Max
1947 *The Theory of Social and Economic Organization,* trans. A. M. Henderson and Talcott Parsons. New York: Oxford University Press.

10 / Historical Analysis

CHAPTER OUTLINE

INTRODUCTION
HISTORY AND CULTURE
HISTORY AND THE GROWTH OF
  KNOWLEDGE
SOURCES OF HISTORICAL DATA
Primary and Secondary Sources
A Comparison of History and Social
  Science
  Generalizability

USES OF HISTORY: SOME
  EXAMPLES
Analyzing Evolutionary Trends
  Changes in Urban Life
The Historical Case Study
Personal Documents
Life History Reports
The Use of Available Records
  Studies of Poverty in America

HISTORICAL ANALYSIS IN
  PERSPECTIVE
SUMMARY
KEY TERMS
EXERCISES
SUGGESTED READINGS
REFERENCES

Introduction

It is a fair assessment of American academic life that the practitioners of the social science disciplines have relatively little contact with one another. Sociologists, psychologists, historians, anthropologists, and economists normally define the boundaries of their respective fields fairly rigorously. In each there is a certain orthodoxy about the relevant questions for investigation and the methodological techniques and modes of analysis central to the particular area of inquiry.

Of course, the disciplines named share a concern with understanding "people in society." They differ from one another in terms of the features of that relationship that they emphasize. We might think of social life as a giant jigsaw puzzle and envision various investigators working on selected parts of it. There is, in other words, a rather extensive division of labor among the social sciences. It is a division of labor brought about by the impossibility of any one discipline being able to attend to the extraordinary number of parts making up the human mosaic.

Each of the social sciences seeks to establish a distinctive paradigm, or model, and to indicate the special problems and issues that are its own. Thus members of an academic field better succeed in affirming their expertise in the minds of others. Naturally, that is useful to one's career; more important, it also de facto establishes the importance of the discipline itself. Sharing a common paradigm facilitates communication among professionals and ensures that there is some knowledge used by the members of a discipline. Therefore, there is some consistency to the socialization of new members.

The division of academic labor exists not only between these "kingdoms" but within them as well. As knowledge grows, specialization within fields becomes nearly inevitable. Just as has been historically the case in professions like medicine, social scientists have become increasingly specialized. It is common in sociology, for example, for one to develop an expertise in a particular substantive area of investigation—deviance, stratification, large-scale organization, medical sociology, or small-group study. The specialization is not just in subject matter; there are also theoretical and methodological concentrations. It is now proper to speak of clear boundaries within each discipline itself.

We can view the development of this separatism between and within social sciences in two ways. From one perspective it is a natural and inevitable consequence of the explosion of knowledge in various fields. From another it may be, in fact, a weakening of our understanding of the human condition. The artificial distinctions maintained prevent us from developing a comprehensive, whole image of social life.

We submit, despite some social scientists' claims that there ought to be greater distinctions between various fields, that in fact psychology, sociology, history, and economics "pour into" one another. At the very least, the members of one discipline ought not to avoid using the concepts, methods, and modes of analysis of other disciplines when these could contribute to an understanding of a particular problem under investigation. This chapter contains a strong argument for the necessity of engaging in *historical analysis*. The inclusion of historical perspectives and methodologies as part of successful social science is not merely a matter of arbitrary choice; it is demanded by the rational acknowledgment that contemporary forms of human behavior all have, by definition, a history.

History and Culture

Researchers are accustomed to studying social phenomena at one point in time—the present. We ask how a particular institution is operating today, or what constitutes deviant behavior in a society today. These are certainly not unreasonable questions, but to answer them only in the form asked may limit our comprehension of contemporary events, situations, behaviors, or institutions.

"Social forms" do not appear spontaneously and autonomously. Every element of a society—from the individual to the complex organization—has a biography, a life history. We cannot escape the judgment that these elements are a product of their pasts. Moreover, social life is constantly in a state of transformation. If we are to expand our understanding of contemporary arrangements, we must look to the transformations through which they have already passed. An example should make our point clear. Let us look at the values held by the members of a society.

Whenever people behave according to their standards of what *ought* to be done—whenever they act according to what they believe is right, proper, decent, or moral—they are expressing their values. The fact that social scientists have found considerable variation between cultures regarding the central values of their members signals the need for historical analysis. We must think of value orientations as representing a society's long-term response to its total historical situation. Sparta's emphasis on militarism and courage, the high premium placed on youth and strength by Eskimos, the place of the work ethic in American society, cannot be understood apart from the historical and environmental factors that shaped those values. Max Weber (1958), in his brilliant historical analysis of capitalism, traces the origin of that economic form to the Protestant work ethic of Calvinist theology.

We may borrow from the writings of C. Wright Mills (1968) to further our claim for the inadvisability of segregating social and historical analysis. An outspoken critic, Mills expressed discontent with the nonhistorical nature of most social science research. As he saw it, the failure to view social phenomena in historical perspective was simultaneously a failure to exercise the "sociological imagination." According to Mills, this imagination is reflected in a concern with "problems of biography, of history, and of their intersections within social structures." He states his case this way:

> The biographies of men and women, the kinds of individuals they variously become, cannot be understood without reference to the historical structures in which the milieux of their everyday life are organized. Historical transformations carry meanings not only for individual ways of life, but for the very character—the limits and possibilities of the human being. . . . Whatever else he may be, man is a social and an historical actor who must be understood, if at all, in a close and intricate interplay with social and historical structures. (Mills, 1968:158)

For Mills the question of whether researchers should engage in historical analysis is one that ought not even be asked: "Unless one assumes some trans-historical theory of the nature of history, or that man in society is a non-historical entity, no social science can be assumed to transcend history" (Mills, 1968:146).

History and the Growth of Knowledge

In calling for a more extended use of historical data as a way of better understanding contemporary societies, we are not asking researchers to engage in analyses foreign to the tradition of their disciplines. Those writers who have provided us with some of the most important theoretical ideas nearly uniformly engaged in historical analysis. Indeed, it was unavoidable for nineteenth-century European scholars because the emergence of modern social science disciplines followed a major historical transformation in the organization of European society. It was the change from peasant agrarian to citified industrial society, a structural upheaval brought about by the French and Industrial Revolutions.

Sociology as an independent, autonomous discipline arose as certain social themes "called out" for analysis after these two revolutions. The themes of power, wealth, status, alienation, the division of labor, and the nature of community life emerged then and are still important today. Speaking of the French Revolution as a catalyst for sociological thought, Robert Nisbet (1966:31) has commented:

> The French Revolution was possessed of a suddenness and dramatic intensity. The stirring Declaration of the Rights of Man, the unprecedented nature of the laws that were passed between 1789 and 1795, *laws touching literally every aspect of the social structure of France*—were sufficient to guarantee to the revolution a kind of millennial character that was to leave it for a whole century the most preoccupying event in French political history. (Italics added.)

Particularly following the Industrial Revolution, the disappearance of the peasant community and the rise of cities caused thinkers to consider the changing basis for social organization. The Industrial Revolution thoroughly altered the condition of labor in society. Karl Marx, still a towering figure in contemporary economics, political science, and sociology, analyzed the developing factory system. His resulting contributions to our understanding of capitalist class structure are, of course, well known. With the growth of technology in large industrial cities, there appeared an extensive and complex system of occupational specialization. This became a theme for the theoretical writings of Emile Durkheim (1947), who, in *The Division of Labor in Society,* examined the changes we have described. Similarly, Sir Henry Maine's (1870) distinction between societies based on status relations and those based on contract relations, Ferdinand Tönnies's (1940) conceptualization of community and society, Robert Redfield's (1947) classification of folk and urban societies, and Max Weber's (1947) discussion of the increasing bureaucratization and rationalization of the modern world are all rooted in analyses of major social, historical trends. In significant respects these works reflect the images of history held by their authors. The concepts they generated remain among the major tools for the contemporary study of social change. Their work stands, therefore, as convincing evidence that the broad contours of modern society are best seen as part of a moving historical scenario.

To summarize the points made thus far, we may say that to study certain features of society in contemporary isolation severely handicaps our ability to answer two questions: (1) How and why have social forms come to assume their present shape? (2) What shapes are they likely to assume in the future? But before we overstate our case for history, its data, and methods, let it be plain that we are not arguing for a naive HISTORICAL DETERMINISM. We would not suppose that *every* present-day aspect of social life stands in a linear relationship to the past. If we try to see every feature of life as a function of historically determined events, we are misusing history.

Neither are we asserting that any research without a historical component to it is somehow improper. It is fully legitimate to study people's present attitudes, values, beliefs, and behaviors. Experimental social psychologists frequently inquire into processes of human behavior—conformity, aggression, patterns of leadership, and the like—many aspects of which can be understood without historical research. It is certainly proper and useful to explain the operation of contemporary large-scale bureaucratic organizations. We need to know how our school systems and mental health programs are functioning; how people adapt to the requirements of such institutions as prisons, hospitals, and homes for the aged; how the present legal system distributes justice; and so forth. We are merely suggesting that scientific researchers not shy away from historical analysis when they believe it could expand their theoretical understanding of whatever they are investigating. Most important, they should not refrain from using historical data merely because the methodologies with which they feel comfortable do not easily equip them to process these data. We must see the worth of adding historical methods to our already established bag of research tools.

The methodologies in use today do not easily allow for historical analysis. The questionnaire, for example, while it does permit researchers to query respondents about their pasts, has its greatest utility in uncovering respondents' present attitudes. Investigators using survey techniques sometimes engage in longitudinal studies, but even these are often of short duration and are not examples of historical research. Participant observation does allow the researcher to acquire a sense of process over time in a particular setting, but again the time frame is normally very limited. Experimental research is nearly always restricted to the investigation of behavior at one point in time. Social scientists do, however, use such techniques as content analysis of literature and inspection of institutional records and personal documents. In these instances they encounter data sources typical of historical research.

Sources of Historical Data

In the remainder of this chapter we shall consider some of the difficulties faced by investigators who choose to base their analyses on personal documents, commercial or confidential records, official government materials, and personal life histories. In order to evaluate the methodological problems one may expect to encounter in the use of such data, we must consider more fully the issues of reliability and validity that they raise.

PRIMARY AND SECONDARY SOURCES

The central methodological question researchers ponder when they work with historical data is: "How much faith can I place in the evidence? To what extent can I believe the data?" Obviously, the closer we are to the events we describe, the more certain we are of the validity of our data. There is a kind of "hierarchy of credibility" when it comes to believing that we have a correct picture of some event or behavior. If we have seen it ourselves—if we have been an eyewitness to the event—we are most confident that we know what went on. If we did not witness the event but heard a report from an eyewitness, our faith in the picture given is somewhat diminished, but we are still likely to find this firsthand account more credible than secondhand or thirdhand information. As the number of steps between the actual event and our hearing of it increases, our faith in the accuracy of the accounting diminishes. Since historical researchers can rarely be eyewitnesses to events extending a long distance into the past, the adequacy of their data becomes a preoccupying concern.

The evaluation of historical data, then, poses special problems of reliability and validity that do not normally confront the researcher who studies contemporary phenomena. A good deal of critical scholarship done by professional historians involves consideration of the validity of data recorded by unseen others. In attending to the distance that data sources stand from the actual events they describe, historians distinguish between PRIMARY DATA and SECONDARY DATA. We shall see that one of the quarrels historians frequently have with social scientists engaging in historical investigation is their overuse of secondary data sources when primary sources are available.

Gottschalk (1950:53) defines a primary data source as

> the testimony of an eyewitness, or of a witness by any other of the senses, or of a mechanical device like the dictaphone—that is, of one who . . . was present at the events of which he tells. A primary source must thus have been produced by a contemporary of the events it narrates.

Primary sources, then, are tangible materials that provide a description of a historical event and were produced shortly after the event took place. They may take many forms: newspaper accounts, letters, public documents, eyewitness verbal accounts, court decisions, and personal diaries. Secondary sources, in contrast, borrow the knowledge they contain from other sources, the evidence contained in them being therefore indirect or hearsay.

Let it be clear that even when social scientists have access to primary data sources, they cannot be certain of their validity. We must recognize that those who produce accounts of events, in any of the possible forms we have named, may do so with their own peculiar perceptions of the situation or with particular ideological or personal-interest perspectives. Journalists, for example, may report events in such a way as to sell the most newspapers. Even a seemingly dispassionate observer may unwittingly have adopted a position on a particular event. In dealing with any historical record, researchers must be aware that every statement or account is written from a definite perspective and for a specific purpose. There are some records, however, that, by their very nature, we can logically assume to be most accurate. We would expect there to be no intentional deceit or error in stenographic or taped records of courts, political bodies, or committees. Notebooks and other memoranda are also high in credibility because they are intimate and confidential records. When journals and diaries are written spontaneously and intimately, they are valuable historical documents. In other words, those documents that we can assume were written by eyewitness observers with no reason to believe that their accounts would be publicly shared are generally thought of as the least biased historical data sources.

A COMPARISON OF HISTORY AND SOCIAL SCIENCE

The major task of historians is "to keep the human record straight." Thus they frequently have a professional investment in establishing facts, for example, by determining the origin or genuineness of a document. In contrast, the social scientist is typically more concerned with *using* historical data than with generating them. Critical historical scholarship may begin and end with the determination that a particular record is authentic, that a document is still in its original form or wording, or that the purported author of a treatise was in fact competent to write it. Extraordinary effort may be expended in determining when or where a document was written. Historians may thus have to become knowledgeable about such fields as paleography (the science of ancient writing), epigraphy (the science of inscriptions and epigraphs), and philology (the science of ancient languages). On the other hand, social researchers, intent on placing the data in a larger framework, would less often be found engaging in this sort of scholarship.

Recently, historians have made use of statistical tools more customarily employed in such fields as economics and sociology. Perhaps they were influenced by the ingenuity of such statisticians as Frederick Mosteller (Mosteller and Wallace, 1964), who studied the disputed authorship of several of the Federalist papers. Hamilton, Madison, and Jay were the known writers, but some of the essays were left unsigned. Who wrote them—Hamilton, Madison, or Jay? Mosteller moved toward a solution this way: he looked at the grammatical structure and word usages in the known writings of each of the three persons. He discovered through this procedure a number of distinctive differences in their literary styles. He then took the disputed papers and subjected them to a statistical analysis designed to establish the frequency of certain stylistic conventions. By so doing, he could provide reasonably convincing evidence that it was one and not the others who wrote a particular essay.

GENERALIZABILITY. The argument has been made that historical events are spatially and temporally specific, that they are unique and nonrecurring. Those who support this idea of HISTORICAL SPECIFICITY point out that there was only one French Revolution and only one American Revolution. Strictly speaking, they contend that it is unwise to compare World War I with the War of the Roses, the Arab-Israeli War, or the Vietnam War. To do so is, as the saying goes, to mix apples and oranges. The supposition underlying this view of the uniqueness of historical events is that the social antecedents of each event are quite dissimilar.

Let us compare this notion of history with the discipline of sociology. Because it seeks after generalization, sociology is resolutely comparative. Sociologists typically center their investigations on recurrent or institutionalized social phenomena, events that repeat themselves in a similar form and thereby allow for comparative analysis. Deviance, for example, occurs in every society, and in every culture people are engaged in patterns of social interaction. In every society people can be compared in terms of their religious, ethnic, race, class, and age statuses. Does this mean that unique, historical data are inherently incompatible with the logic of social science inquiry?

The answer is that history and science, while not identical, are certainly complementary. It is true that events are best understood in terms of their immediate, specific historical contexts. We certainly would not suggest that one outcome of historical analysis ought to be the production of invariant social laws. On the contrary, we realize that one of the values of historical study is to relieve us of our contemporary provincialism. We sometimes tend to see all of social life as understood by looking at contemporary events. Social scientists sometimes write as if they have uncovered unalterable regularities in patterns of human communication, or in the structure of institutions, or in the causes of deviance by investigating their own societies at one point in time. Cross-cultural and historical analyses shake us from this unwarranted faith in the universal truth of much contemporary scientific research. Even if there are no universal historical laws, it is nonetheless possible to use historical data in the search for explanations of contemporary behavior.

One distinction between scientific investigation and historical research involves the scientist's concern with either *testing* hypotheses developed prior to data collection or *developing* theory from collected data. When sociologists or political analysts turn to historical materials, it is usually with the intention of revealing conceptual themes that have an applicability beyond the specific case(s) studied. Historians seem to be much more cautious in their use of data. Rarely do we find them attempting to test theory explicitly. They may offer reinterpretations of events, as did Charles Beard (1935) in his description of the economic motives of the drafters of the United States Constitution; but in few instances are historians willing to claim a wider conceptual significance for their findings. As we turn to a consideration of the types of historical research done by social scientists, keep in mind their claim to be able to move some conceptual distance from the data they collect.

Uses of History: Some Examples

What kinds of research problems warrant, perhaps demand, a historical approach? For purposes of convenience and clarity of organization, we shall examine historically based studies in the following categories:

1. attempts to establish long-term cultural trends
2. the use of historical case studies to test theoretical ideas
3. the use of personal documents and life histories as part of ethnographic reports
4. the use of available records to study institutional change.

We have two goals in mind as we proceed with a selective review of literature utilizing a historical approach. First, we hope to get a better sense of the place and importance of historical evidence for understanding contemporary social life. Second, we shall highlight the methodological problems awaiting the researcher who chooses to consider society in historical perspective. We turn now to social scientists who have endeavored to document long-term processes and regularities in the growth and development of social structures.

ANALYZING EVOLUTIONARY TRENDS

Classical writers were never particularly reticent about postulating global theories of change; such theories are in important respects also theories of history. August Comte (1896), who coined the term *sociology,* is probably most well known for his EVOLUTIONARY THEORY of the human mind, which he believed had passed through three historical stages: the theological, the metaphysical, and the scientific. Each of these stages, Comte thought, grew out of the previous one and would be reflected in the social organization of human life. Another evolutionary theorist, Herbert Spencer (1891), conceived of society as analogous to any other organism, reasoning that societal and organic growth and change could be understood in the same terms.

The failing of early evolutionary thinkers lay in their inability to explain *why* social change took place. Mere explanation by analogy, as in Spencer's case, did not constitute good scientific explanation. For this reason Karl Marx is often considered the first modern theorist of social change because his primary concern was to discover its *source.* For Marx the answer was to be found in an examination of history, an exercise that led him to write in *The Communist Manifesto* (1848) that "the history of all hitherto existing societies is the history of class conflict." Unlike Comte, Marx saw the evolution of society as rooted not so much in ideas as in material conditions. Men made history, Marx insisted, as they transformed these material conditions to their own benefit.

> History does nothing, it possesses no immense wealth, it wages no battles. It is man, real living man, that does all that, that possesses and fights; "history" is not a person apart, using man as a means for its own particular aims, history is nothing but the activity of man pursuing his aims. (Anderson, 1974:7)

As is well known, Marx postulated that the course of human history would be toward the development of a classless society.

An equally comprehensive view of history is to be found in the writings of Max Weber (1947). Weber's lifelong concern with the increasing rationality of the modern world is a theme that runs through his discussions of religion, authority relations between people, and especially his analysis of bureaucratic structure. Marx saw revolution leading to a one-class society as the future course of history. Ever-increasing bureaucratization was Weber's image of history.

CHANGES IN URBAN LIFE. The works of thinkers like Weber and Marx are voluminous and far too complex to analyze within the context of this book. It might be more helpful to turn instead to the recent research of Lyn Lofland. Her work is representative of the type that many modern sociologists are likely to conduct.

In her 1973 book, *A World of Strangers,* Lofland has tried to answer these questions: What is the basis for public social order in cities? How is the potentially chaotic world of biographical strangers transformed into a system of predictable social relationships? Her central thesis is that public urban order is achieved quite differently in modern cities from the way it was achieved in preindustrial and early industrial times. The transition has been from a primarily *appearential* order to the *spatial* order of present-day cities. "In the pre-industrial city, space was chaotic, appearances were ordered. In the pre-industrial city a man was what he wore. In the modern city a man is where he stands" (Lofland, 1973:82). We need not concern ourselves with her argument per se but rather with the kinds of data she must present to convince us of its correctness.

Clearly, Lofland's is a historical argument. She wants to show us through descriptions of both modern and preindustrial cities that there has, in fact, been a transformation in the ordering of city places. To make the comparison necessitated by her thesis, Lofland must reconstruct a situation that she obviously never experienced. She must create for her reader a picture of life in preindustrial and early industrial cities. Her object in one chapter is, as she puts it, to journey backward in time. Before we think about the threats to the validity of her presentation, we might ask why she chose to frame her analysis of modern cities in historical terms at all. Why didn't she simply present data on contemporary cities and leave it at that?

Historical comparison helps us to better see how our own lives are organized. We tend to take our daily routine for granted, and need the "shock" provided by history to see our complacency. Moreover, we should realize that Lofland's book is not just about cities; it is about people's need for order and intelligibility in their lives. It is only through historical comparison that we can see how people have continually adapted to and transformed their environment to produce this order. In a real sense all knowledge is comparative; here, it is the historical reference point that gives Lofland's analysis its power.

Now, however, we must ask the question always posed when historical data are presented. Can we be sure of their accuracy? As Lofland describes modern cities, we are in a position to judge for ourselves the adequacy of the picture given. We can always ask whether the description closely relates to our own experience. We cannot employ this validity criterion when presented with historical data. We must rely on the author's good judgment in piecing together, largely from secondary sources, an image of life in the earlier cities. As a researcher primarily intent on using the preindustrial city as a point of comparison, she cannot invest her energies in the arduous, time-consuming search for primary sources. Her work is, in a manner of speaking, a translation of translations. She selectively produces her picture of preindustrial city life from previously written histories. That selectivity itself suggests other questions.

The problem of validity is complicated as soon as the researcher seeks to do more than transmit the historical message as faithfully as possible. Clearly, Lofland was not merely intent on setting the factual record straight. Her sole objective was not dispassionately to create a picture of the preindustrial city. It was equally to use that picture for a purpose—to show that the most salient basis for order in that type of city was appearential. To do this, the author had to be selective, emphasizing the portion of the historical record that gave support to her thesis. Those who study contemporary events, through whatever method, will also be selective in their data reporting. For researchers who use secondary historical sources, the problem of selectivity is exacerbated somewhat for two reasons: (1) they must draw from the already selective reports of others, and as mentioned earlier (2) their judgment cannot be challenged by our own life experience.

It has not been our goal to question Lofland's rendering of history. We have used her study to illustrate an interesting case of specifying long-term historical transformations. We have also meant to raise some of the problems associated with secondary data analysis.

We urge the reader to examine other works, such as David Riesman's (1961) study of changes in American national character, Pitirim Sorokin's (1928) exposition of cyclical cultural patterns over a 2,500-year period, Karl Polanyi's (1957) description of the rise and fall of market economies, Carr-Saunders and Wilson's (1933) detailed treatment of the growth of professions in modern societies, Seymour Martin Lipset's (1963) analysis of the development of democratic institutions in the United States, and Richard Sennett's (1978) more recent exploration of human personality and the evolution of contemporary capitalism. Although these treatments of historical change and transformation vary considerably in content, you may, in evaluating them, want to raise some of the same questions as have been asked of Lofland's research.

THE HISTORICAL CASE STUDY

The issues confronted to this point should be helpful to you in thinking about the use of *historical case study* materials. The emphasis of this form of research is not so much on documenting trends over time as on examining in detail one reasonably limited set of historical events. Every social situation is a laboratory where some aspect of social life can best be studied. The past provides us some of our best social laboratories.

A superlative example of a historical case study informed by a theoretical perspective is Kai Erikson's *Wayward Puritans* (1966). Ever since classical theorist Emile Durkheim postulated the notion that deviance could serve certain useful social functions in a society, researchers have looked for evidence to support that contention. Erikson finds such evidence in seventeenth-century New England. He echoes Durkheim by showing how Puritan society needed its deviants in order to continually reaffirm the norms of propriety. Functional arguments for the importance of deviance are intriguing. They are a novel way of explaining how certain institutions, if not the society itself, continue to operate. Durkheim maintained, for example, that without sinners a church could not exist. The very existence of sin provides the opportunity for believers to reaffirm the faith that has been offended by the sinner. So, the worst thing that can happen to a church is to completely eliminate sin from the world!

By choosing a specific, dramatic case, Erikson showed how, to the extent that a common morality exists in a society, it comes to depend on its deviants for the maintenance of its social boundaries. These theoretical ideas can be applied to understand the witch hunts in colonial America. Relying most heavily on secondary sources, Erikson described how the "moral entrepreneurs" of early Massachusetts colonial society, in their zeal to maintain religious purity, launched full-scale crusades against alleged Salem witches. Anyone who did not fully identify with Puritanism suffered in these self-conscious attempts to delineate acceptable behavior in the society.

Although Erikson does not draw these parallels himself, we could say, on the basis of casual historical knowledge, that a number of additional cases might be used as illustrations of the functional view of deviance: the McCarthyism of the 1950s, the events leading up to the laws of discrimination against Jews in Nazi Germany, the internment of Japanese-Americans during World War II, and the antipathy expressed toward the hippies of the mid-1960s.

We should be motivated by more than just curiosity about the possible parallels in the historically discrete cases named above; there is an important methodological point to make. We know that no matter how interesting the researcher's rendering of one historical case, we are obligated to question the representativeness of that case. If, however, investigators can show that their theoretical ideas help to explain a number of cases, two things are accomplished: we are allowed to see underlying dimensions of historical events separated in time; and we have greater faith in the generalizations made from any one case. This positive outcome suggests a strategy for social scientists who see value in using history to test their theoretical ideas. They should be willing to conduct a number of case studies as a way of both understanding what happened in the past and continuing to amplify their theories.

Alternatively, historians might expand their own visions by looking at their data from a social scientific point of view. The difficulty of establishing such a reciprocal relationship is, however, considerable. Note the criticisms leveled at Erikson's research by two writers who find fault with *Wayward Puritans* on two related levels. First, they claim that because the author began his inquiry with a specific set of theoretical ideas he wished to test, he was caused to "misquote and misrepresent in his efforts to make the data conform to his theory" (Nelson and Nelson, 1969:149). Second, they maintain that Erikson used secondary sources too frequently when primary sources were available. They argue that he should have made much more extensive use of sermons, available diaries, and the like and that had he done better history rather than stopping "when he finds a secondary source that tells him what he wants to hear" (p. 150), his analysis and interpretation of the historical case would have been far more adequate. We do not consider these criticisms because we want to determine whether or not they are correct, but because they indicate the kinds of issues for which the social researcher utilizing historical data will likely be held accountable.

Erikson's (1969) reply to his critics is equally interesting. He has tried to make clear that his response to the Nelsons ought not be read as a quarrel between professional historians and social scientists. He admits quite readily that he has no training in historiography and that mistakes might have been avoided had he had that kind of training. He also admits to relying heavily on secondary sources but defends himself by saying that social researchers cannot spend their whole lives becoming intimately acquainted with a particular historical period since their goal is to produce comprehensive generalizations.

PERSONAL DOCUMENTS

Not all historical research must extend back a long distance in time. Rather, the period of interest may be quite recent, and the data very far removed from government reports and religious edicts. PERSONAL DOCUMENTS such as diaries, letters, and autobiographical statements have long been used in social research. Perhaps the most well-known example of this form of primary data in sociology is W. I. Thomas and Florian Znaniecki's (1918) study, *The Polish Peasant in Europe and America*. In this research the authors consider a longstanding theoretical problem, namely, how people adapt to new forms of social organization. Polish immigration afforded an excellent opportunity for understanding the modes of adaptation of people transplanted from a largely agrarian culture to a modern industrial one.

The research was based on the letters that immigrants sent to their families in the "old country." Speaking of that data source, Thomas and Znaniecki (1918:1832) wrote, "We are safe in saying that personal life-records, as complete as possible, constitute the perfect type of sociological material." Acquiring the letters through an advertisement in the newspaper, Thomas and Znaniecki were able to document the nature of the interaction between these persons and their distant families. The data, in effect, provided a continuous history of their New World experience. These letters allowed the researchers to assess dynamics of attitude change, changing relations within primary groups, and development of community life.

Much of the presentation in the two-volume work is thoroughly descriptive. Thomas and Znaniecki appear to have included, in an unedited form, every letter they were able to acquire. This is important because it gives their readers an overall feeling for the data, allowing them to judge the adequacy of the researchers' interpretations. At the same time we must be skeptical of the data. First, the letters obtained were necessarily selective. The researchers were able to use only those that the self-selected respondents who answered the advertisement saw fit to show them. Second, we must recognize that the authors of these documents may have had some reason for presenting the quality of their experiences in a particular light.

LIFE HISTORY REPORTS

As part of their effort to see the New World experience from the point of view of the peasants, Thomas and Znaniecki commissioned selected people to record detailed LIFE HISTORIES of themselves. In these documents, which read much like novels, the critical life events responsible for shaping subjects' perspectives were brought into focus. When contemporaries of Thomas and Znaniecki saw how persuasively the life history documents filled out the general ethnographic descriptions of the immigrant experience, they were led to adopt the life history techniques in their own later work. This was especially true of sociologists at the University of Chicago, who, as a group, were committed to discovering people's adaptations to city life. Clifford Shaw's (1930, 1931) recording of delinquents' life histories and Edwin Sutherland's (1937) analysis of the professional thief are two frequently cited examples.

Despite the applause these works have received and the acknowledged importance of the life history method (Allport, 1942; Gottschalk et al., 1945), there was little use of the technique between 1940 and 1970.[1] Perhaps we can account for this hiatus in terms of the historical development of American social science. As research relied more heavily on quantitative procedures after 1940, investigators may have come to feel that life history reports were too journalistic, too impressionistic, and not scientific enough. It is a mark of the maturity of social research today that more life histories are appearing (e.g., Bogdan, 1973; Rubin, 1976; Coles, 1977; Cottle, 1978; Coles and Coles, 1978). The fact that they lack the "hard numbers" that give the appearance of scientific investigation does not render them invalid.

Howard Becker (1970) provides a cogent scientific rationale for the use of life history data. He points out that these data are to be clearly distinguished from the more literary autobiography. When we read autobiographies, we do so with the recognition that authors select their material to present a particular image of themselves. We recognize as well that what an author considers as trivial or unimportant, and therefore chooses not to report, may be quite significant for the social scientist.[2] How then does the life history differ? As researchers gather life history reports, they do not simply rely on subjects to determine fully what will be said. Rather, with their particular theoretical interests in mind, they maintain a continuous dialogue with their subjects. Through this dialogue respondents are oriented toward specific kinds of events in their lives; clarification is demanded where ambiguities exist; and, where necessary, the scientist asks for more extensive descriptions of past events.

The life history must be used in conjunction with other data sources. If we were to rely solely on a few individual case histories to make our generalizations, criticism of our findings would be justified. Just as we must recognize the extent to which historical events are unique, so also must we suppose an individual's life history to be idiosyncratic in some respects. Used in conjunction with other techniques and data sources, however, the life history provides a penetrating, in-depth view of events. It is, in this respect, an extension of the traditional use of "informants" in participant observation research. Used with proper caution, personal documents and life history reports will further our effort to comprehend the intersection of history, individual biography, and social structure.

THE USE OF AVAILABLE RECORDS

As suggested, personal documents and life histories have their limitations as data sources.[3] Although we are able to get an in-depth view of people and events, we usually study only a small number of cases, and the data we acquire are relatively

---

[1]Three notable exceptions are Hughes (1961), Williamson (1965), and Coles (1967).

[2]Researchers may make good use of such works as *The Autobiography of Malcolm X* (1966) and Claude Brown's *Manchild in the Promised Land* (1965), but these sources pose special problems of selectivity that somewhat diminish their sociological value.

[3]For a more detailed discussion of several of the issues taken up in this section, see Chapter 12.

unsystematic. Analysts who wish to comment on the historical experiences of large groups or population aggregates must, therefore, turn to other data sources. AVAILABLE RECORDS have frequently been used by researchers to provide systematic historical data on large numbers of individuals. Although social scientists must live with the fact that records are usually not kept with the expectation that they will someday be used for historical investigation, a variety of official documents do exist that make possible the statistical analysis of sociohistorical trends. To get an idea of the types of records available, we may look briefly at the research concerns of those who do demographic analysis.

Demography is the study of population phenomena. Among other issues, demographers seek to document rates of fertility, patterns of immigration and migration, changing food resources in a society, birth rates, and death rates. They may examine trends or changes in these population parameters on any of a number of levels: for a selected part of society, for a whole society, for several societies—indeed, even for the world. Obviously, in order to produce their aggregate population analyses, demographers must rely exclusively on existing records.

Although the data are sometimes spotty or incomplete, it is possible to document population trends using such materials as census reports; international migration records; population registers; and records of such vital statistics as disease, birth, and death rates. By looking at population trends historically, demographers have shown consistent relationships between a number of these population characteristics and a society's level of economic development. It is by now a well-established "fact" that there is an inverse relationship between a society's level of industrialization and its fertility rate. Generally, as a society becomes more industrialized, people begin to have fewer children. The importance of such a finding for social policy formation needs no elaboration.

Since all their research depends upon existing records, demographers have been particularly sensitive to methodological problems. Although censuses, for example, are considered fairly reliable, we know that they will contain certain types of errors. Many people lie about their age or income. In the compilation of any record some people may be counted twice or omitted altogether. Those responsible for compiling statistics will incorrectly classify some of the cases. For political or ideological reasons "official" statistics may be altered. There may be errors committed unwittingly in *recording* data for official statistics. There can be a temporal problem in certain records: that is, the statuses of a good number of people will change over time (e.g., marital status, citizenship) and the changes will not be reflected in the records we use. Demographers have taken steps to estimate the degree and direction of these various errors in their data. It is impossible to make aggregate data records error free, but it is possible to be cognizant of likely errors in the data and to consider them in assessing the significance of findings.

We have named only a small number of the official record sources employed by the social scientist who wishes to establish statistical trends over time. To those mentioned, we would add the following: voting records; lists of school enrollment; city directories; telephone directories; tax payment records; unemployment figures; sports attendance figures; records of local, state, and national government expenditures; records of police arrests; congressional proceedings; and, of course, codified law. Imagine the kinds of historical trends of potential theoretical significance that could be established using these records. Using telephone directories, it would be conceivable to assess changes in the ethnic composition of an area; records of police arrests may be used to establish how the nature and type of criminal activity have changed over time; the use of voting records to reflect ideological change in the country has been a traditional preoccupation of social scientists.

STUDIES OF POVERTY IN AMERICA. Now that we have some idea of the types of records available for historical analysis, we can illustrate their use in two studies, each one dealing with a different aspect of poverty in America. Both rely on available historical records. Both lend validity to the central point of this chapter—that an understanding of contemporary social forms will be increased by seeing how they stand in a broader historical context.

Much of the literature documenting the degree, nature, and amount of poverty in the United States asserts that the plight of the poor today is of a quite different nature from the poverty of early immigrants. The argument goes that immigrants really were, and perceived themselves to be, in an opportunity-filled society. Consequently, they viewed their poverty status as a temporary one and lived out their lives feeling reasonably certain that if things did not get much better for themselves, certainly their children would be better off economically. Today's poor have been thought to view their disadvantaged economic situation as a permanent one. Although this "new poverty" thesis achieved considerable influence among American academics, the truth of its historical comparison had never been put to the test. Stephan Thernstrom (1968), in an attempt to look at poverty in historical perspective, tried to assess the experience of immigrants to America in the late nineteenth and early twentieth centuries. In doing so, he made use of several data sources.

Thernstrom began his analysis by examining the historical record in Newburyport, Massachusetts, a typical turn-of-the-century manufacturing city that attracted large numbers of immigrants. He combed through census schedules, tax lists, and savings bank records in order to get some general clues about the welfare status of the newcomers. In order to identify this part of a working-class culture, he created a social-class index based on existing records of family property holdings. He was able to uncover records that indicated, for a statewide sample of unskilled laborers in Massachusetts in 1874, the mean annual wage of a family head. Seeing at one point the need to determine the numbers of unskilled workers who left Newburyport, Thernstrom compared the appropriate sections of the census reports over time—in 1850, 1860, and 1870. Part of his task was to look at patterns of occupational mobility. In order to obtain a representative sample of people whose patterns of mobility would be examined, he drew names (presumably in a random fashion) from 1910 marriage license records. He drew another sample randomly from birth certificates. We have given only a portion of the sources from which Thernstrom derived the evidence that allowed him to reject the "new poverty" thesis. To discover exactly how collected data were used to make sense of the historical period, the reader is referred to the original research.

In *Regulating the Poor* (1971), Frances Fox Piven and Richard Cloward also create a historical analysis of poverty. The purpose of their research was, however, quite different from Thernstrom's. Through a combination of history, political interpretation, and sociological analysis, they endeavored to explain the recent, rather dramatic increases in the number of people receiving public welfare. They made it plain at the outset, however, that their concern was not simply with describing the welfare system. Rather, they wished to see how the welfare institution in the United States has been linked to other major social institutions; how it functions today and has functioned in the past to serve the larger political and economic order. Their historical analysis traced the welfare system in the United States from the Great Depression to the present, revealing a distinctive pattern of relief policy; at certain times relief policy has been quite liberal and at other times highly restrictive.

The major thesis, which is convincingly documented through their historical investigation, is that the welfare system has been used to control and regulate the poor. "Historical evidence suggests that relief arrangements are initiated or expanded during occasional outbreaks of civil disorder produced by mass unemployment, and are then abolished or contracted when political stability is returned" (Piven and Cloward, 1971:xiii). It is by examining the operation of the welfare system in historical perspective that we can comprehend the explosion of welfare programs following the civil disturbances of the early 1960s.

Starting out with a comprehensive historical analysis based on the writings of professional historians, Piven and Cloward found that the initiation of welfare systems was a response to the "mass disturbances that erupted during the long transition from feudalism to capitalism beginning in the sixteenth century" (p. 8). In considering the beginnings of the relief system in the United States, the researchers examine a variety of historical data sources: newspaper accounts of the tenor of the society in the 1930s, official unemployment statistics, average wage figures, congressional records, accounts of Senate debates, voting records, and, of course, expenditures for various forms of public relief. As they piece together the relationship between stability in society over time and the expansion or retraction of relief programs, the argument that relief programs have had the function of "diminishing proclivities toward disruptive behavior" (p. 348) becomes compelling.

Historical Analysis in Perspective

A wide range of social problems may indeed be investigated historically. As we may infer from the variety of examples presented, history may be used by researchers in many ways. It is inappropriate to delineate a constant and rationalized set of procedures for collecting or processing data from the past. We find that many of the research methods considered elsewhere in the text can be used in historical analysis, but some (such as content analysis) lend themselves to the enterprise more readily than others (such as experimentation).

Historical research has much in common with such unstructured procedures as participant observation. In both cases the investigator proceeds by making use of any available materials that will enrich insight into the events or processes being examined. As the situations studied change, the available data sources change and so also do the methodological problems. Despite these variations, two questions remain constant in our evaluation of any social scientist's historical investigation: How much faith can we have in the accuracy of the historical picture given? And are the generalizations made from the historical cases legitimate?

Despite these problems, it is undeniable that a comparative historical perspective helps us see with greater clarity both ourselves and the social structures within which we carry out our lives. In recent years considerable progress has been made in the collection and preservation of historical materials. As social scientists begin to acquaint themselves more fully with these data sources, they will benefit from discussions with historians about the historiographic methods that will ensure the proper use of the data. Historians, in turn, can profit by considering how social, political, and psychological theories might inform their interpretations of the past. Such a happy rapprochement depends on the willingness of social scientists to risk looking beyond the "conventional wisdoms" produced through the evolution of their respective disciplines.

Summary

Social scientists' appreciation of history, and of the value of historical data, is a most important interdisciplinary goal. Indeed, it is impossible fully to understand contemporary human behavior without some reference to the evolving cultures from which it emanates. The motives behind human behavior are revealed through history, because culture contains the values, aspirations, and dreams of people, as well as a record of their concrete achievements. The origins of modern social science are found in the attempts of classical writers to wrestle with broad and important historical questions, an important component of the creation of knowledge, which may be forgotten in the ahistorical and narrow thrust of much contemporary investigation. It is wise to steer a path between historical determinism on the one hand and an unwarranted faith in the universal truth of much of today's scientific research on the other.

Sources of historical data include government documents, diaries and personal histories, business records and official demographic surveys. Many of the data are from secondary, rather than primary, sources. Potential validity problems are created whenever events are not directly observed or when accounts are recorded for purposes other than the researcher's. Difficulties in determining the accuracy of data and in generalizing from information obtained selectively are present in all methods of social research. Historical data pose special problems and are most effectively used when combined with other types of information. Professional historians are typically more concerned with "getting the record straight" than with *using* historical data to test or create theory. They have criticized social scientists for using secondary sources when primary data were available. Clearly, to maximize validity, historians and social scientists need to combine their efforts.

Countless social problems may be effectively examined via historical analysis, and the number of different uses of historical data is almost as great. Case studies, personal documents, life history reports, and available records are but four sources of what happened in the past, and why.

Key Terms

available records	historical determinism	personal documents
evolutionary theory	historical specificity	primary data
historical case study	life history reports	secondary data

Exercises

1. Go to the library and read five different newspapers. Choose papers that differ in length and circulation. You might want to include the *Christian Science Monitor, The New York Times,* a local newspaper, and your campus newspaper. Describe how these papers differ. Are there differences in how national events are reported? Does each paper have a distinctive ideological perspective?

Speculate on how a historical research report might be affected if the investigator relied on only *one* of these papers as the data source for a study.

2. Imagine that administrators in your college have an interest in producing a short history of the college (how, why, and when it started; what its growth has been like; and so on) and have commissioned a group of students in your class to begin collecting preliminary data. With two or three other students, work out some division of labor for collecting whatever institutional records might be applicable to this particular problem. Without doing any in-depth analysis, write a brief report indicating the kinds of materials available for such a study. Also indicate the kinds of information you would like to have about the history of the institution that do not appear in available materials.

3. As an exercise in realizing the variability in eyewitness accounts, ask several people to give you an account of what went on in a particular meeting or class you did not attend. Write down the accounts immediately after the class or meeting, and interview a few other people a day or two later.

In what way(s) do the reports of your informants differ? What are the points of similarity? Did those with whom you spoke immediately after the event give more detailed accounts? What do the "data" lead you to say about the difficulties of relying on only one or a few eyewitness accounts in historical research? What methodological recommendations would you make to increase the validity of information acquired via eyewitness reports?

4. Read one or two research reports written by historians and one or two written by sociologists. (You might find it convenient to find these reports in Cahnman and Boskoff's *Sociology and History,* 1964, in the Suggested Readings.) Then answer the following questions:

a. Make a list of the types of historical sources used in the studies. Are they primary or secondary sources?

b. Do the reports differ in terms of the types of generalizations the authors attempted to make from their collected data?

c. What conclusions might be reached about differences in orientation of sociologists and historians?

5. Suppose that one of your roommates was writing a term paper on the segregation of minority groups in large cities and was planning on relying solely on the most recent census data to write the paper. What arguments would you use to persuade your roommate that the term paper could be strengthened if the recent census data were complemented by a broader historical approach?

6. C. Wright Mills is quoted in this chapter as follows: "Unless one assumes some trans-historical theory of the nature of history, or that man in society is a non-historical entity, no social science can be assumed to transcend history." State in your own words what you believe is the significance of Mills's statement. Do you agree or disagree with the statement? Why? Why not?

7. Perhaps you or some fellow students wrote diaries when you were between the ages of 12 and 16. If you can find classmates who have saved these personal accounts and who are willing to share them, construct a social history using the diaries as data. What are the strengths and limitations of this source of information? See Gottschalk et al. (1947) for some guidelines.

Suggested Readings

READINGS ABOUT THE METHOD

Cahnman, Werner J., and Alvin Boskoff
1964 "Sociology and History: Reunion and Rapprochement." In *Sociology and*

History, ed. Werner Cahnman and Alvin Boskoff. New York: Free Press. This article sets the tone for a very worthwhile set of readings on the use of history in sociology. It is a strong, cogent statement of the need for historical sociology. The remainder of the book provides interesting examples of the application of sociological theory and methodology to historical materials.

Denzin, Norman K.
1978   "The Comparative Life History Method." In *The Research Act,* ed. Norman K. Denzin. 2nd ed. New York: McGraw-Hill.

This chapter is the most comprehensive treatment of the methodology of life histories. It includes a discussion of the sources of data; guidelines for collecting data; and sampling, reliability and validity problems associated with the technique.

Gottschalk, Louis, Clyde Kluckhohn, and Robert Angell
1947   *The Use of Personal Documents in History, Anthropology, and Sociology.* New York: Social Science Research Council.

In recent years social scientists have not paid very much attention to personal documents such as diaries as a data source for research. This book deserves to be rediscovered for it systematically presents a discussion of their use and importance.

Lipset, Seymour M., and Richard Hofstadter, eds.
1968   *Sociology and History.* New York: Basic Books.

The authors present some outstanding examples of interdisciplinary research. These essays present further verification of the advantages of combining historical and sociological approaches.

Mills, C. Wright
1968   *The Sociological Imagination.* New York: Oxford University Press.

Of particular interest here is the chapter entitled "The Uses of History," which is well worth reading in full. Mills demonstrates the central

place of a historical perspective in the creation of the "sociological imagination."

Social Science Research Council
1954   *The Social Sciences and Historical Study.* New York: Social Science Research Council.

Recognizing the need for more historical research in the social sciences, the council created a special panel in the early 1950s to discuss and report on points of conjunction in research. Most of the ideas and suggestions still apply today.

Stinchcombe, Arthur L.
1978   *Theoretical Methods in Social History.* New York: Academic Press.

In this lively and provocative book, the author urges social scientists to use history to develop theories of human behavior intead of merely applying already existing theory to history. Four classic studies of revolution and social change are analyzed in order to discredit the idea of historical specificity. Stinchcombe shows how "causally significant analogies" between historical instances were drawn in each of these studies. He argues that it is possible to construct social theories in the process of doing historical research, using sequences of events as a guide.

Winks, Robin, ed.
1969   *The Historian as Detective: Essays on Evidence.* New York: Harper & Row.

The articles in this book deal with the actual mechanics of conducting historical research. Special emphasis is given to the problems involved in the collection and verification of historical materials. Among the topics discussed are: difficulties in obtaining necessary materials, detecting inconsistencies in historical records, and verification of historical evidence. The reader will also find descriptions and discussion of famous historical frauds.

READINGS ILLUSTRATING THE METHOD[4]

Erikson, Kai T.
1976   *Everything in Its Path.* New York: Simon and Schuster.

Erikson uses historical data combined with respondent interviews in order to explain the full impact of a devastating flood in Buffalo Creek, West Virginia. His sensitivity to cul-

---

[4]See the references for this chapter for additional examples of historical research.

ture and the manner in which the historical experience of a people shapes their personal psychology is worthy of the high standard set in his earlier work, *Wayward Puritans*.

Fogel, Richard, and Stanley Engerman
1974   *Time on the Cross: Evidence and Methods*. Boston: Little, Brown.

This book has been controversial because of the methods used by the authors and their findings. Computer technology was employed to analyze a variety of historical documents, and the statistical results led Fogel and Engerman to conclude that slavery was a much more benign institution than is generally thought by most historians. Scholars have engaged in considerable debate over the significance of this work.

Genovese, Eugene D.
1974   *Roll, Jordan, Roll: The World the Slaves Made*. New York: Pantheon Books.

Writing from a neo-Marxist theoretical perspective, the author combines historical data with sociological theory to analyze how slaves constructed a livable world for themselves under very harsh conditions. This book shows the utility of historical analysis for helping us to better understand such contemporary aspects of black culture as its stratification system, its family structure, and its relation to the larger society.

Handlin, Oscar
1968   *Boston's Immigrants*. New York: Atheneum Press.

In this study Handlin attempts to explore the factors influencing the economic, physical, and social adjustments made by immigrants to Boston between 1790 and 1880. Among the data sources used for the study were: newspapers of the period (especially the immigrant press); city, state, and federal census materials; records of town meetings; and immigrant registration records.

Sennett, Richard
1970   *Families Against the City*. Cambridge, Mass.: Harvard University Press.

In this historical study of nineteenth-century city life, Sennett examines such diverse topics as class and mobility patterns, urban power structures, and the relation of these patterns and structures to family life. Sennett tries to show how studying the situation of the family in the nineteenth century gives us a better understanding of contemporary city experiences.

Shaw, Clifford
1931   *The Jack-Roller*. Chicago: University of Chicago Press.

In this early study Shaw used the life history method to understand some of the factors involved in adolescent delinquency. The study focuses on the life of one adolescent and contains fascinating, in-depth descriptive material. Aside from the intrinsic interest of the book, it provides a model for those who would employ this method.

References

Allport, Gordon
1942   *The Use of Personal Documents in Psychological Science*. New York: Social Science Research Council.

Anderson, Charles
1974   *The Political Economy of Social Class*. Englewood Cliffs, N.J.: Prentice-Hall.

Beard, Charles
1935   *An Economic Interpretation of the Constitution of the United States*. New York: Macmillan.

Becker, Howard S.
1970   "The Relevance of Life Histories." In *Sociological Methods: A Casebook*, ed. Norman K. Denzin. Chicago: Aldine.

Bogdan, Robert
1973   *Being Different: The Autobiography of Jane Fry*. New York: Wiley.

Brown, Claude
1965   *Manchild in the Promised Land*. New York: New American Library.

Carr-Saunders, A. M., and P. A. Wilson
1933   *The Professions*. Oxford: Clarendon Press.

Coles, Robert
1967   *Migrants, Sharecroppers, Mountaineers*. Boston: Little, Brown.

1977   *Eskimos, Chicanos, Indians*. Boston: Little, Brown.

Coles, Robert, and Jane H. Coles
1978   *Women of Crisis*. New York: Delcorte Press/Seymour Laurence.

Comte, Auguste
1896 *The Positive Philosophy of Auguste Comte.* London: Bell.
Cottle, Thomas J.
1978 *Private Lives and Public Accounts.* New York: New Viewpoints.
Durkheim, Emile
1947 *The Division of Labor in Society.* Glencoe, Ill.: Free Press.
Erikson, Kai
1966 *Wayward Puritans: A Study in the Sociology of Deviance.* New York: Wiley.
1969 "Response to the Nelsons' 'Case Example.'" *American Sociologist* (May):151–154.
Gottschalk, Louis
1950 *Understanding History: A Primer of Historical Method.* New York: Knopf.
Gottschalk, Louis, Clyde Kluckhohn, and R. Angell
1945 *The Use of Personal Documents in History, Anthropology, and Sociology.* New York: Social Science Research Council.
Hughes, H.
1961 *The Fantastic Lodge.* Boston: Houghton Mifflin.
Lipset, Seymour M.
1963 *The First New Nation.* New York: Basic Books.
Lofland, Lyn
1973 *A World of Strangers.* New York: Basic Books.
Maine, Sir Henry
1870 *Ancient Law.* London: John Murray.
Malcolm X
1966 *The Autobiography of Malcolm X.* New York: Grove Press.
Mills, C. Wright
1968 *The Sociological Imagination.* New York: Oxford University Press.
Mosteller, Frederick, and David L. Wallace
1964 *Inference and Disputed Authorship: The Federalist.* Reading, Mass.: Addison-Wesley.
Nelson, Ann, and Hart Nelson
1969 "Problems in the Application of Sociological Method to Historical Data: A Case Example." *American Sociologist* (May):149–151.
Nisbet, Robert
1966 *The Sociological Tradition.* New York: Basic Books.

Piven, Frances, and Richard Cloward
1971 *Regulating the Poor: The Functions of Public Welfare.* New York: Random House (Vintage).
Polanyi, Karl
1957 *The Great Transformation.* Boston: Beacon Press.
Redfield, Robert
1947 "The Folk Society." *American Journal of Sociology* (January):293–308.
Riesman, David, Nathan Glazer, and Reuel Denney
1961 *The Lonely Crowd.* New York: Anchor Books.
Rubin, Lillian Breslow
1976 *Worlds of Pain.* New York: Basic Books.
Sennett, Richard
1978 *The Fall of Public Man.* New York: Vintage.
Shaw, Clifford
1930 *The Jack-Roller.* Chicago: University of Chicago Press.
1931 *The Natural History of a Delinquent Career.* Chicago: University of Chicago Press.
Sorokin, Pitirim
1928 *Contemporary Sociological Theory.* New York: Harper & Row.
Spencer, Herbert
1891 *The Study of Society.* New York: Appleton.
Sutherland, Edwin
1937 *The Professional Thief.* Chicago: University of Chicago Press.
Thernstrom, Stephan
1968 "Poverty in Historical Perspective." In *On Understanding Poverty*, ed. Daniel P. Moynihan. New York: Basic Books.
Thomas, W. I., and Florian Znaniecki
1918 *The Polish Peasant in Europe and America.* Chicago: University of Chicago Press.
Tönnies, Ferdinand
1940 *Fundamental Concepts of Sociology.* New York: American Book.
Weber, Max
1947 *The Theory of Social and Economic Organization.* New York: Oxford University Press.
1958 *The Protestant Ethic and the Spirit of Capitalism.* New York: Scribner.
Williamson, Henry
1965 *Hustler.* New York: Doubleday.

11 / Content Analysis

CHAPTER OUTLINE

INTRODUCTION
AN OVERVIEW OF THE METHOD
Objective Analysis
Systematic Analysis
Quantitative Technique
Manifest and Latent Content
APPLICATIONS OF CONTENT
  ANALYSIS
Inferences to the Source of
  Communications

Inferences to Populations:
  Communication Content and
  Social Values
Evaluating the Effects of
  Communications
Content Analysis and Structured
  Observation
PERFORMING CONTENT
  ANALYSIS
Specification of the Research Problem
Sampling Items

Choosing the Unit of Analysis
Category Construction
COMPUTER-ASSISTED CONTENT
  ANALYSIS
THE TECHNIQUE IN
  PERSPECTIVE
SUMMARY
KEY TERMS
EXERCISES
SUGGESTED READINGS
REFERENCES

Introduction

The study of communication content has a long tradition in social science. It has revealed significant information about the values of both communicators and their audiences. The extraction of thematic data from a wide range of communications is called *content analysis*. In this chapter we shall consider the major elements of this methodology, offer some examples of its application, and discuss some of the reliability and validity issues that arise for the investigators who use it.

The primary modes of communication in society are words and pictures; these may be expressed in a variety of forms, more or less permanent, persuasive and artistic. It is the extraordinary capacity of humans for symbolic communication (recent research on chimpanzees notwithstanding) that sets us apart from the other animals. Without language human culture would be impossible. Because it allows us to express and to arouse emotion, as well as to convey values, attitudes, and knowledge, language is the key factor in the creation of societies. It is only through language that abstract insights can be formulated as knowledge and then transmitted and shared with others. It is, in other words, through language that knowledge becomes a collective social possession rather than an individual possession. The continuance of culture depends on each generation's communicating its abstract knowledge to the next.

Nearly from the beginning, persons have sought to codify their thoughts and accumulated knowledge. Writing must, in this context, be seen as one of the most profoundly important of human inventions. It is in written communications, from the first stone scratches on cave walls to today's enormous variety of mass-produced printed media, that we find preserved our beliefs, values, under-standings of the world, and images of ourselves. Further, the written word is not merely a record of behavior—it is itself a form of behavior. We may seek through our writing to convince others of a point of view, to change attitudes, to manipu-late others, to motivate action, and so on.

Writing is, of course, only one medium of communication in contemporary society. Our lives are importantly shaped by art and architecture, movies, radio, and most especially television. The power of television to communicate both orally and visually an extraordinary assortment of factual information, ideas, beliefs, and values to millions of people at one time has created revolutionary change in modern society. Television now plays a significant role in the socialization of children. It shapes our knowledge and interpretation of social events. To the extent that it influences our buying habits, it affects the whole economic struc-ture. Some have claimed that television has transformed Americans into a nation of spectators and that it has, thereby, altered our leisure-time activities and the structure of our family lives.

The purpose of content analysis is to study the various forms of communica-tion in order to help us better understand ourselves. It is easy to see that the process of symbol manipulation, our special talent as human beings, is worthy of our attention. Its specific impact upon our behavior, our values, and the world we are creating for future generations represents another necessary and fruitful area for social science inquiry.

An Overview of the Method

The general contours of the method have been summarized by Bernard Berelson (1952:18) in his definition of content analysis as a research technique for "objec-tive, systematic and quantitative description of the manifest content of communi-cation." Let us see what Berelson means by this statement.

OBJECTIVE ANALYSIS

Researchers who use content analysis, Berelson has told us, are *objective* in their evaluation of the content of communications. We have, of course, seen in other chapters that objectivity is a central feature of scientific investigation. How, then, does the idea of objectivity apply to the analysis of human communications? We can best illustrate the need for objectivity through an example.

Were we to hear people comment about the liberal stance of the editorials in a particular newspaper, we might be led to ask them a number of questions to determine the validity of their assertion. What exactly is their definition of liberalism? Have they read all the editorials in the particular paper or has their reading been selective? How long have they been reading the newspaper? To what other newspapers is this one being implicitly compared? We ask these questions because we know that people may interpret the content of any com-munication in terms of their own particular needs, interests, biases, or ideologies. In short, our questions might be directed at uncovering the rules that have been used in categorizing and making evaluations of the contents of a particular written document. The essence of objective, scientific content analysis is that researchers make absolutely explicit the rules they have used in classifying the content of any communication.

We need not agree with the categories that researchers develop for analyzing the content of materials. Nor need we agree with procedures for placing a unit of communication in one or another category. What is important is that, as long as the rules of the game have been spelled out, we can evaluate how conclusions were reached; and we can expect that any researchers who follow those rules, regardless of their own personal values, beliefs, or interests, will document the content of materials in exactly the same way. Content analysis done witb rule-guided objectivity allows researchers using the same procedures to easily replicate the findings of earlier research.

SYSTEMATIC ANALYSIS

Berelson has told us, second, that content analysis is *systematic*. The idea of systematic procedure adds something to our characterization of objectivity. Suppose that we want to compare the editorials in several newspapers. In order for our comparison to be a valid one, we must systematically use the same procedures in documenting the content of each of the separate papers. In comparing the editorial content of *The New York Times, The Washington Post, The Phoenix Sun*, a small local newspaper, and your college paper, it would be contrary to systematic procedure to employ different criteria for each. It should not matter that these papers vary in size and in the nature of the audience they serve. When we commit ourselves to a particular strategy for evaluating data, we minimize considerably any personal biases that might intrude in that evaluation. It is by applying criteria systematically to all cases studied that we avoid collecting only data conforming to our theoretical ideas.

QUANTITATIVE TECHNIQUE

Third, content analysis usually gives us a *quantitative* description of communications. It employs one of several SYSTEMS OF ENUMERATION for gauging frequency and intensity. Perhaps the most common use of content analysis is to detail the frequency with which symbols or themes appear in a written document or series of pictures. But, as we shall see, those who use the technique are also interested in assessing the intensity of particular variables. If we wanted to compare the attitudes of two candidates for office with regard to their position on welfare, we could do a content analysis of their speeches. We might choose at the outset to count the number of times each candidate makes positive or negative comments about public assistance. This relatively simple system of enumeration might be misleading, however. Beyond counting the number of references made, we could devise some set of rules for measuring just *how positive or negative* each of these assertions is. We can imagine that once the researcher chooses to go beyond measuring simple frequencies, the task of setting up adequate categories becomes more difficult. This is an issue to which we shall return.

There are both positive and negative consequences of the quantification of materials demanded by content analysis. On the positive side, the use of rigorous categories yielding quantitative results allows the researcher to characterize a large volume of materials efficiently. Since the meaning of the numbers produced will be clear to any reader, there is no danger that a reader will make impressionistic judgments about the content under investigation. A clear quantitative presentation of the content of materials has another advantage: it can often alert us to themes in those materials that we would otherwise miss.

As we study content analysis, let us keep in mind that we risk missing the overall sense of a body of communications if we do no more than offer statistical summaries of their content. Any communication evokes a feeling, an overall impression, or a sense that cannot be captured simply by counting the frequency with which certain items appear. We might say that any communication is going to be more than the sum of its parts. It is for these reasons that we would claim, as we have done in the past, that qualitative and quantitative techniques must be used in conjunction with one another.

MANIFEST AND LATENT CONTENT

Berelson's final point is that the technique of content analysis deals most effectively with the MANIFEST CONTENT of communication, that is, with what explicitly appears in a text. As an objective, systematic, quantitative procedure, content analysis is highly reliable when researchers restrict their activity to documenting the elements, symbols, or themes that may be enumerated in a communication. By contrast, the LATENT CONTENT, or meanings implied by the written content that do not actually appear in the text itself, is much more difficult to discern. If a group of researchers is assigned the task of "reading between the lines" of a book, continually interpreting the latent impression given off by the manifest, written symbols, there are likely to be numerous disagreements among them. It is easier, and more reliable, to count specific negative adjectives applied to members of an ethnic group in a novel than it is to definitively characterize a variety of situations described in the novel as being examples of prejudiced behavior. To use content analysis to gauge the latent or implied meaning of a communication requires that researchers be trained extensively and that pretesting be done to ensure that they are making their judgments from common premises. To maximize reliability, interpretation of data should not be made as communication content is being enumerated, but at a later stage "at which time the investigator is free to use all his powers of imagination and intuition to draw meaningful conclusions from the data" (Holsti, 1969:12).

Applications of Content Analysis

Now that we have a preliminary sketch of the method's boundaries, let us examine a sample of investigations accomplished using content analysis. Note the data sources employed and the different questions and research goals that frequently motivate the analysis of communications.

Social scientists have analyzed the content of an enormous variety of materials with a number of different purposes in mind. Newspapers, periodicals, government records, personal documents such as letters and diaries, novels, recorded speeches, and children's books are among the written communications that have been used. In addition, researchers have analyzed the content of such diverse media as inscriptions and images on art work, and television and radio programing. Another frequent use of content analysis is as part of structured observation. Robert Bales (1950) has, for example, used standardized observational categories for analyzing the nature of ongoing verbal interaction in small groups.

Whether the data sources are written, visual, or verbal (or some combination), nearly all communications research has been guided by some aspect of the question "Who says what to whom and with what effect?" The concern of the researcher may be to analyze the content of a message in order to understand the motives, goals, intentions, or values of its author or source. Or the investigation may center on the communication itself to determine how larger social phenomena are illuminated by the content. Or the goal may be to assess the effects of communications on particular audiences. We can order our discussion of some representative content analysis studies in terms of these research goals.

INFERENCES TO THE SOURCE OF COMMUNICATIONS

Often the concern of content analysis is to infer from themes uncovered in a communication the characteristics of the people or institutions responsible for creating it. These studies are based on the apparently reasonable assumption that attitudes, values, and beliefs are revealed in symbolic communications. On this assumption researchers have analyzed a variety of documents ranging from diaries to public speeches.

In one well-known study (Paige, 1966) the personal letters of a woman, Jenny Cosgrove, were examined to better understand certain features of personality structure. Although clinicians were able to provide insight into specific features of the series of letters written by Jenny, a widow, to her son, the statistical data produced through content analysis revealed patterns that even a careful reading missed. The analysis, done with the aid of a computer, helped to uncover important themes centering on Jenny's conception of herself, her son, and her job, and her attitudes toward death.

In similar studies researchers have made use of a variety of documents. Suicide notes (Osgood and Walker, 1959) have been examined in order to understand the quality of consciousness of people willing to take their own lives. In another work on the same topic (Ogilvie et al., 1966) the researchers were able to develop a set of categories for analysis sophisticated enough to permit them to distinguish actual from simulated suicide notes.

More recently, Seider (1974) studied speeches in order to assess the ideology of business elites. This example suggests yet another strength of content analysis. It provides the opportunity to study individuals or groups generally inaccessible to social scientists. Elites are one such group. It is nearly impossible to observe the daily activities of "powerful" individuals or to interview them personally. Content analysis partially remedies this problem. We say "partially" because we can analyze only the communications that people consider to be fit for public consumption.

There is something else to take into account in inferring the intentions or values of communications sources. A number of studies have been directed at understanding how the *accuracy* of communications may be affected by the interests of the originating person, or more generally the interests of originating institutions. The concern of this research is often to understand how political, economic, or social interests may affect the content of communications. A study of the kinds of images presented on television constitutes a good example. In 1964, Melvin DeFleur sampled 250 television shows that children might watch during one week. He did so to determine how realistically that medium charac- terized or presented occupational roles to children. His major conclusion was that stereotyped images projected in these programs represented romanticized distortions of the actual occupational world. One might infer that such distortion is done to make the shows more appealing to children. Such a finding assumes considerable importance when we consider that the images presented on televi- sion exert a major influence on childhood socialization.

A number of written communications have been analyzed to illustrate how the coverage of events, phenomena, or social processes might be seen as a function of personal or institutionally based ideological interests. In one cross-cultural study (Wayne, 1956) the content of Russian and American family magazines was com- pared. Consistent with socialist ideology, Russians were most often pictured as engaged in happy and constructive work and leisure activities. The magazines rarely showed people displaying aggression of any sort or engaging in any form of even minor deviance. Magazines in the United States much more frequently pictured Americans engaged in "unflattering" activities. In a related fashion sev- eral studies of newspaper reporting (e.g., Allen, 1922; Lewis, 1960; Blumberg, 1971) suggest that the way events are covered may reflect ideological or sales considerations. These are interesting works because they begin to show how institutional, economic, or political factors can affect the production and distribu- tion of information in a society.

INFERENCES TO POPULATIONS: COMMUNICATION CONTENT AND SOCIAL VALUES

We may distinguish another type of content analysis, in which the purpose is to infer from the data the values of the populations or audiences reached by com- munications. These investigations trace the connection between media content and general social values.

In a number of studies researchers have sought to test hypotheses concerning changes in the value structure of societies. One of the more well known of these works is David McClelland's (1961) examination of the relationship between a society's rate of economic development and the stress it places on achievement values. By correlating achievement themes in 1,300 children's stories from nearly every country in the world with such indicators of economic growth as increases in coal and electricity consumption, he was able to show a greater concern with achievement values in societies with higher rates of economic growth. In other sections of his book, *The Achieving Society,* McClelland demonstrates that a num- ber of additional communications sources may be used to study value changes historically. He makes use of such literary forms as poems, epigrams, legends, tales, and the writings of major authors to measure achievement motivation in societies extending as far back as ancient Greece.

In similar fashion, David Riesman's (Riesman et al., 1950) well-known thesis that there has been a gradual shift in American national character from an "inner directed" stress on personal achievement to an "other directed" concern with group acceptance, has been tested through content analysis. Partial evidence for Riesman's hypothesis was provided through an analysis of advertisements in the *Ladies' Home Journal* over a 66-year period (Dornbusch and Hickman, 1959). The researchers were able to show a significant increase in other-directed advertising at the historical juncture when Riesman suggests the shift began.

Somewhat unusual data sources have been used to assess dominant values in a society. Barcus (1961) studied the themes, type of stories, and type of characters pictured in Sunday comic strips from 1900 to 1959. He found that during that period there was a steady decline in content reflecting domestic or home concerns and an increase in crime and romance themes. Another investigation (Otto, 1963) centered on sex and violence in a sample of newspapers, books, and magazines. The author examined all the issues of 55 magazines and recorded for each the number of violence and sex incidents mentioned. He also measured the column space devoted to stories and pictures with these themes. The information obtained was supplemented with a similar analysis of all the issues of 10 newspapers across the country, and finally with an analysis of the covers of 295 paperback novels published in the same year. Still other researchers have made inferences about cultural values and social change through the analysis of school songbooks (Sebald, 1962), films (Wolfenstein and Leites, 1950), and folk tales (Bradburn and Berlew, 1961).

The concern of this genre of content analysis need not be to document society-wide values. Specific groups or subcultures generate and maintain their own distinctive value structures. Thus we may examine the beliefs and preferences of specific target audiences of communications. Arnheim (1944) tried to discover the values of people listening to daytime radio serials by carefully documenting the themes of these programs and the types of characters portrayed in them. One could imagine an analogous study of daytime television soap operas. In another instance (Albrecht, 1956) the concern was to isolate the distinctive values of different social classes by analyzing periodicals with different class readerships.

In the studies we have been considering in the last few paragraphs the focus is less on the characteristics of those who produce communications and more on how the themes contained in them reflect either comprehensive societal values or the values of specific segments of the population. We acknowledge that some considerable leaps of inference are demanded in these studies, which means that we must weigh very carefully the validity of the interpretations made. Can we know with any certainty that comic strips really do reflect the values of the larger society or that soap operas reflect the ideals of a segment of people in the society? It seems clear that the larger the number of independent sources showing essentially the same findings, the greater will be our faith in any interpretive assertions made.

EVALUATING THE EFFECTS OF COMMUNICATIONS

The content analysis research described to this point is concerned almost exclusively with the themes found in the materials studied. In a significant body of research on the *effects* of communications, the focus is more globally on the *total* process. Questions of the following sort are considered: When are persons persuaded by communications? Do they tend to avoid communications contrary to their preexisting attitudes? In effects-oriented research the specific analysis of content is only a part, albeit a significant one, of the total research effort.

One of the earliest studies designed to assess the effects of communications shows us the utility of combining content analysis with other methodological techniques. We are referring to Herbert Blumer's (1933) examination of the relationship between exposure to movies and people's conduct. A sample of people kept diaries in which they were asked to record their attitudes, feelings, reactions, sentiments, and values concerning the themes, characters, or behaviors in the movies they watched. Researchers analyzed the content of these diaries to determine how various types of people reacted to the medium. Blumer later conducted personal interviews with his subjects to establish still further the effects of the movies on them.

We are all familiar with the ongoing debate in the social sciences on the question of whether violence depicted in the mass media causes people themselves to display violence and aggression. The research evidence around this question is mixed. After doing content analysis to measure the extent of violence portrayed in comic books and other media, Wertham (1972) indicated that a sample of children who had committed violent or criminal acts had more exposure to high-violence materials than a comparative sample of "normal" children. Other researchers, however, have suggested that exposure to violence and aggression usually is chosen by people who do not, themselves, engage in such behavior. Content analysis has been used in combination with other techniques to evaluate the relationship between themes in children's stories and aggressive behavior (Wolf, 1949), protest songs and the creation of countercultural attitudes (Hirsch, 1971), and newspaper editorials and the outcome of elections (Gregg, 1965; McDowell, 1965).

In these studies it is a major methodological problem to determine whether the communications actually *cause* certain behaviors or whether they simply reflect people's previously held attitudes, behaviors, or dispositions. Debate continues around this issue. In the late 1960s there were those who argued that news reports of violence in certain urban ghettos were instrumental in provoking riots in other cities. We can surmise that if there is any relationship between news reports of riots and further rioting it is not a simple one. Perhaps the issue turns on *how* such activity is presented in the news. The validity of this hunch could be tested by doing an analysis of the content and style of news presentations in cities with ghettos that had riots in the mid-1960s and in those that did not. Such an historical study might help to clarify the relationship between media presentations and their effects on audiences. There is a broader point to make: content analysis plays an important role in studies on the effects of communications because it can have substantial implications for the formation of social policy.

CONTENT ANALYSIS AND STRUCTURED OBSERVATION

We have reviewed and grouped studies as source oriented, audience oriented, and effects oriented; these map the general range and variety of applications for content analysis. To these categories we would add one more: the use of content analysis as part of structured observation of behavior.

A criticism frequently made of observational research is that it is difficult to discern just how and why researchers collected the specific information they did. We must often take it as a matter of faith that the data do in fact capture the typical activities, behaviors, or events occurring in a setting. Further, as long as the rules for selecting data cannot be specified, it is virtually impossible to replicate most observational research. When recording structured observational data, it is desirable for researchers to specify precisely the features they will observe and the types of measurements they will make. Observational content categories have frequently been used to document systematically such features of ongoing behaviors as their duration, frequency, and effects. These behaviors need not be only verbal. Researchers have, for example, worked out coding categories to document nonverbal and body movement behaviors (Birdwhistell, 1970) and spatial characteristics of interaction (Hall, 1963). To provide a sense of the types of variables that might be systematically coded in observational research, let us turn to an example.

In one study (Karp and Yoels, 1976) the researchers examined the processes through which both students and teachers formulate definitions of the classroom as a social setting. More directly, they sought to understand the meaning of student participation in college classrooms. Do men talk more than women? Does the frequency of student talk vary with the nature of the subject? How often do students disagree with the comments of their instructors? Is the nature of classroom interaction different at the beginning of class periods from the way it is at the middle or end? Does the nature of interaction change over the course of the semester? Is the sex of the teacher at all influential in the willingness of students to talk? These are some of the research questions with which they began their investigation.

The researchers proceeded systematically to observe behaviors in a number of classrooms over the course of a semester. A codesheet was developed on which observers were asked to note, for every single verbal utterance of every student during each class period observed, the following information:

1. the sex of the student
2. the geographical location of the student (classrooms were divided into nine separate imaginary spatial areas)
3. the stimulus for the student's talk (Was the talk a response to a teacher's question or comment or to another student's question or comment?)

In planning the study, the researchers had decided that it would not be sufficient simply to document the *number* of interactions occurring; they wanted to evaluate the *nature* of those interactions. They had available to them a number of established and widely used category systems for coding the nature or content of verbal interaction. In this case they decided to make use of the coding categories developed by Robert Bales (1950). Considerable observation of small-group interaction had led Bales to believe that it could all be placed into one of three classes: interactions involving positive social or emotional attitudes and feelings, those involving negative social or emotional feelings, and those explicitly related to group tasks. The elaboration of these three dimensions resulted in the construction of the following coding categories:

a. *Social-Emotional Area: Positive*
   1. Shows solidarity.
   2. Shows tension release.
   3. Agrees.

b. *Task Area: Neutral*
   1. Gives suggestions.
   2. Gives opinions.
   3. Gives orientation.
   4. Asks for suggestions.
   5. Asks for opinions.
   6. Asks for orientation.
c. *Social-Emotional Area: Negative*
   1. Shows antagonism.
   2. Shows tension.
   3. Disagrees.

Observers were asked to make fairly detailed qualitative comments on events not covered by coding categories, such as special or unusual events that may have occurred in the class, the general demeanor of teachers and students, the nature of material discussed in class, and nonlinguistic gestures made by teachers and students. This qualitative information was helpful to the researchers in complementing their understanding of the "objective" data collected. The researchers accumulated much information about what went on in the observed classes. At the end of the semester they supplemented the content analysis data by having students and faculty fill out questionnaires. They were, thereby, able to examine the relationship between the perceptions that students and teachers had of classroom behavior and the kinds of behaviors that actually occurred in the classrooms.

This example of classroom observation shows that content analysis need not be restricted to the study of standard communications media and may be used to record the content of behaviors in a variety of natural behavioral settings. Moreover, you should now have some sense of the research problems for which structured observation might be appropriate and the types of variables or behaviors that can be systematically tabulated. In addition, it is apparent that content analysis is particularly useful in conjunction with other methodological techniques. Now, let us fill out the details of the picture we have been creating by describing some of the specific mechanics of the method.

Performing Content Analysis

A general overview of the type provided thus far cannot fully express the complexities of content analysis when actually applied to a research problem. The manner of its application will vary somewhat, depending upon the topic for research. It is nonetheless possible to describe the types of decisions and judgments that need to be made in the process of any content analysis investigation. One way to do this is to consider how social scientists might plan and carry out a specific study. We will imagine, therefore, a group of researchers with a general interest in investigating changing women's roles in the United States. Their first task is to specify the research problem.

SPECIFICATION OF THE RESEARCH PROBLEM

Our researchers begin by asking: Has the women's movement had any effect in altering images and stereotypes of the female role? From that general question flow a number of other, more specific questions. Have there been any changes in the kinds of activities thought proper for men and women? Have there been any changes in the kinds of occupations thought appropriate for men and women? Are females pictured in more egalitarian relationships with men today than they were in the past?

As the researchers continue to spell out these and similar questions, they begin to consider how their focus ought to be narrowed so that they can actually begin to collect data. Let's imagine they decide that one way to focus their problem would be to study changes in the kinds of gender images that children perceive. One rationale for such a choice might be that if women's roles really change, there have to be corresponding basic alterations in the gender role socialization of children. The theoretical literature on socialization has convinced the researchers that gender roles are learned and become deeply ingrained during childhood.

Once the problem has been specified theoretically to consider only the images and stereotypes taught to young children about female roles, the attention of the researchers logically turns to the kinds of data sources that can be used to assess any changes in the content of socialization over time. We can imagine several options. It would be possible to consider how males and females are portrayed to children in such mass media sources as television or movies. One could, for example, do a content analysis of such children's shows as "Sesame Street" or "Mister Rogers," and compare them with the tapes of children's shows from several years ago.

After considering all the means by which they could study socialization changes over time, the researchers decide to restrict their data source to children's books. There are several good reasons for this choice. First, as we have seen, there is considerable precedent in the literature for using children's books to establish social trends (McClelland, 1961). Second, and a more pragmatic reason, children's books are easily accessible. The researchers might also conclude that the use of children's books provides the opportunity for more rigorous comparative analysis than do other data sources. If they choose to, they can compare books that are of a particular length; they can limit their analysis to works of fiction; and so on. Having specified the problem to this point, the investigators must begin to think how they will use the chosen data source to answer their research question, which is:

> Has the women's movement had any effect on the female stereotypes or images found in children's books?

We can see that there are many procedural decisions still to be made. The first of these is to determine just how the children's books will be sampled.

SAMPLING ITEMS

The stated problem demands a research design allowing comparison of past and current books. At a bare minimum, two samples of books are required: one sample from before the beginning of the women's movement and another from contemporary books. Assuming it is historically accurate that the women's movement began in the mid-1960s, the researchers could choose to sample books published each year from about 1960 (four or five years prior to the emergence of the movement) to the present. If there have been any changes in sex role images, such a sampling design would allow the investigators to say more surely just when these changes began to take place. If they have the money and staff to sample materials in this way, they might be in a position to make some elegant theoretical statements concerning the length of time before a movement begins to have any discernible effect in changing the content of published materials. In order to simplify our analysis somewhat, however, we will assume that the researchers choose to compare two samples of books. One sample will be of books published in the three years immediately prior to the emergence of the women's movement. The second sample will be composed of books published during the past three years.

Even if the researchers opt for this relatively simple design, their sampling problems are not resolved. After all, there are literally thousands of children's books published each year. Sampling is, in the case of content analysis, nearly always a multistage process. Once researchers make some preliminary determination of the UNIVERSE of materials applicable to their problem (in our case, *all* children's books), they are still left with many more materials than are manageable. In virtually all content analysis investigations it would be literally impossible to analyze all the items applicable to the problem. Our investigators might, therefore, restrict their attention to only those schoolbooks used in grades 1 and 2. If asked why, they could argue that (1) children are likely to become most intimately acquainted with the books they use in school, and that (2) children in the early grades are at a formative age, an age when sex role socialization will have its greatest impact.

If, after having made this decision, the researchers still feel that the universe is unmanageably large, they would likely consider analyzing only those books used in a particular area of the country, a single city, or perhaps even one school district. They must recognize, however, that as they restrict the universe of books, they also restrict the generalizability of their findings.

Once the universe is clearly determined, there are a number of ways in which the final items for analysis might be drawn. If the total number of items is small enough, they may all be included in the final study. Our researchers, however, decide that it would be unfeasible, given resources and staffing, to analyze more than one hundred books, fifty in each of their two samples. It might be possible for them to construct their two samples by choosing the one hundred books at *random*. Simple random sampling can be used, however, only if *all* the appropriate items that it is possible to include in the sample can be clearly identified.

Sometimes simple random sampling is not possible because one cannot identify all the elements of the universe or because such a sampling procedure does not meet the demands of the research problem. Our researchers might decide, for example, that all children's books do not have an equal influence because some are more widely read than others. Consequently, they would fashion a sampling procedure to put them in contact with those books likely to have greatest influence because they are the most widely circulated. Were they to make this decision, they might use judges or experts to help them determine the most useful books for their research problem. They could consult with a number of primary school teachers or publishing company representatives who would be asked to submit lists of the most frequently used books. If possible, this information could be supplemented with school records of books ordered. It might even be reasonable to tabulate the books most frequently checked out of school libraries. The wisest course of all might be to use a combination of the procedures mentioned.

However accomplished, we can assume that the researchers now have in hand the one hundred books that will be the basis for their analysis.

At this point the investigators must decide which aspects of gender image they wish to measure and how that measurement shall be done. Will they consider the images portrayed in each book as a whole? Will they code the images portrayed in particular stories within each book? Will they code the images presented in the books paragraph by paragraph? sentence by sentence? Might it be possible, indeed, to code specific words (for example, adjectives) related to female images in the books?

There are, then, two decisions that must be made at this juncture: (1) Which dimensions of female role image are going to be assessed? Which *categories*, in other words, should guide the coding of the data? (2) What exactly ought to be the UNIT OF ANALYSIS in the study (words, sentences, paragraphs, stories, the book as a whole)? In any content analysis these decisions must be made in terms of the research questions, hypotheses, and theoretical ideas guiding the study, as well as the peculiarities of the data source used. There are, however, some general methodological considerations that ought to guide both of these interrelated decisions. We shall say a few words about units of analysis and then consider in greater detail the problems of category construction.

CHOOSING THE UNIT OF ANALYSIS

In our earlier discussion of the kinds of research done using content analysis, we saw that the specific unit of content tabulated, or the RECORDING UNIT, can vary considerably. In some studies researchers will tabulate the simplest content unit constituting any communication—the *single word*. One way that our researchers studying female role images could proceed would be by coding every adjective used to describe males and females in the books examined. They could create procedural rules for classifying each of the adjectives attached to gender. The choice of the single word or symbol as the unit of analysis has some distinct benefits. The primary benefit is that coders must make relatively few judgments in the classification of this recording unit and in the usual case few inferences about its meaning. Instructions can be so explicit that virtually all decisions about proper coding are made ahead of time. Coders could be told, for example, that every time they see the adjective *aggressive* it is to be classified in category X. The researchers could even provide the coders with an exhaustive list of adjectives, with directions concerning the category into which each should be coded. As coders confront each adjective in the textual material, they simply consult this prepared coding list and are, therefore, relieved of any interpretive decisions. The use of this simplest unit thus has the advantage of increasing reliability.

On the other hand, the materials to be analyzed, the variables of interest to the researchers, the hypotheses to be tested, and the theories to be evaluated may make the single word an inappropriate unit of analysis. Researchers may need to work with more comprehensive units—such as the content of sentences, paragraphs, or chapters, or the entire item (a whole book, a whole film, a whole newspaper). Using any of these units, categories will be devised to tabulate the themes, types of people or characters, or types of behaviors represented.

As researchers move to the analysis of more comprehensive units with the idea of extracting specific themes from them, the coding task becomes more complicated. Unlike the situation in which coders can simply consult a list to determine exactly how a particular word ought to be categorized, the analysis of themes in sentences, paragraphs, or whole books cannot be achieved by reference to comprehensive coding rules; interpretive judgments are an integral part of these analyses.

CATEGORY CONSTRUCTION

The most critical step in content analysis is the construction of the categories that will direct the coding of the content. In the construction of categories the researchers indicate just how they will classify the materials being investigated. If the categories are to be successful, they must bear a close relationship to the problem as originally stated. They must faithfully reflect the major theoretical concepts on which the study is based.

Procedurally, researchers normally begin to construct coding categories by exhaustively listing all aspects or dimensions of the phenomenon being investigated. In our research example the types of behaviors, themes, ideas, or symbols on this preliminary, tentative listing might include: power in interaction, personality characteristics, expressed occupational aspirations, leisure-time activities, sexual divisions of labor, types of children's play activities, the number of males and females appearing in the items, and the type of dress of male and female characters.

As the researchers continue to list the dimensions of gender role image, they will find it necessary to specify subdivisions within each broad category they propose. They could, for example, elaborate the interactional power dimension mentioned above by distinguishing whether females when in interaction with males are pictured in *subordinate, egalitarian,* or *superordinate* power positions. As the researchers continue to refine their categories, they will likely consider at the same time the procedural rules that will guide the classification of unit contents into one or another of the proposed categories. Coders might be provided rules of the following sort for classifying each instance of male/female power interaction.

1. Each time a female is pictured interacting with a male, classify the female as in a subordinate power position if she is asking the male for advice of any kind.
2. If the male and female are pictured as talking approximately the same amount and neither is giving advice to the other, classify this as an instance of an egalitarian role relationship.
3. If the male is asking the female for advice, classify this as an instance of the female in a superordinate power position.

Researchers also frequently find it useful to imagine just how their collected data will eventually be arranged in tabular form. If in their final report they are to have a section on "changing images of female/male power relations" (see Figure 11.1) and if the principles for constructing categories are well laid out and unambiguous, those coding content data will achieve a high degree of consistency or reliability.

Before finally committing themselves to particular coding categories, researchers will normally conduct a pretest. They will ask a number of people to

FIGURE 11.1   Changing Images of Female/Male Power Relations

Female Role Position	*Premovement Books (N = 50)*		*Current Books (N = 50)*	
Subordinate	No. of Cases	%	No. of Cases	%
Egalitarian	No. of Cases	%	No. of Cases	%
Superordinate	No. of Cases	%	No. of Cases	%
	Total No. 100%		Total No. 100%	

code the same body of data independently. If they find that there is little consistency in the classification of the data, they will have to rework the categories. Researchers typically find it useful to put coders through a short training program on the use of the categories. Coding reliability must be high if we are to have any faith in the accuracy of the final data tabulations.

It should be apparent that every single case of male/female interaction noted in the books studied will fit into one of the categories proposed. Categories are EXHAUSTIVE when every specimen of data or every case under investigation will fit into at least one of the categories developed. They must be reconstructed if certain types of data necessary for testing research hypotheses cannot be coded.

It is often difficult, in fact, to create categories that are completely exhaustive. Unexpected or idiosyncratic units may turn up that do not clearly fit into one of the categories developed at the outset of the study. In much the same way, the criterion of MUTUAL EXCLUSIVITY is often harder to maintain in practice than to state in theory. To the extent that any symbolic communication will allow for a number of interpretations, it could potentially fit into more than one coding category. The safest assertion to make is that high reliability in any content analysis is dependent on the production of clear, rule-guided categories.

The fewer the number of decisions, interpretations, or judgments coders must make as they classify data, the greater will be the overall reliability of the study. This general rule has implications for the number of categories researchers may wish to use in their studies. The coding task will generally become more complicated as the number of categories increases. Theoretically, the number of categories that can be used in a study is limitless.

In the example we have been using, the researchers simply classified male/female interactions into one of three power categories—female subordinate, female equal, female superordinate. They might decide, however, that it would be theoretically useful to know not only the power positions most frequently experienced by females but also the particular *contexts* of these relations. Are females shown more frequently in subordinate positions when in the work world than when engaged in leisure activities? In male/female interactions in leisure activities, are females more often subordinate in sports than in parlor games? They might, therefore, choose to elaborate their categories to include this context variable. By doing so, they will be able to make many more comparisons of different features of the data in their final analysis. In sum, as the number of categories used in a study increases, researchers provide themselves the opportunity for more extensive analysis of their data, but they may do so at the expense of the accuracy or reliability of the data coded.

We have been assuming that researchers using content analysis are concerned only with tabulating how often or how frequently themes appear in a given communication. There are, however, occasions when researchers will consider it theoretically appropriate to determine as well the intensity or degree of a theme or variable in the communications studied. We will look at a brief example to illustrate how the decision to measure the intensity of variables in content analysis necessarily complicates the coding task.

Suppose our sex role researchers have come to feel that an important theme for analysis in the children's books is females' *expression of dissatisfaction* with their expected roles. It then follows that one coding task will be to identify and tabulate each instance where a female is shown expressing dissatisfaction. Beyond that, however, the researchers want to know the intensity of the dissatisfaction females are shown to express. Once this decision is made, the number of judgments that coders must make as they seek to classify the contents of a unit will at least double. The coder must first decide whether the theme of dissatisfaction is present or not. Once the theme is determined to be present, the coder must employ another set of rules to rate the degree of its existence. Coders may be provided rules for placing instances of expressed dissatisfaction into *ordinal* categories (for example, high dissatisfaction, medium dissatisfaction, or low dissatisfaction).

Our example on the issue of intensity shows that content analysis need not be limited to the simple tabulation of word or theme frequencies. It is possible to develop more sophisticated measures, but there is a cost in doing so. As the number of categories and coding rules increases, the analysis of data becomes much more time-consuming, the number of interpretive judgments we ask coders to make increases substantially, and there may be a consequent decrease in coding reliability.

When researchers have defined their problem, decided on their unit of analysis, created coding categories, and made explicit the rules for classifying data, they have completed the major technical steps for their investigation. By now you may infer that the actual tabulation of data is likely to be a laborious, tedious process. A significant number of classification errors inevitably result simply because coding is often a fatiguing job. The problem of fatigue and boredom is greater, of course, with large samples of items for analysis. In cases where the number of items makes hand tabulation of data nearly impossible, researchers might use a computer to do the coding. As social scientists increasingly use computers, serious efforts are being made to create programs designed explicitly for certain types of content analysis.

Computer-Assisted Content Analysis

We suggested earlier that as the unit of analysis becomes larger and more comprehensive, coders must make a greater number of interpretive judgments about the meaning of the content before a particular unit can be assigned to a category. Human beings can recognize meanings by reading complete phrases, sentences, or paragraphs in a text. As we read textual material, we do not split up a sentence or paragraph into its component parts. We do not separate out nouns, adjectives, and the like. Rather, we consider the communications read as a whole, as a single meaningful picture. Human beings are, in other words, capable of high levels of symbolic abstraction. In studies where researchers must make subtle decisions about thematic meaning in a communication, computers have relatively limited use.

Computers will, however, perform with unerring accuracy any coding task in which the classification rules are absolutely unambiguous. Such was the case in the study to determine the authorship of several of the unsigned Federalist papers (Mosteller and Wallace, 1964). The researchers first looked at the known writings of the three authors—Hamilton, Madison, and Jay—and tabulated the frequency with which each of the authors used 265 key words. They then programed a computer to tabulate the frequencies of these words in the twelve papers of unknown authorship. The data produced clearly suggested Madison as the author of those papers. In studies such as this, where coding judgments about the specific meaning of items is not demanded, computers can facilitate the research process enormously. This is most often the case in studies where the single word is chosen as the most appropriate unit of analysis.

The first widely used computer programs for content analysis were developed by Philip Stone and his colleagues (1966). The General Inquirer system provides a set of computer procedures for tabulating a variety of textual characteristics. This ever-expanding system has been adapted to meet the needs of a variety of specific research problems. Special-purpose programs have been created to study achievement themes, cross-cultural folk tale themes and class-related language themes in written materials.

Following these programs, the computer is capable of "reading" a communication word by word and comparing each word to categories specified by the researcher. The total set of words earmarked by the investigator as applicable to the particular research is often referred to as the DICTIONARY. Each word included is called a TAG WORD or tag. The computer is programed to identify tag words and to place them into preestablished theoretical categories. It is not unusual for variations of the General Inquirer program to include several thousand tag words and eighty or more categories. After the computer has read all the materials, it will print out such information as a list of tag words and the frequency with which each appears, the proportion of sentences in the text containing tag words, and graphs indicating the number of tag words appearing in each category used in the study.

One of the difficulties in any content analysis of word items is that words have different meanings in different contexts. Think about the meaning of the individual words in an expression such as "time flies like an arrow." In response to this problem, work has been directed at creating programs that allow the computer to distinguish between alternative meanings for the same word, on the basis of the context in which the word is used. By instructing the computer to look at the way words appear in pairs or clustered together in CONTEXT UNITS, we can have it make more sophisticated meaning distinctions as it places the words into theoretical categories. Even with these advances, however, we cannot yet rely on the computer to make sophisticated judgments. Because of the intricate symbolism of language, coding validity remains a substantial problem. This is not to suggest that manual coding eliminates validity problems, but that direct contact with the data makes it easier to evaluate the tone and inflection of materials, and being able to evaluate these features is crucial to assessing intended meaning.

Although the computer will eliminate coding errors stemming from fatigue or boredom, it cannot altogether eliminate the need for highly routinized work. Researchers must prepare the text as demanded by the particular computer program used, which entails the transfer of textual information to computer cards. They must not use existing computer programs simply because they are available. If, because of the nature of the communications to be analyzed or the researchers' particular theoretical ideas, none of the established dictionaries or theoretical categories satisfies the researchers' needs, they will have to create their own computer program. The creation of new dictionaries and coding categories can itself be time-consuming. But if the researchers work with ill-conceived research problems or categories inapplicable to their theoretical concerns, the computer will only function to rapidly tabulate a large volume of insignificant data.

In sum, computers can be a valuable tool for social scientists who wish to analyze a large volume of written communication. By saving researchers the countless hours ordinarily involved in manual data coding, rating, and tallying, machine data processing makes possible content analysis projects that would have been unthinkable only a few years ago. As more social scientists see the potential of computers for facilitating the coding of content data, we would expect a continued growth of standard computer programs based on frequently used theoretical categories in the social sciences. However, we must emphasize again that a computer is only a tool. And it is valueless without the sound theoretical reasoning of the social scientist, who must choose meaningful problems, determine the materials to be used for analysis, construct categories that reflect the theoretical issues at hand, and finally make sense of the collected data.

The Technique in Perspective

One of the most significant strengths of content analysis is that it is a thoroughly *unobtrusive* method. Nearly all the methods employed by social scientists necessitate a direct involvement with subjects. This is certainly so in survey, experimental, and participant observation research. But content analysis, which makes use of available materials, eliminates a source of troublesome bias that threatens our research whenever the subjects of investigation are directly questioned or observed. We do not have to bother with the potential response biases of subjects who are influenced by the presence of an investigator or by the knowledge that they are participating in a study. In this respect, content analysis may complement the findings of the more obtrusive methods discussed elsewhere in this book.

While content analysis may serve as the central method in an investigation, it can also be used to test preliminary ideas, hypotheses, hunches, or theories prior to a more complete investigation. By conducting a pilot study through the content analysis of a few selected communication sources, researchers may generate hypotheses and discover important variables. The findings of such initial research may then guide further work where perhaps surveys or participant observation become the primary data collection methods. Although content analysis is a powerful tool for evaluating personal or social values, investigators may want to employ intensive interviewing, survey research, or direct observation to check the validity of inferences made from the communication sources used in a study. This is especially likely when the specific goal of the research is to evaluate the effects of communications.

Content analysis is an adaptable research method. It is an economical and time-efficient procedure. It sometimes becomes the central technique in historical research concerned either with a particular period or with trends over time. It also makes possible a variety of cross-cultural studies that would likely be unfeasible using other methods. In addition, because of the availability of data sources and (as shown in our hypothetical example) the relative simplicity of the mechanics involved, students with little research experience can easily make use of the method. Content analysis will often be a useful research strategy when our interests lead us to inquire into the values, ideologies, sentiments, or beliefs motivating behavior in a society.

Summary

Words and pictures are valuable sources of social science data. The primary intent of content analysis is to uncover themes in these sources of communication—themes that are representative of an entire culture, a specific group of people, or the life of an individual. In some studies the discovery of these themes may be accomplished through the tabulation of specific words. Alternatively, the thematic content in sentences, paragraphs, or perhaps an entire essay or book may be ascertained. Regardless of the particular unit of analysis employed, the underlying goal of the research remains constant: to find a logic in the themes uncovered such that the characteristics of authors or their audiences may be better understood.

Realization of this central goal rests on the objective, systematic, and quantitative collection and processing of data. Strict rules for the categorizing of the manifest content of communication must be adopted and followed. Categories for the classification of data must reflect the major theoretical concepts being used in a particular study. The validity of the judgments made about the values, motives, beliefs, or ideologies of individuals, populations, and societies depends on the nature of the theoretical categories generated at the outset. Two basic requirements are that categories be mutually exclusive and exhaustive, in order to minimize problems of reliability in coding. Of course, even the most complete and valid set of categories is useless without proper sampling procedures.

Increasingly, the time-consuming and intricate routine of data processing in content analysis has been taken over by computers. At present, machines are superb at enumerating content but less reliable in assessing its contextual meaning. Content analysis has a bright future as an unobtrusive technique that eliminates respondent bias and that has wide practical application in all of the social sciences. There are some potential difficulties in the method, threats to the reliability of its coding procedures and to the validity of its classificatory categories, but these are readily recognized and are being continually addressed.

Key Terms

context unit	exhaustive categories	manifest content
dictionary	latent content	mutually exclusive categories

recording unit   tag word   universe
system of enumeration   unit of analysis   unobtrusive technique

Exercises

1. Reread the section of this chapter on structured observation and then construct coding categories so that you may gather data to accept or reject the following hypotheses:

   a. There is no difference in male and female participation in college classrooms.

   b. The area of the classroom in which a student sits is unrelated to the likelihood of his or her participation in class.

   You may offer a preliminary test of these hypotheses by randomly choosing two or three classes at your college and observing them for a week. To increase the sample size of observed meetings of the classes, it is possible for a number of students in your class to operate as a research team with each member observing a couple of meetings. If you choose to work as a group, it will be important to discuss just how the coding will be done so as to ensure a high intercoder reliability. After the data relative to these two hypotheses have been tabulated, try to offer some explanation of the findings.

2. Do different communications sources "make" news? Answer this question by comparing coverage in a major newspaper to that in a neighborhood newspaper on any political, social, or economic event that has been in the news recently. It will probably be best to restrict your content analysis to one week's reporting and analysis of the event in the respective newspapers. Decide on the features of the coverage you will document (for example, column space devoted to the event, the kinds of details reported, the position taken by the paper on the event). Be sure to include in your brief report some description of the categories constructed for analyzing the reports and the unit of analysis used. Speculate from your collected data on the values of the audiences served by the two newspapers. If you expected a difference in coverage between the papers but found none, explain why this happened.

3. We reported in this chapter that Barcus (1961) studied the themes, types of stories, and types of characters pictured in Sunday comic strips. This study was done for the years 1900 to 1959. During that period Barcus noted an increase in violence and romance themes. Has there been a significant change in the content of comics since 1959? After constructing appropriate categories (you may want to read Barcus's study in this regard), do an analysis of the comic strips in any major Sunday paper for the last four months. Does your study indicate that there may have been shifts in the content of comics since 1959?

4. Write a brief essay indicating what you consider to be some of the validity problems involved in assessing the values of communicators or their audiences, using the method of content analysis. How could content analysis be used in conjunction with other methods to increase the validity of the research findings?

5. Compare content analysis and any other method you have read about in this book in terms of the potential sources of bias that are avoided by using content analysis. It would probably be easiest to make this comparison by choosing a relatively unstructured technique such as participant observation. What would be the disadvantages of using content analysis instead of the method with which you are comparing it?

6. Imagine that you want to conduct a study to discover the typical values of people in different social classes in the United States. Assuming that you choose to do a content analysis study to assess class values, indicate the kinds of problems you would likely face in selecting sample items for the study.

7. Watch television from seven o'clock in the evening until midnight. Do a content analysis of all the commercials you see, according to the explanation given in each for buying the product or service being offered. It will help you to devise your categories in advance. Try to think of at least five mutually exclusive reasons for buying a product or using a service (quality, price, etc.). After you have collected your data, draw some inferences about the preferences and motivations of the viewing public. How do the advertisers see the public to whom they are trying to appeal?

Suggested Readings

READINGS ABOUT THE METHOD

Carney, Thomas F.
1972 *Content Analysis: A Technique for Systematic Inference from Communications.* Winnipeg, Canada: University of Manitoba Press.

Written for the beginning student, this is a highly readable text on content analysis. Carney provides full illustrations of the issues and problems typically faced in using the method.

Cartwright, Dorian
1953 "Analysis of Qualitative Material." In *Research Methods in the Behavioral Sciences,* ed. Leon Festinger and Daniel Katz. New York: Holt, Rinehart and Winston.

Cartwright's essay is more critical than most concerning the use of content analysis. Although not denying the utility of the method, he is concerned that many content analysis studies are substantively unimportant since they are preoccupied with the mere counting of items or themes. Cartwright disagrees with the idea that content analysis can be used only to describe the manifest content of communication. His criticism points to the central place of "meaning" in the analysis of communication.

Holsti, Ole R.
1968 "Content Analysis." In *The Handbook of Social Psychology,* ed. Gardner Lindzey and Elliot Aronson. Reading, Mass.: Addison-Wesley.

In a relatively short space Holsti defines content analysis and describes its several uses; he also offers several reasonably detailed examples of actual research done using the method. He discusses many possible research designs and some advances in the use of content analysis.

1969 *Content Analysis for the Social Sciences and the Humanities.* Reading, Mass.: Addison-Wesley.

This is a comprehensive review of content analysis in the various social sciences and humanities. It contains an extended treatment of each of the stages in a content analysis study discussed in this chapter. In addition, Holsti offers several examples

of the kinds of categories that have been constructed in various studies, which may be used as models by any researcher. There is also a complete discussion of the uses of the computer in content analysis research.

Krippendorf, Klaus
1980 *Content Analysis: An Introduction to Its Methodology.* Beverly Hills, Calif.: Sage.

An advanced text that sets forth the history and conceptual assumptions of content analysis and enumerates its advantages and limitations.

Markoff, John, et al.
1974 "Toward the Integration of Content Analysis and General Methodology." In *Sociological Methodology 1975,* ed. David R. Heise. San Francisco: Jossey-Bass.

This chapter is a recent summation of the potential contribution of the technique to social investigation. It attacks routine enumeration in content analysis and calls for the increased use of the computer to draw important information from human speech and behavior.

Pool, Ithiel de Sola, ed.
1959 *Trends in Content Analysis.* Urbana, Ill.: University of Illinois Press.

In this series of essays a number of problems involved in content analysis are discussed. Of particular importance are the questions concerning the types of errors likely to be made by human coders who must often use commonsense judgments in trying to ascertain the meanings transmitted in communications of all sorts. The implication is that techniques must be developed for going beyond the manifest content of communication.

Stone, Philip, et al.
1966 *The General Inquirer: A Computer Approach to Content Analysis in the Behavioral Sciences.* Cambridge, Mass.: MIT Press.

In this very important book, two central goals are met. First, the authors present the logic and techniques developed for computer content analysis. Second, they present a series of studies illustrating the value of computer techniques in extracting thematic data from communications sources. This book presents the most sophisticated treatment available of the potential and limits of computer technology for conducting content analysis studies.

READINGS ILLUSTRATING THE METHOD

Berger, Arthur A.
1973   *The Comic Stripped American: What Dick Tracy, Blondie, Daddy Warbucks and Charlie Brown Tell Us About Ourselves.* Baltimore: Penguin Books.

In an intriguing use of content analysis, Berger gauges changing American values by probing the themes found in comic strips over three generations. As the subject matter suggests, it is fun to read.

Birdwhistell, Ray L.
1970   *Kinesics and Context: Essays on Body Motion Communication.* Philadelphia: University of Pennsylvania Press.

Most studies of communication have centered on written or verbal communication. A growing area of interest in the social sciences is nonverbal, gestural communications. Kinesics is the label that has come to be attached to the study of gestural communication. In this book the author not only illustrates the importance of such study but also develops a system for coding nonverbal communications.

Hesse-Biber, Sharlene, et al.
1979   "Sex Role Bias in Public Opinion Questionnaires." *Social Policy* (November–December):51–56.

The authors analyze the manifest content of opinion questionnaires. They conclude that the sex-loaded manner in which many questions are worded may have significant impact on the reliability of poll results.

Levin, J., and James L. Spates
1971   "Hippie Values: An Analysis of the Underground Press." In *Mass Culture Revisited,* ed. Bernard Rosenberg and David M. White. New York: Van Nostrand Reinhold.

An interesting example of content analysis that compares the values of conventional society with those central to the hippie movement of the mid-1960s. To assess hippie values, the researchers analyzed a sample of underground press periodicals known to have wide circulation. From these they chose a subsample of nonfiction articles; they then selected a comparable sample of nonfiction articles from *Reader's Digest.*

Lewis, Lionel S., and Dennis Brissett
1969   "Sex as Work." In *Social Problems: Persistent Challenges,* ed. Edward C. McDonagh and Jon E. Simpson. New York: Holt, Rinehart and Winston.

Major social changes are occurring in American society. As the society becomes less production oriented and more consumption oriented, people have increasing leisure time. Yet, the authors argue, Americans are so deeply imbued with the Protestant work ethic that they consider even their leisure as a job; even play is becoming work in mass society. In this article the authors extend this broad theoretical notion to a particular leisure-time activity—sex. A content analysis of marriage manuals reveals that sexual activity is presented as a kind of work in which certain techniques must be mastered to ensure success.

McGinnis, Joe
1970   *The Selling of the President, 1968.* New York: Trident Press.

In this provocative study of the political control of information, the author discusses the central place of the mass media in creating an image of political candidates. A significant portion of this book describes the relationship between television "spot" commercials and the motives of political strategists.

References

Albrecht, Milton C.
1956   "Does Literature Reflect Common Values?" *American Sociological Review* 21 (December):722–729.

Allen, Frederick
1922   "Newspapers and the Truth." *Atlantic Monthly* 129 (January):44–54.

Arnheim, Rudolf
1944   "The World of the Daytime Serial." In *Radio Research: 1942–1943*, ed. Paul F. Lazarsfeld and Frank N. Stanton. New York: Duell, Sloan & Pearce.

Bales, Robert F.
1950   *Interaction Process Analysis.* Reading, Mass.: Addison-Wesley.

Barcus, Francis E.
1961   "A Content Analysis of Trends in Sunday Comics, 1900–1959." *Journalism Quarterly* 38 (Summer): 171–180.

Berelson, Bernard
1952   *Content Analysis in Communication Research.* Glencoe, Ill.: Free Press.

Birdwhistell, Ray
1970   *Kinesics and Context.* Philadelphia: University of Pennsylvania Press.

Blumberg, Nathan B.
1971   "The 'Orthodox' Media Under Fire: Chicago and the Free Press." In *Mass Culture Revisited*, ed. Bernard Rosenberg and David M. White. New York: Van Nostrand Reinhold.

Blumer, Herbert
1933   *Movies and Conduct.* New York: Macmillan.

Bradburn, Norman N., and David E. Berlew
1961   "Need for Achievement and English Economic Growth." *Economic Development and Cultural Change* 10 (October):8–20.

DeFleur, Melvin L.
1964   "Occupational Roles as Portrayed on Television." *Public Opinion Quarterly* 28 (Spring):57–74.

Dornbusch, Sanford M., and Lauren C. Hickman
1959   "Other-Directedness in Consumer-Goods Advertising: A Test of Riesman's Historical Theory." *Social Forces* 38 (December):99–102.

Gregg, James E.
1965   "Newspaper Editorial Endorsements and California Elections, 1948–1962." *Journalism Quarterly* 42 (Winter):532–538.

Hall, Edward
1963   "A System for the Notation of Proxemic Behavior." *American Anthropologist* 65 (October):1003–1026.

Hirsch, Paul M.
1971   "Sociological Approaches to the Pop Music Phenomenon." *American Behavioral Scientist* 14 (January-February):371–388.

Holsti, Ole R.
1969   *Content Analysis for the Social Sciences and Humanities.* Reading, Mass.: Addison-Wesley.

Karp, David A., and William C. Yoels
1976   "The College Classroom: Some Observations on the Meanings of Student Participation." *Sociology and Social Research* 60 (July):421–439.

Lewis, Howard
1960   "The Cuban Revolt Story: AP, UPI, and Three Papers." *Journalism Quarterly* 37 (Winter):573–578.

McClelland, David C.
1961   *The Achieving Society.* New York: Free Press.

McDowell, James L.
1965   "The Role of Newspapers in Illinois' At Large Election." *Journalism Quarterly* 42 (Summer):281–284.

Mosteller, Frederick, and David L. Wallace
1964   *Inference and Disputed Authorship: The Federalist.* Reading, Mass.: Addison-Wesley.

Ogilvie, Daniel M., Philip J. Stone, and Edwin S. Schneidman
1966   "Some Characteristics of Genuine Versus Simulated Suicide Notes." In *The General Inquirer: A Computer Approach to Content Analysis in the Behavioral Sciences*, ed. Philip Stone et al. Cambridge, Mass.: MIT Press.

Osgood, Charles E., and Evelyn B. Walker
1959   "Motivation and Language Behavior: A Content Analysis of Suicide Notes." *Journal of Abnormal and Social Psychology* 59 (July):58–67.

Otto, Herbert A.
1963   "Sex and Violence on the American Newsstand." *Journalism Quarterly* 40 (Spring):19–26.

Paige, Jeffrey M.
1966   "Letters from Jenny: An Approach to the Clinical Analysis of Personality Structure by Computer. In *The General Inquirer: A Computer Approach to Content Analysis in the Behavioral Sciences*, ed. Philip Stone et al. Cambridge, Mass.: MIT Press.

Riesman, David, Nathan Glazer, and Reuel Denney
1950 *The Lonely Crowd.* New Haven, Conn.: Yale University Press.

Sebald, Hans
1962 "Studying National Character Through Comparative Content Analysis." *Social Forces* 40 (June):318–322.

Seider, Maynard S.
1974 "American Big Business Ideology: A Content Analysis of Executive Speeches." *American Sociological Review* 39 (December):802–815.

Stone, Philip, et al., eds.
1966 *The General Inquirer: A Computer Approach to Content Analysis in the Behavioral Sciences.* Cambridge, Mass.: MIT Press.

Wayne, Ivor
1956 "American and Soviet Themes and Values: A Content Analysis of Pictures in Popular Magazines." *Public Opinion Quarterly* 20 (Spring): 314–320.

Wertham, Frederick
1972 *Seduction of the Innocent.* Port Washington, N.Y.: Kennikat Press.

Wolf, Bernard
1949 "Uncle Remus and the Malevolent Rabbit." *Commentary* 8 (July):31–34.

Wolfenstein, Martha, and Nathan Leites
1950 *Movies: A Psychological Study.* New York: Free Press.

12 / Aggregate Data Analysis

CHAPTER OUTLINE

INTRODUCTION
APPLICATIONS OF AGGREGATE
 DATA ANALYSIS
Using Census Materials to Study
 Geographical Social Groupings
Estimated Rates and True Rates: The
 Case of Crime Statistics

Development of Social Indicators
Forecasting
Simulation
FALLACIES IN THE
 INTERPRETATION OF
 AGGREGATE DATA
The Ecological Fallacy

The Atomistic Fallacy
SUMMARY
KEY TERMS
EXERCISES
SUGGESTED READINGS
REFERENCES

Introduction

Social scientists are concerned with understanding the factors influencing the behavior of *individuals* and how this behavior is affected by membership in social groups. In a great variety of research, individuals constitute the UNITS OF ANALYSIS; that is, the data originate with people. Many of the methodologies we have discussed (for instance, survey research, experimentation, participant observation) are employed to understand peoples' attitudes, beliefs, and values. If we want to discover why people vote as they do, exhibit prejudice, or engage in criminal behavior, we often proceed by interviewing or observing an appropriate sample of individuals. We try to show the distinctive characteristics of people who engage in these behaviors.

It is a mistake, however, to believe that individuals are always the focus of social analysis. We may want to understand the nature, character, and dynamics of social structures, as well. We frequently wish to compare institutions according to some attribute. Social scientists sometimes take as their unit of analysis such organizations as universities, business corporations, prisons, or hospitals. As we shall see, much investigation is also concerned with geographical, or AREAL GROUP-INGS, of people. We might be interested in comparing rates of suicide in various countries. While it is true that individuals are responsible for taking their own lives, the focus of our research need not be on the particular or separate motives, beliefs, or personal life conditions of these individuals. Rather, it may be directed at understanding the characteristics of societies where, relatively speaking, large or small numbers of persons commit suicide. It is clear that there are a great many research problems for which data on individuals are used primarily to arrive at a comprehensive characterization of social structures.

Whenever we combine information about the behaviors, attitudes, or other attributes of individuals in order to represent statistically some social unit comprising those people, we are using AGGREGATE DATA. These social units will vary in size and comprehensiveness. Researchers might, for example, study the same phenomenon at progressively higher LEVELS OF AGGREGATION. They might investigate how rates of mental illness vary in different neighborhoods, then combine, or aggregate, these data to examine mental illness rates in entire cities. Information from various cities, in turn, could be aggregated to generate data on counties, and so forth. As a logical extension of this aggregation process, researchers could compare countries concerning their mental illness rates.

The procedure of combining or aggregating information on individuals to produce an overall group rating should not be unfamiliar to us. College administrators may boast in their public relations literature that students' average Scholastic Aptitude Test score is over 600. This one score is used to characterize the whole student body and is produced by combining data on each student in the school. In much the same way we make judgments about society's condition and the quality of our own lives using "official statistics" computed by aggregating data on individuals. These statistics, we should note, are often the basis for the creation of social policy.

Some people are willing to measure the morality of a society in terms of suicide statistics or rates of divorce or church attendance. Politicians promise us that if elected they will institute programs to reduce the frequency of crime in our major cities. We weigh our economic futures by monitoring unemployment statistics. Ecologists and environmentalists ask us to consider seriously the implications of population growth rates. Comparisons are often made between cities, counties, states, and nations in terms of juvenile delinquency, infant mortality, literacy, average income, and migration. Clearly, aggregate data comprise a significant portion of the information that both professionals and nonprofessionals need to assess social, economic, and political behavior in relative terms.

Our goal in this chapter is to discuss some of the methodological issues raised when aggregate data are used in research. Among the questions that will occupy our attention are: How do researchers decide on the appropriate unit of analysis in their studies? How closely do the rates reflected in aggregate data approximate the true extent of the phenomenon studied? Do crime rates, for example, really tell us how much criminal activity actually exists? Can we ever make statements about individuals from aggregate data? If we find, for example, that rates of delinquency are highest in areas where the divorce rate is highest, can we then infer that family disorganization causes *specific* individuals to engage in delinquent behaviors? Under what conditions might it be misleading to characterize an institution by summing up the characteristics of the people composing it? Are there situations where the whole is more than, less than, or at least different from the sum of its parts? Are there any differences in the nature of the information obtained as we move from one level of aggregation to another?

Before we tackle some of these issues, let us consider some applications of aggregate data analysis.

Applications of
Aggregate Data Analysis

Aggregate data analysis is not restricted to one or a few areas of social science inquiry. Those studying such diverse subjects as deviance, stratification, race relations, urban life, large-scale organizations, occupations and professions, and mass communications will frequently formulate research problems that require aggregate data analysis. But there are certain topics for investigation where it is nearly always necessary. All demographic analyses of population trends rely on official statistics already aggregated. A good deal of research in urban sociology makes use of census data collected periodically by the federal government. As might be expected, criminologists must rely heavily on available crime statistics. Recently, social scientists have made considerable progress in developing indicators for evaluating the "social well-being" of nations. In this research, aggregate statistics are used for assessing changes in such social rates as poverty, public safety, health, and employment.

Because of the extraordinary range of applications for aggregate data analysis, we must be selective in our discussion. We have chosen to examine some research problems that call for extensive, if not exclusive, use of aggregate data analysis and that also highlight the methodological problems connected with its use. We shall treat, in turn, studies employing census materials and crime statistics, as well as research devoted to the development of social indicators and the forecasting of future social trends.

USING CENSUS MATERIALS TO STUDY
GEOGRAPHICAL SOCIAL GROUPINGS

Suppose we had the idea that there have been major changes in the structure and composition of American cities over the past fifty years. We have a theory that suggests that the growth of suburbs has affected the age, ethnic, racial, and income characteristics of city dwellers. We want to show that large cities are increasingly inhabited by younger, lower-income minority groups, especially blacks. Consider the kind of data we need to establish the validity of our contention. We need information on the attributes of people in each major city, collected periodically and regularly over a long period of time. Aggregate census statistics are indispensable to social scientists because they contain precisely the kind of demographic data often used to characterize the population attributes of distinctive territorial groupings of people.

The data available in census reports refer to other territorial groupings besides cities, some less and some more comprehensive. A territorial grouping, or geographical unit, that may include fewer than a hundred households is called a CENSUS BLOCK. Traditionally, however, social scientists have made greater use of aggregate census data reported for a somewhat broader areal unit called the CENSUS TRACT. Although bigger than the census block, the census tract is still a relatively small area containing a population of between 3,000 and 6,000 persons. Each city is divided into a number of census tracts. Although there is certainly an arbitrary component to the specification of census tract areas, they are reasonably uniform in terms of population and size. As noted earlier, social scientists sometimes want to make comparisons between geographically defined social structures larger than census blocks, census tracts, or cities. Census data can be obtained to characterize counties, states, areas of the country, and the nation as a whole. Moreover, nearly all nations maintain census records, and this makes it possible to engage in CROSS-CULTURAL COMPARISONS.

The population characteristics mentioned earlier (age, race, ethnicity, and income) are only a few of those collected and reported in census statistics. Among other aggregate data reported for each of the territorial levels mentioned are the following: place of birth, occupational level, educational attainment, marital status, and family size. Without the data contained in census reports much social investigation would be impossible. On a simple descriptive level we could not determine with any accuracy how different groups (ethnic, racial, class, and so on) are distributed geographically throughout cities. We could not determine rates of urban population growth and decline. We could not easily assess income differentials among city groups. Nor could we specify the relationships between such variables as population growth and economic development, or residential location and occupational status.

As an example of important research relying on the aggregate data provided in census reports, we will examine Karl and Alma Taeuber's (1966) study of one of our most difficult social problems: racial residential segregation in American cities. In their research the authors used census data to investigate various aspects of segregation in United States metropolitan areas, focusing on the period from 1940 through 1960.

The Taeubers reasoned that if race made absolutely no difference in determining where a person chose to live, or was allowed to live, then no area of a city would be all black or all white. If, for example, blacks constituted 25 percent of a city's population, it would be expected that in each city block examined they would comprise 25 percent of the residents. Similarly, if blacks made up 50 percent of a city's population, it would be expected that one out of every two households would be black. These assumptions would hold only if there were absolutely no residential segregation.

To compare one metropolitan area with another, the authors devised an index of housing segregation, ranging from 0 to 100. If a city had no racial segregation, it could theoretically be assigned a score of zero. On the other hand, if each block examined were all black or all white, the index score would be 100.[1]

Using census materials to compute a segregation index for 207 cities, the Taeubers were able to show convincingly that "a high degree of residential segregation is universal in American cities" (1966:2). For all areas examined, the lowest index was 60.4 and the highest was 98.1, with half the cities having values above 87.8, and one-fourth above 91.7.[2]

It is not possible in a short review to present all the findings in this study. It is important to note, however, that by beginning with census data and processing

---

[1]For a discussion of the major issues in index construction, see Chapter 15.

[2]It is noteworthy that as long as race is correlated with income, it would be possible for there to be differences in the distribution of the races even if there were no racial discrimination in the allocation of residence. The evidence, however, indicates that economic factors "cannot account for more than a small portion of observed levels of racial residential segregation" (Taeuber and Taeuber, 1966:2).

them, the authors were able to present: comparisons in residential segregation between areas of the country, statistics on *changes* in segregation rates for cities and areas of the country between 1940 and 1960, data on the economic and social characteristics of black residential areas, an analysis of the factors involved in the flight of whites as blacks move into an area, and data describing the economic characteristics of blacks in racially mixed census tracts.

The wide-ranging information reported in this study is valuable for two related reasons. First, the descriptive aggregate rates of segregation for separate cities and areas of the country allow us to see exactly the parameters of the problems we face. The data presented in this study certainly laid to rest the stereotype held by many that segregation is primarily a Southern problem. Second, it is only through a comprehensive understanding of the kinds of patterns uncovered in research of this sort that we can begin to formulate intelligent social policy. Assuming that we can agree on the value of integration, we must know just how and why city neighborhoods change or remain stably mixed racially before we can begin to create the kind of change we want.

Available sources of aggregate data such as censuses are indeed valuable, but we must also recognize the limitations and methodological problems involved in the use of such "official" statistics. Certain errors may creep into the aggregate data with which we often work. First, there may be ERRORS OF COVERAGE. Inevitably, counting mistakes will be made in the original collection of data from individuals. Some people are invariably missed and therefore not represented in the aggregate figures compiled, and some may be counted twice. (Those who work frequently with census materials suggest that coverage errors result much more often in undercounts than in overcounts.)

Second, there will be unavoidable CLASSIFICATION ERRORS. Census data, collected every ten years, is obtained using self-administered questionnaires delivered through the mail or by enumerators hired to conduct personal interviews. As would be the case in evaluating the quality of any data collected via questionnaire, we know that respondents will lie about certain issues. People may want to "look good" in their own eyes and in the eyes of the interviewer and consequently give false information about such items as their education, income, and occupational levels. Common sense would lead us to expect that the direction of the error will be toward the higher education, income, and occupational categories. It is always possible, further, that people will not understand the questions asked by census enumerators or that those collecting the data will themselves make systematic classification errors. There will also inevitably be a number of mistakes made in the final processing, tabulating, or aggregating of the data collected on millions of people.

There are still other problems that the researcher using census data may face. As indicated in our review of the Taeubers' research, investigators frequently want to compare changes over time in particular areal units. We might be interested in how the income distributions for particular towns have varied over a fifty-year period. Unfortunately, town boundaries may expand during the ten years intervening between census tabulations, making the desired comparison difficult. For researchers who wish to make cross-cultural comparisons using census data, there will be other problems: certain types of data collected in one country may not be collected in another; data for certain countries may be incomplete; there may be special cultural factors in a society that induce individuals to misrepresent themselves; ideology or politics might affect the way that statistics are reported; the individuals' categories used for classifying (say, by education or income) will vary from country to country and again hinder comparative analysis.[3]

Some of the types of problems we have been discussing with reference to census data are more strongly highlighted when we consider other official statistics that social scientists frequently employ in their research. To extend our comments on the possible errors contaminating available aggregate data—errors that, in turn, may lead us to false conclusions and inferences—we shall consider briefly some of the methodological dilemmas of those who rely on official crime statistics.

ESTIMATED RATES AND TRUE RATES: THE CASE OF CRIME STATISTICS

Of all the aggregate data available to social scientists, official crime rate statistics are among the most unreliable. While the problems in the use of these figures may be especially severe, they are nevertheless the types of difficulties with which we must cope when we use any aggregate data previously prepared by others. Because of a variety of errors in the compilation of any data, there will always be a discrepancy between the REPORTED RATE of some phenomenon and the TRUE RATE. We would do well to consider just how great this discrepancy is likely to be in the data we use.

In the case of criminal behavior we know that there are many more crimes committed than appear in official statistics. The statistics do not accurately reflect the commission of crimes that are rarely reported by victims, such as rape. In other words, the number of crimes known to the police is always substantially smaller than the total actually committed. Of equal importance in making us suspicious about the validity of crime statistics is the knowledge that the tabulation varies with local police policies, court policies, and public opinion. If the statistical data presented have not been compiled in a uniform fashion (that is, according to the same rules or criteria), comparative analysis of rates in different jurisdictions is very misleading.

The criteria used to classify crimes vary widely in different geographical areas. There is even disagreement between various jurisdictions as to the definition of *crime* itself. Crime rates vary widely because local administrators may interpret the law differently. If we were to treat the statistics at face value, we might be led to believe that there is more crime in Berkeley, California, than in Palo Alto, when in fact the difference is simply an artifact of the methods used in compiling the statistics. If law enforcement officials began systematically to arrest people for vagrancy, prostitution, and speeding, where they had previously been lenient toward these crimes, it would be incorrect to conclude that there had been a substantial upsurge in the crime rate. Because of political pressure from government leaders or citizens' groups, police officials may periodically "crack down" on certain kinds of activities. On the other hand, we could imagine officials not reporting in their records all the crimes they know occur in their areas so that it

---

[3]For a discussion of some of the problems encountered in comparative research using aggregate data, see Chapter 13.

will appear that they are succeeding in keeping the crime rate down. Such biasing factors affecting the reporting and maintenance of statistics make the study of changing rates of crime very difficult. We cannot easily know whether differences from year to year in a given jurisdiction are real.

Some have argued that crime rate statistics are badly flawed because police officials differentially enforce the law. There is compelling evidence that blacks are much more likely than whites to be arrested for the same behaviors; that middle- or upper-class youngsters are likely to only be warned by local police when engaging in behaviors that would lead to the arrest of adolescents in working-class areas. There are, in addition, certain kinds of crimes for which people are very unlikely to be arrested. This is perhaps most true of white-collar crimes, such as income tax evasion, bribery, and kickback schemes (Sutherland, 1961).

The factors mentioned, taken together, conspire to make the validity of statistical crime rates highly questionable. It has not been our intention, however, merely to comment on one substantive area of social investigation. Crime statistics stand as a convenient example to raise a larger point. Whenever we use aggregate data already compiled by others, we need to be skeptical about the extent to which the rates presented reflect the actual volume of behaviors, events, or demographic attributes in the groups studied.

DEVELOPMENT OF SOCIAL INDICATORS

A country cannot chart its own progress, change, or growth by looking at the behavior or life conditions of only a few individuals. Aggregate analysis is required if we wish to develop yardsticks for evaluating the social state and well-being of a nation. Just as economists have charted trends using such economic indicators as gross national product, median family income, and unemployment rate, so too have social scientists developed SOCIAL INDICATORS.[4] Social indicators are used to measure change in such conditions as: poverty, public safety, education, health, and housing. They are also used to produce knowledge that will be of use in social planning and the formulation of public policy. Such information can be of help in the determination of where our money, programs, and general efforts at creating social change are most needed. Social indicators are generally presented as TIME-SERIES DATA; this makes it possible to chart changes over time. Not all time-series statistics would be classified as social indicators. Typically, social indicators are quantitative aggregate measures used to assess trends in various aspects of the quality of social life (Land, 1975).

The widespread use of social indicators is relatively recent. Some work was done in the 1930s (for example, President's Research Committee on Social Trends, 1933), but the effort did not really mature until the mid-1960s. Some who do social indicators research focus on the production of longitudinal statistics, documenting trends in various aspects of the quality of social life. Others apply these statistics to the study of social mobility, to changes in the female occupational structure, to changes in degree of racial segregation, and so on—that is, to studies based on social indicator trend data.

---

[4]Presentation of social indicators is always in the form of aggregate data, but it is sometimes the case that the information was obtained from a nonaggregate source, such as survey research data.

Suppose we were to ask the question: Is the health status of the United States improving? We might turn to a source such as *Social Indicators 1976,* which presents graphs and tables of trends in eight areas: employment, income, leisure and recreation, housing, public safety, population, and health. Given our research question, we would be particularly interested in the data for the various health indicators. Among the statistics available would be life expectancy at birth (by sex and race), death rates (by age, sex, race, and cause of death), and infant mortality rates. Also included are several indicators assessing various forms of disability and access to medical care. Some of these statistics are available for each year since the turn of the century; others for the last fifteen years or so. To answer our research question, we might decide to limit ourselves to a particular aspect of health status, or we might attempt a synthesis based on all the measures.

Our discussion of social indicators may be used as a platform for thinking about the implications of the level of aggregation on which we carry out our research. Social indicators typically represent rates for a whole nation or society but what information is gained or lost as the level of aggregation becomes more comprehensive? In order to deal with this question, it is best to start with a concrete example. As previously mentioned, one social indicator of health at the national level of aggregation is average life expectancy. This indicator will tell us of changes, up to the present, in the average life expectancy of individuals at birth. Let us look at some actual data on life expectancy rates broken down by sex and race in Figure 12.1.

These data indicate that average life expectancy has generally increased continuously since 1900. We should note, also, the substantial differences between

FIGURE 12.1   Life Expectancy at Birth by Sex and Race, 1901–1971

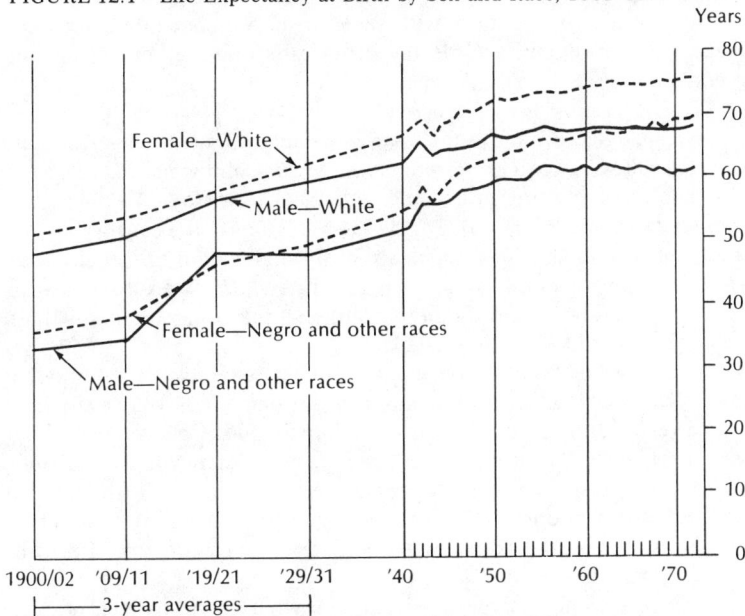

Source: Executive Office of the President: Office of Management and Budget, *Social Indicators, 1973* (Washington, D.C.: U.S. Government Printing Office, 1973).

men and women and the even more startling variation between whites and non-whites. White women can expect to live longer than white men. Nonwhite women can expect to live longer than nonwhite men. In all cases, until very recently, whites (men and women) could expect to live longer than nonwhites. Only since about 1965 has the average life expectancy of nonwhite women become greater than that of white men. As recently as 1971 white women could expect to live about fifteen years longer than nonwhite men.

As we consider these figures on life expectancy, there are a number of questions worth raising. The most basic of these is: What potentially important information is unavailable to us—given that the data are presented on the *national level* of aggregation? Imagine that we are administrators responsible for the allocation of monies to various health improvement programs around the country. We would say that these national figures are interesting but that they do not tell the whole story. We might comment that the national statistics do not allow us to see variations between areas of the country (West, Midwest, Northeast, etc.) in life expectancy rates. It could be that life expectancy rates are quite high in one area but relatively low in another. If we knew this to be so, we would have a better idea of where to allocate available funds.

Suppose it would be possible to DISAGGREGATE the available data so that we could see differences between areas of the country in life expectancy rates. When we disaggregate, we take an existing unit of data and break it into finer or less comprehensive units. If we could disaggregate the national data, we would have more information because it would be possible for us to see differences between smaller units (regions of the country), differences that were masked in the national-level data. Even now, however, we might not be altogether satisfied because individual states can vary widely in life expectancy rates. If we could see such variations, it would further facilitate our decision making; we would give more money to programs in the states with lower life expectancy rates. Since the data aggregated at the region level do not provide us information on separate states, we could ask that the data be disaggregated to this less comprehensive unit.

With the available data from the fifty states, we might have the idea that life expectancy rates will still vary for different cities. At this point we have to face the fact that the data are beginning to become somewhat unwieldy. We have gone from one rate (the national level) to five or six rates (regions of the country) to fifty rates (states), and we must now recognize that disaggregation to the city level would mean looking at several hundred separate rates. If we were to move this one step lower, it would become difficult to examine intelligently the many thousands of statistics that would be generated.

There is an important point to be made from our example of information gained and lost as we aggregate and disaggregate data. It is that each time researchers move to a higher level of aggregation they lose information about levels immediately below. At the same time there is an efficiency to the statistics on higher levels of aggregation. At the national level we need deal with only one rate, at the state level it increases to fifty rates, and so forth, until it would be literally impossible to manage or interpret the extraordinary amount of data at lower levels of aggregation.

There is, then, no easy answer to the question: At what aggregate level ought a researcher to carry out analysis? We want to maximize both information and efficiency. In some cases, however, there is little choice in the matter. We simply must work at the level for which available statistics have already been aggregated. This is so when we make use of census data. Here we are constrained by the geographical units for which census data are reported. In other words, whenever available statistics are used, they can always be aggregated to higher levels but not disaggregated to levels lower than the one presented in the available data. Where researchers do have a number of options relative to level of aggregation in a study, their choice must be made in terms of the research goals and theories guiding the investigation.

FORECASTING

Social indicators, we have noted, allow researchers to evaluate changes in the condition of a nation over time, from some point in the past to the present. It is a somewhat different task to adequately *forecast* future trends in a society. We know that it is important for planning purposes to estimate with some accuracy what the population will be in the United States in fifty years or more. It is vital to know what our energy needs and natural resources will be in the future. We might also want to know whether welfare caseloads will increase or decrease or whether there will be significant changes in employment opportunities. Typically, those who do such social forecasting must rely on aggregate data.

Forecasting is often done by looking at aggregate trends in the factors of interest (birth rates, welfare expenditures, and so on) from some point in the past to the present. If we assume that the rates of increase or decrease we see will not change substantially, we can estimate future trends or growth. In their simplest form, forecasting models can be depicted as shown below:

Suppose we wanted to forecast population trends in the United States. We could look at data from, say, 1930 to the present. Clearly, we could not simply look at regular increases or decreases in birth rates; total population growth is a function of several variables, and birth rates alone would not provide enough data for us to make an adequate forecast. In order to estimate future population growth, we would have to take into account such additional factors as national death and migration rates. We might, then, begin our analysis by looking at the data collected by the Bureau of the Census (see Figure 12.2).

Examination of the aggregate data in Figure 12.2 reveals some of the difficulties in forecasting population trends. We can see in this particular case that fertility (birth) rates do not increase or decrease with any apparent regularity. There was a sharp decrease in fertility between 1968 and 1972. We wish to project population trends into the future, but we must acknowledge that these

FIGURE 12.2   Estimated Births, Deaths, Net Civilian Immigration and Net Population
Growth, United States, 1930–1972

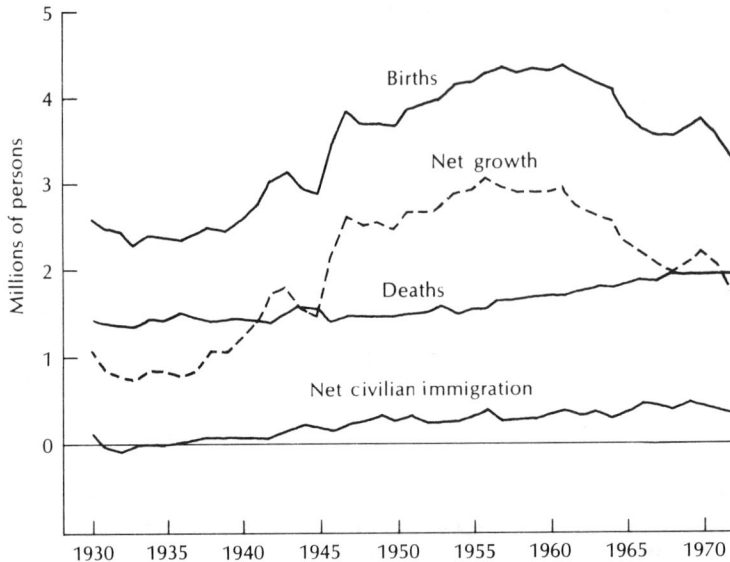

Source: U.S. Bureau of the Census, Current Population Reports, Series P-25, No. 499,
"Estimates of the population of the United States and components of change, 1972"
(Washington, D.C.: U.S. Government Printing Office, 1973).

abrupt, apparently unpredictable rate changes seriously hinder clear predictions.
As a consequence, DEMOGRAPHERS (those who study population trends) cannot
make flat predictions about future population growth rates. Instead, they must
talk about *ranges* of growth or decline that are based on a number of forecasts;
and each forecast rests on a different assumption about future fertility rates. The
demographer may say, "If the fertility rate is 2.8 births per woman, we can expect
the population to grow this way; if the rate is 2.5 births, population growth will
assume a different direction," and so forth. In other words, demographers will not
make one flat prediction but rather will lay out a number of scenarios based on
alternative assumptions about key rates.

While we cannot know for certain which of the several assumptions is correct,
we can still extract important information from the kind of research we have been
describing. We might find that for the lowest plausible estimate of future fertility,
the population will double during the next thirty years; that is, we can be sure
that at the very least the population will grow to a certain size within this specified
time period. Informed social planning and public policy is dependent upon information of this kind.

SIMULATION

We have been talking about some of the difficulties in forecasting trends for a
single variable—population. Problems of forecasting become more formidable
when researchers wish to consider the interplay of *several variables simultane-*

ously in predicting future social conditions. In these cases social scientists increasingly use computer technology to *simulate* future social trends. To obtain a clearer picture of how computer simulations are done, we shall consider the research of Donnella Meadows and her colleagues (1972), who, in *The Limits To Growth,* have attempted to predict world trends in population size and in the use of resources.

Meadows raises no less a question than: What will happen to the world if current economic and demographic trends continue at present rates? Note that the research question does not refer to a single variable but to a total social system—the world's total ecological system. The first step is to construct a SIMULATION MODEL describing the system under investigation. Since the success of any computer simulation depends on the model constructed at the beginning of the research, we shall find it useful to look quite carefully at this process. More particularly, we need to distinguish between static and dynamic models.

In Chapter 1, we examined the development and use of models in social science. As an example we looked at a model showing the key or major variables most predictive of an individual's present occupational position. They were: father's educational achievement, father's occupational status, respondent's educational achievement, and the status of the individual's first job. We can review two major characteristics of this type of model:

1. It is composed of the relatively few factors deemed most influential in describing or explaining the system, phenomenon, or events investigated.
2. The causal relationships assumed to exist among the variables constituting the model are clearly specified.

It is important to point out, however, that it is a STATIC MODEL which means it is designed solely to predict events at one point in time. Its success is evaluated primarily on how accurately the variables named predict a person's present occupational position. The model is not designed to predict features of the stratification system in the future. It could happen, for example, that in fifty years educational achievement will be inconsequential in predicting a person's occupational position. Such potential changes in the causal influence of variables is not troublesome if our goal is only to predict an event in the present in terms of events in the past.

Where the research goal is to simulate or forecast future events, static models are not sufficient. Consider again the research problem faced by Meadows. She wanted to look at the likely condition of the world's ecological system at a number of different points in the future. The model she used had to allow her to make accurate predictions about the conditions of the ecological system in one, five, ten, twenty, thirty, fifty, or one hundred years. Clearly, her model had to be one that not only specifies the variables most influential in describing the present ecological system but specifies as well the generic processes through which the variables in the model will continue to interact with each other over time. Models that account for the processes governing the interaction between variables in predicting certain outcomes (for example, changes in an ecological system) are called DYNAMIC MODELS.

On the basis of aggregate data trends from 1900 to 1970 and her own theoretical reasoning, Meadows constructed a model composed of five key variables central to the world's ecological system—population, food supply, natural resources, industrial production, and pollution. Meadows then produced a set of mathematical equations detailing the processes through which the five variables interact with each other. These equations, constructed from available aggregate data, describe a FEEDBACK SYSTEM wherein a change in any one of the variables causes changes in the other variables, which in turn modify the variable that started the change process. One of the several equations describing the dynamic interactions between the variables might detail the feedback process shown below which is set in motion by a change in population growth rates:

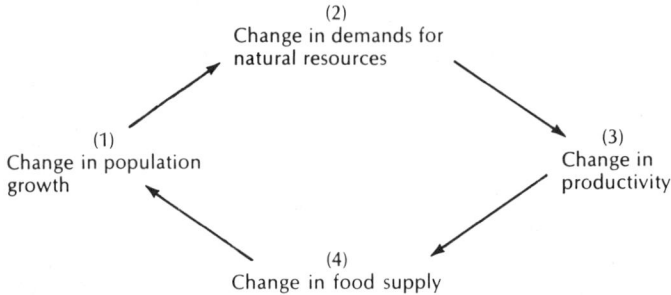

```
                            (2)
                    Change in demands for
                     natural resources

     (1)                                              (3)
  Change in population                            Change in
  growth                                          productivity

                            (4)
                    Change in food supply
```

After describing mathematically how the variables interacted with each other in the past, Meadows projected that same process into the future. As mentioned, the most immediate research requirement was to simulate the condition of the ecological system for different points in the future, assuming that growth rates in the key variables remain as they have in the past. The results of this simulation are quite gloomy. Meadows et al. (1972:23) report:

> If the present growth trends in world population, industrialization, pollution, food production and resource depletion continue unchanged, the limits to growth on this planet will be reached sometime within the next hundred years. The most probable result will be a rather sudden and uncontrollable decline in both population and industrial capacity.

The utility of Meadows's simulation model does not, however, end with this one prediction. We might ask what would happen to the ecological system at different points in the future if we were able to institute immediately a program to increase food production by a specified amount over its present rate. Researchers can do any of a number of simulations by assuming a different hypothesized value or rate for the dimensions in the model. It is referred to as SENSITIVITY TESTING each time the researchers try out different values or rates for a variable in the model. Through sensitivity testing researchers can produce a large number of future scenarios, each of which is generated from alternative assumptions about key rates in the parameters of the model. For this reason computer simulation models are valuable aids in designing and then testing the likely effects of alternative policies. Indeed, Meadows has been able to propose from the variety of sensitivity tests done with her model just how growth rates must be reduced in order for the ecological system to reach a state of equilibrium. She has advocated that social planners immediately design programs to achieve global aggregate rates compatible with the survival of the environment.

There are those who have soundly criticized the type of computer modeling we have been describing. A basic criticism raised suggests that because models used in computer simulation can encompass only a relatively few variables they simply are not a very good representation of reality. A critic might argue that if a few different variables were included in the models, the simulated outcomes would be radically altered. We might say that one of the flaws in Meadows's model stems from the failure to include any *cultural* or *social value* variables. Certainly people's values, outlooks on the world, beliefs, and attitudes will determine how they will respond to environmental changes. Since it is virtually impossible to predict just the part that such values would have in the total environmental change process, it is also virtually impossible to include them in a model in which variables must be restricted to those with known rates and known effects. It is worth repeating that the validity of computer simulation findings must be evaluated in terms of the model used to generate them. We must insistently question whether potentially important variables have been excluded from the models used in any research.

Others have quarreled with the findings of Meadows's research because it was based only on *global aggregate* data for each of the five variables in the model. These critics suggest that if the researchers had been able to analyze data on lower aggregate levels (for example, countries or communities), they would have produced a model that made quite different predictions. They reason that the variables named in the model interact first at local levels in a society and that once these changes are seen to be occurring, there is likely to be corrective social planning at these lower aggregate levels. Should such corrective measures be taken, global failure of the ecological system, as predicted by Meadows, would not occur. The criticism recalls two points from previous discussion. First, social scientists are often constrained in their research because they must use available aggregate data. Second, the aggregate level on which data are analyzed may considerably influence the kind of information obtained and hence the conclusions reached in the research.[5]

---

[5]Following the central concern of this chapter, we have chosen as an example of a study using simulation techniques one employing aggregate data. It would, however, be misleading for the reader to assume that all simulations depend on aggregate data or are always done to project further events, as in the case of Meadows's research. Simulations do, in fact, have broader applications. Any time we try to imitate the outcomes of a process in order to understand, explain, or clarify the mechanisms of some phenomenon, we engage in a simulation.

Given this broad definition, not all simulations rely on computer technology. When soldiers play "war games" during basic training, they are engaging in a simulation of the process of war. Social scientists have devised games to simulate some of the major components of a society. In one such game a model is created of a small community. Individuals participating in this simulated society are given certain personal, social, and political goals to realize during the course of the game. While the model on which the game is based is certainly a simplification of society (any model is a simplification), it is nevertheless possible to learn about the basic processes of social organization using the model. Simulations in which human beings are the essential interacting components are called *man-model* simulations.

A second major type has been called *man-machine* simulation. A simple example would be programing a computer to play chess against a person. Man-machine simulations have been used to play out complex international diplomacy scenarios based on historical data fed into the computer. Programed with appropriate information, the computer can print out likely responses of foreign governments to various diplomatic positions taken by an individual representing the United States. Man-machine simulations can be used to train persons for situations too costly or dangerous for them to actually experience during training. They may also be used to test the viability of different strategies for solving practical problems.

Finally, there are *machine* simulations where the whole process of interest to re-

Fallacies in the Interpretation of Aggregate Data

We have provided examples of aggregate data analysis and pondered some of the questions and problems faced by researchers who do it. They must worry about errors in the available data with which they work. In some cases aggregate rates are poor estimates of true rates. Researchers must also be certain that the data describing each of the units they compare have been collected according to the same criteria. Even if we could assume ideal research conditions where none of these problems existed, it would still be possible to commit certain logical errors in making inferences from aggregate data.

Methodologists have pointed out a number of fallacies that may trap researchers as they try to interpret information. In nearly all cases where such logical errors occur, data have been collected at one level of aggregation (say, at the individual or small-group level), but the researcher has tried to use the data to make statements about phenomena at a different level. Keeping in mind that the level of aggregation influences the specific interpretations one can make, let us examine two common errors of inference, the ecological fallacy and the atomistic fallacy.

THE ECOLOGICAL FALLACY

We must be wary about employing data collected from and about groups in order to impute motives to individuals. The ECOLOGICAL FALLACY involves making such an illegitimate shift of inference. Suppose that a jury is deciding a case and after much deliberation reports to the judge that it cannot as a group decide the guilt or innocence of the defendant. The jury is hung; as a *group* it is undecided. Although the jury is composed of twelve individuals, we can make reference to the group as a whole (this is essentially what we do when we aggregate data). We can say that the jury is undecided.

Now to the important point. Can we move from our statement that the jury is undecided to say that *individual jurors* are undecided? Certainly not! Indeed, it may very well be that none of the twelve jurors is undecided; they are simply individually decided in different directions. The conceptual, logical point to be made here is that *one cannot properly make inferences about individuals in groups on the basis of data about the group as a whole.* To do so is to commit the aggregative, or ecological, fallacy. Let us proceed from our simple example to a somewhat more complicated one.

Suppose that a group of researchers is interested in seeing whether there is any relationship between crime rates and the racial composition of some selected areas. The researchers decide to use census data in order to discover any connection that might exist between these two variables. Note that they will be using

---

searchers is simulated by the computer. The Meadows et al. (1972) study is representative of this third type. As one further point of clarification, computer simulations need not focus only on world, or global, processes. It is certainly possible to use computers to simulate the process through which such small systems as social groups operate.

aggregate group-level data in their analysis. They will not be collecting data from specific individuals. Further, they will be relying on data already available. We shall assume that they choose to examine the aggregate data for census tracts and then to look at crime rates in those same tracts. They are wondering, most particularly, if there is any relationship between the percentage of blacks in a census area and the crime rate. After examining the appropriate figures, the researchers display their findings in a SCATTERGRAM, as in Figure 12.3.

An examination of these data shows a clear pattern. There is a positive correlation between the percentage of black persons in an area and the crime rate; as the percentage of black persons increases, there is a general corresponding increase in the amount of crime. Now, remember that the data represented in Figure 12.3 are aggregated, group, or ecological data. Is it appropriate for these researchers to say, on the basis of these data, that black *persons* are much more likely than white persons to commit crimes? Again, certainly not! For the same reason that we cannot say anything about the individual jurors in our previous example, we cannot say anything about the propensity for crime of individual black persons. It could be, for example, that as the percentage of black persons in an area increases, the whites still remaining in the areas are more and more marginal or alienated; and that it is these relatively few alienated white persons who are committing most of the crime in the heavily black areas. Or to use the kind of extreme example offered by Galtung (1967), what if the crimes committed are assaults on blacks by whites or even the lynchings of blacks? In other words, it could be that blacks are not committing the crimes at all, but that the crimes are performed against them and that the percentage of crimes depends on the high availability of blacks.

Given the same logic presented here, we cannot say that because there is, for example, a high correlation between the percentage of divorced persons in an area and rates of juvenile delinquency that family disorganization is the cause of delinquency. In the cases we have mentioned, it might immediately seem reasonable to make inferences about individuals from aggregate data, but there is a grave danger in doing so.

The most important idea that the ecological fallacy alerts us to is that the level on which we conduct our analysis must correspond to the level of the units referred to in our hypotheses and at issue in our theories. If the conceptual model focuses on the differences between individuals, we must be certain that we use individual-level data. If we are certain that the data level used in a study corresponds to the units of analysis referred to in our hypotheses and theoretical constructs, we can be confident we have avoided the ecological fallacy.

THE ATOMISTIC FALLACY

It is possible to commit the ecological fallacy in reverse—to make incorrect statements about groups on the basis of data from individuals. When we try to test hypotheses about groups when we have only individual-level data, we risk committing what has been called the ATOMISTIC FALLACY.

Suppose we had in mind the hypothesis that there is a relationship between rates of residential mobility in cities and rates of mental illness. More specifically, we believe that the higher the rates of residential mobility, the greater the inci-

FIGURE 12.3   Scattergram Showing Relationship between Race and Crime in a Hypothetical City, 1979–1980

Percentage black

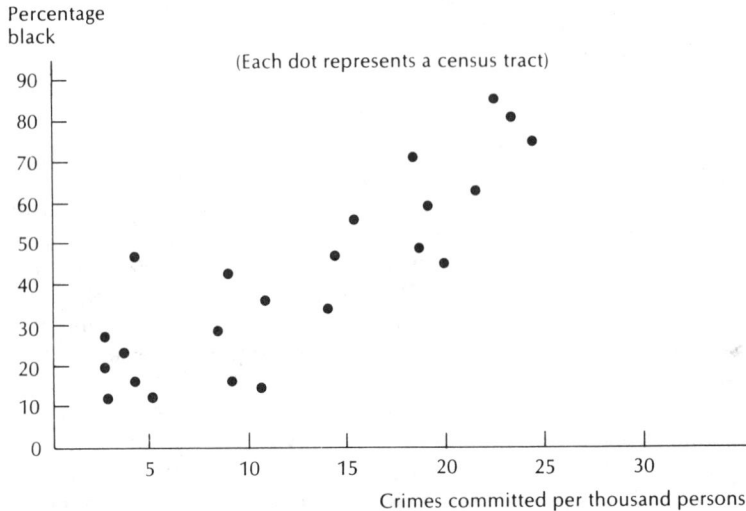

(Each dot represents a census tract)

Crimes committed per thousand persons

dence of mental illness. Please note that this hypothesis refers to the characteristics of cities as social systems. *It is not an hypothesis about differences between individuals.* Consider now the inferential error we would make if we were to mistakenly test this group-level hypothesis with individual-level data.

We might begin the research by collecting data on individuals. We could do this by getting the names of all people in a particular city who were committed to mental hospitals within the last year. We might then interview these people or check records to determine how many times they had moved (a measure of residential mobility) during the five years prior to entering the hospital. We might find that the people studied move very infrequently and therefore conclude that our original hypothesis—that high rates of residential mobility will be strongly related to mental illness rates—is incorrect. We will have rejected an hypothesis about spatial groupings or structural units by examining data from individuals. Will we have properly rejected our original hypothesis, or will we have committed a logical error of inference?

It could be that the individuals who become mentally ill in cities are precisely those who are left behind when their friends move out of the immediate neighborhood. There is, in other words, a *structural effect* operating. The likelihood of individuals becoming mentally ill may not be a function of what they themselves do but of what is happening around them. Indeed, it could be that there is quite a strong relationship between rates of residential mobility in cities and rates of mental illness, which has not been seen because our researcher looked only at individual-level data. The researcher has simply assumed that what the individuals studied do is sufficient data on which to characterize the social groupings of which they are a part.

Whether we commit the ecological or the atomistic fallacy, the underlying reason for the mistake remains the same. We have, in both cases, committed what Galtung (1967) calls "the fallacy of the wrong level."

Summary

When we combine data on individuals in order to represent some social unit comprising these people statistically, we are using aggregate data. The possible levels of aggregation vary considerably, from relatively small census tracts to cities, states, and nations. The proper use of aggregate data involves taking these entities as units of analysis in order to make generalizations about the character of social structures.

Aggregate data analysis has wide applicability in the social sciences, for example, in demography, criminology, and urban planning. It is also useful in studies that compare neighborhoods, counties, or countries, as well as those that assess trends in poverty, health, education, and public safety. Census data are particularly helpful, but in working with them, errors of coverage, classification, and processing typical of all existing data are liable to occur. We know that the reported rates in crime statistics vary considerably from the true incidence of crime within a population and that criteria for data collection differ according to jurisdiction. We must recognize that aggregate data offer only an estimate of the group characteristics of interest to us. We need to take this into account as we interpret the information collected.

Researchers must conduct their investigations on the aggregate level for which data are available. Further, the level of aggregation at which they carry out their analysis affects the nature of the generalizations they can make. In devising social indicators (yardsticks for measuring the well-being of large groups of people), important information regarding differences between units at lower levels of aggregation may be lost or unavailable. This principle applies also to another application of group data—forecasting trends. We must be careful not to assume that variables at the level of aggregate data we have available are the most important ones for determining future events. It is possible to simulate the behavior of aggregates using a computer, but this technique is subject to the same potential validity errors as is standard aggregate data analysis.

Finally, we must avoid mixing levels of aggregation by making inferences about individual behaviors from group data (the ecological fallacy) and by drawing conclusions about groups from individual data (the atomistic fallacy). The better we know the potential flaws or biases in dealing with specific kinds of data, the more likely we are to correct these errors and thus improve the quality of our findings.

Key Terms

aggregate data	disaggregation	sensitivity testing
areal groupings	dynamic model	simulation model
atomistic fallacy	ecological fallacy	social indicator
census block	error of coverage	static model
census tract	feedback system	time-series data
classification error	level of aggregation	true rate
cross-cultural comparison	reported rate	unit of analysis
demographer	scattergram	

Exercises

1. Using the most recent census data in your school or public library, construct an *index of segregation* for the city in which you live or the city closest to you. As an aid in creating your index you may want to read the Appendix in Taeuber and Taeuber's *Negroes in Cities* (1966). The Appendix is titled "The Measurement of Residential Segregation."

Describe in some detail the data used and the steps taken in the construction of your index. Following our discussion in this chapter, briefly outline some of the errors in census data that may affect the validity of your index.

2. Working alone or with another student in your class, collect data to show whether there is any association between the percentage of population that is black and the crime rates in cities. Collect data for both variables on ten cities of your choice. The percentage of black persons in each case can be determined using available census materials. An overall crime rate for the same cities can be obtained from the most recent edition of the *Uniform Crime Reports for the United States*. Arrange your data in a scattergram, as for the hypothetical study cited in this chapter.

What trends are you able to note in your data? Is there a positive relationship between the two variables (i.e., does the crime rate increase as the percentage of black persons in the population increases)? If you do find a positive relationship, can you draw the inference that black persons are more likely to commit crimes than white persons? Why? Why not?

3. Examine the extent to which your college has changed over the last twenty years. You might be interested in looking at one or more of the following variables: average college board scores of entering freshmen, the proportion of persons majoring in the natural sciences, the winning percentage of the school football team, or the percentage of seniors graduating with honors. What other variables interest you?

Choose two variables for which you can obtain data for each of the last twenty years. After constructing tables presenting your collected data, try to offer an explanation of any changes discovered.

4. There is a hypothesis that individuals who come from broken homes are more likely to commit delinquent acts than individuals who come from "stable" homes. Could you test this hypothesis by comparing delinquency rates in city areas with high and low divorce rates? Why not? Explain the kind of fallacy you might be committing if you use these suggested data. What kind of data would you need to test your hypothesis?

5. Suppose you get into a discussion with someone who points out that the average life expectancy rate in the United States as of 1970 was 70.8 years. Imagine the person uses this national-level social indicator to argue that all Americans experience very good health. Would you accept his or her judgment based on this one national-level statistic? In what ways might differences between segments of the American population in life expectancy be masked at the national level of aggregation? What additional information can be gained by disaggregating, if possible, these national-level data? What would be the advantages and disadvantages of looking at data for a number of different aggregate levels?

6. Reread the sections of this chapter on forecasting and simulation and then briefly answer the following:
   a. Distinguish between static and dynamic models.
   b. Indicate why simulations must use dynamic models.
   c. Describe the potential importance of sensitivity testing for the creation of social policy.
   d. Indicate why social scientists cannot forecast social trends with perfect accuracy.

Suggested Readings

READINGS ABOUT THE METHOD

Armstrong, J. Scott
1978 *Long-Range Forecasting*. New York: Wiley.
A discussion of numerous techniques of social and economic forecasting used in various social science disciplines. Particularly helpful are the sections comparing different techniques and the annotated bibliography.

Borgata, Edgar F., and David J. Jackson
1979   "Aggregate Data Analysis: An Overview." *Sociological Methods and Research* 7, 4 (May).
    This is the lead article in an entire issue devoted to analysis and interpretation of aggregate data.

Dogan, Mattei, and Stein Rokkan, eds.
1969   *Social Ecology*. Cambridge, Mass.: MIT Press.
    In this book various aspects of inference from aggregate data are discussed. Part I includes essays on the ecological fallacy. These essays carry the analysis of inference from aggregate data beyond what is found in most introductory methods books. The essays should be read by the student who wishes to acquire a more sophisticated understanding of the issues involved in ecological and atomistic fallacies.

Hannan, Michael T.
1971   *Aggregation and Disaggregation in Sociology*. Lexington, Mass.: D. C. Heath (Lexington Books).
    This book is written at a fairly sophisticated level. Its major focus is on assessing the effects of changes in levels of aggregation on parameter estimates in linear causal analysis (path analysis and multiple regression are examples of linear causal analysis). The author considers the problem of making inferences from the level of aggregation at which the data were collected to some other level. This includes efforts to make inferences from lower to higher levels (aggregation) as well as from higher to lower levels (disaggregation).

Land, Kenneth C., and Seymour Spilerman, eds.
1975   *Social Indicator Models*. New York: Russell Sage.
    The introductory essay by Land covers such topics as: rationales for social indicators (social policy, social change, and social reporting), defining characteristics of social indicators, types of indicators and social indicator models, and the content of social indicators.

Langbein, Laura Irwin, and Allan J. Lichtman
1978   *Ecological Inference*. Beverly Hills, Calif.: Sage.
    This book summarizes the efforts of researchers to challenge the idea of the ecological fallacy first put forth by W. S. Robinson (1950). It explains the conditions under which the results obtained from aggregate data *converge* with those obtained from individual-level data. This is a shorter and less technical treatment of general issues in aggregate data analysis than Hannan (1971).

Peterson, William
1975   *Population*. New York: Macmillan.
    This is a basic textbook in demographic population analysis. Peterson shows how demographers relate population phenomena to sociological, historical, and economic variables. In Chapter 2 the author discusses the aggregate data sources used most frequently in population studies and the types of errors found in those sources.

Raser, John R.
1969   *Simulation and Society*. Boston: Allyn & Bacon.
    Raser's book is a readable, nontechnical introduction to simulation and gaming techniques. The author shows their utility in a number of social science disciplines. He demonstrates how simulation can be used as a means for developing and testing social science theories.

Robinson, W. S.
1950   "Ecological Correlations and the Behavior of Individuals." *American Sociological Review* 15 (June):351–357.
    The nature of the ecological fallacy is described in this classic article. It is not difficult to follow Robinson's argument and the data presented show that it is fallacious to assume that properties associated at the group level are also associated at the individual level.

Wilcox, Leslie D., et al., eds.
1972   *Social Indicators and Social Monitoring: An Annotated Bibliography*. San Francisco: Jossey-Bass.
    This volume contains an annotated bibliography of more than 600 books, articles, and papers related to social indicators and social monitoring. The book is introduced with an historical overview of the social indicators movement, starting with the commission initiated by President Hoover in 1929, which published its findings four years later in *Recent Social Trends*. Of particular interest in this essay is the discussion of the various criticisms that have been made of the social indicators movement.

READINGS ILLUSTRATING THE METHOD

Davis Kingsley
1965   "The Urbanization of the Human Population." *Scientific American* 213 (September):41–53.

This study of urbanization places a heavy reliance on the official government statistics of countries around the world (especially national censuses). Davis uses aggregate data on urbanization in a number of fascinating ways. He presents the degree of urbanization for the major regions of the world and charts the historical development of urbanization in Europe. He considers the urbanization of today's developing countries. Davis then contrasts the causes of city growth in the developed and developing countries.

Executive Office of the President, Office of Management and Budget
1976   *Social Indicators, 1976*. Washington, D.C.: U.S. Government Printing Office.

In this sequel to *Social Indicators, 1973* a wide variety of measures are recorded for the purpose of aiding community needs assessments; determining priorities for, and monitoring, social programs; and program evaluation.

Faris, E. L., and H. Warren Dunham
1939   *Mental Disorder in Urban Areas*. Chicago: University of Chicago Press.

This is a classic study in urban ecology. Faris and Dunham show in their research that mental illness rates consistently vary in different geographical areas of the city. More directly, they show that there is a steady decline in mental illness rates as one moves toward the periphery of the city. One of the most significant features of this research is that the authors also carry out an individual level of analysis. They do this to determine whether rates of mental breakdown are, in fact, a function of the structural characteristics of the city or a function of the personal attributes of individuals living in different city areas. This work clearly shows the value of conducting research on both group and individual levels of analysis.

Forrester, Jay W.
1969   *Urban Dynamics*. Cambridge, Mass.: MIT Press.

In this book by a leading figure in the development of simulation models for social science research, a model is created to represent the growth process of an urban area through its first 250 years of life. At what point in a city's history will it reach a point of equilibrium? At what point will unemployment rates increase to a dangerous level? These are some of the questions Forrester tries to answer using simulation techniques.

Jackman, Robert W.
1975   *Politics and Social Equality: A Comparative Analysis*. New York: Wiley.

Jackman presents a causal model of cross-national variations in the degree of within-nation social equality as measured by three indicators: an index of social insurance program experience, an index of social welfare based on health and nutrition indicators, and an index of inequality in the distribution of income. The study is based on aggregate data from sixty countries.

Marshall, Harvey
1979   "White Movement to the Suburbs: A Comparison of Explanations." *American Sociological Review* 44 (December):975–994.

In this study of "white flight" from central cities to suburbs, the units of analysis are 112 metropolitan areas in the United States. The author utilized census data to discover whether the outmigration was caused by urban problems (such as crime, taxes, race riots) or by the attractiveness of suburbs in employment and housing.

Miller, Herman P.
1971   *Rich Man, Poor Man*. New York: Crowell.

This book is about the distribution of income in the United States. Some comparisons are made with other countries; for example, there is a discussion of the amount of time the average worker must work to earn enough to buy a meal in the United States and in eight other countries. The data used are drawn from a variety of government publications, particularly those of the Department of Labor and the Bureau of the Census.

References

Executive Office of the President: Office of Management and Budget
1976   *Social Indicators, 1976.* Washington, D.C.: U.S. Government Printing Office.

Galtung, Johan
1967   *Theory and Methods of Social Research.* New York: Columbia University Press.

Land, Kenneth C.
1975   "Social Indicator Models: An Overview." In *Social Indicator Models,* ed. Kenneth C. Land and Seymour Spilerman. New York: Russell Sage.

Meadows, Donnella H., et al.
1972   *The Limits to Growth.* New York: Universe Books.

President's Research Committee on Social Trends
1933   *Recent Social Trends.* New York: McGraw-Hill.

Sutherland, Edwin
1961   *White Collar Crime.* New York: Holt, Rinehart and Winston.

Taeuber, Karl E., and Alma F. Taeuber
1966   *Negroes in Cities: Residential Segregation and Neighborhood Change.* Chicago: Aldine.

U.S. Bureau of the Census
1973   *Current Population Reports,* Series P-25, No. 499, "Estimates of the Population of the United States and Components of Change, 1972." Washington, D.C.: U.S. Government Printing Office.

13 / Comparative Research Methods

CHAPTER OUTLINE

INTRODUCTION
A Brief History
WHY DO COMPARATIVE
    RESEARCH?
Extending and Qualifying Existing
    Theory
Testing Theory Cross-Culturally
Specifying the Conditions Under
    Which Theory Applies
Discovering the Relationships Among
    Macrolevel Variables

OBSTACLES TO RELIABLE AND
    VALID COMPARISON
Field Work
    Ethnographic Data Files
Survey Research
    Conceptual and Measurement
        Equivalence
    Comparative Sampling and
        Interviewing
    Secondary Data Analysis

Aggregate Analysis
    Two Examples
    Warning: Use with Care
Other Comparative Techniques
ETHICAL CONSIDERATIONS
SUMMARY
KEY TERMS
EXERCISES
SUGGESTED READINGS
REFERENCES

Introduction

A major goal of social science is to make universal generalizations about social structure and behavior. In view of this goal it is surprising that most research is confined to one country. Studies that offer comparison with other settings are rare. Because much of our knowledge is CULTURE SPECIFIC, it may be difficult or impossible for us to generalize from our own experience to the experience of other nations and peoples.

In this chapter we shall outline the principal advantages of using comparative data. The value transcends the issue of improving the validity of our generalizations; there are some research questions that simply cannot be answered except through comparative analysis. But there are a host of potential pitfalls confronting researchers who employ data from other societies. We shall examine these as we illustrate a variety of applications of the comparative method.

A BRIEF HISTORY

Despite the limited extent to which the comparative method is used today, the approach has a long history. Herodotus (495–424 B.C.) was one of the first to use systematic observation across societies as a basis for generalizing about human behavior. Many of the topics he considered in his *Nine Books of History* would today be classified as anthropology, political science, or sociology. At one point he compared the Egyptians with the Lacedaemonians with respect to interaction between young men and their elders. In both societies when they met on the street, the young men gave way to their elders by stepping aside; and when an elder came into the room, the young men rose from their seats. In the *Peloponnesian War* Thucydides (460–400 B.C.) made a number of cross-societal comparisons. He pointed out that Sparta controlled its allies by establishing oligarchies to rule them; in contrast, Athens tended to focus on exacting tribute from its allies. Aristotle (384–322 B.C.) collected and analyzed data on 158 political constitutions. His concern with cross-societal similarities and differences in governments, and particularly in constitutions, is extensively documented in *Politics*.[1]

The comparative method as practiced today may be traced most directly to the work of Herbert Spencer and other nineteenth-century evolutionists. The proponents of EVOLUTIONARY THEORY viewed society as passing through a series of stages. Evidence from existing primitive societies could be used to make inferences about what more advanced societies were like at earlier stages in their evolution. Karl Marx also drew heavily on comparative historical data. One example is his discussion of the various epochs characterized by differences in the "modes of production," ranging from primitive communism, to ancient society (slavery), to feudal society (serfdom), and finally to modern capitalism (wage labor).

Following World War I there appeared much criticism of the evolutionist perspective, with a consequent movement away from cross-cultural analysis. The revival of the method is due, in part, to the work of George Murdock (1937), who was interested in the relationship between kinship structure and other aspects of culture. He based his analysis on a sample of 230 societies (predominantly primitive) drawn from around the world. After 1945 improvements in transportation and communications, as well as the more assertive role of the United States in world affairs, produced new generations of comparativists, not only in anthropology but in sociology, political science, and psychology as well. Some of these comparativists have analyzed the industrial democracies of Western Europe and North America. Others have concentrated on the centrally planned economies of the communist bloc. Beginning in the early 1960s the newly independent countries of Asia, Africa, and Latin America became a third major focus for comparative investigation.

Why Do Comparative Research?

The most immediate benefit of the increase in comparative research over the past thirty-five years has been the accumulation of a rich storehouse of information about social and political structures and the process of personality formation in foreign cultures. Two more enduring benefits of the growing contemporary interest in comparative social science are its value in creating new theory and in extending and confirming existing theory.

---

[1]This historical summary draws upon Warwick and Osherson (1973:3–6).

EXTENDING AND QUALIFYING EXISTING THEORY

In research conducted in Kansas City, Sears and Wise (1950) found a positive relationship between the variables *age of weaning* (the age at which an infant ceases to be breast-fed) and *degree of emotional disturbance* the infant displays in response to the weaning. Most of the babies in the sample of eighty were weaned between birth and 7 months. It was found that as the age of weaning increased there was a tendency for the infant to show more emotional disturbance. Such a finding is quite inconsistent with Blackwood's (1935) report that among the Kurtatchi in the Solomon Islands mothers do not wean their children until they are over 3 years old, and these children show no signs of emotional disturbance. Presented with these seemingly inconsistent results, we might decide to search for a possible explanation. Do the results for the Kurtatchi represent an exception

FIGURE 13.1   Relation between Age at Onset of Weaning and Amount of Emotional Disturbance Shown by Child. Comparable Data from Eighty Individual Children from Kansas City (Sears and Wise, 1950) and from Thirty-Seven Societies (Whiting and Child, 1953).

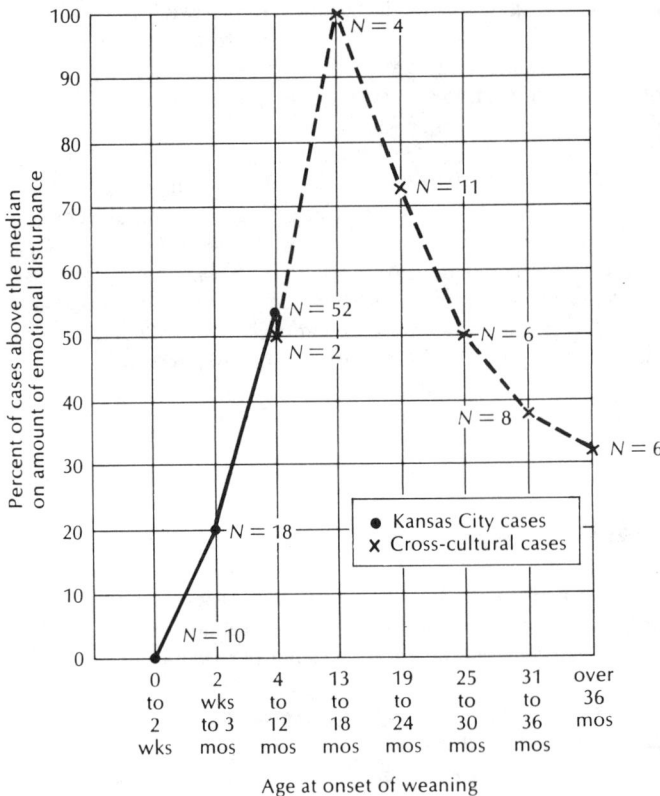

Source: John W. M. Whiting, "Methods and Problems in Cross-Cultural Research" in Gardner Lindzey and Elliot Aronson, eds., *Handbook of Social Psychology*, 2nd ed. (Reading, Mass.: Addison-Wesley, 1968), p. 695.

to the general trend established by Sears and Wise, or is there some more systematic way to account for the data from the Kurtatchi?

One way to address this question is to examine the relationship between the two variables for a large number of very diverse societies. Whiting and Child (1953) did just this. They considered seventy-five societies and found that relevant data were available for thirty-five of them. Their results are presented along with those from Sears and Wise in Figure 13.1. The data points from the Kansas City sample are connected by solid lines, and the data from the thirty-seven societies studied by Whiting and Child are connected by broken lines.

Before placing too much faith in these results, we would want to take a very careful look at the way in which the concept of emotional disturbance has been measured in the Kansas City study as well as in the thirty-seven societies Whiting and Child considered. But for the present we shall assume that they were able to define and measure emotional disturbance in a way that we would find acceptable, and we shall focus on the actual results. One interpretation of these data is that there is a tendency for the extent of emotional disturbance to increase as age of weaning increases from birth up to approximately 18 months, and then to decline steadily from that point to at least age 3. These data do not tell us why the relationship is CURVILINEAR (U-shaped) rather than linear, but they do suggest that the results for the Kurtatchi are more than an exception or a statistical fluctuation.

This example illustrates in a very dramatic way how cross-cultural analysis may be used to extend and to qualify the results obtained from a study in one society. In the United States weaning tends to occur at a very early age. To find out how the level of emotional disturbance varies with age of weaning for those weaned at 2 and 3 years of age, we would have to use cross-cultural evidence.

In some societies it is not unusual for children to be weaned at age 3; in the United States this would be characterized as deviant. In the unlikely event that we were interested in the relationship between late weaning and emotional disturbance in a cultural setting in which late weaning was considered deviant, we might want to consider the few cases of late weaning we could find in the United States. But if we wanted to discover the relationship between late weaning and emotional disturbance in a society for which late weaning was culturally acceptable, we would have to turn to cross-cultural data.

TESTING THEORY CROSS-CULTURALLY

One of the most noteworthy strengths of the comparative method is that it can be used to test the generalizability of a finding based on data from one society. It is not at all uncommon for propositions to be stated as if they applied to all societies, but rarely have such propositions actually been put to the test cross-culturally. We might want to ask whether the Oedipus complex first explained by Sigmund Freud is a universal phenomenon or whether it tends to be restricted to a small group of Western societies.

In European-American culture the father role includes being both the mother's lover and the child's disciplinarian. It is reasonable to argue that for most of Freud's patients the mother's lover and the child's disciplinarian were the same person. This suggests two possible explanations for any hostility boys might show toward their fathers. One is that the boy resents his father because the father is the mother's lover and therefore the boy cannot become the mother's lover (the Oedipal theory). The other explanation is that the boy resents his father because the father is the disciplinarian. These alternative theories cannot be adequately tested in a society in which both of these roles are filled by one person. One way we can test these alternative propositions is to consider comparative data from societies in which the roles are separated. Malinowski (1927) found that among the Trobriands the mother's brother acted as the disciplinarian. In this society hostility tended to be directed toward the disciplinarian rather than toward the mother's lover, casting doubt on the Oedipal theory. We would want to consider evidence from other societies in which the roles of mother's lover and son's disciplinarian are separated before coming to a firm conclusion with respect to the generalizability of Freud's theory, but the logic of the analysis should be evident from this example.

We know from earlier chapters that replication is a fundamental aspect of the scientific enterprise. Studies are most typically replicated in the same society, but it is often of great value to be able to replicate a finding across several societies. When we turn to comparative data to test the generalizability of a finding based on one society, we can argue that the original finding has been replicated if it holds up for the other societies we consider.

A particularly clear illustration of the use of cross-societal comparisons for replication is the Inkeles and Smith (1974) study of the process by which people move from a traditional to a modern orientation in a developing country. The researchers interviewed industrial workers, peasants, and urban nonindustrial workers in six developing nations. Basically the same questions were asked in each country. Many of the questions were designed to measure *individual modernity* as reflected in respondents' values, beliefs, attitudes, and behavior. Other items were used to assess *degree of exposure to a variety of modernizing institutions* such as the factory, the school, the mass media, and so on. The researchers found a consistent trend across all six societies for those who are most exposed to these modernizing institutions to be the most modern in their outlook.

The Inkeles and Smith study is a replication in two different ways. Prior to their research a great deal of work had been done showing a relationship between certain institutions found in industrial nations (for example, factories and schools) and the attitudes of people living in these nations. One way in which the Inkeles and Smith study is a replication is that it represents an effort to establish for *developing* nations the connection between several of these institutions and the attitudes of those in contact with them. A second way in which the study is a replication is that the research design was the same in each of the six countries considered, so that each can be used as an independent test, or replication, of the theories being tested.

Specifying the Conditions Under Which Theory Applies

When we use comparative data to test findings cross-culturally, we sometimes find that the results for the original society will hold up in some settings but not in others. If we can find some characteristic that differentiates those societies for which the original relationship holds from those for which it does not, we shall have specified the conditions under which the original relationship exists. This is another strength of the comparative method.

The SPECIFICATION of theory is illustrated by the Lipset et al. (1954) study of voter participation in the United States and in various European cities. The research focused on the rate of participation of the working class in relation to that of the middle class. A higher rate of turnout for middle-class voters than for working-class voters was found in the United States. This pattern was confirmed in Great Britain but was reversed in some Austrian and German cities. When they looked more closely at these cities, the researchers found that the labor movement there had created a network for indoctrination of workers; such networks were less developed in Great Britain and in the United States. The Lipset research had thus identified the condition under which the relationship originally found for one country held true for others and the condition under which it failed to hold true.

For some purposes it is useful to make comparisons between societies that are similar in many respects. For other purposes it is useful to select societies that are as diverse as possible. When our objective is to argue for the generalizability of a relationship between two variables, the case is strongest when it can be shown to hold up across a very diverse range of societies.

Nadel (1952) selected two cultures that exist side by side for a study of beliefs about witchcraft. The Nupe believe that witches are female; their neighbors, the Gwari, believe that witches may be of either sex. Nadel's work illustrates the strategy of selecting for comparison societies which have minimal differences between them. In this way it is easier to isolate just those differences which might be relevant to an explanation of the divergent beliefs of the two people.

DISCOVERING THE RELATIONSHIPS AMONG MACROLEVEL VARIABLES

Another strength of the comparative method is that it allows us to test theories that specify MACROLEVEL structures or behaviors—that is, characteristics of entire societies—as variables. If a theory states that the political or economic structure of a country has a causal impact on the way in which income and wealth are distributed, we encounter problems in attempting to verify this proposition on the basis of data from that one country alone. It is not possible to assess the impact of a variable such as economic structure, which is a constant for any one nation. But if we compare income inequality in several societies having different types of economies, we will be in a position to draw some conclusions about the impact of economic structure on the distribution of wealth. Generally, it is not possible to obtain a quantitative estimate of the effect of any society-wide characteristic on the basis of data from just one country. But if we base our study on several societies and select them in such a way that there is variation in the macrolevel characteristic of interest to us, it is possible to estimate the impact of this variable.

This use of comparative data is well illustrated in the work of Robert Jackman (1975), who constructed a model to account for income inequality. Among the variables of interest to him were *strength of socialist parties, strength of unions,* and *degree of freedom of the press.* By basing his study on data from sixty countries, he was able to make some quantitative estimates of the causal impact of these characteristics on the extent of income inequality within nations. However, since he did not include any communist states in his sample, he was not in a position to estimate the effect of a nation's being communist on the extent of its income inequality.

Obstacles to Reliable and Valid Comparison

There are a number of very strong reasons for doing comparative research. In view of this we might ask why such a small fraction of all research is indeed comparative. One reason is the variety of obstacles facing those who use cross-cultural data. Many of these difficulties are the same as those we face when doing research in one society, but in the context of comparative research they are even more problematic.

Most of the research methods considered in preceding chapters may be used comparatively, but some are employed more extensively than others. A great deal of cross-national research has been done using survey techniques, but comparative experimentation is still quite rare. In this section we discuss in detail the three most frequently used methods of data collection in comparative research: ethnographic field work, survey research, and aggregate data analysis; and we look briefly at three other methods: experimentation, content analysis, and historical analysis. We shall illustrate some ways in which these six research methods have been used comparatively. In addition, we shall outline some of the problems that must be dealt with when using each method in a comparative context. Some of these difficulties are unique to a specific technique; others tend to appear in all forms of comparative research.

FIELD WORK

Some studies of other cultures have been carried out by sociologists using observational techniques, but most of this work has been done by anthropologists. Typically, an anthropologist goes to live with a tribe (for example, the Kurtatchi in the Solomon Islands) for a year or two and then writes a book (referred to as an ETHNOGRAPHY) based on this field work. The ethnography describes the society's organizations, kinship system, language, religious beliefs, and so forth.

Is such an ethnography an example of comparative research if it is based on only one society? Although the research report describes only one setting, there is a sense in which it is comparative. The anthropologist is almost always from a different society, and consequently there will often be some explicit, and always many implicit, contrasts with that society. We can raise a similar question about much of the social and political research carried out in a single foreign country (often referred to as AREA STUDIES). An American sociologist examined the status of women in Senegal (Barthel, 1975). Her study contained few if any explicit contrasts between Senegal and the United States, but the choice of issues for emphasis was unavoidably based on a number of implicit comparisons with the United States. We do not seek to resolve the debate as to whether ethnographic reports and other single-society area studies should be considered de facto comparative. Some unquestionably fit the label better than others. When data from several area studies or ethnographies are combined, the product is unquestionably an example of comparative research.

A major barrier to the use of ethnographic data is that each researcher selects different aspects of a society on which to focus. Therefore, if we wish to use a variety of separate case studies in order to confirm a particular hunch or hypothesis, we may find that the investigator has failed to comment upon issues relevant to the solution of our problem. Thus many cases cannot be used because they lack adequate data. Even if the variables in which we are interested have been considered, we cannot be sure that differences in emphasis given to them in different societies reflect true variation rather than selectivity on the part of the researcher(s) involved.

Ethnographic data depend heavily on the observations, judgments, and interpretations of the small number of social scientists (often only one) conducting the research. It is, for example a common practice among anthropologists to develop a certain territoriality about the group they have studied. The same anthropologist may return to a community several times over the years; it is uncommon for another person to study exactly the same community. When independent studies are made of the same setting, the observations and conclusions can be quite inconsistent. In 1930 Robert Redfield published *Tepoztlan: A Mexican Village,* which was based on his personal observations. Having observed, for example, a great deal of harmony and cooperation among the people, he stressed in his report the positive aspects of "folk" life as opposed to "modern" life in the community. Oscar Lewis (1951) later went to the identical town; he presented his description in *Life in a Mexican Village.* He drew an almost totally opposite portrait, including reports of discord among villagers and a description of interpersonal relationships more characteristic of the negative stereotype of the city dweller who fears even the next-door neighbors.

It could be that one of these researchers was an unusually poor observer, and that this explains their widely divergent findings. A more likely explanation is that each one expected to find different things and behaved differently in the research setting. The variety of community experiences to which each investigator was exposed was not identical; in fact, these experiences probably overlapped only partially. Examples such as this cast doubt on the reliability of comparative ethnographies. Studies based on field work data are difficult to replicate, even more so when they have occurred in exotic settings. Moreover, the traditional strength of the ethnographic technique, the validity that comes from a lengthy stay in a particular setting and from participant observation, may be mitigated or compromised in comparative work. Dealing with an unfamiliar language and culture, the investigator may not even realize that he or she is misinterpreting events or being fed inaccurate information by respondents because they resent the intrusion or because they themselves do not understand what the researcher wants to know.

ETHNOGRAPHIC DATA FILES. In 1938 George Murdock initiated a major attempt to codify and rationalize comparative field data in the Human Relations Area Files (HRAF). The data base for these files is observational ethnographic reports from anthropologists and sociologists prepared for more than 200 societies. These ethnographies have been photocopied, taken apart, and organized into a set of categories, which is described in the *Outline of Cultural Materials* (Murdock et al., 1971); there are over 700 such categories, including: infant feeding, childbirth, independence training, cosmology, and suicide. A single page from an ethnography may be filed in more than one place if it contains information relevant to more than one topic.[2]

Numerous studies have been based on these data. One example is Whiting and Child's (1953) examination of the relationship between personality and various aspects of child training. This study considered a number of hypotheses derived from psychoanalytic theory about fixations. One proposition is that a child can develop an oral fixation as a result of certain types of socialization practices relating to nursing and weaning. A person is said to have an oral fixation if various behaviors that involve eating, drinking, smoking, and the like have greater importance than is usual for people who have not undergone this same socialization experience. The research cited earlier concerning the relationship between age of weaning and emotional disturbance is part of this larger study.

The HRAF files have proven a valuable source of information for cross-cultural research. In view of their importance it is of interest to consider a few of the major problems that must be faced by those who choose to work with this source and with less elaborate data bases.

One of the most common difficulties is that the researcher's categories do not correspond to those by which the ethnographic data have been classified. If we are lucky, it is possible to find the relevant material by looking under two or three existing categories or by shifting to a more general heading. But there are always some issues for which the standard categories are inappropriate. In such instances we run the risk of missing information that is actually available in the file.

Another issue that all users of ethnographic data files must face is the selection of a unit of analysis. Some reports may describe a nation, others a tribe or society, but by far the most common are ethnographic descriptions of a specific community within a tribe or a society. This fairly small unit of analysis reflects the emphasis in the ethnographic work that anthropologists have done over the past century. The Kwoma, for example, is a tribe numbering approximately 900 in central New Guinea. It is divided into four subtribes. Each of these is in turn divided into hamlets. In his book, *Becoming a Kwoma,* Whiting (1941) reports on one hamlet; he did not conduct a systematic analysis of all those who call themselves Kwoma. The anthropologist will generally be explicit as to whether a hamlet or a society is being studied, but the researcher must track down such information so as to ensure consistency, or equivalence, in the level of the cases studied.[3]

One of the most difficult exercises confronting those who choose to use resources like the HRAF files is sampling. The major problem is in deciding which communities, tribes, societies, or cultures are sufficiently distinct as to represent independent observations. There is heated debate among anthropologists over the criteria for defining a society or a culture; we could not hope in this brief discussion to present, let alone resolve, the debate. One of the reasons there is so much disagreement is that in many instances there is considerable overlap between

---

[2]Many universities have the HRAF files available on microfilm; a smaller number have actual photocopies of the files available.

[3]The issue of consistency in the level of the unit of analysis is sometimes solved by restricting the study to nation-states. But even this strategy has its problems. Some nation-states have a population of less than 100,000 persons and for many purposes would be more equivalent to one state in a larger nation such as the United States.

tribes with respect to language and other aspects of culture. This diffusion makes it more reasonable to talk about criteria for measuring degree of independence between societies than to look for criteria for complete independence. This problem of lack of independence between units is referred to as GALTON'S PROBLEM in honor of Sir Francis Galton, who in 1889 was the first to raise the issue. It is important because it creates the possibility that what appear to be a large number of societies in which the researcher's hypothesis is supported may turn out to be duplicate observations of what would more appropriately be considered one society. To date there has been no adequate mechanism for solving Galton's problem although several methods have been proposed.

One approach is to use the criterion of LINGUISTIC RELATEDNESS. The researcher considers a set of common terms for which all cultures have words (for example, sun, moon, water) and, using a technique known as lexico-statistics, makes estimates of how much time has elapsed since two languages split off from a common root. The fewer words the two languages have in common, the longer it has been since the split occurred. Thus, in constructing a sample for the HRAF, we could use as one criterion that no two societies be included that derived from the same language within the last 1,000 years. A world linguistic sample containing 136 cases has in fact been selected (Whiting, 1968:705–706).

Although there are a variety of methodological problems awaiting those who work with the HRAF files, these are minor when contrasted with the difficulties that would be involved in trying to collect the relevant data for twenty-five, fifty, or seventy-five societies each time we want to carry out a comprehensive, comparative ethnographic study. More to the point, the existence of these data files makes possible the testing of a variety of hypotheses that could not be tested without them.

SURVEY RESEARCH

Ethnographic data in the form of the HRAF files have been available for *secondary analysis* since the late 1930s. More recently a number of repositories have also been established for comparative survey data. One of the largest, the Roper Public Opinion Center, has on hand data from over 1,000 survey research studies conducted in more than sixty countries. While such repositories (referred to as DATA BANKS) can be very useful to those interested in the secondary analysis of survey research data, there are again a set of problems that users must confront. But it is more appropriate to review these after discussing the use of survey research as a method for *primary* data collection.

Since survey data are used extensively in social research, it should not surprise us to find that much comparative work is based on survey data. One of the most ambitious comparative survey research studies to date was carried out under the direction of Inkeles and Smith (1974). As will be recalled from the brief description given earlier, it was an examination of the process by which people undergo change from a traditional to a modern orientation in their beliefs, values, and attitudes. The researchers hypothesized that similar processes would be involved in any developing nation; with that in mind they selected six different countries. A question of particular interest to them was whether there is a fairly coherent syndrome that can be meaningfully referred to as "modern man" across countries, or whether the various hypothesized components of such a syndrome are unrelated. One of the major conclusions of this survey of almost 6,000 respondents from Argentina, Chile, India, Israel, Nigeria, and Bangladesh is that it *is* possible to develop a composite measure of "individual modernity" that can be applied cross-culturally.

Some of the methodological problems that confront those who seek to carry out comparative survey research studies relate to conceptual equivalence, measurement equivalence, sampling, and interviewing. We will look at each in turn.

CONCEPTUAL AND MEASUREMENT EQUIVALENCE. The issue of CONCEPTUAL EQUIVALENCE is central to all cross-societal research; the concepts used must be meaningful in all the cultures being compared. Some concepts—such as unemployment, bureaucracy, and civil service—have meaning in some societies but not in others. Obviously, we cannot attempt a comparison between one society in which a concept does have meaning and another in which it does not. But social scientists often find themselves working with such variables as *individual modernity, achievement motivation, fatalism,* and *alienation*; it is most difficult to say with certainty that these have no meaning in a particular setting. We are much more likely to conclude that a construct such as achievement motivation has a very different meaning in two given societies, or to conclude that it is much less important in one of those societies, than to conclude that in one it has no meaning at all. Perhaps the goals toward which achievement motivation is directed are widely divergent, perhaps antithetical, in the societies being compared. The same comparison is true of, say, alienation. We must know each society well in order to comprehend the forms that alienation takes. We must then determine an appropriate way to define and measure it in each setting.

Equivalence in definition can be very difficult to achieve. We know that there may be some variation from one society to another with respect to the specific components of a concept. It does not make sense to use a concept that has not been adjusted to take cultural context into consideration, but we can never be sure that the adjustment has been done in such a way that the resulting measure is equivalent across the societies being compared.

The problem of MEASUREMENT EQUIVALENCE, that is, of operationalizing theoretical concepts in such a way that the resulting measures are comparable across all societies being considered, must be confronted by all who engage in comparative research. Suppose our theory calls for a measure of upper-class membership. Clearly, the criteria for upper-class membership vary from one society to another. The variety of possible criteria makes the task of constructing equivalent measures difficult. Let us assume for the sake of the present discussion that one criterion that is important for each of the societies being considered is family assets. We select one society and determine that the most appropriate lower limit for upper-class membership is assets in excess of $10,000. For that society only 1 percent of the population is classified as upper class. Now suppose we want to construct an equivalent measure of upper-class membership for a second society, which is at a substantially higher level of economic development. If we again used the figure of $10,000, it would result in 20 percent of the population being classified as upper class. If, alternatively, we propose a different criterion, such as $50,000, we would again restrict the upper class to 1 percent of the population. But, in effect, we are shaping the criterion for upper-class memberships: we are making it financial elitism rather than, say, what some given amount of money can buy or how long the money has been in the family.

So far we have considered only one criterion for upper-class membership. The task becomes even more complicated as we attempt to introduce other criteria, such as occupation, education, and annual income. Our goal is simply to obtain a measure of upper-class membership that is equivalent across each of the societies being considered. But in the process we must confront choices between alternative dimensions of equivalence. We can get more equivalence in one respect, but at a cost of reduced equivalence in another. For this reason regardless of how careful we are in constructing our measure of upper-class membership, we will be vulnerable to the criticism that our indicator shows a lack of comparability in at least some respects.

Although the problem of measurement equivalence will never be entirely resolved, a number of techniques have been developed to deal with it. Suppose we want to measure a concept such as *fatalism* for respondents in several countries. Typically, we would start with an English version of the questionnaire and then translate it into each of the local languages needed. But how can we be sure that we have not lost something important in the translation? One strategy that has been developed for dealing with this problem is BACK TRANSLATION. First, we have one bilingual person translate the questionnaire from English into the language of the society we are considering. Then, we have a second bilingual person, who has no knowledge of the original English version, translate the questionnaire back into English. Then, the original version and the back translation can be compared. When there are major discrepancies, the questionnaire is rewritten and the process is repeated.

We now turn to a procedure that is sometimes used when the goal is to obtain equivalent measures of an abstract psychological concept such as *alienation*. Typically, alienation is measured using an index constructed by combining the answers for several individual attitudinal questions. The researcher often writes a set of general questions that do not make any reference to a specific cultural context, assuming that if the question is sufficiently abstract, the resulting measure will be equivalent across cultures. A criticism of such measures is that many respondents either do not understand these abstract questions or interpret them in ways that the researcher has not anticipated. One way to deal with this is to base the measure instead on questions that are very concrete and have been tailored to each cultural context; that is, the concrete situation described will differ from one society to another so as to take into consideration cultural variation. But we will still be faced with the possibility that these questions may not yield a measure that is in all ways comparable across each of the societies being considered.

One way to resolve this dilemma is to combine the two approaches. For each society being considered, we write two types of questions. One set of questions attempts to measure the concept of interest, in this case alienation, in very general terms. Our objective is to formulate questions that are sufficiently abstract to be free of specific cultural content. The second set of questions prepared for each society attempts to assess the same concept but in more concrete terms specific to that society.

COMPARATIVE SAMPLING AND INTERVIEWING. The quality of a survey research study depends in large measure on the quality of the sampling. For this reason efforts to obtain equivalent samples receive considerable attention in comparative studies. Few countries have the experienced survey research organizations available in the United States. Therefore, considerable variability exists in the quality of the sampling from one country to another; this is particularly true if studies have been set up independently by different investigators.

There are a variety of ways in which sampling occurs in comparative survey research studies. One is the selection of countries to be included. Given the expense of such an investigation, it is unusual to survey more than five or six countries if primary data are being collected; studies based on secondary analysis can extend the number of countries. It is not uncommon for the researcher's prior contacts to have some bearing on the final selection of settings, a fact that has obvious implications for the representativeness of the countries selected. With awareness of cost considerations, the researcher sometimes restricts the study to a specific community or region of each nation being studied; national samples are typically much more expensive to administer. Another factor that can influence the quality of the sample is the nonresponse rate, which can vary considerably from one culture to another.

Interviewing is another area in which problems may arise in comparative survey research. The pollster or interviewer is not an ordinary part of a person's life in most societies. The interview situation is a strange and frightening experience for many people. When this is compounded by differences in dress, status, and manner (and possibly in native language) between surveyor and subject, the validity of the results obtained can be seriously questioned. The interviewer is often a stranger and is sometimes suspected of being a government agent. When such fears are present, we can expect less than candid responses on a number of issues—such as political alienation, degree of support for the government, and personal income.

For a variety of reasons it is often necessary to conduct an interview in the presence of a third party. Women, for example, require a chaperone in some societies. The presence of a third party can be positive in the sense that the person may help keep the respondent honest or help the respondent to remember required information, but the impact is more typically to reduce the validity of responses given. The presence of others may force the respondent to give culturally approved answers; it may also keep the subject from openly discussing personal matters.

A final factor that can affect the interview situation is *courtesy bias*. This occurs when respondents provide information that they feel will please the interviewer or that they feel is befitting to people of their status. There is some evidence that the direction of courtesy bias differs from country to country. It has been observed that Japanese humility has resulted in an understatement of personal achievement, class position, and income level; in other countries respondents have exaggerated their wealth and social position in response to survey questions (Mitchell, 1968).

SECONDARY DATA ANALYSIS. Earlier, we mentioned that there exist a number of repositories that have on file data from survey research studies conducted in countries around the world. As was the case with the Human Relations Area Files, these data banks make possible the testing of a variety of hypotheses that would otherwise be extremely difficult to test. They make comparative survey research data available to many who could not otherwise afford to obtain it. There are, however, special problems for those who seek to carry out a secondary analysis using these data banks. One is that there is usually a lack of documentation of the various sources of irregularity in the study, particularly in the area of sampling. The quality of the data varies considerably, but it is often quite difficult to assess quality on the basis of the information provided.

Other difficuties relate to the issue of measurement equivalence. Typically, the researcher will be attempting to compare the results for several countries, each of which may measure concepts in a somewhat different way. There are serious problems of equivalence with respect to such variables as *occupation* and *income*. In the case of foreign-language questionnaires, we are occasionally able to check an English version to verify that the same questions have been asked, but we know from our earlier discussion that it is dangerous to assume nothing was lost or changed in the process of translation into the relevant local language.

These are only some of the obstacles we face if we choose to engage in secondary analysis of comparative survey data. Briefly, some of the others are: variation in the training of interviewers and in the quality of the supervision of interviewers, variation in nonresponse rates and in ways of dealing with nonresponse, and specific national events that may have produced a temporary shift of opinion on certain issues. These obstacles are in most cases extensions of related problems that occur when a survey research study is carried out in the context of one society. But the problems are exacerbated in the context of comparative research. Much the same argument can be made about the use of national-level aggregate statistics, a topic to which we now turn. Many of these statistics are based on survey data and thus are subject to some of the same sources of bias.

AGGREGATE ANALYSIS

Aggregate analysis can be carried out at a variety of levels.[4] In the present discussion we are concerned with data for which the unit of aggregation is the nation. A major source of such data is the various publications of the United Nations, such as the *Demographic Yearbook* and the *Statistical Yearbook*. There are also a number of social science programs that were devised to collect various types of aggregate statistics and to organize them in a form permitting comparisons among nations. The National Bureau of Economic Research and the Cowles Commission are two examples of such longstanding projects in the field of economics. Data are gathered on national income, economic development, and economic stability. Similar programs have been established in other fields. The Yale Political Data Program collects, analyzes, and evaluates aggregate statistics from many nations on social conditions related to political development and change. Much of this information has been published in the *World Handbook of Political and Social Indicators* (Taylor and Hudson, 1972) and in other similar volumes.

Our social theories sometimes specify *structural characteristics of nations* as independent variables: the political structure (for example, representative democracy versus totalitarianism) or the economic structure (for instance, capitalism versus communism) are acknowledged to be important determinants of a range of social phenomena within a nation. Such factors cannot be used in an analysis

---

[4]Recall from the discussion in Chapter 12 that aggregate data at one level, such as the nation, are obtained by combining data for units at a lower level of aggregation, such as the state or the individual.

based on one country because they are constant for that country. When we shift to the nation as the unit of analysis, these factors can be included as variables as long as there are differences between countries with respect to them. Note that these variables are not based on aggregate data, but they can be used along with other variables that are (for example, infant mortality rate, percentage illiterate, percentage over age 65). In recent years a number of very interesting studies have been conducted that combine national-level aggregate statistics with measures of structural characteristics of nations.

TWO EXAMPLES. In Harold Wilensky's (1975) study, *The Welfare State and Equality,* the major dependent variable is *social welfare effort,* which is measured by the *ratio* of government expenditures for various social security programs (using a rather broad definition of social security) to the Gross National Product (GNP). Wilensky was able to measure his key variables, some of which were based on aggregate data and others of which were structural, for sixty countries. One question of particular interest to him was the relevance of the political structure of a country to the level of social welfare effort. For each of the countries considered, he classified the political system into one of the following four categories: liberal democratic (for example, United States, Sweden), totalitarian (for instance, Poland, USSR), authoritarian oligarchic (for example, Taiwan, Honduras), and authoritarian populist (for instance, Mexico, Iraq).

On the basis of a cross-sectional (that is, at one point in time) analysis of these comparative data, Wilensky concluded that political structure has little impact on the level of social security effort. He also reported that ideology of the elite and the proportion of the GNP spent on defense have little impact on social security effort. His major conclusion was that the level of economic development, as measured by GNP per capita, has a strong indirect effect on social security effort. These findings are consistent with the thesis that modern societies are converging toward a common form of postindustrial welfare state that is independent of variation in political system.

In a related study, Robert Jackman (1975) selected several indicators of social inequality as his major dependent variables. One is a measure of income inequality. Another is a composite index of social welfare based on a variety of health and nutrition indicators. As in the Wilensky study, Jackman considered sixty countries; again some of the variables are based on national-level aggregate data while others are based on structural characteristics of the country. One of the more interesting conclusions in Jackman's work was that high rates of population growth and high rates of economic growth tend to increase the amount of inequality in a society. A variety of other topics have also been investigated by means of techniques similar to those used by Wilensky and Jackman, for example: mass political violence (Hibbs, 1973); economic development (Adelman and Morris, 1967, 1973); and CONVERGENCE THEORY, the idea that all industrial nations are becoming increasingly alike (Williamson and Fleming, 1977; Williamson and Weiss, 1979).

WARNING: USE WITH CARE. An attractive aspect of comparative aggregate analysis is that the data can generally be obtained easily; they are often as close as the nearest major library. While the cost of obtaining primary data of this sort would be prohibitive, the fee for available secondary data is usually nominal. In recent years the number of countries for which these data are available has been increasing, as has the quality and comprehensiveness of the information. It is likely that the number of such studies will continue to increase. For this reason among others, it is important that we keep in mind some of the potential pitfalls of using comparative aggregate data.

The United Nations, which is a major source, has very little control over the quality of the data provided by member nations. For some countries the data are quite reliable, but for others they are quite poor.[5] To further complicate matters, there is usually little documentation with which we could judge the quality of the data for individual countries. In general, there is a tendency for the reliability of the data to rise with the level of economic development. Since collection and evaluation of such information are expensive and require skilled personnel, the more industrialized countries are better equipped to do them.

One of the most serious problems is that the categories used in collecting aggregate data vary from one country to another. There is little uniformity in the definition of such basic concepts as unemployment, family size, family income, literacy, and cause of death. Take, for example, the definition of *literacy*. Most nations define it as "the ability to read and write," but some countries define it simply as "the ability to write." There is also considerable variation in the minimal level of reading and writing required of those classified as literate. Another factor in literacy rates is the section of the population for which literacy is determined; most countries base estimates on the population over age 15, but some countries select a different age criterion.

As a second example we can consider statistics on *cause of death*. Often, one death could be classified under any of several possible categories. Death sometimes results from a variety of factors; in such situations the selection of the one primary cause can be quite misleading. Suicide is one cause of death for which the definition varies from one country to another. Even when the definition is the same, there is a potential lack of comparability in the statistics because of variation in the willingness to use the category of suicide; there are often other categories, such as drug overdose or automobile accident, under which a death might be classified (Atkinson, 1978).

Another source of error in statistics provided to the U.N. and other international organizations is *distortion* of data for political purposes. A country might decide to slant the economic figures so that it appears more stable economically than it actually is. This might be done for a variety of purposes, one of which would be to attract foreign investment capital. There are often internal political reasons for distorting data. Representation in the national assembly may be based on population estimates provided by a national census. Such data sometimes are intentionally inflated for certain regions of the country in an effort to obtain more seats in the assembly for those regions.

The aggregate data provided to the U.N. by member nations are not collected with the idea of social research in mind.[6] The researcher who attempts to use secondary data collected for entirely different purposes runs the risk of attempt-

---

[5]When a regional office is faced with a demand for data that it is incapable of collecting, it may find ingenious ways of fabricating the desired information.

[6]Governments have many reasons for collecting aggregate statistics. Planning for the future, assessing the needs of the population, and administering existing governmental programs are just a few of these. Data that satisfy these needs do not always have relevance for social science research.

ing to make the data into something they are not. There is a fine line between the creative use and the misuse of such data. It is common for the researcher to find that the exact data called for by theory are simply not available. One response is to select one or more available variables as indicators or PROXIES for the variable of actual theoretical interest. If the proxy selected is too different from the theoretical variable, the results obtained will be useless. Another related problem is that some researchers start with the variables for which aggregate data are available and then attempt to construct a theory that justifies using these variables. All too often, the result is a very lame theory and a study devoid of theoretical merit.

OTHER COMPARATIVE TECHNIQUES

So far we have discussed three categories of comparative analysis—ethnographic, survey, and aggregate. Although these approaches account for a substantial proportion of the comparative studies that have been done in recent years, other techniques—such as historical analysis, content analysis, and experimental approaches—are also used extensively. The three examples to which we now turn illustrate these alternative approaches.

In *Regulating the Poor,* Piven and Cloward (1971) argued that relief-giving is a mechanism for controlling the indigent. They pointed out that relief rolls are expanded during periods of civil disorder to contain the disorder and restore calm; they are then contracted when the threat of civil disorder subsides, thus assuring an adequate supply of low-wage labor. To document their thesis, the authors drew on historical materials from sixteenth-century England and France as well as on more recent materials from the United States. These comparative historical data lend credibility to the claim that the use of relief as a mechanism of social control is not confined to contemporary United States.

In *The Achieving Society,* David McClelland (1961) argued that there is a positive relationship between the level of achievement motivation that existed in 1925 and the rate of economic expansion during the following twenty-five years. His measure of achievement motivation was based on a content analysis of a sample of children's stories that appeared in books available in 1925. He was able to obtain these data for twenty-three countries. As hypothesized, he did find a positive relationship between the level of achievement motivation and the rate of economic growth.

Stanley Milgram (1961) was interested in an experimental investigation of differences between countries with respect to conformity behavior. He adapted for the purpose Solomon Asch's (1952) now-classic study of conformity in small groups. In the original experiment a group of six students was shown several lines of different lengths. Each student was then asked to make a judgment as to the relative length of these lines. The group was set up so that the students who were actually confederates of the experimenter would speak first and give what was clearly an incorrect answer. Asch found that in response to this group pressure a very high percentage of the experimental subjects conformed to the obviously incorrect judgments of others.

In Milgram's adaptation, subjects made judgments as to the length of auditory signals (tones). The other members of the listening group were simulated rather than actually being present; that is, the experimental subject went into one booth and was led to believe that the people he heard talking over his earphones were in the other booths, but in reality he was only hearing their voices on a tape record-ing. Milgram conducted his experiment in both Oslo and Paris. He ran several variations on the basic design, but in all of them he consistently found: (1) a tendency for a substantial percentage of the subjects to conform to the group pressure—a replication of Asch's findings—and (2) a consistent trend for the Norwegian subjects to conform more frequently than the French subjects.

When we use historical methods, content analysis, or experimentation com-paratively, we face methodological issues that are unique to each of these ap-proaches. At the same time we encounter other difficulties that are generically comparative, in defining units of analysis, selecting samples cross-nationally, and in attempting to establish conceptual and measurement equivalence. One longstanding debate is over the issue of whether there is a body of procedures properly identified as the "comparative method" or whether it is more appropriate to consider comparative research merely as a specific application of a variety of techniques such as survey research and experimentation. To the extent that there is a common set of problems with which comparativists must cope, it is legitimate to conclude that in spite of the many forms it takes, the comparative method is a separate entity in social science, requiring its own special expertise and exposing its practitioners to many similar research experiences.

Ethical Considerations

Let us close this chapter by noting some important ethical issues that arise in the context of comparative research.[7] Some relate to the sponsorship, and anticipated application, of the research results. This is well illustrated by the example of Project Camelot (see Chapter 4). Because of the sums of money involved, many social scientists were more than willing to avoid explicit questions as to what the Department of Defense, the sponsoring agency for the project, was really in-terested in finding out. The prevailing counterinsurgency policy of the Defense Department was founded less on the best interests of the nations under scrutiny than on the perceived need to defend our own nation from the encroachment of communism among our neighbors, near or far. One small part of the study was to be carried out in Chile by an investigator who lied about the source of his funding. When he was found out, there was a reaction of extreme outrage, which led to the entire project being canceled.

Other ethical considerations relate to collaboration with local researchers in the host country. Such collaboration can be invaluable, but there has been an unfortunate tendency for at least some Americans to use their foreign associates as assistants in their own research projects rather than as colleagues working on a joint endeavor. The problems with this attitude are well summarized by Kelman (1968:81):

> Many of us have assumed, implicitly and without questioning, that the other society is simply there for us to research upon it, and that we can take what we wish from it as long as we pay the fair market price. In the process, we have too often displayed a lack of respect for the values of the society, the sensitivities of its members, the dignity of our respondents, and the personal and professional aspirations of our colleagues. Such an attitude simply will not do.

---

[7]See Chapter 4 for a general discussion of ethics in social research.

Summary

Although there has been increased interest in comparative social research over the past generation, it is obvious that relatively few studies employ data from other countries and cultures. This is surprising when we consider that the goal of social science is to make universal generalizations. In this chapter we have considered the many benefits of comparative analysis, as well as some of the obstacles to making valid and reliable comparisons across national boundaries.

Comparative social science has a unique role in extending and qualifying existing theory in psychology, political science, and sociology. Data from one society may be tested in another, and the specific circumstances under which existing theory applies may be uncovered. Replications of studies in other cultures are useful because they make us aware of those aspects of our behavior that are unique to our culture, and of those that are found in most, or all, settings. Much of our theorizing is a product of a given cultural milieu. Comparative research forces us to realize the limitations of theories that are often accepted uncritically or thought to be universally applicable. As social problems become truly worldwide, and as improvements in communication make possible increased contact and mutual education of peoples, the need for methodological techniques to analyze macrolevel variables increases. Because social structures are typically constant in one country, it is impossible to gauge their impact without recourse to cross-national data.

It is possible to use a variety of data gathering methods comparatively. Much field work in foreign countries is implicitly comparative, even when it does not specifically mention the United States or its institutions. The major problem in using cross-national ethnographic data is the idiosyncratic nature of these data. The experiences of field workers may not be similar enough for reliable comparison. The categories used for description and analysis, even in similar settings, are likely to differ. To help resolve these and other difficulties, files of ethnographic data have been created, which combine reports from hundreds of countries and regions. These files are a boon to research, but it is sometimes difficult to find a workable unit of analysis and sampling procedure.

Secondary data bases of survey research suffer from similar problems, and in addition serious validity questions must be raised regarding the use of survey instruments cross-culturally. Equivalence of measurement and meaning must be established. Sampling procedures are often not as sophisticated as are required for reliable results. The survey interview, a cultural institution in the Western world, may provoke bewilderment or hostility in other settings. A variety of techniques have been employed to reduce the Western bias of comparative surveys and to thus improve their reliability and validity.

Another popular technique for comparative analysis is the use of aggregate data. Although official statistics can be unrealiable, this method has great promise, particularly when statistics are combined with national-level structural variables to explain differences between nations. Care must be taken to avoid the temptation to use data merely because they are available or because they are assumed to be reliable. This pitfall of research leads to studies that are theoretically vacuous and, most likely, useless.

Because these and a variety of other techniques have been used comparatively, there is a tendency to see cross-national research as just another specific application of the methodological tools that have been described in other chapters. Since comparative social science in all disciplines requires common skills of researchers, including sensitivity to ethical issues of honesty and exploitation, a case may be made that the "comparative method" deserves attention as a separate social science interest and specialty.

Key Terms

area studies	curvilinear relationship	linguistic relatedness
back translation	data banks	macrolevel variable
conceptual equivalence	ethnography	measurement equivalence
convergence theory	evolutionary theory	proxy variable
courtesy bias	Galton's problem	specification
culture specific		

Exercises

1. Select two or three anthropological monographs that have sections on child rearing, marriage practices, or any other topic in which you are interested. Reading just those sections that deal with the topic you are investigating, compare the reports in terms of their degree of comprehensiveness and completeness. In what way do the practices in these societies differ? How are they similar? Are there any social phenomena that are discussed in only one of the reports? Can you conclusively determine that their absence in the other report(s) is not the result of the failure of the observer to either record or observe their occurrence? What reasons can you give to support your answer?

2. Using one of the publications of aggregate international statistics mentioned in the text, such as the *Demographic Yearbook of the U.N.,* select a small sample of societies (five to ten). Choose an abstract characteristic such as industrialization or modernization and select a series of indicators for that dimension, for example, statistics on production, gross national product, type of industry, and distribution of the work force. Are statistics available on every indicator you selected for each society in your sample? How do these societies compare with one another on each of the selected indicators? What can be said about each society in terms of the overall problem being explored? What solution can you offer to include the societies that did not have information available on every indicator in your comparative analysis?

3. As a class project, work in groups of five to compose a questionnaire on some general topic to be administered cross-culturally. Select a topic that is broad and has universal reference, such as attitudes toward education, marriage practices, or rural versus urban life. The questionnaire should be short and written in a format that will make it easy to administer it to people from other countries. Administer the questionnaire to a sample of native-born students and foreign students. What are the results? Were the questions equally relevant to both groups of students? Were there any difficulties experienced in administering the questionnaire? Were some questions embarrassing to the foreign students? Why?

4. Consider a research area that you would like to pursue by comparative international research. What countries would you examine? Why? What type of comparative approach would you use to study this problem? What factors would be important to consider in selecting a particular approach?

5. In "The Urbanization of the Human Population" Kingsley Davis (1965, in Suggested Readings) approaches the concept of urbanization by considering the percentage of the total population that is concentrated in urban settlements as a measure of the level of urbanization in the country. How adequate do you think the percentage of people living in urban settlements is as a measure of urbanization? Is it a good measure for comparative purposes? Are there other aspects to urbanization that should be considered? If there are, how would you tap these dimensions?

6. Discuss the ways in which sponsorship may affect a comparative international research project in terms of the goals, scope, issues investigated, and objectivity in inter-

preting and reporting the results. How might knowing that the sponsor is the government affect the answers of the respondents in a totalitarian country? What are the advantages of sponsorship? Are there certain types of research efforts that require some form of sponsorship if they are to be performed at all?

7. One ethical and political consideration connected with comparative international research is the issue of exploitation in collaborative research efforts. The chapter has pointed to the exploitation of researchers from other countries as one example. What other kinds of potential exploitation can you think of in comparative international research? What would you do about them? What other ethical and political problems can you foresee arising in comparative international research? What would you do to avoid these problems? You may wish to refer to Chapter 4 in formulating your answer.

Suggested Readings

READINGS ABOUT THE METHOD

Amer, Michael, and Allen D. Grimshaw, eds.
1973 *Comparative Social Research: Methodological Problems and Strategies.* New York: Wiley.
The volume considers a range of issues, including: the definition of comparative sociology, how comparative sociology differs from "area" sociology, and the benefits of comparative analysis.

Brislin, Richard W., Walter J. Lonner, and Robert M. Thorndike
1973 *Cross-Cultural Research Methods.* New York: Wiley.
This monograph discusses a number of issues of particular interest to psychologists doing cross-cultural research. Some of them are: a working definition of cross-cultural psychology, questionnaire wording, translation, survey methods, the conduct of experiments, and the cross-cultural use of psychological tests.

Holt, Robert T., and John E. Turner, eds.
1970 *The Methodology of Comparative Research.* New York: Free Press.
The articles in this anthology emphasize a variety of issues of particular interest to comparative political scientists. Among the issues considered are: the question of what comparative politics is, the control of background factors by randomization, the control of background factors by specification, non-culture-bound concepts and operational definitions, and problems of comparability in sampling.

Kelman, Herbert C.
1968 *A Time to Speak: On Human Values and Social Research.* San Francisco: Jossey-Bass.
The ethical and political considerations involved in doing foreign research are discussed fully in this book. Of particular interest are Kelman's observations regarding research in developing countries. There are important discussions of Project Camelot, the problem of government influence, and the temptation on the part of foreign researchers to exploit the countries in which they conduct their work. In all of these discussions Kelman argues forcefully and humanely for ethical comparative international research.

Marsh, Robert M.
1967 *Comparative Sociology.* New York: Harcourt, Brace & World.
This book begins with a consideration of the theoretical and methodological schools of thought in comparative international research. It then turns to a codification of ninety comparative studies. The topics include family structure, bureaucracy, stratification, and cultural values. Propositions from the studies are extracted and codified. Finally, a special section is devoted to a discussion of problems of methodology in comparative international research. The book contains a very extensive bibliography.

Przeworski, Adam, and Henry Teune
1970 *The Logic of Comparative Social Inquiry.* New York: Wiley.

This is a theoretical book about comparative research. One of the arguments made is that the goal of comparative analysis is to substitute the names of variables for the names of societies in our explanation. We may report that there is a difference between two countries with respect to some phenomenon. This is fine as a first step, but we must then turn to an analysis of what it is about the countries that can be used to account for the difference found. The book considers in some detail issues related to measurement and to criteria for establishing equivalence.

Vallier, Ivan, ed.
1973   *Comparative Methods in Sociology.* Berkeley and Los Angeles: University of California Press.

A collection of essays by prominent social scientists who have done comparative analysis, this volume focuses on the contributions of classical comparativists (Alexis de Tocqueville, Karl Marx, Max Weber) as well as on those of contemporary researchers. There is also a useful bibliography.

Warwick, Donald P., and Samuel Osherson, eds.
1973   *Comparative Research Methods.* Englewood Cliffs, N.J.: Prentice-Hall.

This edited collection of articles focuses on conceptual, measurement, and linguistic equivalence in comparative research. A final section covers the relative merits of surveys and participant observation for comparative international research.

Whiting, John W. M.
1968   "Methods and Problems in Cross-Cultural Research." In *Handbook of Social Psychology,* ed. Gardner Lindzey and Elliot Aronson. 2nd ed. Reading, Mass.: Addison-Wesley.

This is a very well-written introduction to the anthropological literature on cross-cultural research. The discussion is focused on the tradition of George Murdock. Some of the issues considered are: advantages of the cross-cultural method, the definition of a case, sampling, and transcultural definitions of variables.

READINGS ILLUSTRATING THE METHOD

Almond, Gabriel, and Sidney Verba
1963   *The Civic Culture: Political Attitudes and Democracy in Five Nations.* Princeton, N.J.: Princeton University Press.

This is a comparative survey conducted in the United States, Great Britain, Germany, Italy, and Mexico. The focus was on the conditions that encourage the development and maintenance of democracy in the political system of a country. The nations were chosen because of their differing routes to democracy. The research was based on approximately 1,000 representative interviews conducted by native interviewers in each of the countries.

Davis, Kingsley
1965   "The Urbanization of the Human Population." *Scientific American* 213 (September):41–53.

This study of world urbanization relies heavily on the official government statistics of countries around the world (especially national censuses). Davis uses aggregate data on urbanization in a number of fascinating ways throughout the article. He presents the degree of urbanization for the major regions of the world and charts the historical development of urbanization in Europe. Finally, Davis examines the urbanization of today's developing societies, contrasting the causes of city growth in the developed and the developing societies.

Gray, Paul S.
1980   "Collective Bargaining in Ghana." *Industrial Relations* 19, 2 (Spring): 175–191.

The author traces the growth of a Western institution, collective bargaining between labor and management, in an African country. It is more than an implicit comparison because specific contrasts and parallels are drawn with the experience of the United States. Data were gathered through participant observation and from union, government, and employers' statistics.

Inkeles, Alex, and David H. Smith
1974   *Becoming   Modern: Individual Change in Six Developing Countries.* Cambridge, Mass.: Harvard University Press.

This book explores how individuals change their personalities from traditional to modern. The basic comparative data for the study were gathered by interviewers from approximately 6,000 people in Argentina, Chile, India, Israel, Nigeria, and Bangladesh. Among the variables examined for their impact on individual modernization were *education, exposure to an urban environment,* and *employment in a factory setting.*

Myrdal, Gunnar
1968   *Asian Drama: An Inquiry into the Poverty of Nations.* Vols. 1–3. New York: Twentieth Century Fund.

This comparative international research represents a massive effort. South Asian developing countries were examined over a long period of time through a variety of data collection techniques (which included surveys and official government statistics). The broad range of topics covered include political problems, particularly those related to independence; economic dilemmas, such as how to rationally plan the economy; and trends in population growth and composition.

Williamson, John B., and Joseph W. Weiss
1979   "Egalitarian Political Movements, Social Welfare Effort and Convergence Theory: A Cross-National Analysis." In *Comparative Social Research.* Vol. 2, ed. Richard F. Tomasson. Greenwich, Conn.: JAI Press.

This study, based on national-level aggregate data and structural characteristics of nations, examines two interpretations of the convergence theory that all industrialized countries are becoming increasingly alike.

Wolf, Eric R., and Edward C. Hansen
1972   *The Human Condition in Latin America.* New York: Oxford University Press.

One of the best comparative introductions to Latin American countries, this text synthesizes a variety of data—aggregate statistics, field interviews, and secondary sources. The authors are particularly sensitive to common cultural themes that are focal points for comparison.

The World Bank
1978   *World Development Report 1978.* Washington, D.C.: World Bank.

This volume is a good source of aggregate data on 125 reporting countries of low, middle, and high income. Data are presented for 1960 and 1976 in a format that allows easy assessment of trends in development. Indicators include gross national product, the extent and direction of trade, and various measures of health, education, and welfare.

References

Adelman, Irma, and Cynthia Taft Morris
1967   *Society, Politics and Economic Development.* Baltimore: Johns Hopkins Press.
1973   *Economic Growth and Social Equity in Developing Countries.* Stanford, Calif.: Stanford University Press.

Asch, Solomon
1952   *Social Psychology.* Englewood Cliffs, N.J.: Prentice-Hall.

Atkinson, J. Maxwell
1978   *Discovering Suicide.* Pittsburgh: University of Pittsburgh Press.

Barthel, Diane L.
1975   "The Rise of a Female Professional Elite: The Case of Senegal." *African Studies Review* 18 (December):1–17.

Blackwood, B.
1935   *Both Sides of Buka Passage.* Oxford, England: Clarendon Press.

Hibbs, Douglas A., Jr.
1973   *Mass Political Violence: A Cross-National Causal Analysis.* New York: Wiley.

Inkeles, Alex, and David H. Smith
1974   *Becoming   Modern.* Cambridge, Mass.: Harvard University Press.

Jackman, Robert W.
1975   *Politics and Social Equality: A Comparative Analysis.* New York: Wiley.

Kelman, Herbert C.
1968   *A Time to Speak: On Human Values and Social Research.* San Francisco: Jossey-Bass.

Lewis, Oscar
1951   *Life in a Mexican Village.* Urbana, Ill.: University of Illinois Press.

Lipset, Seymour M., et al.
1954   "The Psychology of Voting: An Analysis of Political Behavior." In *Handbook of Social Psychology,* ed. Gardner Lindzey. Reading, Mass.: Addison-Wesley.

Malinowski, Bronislaw
1927   *The Father in Primitive Psychology.* New York: Norton.

McClelland, David C.
1961   *The Achieving Society.* New York: Free Press.

Milgram, Stanley
1961   "Nationality and Conformity." *Scientific American* 205 (December): 45–51.

Mitchell, Robert E.
1968   "Survey Materials Collected in Developing Countries: Obstacles to Comparison." In *Comparative Research Across Cultures and Nations,* ed. Stein Rokkan. The Hague: Mouton.

Murdock, George P.
1937   "Correlations of Matrilineal and Patrilineal Institutions." In *Studies in the Science of Society,* ed. George P. Murdock. New Haven, Conn.: Yale University Press.

Murdock, George P., et al.
1971   *Outline of Cultural Materials.* 4th rev. ed. New Haven, Conn.: Human Relations Area Files.

Nadel, Siegfried F.
1952   "Witchcraft in Four African Societies." *American Anthropologist* 54 (January):18–29.

Piven, Frances Fox, and Richard A. Cloward
1971   *Regulating the Poor.* New York: Random House (Vintage).

Redfield, Robert
1930   *Tepoztlan: A Mexican Village.* Chicago: University of Chicago Press.

Sears, Robert R., and George W. Wise
1950   "Relation of Cup Feeding in Infancy to Thumbsucking and the Oral Drive." *American Journal of Orthopsychiatry* 20 (January):123–138.

Taylor, Charles L., and Michael C. Hudson
1972   *World Handbook of Political and Social Indicators.* New Haven, Conn.: Yale University Press.

Warwick, Donald P., and Samuel Osherson, eds.
1973   *Comparative Research Methods.* Englewood Cliffs, N.J.: Prentice-Hall.

Whiting, John W. M.
1941   *Becoming a Kwoma.* New Haven, Conn.: Yale University Press.
1968   "Methods and Problems in Cross-Cultural Research." In *Handbook of Social Psychology,* Gardner Lindzey and Elliot Aronson. 2nd ed. Reading, Mass.: Addison-Wesley.

Whiting, John W. M., and Irvin L. Child
1953   *Child Training and Personality: A Cross-Cultural Study.* New Haven, Conn.: Yale University Press.

Wilensky, Harold L.
1975   *The Welfare State and Equality.* Berkeley, Calif.: University of California Press.

Williamson, John B., and Jeanne J. Fleming
1977   "Convergence Theory and the Social Welfare Sector." *International Journal of Comparative Sociology* 18:242–253.

Williamson, John B., and Joseph W. Weiss
1979   "Egalitarian Political Movements, Social Welfare Effort and Convergence Theory: A Cross-National Analysis." In *Comparative Social Research.* Vol. 2, ed. Richard F. Tomasson. Greenwich, Conn.: JAI Press.

14 / Evaluation Research

CHAPTER OUTLINE

INTRODUCTION
An Example
The Social Significance of Evaluation
    Research
EVALUATION RESEARCH
    PROCESS
Formulation of the Problem

Research Design
    Experimentation and Evaluation
    Observation and Evaluation
Plans for Data Collection, Sampling,
    and Measurement
Difficulties in Implementing Research
    Design

Utilization of Results for Decision
    Making
SUMMARY
KEY TERMS
EXERCISES
SUGGESTED READINGS
REFERENCES

Introduction

The goal of APPLIED SOCIAL RESEARCH is to solve real problems for individuals and organizations. It accomplishes this by assessing the need for, and devising particular strategies of, social action programs. An important requirement that complements this problem-solving effort is the evaluation of programs once they are implemented. In effect, *evaluation research* is a type of experiment (see Chapter 9) conducted in a real-world setting. Its purpose is to discover whether a strategy implemented in order to improve the quality of life for a specific group of people has in fact achieved its goal. Evaluation research assesses the effectiveness of a program by comparing its original goals with its subsequent, actual accomplishments. The findings from this comparison are then used to determine the value of the program and perhaps how to change it in the future.

AN EXAMPLE

The major components of evaluation research are illustrated in the following example: A group of citizens, The Committee on Civil Rights in East Manhattan, decided to launch a program to investigate, and then to reduce, discrimination against blacks in restaurants surrounding the United Nations building. To arrive at a baseline measure of the amount of discrimination, C.C.R.E.M. sent survey teams of blacks and whites into the same sample of restaurants. After leaving the restaurants, members of each team answered questionnaires designed to evaluate differences in the treatment they had received. As a result of this evaluation of the amount of discrimination, C.C.R.E.M. had data showing that over 40 percent of the black teams had indeed experienced treatment inferior to that experienced by their white counterparts (Selltiz, 1955).

The next step taken by C.C.R.E.M. was to design an action program to reduce discrimination. The program agreed upon involved a two-part approach: (1) contacting people who operated the restaurants, in order to get pledges of equal treatment, and (2) notifying the news media about the questionnaire findings of widespread discrimination and about the restaurants' subsequent pledges of equal treatment.

After implementing its action program, C.C.R.E.M. wanted to know how effective it had been in solving the problem. To gain this knowledge, it reevaluated the previously sampled restaurants by again having teams visit them and then fill out questionnaires that measured discriminatory treatment. This second set of questionnaires revealed that in 16 percent of the restaurants the black team was given treatment clearly inferior to that given the white team. Comparing the amount of discrimination found in the survey conducted before the program (42 percent) with that found afterward (16 percent), the committee concluded that its program was indeed of value in creating change toward the equal treatment of blacks.

The C.C.R.E.M. experience contains the three elements that, when they occur together, define a problem-solving effort as evaluation research. First, the effort must occur in a *real-world setting*. In accordance with this requirement, C.C.R.E.M. conducted its project in restaurants surrounding the United Nations building. In evaluation research the focus is on practical applied problems that may or may not be relevant to the more general theoretical issues that often concern academic social science researchers.

Second, evaluation research must involve a *program design aimed at improving the life situation* of a specified group of people. The C.C.R.E.M. project, with its program of contacts with restaurants and the news media, was set up to effect reduced discrimination toward blacks, a goal seen as an improvement in the life situation of blacks.

Third, provisions must be made for an *evaluation* of the program's success. C.C.R.E.M.'s evaluation was a comparison of the amount of discrimination before its program with the amount occurring afterward. Because discrimination was reduced, the committee evaluated its program as a success.

THE SOCIAL SIGNIFICANCE OF EVALUATION RESEARCH

Since the 1930s both the public and private sectors of American society have instituted numerous programs to eliminate some negative condition, or to create some positive condition, affecting the lives of people. The federal government, for instance, initiated a wide variety of programs during the 1960s that had the ultimate goal of eliminating poverty. Other programs have been initiated in the areas of corrections, mental health, and population policy. Scientific evaluation research measures the degree to which such improvement-oriented programs achieve what they set out to achieve:

> Does encouraging local citizens to participate in decision making really make them less likely to engage in violent or other antisocial behavior?

Does increasing the penalty for violation of a law really deter potential criminals?

Does "tracking" of students in high school according to their tested ability have a beneficial effect on learning?

Is psychotherapy an effective treatment for alcoholism?

Each of these questions and countless others may be examined through evaluation research. The findings of these studies may be used in decision making that affects social policy: Which programs should be altered, and in what way? Which programs should be eliminated?

We might well ask how evaluation research differs, if at all, from nonevaluation research. One difference relates to an accusation sometimes made against one or another project—that it seems to have little relevance to the "real" social world. In other words, some research may seem to be of little interest except to other social scientists. Since evaluation research is used for decision making about programs designed to deal with social problems or about the delivery of various services, it is less susceptible to this criticism. The more abstract research carried out in the halls of academia certainly has a role to play in the ultimate resolution of societal problems, but evaluation research seeks such solutions more immediately and concretely.

A point in common for both evaluation and nonevaluation studies is that the same basic steps of the research process must be followed. It should be emphasized, however, that there are special problems associated with the attempt to do rigorous evaluation research. There may be resistance by program administrators who fear that negative findings might terminate their programs. Or there may be difficulty in getting a representative sample if those not sampled are thereby deprived of gaining something positive from the program. We shall consider these issues in some depth, but it is best to begin by describing the overall research process in an evaluation study.

Evaluation Research Process

In the discussion that follows, we offer a general outline of how evaluation research is done. In actual practice there are usually some deviations from this outline. It would be wisest to think of it as a checklist of important points to consider rather than as a fixed list to be adhered to at all costs. The first stage in the process is the formulation of the problem, which includes identifying and specifying it. The formulation stage also includes the designation of a program that has the purpose of either ameliorating or eliminating the selected problem. A second broad phase in the evaluation process is the development of a research design for determining the effectiveness of the program. The final stage involves the implementation of the research design and the preparation of the results for decision making.

FORMULATION OF THE PROBLEM

Social scientists who do evaluation research are usually hired by an organization (examples are community groups, private and public service agencies, state and federal governments). The organization is either sponsoring or contemplating the sponsorship of a program designed to deal with some problem that usually has already been defined when the researcher arrives on the scene. The organization may have decided to address the issue of unequal education, juvenile delinquency, or teenage pregnancy. Although it is to be expected that the general problem has already been chosen by the organization, it would be better if the group concerned contacted the evaluation researchers before the issue was narrowed down, the goals of the program established, and the specific helping strategy selected. When the organization does not recruit evaluators until after its program has been put into operation, the researchers must reconstruct the objectives of the program. Sometimes this leads to a situation where an educated guess has to be made to determine what decision makers *really* want to find out.

Let us assume that the ideal situation exists; the evaluation researcher is consulted from the outset. The first aim should be to narrow down the general problem in such a way that a program can be planned. If the issue is discrimination against women, the researcher must decide what kind of discrimination to focus on—discrimination in employment? discrimination in education? Suppose that discrimination in employment is settled on. Once again, is it discrimination in hiring or in promotion? It is through such questioning that a concrete and manageable problem area is eventually pinned down.

Another aspect of this process is that a careful inquiry should be made about the perceived cause of the problem that is eventually to be dealt with by the program. Assume that a large corporation has decided it wants to reduce discrimination against women in job promotions. Does the organization see the problem as caused by prejudiced behavior on the part of male administrators in the business world or, possibly, by undesirable behavior on the part of employed women? It is precisely this kind of focusing that is needed at the outset in order for the researcher to be able to decide whether or not the project is desirable from a personal and ethical point of view. If the answer is that the problem is being articulated in an unethical (for example, racist or sexist) manner, the investigator may decide not to work with the sponsors of the research. In our example let us assume that the organization and the evaluation researcher decide to pursue the problem of discrimination against women in job promotions as a function of the prejudiced behavior of businessmen. Now, the researchers can specify a program for intervention and clarify its purposes.

Usually, many different kinds of programs may be implemented to attain a particular goal. One possibility in this case might be a series of consciousness-raising seminars on discrimination against women in the major institutional sectors of American life (education, religion, the family, the economy, and the political system). A teaching team composed of a psychologist, a sociologist, an American historian, and an economist—all with special knowledge in the area of women's studies—could be contracted to organize and conduct the seminars. There would be many practical issues to resolve if such a program were implemented. Which businessmen would be selected to participate, and how would their cooperation be secured, for example?

It is, of course, important to spell out in detail the purposes of any program. Suchman (1967:39–41) provides a guideline of questions to be considered:

1. *What* is the nature of the content of the objective? Are we interested in changing knowledge, attitudes, or behavior? Are we concerned with producing exposure, awareness, interest, or action?

2. *Who* is the target of the program? At which groups in the population is the program aimed?
3. *When* is the desired change to take place? Are we seeking an immediate effect, or are we gradually building toward some postponed effect?
4. Are the objectives UNITARY or MULTIPLE? Is the program aimed at a single change or at a series of changes?

How would these considerations shape the contemplated program of consciousness-raising seminars?

1. The nature of the objective is to diminish the prejudiced behavior of businessmen in the area of job promotions for women. Any seminar program would most likely seek to inform businessmen of certain facts about the condition of contemporary women in America and the ways in which institutional sexism operates. Hopefully, this would lead to a reduction of prejudiced attitudes about women who work. The final goal would be for the businessmen to change their attitudes and to reduce prejudiced behavior with respect to job promotions for women.

2. The target of the program would be male administrators in the business world who make decisions about job promotions for women. But which ones? The decision might ultimately be reached to concentrate on one or two large branches of the corporation sponsoring the research.

3. The question of timing of the changes might be handled by agreeing that it is desirable for change to occur in both the short term and the long run. Some significantly different behavior in the area of job promotions might be expected from businessmen who had been exposed to consciousness-raising seminars over a period of six months to a year. More dramatic changes would probably be expected over a longer period of time.

4. The changes created by any program are rarely unitary. We have already agreed that any program would most likely have the purpose of changing knowledge, attitudes, and behavior about job discrimination toward women. It is also likely that such a program would not be concerned solely with changes in the area of job promotions. There would probably also be interest in diminishing discriminatory behavior toward women in the day-to-day work process. Furthermore, thought should be given to the unintended effects, as well as to the stated objectives of any program. Strategies for change carry the potential for LATENT CONSEQUENCES, which may or may not work against the original rationale for intervention. In this example, improving promotion chances for women in the firm may in fact have a negative effect on the hiring of new female employees at relatively high positions. This possibility should be recognized early on so that it may be addressed.

It should be clear that the formulation of the problem is a critical phase in the evaluation research process. Many commentators have noted that when investigators are not careful at this initial stage, they plan social programs with unclear goals, a failing that consequently makes evaluation research almost impossible to carry out. Moreover, in developing plans for social intervention that have both short- and long-term effects, care must be taken to measure both. It is possible for a program to produce immediate positive results but ultimately to fail because the theory underlying the formulation of the problem was faulty. An example of such THEORY FAILURE might be a training program that succeeds in producing competent building tradespeople but does not result in the participants' finding employment, as had been expected (Finsterbusch and Motz, 1980).

RESEARCH DESIGN

Assuming that the issues involved in the formulation of the problem are handled effectively, the next task of the evaluation researcher will be to develop a design that tests the effectiveness of the specified program. This design is essentially the game plan that the researcher spells out in detail before data collection commences. The basic elements of research design are the same for both nonevaluation and evaluation research. What we shall consider here is their particular relevance for evaluation research.

There are many possible overall strategies for evaluating a program. One technique is to study a group of people from the target population after it has been exposed to a program that has caused some change. This approach is called the ONE-SHOT STUDY. In our example, a group of businessmen who attended the seminars on the condition of women in America would be examined to see if in fact their knowledge, attitudes, and behavior toward women had changed in a nondiscriminatory direction. There are some obvious difficulties with this approach. One is that there is no BASELINE MEASUREMENT—no measurement of the knowledge, attitudes, and behavior of the businessmen toward women *before* their exposure to the seminars. What are the findings of such a study to be compared with? One way out of this dilemma is to ask the participants of programs, after the fact, about their prior knowledge, attitudes, and behavior. One of the many potential sources of error here is the inaccuracy generated by the fallibility of the human memory.

An alternative technique is to study a group of people both before and after exposure to a particular program. This circumvents many of the problems of the one-shot study. BEFORE-AND-AFTER STUDIES, however, suffer from another potential flaw. Suppose that positive findings (a change in the direction in which the program is aiming) emerge from such a study. These findings could be explained by experiences other than participation in a given program. Returning to our example, a group of businessmen could show changes in the direction of nondiscrimination toward women. We may ask whether these findings could have been produced by the men having had their consciousness raised through people they had met who were strong feminists. What is needed to avoid this difficulty is some means of taking such extraneous factors into account. (It should be apparent that the one-shot study also suffers from this deficiency.) The CONTROLLED EXPERIMENT provides such a check and is therefore considered to be an ideal research approach for evaluation research.

EXPERIMENTATION AND EVALUATION. There are many different kinds of controlled experiments. The simplest for purposes of evaluation research is set up in the following way. We select a number of people from the target population (when possible, we would want to use probability sampling). Our goal is to create two groups as nearly alike as possible. The usual way to do this is through the random assignment of half of the selected people to one group and half to the other group (the technical term for this process is RANDOMIZATION). The key aspect to experimentation is that one group, the experimental group, participates in the program under consideration while the second group, the control group, does not.[1]

Measurements of the desired goals and outcomes of the program are made both before and after the program is conducted to see whether the program produces the desired changes. This is done for both the experimental group and the control group. The measurements should show no difference between the two groups before the program commences. If the program is effective, the "after" measurements should show that the experimental group has experienced a change in the desired direction that is significantly greater than any change registered for the control group. The "after" measurement for the control group is the means by which we take into account any of the extraneous factors related to the desired outcome of the program that may be occurring for both the experimental and the control groups. If we subtract the change experienced by the control group from the change evidenced in the experimental group, the result is a measure of the program's impact.

A controlled experiment is clearly superior to either a one-shot study or a before-and-after study. The control group in an experiment eliminates the possible interpretation that extraneous factors are not accounted for in the one-shot and before-and-after approaches. The "before" measurement in an experiment provides the baseline that is lacking in the one-shot study. Yet, with all these advantages, experiments are used *less* frequently in evaluation research than in either of the other two research approaches. The reason for this is that there are a number of problems involved in experimental evaluation research.

A general source of resistance to using the controlled experiment is that the research on the effectiveness of a particular program is often considered to be secondary to the program itself. The prime concern of the sponsoring organization and its administrators is the successful operation of the program itself, not the research. This means that the more ideal conditions under which an experiment can be conducted in a laboratory usually cannot be duplicated. Most administrators are reluctant to allow a research approach that makes it possible for any members of the target population to be excluded from the services of the program. But the random assignment of people from the target population to experimental and control groups requires this exclusion.

One possible solution to this dilemma is to compare groups of people who have self-selected themselves into one group that participates in a social program voluntarily and another group that has decided not to participate. If the two groups are similar in important background variables, and if differences emerge between them after the program is completed, there is some justification in attributing the differences to the impact of the program. Even if both these conditions are satisfied, there is still the gnawing question of whether or not the selectivity involved has operated in such a way as to make the two groups actually nonequivalent. But the use of somewhat nonequivalent groups is better than having no comparison group at all.

Another strategy is to shift the emphasis from testing the effectiveness of one program to examining the effectiveness of alternative programs. What is involved

---

[1]For a more detailed discussion of experimental designs, see Chapter 9. In that chapter we describe the *true experiment* in which subjects are randomly assigned to either the control or the experimental group. We also discuss the *quasi-experiment* in which a control group is used but without random assignment of subjects. Both the true experiment and the quasi-experiment are forms of what we refer to in this chapter as the *controlled experiment*.

here is a variation of the simple controlled experiment wherein different groups are exposed to different programs. The issue of control groups not having the opportunity to share in the benefits of a program disappears, as should some of the resistance of program administrators. An example of this solution in our hypothetical example would be to compare the relative merits of three types of consciousness-raising seminars. Note that a pure control group (participating in no program) is not included in this research approach. If a pure control group is added to the groups that are exposed to different programs, some of the resistance to "experimentation" is likely to reappear.

A third solution to the difficulties involved in employing the controlled experiment in evaluation research is perhaps the most obvious: randomly assign members of the target population to the experimental and control groups in such a way that it will not meet with resistance. If, for example, there are not enough funds to allow all interested people in the target population to participate in a program, a random basis for selection may be possible. The sponsoring organization may be promised that people who are not selected initially may be able to participate in a program at a later time. In the meantime these people can function as a control group for the people who are selected first. It should be apparent that such situations do not always occur. The evaluation researcher is usually forced to accept some form of compromise with the desired goal of a controlled experiment.

Although experimentation is an ideal model for evaluation research, other approaches can be quite appropriate. Rossi (1972), for example, ranks several possible techniques for data collection from "soft" to "hard" in the following way: program administrators' narrative reports concerning the program (least desired), program audits based on the qualitative judgments of outside observers, correlational designs in which statistical controls are used, quasi-experiments with impure control groups, and controlled experiments (most desired). Rossi argues that nonexperimental designs can be validly used to see if a particular program creates a *large* impact. If they do not reveal such an impact, it is unlikely that harder approaches will; but if significant results do appear in research using the softer techniques, it is approriate to pursue evaluation by more quantitative means.

OBSERVATION AND EVALUATION. Under certain circumstances the softer techniques (such as observational field work) are the most valid approaches to evaluation. This is particularly the case when the organization sponsoring the study has made some faulty assumptions in developing the rationale for carrying it out, even before data are collected. Sophia McDowell (1977) conducted research on race relations for the United States Army. The sponsors were initially concerned that polarization of blacks and whites into racially exclusive groupings was producing a hostile social environment in the military. They asked McDowell to investigate this polarization and to recommend policies to promote social groups that were racially mixed. Using participant observation at a military post where race relations were defined as relatively cordial, McDowell discovered, contrary to the sponsors' premise, that many positive effects resulted from "voluntary racial separation," particularly improvement in black pride and confidence. The perception of separation as invariably dangerous and polarizing was discovered to be invalid. This finding greatly enhanced the usefulness of the recommendations the researcher was able to make, but it would not have been possible without the collection of observational data.

Another context where field work greatly improves the validity of evaluation research is one in which the statistics to be used in experimental design are problematic. If the difference between the control group and the experimental group is to be measured using inflated or falsified figures, the evaluation is doomed. Often, the only way to discover whether an agency or organization is supplying the evaluator with reliable data is to learn how the data are produced and for what purpose; field work is an effective way of doing this.

John Johnson researched the welfare bureaucracy, specifically Child Welfare Services. The following remarks from supervisors and social workers have a direct bearing on the statistics generated by the welfare system:

> "I think, really though, that the paperwork mill has become a disaster. I can't even keep up with it myself anymore. Half the time I'm not sure what I've just signed."

> "We really don't have any idea of what we're doing. . . . But we never say so publicly, of course. . . . Yeah, the [classification] forms are always neat; it's always this or that, and it's never in between."

> "It isn't what you actually do that makes a goddam bit of difference around here, but only what you *appear* to be doing. That's where it's at, just the numbers. They just say what you want 'em to say." (Johnson, 1975:44–45)

The amount of records, reports, and other documentary evidence that is required in most evaluations of welfare and other human services delivery programs has ballooned in recent years. One result of this trend has been an increase in the number of personnel whose duties relate directly to the collection and processing of information. Although this monitoring is potentially beneficial to social research, there is also a danger that the statistics are conveying an inaccurate impression of the need for programs and/or the level of their performance. Observational research provides a way of checking on and improving the validity of such data. We are not suggesting that field work replace experimentation that employs hard survey data. In the process of evaluation, as in many other types of research, a combination of methods is, however, undeniably beneficial.

PLANS FOR DATA COLLECTION, SAMPLING, AND MEASUREMENT

After the general game plan for program evaluation has been chosen, procedures are devised for the collection of data, sampling, and measurement of variables. It is important not to exclude any potential sources of evidence that a program is either succeeding or failing. The following is a list of sources proposed by Weiss (1972:53):

> Interviews, questionnaires, observation, ratings (by peers, staff, experts), psychometric tests (of attitudes, values, personality, preferences, norms, beliefs), institutional records, government statistics, tests (of information, interpretation, skills, application of knowledge), projective tests, situational tests (presenting the respondent with simulated life situations), diary records, physical evidence, clinical examinations, finanical records, and documents (minutes of board meetings, newspaper accounts of policy actions, transcripts of trials).

Some of these sources overlap with one another. Nevertheless, it is plain that there are many alternatives. The selection of a combination of data sources may be appropriate for a given evaluation study. There is usually a connection between the general research approach and the data source. If one wishes to approximate a controlled experiment, for example, the usual data sources are observation, interviews, and questionnaires.

We have already briefly considered some sampling plans for evaluation research. Probability sampling is generally preferred for selecting people from the target population, but it is often not possible in evaluation research. It is more likely that a sample will be composed of self-selected volunteers. In such cases allowances and corrections must be made for the possible bias in the sample.

Some other difficulties frequently connected with samples in evaluation research are illustrated by the income maintenance experiment sponsored by OEO, the federal Office of Economic Opportunity (Kershaw and Fair, 1976). The purpose of this study was to examine what effects an income subsidy would have on the attitudes and behavior of low-income families. A problem encountered in the research was the pressure of local community groups on the sample selection process. When the experimental group to be studied is going to receive something beneficial, such as an income subsidy, the pressure on sample selection is difficult to avoid. One way for the evaluation researcher to deal with this problem is to stress the scientific demands of the research process. Another potential difficulty is the attrition of members from the groups being studied, which can result in a loss of representativeness. It may not be easy to keep people in the control group interested in an experiment that runs several months or years, as was the case with the income maintenance study.

A fundamental part of all research is the development of reliable and valid measures of variables. This is only possible in evaluation research if a program has clearly and explicitly defined goals. Otherwise, the evaluator will find it impossible to gauge success or failure. Consider the following dialogue between a researcher and the administrator of a job training program:

RESEARCHER: What are the goals of your program?

ADMINISTRATOR: We seek to teach our students the kind of knowledge that will be useful to them wherever they go in life.

Clearly, this answer is too general for purposes of measurement in research because it does not suggest specific variables.

RESEARCHER: Could you give me more details?

ADMINISTRATOR: Certainly. We take juvenile delinquents and turn them into productive, contributing, self-supporting citizens.

This is a more useful answer because the researcher may begin to have an idea how to measure *productivity*. But the goals of the program can be expressed even more concretely.

RESEARCHER: In what sense do you mean, "contributing citizens"?

ADMINISTRATOR: Well, the program is designed to teach each boy a skill, to help him get a job, to follow his progress in the job to see how he's doing and to provide advice and support where needed.

Here we have four explicit goals that can be measured effectively. Have participants learned a skill? Have they obtained employment? Have they adapted well to work routine? And is the counseling provided by the program effective?

If administrators understand and are in agreement with how goals are to be measured at the beginning of a study, they are more likely to be persuaded of the validity of the findings at its conclusion. From the point of view of the researcher, however, it is unfortunate that a detailed and explicit statement of program objectives is often difficult to obtain. One obvious reason is that the more specific are the stated goals of an organization, the more accountable it must be for their accomplishment. Administrators may have a vested interest in deflecting criticism of their own performance by being vague about the objectives of their agency or program. A second reason is that to obtain funding or authorization in the first place, a social program may have only the most general mandate or statement of purpose. One consequence of the political process, whether in government or in the politics of smaller organizations, is that specific proposals that might provoke disagreement are often whittled down or softened. Therefore, programs that do receive the go-ahead are sometimes so noncontroversial in purpose that they are difficult to criticize or evaluate in practice.

This is certainly an instance where the administrator may be at odds with the researcher, who is attempting to carry out a GOAL-BASED EVALUATION. The social scientist typically wants to express the objectives of an organization in terms specific enough to permit the organization's behavior to be measured; the administrator may simply want the program or agency to remain in operation. One argument the researcher may use to encourage greater specification of program goals is that if evaluation measures are vague, critics can claim that it was not the program itself that succeeded, but rather an invalid measure that produced the positive results.

An alternative strategy that may reduce the potential for distrust between a researcher and program personnel is the so-called GOAL-FREE EVALUATION (Scriven, 1972). Proponents of this model believe that information should be gathered that reflects a broad array of actual program accomplishments in response to general social needs, and that data collection must not be confined soley to the more narrow and specific list of goals that may appear in a program's official statement of purpose. A program is then judged according to its observed impact on the setting in which it functions, and there are no a priori restrictions on the range of data to be obtained. If conducted adroitly, goal-free evaluation may reduce the anxiety of administrators that their organizations are "on trial." At the same time, important, unanticipated benefits of program operation may be uncovered and assessed.

DIFFICULTIES IN IMPLEMENTING RESEARCH DESIGN

Our discussion of data collection and measurement highlights the fact that the realities of the setting under investigation often make it difficult to do evaluation research exactly as one may have been taught to do it. We have noted that researching the effectiveness of a program is often considered by administrators and program personnel to be secondary to the implementation of the program. There are obvious conflicts between the two goals. It is common to find a SHIFTING PROGRAM, one that is not executed in a perfectly predictable manner. It is not unusual for strategies dealing with the problem area to be altered as a result of the decisions of program administrators. Program personnel may change through the resignation of staff members. Participants may drop out and others may join the program while it is in progress. How is the evaluation researcher supposed to cope with such difficulties and still adequately evaluate how successful a program is in attaining its objectives?

Some concrete suggestions for dealing with these issues have been offered by Weiss (1972:98):

1. Take frequent periodic measures of program effect (for example, monthly assessments in programs of education, training, therapy), rather than limiting collection of outcome data to one point in time.
2. Encourage a clear transition from one program approach to another. If changes are going to be made, try to see that A is done for a set period, then B, then C.
3. Clarify the assumptions and procedures of each phase and classify them systematically.
4. Keep careful records of the persons who participated in each phase. Rather than lumping all participants together, analyze outcomes in terms of the phase(s) of the program in which each person participated.

Another problem in executing an evaluation research design is that investigators and program personnel are not in a naturally cooperative situation. One area of difference between the two relates to the scientific versus the practical objectives of an evaluation study. The researcher is at least somewhat concerned with the relationship of the study's findings to the growth of knowledge in a particular academic discipline. (Will this research contribute to the long-run development of understanding in this field?) Program personnel, on the other hand, have a more nuts-and-bolts attitude toward the program. There are also bound to be personality differences between the two. The researcher is likely to be detached and analytical—a person who is interested in ideas and abstractions. Program personnel may be more sensitive to the issue of servicing people's needs right now (Rodman and Kolodny, 1965). Closely associated with these potential personality conflicts are differences in the respective roles. Program personnel are usually committed to the policies and strategies currently in use, while the researcher is in the position of asking how effective these strategies are. Indeed, evaluation researchers are probably always viewed suspiciously, and often as a threat. The personnel see the researcher as taking time and money from the program while offering a possibly negative report in return. Furthermore, they may perceive the researcher as unfavorably judging their work, competence, and personalities. These conflicts of interest are compounded when the investigator is not actually hired by the agency or program concerned, but by the government or another supervisory body.

What are the solutions to these problems? One is to involve the program personnel in the evaluation research process. This will enable them to better understand the nature of the research and to reduce their uneasiness about why so many questions must be asked. A further benefit of personnel involvement is that they may become more committed to the research if they contribute to its implementation. A different, more traditional solution to relational problems between researcher and personnel is to clarify role definitions and lines of authority. This solution entails spelling out the role expectations of all parties prior to the beginning of the program so that it is known who makes which decisions and what channels of appeal exist.

One way of dealing with the fears and suspicions of program personnel is to design an evaluation in which the focus is on providing feedback as the program progresses. Here the idea is to offer suggestions for improvement along the way, rather than making one final pro or con judgment. One advantage of such a focus is that personnel can see the benefits to the program and get some evidence that the research is of value to them. Another advantage is that the results are more likely to be put to use. A disadvantage is that such a process may make an overall pro or con judgment all but impossible because there have been so many changes in the program along the way.

There are many other problems in executing an evaluation research design. One is deciding who should know about the program and about the research in the community where they are being conducted. It is important to get community leaders and experts on one's side in order to initiate and successfully carry out evaluation research. Of course, one cannot always predict what obstacles will lie in the path of implementing a research design. One such dilemma was experienced in the income maintenance study we were looking at previously when the United States Senate made a request for information from the study while the research was still going on (Kershaw, 1972). Obviously, the public release of information regarding a study before it is over can have the effect of biasing results or of bringing the study to a premature conclusion.

UTILIZATION OF RESULTS FOR DECISION MAKING

Ideally, the results of evaluation research are used to make social policy. There are, however, some crucial potential obstacles to the fulfillment of this goal. One is that the organization under consideration may react negatively to the research conclusion. It may either resist implementing the recommendations of the researcher or use the findings selectively for its own purposes. Suchman (1967:143) points out that an organization that is responsible for a particular social program may misuse evaluation research in the following ways:

1. *eyewash:* an attempt to justify a weak or bad program by deliberately selecting only those aspects that "look good." The objective of the evaluation is limited to those parts of the program that appear successful.
2. *whitewash:* an attempt to cover up program failure or errors by avoiding any objective appraisal. A favorite device here is to solicit "testimonials" that divert attention from the failure.
3. *posture:* an attempt to use evaluation as a "gesture" of objectivity and to assume the pose of "scientific" research. This "looks good" to the public and is a sign of "professional" status.
4. *Postponement:* an attempt to delay needed action by pretending to seek the "facts." Evaluative research takes time and, hopefully, the storm will blow over by the time the study is completed.

What is common to all these techniques is the effort of an organization to manipulate evaluation research for its own interests. Researchers must always be on their guard against the possibility of being co-opted as a "servant of power." They must be concerned about this possibility from their first contact with a particular evaluation research situation until the entire process is completed. If it appears that any of the manipulations suggested above are being planned or executed, researchers should attempt to correct the situation or disassociate themselves from the specific research enterprise.

Another possible negative reaction to the results of evaluation research is that the organization whose social program has been found lacking will disregard unfavorable findings. Let us consider the following list of rationalizations used by professionals in the field of corrections:

> The therapeutic relationships examined or the impact of the program is "too subtle to measure with statistics."
>
> "The presence of outsiders disturbs the normal conduct of the program or the group or the session."
>
> "Even through they may come back to prison, they are better or happier or more emotionally stable people for having participated in the program."
>
> "The effects of the program can only be measured in the long run, not just during the first six months or year after release."
>
> "The program or the technique is OK but it is not designed for this particular individual."
>
> "The reason that the program failed is that it wasn't extensive enough or long enough or applied by the right people."
>
> "The program is worth it if it saved one man." (Ward and Kassebaum, 1972:302)

It is probably sensible to expect such rationalizations from people and organizations whose programs are subjected to criticism as a result of evaluation research. One commonly offered solution to this problem is for investigators to shift their attention away from determining whether or not a specific social program should be totally accepted or totally rejected. Evaluation research is much more likely to be well received if its concern is to examine the relative merits of different programs sponsored by the same organization or if its emphasis is to examine possible modifications in any given program. An example of such research is the evaluation done on the Sesame Street television show for children. Different presentations were shown to a sample of children; the program was changed on the basis of the children's reactions (McDill, McDill, and Spehe, 1972).

Another potential obstacle to the proper utilization of results from evaluation research is the relationship between the researcher and the sponsors. Most researchers are primarily oriented toward the academic community for acceptance of their efforts. Rewards are more frequently reaped via publication than through taking extra time to carefully interpret the research results for decision makers. In addition, evaluation researchers are often encouraged by those who hire them to say nothing or to stay uninvolved in the application of results.

It is unfortunate that so much of what passes for evaluation research is based on faulty premises or improper investigative procedures. As Weiss (1971:138) notes: "A ... major limitation on the use of evaluation results is the current state of evaluation practice. Much evaluation is poor; more is mediocre." When two investigators rated a sample of evaluation research reported between 1969 and 1973, they found that less than one-fourth of the studies met even the most elementary scientific criteria (Gordon and Morse, 1975). The investigators discovered that most of the competent research had reported a negative evaluation of a program. Moreover, the most rigorous standards of research tended to be employed by investigators who were outsiders, that is, not officially connected with the agency or program being evaluated. These findings have important implications for the utilization of research findings. Favorable evaluations may be, in effect, little more than sophisticated public relations tactics. Negative conclusions may be suppressed or attributed to unresolvable differences of values and opinion between the academics who do research and the personnel who work in the programs being studied.

A conservative interpretation of the scientific canon of objectivity can lead one to the position that researchers should not become involved in advocating any particular use of their findings. This interpretation is often heard, but we do not agree with it. To fail to take an active role in pressing for the constructive application of one's findings is to relegate much evaluation research to a graveyard of useless or misleading information. Those who follow up their work to see that it is correctly and completely reported and that it is used for the solution of human problems contribute to the overall quality of evaluation research and to the relevance of science for society.

Summary

Evaluation research is a form of applied social science. Its purpose is to determine whether social programs have indeed achieved the goal of improving the quality of life for the specific public they serve, whether it be welfare recipients, schoolchildren, military personnel, or any other group affected by a program. The original goals of an agency or organization are compared with its subsequent, actual accomplishments in a real-world setting. In this sense, evaluation research makes scientific methodology and a variety of data collection techniques directly relevant to social life. A number of problems, however, typically occur in implementing even the most thorough study design. These include the following:

1. The organization that hires the evaluation researcher may perceive the problem for investigation quite differently from the way it is perceived by the evaluator. The organization may not be bound by the same ethical principles.
2. The purpose of the study, from the sponsor's point of view, may not be to present a scientifically valid picture of what transpires in the organization. Motives for evaluation research that are potentially antithetical to science include the mechnical and uninspired satisfaction of red-tape requirements for program monitoring or the desire to depict a program in the most favorable light, regardless of the evidence.
3. Any program may have unintended, hidden consequences that may or may not negate its original purpose. These must be accounted for in an effective study design; yet they are often difficult to discover, particularly in the short run.
4. It is often difficult to sample effectively or to maintain other necessary procedures of controlled experimentation because program administrators are typically more interested in getting on with their work than in producing a scientifically rigorous study.
5. The data supplied by an organization for purposes of evaluation may be unreliable.

It is possible to anticipate and correct some of these problems by encouraging program administrators to be as specific as possible in delineating their goals and the rationale behind them, by using observational techniques to check on the validity of data provided by the organization under study, by using quasi-experimental designs that take into account actual conditions in the field, and by remaining as flexible as possible, both in choosing data collection strategies and in deciding what the sources of the data will be. In many cases, however, these tactics are less than completely successful. The overall scientific quality of evaluation research remains low because of the many methodological problems that must be addressed and because of the relationship between researchers and program personnel, which is often less than fully cooperative. In order to improve the scientific quality of evaluation research, as well as its usefulness in solving human problems, researchers should exercise their responsibility to see that their work is fully and fairly reported by the sponsors and that improper use of research results is brought to light.

Key Terms

applied social research	goal-free evaluation	shifting program
baseline measurement	latent consequences	theory failure
before-and-after study	multiple objectives	unitary objectives
controlled experiment	one-shot study	whitewash
goal-based evaluation	randomization	

Exercises

1. By yourself or with another student, choose a group known to be subject to discrimination and design a project that will both reduce the discrimination and measure its reduction. As part of your design, set up control and experimental groups, and tell how you would actually select people to be in those groups. Elaborate on how the design you have chosen would control for outside events or extraneous factors that you feel could influence the results. Claire Selltiz's article "The Use of Survey Methods in a Citizens' Campaign Against Discrimination" (1955) should be useful for this project.

2. James Coleman et al.'s controversial study, *Equality of Educational Opportunity* (1966, in Suggested Readings), indicated that the average achievement scores of racial and ethnic minorities were significantly lower than those of whites. It further stated that achievement scores were directly influenced by the students' social and cultural background. Part of the definition of evaluation research indicated that this research involves a program designed to improve the lot of people. Can you imagine how Coleman's evaluation research findings could be used in a harmful way? Who is responsible for preventing their misuse? How could their misuse be prevented?

3. Suppose you were given the assignment of helping your professor study the effects of desegregated schooling on student achievement. During the process of the study, certain social events occurred: some students dropped out of school, you were unable to randomly select the students to be studied, and the students who were studied were aware they were being studied. Given this tough but realistic situation, how would you advise your professor about the way to establish that the extraneous variables mentioned above did not influence your measurement of students' achievement? What steps may be taken, if any, to ensure that the achievement that did occur would be generalizable to similar attempts at desegregation? To get ideas for answering this question, see Campbell and Stanley's *Experimental and Quasi-Experimental Designs for Research* (1963, in Suggested Readings).

4. Consider an established program located in your college or residential community that has the goal of improving the human condition in some way. Assess the effectiveness of the program by any means of your own choosing as long as it takes less than two hours to collect the data.

5. After exercise 4 is completed, each student in the class should be asked to contact one other student in the class. If it is possible, this should be done in a random fashion. Once the identities of the student pairs (dyads) are established, the students should inform one another of the programs that they evaluated for exercise 4. Discussion should cease at this point. Then, each student should do exercise 4 for the program chosen by the other student in the dyad. When this is accomplished, the two students should compare their evaluation research experiences.

6. Work with another student on this question. Consider various problems currently of significance in American society.

Settle on one problem you both will work on independently. Each of you should develop a program addressed to the problem. Discuss the advantages and disadvantages of the programs that the two of you have devised.

7. You and your partner from exercise 6 are now faced with the problem of making research design decisions about how you would evaluate your programs. Make these decisions. Be sure to discuss whether or not

the option of using a research approach that compares the effectiveness of your two programs makes the most sense.

8. Assume that you were hired to evaluate the programs on which you collected data for exercises 4 and 5. Do you see any possibility of your findings being manipulated by the organization responsible for the program under consideration? How would you try to combat the possible negative utilization of your findings?

Suggested Readings

READINGS ABOUT THE METHOD

Asher, J. W.
1976 *Educational Research and Evaluation Methods.* Boston: Little, Brown.
       A review of several evaluative techniques applied specifically to educational settings and research.
Campbell, Donald, and Julian C. Stanley
1963 *Experimental and Quasi-Experimental Designs for Research.* Chicago: Rand McNally.
       This book is one of the best treatments of experimental designs available. Five research approaches are examined in detail: pre-experimental, true experimental, quasi-experimental, correlational, and ex post facto designs. The major emphasis is on true experimental designs. This work is somewhat complex but well worth the time and effort required.
Klein, Malcolm W., and Katherine S. Teilmann, eds.
1980 *Handbook of Criminal Justice Evaluation.* Beverly Hills, Calif.: Sage.
       A review of evaluation models and outcomes specifically from studies of the criminal justice system.
Moursund, Janet
1973 *Evaluation: An Introduction to Research Design.* Monterey, Calif.: Brooks/Cole.
       This is a good general introduction to the field of evaluation research for the beginning student. Major attention is given to the type of research design that should be employed. Other questions addressed are: What kinds of data should be collected? How should the data be analyzed?

Orlans, Harold
1973 *Contracting for Knowledge.* San Francisco: Jossey-Bass.
       This book addresses the value and limitations of applied social science research. The author's position is that although considerable benefit is derived from the knowledge provided, the case has often been overstated. The chapter on evaluation research discusses the tension that exists between good programs and good evaluations.
Patton, Michael Quinn
1980 *Qualitative Evaluation Methods.* Beverly Hills, Calif.: Sage.
       A complete explication of the role of field work data collection techniques in the process of evaluation research. This book describes the particular strengths of qualitative methods for making evaluations and gives examples from actual studies.
Rossi, Peter H., et al.
1979 *Evaluation: A Systematic Approach.* Beverly Hills, Calif.: Sage.
       One of the most comprehensive overviews of the evaluation process, this book is especially useful because of its many concrete examples and definitions of key terms. Topics covered include: uses of evaluation research, monitoring program implementation, a framework for assessing the impact of programs, and measuring program efficiency.
Suchman, Edward
1967 *Evaluative Research.* New York: Russell Sage.
       A very sound and sophisticated treatment of the key methodological issues in evaluation research is pre-

sented in this now-classic book. The presentation tends to be somewhat formal and abstract, but it is well worth the attention. The author is particularly effective in describing the possible types of research designs for evaluation research and the difficulties that can emerge in the relationships between researchers and those whose programs are evaluated.

Weiss, Carol
1972 *Evaluation Research*. Englewood Cliffs, N.J.: Prentice-Hall.

This is a good, sophisticated introduction that does not use excessively technical jargon. The heart of the text is concerned with how one would design a piece of evaluation research. The beginning and end of this text contain thoughtful discussions of the ethical issues involved.

Weiss, Carol, ed.
1972 *Evaluating Action Programs: Readings in Social Action and Education*. Boston: Allyn & Bacon.

This is a collection of readings by prominent evaluation researchers. The topics include the issues of experimentation and organizational resistance to evaluation research. There is a healthy mixture of theoretical discussion and actual examples of research. Weiss provides an excellent bibliography.

Williams, Walter, and Richard F. Elmore, eds.
1976 *Social Program Implementation*. New York: Academic Press.

This volume contains commentaries on a variety of evaluation studies, particularly in education and community-oriented programs.

READINGS ILLUSTRATING THE METHOD

Abert, James G., ed.
1979 *Program Evaluation at HEW: Research Versus Reality*. Parts 1, 2, and 3. New York and Basel: Marcel Dekker.

This series of books presents reports of two dozen evaluation studies done for the Department of Health, Education and Welfare, arranged in a format that makes it easy to analyze each. Of particular interest are some of the reports in which the authors speculate on the reasons for the incomplete success of their study designs.

Coleman, James S., et al.
1966 *Equality of Educational Opportunity*. Washington, D.C.: U.S. Government Printing Office.

The Coleman report helped to inaugurate a series of laws and court decisions to address racial imbalance in American education.

Deutsch, Morton, and Mary Collins
1951 *Interracial Housing: A Psychological Evaluation of a Social Experiment*. Minneapolis: University of Minnesota Press.

This study examines an integrated, interracial housing project in the New York metropolitan area. The emphasis is on whether or not the integrated project encouraged

closer contact and improved relationships between blacks and whites. In order to test this idea, interviews were conducted with residents of both the integrated project and another project in the area that had a segregated housing policy.

Goodwin, Leonard
1972 *Do the Poor Want to Work?* Washington, D.C.: Brookings Institution.

This book is an extensive exploration and comparison of the attitudes toward work held by welfare families and people who participate in federal work-training programs and the attitudes of middle-class families. Goodwin finds that there are no differences between the poor and the nonpoor with respect to their desires to work and to succeed. This leads to the suggestion that welfare policy should not be articulated with the goal of punishing those on welfare for not working.

Pechman, Joseph, and P. Michael Timpane
1975 *Work Incentives and Income Guarantees*. Washington, D.C.: Brookings Institution.

This work analyzes the negative income tax experiment that was carried out in New Jersey and Pennsylvania between 1968 and 1972. A close look is given to the impact of income guarantees on the behavior of the people who participated in the program. The results of this research have important implications for policy decisions regarding the welfare system in the United States.

Pfohl, Stephen J.
1978   *Predicting Dangerousness*. Lexington, Mass.: Lexington Books.

In this evaluation of a hospital for the criminally insane, the author used participant observation to study patients, doctors, psychologists, and social workers. The major finding was that there is wide variation in the diagnoses, or labels, attached to the same patient behavior. The labeling process was related more to the status of the mental health professionals than to the actual condition of patients.

Rist, Ray
1970   "Student Social Class and Teacher Expectations: The Self-Fulfilling Prophecy in Ghetto Education." *Harvard Educational Review* 40 (August):411–451.

Many studies have shown that minority students achieve less than other students. Rist's research evaluated *how* this phenomenon developed. He discovered that teachers grouped students, according to their social class, into groups expected to fail or succeed. By the time the student who was expected to fail reached the higher grades, his academic achievement began to match his various teachers' expecta-

tions. On the basis of his evaluation, Rist was able to recommend that systems of education not permit differential treatment of students.

Vanecko, James
1969   "Community Mobilization and Institutional Change: The Influence of the Community Action Program in Large Cities." *Social Science Quarterly* 50 (December):609–630.

This is an evaluation of the Community Action Program sponsored by the U.S. Office of Economic Opportunity. Vanecko analyzes data from fifty large U.S. cities that show that community action agencies that stress the mobilization and organization of the poor are more effective than agencies geared toward the delivery of employment, welfare, and educational services.

Williamson, John B., et al.
1975   *Strategies Against Poverty in America*. New York: Wiley (Halsted).

The authors systematically evaluate the gamut of antipoverty programs instituted in the United States from the 1930s through the 1960s. Six general categories are considered: income-in-kind, income, manpower, education, economic development, and organization. The various strategies within each of these approaches are rated using a set of twenty-six criteria such as: proportion of the poor who benefit, impact on the distribution of income, and extent to which recipients of the programs are stigmatized.

References

Finsterbusch, Kurt, and Annabelle Bender Motz
1980   *Social Research for Policy Decisions*. Belmont, Calif.: Wadsworth.

Gordon, Gerald, and Edward V. Morse
1975   "Evaluation Research." In *Annual Review of Sociology*. Vol. 1, ed. Alex Inkeles et al. New York: Free Press.

Johnson, John M.
1975   *Doing Field Research*. New York: Free Press.

Kershaw, David, and Jerilyn Fair
1976   *The New Jersey Income Maintenance Experiment*. New York: Academic Press.

McDill, Edward L., Mary S. McDill, and J. Timothy Sprehe
1972   "Evaluation in Practice: Compensatory Education." In *Evaluating Social Programs,* ed. Peter Rossi and Walter Williams. New York: Seminar Press.

McDowell, Sophia F.
1977   "Race Research in the Army: The Problem of Defining the Problem." Paper presented at the 72nd Annual Meeting of the American Sociological Association, Chicago.

Rodman, Hyman, and Ralph Kolodny
1965   "Organizational Strains in the

Researcher-Practitioner Relationship." In *Applied Sociology,* ed. Alvin Gouldner and S. M. Miller. New York: Free Press.

Rossi, Peter H.
1972   "Testing for Success and Failure in Social Action." In *Evaluating Social Programs,* ed. Peter H. Rossi and Walter Williams. New York: Seminar Press.

Scriven, Michael
1972   "Prose and Cons About Goal Free Evaluation." *Journal of Education Evaluation* 3, 4 (December):1–7.

Selltiz, Claire
1955   "The Uses of Survey Methods in a Citizens' Campaign Against Discrimination." *Human Organization* 14 (Fall):19–25.

Suchman, Edward
1967   *Evaluation Research.* New York: Russell Sage.

Ward, David, and Gene Kassebaum
1972   "On Biting the Hand That Feeds: Some Implications of Sociological Evaluations of Correctional Effectiveness." In *Evaluating Action Programs,* ed. Carol Weiss, Boston: Allyn & Bacon.

Weiss, Carol H.
1971   "Utilization of Evaluation: Toward Comparative Study." In *Readings in Evaluation Research,* ed. Francis G. Carr. New York: Sage.
1972   *Evaluation Research.* Englewood Cliffs, N.J.: Prentice-Hall.

Part III

Quantitative Analysis

15 / Indexes and Scales

CHAPTER OUTLINE

INTRODUCTION
An Example: The Consumer Price
   Index
INDEX CONSTRUCTION
Item Selection
  Face Validity
  Unidimensionality
  Achieving Conceptual Balance
  Statistical Relationship Among
   Items
Index Scoring
  The Range and Numbering of
   Response Categories

Weighting of Index Items
  Coping with Missing Data
Index Validation
  Internal Validation
  External Validation
THE SCALING OF RESPONSES
Measuring Intensity and Response
  Patterns
Some Well-Known Scaling
  Techniques
  The Bogardus Distance Scale
  Thurstone Scaling
  Guttman Scaling

STANDARDIZATION OF
  COMPOSITE MEASURES
A Comparison of Two Measures
The Politics of Measurement
SUMMARY
KEY TERMS
EXERCISES
SUGGESTED READINGS
REFERENCES

Introduction

The subject of this chapter is the measurement of complex behaviors and attitudes. We know from earlier discussions that many of the variables that researchers manipulate are multifaceted; for example, a number of separate mental and physical operations are required to produce the attitude of prejudice as well as discriminatory behavior, or the attitude of religiosity as well as pious behavior. *Indexing* and *scaling* are techniques for measuring these and other complex phenomena in social science.

Before we offer some concrete examples and explain the logic of index and scale construction, let us recall the basic principles of measurement outlined in Chapter 3 and the illustrations of questionnaire items in Chapter 6. An important way to increase both the reliability and the validity of abstract constructs—such as happiness, alienation, tolerance, and anxiety—is to operationalize them by using MULTIPLE INDICATORS of the same phenomenon. A number of survey questions may be combined to assess the strength of a particular variable, the degree to which it is present, or its intensity. Here we shall explore this idea in more detail.

Indexes and scales are devices for creating a single COMPOSITE MEASURE of behavior and attitudes out of a number of related indicators. Thus they are particularly useful for summarizing complicated activities and orientations such as human mental capacity and peoples' perceptions, interests, and intentions. An index composed of several items elicits a greater *range* of responses than does a single question and therefore may reflect a more comprehensive and accurate picture of the respondent. To discover how liberal a person is politically, we may elicit opinion on deficit spending or gun control alone, but if we create an "index of liberalism" containing, say, twenty-five items, with topics including abortion, national defense, nuclear power, and so forth, we shall obtain a much more complete impression of the person's political attitudes. We shall also have greatly reduced the chances that the responses given to one or two questions were a fluke or atypical of the person's positions on most issues.

As explained in Chapter 3, an INDEX SCORE is obtained by assigning numbers to the answers given, in relation to the presence or absence of the variable under investigation. If we have decided that a "liberal" is someone who approves of abortion, the Equal Rights Amendment, and reduced military expenditures, then these responses might each be assigned a score of 1, and the opposite answers may each receive a score of zero. Because indexes and scales can convert a wide variety of qualitative variables to *ordinal* measures, they make possible a ranking of each respondent, relative to others. In our example, the liberals will have higher index scores than the moderates or conservatives; the higher the score, the more liberal the respondent.

The index score makes comparison easier, but it is also useful for purposes of DATA REDUCTION; that is, it expresses a wide range of data in abbreviated, numerical form. This is important not only for the measurement of attitudes but also for gauging the behavior of large organizations that are composed of many subunits. Consider the problem of assessing the performance of the New York Stock Exchange, with thousands of firms represented, on any given day. Information concerning the stock market is vital for the graphing of trends, for the measurement of business cycles, or for tracing the impact of government decisions and international events on investors' behavior. Yet, it is far too cumbersome to use figures for every firm on the stock exchange in order to achieve these goals. Furthermore, many stocks are inactive because they are not traded in large quantities or because their firms are not located in volatile sectors of the economy. Assessing economic trends by looking at these firms might cause an observer to underestimate an upward or downward direction in the market as a whole. The solution is the development of composite measures of the market, for example, Standard and Poor's Index or the Dow-Jones Industrial Index. These measures are obtained by looking at the behavior of carefully selected stocks of varying degrees of volatility and in different sectors of the economy.

The example of the stock market helps to illustrate a final, important point about indexes and scales. On a given day, the Dow-Jones Index may go down, while Standard and Poor's may go up or remain the same. The reason is that each is composed of different indicators. The value and overall representativeness of each measure depends on the validity of item selection for each index (in this case, the choice of business firms). Later we shall discuss the validation of indexes and scales. For now, let us recall that there is always the danger of *information loss* when numbers are substituted for qualitative impressions or when relatively few numbers are taken to represent many. An index will be meaningless if the indicators comprising it are invalid. A composite measure of political liberalism, stock market behavior, or any other phenomenon must be judged on the quality of the items that contribute to it. Index scores may appear precise and therefore accurate, but they may be quantifying misinformation. As we shall see, there are steps that can be taken to maximize validity, enabling the researcher to use scales and indexes with confidence to reduce data to manageable size, to increase the range and accuracy of measurement, and to compare people's complex behavior and attitudes.

AN EXAMPLE: THE CONSUMER PRICE INDEX

Now that we have outlined the major benefits and potential problems of composite measures in social science, let us examine one that has an impact on all of us in the real world. The Consumer Price Index (CPI), devised by the U.S. Bureau of Labor Statistics, has appeared in various forms continuously since 1919. Its history and composition, as well as its many uses, demonstrate how research methodology may influence public policy and meet national needs for reliable information. Indeed, largely because of the publicity that the CPI receives through the media as well as from government and trade union officials, economics has become dinner-table conversation in millions of homes across the country.

The CPI compares the cost of a market basket of goods and services each month with its cost a month ago, last year, or ten years ago (U.S. Department of Labor, 1978). The point in time to which today's prices are compared is called the BASE PERIOD. The base period for the current CPI is 1967. This means that the cost of today's market basket is measured in 1967 dollars (1967 = 100). In January 1981, for example, the CPI was 260.5; that is, the same combination of goods and services that cost $100.00 in 1967 cost $260.50 fourteen years later. Almost 400 items are priced regularly, ranging from cookies and canned ham to infants' underwear, to the cost of rent, heat, and electricity, to fees for lessons or instructions and sporting events.

You can imagine that great care must be taken both in selecting the items for the CPI and in determining what prices people are paying for them. If items are sampled at unusually expensive stores of a sort that only a small percentage of the buying public patronizes, the overall index score will be unrealistically inflated. If the cost of specific goods (such as caviar and champagne) is increasing, but few consumers buy these items regularly, it may be unwise to include them in the index. We shall examine item selection and the determination of prices for the CPI later in the chapter.

CPI scores are widely used by government and the public. The CPI measures price changes and is therefore an index of inflation during times of rising prices; it serves as an indicator of the success or failure of government attempts to control inflation; and it has an influence on income payments to pensioners, welfare recipients, and a multitude of workers whose salaries are pegged to the CPI. When the index rises, payments to more than 50 million people increase automatically. In fact, even the operational definition of *poverty* changes as the CPI rises, since the official federal poverty line is kept current in relation to the index.

Because it has such important policy applications, the reliability and validity of the Consumer Price Index are even more crucial than for most composite measures. A mere 1 percent increase in the CPI can trigger payment of over $1 billion in income; therefore, an error of only one-tenth of 1 percent "can potentially lead to the misdirection of about $100 million" (U.S. Department of Labor, 1978:2). It is doubtful that any index or scale you would be called upon to devise would involve such responsibility. Nonetheless, as we examine how indexes are put together, scored, and validated, it is important to recognize that any one of a series of seemingly minor research decisions could have subsequent, major consequences.

Index Construction

ITEM SELECTION

An index is a device for "adding the unaddable" (Simon, 1978:258). Everyone knows you cannot add apples and oranges, yet that is precisely what the Consumer Price Index does—it reduces the various commodities to what they have in common, their cost. Similarly, an index of liberalism may bring together opinions on disparate social issues by boiling them down, conceptually, to positions on a common spectrum of political ideas. To guide the researcher in what is often a sensitive and time-consuming procedure, there are several basic criteria for item selection: face validity, unidimensionality, achieving conceptual balance among the index items, and establishing a statistical relationship between them.

FACE VALIDITY. Let us say that we want to devise a composite measure of *authoritarianism* in a number of families, such that we could rank them on a continuum like the one below.

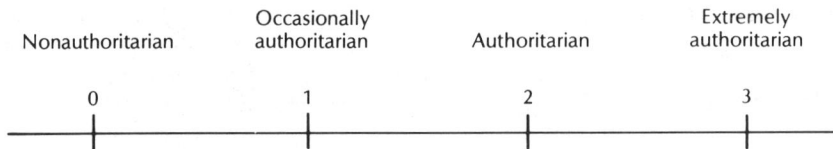

Nonauthoritarian	Occasionally authoritarian	Authoritarian	Extremely authoritarian
0	1	2	3

To position a given family on the continuum, we would have to assign it an index score; the more authoritarian, the further to the right it would be placed. But to produce the index score, we need to create specific indicators of the concept.

At this point we must ask: What are the major aspects and components of "authoritarianism in the family?" Clearly, it is a complex constellation of behaviors and attitudes, some directly observable by an outsider and some that only become apparent by getting to know the context of family life. Adorno et al. (1950) defined the authoritarian personality syndrome as comprising several variables, including aggression, superstition and stereotyping, power and toughness, destructiveness and cynicism. In this case, we might develop indicators from the following three general components of authoritarianism: *physical, moral,* and *political.*

These indicators, which could be operationalized via intensive interviews, questionnaires, or psychological tests of personality, have FACE VALIDITY. They are logically related to the overall concept being measured. This is the most elementary criterion for item selection, but an important one. There are an infinite

Component	Indicators
Physical	Family members show signs of bodily abuse—bruises, cuts, burns, etc. They report that these injuries have been inflicted by others in the family.
Moral	Family members of all ages maintain inflexible attitudes toward "right" and "wrong" behavior. There is a high degree of intolerance for weakness and error, and family members manifest considerable guilt for failure to live up to expectations.
Political	The family is run in a highly autocratic manner. The head(s) of the household rarely consult(s) with others before announcing decisions or priorities with regard to family finances, the home routine, or outside activities. Little or no open opposition to or appeal from these decisions is tolerated.

number of variables that do not seem to be logically related to authoritarianism at all (for example, whether a family member was born on a Wednesday, the city in which a family is located, the color of the living room). These may immediately be excluded from consideration as index items.

UNIDIMENSIONALITY. An index may contain a set of questions designed to tap different components of a concept, but it is important to remember that just *one* construct, albeit a complex one, is being measured. Indexes must have UNIDIMENSIONALITY in that they must adhere to one topic only. It may be the case that there is much boisterous vocal behavior (loud talking, yelling, etc.) in a highly authoritarian family, but this could also be the case in a democratic household where family members were defending their points of view vociferously. If we include such evidence as part of an index of *authoritarianism,* we risk losing unidimensionality; we could instead be measuring *argumentativeness.*

ACHIEVING CONCEPTUAL BALANCE. Item selection for composite measurement is an exercise in sampling. The researcher needs to select relatively few items: those that will reflect most efficiently the full range and variability of consumer prices, political attitudes, or any other phenomena present among the universe being examined. The CONTENT VALIDITY of an index is established by ensuring that a representative sampling of all possible items has been achieved. To do this, the concept we are measuring has to be operationally defined; then, index items that reflect a balance between the various aspects of this operational definition should be included. We defined authoritarianism as a physical, moral and political phenomenon within the context of the family. Therefore, we need indicators of each of these three components of the concept in our index in about equal proportions (that is, if the index contains thirty items or questions, ten might be designed to obtain evidence for each component of the concept).

TABLE 15.1   A Pacifism Scale

---

*1. The United States must be willing to run any risk of war that may be necessary to prevent the spread of communism.

2. If disarmament negotiations are not successful, the United States should begin a gradual program of unilateral disarmament—i.e., disarm whether other countries do or not.

*3. Pacifist demonstrations—picketing missile bases, peace walks, etc.—are harmful to the best interest of the American people.

4. The United States has no moral right to carry its struggle against communism to the point of risking the destruction of the human race.

5. It is contrary to my moral principles to participate in war and the killing of other people.

6. The real enemy today is no longer communism but rather war itself.

*7. Pacifism is simply not a practical philosophy in the world today.

---

*Reverse scoring item.

Source: Adapted from Snell Putney and Russell Middleton, "Some Factors Associated with Student Acceptance or Rejection of War," *American Sociological Review* (Washington, D.C.: The American Sociological Association), vol. 27, 1962, p. 658.

STATISTICAL RELATIONSHIP AMONG ITEMS. The last major criterion for the selection of items in an index is that they be statistically related to each other. If a composite measure is truly unidimensional, then each respondent's answers will be consistent. Let us examine how to verify a statistical relationship between and among items in a nontechnical way.[1]

For the scale of *pacifism* depicted in Table 15.1, the concept is defined as "a tendency to regard war as inherently unacceptable in the modern world" (Robinson et al., 1972:360). Notice that three of the seven items (those marked with an asterisk) are measures of antipacifist attitudes and thus are to be scored in reverse. The most pacifistic respondents would therefore answer statements 1, 3, and 7 in the negative and the remaining items in the affirmative. Note also that the various aspects of the concept pacifism, as operationally defined, are reflected in the seven items. These include: absence of fear about communism, support for pacifist demonstrations, and belief in the morality of pacifism.

To establish a statistical relationship among the seven items, we could record the percentage of respondents who answered "no" to statements 1 and 3, and those who answered "yes" to statements 4 and 5, and so forth. If, for example, 85 percent of those who gave a negative answer to item 1 also gave a negative answer to item 3, we may say that a strong, positive statistical relationship exists between these two items.

In a good composite measure, all items will correlate highly with one another. We should be wary of items that correlate poorly. In our example, suppose that only 10 percent of respondents who answered "yes" to statements 4 and 5 also answered item 2 in the affirmative. This should warn us that the scale may not be unidimensional. Perhaps respondents are making a substantive distinction be-

---

[1]In practice, the techniques of bivariate and multivariate analysis are frequently used for this purpose. See Chapter 16.

tween upholding the morality of pacifism and supporting protest demonstrations, which they may construe as improper. In order to determine whether support for such demonstrations is really an integral part of the total idea of pacifism, we might sample other populations, and if our findings are repeated, the item that correlates poorly should be discarded.

Another principle in establishing statistical relationships between and among index items is that every question asked should add something to the evaluation of each respondent. In our attempt to achieve unidimensionality, we must be careful that we do not simply repeat the same question again and again in different items, using synonyms or different ways of phrasing the identical ideas. To ensure the usefulness of each item, there is usually a *pretest* phase of index construction, in which statements or questions are tried and discarded. In addition, there is frequently a *retest* phase, in which the index items that appear to be unidimensional for one population are used to elicit data from another population. In recent years sophisticated computer programs have been devised to assess the correlation between index items. The time and effort are indeed worth it, because composite measures that are painstakingly perfected have the widest applicability. Some IQ tests and various psychological measures of personality and aptitude have been used for decades with only minor modifications because the initial research that helped to devise them was so thorough.

INDEX SCORING

As intricate and sensitive as item selection may be, it is only part of the process of index construction. Four critical decisions must also be made regarding the *scoring* of a composite measure once the items are selected. These are: (1) determining the range of response categories, (2) deciding how to assign numbers to responses and what the range of scores will be, (3) deciding whether responses to all items will be weighted equally, and (4) coping with missing data. Let us look at each of these issues.

THE RANGE AND NUMBERING OF RESPONSE CATEGORIES. When determining the appropriate response categories for a composite measure, we need to keep in mind the general principles for creating answer formats explained in Chapter 6. Categories must be *exhaustive, mutually exclusive,* and *clear* to the respondent. A great variety of index scoring formats are commonly used in social research. We have already illustrated the SUMMATED-RATINGS index, in which a positive answer (one indicating the presence of the variable under investigation) might be assigned a score of 1, and a negative answer, a score of zero. As the range of possible answers increases, more intricate numbering schemes are called for.

The *forced-ranking* scale asks respondents to arrange a fixed set of items in order of importance. Rokeach (1968) showed subjects a list of seventeen values, including: equality, freedom, salvation, happiness, and security. Respondents were requested to number them, beginning with 1 (the most important). The advantage of this format is that each of the items may be ranked against the others (Philliber et al., 1980). But although we can determine whether a respondent thinks that freedom in the abstract sense is more important than salvation, or vice versa, the forced-ranking format does not enable us to discover the importance of each item for the respondents in a personal sense. Perhaps the value ranked most important is still not very meaningful for them. RATIO SCALING is a technique for dealing with this dilemma. It is a response format that uses a fixed set of items but that allows the subject some autonomy in scoring.

In a study of the stigma, or negative image, attached to various forms of public aid to the poor, Williamson (1974) employed such a ratio scale. A list of actual and proposed programs was prepared and shown to each respondent. The list included the following forms of public assistance:

Aid to Families with Dependent Children (AFDC)
Aid to the Permanently and Totally Disabled
General Relief
Guaranteed Annual Income
Head Start
Old-Age Assistance
Public Housing
Social Security
Unemployment Compensation

Unemployment compensation, a program with which most respondents were familiar, was assigned a score of 100, because it proved to be relatively acceptable in a pretest. Subjects were then asked to rate the amount of stigma associated with being a recipient of each of the other kinds of aid, relative to that associated with unemployment compensation. A respondent scored a particular program 50 if it had half the stigma; 300 if it had three times the stigma, and so on. To make sure that subjects understood this ratio-scaling system, they were given practice exercises as part of the interview.

Perhaps the most common type of response format for composite measures is the LIKERT SCALING TECHNIQUE. Examples of two items together with Likert response

TABLE 15.2   Likert Response Formats

Overall, I would rate the quality of instruction I have received in this course as:

_____ Excellent	_____ Excellent	_____ Above average
_____ Good	_____ Good	_____ Average
_____ Fair	_____ Average	_____ Below average
_____ Poor	_____ Fair	
	_____ Poor	

I would recommend that others take this course.

_____ Strongly agree	_____ Strongly agree	_____ Agree
_____ Agree some-what	_____ Agree	_____ No opinion or don't know
_____ Disagree somewhat	_____ Neither agree or disagree	_____ Disagree
_____ Strongly dis-agree	_____ Disagree	
	_____ Strongly disagree	

Source: Adapted from Susan G. Philliber et al., *Social Research: Guides to a Decision-Making Process* (Itasca, Ill.: Peacock, 1980), p. 40.

options appear in Table 15.2. These formats offer a wider range of response alternatives than do simple summated ratings, but they display ordinal response categories that can then be assigned a score. In an index of *teacher quality,* one of the statements in Table 15.2 might be used. The response "strongly agree" could be given a score of 5, "agree" a score of 4, and so on. This technique elicits a great deal of information because people will make relative judgments more readily than absolute ones.

Usually, Likert response formats contain between three and seven alternatives. More choices might be confusing to subjects and also probably futile, since there is a limit to the subtleties of opinion that people have, or think they have. The number of categories for responses should always reflect as closely as possible the estimated or expected variation in the answers given. The choice of answer format can be difficult. If the range of answers is too restricted, information loss may result; on the other hand, generating a large number of response options that are not chosen does not usually add much to what we know about the respondents.

WEIGHTING OF INDEX ITEMS. In most scoring strategies that use summated ratings, each index item contributes equally to the overall score. In the indexes of political attitudes, pacifism, or authoritarianism that we have thus far used as examples, the various questions asked may be designed to tap different components of the concepts, but no one component is deemed to be more important than the rest. Similarly, the forced-ranking, ratio-scaling, and Likert-type formats may score various response options differently, but each item in the index has an equal chance of contributing to the total. Sometimes some questions or parts of the composite measure are judged to be worth more than others. In such cases WEIGHTING of index items is desirable.

The judgment for the assignment of weights is made by the researcher, based on theory or on prior estimates of the behavior that the index is designed to measure. If we were creating an index of *socioeconomic status,* we might include indicators of three major components: respondents' income, occupational position, and education. Suppose that income was thought to be more important than the other variables. We could score the income indicators so that they would count double. Table 15.3 compares a three-item weighted index with an unweighted index. Note that as the result of weighting, the variable *income* receives a greater proportion of the total score.

COPING WITH MISSING DATA. Missing data are a problem common to all social research, especially large surveys, but this problem is particularly critical in the

TABLE 15.3   Comparison of Two Scoring Procedures for Three Indicators of Socioeconomic Status

Summated ratings index		*Weighted index*	
	Score Range		Score Range
Income	1–5	Income	2–10
Occupation	1–5	Occupation	1–5
Education	1–5	Education	1–5
Total Score Range	3–15	Total Score Range	4–20

development of composite measures that have wide application but that depend on a one-shot observation. To see how researchers deal with incomplete data, let us return to the example of the Consumer Price Index.

The Bureau of Labor Statistics employs enumerators who visit or contact by telephone about 2,300 food stores as part of the nationwide data collection process. What do these researchers do when they attempt to price an item, such as skimmed milk in quart containers, and find that it is missing from the dairy compartment? In such cases, the CPI enumerators adopt the principle of *imputation*: they ascribe to missing sample items the change in price for groups of goods and services presumed to have similar price movements. It would be impractical to wait until the next milk delivery or to return to the store again and again in hopes of finding the specific sample item, given the expense and intricate scheduling of data collection involved in the research.

Imputation is just one of the strategies that have been devised to deal with the problem of missing data. Another is to *infer* the respondent's answer. Suppose a person is asked whether or not he or she belongs to any of ten voluntary organizations on a list, and the person answers "yes" to the Rotary Club and the Junior Chamber of Commerce, leaving blank the negative options for the other organizations. In such a case it is proper to assume that membership is limited to those groups for which an affirmative response was given.

An additional tactic used for index items where there is a range of scores—say, from 1 to 5—is to count missing data as the midpoint score of 3. This approach is particularly helpful when the midpoint signifies "neutral" or "unsure." In a summated-rating index a similar procedure is often followed, wherein the missing score is assigned as the equivalent of the average of the other scores, so that if an index contains ten items, and the scores for nine of them average .78, then the missing tenth item is given a score of .78 as well. In other words, the value of what is *not* observed is based on the value of what *is* observed.

INDEX VALIDATION

The rigorous concern with reliability and validity that is a guiding principle of all science is an integral part of the construction of indexes. Many composite measures are developed over a period of months or years by eliminating the less reliable and valid index items and replacing them with better ones. A variety of analytic techniques exist to assess the worth of each question or indicator and its contribution to the total index score. These techniques are of two types: those *internal* to the measure itself and those that are *external*.[2]

INTERNAL VALIDATION. If questions and indicators have been carefully selected initially to meet the criteria of face validity and statistical relatedness, the result is likely to be both a valid index (which measures what it purports to measure) and a reliable one (which may be used in replicated studies with consistent results). Often, researchers attempt to demonstrate how appropriate their choice of items is by performing statistical tests on a particular composite measure after data have been collected.

---

[2]See Chapter 3 for a general discussion of validity, reliability, and systematic measurement error.

The process of INTERNAL VALIDATION is accomplished through ITEM ANALYSIS, in which the effects of each of the many parts of an index are assessed. In ITEM-TO-SCALE CORRELATION, for instance, the results for each statement or question are compared with those for the entire instrument. For each person from whom data are collected, scores on individual questions should conform to the overall score. The extent to which this occurs when an instrument is administered to a sample or series of samples is reflected by an item-to-scale RELIABILITY COEFFICIENT.[3] The consistency of results obtained when an index is used repeatedly is referred to as STABILITY. The item-to-scale reliability coefficient may be used to assess stability from one administration of a test to the next.

Another type of item analysis is the SPLIT-HALF CORRELATION. Here, all the items in the instrument are divided into two groups (say, by selecting odd- and even-numbered questions). The comparison of the scores from these two subscales is then reported as a split-half reliability coefficient.[4] This coefficient shows the extent to which each of the two halves measures the same thing. It can also be used to determine the stability of responses to tests over time. Another use of the split-half correlation is to assess the effectiveness of a revision of a previously employed data collection instrument. Scores for the "established" half are compared with scores for the "new" half that is being considered for adoption (Hull and Nie, 1979:126).

These and other procedures for assessing internal validity are quite sophisticated, but they are not sufficient to prove that researchers have in fact done what they set out to do. Reliability coefficients may be quite high even when ITEM-TO-ITEM CORRELATIONS are low, showing that although a measure may be stable, this does not necessarily imply that it is unidimensional. To establish definitively the validity of a composite measure, some *outside* source of information about identical or related variables must be consulted.

EXTERNAL VALIDATION. The most common form of EXTERNAL VALIDATION involves the creation of a composite measure out of a portion of the items in a questionnaire and then comparing the results for this measure with answers to questions that were not included in the index being validated. In their research on anti-Jewish sentiment, Levinson and Sanford (1944) used fifty-two Likert-type items. They divided these questions into five separate SUBSCALES, according to various aspects of anti-Semitism. These groups of items were designed to measure both whether respondents believed Jews to be personally offensive, socially threatening, too intrusive or clannish, and/or too aggressive, and general attitudes about what should be done to or against Jews (Robinson and Shaver, 1972:287). By comparing responses to each of these measures, the five subscales were used to validate each other externally.

The responses to each subset of questions were, of course, descriptively different, but the answers to all of the items in the questionnaire, taken together, painted a coherent, composite picture of anti-Semitism. Discovering the extent to

---

[3]Perhaps the most common reliability coefficient is called *alpha* (Hull and Nie, 1979). It is expressed in scores from .01 to .99; the higher the coefficient, the greater the reliability of index items. If data are dichotomous, that is, if there are only two response alternatives, *alpha* is equivalent to the reliability coefficient KR-20, another commonly used measure for assessing reliability.

[4]The most common such measure is the Spearman-Brown coefficient.

which this sort of coherence is present is the goal of external validation. Often, the outside corroboration for a particular index will not be another measure of the same variable that that index was designed to measure but rather a measure of a related variable, its causes and consequences.

The information against which an index is checked is not necessarily contained in separate items from the same questionnaire. Levinson and Sanford also validated their measure of anti-Semitism externally by conducting in-depth interviews, eliciting attitudes concerning Jews from the interviewees, and comparing these with index scores achieved by the same subjects. In validating the Consumer Price Index, researchers conducted quarterly intensive interviews with about 20,000 families during 1972–1973 to determine what people were actually buying. Another group of consumers was asked to keep a diary, recording in it expenditures for frequent, small purchases. And in 1974 a third large sample participated in a "point-of-purchase" survey, the object of which was to determine *where* people actually buy the goods and services listed in the CPI (U.S. Department of Labor, 1978). These supplementary activities are all examples of attempts to establish external validity.

Before we leave this topic, a word of caution is in order. Suppose that an outside source of information correlates poorly with a particular composite measure of a related phenomenon. Does this necessarily mean that the index is poor? The answer is that it does not. Researchers are often faced with a dilemma in this regard, because it is as difficult to establish the validity and reliability of the outside measure as it is to evaluate the quality of the index itself. Perhaps the index or scale is valid, but the external validator is poor! This dilemma underscores the researcher's obligation to be ever vigilant in the selection of measures.

The Scaling of Responses

We have thus far considered only those indexes for which there is an accumulation of the scores assigned to individual attributes. There is another type of composite measure in social science that is created by assigning different scores to behaviors and attitudes according to the part each plays in a *pattern* of attributes. In this section we shall compare these two measurement strategies.

If we were interested in gauging people's *tolerance of homosexuals*, we might devise a series of questions such as those in Table 15.4 asking respondents to say whether or not it was proper for a homosexual to work in a number of occupations. If we scored an affirmative response to each item as 1, we could compare index scores for a sample of respondents. The more occupations deemed appropriate for homosexuals, the more tolerant the subject.

As we have noted in discussing numerous, similar illustrations, this is a useful measuring strategy, and it is commonly employed in social science. It does have certain drawbacks, however. Two respondents for whom the same total index score is obtained may in fact have divergent patterns of response. A person who replied affirmatively to items 1, 3, 5, 7, and 9 only would net the identical overall score as a person who replied affirmatively to items 2, 4, 6, 8, and 10 only. Thus there is considerable information loss connected with this indexing procedure. Similar total scores can mask the real differences among respondents' attitudes. Another shortcoming of this indexing technique is its failure to gauge the *intensity* of subjects' feelings. Perhaps in a particular respondent's view certain occu-

TABLE 15.4   Measure of Tolerance for Homosexuals

		(check one)	
Item	*Occupation*	*Proper*	*Not proper*
1	Bricklayer	_____	_____
2	Law enforcement officer	_____	_____
3	Stage performer	_____	_____
4	Dishwasher	_____	_____
5	Schoolteacher	_____	_____
6	Interior decorator	_____	_____
7	Insurance salesperson	_____	_____
8	President of a major corporation	_____	_____
9	President of the United States	_____	_____
10	Telephone operator	_____	_____

"Proper"   = 1
"Not proper" = 0

pations are just barely unacceptable, while others are completely out of the question. Because each item contributes to the total score in equal proportion, we have no way of judging the degree of conviction with which a given attitude is held.[5]

MEASURING INTENSITY AND RESPONSE PATTERNS

The terms *indexing* and *scaling* are often used interchangeably, but for the sake of convenience we shall refer to the scoring of *patterns* of response as *scaling*. Scaling enables the different total scores obtained on a composite measure to reflect the varying intensity of respondents' feelings. In addition, it ensures that divergent patterns of response will be reflected in divergent total scores. To accomplish these aims, the researcher arranges index items in a logical order for the purpose of analysis, such that the most intense or powerful indicators gradually give way to the less powerful ones. Table 15.5 shows how the items in Table 15.4 might be scaled.

In Table 15.5 the occupations have been arranged to reflect reasonably expected intensity of feeling. A person who would not object to an actor or actress being a known homosexual (item 7) may be expected to accept items 8 through 10 with equanimity. Similarly, most respondents who would think it proper that a schoolteacher (item 3) be a homosexual would likely accept a homosexual as a police officer (item 4) or bricklayer (item 5). A respondent who is completely tolerant of homosexuals would answer in the affirmative to all items. A moder-

---

[5]We could use a more sophisticated answer format such as Likert alternatives (Strongly agree . . . Strongly disagree), but this approach measures a respondent's intensity of feeling for each item separately, not comparatively among items. The Likert format assumes that each item has approximately equal intensity. If we used the *ratio-scaling* technique, we would learn the *relative* importance of each item to the respondent but not the *absolute* value of any one item.

TABLE 15.5   Scaled Measure of Tolerance for Homosexuals

Item	Occupation	(check one) Proper	(check one) Not proper
1	President of the United States	_____	_____
2	President of a major corporation	_____	_____
3	Schoolteacher	_____	_____
4	Law enforcement officer	_____	_____
5	Bricklayer	_____	_____
6	Insurance salesperson	_____	_____
7	Stage performer	_____	_____
8	Interior decorator	_____	_____
9	Telephone operator	_____	_____
10	Dishwasher	_____	_____

ately tolerant individual might find all occupations acceptable except the top two or three. A highly intolerant respondent whose prejudice against homosexuals was extreme might find even items 9 and 10 (representing occupations that are relatively remote from the public) nonetheless unacceptable.

The scoring of a scaled sequence of index items is a type of weighting that always follows their assumed intensity structure. The "hardest" or most potent measure of a variable (in this case, tolerance for homosexuals) is scored the highest, followed by the remainder in descending order. In our example, because there are ten items, we might want to give the affirmative response to item 1 a score of 10, to item 2 a score of 9, to item 3 a score of 8, and so on. The total score thus reflects a pattern of answers, not just the sum of individual responses.

SOME WELL-KNOWN SCALING TECHNIQUES

As examples of the actual application of the logic of scaling, we shall consider three important measures: the Bogardus Social Distance Scale, the Thurstone Scale, and the Guttman Scale.

THE BOGARDUS SOCIAL DISTANCE SCALE. There are many variations on this measure of the "distance" that respondents perceive between themselves and members of different social categories (nationalities, racial groups, deviants, etc.). The Bogardus Social Distance Scale, for example, is weighted according to the type of interaction that the subject is willing to engage in with members of a group or of different groups. (See Figure 15.1.) The logic of the increment in intensity is the perceived threat to respondents of each situation described by the scale items.

Theoretically, an individual who would readily accept a member of another ethnic group as a relative would have no objection to working alongside that person or to that person's becoming an American citizen. Because scores for each item vary with its potency, we can tell *which* relationships a respondent is willing to accept by knowing *how many* relationships were acceptable and the total scale

FIGURE 15.1   A Bogardus Social Distance Scale

1. Remember to give your *first feeling reactions* in every case.
2. Give your reactions to each nationality as a group. Do not give your reactions to the best or the worst members that you have known, but think of the picture or stereotype that you have of the whole group.
3. Put a cross in as many of the boxes as your feelings dictate.

Scoring Weights	Category	Mexicans	Vietnamese	Nigerians	Chinese
7	Close kinship by marriage				
6	In my club as personal chums				
5	On my street as neighbors				
4	Working alongside me in my occupation				
3	As citizens in my country				
2	As visitors only to my country				
1	Would exclude from my country				

Source: Adapted from E. Bogardus, *Social Distance* (Yellow Springs, Ohio: Antioch Press, 1959).

score.[6] Therefore, the SOCIAL DISTANCE scaling technique is an effective means of data reduction.

Although social distance scales appear to have reliability and validity, a possible objection to their use is that the response categories are not, in reality, "equidistant" from each other although the numbers assigned to each category (1, 2, 3, 4, etc.) are. The Bogardus scale is scored as if it were interval; yet, the distances between items are unknown and are likely to differ (for example, the distance between marrying a person and having him or her as a neighbor seems greater than the distance between having someone as a neighbor and knowing him or her only casually (Eckhardt and Ermann, 1977).

THURSTONE SCALING. The Thurstone scaling technique is an attempt to deal with the problem of making an ordinal series of numbers fit phenomena that are more difficult to arrange intuitively than is social distance. Thurstone created a DIF-FERENTIAL SCALE, in which the relative positions of the many indicators of a single variable are determined from the ratings or rankings produced by a panel of

---

[6]If a subject reacting to Mexicans as a group achieves a score of 15, and we know that five categories have been checked, then we know automatically *which* categories they are (the bottom five) because the only combination of five numbers totaling 15 is 1, 2, 3, 4, and 5.

judges. The issue of distance between each indicator is resolved by constructing the scale in such a way that the intervals *appear* equal.[7]

There are four basic steps in Thurstone scaling. First, the researcher makes a *list of the possible indicators* for the variable under investigation. Sometimes the list is in the form of attitude statements (possibly as many as 100 or 200). Then, a large number of *evaluators,* perhaps hundreds, are asked to *classify these indicators* by scoring them independently, according to how well they measure the variable. There may be as many as eleven or more scoring categories, ranging from "extremely powerful" indicator of the phenomenon being examined to "barely related." If sexism were being measured, one judge might find the statement: "Women should think of their children before thinking about a career" to be a potent indicator, and assign it a score of 9 or 10 out of a possible 11. Another evaluator might see the statement as denoting less sexism and assign it a score of 5 or 6.

Next, the *scale value of each indicator is determined* by calculating the average score obtained for each. Indicators on which there is too little consensus are eliminated. Finally, the *specific indicators* that will be used to measure the variable are chosen from among those that fall along the scale from one extreme to the other. These indicators may later be incorporated in a questionnaire or other data gathering instrument.

The Thurstone scaling technique is ingenious in that random errors in rating the indicators tend to cancel each other out when a large number of independent judgments are made. The result is a valid set of components for each complex variable being measured. Unfortunately, the four-step procedure is quite time-consuming and expensive, so that actual examples of research using Thurstone scaling are rare. Its major utility is for illustrating the logic of scale construction.

GUTTMAN SCALING. Like the other scaling techniques we have discussed, the procedure developed by Guttman (1950) relies on the fact that some indicators are more vivid or powerful reflectors of a variable than are others. But in Guttman scaling, *both* respondents and index items are ranked, according to the actual answers given. As a result we may verify that items already scaled have been ranked correctly for a given population. Alternatively or in addition, Guttman scaling may be used to rank responses to indexes that were originally scored using summated ratings.

To show the logic of the technique, let us assume a variation on the Bogardus Social Distance Scale, in which twelve subjects are asked to respond "yes" or "no" to a series of four items[8]:

A. I would marry an ex-convict.

B. I would have an ex-convict for a friend.

C. It would be acceptable for an ex-convict to live on my street.

D. It would be acceptable for an ex-convict to live in my community.

---

[7]By contrast, note that most other scales in social science, including those reviewed in this chapter, are *ordinal* rather than *interval.*

[8]It is possible to use Guttman scaling when more than two response alternatives are provided, but the procedure is more complex.

TABLE 15.6   Scores on Four Attitude Items, by Item and by Respondent

Respondent	Item A	Item B	Item C (1 = yes, 0 = no)	Item D	Respondent score
1	1	0	0	1	= 2
2	0	0	0	1	= 1
3	0	0	0	1	= 1
4	0	0	0	0	= 0
5	1	1	1	1	= 4
6	1	1	0	1	= 3
7	1	1	0	1	= 3
8	0	0	1	0	= 1
9	0	0	0	1	= 1
10	1	0	0	1	= 2
11	1	1	1	1	= 4
12	1	1	0	1	= 3
Item Score	7	5	3	10	

Each affirmative response will receive a score of 1; each negative response will receive a score of zero. Table 15.6 shows how the data, once collected, could be summarized. The item score is the sum of all positive responses for each item. The respondent score is the sum of all positive responses for each respondent.

The next step in the procedure is to construct a SCALOGRAM, a table formed by rearranging the data to reflect the ranks of respondent scores together with item scores.[9] The scalogram in Table 15.7 tells us the degree to which the social distance scale we used reflects the actual intensity of attitudes among the twelve respondents. It also shows us the extent to which knowledge of a respondent's score helps us to discover the patterning of answers that contributed to it.

If we look at the extent of variation in the patterns that produced each respondent score, we may select the one pattern for which each score is the best predictor. The most frequent (in this case the only) pattern that produced a respondent score of 4 is 1 1 1 1. Thus, if we use the respondent score alone to predict the actual responses for respondents 11 and 5, we would make no errors. Similarly, a respondent score of 3 predicts an answer pattern of 1 1 1 0 with no errors; a score of 2 predicts the pattern 1 1 0 0 with no errors; a score of zero, of course, predicts the pattern 0 0 0 0 with no errors.

The answers from subjects who obtained a score of 1 are harder to analyze. In this case the respondent score 1 is a MIXED TYPE. Respondents 2, 3, and 9 show the pattern 1 0 0 0; therefore, if we use the score of 1 to predict their answers, we shall make no errors. But respondent 8 shows a pattern in which the score of 1 was obtained by the sequence 0 0 0 1. Therefore, if we used the most frequent

---

[9]The process of Guttman scaling analysis is often more intricate than this example, which is meant only to be illustrative. Many more index items and a much larger sample are typically employed in actual data collection; the computer may be programed to create the Guttman scalogram in such cases.

TABLE 15.7   Scalogram of Four Attitude Items

Respondent	Item D	Item A	Item B	Item C	Respondent score
11	1	1	1	1	= 4
5	1	1	1	1	= 4
6	1	1	1	0	= 3
7	1	1	1	0	= 3
12	1	1	1	0	= 3
1	1	1	0	0	= 2
10	1	1	0	0	= 2
2	1	0	0	0	= 1
3	1	0	0	0	= 1
9	1	0	0	0	= 1
8	0	0	0	1	= 1
4	0	0	0	0	= 0
Item Score	10	7	5	3	

response pattern for score 1 to predict the exact answers of respondent 8, we would make *two* errors (the replies to items C and D would not match our prediction).

This scalogram analysis shows that we were able to make forty-eight separate predictions (12 respondents × 4 items) and that by taking the most frequent pattern of answers for each respondent score as a guide, we would make two errors. The relationship between predictions and errors is called the COEFFICIENT OF REPRODUCIBILITY and is expressed in the following formula:

$$\text{Coefficient of reproducibility} = \frac{\text{correct predictions}}{\text{total predictions}}$$

$$\text{or in our example: } \frac{46}{48} = .96 \text{ or } 96\%$$

In social research a Guttman scale is acceptable if its coefficient of reproducibility exceeds 90 percent. Over 95 percent is considered excellent.

Barring errors of prediction, there is only one way to obtain each Guttman scale score. Therefore, the coefficient of reproducibility measures the extent to which the total score is an accurate data-reduction device. Like any measuring tool, this one must be used with care. There is no automatic guarantee that valid indicators have been selected for inclusion in a Guttman scale. Indeed, the coefficient of reproducibility may be high; yet the possibility remains that the items or questions do not really measure the variable of interest. Moreover, it is important to note that SCALABILITY, the extent to which a set of items may be arranged according to a logical order of intensity, is *sample dependent*. The identical set of questions may result in two different coefficients of reproducibility when scaled for different groups of respondents. Thus the Guttman scaling technique is not a way to devise once-and-for-all, reliable measures, but a tool for analyzing the answers given by a particular group of respondents.

Standardization of Composite Measures

Not all measures are necessarily as sample dependent as are Guttman scales, but there is the unfortunate tendency to regard some frequently used indexes of complex variables as being "etched in stone" because their reliability coefficients are high or because their predictive validity seems to have been proven over the years. In fact, researchers should pay careful and continuous attention to the circumstances (time, place, and population) for which composite measures were originally validated, or *standardized*.

Previous sections of this chapter have amply demonstrated the usefulness of composite measures, especially when they are asked to do no more than they were designed to do. This final section supplements our discussion in Chapter 3 by emphasizing once again the problematic nature of the search for "truth" in social science and the impossibility of knowing which specific measuring tool is best without also knowing the purpose of the research for which that tool is to be used. As our example of the Consumer Price Index shows, it is possible for measures to become dated and therefore to be less than fully useful or downright misleading, unless they are periodically updated to account for demographic trends. Even Thurstone scaling, which attempts to maximize validity of measurement via a lengthy and elaborate procedure, can result in biased research findings if the judges who rank the indicators or scale items are atypical of the population about which the research seeks to generalize.

A COMPARISON OF TWO MEASURES

In a classic methodological analysis, Lundberg and Friedman (1943) offered vivid evidence that the process of index standardization may influence research findings every bit as much as the specific questions asked of respondents or the types of observation made during data collection. A small rural township in Vermont provided the setting for a comparison of two measures of socioeconomic status. Figure 15.2 shows the results when two scales, the Chapin and the Sewell, were applied to the same Vermont population. The vertical axis represents the frequency with which families (out of a sample of 233) were classified at various points on the scoring continuum for socioeconomic status (the horizontal axis). A score of 100 is deemed to represent poverty. A score of 200 represents a relatively comfortable, middle-class standard of living.

Clearly, the Chapin Social Status Scale gives the impression that the small community being examined is very poor indeed. The mode of the Chapin distribution (the highest point) falls just about at the poverty line. Only a small proportion of the households, according to this scale, are middle class. If we compare these findings with those obtained using the other measure of socioeconomic status, we notice a marked difference. In fact, the Sewell scale gives an almost totally different picture. It seems to reflect a more homogeneous population, and one that is almost entirely middle class in its standard of living. But these inconsistent results were obtained for the *same* population! How can we explain the inconsistency?

FIGURE 15.2   A Comparison of Two Scales of Socioeconomic Status

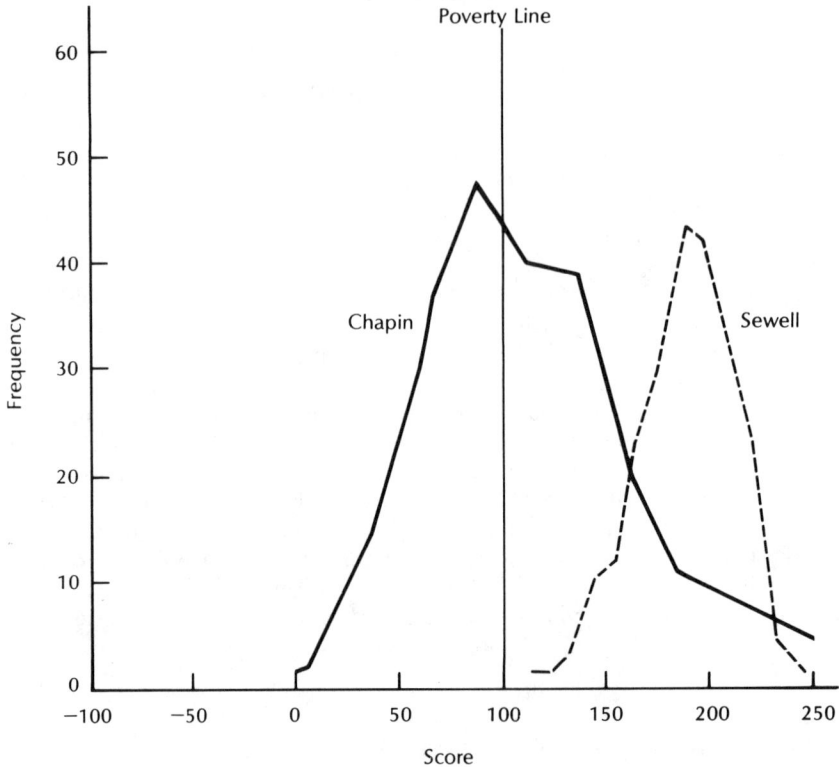

Source: Adapted from George A. Lundberg and Pearl Friedman, "A Comparison of Three Measures of Socioeconomic Status" in *Rural Sociology* (Auburn, Ala.: The Rural Sociological Society, 1943), vol. 8, p. 229.

It could be that the items contained in each scale were so dissimilar that they were not measuring the same thing. This is a plausible explanation for the disparity in the distributions of scores, but in this case it is not correct. The Sewell and Chapin scales are substantially the same in content. For both measures researchers visited each household in the sample and were instructed to make systematic observations of a variety of items, including the number of rooms and the amount and condition of furniture in each, whether there was a fireplace, a telephone, indoor plumbing, a washing machine. Data collectors also looked for books and periodicals and noted their titles. They supplemented their observations by questioning family members about their employment and leisure-time activities, the clubs or organizations to which they belonged, and so forth. In only a few cases were the scales actually eliciting information about different phenomena.

The explanation for the disparity in research results for the Vermont community lies not in the index items, but in the manner in which they were scored and weighted. The weightings were based on two totally different environments for validating composite measures. The Sewell scale was standardized for farm families in Oklahoma; the Chapin scale was standardized for urban working-class families in Minneapolis, Minnesota, an inherently wealthier environment that enjoys a much higher standard of living. Thus, because having a kitchen sink, running water, and a separate living room and dining area were unusual in many of the Oklahoma homes, they were assigned positive values in the Sewell scale. These and many other items were taken for granted in the Chapin scale, which deducted index points only if they were *not* present but did not assign any points if they *were*. Judging by Minneapolis standards, farm life in Vermont in the 1930s and early 1940s was rather spartan. But by Oklahoma standards, the Vermont farmers were doing quite well.

THE POLITICS OF MEASUREMENT

An important lesson to be learned from this example is that researchers need to investigate the original purpose of measures that they adapt for their own use. It is clear in this case that neither scale of socioeconomic status is perfectly suited to the environment in which it was used. On balance, the Sewell scale was standardized in the more similar setting and therefore may be judged to be more valid. The significance of this example, however, transcends the social scientist's search for valid knowledge. It has potential political implications as well.

Suppose a governor or other elected official wanted to justify spending a large amount of money to revitalize the rural areas of a state. Which research tool, the Sewell scale or the Chapin scale, would be most desirable to use to investigate conditions in farm communities? How may we answer this question to the governor's satisfaction, and to our own, keeping in mind the canon of objectivity in science? Does it matter whether farm conditions are actually bad and whether they could be improved more as a result of using a scale that was standardized in an urban area to conduct the investigation?

It is at this juncture that the goals of politics and science may be in conflict and that the researcher, realizing that it would probably not be worth the effort to explain the difference between the two scales to the voting public as we have done in this chapter, must act responsibly. Similarly, analysts who have the power to change the elements in the Consumer Price Index should not allow themselves to be influenced by politicians or special interests. In fact, each time the basis for computing the CPI has been altered in recent years, the changes have been greeted with considerable apprehension by trade union leaders and representatives of the elderly and others on fixed incomes. Can we really expect them to be as concerned about the scientific quest for reliability and validity as they are about the potential reduction of income that tinkering with the index could bring?

These are hard questions to grapple with, but one thing is clear. Social scientists, having devised immensely beneficial composite measures, must not misuse them or allow them to be misused. By standing for the integrity of their measures, we show our own integrity.

Summary

Indexing and scaling are techniques for measuring complex phenomena in social science. They create a single, composite measure of behavior and attitudes out of several related indicators. Index items are then scored or assigned numbers to enable us to compare respondents and to provide a means of reducing data. Any composite measure is only as good as the validity of the items that comprise it. For this reason much attention is given to the composition of indexes and scales; researchers pretest and retest them in an attempt to eliminate items that are not unidimensional or that do not relate well enough to one another statistically. Every item in a composite measure should add something to our ability to understand respondents, so items that nearly duplicate one another are also removed or altered.

There are a variety of ways to score composite measures. Summated ratings, forced rankings, and ratio scaling are three of these. Perhaps the most commonly used in situations where it is desirable to offer a range of responses for each question is the Likert format. Each of these ways of categorizing answers differs with regard to the number of options given and the autonomy allowed respondents in answering. They share the attribute that each item has an equal chance of contributing to the overall score of the composite measure, unless the index items are weighted.

Weighting is desirable in some indexing exercises, but it is essential in scaling, the purpose of which is to gauge the intensity of subjects' feelings and to be able to reflect patterns of response in composite measure scores. Three important scaling techniques are the Bogardus Social Distance Scale, the Thurstone Scale, and the Guttman Scale. These measures may be efficient ways of reducing data, since the scale score implies more than does a summated rating. Guttman scaling techniques rank respondents as well as scale items, resulting in a mechanism for measuring how efficient a predictor of actual responses the scale score is.

As sophisticated as some scaling procedures are, they do not guarantee validity. Both the reliability and validity of composite measures are checked internally (by comparing responses to the separate items in the measure) and externally (by comparing responses to some outside source of information on a similar or related variable). Despite this continued effort, composite measures are sometimes used inappropriately. Researchers may not be sufficiently aware of the specific environment for which the measure was standardized and may engage in unwarranted extension of a scale beyond its limits. Because the results using different composite measures may vary significantly, it is possible for the process of measurement to be subverted for political or pecuniary motives. The researcher must be aware of these possibilities and work to minimize them.

Key Terms

base period	internal validation	scalability
coefficient of reproducibility	item analysis	scalogram
	item-to-item correlation	summated ratings
composite measure	item-to-scale correlation	social distance scale
content validity	Likert scaling	split-half correlation
data reduction	mode	stability
differential scale	mixed type	subscale
external validation	multiple indicators	unidimensionality
face validity	ratio scaling	weighting
index score	reliability coefficient	

Exercises

1. Select one of the following complex concepts—*love, leadership,* or *jealousy*— and develop a list of its various aspects or components. Operationalize each compo-

nent that you have identified by creating an appropriate statement or question for inclusion in an index.

2. Develop a ten-item scale designed to measure *alcoholism*, and specify the scale items in increasing order of intensity or potency.

3. A researcher wants to develop an index of occupational prestige in the United States by asking respondents to rank ten selected occupations. But the specific occupational categories need to be chosen. Suppose you were assisting this researcher. If you could pick only ten occupational titles as a sample of the full range of jobs in America, which ones would you select? Make such a list and give the reasons for your choices.

4. Participate with your class in a Thurstone-type rating of indicators. Some students should be responsible for devising the list of indicators, and a larger group should be the judges. Some suggested variables for investigations are: *sex appeal, patriotism,* and *racism.* What major differences, if any, appear in the rankings made by the evaluators? What do the ranking patterns reveal about the group of judges and about the difficulty of achieving validity in social science measurement?

5. Conduct a study of student reaction to campus political and social issues using the *ratio-scaling* response format. First, devise a list of ten issues. Next, assign a score of 100 to an issue that you estimate to be of

medium importance. Then, ask a sample of twenty students to score the other issues in proportion to 100. Summarize your findings. In your experience what were the advantages and disadvantages of the ratio-scaling technique?

6. You have developed a ten-item scale of political conservatism and have arranged the scale items according to their estimated potency or intensity. When you present these items to respondents in a questionnaire, should you retain the scaled order from most intense indicator to least? Why, or why not?

7. Think of a concept that might be operationalized and Guttman-scaled. (You might look in the tables of contents of volumes such as Robinson et al., 1972, and Robinson and Shaver, 1972, for inspiration.) Create five scale items and administer them to five respondents. Summarize your findings in a format similar to that used in Table 15.7. Did the items scale as you expected they would?

8. What problems occur if an acceptable Guttman scale emerges from the data, but it is not the same one that the researcher expected to find? What solutions to these problems would you suggest?

9. If today you were restudying the Vermont community originally analyzed by the Sewell and Chapin scales (see Lundberg and Friedman, 1943), would you use either measure again, or would you use some other measure? Why?

Suggested Readings

Edwards, Allen L.
1957   *Techniques of Attitude Scale Construction.* New York: Appleton-Century-Crofts.

   Still one of the best sources on the topic. Particularly useful is the section on Guttman scaling in Chapter 7.

Inkeles, Alex, and David Horton Smith
1974   *Becoming Modern: Individual Change in Six Developing Countries.* Cambridge, Mass.: Harvard University Press.

   This award-winning cross-cultural analysis relies on a composite measure of *modernity,* the O-M scale. Part II presents a detailed but nontechnical explanation of how the scale was constructed.

Miller, Delbert C., ed.
1977   *Handbook of Research Design and*

Social Measurement. 3rd ed. New York: David McKay.

   Pages 86–96 are a resource for students planning to use indexes and scales in their own work. This section abounds with examples and suggestions for the application of composite measures.

Robinson, John P., and Phillip R. Shaver
1972   *Measures of Social Psychological Attitudes.* Ann Arbor, Mich.: Institute for Social Research, University of Michigan.

   This volume is packed with illustrations of composite measures of variables such as *life satisfaction, self-esteem, authoritarianism,* and *religious attitudes.* For each measure cited, a summary of the rationale for its use is given, as well as the results of tests of validity and reliability and additional topical references.

Robinson, John P., et al.
1972   *Measures of Political Attitudes*. Ann Arbor, Mich.: Institute for Social Research, University of Michigan.
    Similar in format to Robinson and Shaver (1972), this volume covers measures of public reaction to politi-

cal issues, liberalism and conservatism, racial and ethnic attitudes, and orientation toward the political process.

Shaw, Marvin E., and Jack M. Wright
1967   *Scales for the Measurement of Attitudes*. New York: McGraw Hill.
    A comprehensive summary of composite attitude measures.

References

Adorno, T. W., et al.
1950   *The Authoritarian Personality*. New York: Harper.

Bogardus, E.
1959   *Social Distance*. Yellow Springs, Ohio: Antioch Press.

Eckhardt, Kenneth W., and M. David Ermann
1977   *Social Research Methods: Perspective, Theory, and Analysis*. New York: Random House.

Guttman, Louis
1950   "The Basis for Scalogram Analysis." In *Measurement and Prediction*, ed. Samuel A. Stouffer et al. Princeton, N.J.: Princeton University Press.

Hull, C., Hadilai, and Norman H. Nie
1979   *SPSS Update*. New York: McGraw-Hill.

Levinson, D. J., and R. N. Sanford
1944   "A Scale for the Measurement of Anti-Semitism." *Journal of Psychology* 17, 2:339–370.

Lundberg, George A., and Pearl Friedman
1943   "A Comparison of Three Measures of Socioeconimic Status." *Rural Soiology* 8:227–236.

Philliber, Susan G., et al.
1980   *Social Research: Guides to a Decision-Making Process*. Itasca, Ill.: Peacock.

Robinson, John P., and Phillip R. Shaver
1972   *Measures of Social Psychological Attitudes*. Ann Arbor, Mich.: Institute for Social Research, University of Michigan.

Robinson, John P., et al.
1972   *Measures of Political Attitudes*. Ann Arbor, Mich.: Institute for Social Research, University of Michigan.

Rokeach, M.
1968   *Beliefs, Attitudes, and Values*. San Francisco: Jossey-Bass.

Simon, Julian L.
1978   *Basic Research Methods in Social Science*. 2nd ed. New York: Random House.

United States Department of Labor
1978   *The Consumer Price Index: Concepts and Content Over the Years*. Washington, D.C.: U.S. Bureau of Labor Statistics.

Williamson, John B.
1974   "The Stigma of Public Dependency: A Comparison of Alternative Forms of Public Aid to the Poor." *Social Problems* 22, 2 (December):213–228.

16 / Basic Statistical Analysis

CHAPTER OUTLINE

INTRODUCTION
UNIVARIATE ANALYSIS
Marginals
Central Tendency and Levels of
    Measurement
Measures of Variability
Grouping and Recoding Data
BIVARIATE ANALYSIS
Cross-Tabulation

Computing Percentages for
    Cross-Tabulations
Measures of Association
    Correlation
    Other Measures of Association
STATISTICAL CONTROL
The Elaboration Paradigm
    Explanation
    Interpretation

Specification
Suppressor Variables
Partial Correlation
SUMMARY
KEY TERMS
EXERCISES
SUGGESTED READINGS
REFERENCES

Introduction

Social scientists are almost constantly in contact with quantitative data that have been summarized and presented in statistical form. Published reports of the results of quantitative research usually include tables, graphs, and diagrams. In order to evaluate the work of other social scientists or to analyze one's own data, a thorough understanding of statistical procedures, including their underlying assumptions and their limitations, is essential. The goal of this chapter is to present a nontechnical overview of the basic techniques, concepts, and issues involved in one of the most challenging phases of the research process—the analysis of quantitative data.

Univariate Analysis

A distinction is often made between DESCRIPTIVE RESEARCH, which delineates the outstanding characteristics of a sample, or of the population from which the sample was drawn, and EXPLANATORY RESEARCH, which concentrates on cause-effect connections among those characteristics. In practice most quantitative studies involve elements of both description and explanation, beginning with a descriptive statistical summary of the data and progressing toward testing hypotheses and causal relationships. Descriptive analysis typically involves consideration of one variable at a time rather than the relationship between two or more variables. For this reason it is often referred to as UNIVARIATE ANALYSIS.

MARGINALS

Suppose we were to draw a representative state sample of 1,500 people for a study of the characteristics of people who belong to different religions. We might want to start by looking at the proportion of the sample belonging to each of the major religions. Responses to the question "What is your present religious affiliation?" are placed in four categories: "Protestant," "Catholic," "Jewish," and "Other or none," a residual category for all those who either profess atheism or who belong to a group that is numerically small in the state being considered. A table that presents the FREQUENCY DISTRIBUTION (count of cases) and the percentage distribution (proportion of all cases) for each response category associated with the variable is referred to as a table of MARGINALS. Table 16.1 presents marginals for the variable *religion*.

Notice that percentages are computed twice in Table 16.1, and the results depend on which cases we take to represent the whole, or 100 percent. The first row indicates that the sample included 720 Protestants, who comprise 48 percent of the total of 1,500 persons surveyed. If the researcher were interested only in making comparisons among the major religious groups, the 180 persons who indicated that they belong to no religious group or to a small one, and the 120 persons who refuse to disclose their religion, could be excluded from subsequent analysis. This would leave 1,200 cases; the third column, labeled ADJUSTED PERCENTAGES, presents the recomputed figures for this working sample. Hence the 720 Protestants constitute 48 percent (720/1,500) of all persons polled, but they constitute 60 percent (720/1,200) of the cases to be analyzed. Percentages are routinely adjusted in this way whenever the researcher intends to exclude missing data (or responses not considered appropriate) from the analysis.

The data presented in Table 16.1 can also be summarized graphically. In Figure 16.1 the adjusted percentages are presented in the form of a BAR GRAPH; in Figure 16.2 they are presented in the form of a PIE DIAGRAM. Although they convey somewhat less information than the table from which they were extracted, these alternative ways of presenting the same data can often be useful in highlighting some especially important point.

Marginals are particularly useful for summarizing the responses of a large sample to a question that has only a few response categories—such as about race, religion, or gender. But what if we were to construct marginals for variables such as *years of education* or *income*? The number of possible response categories for

TABLE 16.1   Marginals for the Variable *Religion*

"What is your present religious affiliation?"

Category	Frequencies	Percentages	Adjusted percentages
Protestant	720	48	60
Catholic	360	24	30
Jewish	120	8	10
Other/none	180	12	—
Missing data	120	8	—
Total	1,500	100%	100%

FIGURE 16.1   Bar Graph for Data in Table 16.1

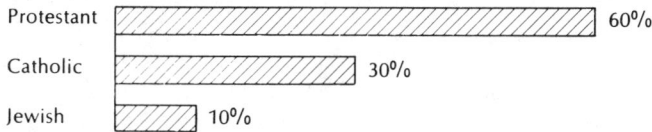

FIGURE 16.2   Pie Diagram for the Data in Table 16.1

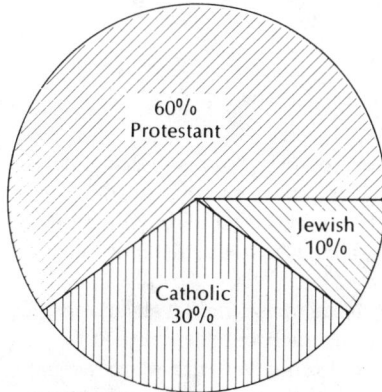

these variables can be so unwieldy that the marginals table no longer constitutes a succinct summary. One solution to this problem is the use of summary statistics that measure important characteristics of the distribution. Measures of central tendency and measures of variability are useful for this purpose.

CENTRAL TENDENCY AND LEVELS OF MEASUREMENT

MEASURES OF CENTRAL TENDENCY are statistics used to represent an average or typical respondent. The actual statistic used to represent the average depends on the level of measurement that has been reached for the characteristic being considered. As will be recalled from the discussion in Chapter 3, we can distinguish between four levels of measurement: nominal, ordinal, interval, and ratio.

For a *nominal-level variable* such as sex, race, or religion we must be able to classify all our respondents into a set of categories that are mutually exclusive and exhaustive. It must be possible to find a category that each respondent in the sample will fit into (the categories must be exhaustive), and no respondent should be able to fit into more than one of the categories (they must be mutually exclusive). The variable *religion,* considered in Table 16.1, meets both of these criteria.

An *ordinal-level variable* shares the properties of a nominal-level variable (i.e., the categories must be mutually exclusive and exhaustive), but the categories must also be ranked—that is, put into some order of progression, such as from high to low, or from very strong to very weak. Each category represents more of the variable's characteristic than the next-lower category, but we cannot measure the distance between categories. In Table 16.2 we can say that persons in category 1 favor handgun control more than do persons in any other category. But we

TABLE 16.2   Marginals for an Ordinal-Level Variable

"The private ownership of handguns
should be made illegal."

Category	Frequency	Percentage
1. Agree strongly	400	40
2. Agree	250	25
3. Disagree	150	15
4. Disagree strongly	200	20
Total	1,000	100%

cannot say they favor handgun control twice as much as persons in category 2 or three times as much as persons in category 3. Nor can we say that the difference in sentiments between persons in categories 1 and 2 is equal to the difference in sentiments between persons in categories 2 and 3, because the distance between categories is subjective and unknown.

An *interval-level variable* has all the properties of an ordinal-level variable, but it has the additional capacity to measure the distance between categories. An example is temperature measured in degrees Fahrenheit. A *ratio-level variable* has all the properties of an interval-level variable and also has a zero point that represents the total absence of whatever the variable measures (0 years of education, 0 dollars of income, and so on.).[1] For most social science research, the distinction between interval and ratio measures is not important, since most statistical procedures require only an interval-level measure.

At the nominal level of measurement, the only appropriate measure of central tendency is the MODE, defined as the category of a variable with the largest number of cases in it. In Table 16.1 the mode is the Protestant category, with 48 percent of the respondents. Note that the modal category, though it is the most typical response in the sample, does not necessarily contain a majority of the cases. For this reason, and because there is no reason to consider cases in any other categories to be near or similar to cases in the modal category, the mode is a very weak indicator of central tendency.

For variables that reach the ordinal level of measurement there is a stronger measure of central tendency, the MEDIAN. The median is the category in which the middle observation falls; it is the point in the distribution where half of the cases have less, and the other half of the cases have more, of the characteristics being measured than does the median. For the following set of numbers—7, 3, 5, 17, 2, 20, 17, 5, 3, 17, 14—the median is 7 because it is the value that falls in the middle of the distribution. For the data in Table 16.2 we would start at either end of the distribution and count to the 500th person. Since this person would be found in the "agree" category, this becomes the median for the variable. Note that the mode can also be determined and used, but the mode and the median do not necessarily coincide. The median is generally considered a better measure of

---

[1]Note, by contrast, that a reading of 0 in degrees Fahrenheit does not represent a total absence of heat or temperature.

TABLE 16.3   Computations of Mean, Median, and Mode for a
Set of Eleven Observations

Observations: 7   3   5   17   2   20   17   5   3   17   14

Mode = most frequent value = 17

Median = middle of the distribution = 7
Distribution of scores from lowest to highest:
    2   3   3   5   5   7   14   17   17   17   20
                         ↑   ↑
                      median   mode

$$Mean = \frac{\text{sum of all observations}}{\text{number of observations}}$$

$$= \frac{2 + 3 + 3 + 5 + 5 + 7 + 14 + 17 + 17 + 17 + 20}{11}$$

$$= \frac{110}{11}$$
$$= 10$$

Mode: 17   Median: 7   Mean: 10

central tendency than the mode because it takes into consideration the order that exists between response categories.

For interval-level and ratio-level variables, the MEAN can be used as a measure of central tendency. The mean is simply the arithmetic average—the sum of all observations divided by the total number of observations. Table 16.3 presents the computation of the mean for the set of numbers cited earlier and a comparison of this to the median and the mode. The mean is often used with such variables as *income, years of schooling completed,* and *age.* The more closely the mean, median, and mode correspond when they are all computed for the same variable, the more confident you can be of having found a value that is typical or average. In Table 16.3 the wide divergence among these three statistics indicates a distribution of observations that fails to converge on any central point.

For interval and ratio levels of measurement it is always possible to compute both the median and the mode in addition to the mean. The mode, however, is rarely used with interval-level data; but the median is used, particularly when the researcher wants to deemphasize the impact of a few extremely high or extremely low observations. The mean can be very strongly influenced by even one observation at a very high or low value; in this sense the mean is less stable than the median. For the set of numbers 1, 5, 7, 12, 275, the mean is 60 and the median is 7.[2] If we have any reason to believe that there might be error in the one extremely high observation, or if we know it to be an accurate but DEVIANT CASE (an extremely unusual observation that should not be allowed to so heavily influence the com-

---

[2] Note the extreme discrepancy between the median and the mean. Which value seems more "typical" of the set of observations?

TABLE 16.4   Central Tendency Within Two Distributions with Differing Degrees of Variability

Distribution A	8	8	9	9	10	10	10	11	11	12	12
	Mean: 10		Median: 10								
Distribution B	1	2	2	4	8	10	13	16	16	18	20
	Mean: 10		Median: 10								

putation of an average value), then the median would be a more appropriate measure of central tendency than the mean.

The measures of central tendency that we have considered can be used to describe the average or typical respondent, but they tell us nothing about the degree of DISPERSION (variability) of the data around this average or central point. Table 16.4 presents two sets of observations that have identical means and medians but that are dispersed in quite different ways. Distribution B is much more dispersed than Distribution A. We can get some idea of the degree of variability in a distribution by simply examining its marginals, but we often need a more concise way to compute and summarize this variability. For this purpose a number of statistics have been developed that measure variability.

MEASURES OF VARIABILITY

There are no generally accepted measures of variability for either nominal-level or ordinal-level variables. In this section we shall consider the range, standard deviation, and variance, each of which is an appropriate MEASURE OF VARIABILITY for data at the interval-level or ratio-level of measurement.

The RANGE is the simplest measure of variability: it is the difference between the largest and the smallest observations in the sample. If in a sample of 1,000 respondents the lowest reported income is \$1,500 and the highest is \$76,500, then the range is \$75,000. The range is very easy to compute and to understand. It is, however, highly unstable, since it is based on extreme observations at each end of the distribution.

The STANDARD DEVIATION is the most frequently used measure of variability and is based on calculating how far each individual observation (X_i) deviates from the mean $\bar{X}$. The formula for the standard deviation is:

$$\text{Standard deviation} = s = \sqrt{\frac{\sum (X_i - \bar{X})^2}{N}}$$

where X_i = a score on variable X
$\bar{X}$ = the mean for all scores on variable X
N = the number of observations

To compute the standard deviation, first compute the mean, and then subtract this mean from each individual observation. Next, square the results of each of these individual subtractions, and then add all these squares together. Divide the total sum of the squares by N, the number of observations, and take the square root of the resulting quotient. Table 16.5 illustrates these steps in computing the standard deviation for a set of observations from a sample of five cases.

The squaring of deviations from the mean gives a heavy emphasis to the larger (more extreme) deviations from the mean. To check this point in Table 16.5, compare the relative magnitudes of the values in the $(X_i - \overline{X})$ column to those in the $(X_i - \overline{X})^2$ column. A small standard deviation indicates that the observations tend to cluster closely around the mean; a large standard deviation indicates a great deal of dispersion in the data, with relatively few observations close to the mean. Hence, when the standard deviation is small, the mean can be interpreted as a fairly accurate description of most respondents in the sample. To better understand this important relationship between the mean and the standard deviation, you might find it helpful to compute for yourself the standard deviations for each of the two sets of observations presented in Table 16.4.

Although the standard deviation is somewhat more complicated than other measures of dispersion, and more difficult to calculate, it is used frequently be-

TABLE 16.5   The Computation of the Standard Deviation

The following computations give the
standard deviation for the five observations
of the variable X: 0, 50, 100, 150, 200.

Observed value (X_i)	Deviation from sample mean $(X_i - \overline{X})$	Square of deviation from sample mean $(X_i - \overline{X})^2$
0	-100	10,000
50	-50	2,500
100	0	0
150	50	2,500
200	100	10,000

N = sample size = 5

$$\overline{X} = \text{mean} = \frac{\Sigma X_i}{N} = \frac{(0 + 50 + 100 + 150 + 200)}{5} = 100$$

$$\text{Standard deviation} = s = \sqrt{\frac{\Sigma(X_i - \overline{X})^2}{N}}$$

$$= \sqrt{\frac{(10,000 + 2,500 + 0 + 2,500 + 10,000)}{5}}$$

$$= \sqrt{5,000}$$

$$= 70.71$$

The symbol "X_i" is used to refer to the observations for the variable X. In this case $X_1 = 0$, $X_2 = 50$, $X_3 = 100$, $X_4 = 150$, $X_5 = 200$. The symbol "$\overline{X}$" is used to refer to the mean of the observations for the variable X. In this case it is the mean of X_1, X_2, X_3, X_4, and X_5. The symbol N refers to the number of observations the mean is based on. In this case, N = 5. The symbol "ΣX_i" is used to indicate that we are to sum the observations of the variable X for all values of the subscript "i." In this case we sum X_1, X_2, X_3, X_4, and X_5.

cause it has a special meaning in relation to the NORMAL CURVE and hence also in relation to variables whose distributions approximate the normal curve. When plotted, some variables, such as *SAT* (Scholastic Aptitude Test) or *IQ scores,* closely approximate the normal curve's distribution—with most cases falling close to the mean and the more extreme scores tapering off and becoming less common as we move farther and farther from the mean value. This tendency to approximate a normal distribution is true of a wide variety of variables used in social research, such as years of education and various political attitudes. Errors in sampling also tend to be normally distributed. When a variable is distributed normally, we can use its mean and standard deviation directly to determine what proportion of all observations fall within a specified distance of the mean.

As we see in Figure 16.3 for the normal curve, approximately 68 percent of all observations fall within one standard deviation on either side of the mean; approximately 95 percent fall within two standard deviations; and approximately 99 percent fall within three standard deviations on either side of the mean. If we know that the mean of a distribution is 100 and the standard deviation is 15, then 68 percent of the cases will be between 85 (100 − 15) and 115 (100 + 15); 95 percent of the cases will fall between 70 (100 − 30) and 130 (100 + 30); and 99 percent will lie between 55 (100 − 45) and 145 (100 + 45). This property of the normal curve (and of variables or statistics that we can assume are normally distributed) allows us to specify the chance (probability) of any score deviating from the mean by a given magnitude. Another noteworthy property of the normal

FIGURE 16.3   Percentages of Observations within Various Standard Deviation Units of the Mean for the Normal Curve

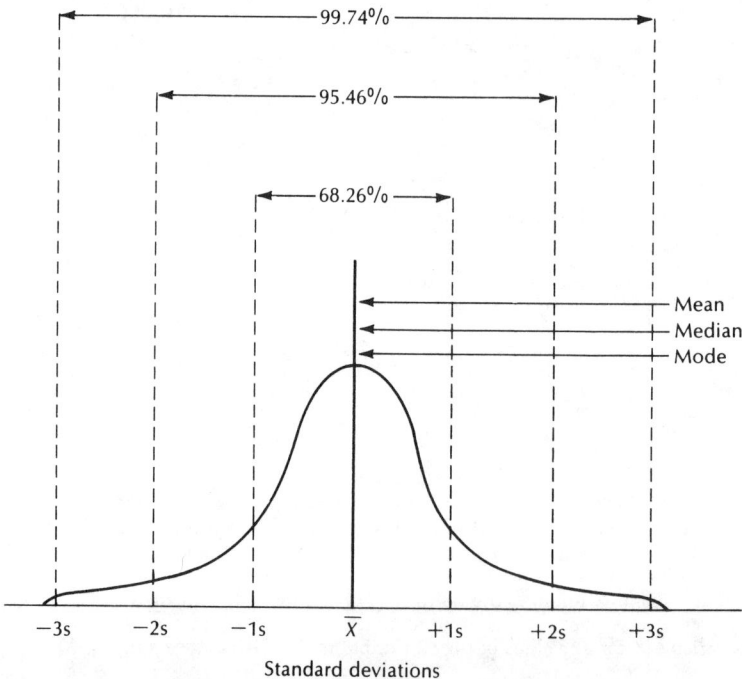

distribution that can be seen in Figure 16.3 is that the mean, median, and mode all coincide.

You will recall that the procedure for determining the standard deviation requires us to take the square root as our last step. Omitting this last step produces a third measure of variability, referred to as the VARIANCE, which is equal to the square of the standard deviation:

$$\text{Variance} = s^2 = \frac{\sum (X_i - X)^2}{N}$$

The standard deviation is used more extensively than the variance in descriptive analysis because of its special relationship to the normal curve. Variance, however, becomes very important in more complex statistical procedures, such as correlation and regression, which are based upon an analysis of the variance.

GROUPING AND RECODING DATA

Many variables, especially those measured at the interval or ratio levels, have a large number of categories. In a large sample of adults whose ages range from 21 to 95, it is quite conceivable that scores on the age variable might fall into more than seventy different categories. When this happens, it is very inconvenient to present the data as a set of marginals without first consolidating groups (ranges) of values into broad categories. With a variable such as *income,* if we had no such broad categories and instead recorded each individual's exact income, we might end up with as many different values as we had persons in the sample. Although for some purposes such accuracy and precision in measurement might be very desirable, it is not a strategy that lends itself to summary presentation of the data. To present data succinctly in tables, we need to use a grouping scheme for such variables. Table 16.6 shows one possible categorization of the income variable.

Every scheme for grouping data has to conform to the needs of the research project, keeping in mind how the data will later be used. When an interval-level or ratio-level variable is being coded, a grouping scheme can be devised and built directly into the coding process. When devising your coding scheme, remember that the more categories you allow for a variable, the more precise your measurements will be; on the other hand, the fewer categories you use, the easier it will be to present the data in a table. Often, however, computer programs such as SPSS (Statistical Package for the Social Sciences)[3] allow you to take data that were originally coded into a very large number of categories and easily reduce them to a more manageable form, thereby achieving both precision and convenience. You can then put your data into different forms according to the needs of the various phases of your analysis.

When we take a ratio-level variable such as *income* and categorize its values as we have done in Table 16.6, what level of measurement can we now assume for the newly recoded variable? In going from uncollapsed income data to the summary categories presented in this table, we have lost information. In sacrificing precision for convenience, we are always giving up information, and this happens

---

[3] For a brief discription of SPSS, see Appendix H in Babbie (1979).

TABLE 16.6   A Categorization of the Income Variable

Income	Frequency	Percentage
$ 0–$ 5,000	50	5
$ 5,001–$10,000	300	30
$10,001–$15,000	400	40
$15,001–$20,000	200	20
Over $20,000	50	5
Total	1,000	100%

every time we collapse the categories of a variable. As a result, what was a ratio-level variable is now only an ordinal-level variable. Why? Because the difference in income between respondents in adjacent income categories in Table 16.6 might be $4, $40, $400, or any amount ranging between $1 and $5,000. Whenever an interval-level or ratio-level variable is categorized into ranges, the resulting variable drops to the ordinal level of measurement. Furthermore, procedures for computing either a mean or a standard deviation become both more complex and less precise than those we have outlined above.

Marginals, measures of central tendency, and measures of variability are the main tools of univariate analysis. Marginals provide a great deal of descriptive information, but for some purposes it is useful to summarize this information more concisely, using measures of central tendency and variability. Such measures give us an idea of what the average case or respondent is like and how similar other cases or respondents are to the average. Although some quantitative studies stop with univariate analysis, seeking only to describe the characteristics of their samples, most studies go beyond this to look at the interrelationships among the variables examined.

Bivariate Analysis

BIVARIATE ANALYSIS refers to any presentation of data in which an attempt is made to relate two variables to one another. Table 16.6 presented data only for the variable *income*, describing what proportion of a sample of 1,000 persons fit into each of several income categories. After we have examined this overall income distribution, it would seem reasonable to divide the sample into distinct subgroups whose income distributions we suspect will be different from the overall figures of Table 16.6 and also different from one another. We might divide the sample into men and women and compare their income distributions. Or we might divide the sample into three religious groups—Protestants, Catholics, and Jews—to compare them with respect to income. Table 16.7 illustrates this technique; the sample is divided into whites and nonwhites.

CROSS-TABULATION

Table 16.7 exemplifies a technique called CROSS-TABULATION, on which most bivariate analysis is based. In cross-tabulation the categories of two variables are used simultaneously to define subgroups into which the total sample is divided. A

TABLE 16.7   A Bivariate Frequency Distribution of Income
                        by Race

Income category	White	Nonwhite	Total
$ 0–$ 5,000	20	30	50
$ 5,001–$10,000	180	120	300
$10,001–$15,000	300	100	400
$15,001–$20,000	155	45	200
Over $20,000	45	5	50
Total	700	300	1,000

table (cross-tabulation) is made up of all possible combinations of the categories of one variable with the categories of the other variable. This provides us with a more elaborate description of the data by transforming the univariate frequency distribution of Table 16.6 into the bivariate frequency distribution of Table 16.7, and to this extent cross-tabulation serves the purposes of purely descriptive research. We can now describe separately the income distribution for whites and for nonwhites.

Bivariate analysis, however, has important uses besides making descriptions more elaborate. Cross-tabulations allow comparisons to be made between subgroups within the sample, and when such comparisons are made, the relationship between one variable and another begins to emerge. By comparing the income distribution for whites to that for nonwhites, our attention is drawn to the way in which race affects income. If the two distributions were nearly identical, then we might conclude that race does not affect income (for the population from which our sample was drawn). But the two distributions in Table 16.7 appear to be quite different, so we have preliminary evidence that race is an important factor affecting a person's income. Because the sample of whites in Table 16.7 is much larger than the sample of nonwhites, it is difficult to compare the two distributions. Such comparisons are much easier to make when we convert these frequencies into percentages, as is done in Table 16.8.

COMPUTING PERCENTAGES FOR CROSS-TABULATIONS. The simplest form of explanatory research involves testing for the existence of a relationship or association between an independent variable (cause) and a dependent variable (effect). In this case it is logical to consider *race* the independent variable affecting *income,* the dependent variable. As Table 16.8 illustrates, percentages are computed by considering the categories of the independent variable one at a time. Starting with whites, for example, divide the frequency in each income subcategory ($0–$5,000, $5,001–$10,000, and so forth) by the total number of whites (700). Follow the same procedure for each category of the independent variable until you have computed an appropriate percentage for each cell in the table. The end result allows direct comparisons between the percentage of whites and the percentage of nonwhites in each income category.

In a cross-tabulation there are several possible ways to compute percentages, and each method of calculation serves a different analytical purpose. Percentages may be calculated across ROW totals, down COLUMN totals, or in other ways; the

TABLE 16.8   A Cross-Tabulation of Income by Race, with
               Frequencies and Column Percentages

Income Income category	White	Nonwhite	Total
$ 0–$ 5,000	3% (20)*	10% (30)	5% (50)
$ 5,001–$10,000	26% (180)	40% (120)	30% (300)
$10,001–$15,000	43% (300)	33% (100)	40% (400)
$15,001–$20,000	22% (155)	15% (45)	20% (200)
Over $20,000	6% (45)	2% (5)	5% (50)
Total	100% (700)	100% (300)	100% (1,000)

*Numbers in parentheses represent the number of cases.

manner in which they are calculated defines and restricts the statements and comparisons that can legitimately be based on the percentages. It follows, therefore, that you should never compute percentages in a cross-tabulation until you are certain that the direction in which they are computed is suited to your research questions and the comparisons you need to make.

Reexamine Table 16.8, and see how the percentages were calculated. Noticing for example, that there are 20 whites with incomes of $5,000 or less, we could have calculated *across the row* that 40 percent (20 of 50) of all the persons with incomes of $5,000 or less are white. Instead, we calculate *down the column* that 3 percent (20 of 700) of all whites have incomes of $5,000 or less. The difference between these two statements is a crucial one that exposes the essential logic of computing percentages. *Percentages must be computed in a way that allows us to make intergroup comparisons that are unaffected by differences in the sizes of the groups.* To state that 40 percent of the persons with incomes under $5,000 are white and that 60 percent are nonwhite is to make an almost meaningless comparison between whites and nonwhites, since the percentages are mainly a function of the larger number of whites in the sample. It is far more useful, in this context, to state that only 3 percent of whites in contrast to 10 percent of nonwhites have incomes of $5,000 or less.

Using column percentages throughout the table to compare whites against nonwhites systematically with respect to their incomes, a general pattern becomes clear. Whites are more likely than nonwhites to be in high-income categories; conversely, nonwhites are more often found in low-income categories. Half of all nonwhites (50 percent) but less than a third of whites (29 percent) have incomes of $10,000 or less. We conclude, therefore, that the independent variable race does indeed affect income—with a substantial income advantage accruing to whites. The cross-tabulation has shifted our focus away from either race or income individually; we are now squarely confronted with the *relationship* between the two variables.

MEASURES OF ASSOCIATION

Cross-tabulations are a useful and compact way to illustrate relationships between variables, but they require that the variables be expressed in only a few categories. As the number of categories for each variable increases, the size of the resulting table increases geometrically. The larger the table, the more difficult it is to interpret. Should the table exceed, say, twenty-five cells, the pattern of relationship between variables will very likely no longer be discernible. One solution to this problem is to group data, recoding and thereby reducing the number of categories so that the cross-tabulations remain manageable. Unfortunately, as we saw earlier, data reduction by grouping inevitably diminishes the amount of information by sacrificing precise measurement for the sake of convenience. Happily, there is another solution to the problem of large tables.

CORRELATION. Suppose we have data from a large sample of college graduates on their verbal SAT scores prior to college entry and on their grade-point averages during college. We would like to know whether or not the *SAT scores* (the independent variable) are correlated with *grade-point averages* (the dependent variable). One way to test for an association between these two variables might be to reduce each variable to only three categories (low scores, moderate scores, and high scores) and then to cross-tabulate them, as in Table 16.9. The results show a fairly clear pattern: persons with high SAT scores tend to do well in college, while those with low SAT scores tend to do poorly. Sixty percent of those with SAT scores above 600 achieved a college grade-point average of over 3.3, while only 10 percent of those whose SAT scores were below 400 achieved as well.

CORRELATIONS are complex computations that measure the degree of association between two variables, utilizing exact scores instead of rough categories. The computation produces a single number, called a CORRELATION COEFFICIENT, which

TABLE 16.9   Cross-Tabulation of Grade-Point Average in College by Verbal SAT Scores

Grade-point average	Verbal SAT score			
	Low (below 400)	Moderate (400–600)	High (above 600)	Total
High (above 3.3)	10% (25)	25% (125)	60% (150)	30% (300)
Moderate (2.5–3.3)	40% (100)	55% (275)	30% (75)	45% (450)
Low (below 2.5)	50% (125)	20% (100)	10% (25)	25% (250)
Total	100% (250)	100% (500)	100% (250)	100% (1,000)

summarizes the relationship. A coefficient of 0.0 means that the independent variable's value does not help us to predict or explain anything about the dependent variable. At the other extreme a coefficient of ± 1.0 signifies a perfect correlation between the two variables: if we know someone's score on the independent variable, we can exactly predict their score on the dependent variable. To illustrate the correlation between SAT scores and grades, we will graph the data from Table 16.9, using exact scores instead of summary categories. The type of graph depicted in Figure 16.4, in which each case is plotted according to its values on the independent and the dependent variable, is called a scattergram. Note the similarities between Table 16.9 and Figure 16.4, which present the same data in different ways.

One way to think of the correlation coefficient is in terms of the relationship between a set of data points and a line that has been drawn through these points in such a way as to minimize the sum of the square of the distances between each point and the line. The closer the points fall to this line, the higher the correlation. The Pearson correlation coefficient (r) will be positive if the line through the points slopes upward as we move to the right (as in Figure 16.4), that is, if the

FIGURE 16.4   Scattergram of the Relationship Between Grade-Point Average in College and Verbal SAT Score

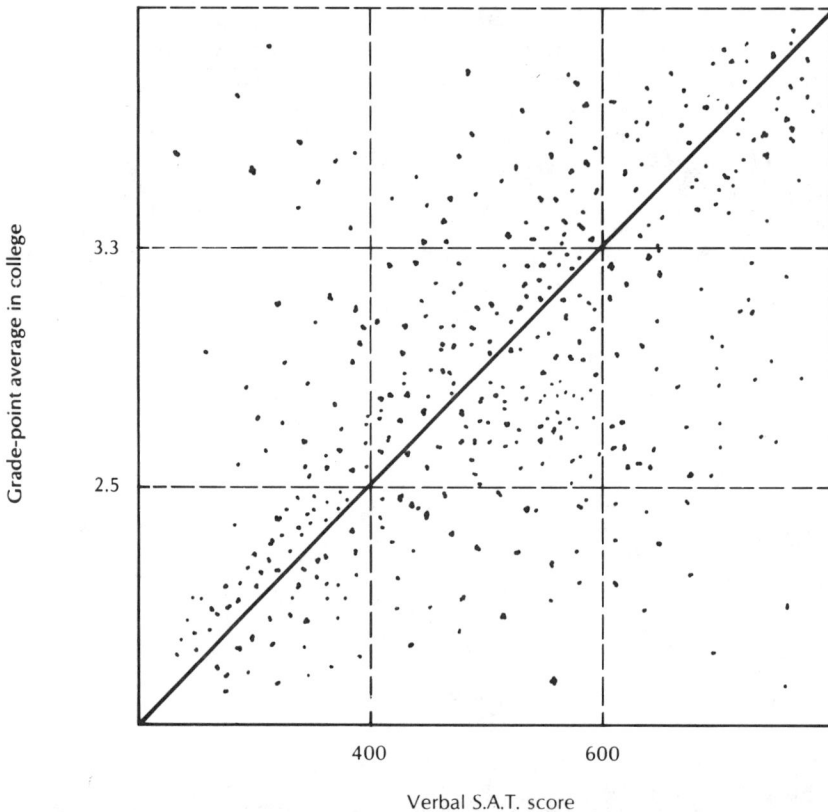

Verbal S.A.T. score

values of the dependent variable get larger as the values of the independent variable increase. Conversely, the coefficient will be negative (ranging from 0.0 to −1.0) if the line through these data points slopes downward as we move to the right, indicating that as the values of the independent variable increase, the values of the dependent variable decrease. Figure 16.4 illustrates a strong positive correlation ($r = +.70$).

The scattergrams in Figure 16.5 illustrate several alternative relationships between the independent variable X and the dependent variable Y. The following observations can be made on the basis of the information in Figure 16.5:

(A) the data for this scattergram illustrate a moderately strong positive correlation that would be approximately .60. You will note that in this scattergram, as in the others, the X values increase from left to right, that is, from L (low) to H (high); and the Y values increase from bottom to top (also from low to high). As with all positive correlations, there is a tendency for the Y values to increase as the X values increase.

(B) Here all the data points fall along a straight line; this is what happens when there is a perfect positive correlation between X and Y ($r = 1.00$). The correlation is perfect only in the sense that it represents the upper limit for the correlation coefficient. In actual social research applications we do not get correlations of 1.00 unless we have somehow managed to correlate a variable with itself.

(C) Here there is no relationship between X and Y ($r = .00$).

(D) Here there is a weak positive correlation ($r = +.20$) between X and Y.

(E) Here there is a very strong positive correlation ($r = +.90$).

(F) Here there is a perfect negative correlation ($r = -1.00$). Note that for a negative correlation Y decreases as X increases.

(G) Here there is a strong negative correlation ($r = -.90$). An example of a negative correlation would be the relationship between cigarette consumption (X) and life expectancy (Y). As cigarette consumption increases, life expectancy decreases. (Undoubtedly, the actual correlation between these two variables is weaker than −.90.)

(H) Here there is a strong NONLINEAR RELATIONSHIP between X and Y ($r = .00$). It is not appropriate to use the correlation coefficient to summarize this relationship. The low correlation masks the evidence of its pronounced nonlinear shape.

OTHER MEASURES OF ASSOCIATION. The correlation coefficient, r, is a statistic designed to measure the strength of association between two interval-level or ratio-level variables. When one (or both) of the variables whose strength of association you are testing fails to reach at least the interval-level, some measure of association other than r should be used (although many researchers violate this rule and apply r to ordinal-level data). Alternative coefficients have been designed to suit almost any situation, and they are described in most statistics texts. Although all of these coefficients appear at first to be similar in form to r and to one another, each is calculated in a different way, and each needs to be interpreted with great caution.

Not all coefficients vary between −1.0 and +1.0; some never take negative values, and others never reach ±1.0. A number of coefficients cannot distinguish between a positive and a negative association. In general, the varying methods of calculation make it impossible to compare one coefficient directly with any other

FIGURE 16.5   Scattergrams for Alternative Correlations between X and Y

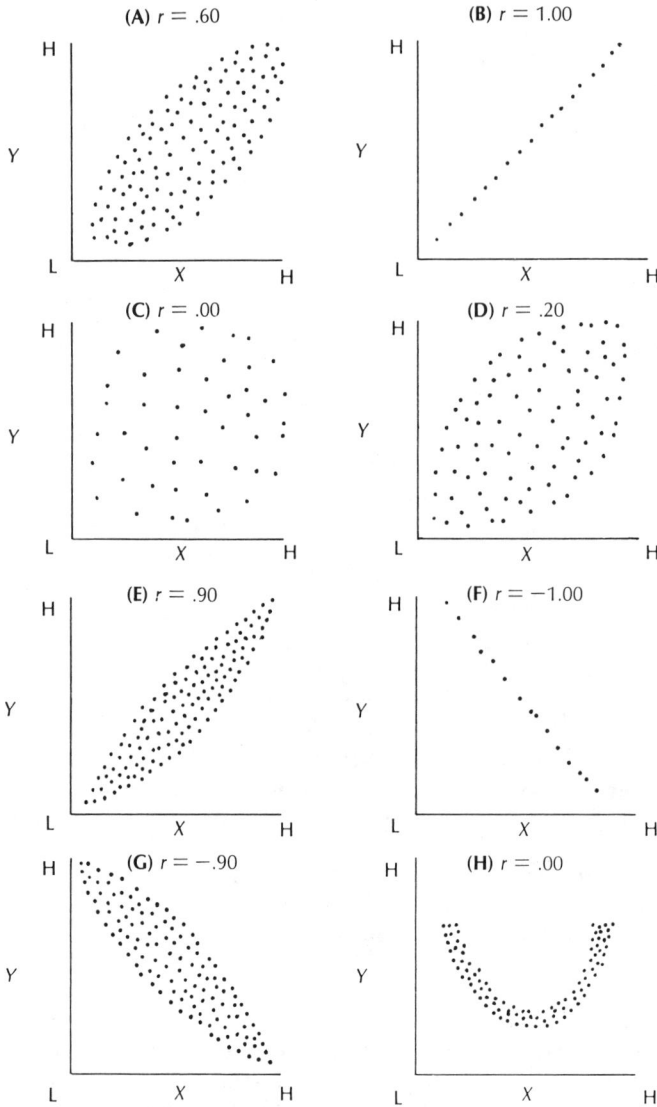

coefficient; each must be interpreted according to its own standards.[4] It is thus imperative that the researcher become thoroughly familiar with the purposes of, and the calculations behind, any coefficient before using it.

_____

[4]Thus it is risky to compare the results in one study reporting an association of .40, using one measure, to the results of a second study reporting an association of .60 using a different measure.

FIGURE 16.6   The Bivariate Relationship Between Birth Rate and Stork Count

| | | Stork Count | |
		High	Low
Birth Rate	High	82% (82)	18% (18)
	Low	18% (18)	82% (82)
	Total	100% (100)	100% (100)

Statistical Control

Bivariate procedures allow us to assess the impact of one variable on another by using measures of association or by constructing a TWO-WAY TABLE (a cross-tabulation involving two variables). These procedures are adequate for relatively simple relationships between variables, but many problems that we wish to analyze involve more complex relationships. Table 16.8 presents hypothetical data on the relationship between race and income, but the two-way table itself does not explain this relationship. In an effort to increase our understanding of this relationship, we might want to consider a series of TEST FACTORS—such as age, education, years of experience, type of occupation, area of residence, and union membership—to see what effect each has on the association between race and income. Testing the effects of outside influences on the original, bivariate relationship is referred to as *introducing statistical controls*, and it is accomplished by extending the basic principles of cross-tabulation and correlation. The following example illustrates how statistical control can be brought about by introducing a third variable in a cross-tabulation.

Figure 16.6 presents the two-way (bivariate) relationship between the variables *birth rate* and *stork count*, for a sample of 200 counties. The table presents a surprisingly strong association between the number of storks and the number of births, supporting a popular but whimsical (and heretofore implausible) theory of where babies come from. Eighty-two percent of the counties where storks are found in abundance show a high birth rate, whereas only 18 percent of the counties where storks are seldom seen have a high birth rate. What can account for this mysterious relationship? Unless modern biology is totally misinformed, there must exist some hidden third factor that can account for this apparent connection between storks and births.

THE ELABORATION PARADIGM

The ELABORATION PARADIGM is a set of procedures for introducing a CONTROL VARIABLE (or test factor) into a cross-tabulation and analyzing the causal relationships in the resulting three-way table, called a contingency table.[5] We refer to the process

---

[5] Much of the work on the paradigm was originally done by Paul Lazarsfeld, and his name is still identified with it. For an early treatment of the work, see Kendall and Lazarsfeld (1950). For more recent extensions of the paradigm, see Hyman (1955) and Rosenberg (1968).

FIGURE 16.7   The Relationship between Birth Rate and Stork Count Controlling for Population Density: an Example of Explanation

		Population Density					
		Rural Counties			Urban Counties		
		Stork Count			Stork Count		
		High	Low		High	Low	
Birth Rate	High	90% (81)	90% (9)		10% (1)	10% (9)	
	Low	10% (9)	10% (1)		90% (9)	90% (81)	
	Total	100% (90)	100% (10)		100% (10)	100% (90)	

of introducing a third variable as *controlling* for the variable, because it results in a series of SUBTABLES for each of which the third variable takes a constant value (i.e., its value is controlled instead of being allowed to vary, as in most tables). The control variable takes on different values for each subtable, but within any single subtable its value remains constant. Figure 16.7 reexamines the relationship between stork count and birth rate while controlling for the effects of a third contingency, or variable, *population density* (i.e., whether the county is urban or rural). Two subtables are generated, one for each value of the control variable.

The elaboration paradigm is simply an organized approach to analyzing what happens to the relationship between two variables when a third variable is controlled. There are three major categories of elaboration: explanation, interpretation, and specification. Figure 16.7 is an example of explanation, the type of elaboration we shall consider first.

EXPLANATION. We may suspect that Figure 16.6 presents a SPURIOUS RELATIONSHIP because we do not believe either that storks cause births or that births cause storks. To demonstrate that the relationship is spurious, we must show that it can be accounted for through some other variable that is: (1) causally prior to both birth rate and stork count and (2) related to both birth rate and stork count. If we are successful in locating a control variable that meets these two conditions and also makes the original, bivariate relationship substantially decrease or disappear, we shall have carried out the form of elaboration known as EXPLANATION.

We may test a series of control variables in an attempt to show that the relationship between birth rate and stork count is spurious. Figure 16.7 presents one of these tests. If the original relationship is spurious, then it will disappear in the subtables. Recall that the original table (Figure 16.6) showed high birth rates associated with high stork counts, and low birth rates with low stork counts. Subtable 1 of Figure 16.7, comprised of all counties whose population density is rural, shows no such association; high birth rates are found in 90 percent of rural counties, irrespective of the number of storks in the county. Similarly, subtable 2 (all urban counties) shows a 90 percent likelihood of low birth rates, irrespective of the number of storks. Hence, since the stork count becomes irrelevant when

FIGURE 16.8   The Bivariate Relationship between Abortion Attitude and Size of Birth Place

		Size of Birthplace	
		Town	City
"Should it be possible for a woman to obtain an abortion on demand?"	No	82% (410)	18% (90)
	Yes	18% (90)	82% (410)
	Total	100% (500)	100% (500)

we control for population density, the original bivariate association of Figure 16.6 has been explained.

INTERPRETATION. Figure 16.8, a cross-tabulation of the relationship between *attitudes toward abortion* and *size of one's birthplace,* shows persons from cities much more likely (82 percent) to endorse the right of women to obtain an abortion than are persons from towns (18 percent). Suppose, as in the previous example, we try to explain away the relationship but fail to discover any control variable that meets both requirements (i.e., associated with and causally prior to both original variables). When explanation fails to reduce such a nonobvious relationship between two variables, there still exists the possibility that we can uncover a third factor to help clarify the chain of circumstances that connects the two variables to one another.

FIGURE 16.9   Models Illustrating the Distinction Between Explanation and Interpretation

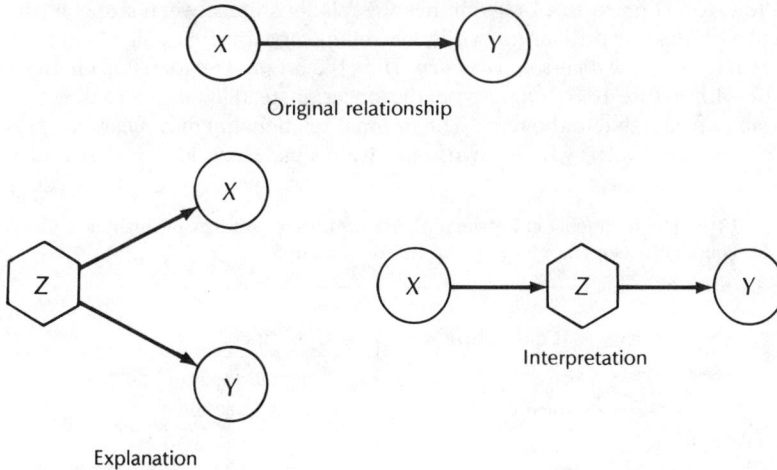

Original relationship

Explanation

Interpretation

X = Independent variable
Y = Dependent variable
Z = Control variable

INTERPRETATION, the second part of the elaboration paradigm, is the search for a control variable (Z) that *causally intervenes* between the independent variable (X) and the dependent variable (Y). Figure 16.9 diagrams the differences between explanation and interpretation as they modify the original relationship between the independent and dependent variables. An INTERVENING VARIABLE must be related to both the independent and the dependent variable, and it must be plausible to think of it as somehow a result of the independent variable that, in turn, affects the dependent variable. Figure 16.10 illustrates the effects of an intervening variable.

Searching for an intervening variable that might explain the relationship between abortion attitude and size of birthplace (Figure 16.8), one might hypothesize that towns and cities promote very different kinds of political and social ideologies, which in turn might account for the city/town differences in abortion attitudes. In effect, people born in towns are more likely to be conservative than are people born in cities, and conservatives are more likely than liberals to oppose abortion. Note in Figure 16.10 that there are no longer any differences in abortion attitudes between town people and city people in either subtable; all town/city differences have been accounted for by subdividing the sample into *conservatives* and *liberals*. Hence we have successfully interpreted the relationship by locating an intervening variable.

Compare Figure 16.7 with Figure 16.10. Notice that the results have the same statistical form; that is, the introduction of a control variable makes the original relationship disappear. Hence the difference between explanation and interpretation rests in the underlying logic, not in the statistics. We now turn to a third form of elaboration, referred to as SPECIFICATION, in which the objective is not to make the original relationship disappear, but rather to specify the conditions under which the strength of the original relationship varies in intensity.

SPECIFICATION. Figure 16.11 reexamines the relationship between size of birthplace and attitudes toward abortion while controlling for a third variable, the *region of the country in which a person was born*. Here the original relationship changes (compare with Figure 16.8) but does not disappear; instead, it takes on a different form from one subtable to the next. The original relationship disappears for persons born in the South, where town and city people show identical attitudes

FIGURE 16.10   The Relationship Between Abortion Attitude and Size of Birthplace Controlling for Political Ideology: an Example of Interpretation

		Political Ideology			
		Conservative		Liberal	
		Size of Birthplace		Size of Birthplace	
		Town	City	Town	City
"Should it be possible for a woman to obtain an abortion on demand?"	No	90% (405)	90% (45)	10% (5)	10% (45)
	Yes	10% (45)	10% (5)	90% (45)	90% (405)
	Total	100% (450)	100% (50)	100% (50)	100% (450)

toward abortion; it remains strong in the West, where town people are more likely than city people to oppose abortion (86 percent versus 21 percent); and it intensifies in the North, where differences between town and city people regarding abortion attitudes are most pronounced (89 percent versus 0 percent oppose abortion). Introducing a control variable has enabled us to analyze the relationship between size of birthplace and attitude toward abortion more precisely, pinpointing the circumstances under which the association holds. This is an example of specification.

It is entirely possible that the use of a control variable for specification of a relationship, as in Figure 16.11, may produce fundamentally different relationships in different subtables. It is conceivable that town persons might favor abortion more than city persons in one region, and yet the opposite might be true in another area. When this occurs, there is good reason to suspect that other, undiscovered factors are affecting the relationship. A specification that results in such markedly different subtables is an invitation to pursue the analysis further, as the following case illustrates.

SUPPRESSOR VARIABLES. Suppose we have a table in which no relationship appears, even though we had good reason to expect to find an association. In Figure 16.11 the data for the West and the North indicate a strong association between size of birthplace and abortion attitude; yet the association disappears in data for the South. Why? It is possible that some hidden third factor is *suppressing* the true relationship between the two original variables. Such a factor is referred to as a SUPPRESSOR VARIABLE, because it hides the actual relationship until it is controlled.

Figure 16.12 reanalyzes this data for the South, controlling for another variable, *percentage of persons in the community who are black*. Whereas the original data showed no relationship between size of birthplace and abortion attitude, these two subtables each show strong (but opposite) associations. Subtable 2 shows data that are consistent with the overall findings presented in Figure 16.11, while subtable 1 isolates the deviant cases. When the two subtables are combined, as they were in Figure 16.11, the relationship is no longer discernible.

FIGURE 16.11   The Relationship Between Abortion Attitudes and Size of Birthplace, Controlling for Region of Birthplace: Example of Specification

Region of Birthplace

		South			West			North	
		Size of Birthplace			*Size of Birthplace*			*Size of Birthplace*	
		Town	City		Town	City		Town	City
"Should it be possible for a woman to obtain an abortion on demand?"	No	50% (40)	50% (40)	No	86% (160)	21% (50)	No	89% (210)	0% (0)
	Yes	50% (40)	50% (40)	Yes	14% (25)	79% (190)	Yes	11% (25)	100% (180)
	Total	100% (80)	100% (80)		100% (185)	100% (240)		100% (235)	100% (180)
		(Subtable 1)			(Subtable 2)			(Subtable 3)	

FIGURE 16.12   A Three-Way Table Illustrating the Effect of Introducing a Suppressor Variable

Percent Black in Community of Birth
for Respondents Born in South

		High			Low	
		Size of Birthplace			*Size of Birthplace*	
		Town	City		Town	City
"Should it be possible for a woman to obtain an abortion on demand?"	No	100% (40)	0% (0)		0% (0)	100% (40)
	Yes	0% (0)	100% (40)		100% (40)	0% (0)
	Total	100% (40)	100% (40)		100% (40)	100% (40)
		(Subtable 1)			(Subtable 2)	

The data we have presented in this discussion of various methods of elaboration (Figures 16.6 to 16.8 and 16.10 to 16.12) are hypothetical and exaggerated to illustrate points of analysis. In actual research, relationships are seldom so strong, nor are distinctions between types of elaboration so clear. However, the logic that underlies these idealized examples embodies the range of possibilities for analysis that you will encounter in real research, and a thorough knowledge of these classifications will serve as a useful guide.

For the sake of simplicity we have developed elaborations around *dichotomies* — variables with only two values. The same logic applies to more complex variables, but when tables get larger, the elaborations soon become unwieldy. Indeed, it is often desirable to control for the effects of more than one variable, but we find ourselves confronted with the same practical difficulty. Just as correlation analysis was introduced to solve the analogous problem for two-variable tables with many cells, a technique called partial correlation exists to aid in the analysis of more complex elaborations.

PARTIAL CORRELATION

Earlier in this chapter we discussed the correlation coefficient as a measure of association between two variables. There is also a MULTIVARIATE[6] form of this measure, referred to as PARTIAL CORRELATION. It may be used to analyze more than two variables in many ways similar to the bivariate contingency-table elaboration

---

[6]When we analyze data for one variable at a time, we call it *univariate analysis*. When we consider the relationship between two variables, we call it *bivariate analysis*. When we consider the relationship between two variables controlling for the effects of one or more other variables, we call it *multivariate analysis*.

discussed above. The partial correlation between variable X_1 and variable X_2, controlling for X_3, is designated symbolically as "$r_{12.3}$," and conceptually it can be thought of as the mean of the correlations between X_1 and X_2 for each of the scattergrams that would result if a separate scattergram were plotted between X_1 and X_2 for each value of X_3. It is a measure of the average correlation between X_1 and X_2 when X_3 is controlled. It has the same range and interpretation as the two-variable (Pearson) correlation.

Suppose we are presented with a correlation between X_1 and X_2 that we suspect is spurious. To check for this possibility, we introduce several control variables that are causally prior to both X_1 and X_2. Eventually we hit on a causally prior control variable X_3 for which the partial correlation drops to zero (or nearly zero). In so doing, we have demonstrated that the original relationship was spurious.

To be more concrete, suppose we are doing a study in which the census tract is the unit of analysis (a census tract is an area made up of a cluster of blocks and includes approximately 3,000 residents). Suppose that we find a high correlation ($r_{12} = .60$)[7] between our measure of *delinquency rate* (X_1) and *percent broken homes* (X_2). If we suspect that this correlation is spurious, we might attempt to locate a causally prior control variable that can account for this relationship. Suppose we eventually hit on the variable *percent poor* (X_3). When X_3 is controlled for, the partial correlation turns out to be very close to zero ($r_{12.3} = .05$). On the basis of this evidence, we would conclude that the original correlation ($r_{12} = .60$) was spurious. This outcome is illustrated in Figure 16.13B. It should be clear that there is a very close parallel between what we have done here and the form of elaboration we earlier referred to as *explanation*.

Suppose we are presented with a strong correlation ($r_{14} = .60$) between the variable *percent black* (X_4) and *delinquency rate* (X_1). As part of our analysis of this relationship, we might decide to search for possible variables that intervene between percent black and delinquency rate. Suppose we eventually try the variable *percent poor* (X_3) and find that when this variable is controlled, the partial correlation is much below the original correlation. With such results we would conclude that percent poor is an intervening variable between percent black and delinquency rate. This outcome is illustrated in Figure 16.13D. The parallel between this example and the form of contingency-table elaboration referred to as *interpretation* should be evident.

Thus far we have considered only examples in which one control variable is introduced. It is possible to control for several variables simultaneously, using higher-order partial correlations. Thus we may compare the partial correlation between X_1 and X_2, controlling for X_3, X_4, X_5, X_6 ($r_{12.3456}$). In partial-correlation analysis, the Pearson correlation is often referred to as the ZERO-ORDER CORRELATION to distinguish it from a *first-order partial correlation* (for example, $r_{12.3}$), a *second-order partial correlation* (for example, $r_{12.34}$), and other, *higher order partial correlations* in which the order of the partial correlation corresponds to the number of variables being controlled.

An advantage of partial correlation as a statistical technique, relative to contingency-table analysis, is that the controlling operation is based on statistical

---

[7]What we refer to here as r_{12} is the same (Pearson) correlation we referred to earlier in the chapter as r where we omitted the subscripts.

FIGURE 16.13   Models Illustrating Alternative Interpretations of Partial Correlation Results

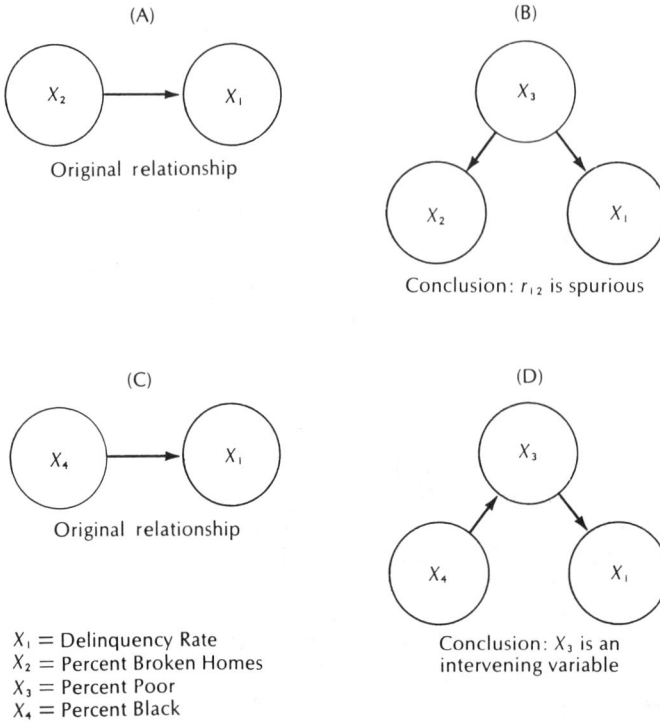

(A)

$X_2 \longrightarrow X_1$

Original relationship

(B)

X_3

X_2 X_1

Conclusion: r_{12} is spurious

(C)

$X_4 \longrightarrow X_1$

Original relationship

X_1 = Delinquency Rate
X_2 = Percent Broken Homes
X_3 = Percent Poor
X_4 = Percent Black

(D)

X_3

X_4 X_1

Conclusion: X_3 is an intervening variable

adjustments of the scores for the original two variables rather than on the construction of physically separated subtables. Partial correlation is very useful when the investigator wants to control simultaneously for several factors, particularly if the sample is relatively small. In contrast, attempts to control for several variables simultaneously in contingency-table analysis become awkward because some of the partial tables end up with few, if any, respondents.

This advantage of partial correlation analysis also has its costs. A major disadvantage is the loss of information about variation in the strength of the relationship between the original two variables for the various categories of the control variable. The strength of the relationship may fluctuate considerably for the different categories of the control variable. If we were to construct separate scattergrams (and compile separate zero-order correlations) for the same data, we would be able to see this fluctuation. But with partial-correlation analysis all we get is one summary number that averages the relationship for the various subcategories. If these fluctuations are of no interest to us, or if there is very little fluctuation in the strength of the relationship for the various categories of the control variable, then this loss of information is not a major problem. It is of interest to note that the contingency-table alternative to partial correlation also involves a loss of information—albeit in a different form; that is, information is lost when interval-level variables are recoded into a relatively small number of categories for tabular analysis.

Summary

This chapter has presented some of the most commonly used techniques of basic quantitative analysis. Univariate analysis is a description of the characteristics of a set of scores (measures) for a single variable. For variables with a small number of categories, univariate analysis usually begins with a presentation of the distribution of scores. For more complex variables, summary univariate statistics exist that are designed to estimate two major characteristics of the variable's distribution—its central tendency and its dispersion. In order to decide what summary statistics are most applicable in any situation, one must first determine the variable's level of measurement.

Bivariate statistics are useful for analyzing the relationship between two variables. The simplest and most easily understood form of bivariate analysis is the cross-tabulation. Since cross-tabulations usually involve comparisons of unequally sized subgroups, figures must be converted into percentages before proper comparisons can be made. But since percentages can be computed either across row totals or down column totals in a cross-tabulation, great care must be taken to specify the logic of the group comparisons you wish to make before deciding how to compute percentages.

When there are a large number of categories for one or both of the variables being considered, it is often convenient to summarize the relationship in terms of one or more of the standard measures of association. The one most commonly used is the Pearson correlation coefficient, but there are many other measures of association. Some are most appropriate for interval-level data, some for ordinal-level data, and some for nominal-level data.

Bivariate associations can be further analyzed using statistical procedures that are extensions of correlation analysis and cross-tabulation analysis. The technique of cross-tabular analysis that involves the introduction of a third control variable is referred to as the elaboration paradigm. Correlation with statistical controls is referred to as partial correlation; it follows a logic that is very similar to that in the elaboration paradigm.

Key Terms

adjusted percentage	explanatory research	partial correlation
bar graph	frequency distribution	pie diagram
bivariate analysis	interpretation	range
column	intervening variable	row
contingency	marginals	specification
control variable	mean	spurious relationship
correlation	measure of central	standard deviation
correlation coefficient	tendency	subtable
cross-tabulation	measure of variability	suppressor variable
descriptive research	median	test factor
deviant case	mode	two-way table
dispersion	multivariate analysis	univariate analysis
elaboration paradigm	nonlinear relationship	variance
explanation	normal curve	zero-order correlation

Exercises

1. Compute the mean, the median, and the mode for the following set of numbers: 5, 10, 6, 5, 10, 1, 4, 10, 7, 5, 10, 3, 5, 8, 10, 10.

2. Compute the standard deviation for the set of numbers in exercise 1.

3. In Table 16.1 the largest category includes only 48 percent of the sample. Is it possible for the modal category to include less than 50 percent of the sample? What is the smallest percentage of the sample that a category can include and still be classified as the mode?

4. On the basis of the data presented in Figures 16.8 and 16.10, would you conclude that the original relationship between size of birthplace and attitude toward abortion was spurious? Explain.

5. Compute percentages across the rows of Table 16.7, and then use these per-centages to discuss the data in the table. Now compare these percentages with those in Table 16.8. Which set of percentages is more useful? Explain.

6. Using the data presented in Figure 16.7, construct the tables you would need to demonstrate that the control variable is related to both of the variables in the original table (Figure 16.6).

7. Using the data presented in Figure 16.10, construct the tables you would need to show that the control variable is related to both of the variables in the original table (Figure 16.8).

8. There is a partial-correlation equivalent of *explanation* as the term is used in the elaboration paradigm. There is also an equivalent of *interpretation*. Explain why there is no partial-correlation equivalent of *specification*.

Suggested Readings

Blalock, Hubert M., Jr.
1979 *Social Statistics*. 2nd rev. ed. New York: McGraw-Hill.

A very useful advanced introduction to statistical analysis. It includes the same material covered in the more elementary texts but in addition considers topics such as two-way analysis of variance, intraclass correlation, nonlinear correlation and regression, dummy variable analysis, analysis of covariance, and tests of significance for correlation coefficients. It also includes a thorough chapter on sampling.

Campbell, Stephen K.
1974 *Flaws and Fallacies in Statistical Thinking*. Englewood Cliffs, N.J.: Prentice-Hall.

This book is longer than, but in many ways similar to, Huff's (see below). Its objective is to sensitize the reader to the various ways in which statistics are used in the mass media and in other popular sources of information to mislead the audience. This is particularly the case with statistical analysis presented in advertisements.

Goehring, Harvey J.
1980 *Statistical Methods in Education*. Arlington, Va.: Information Resource Press.

A basic introduction to the value and use of statistical procedures in the field of education.

Huck, Schuyler, W., William H. Cormier, and William G. Bounds, Jr.
1974 *Reading Statistics and Research*. New York: Harper & Row.

The focus of this book is on learning to understand and critically evaluate statistically oriented articles and research reports. The applications are for the most part drawn from psychology. The book begins with a very competent discussion of the typical format of a journal article. Then it considers one-way analysis of variance, factorial analyses of variance, analysis of variance with repeated measures, analysis of covariance, multiple correlation, and discriminant function analysis.

Huff, Darrell
1954 *How to Lie with Statistics*. New York: Norton.

A very simple introduction to descriptive statistics with many cartoons. This book is appropriate for use during the first weeks of an undergraduate course in social statistics. It is written for a lay audience. Like Campbell, Huff alerts us to the deceptive uses of statistics in the mass media. Considered are sampling bias, the well-chosen average, and making small differences or changes appear large.

Malec, Michael A.
1977   *Essential Statistics for Social Research.* New York: Lippincott.

A very clearly written introduction to descriptive and inductive statistics for the undergraduate social science major. The book deals with such topics as: measures of centrality, measures of dispersion, the logic of hypothesis testing, measures of association, multivariate table analysis (elaboration), and partial correlation.

McCollough, Celeste
1974   *Introduction to Statistical Analysis.* New York: McGraw-Hill.

An introduction to descriptive and inductive statistics that combines aspects of the standard textbook format with the programed learning approach. Correlation analysis, regression analysis, one-way analysis of variance, the chi-square test, measures of dispersion, measures of central tendency, and conditional probability are considered.

Rosenberg, Morris
1968   *The Logic of Survey Analysis.* New York: Basic Books.

This is a book-length treatment of the issues considered in the section of this chapter on the elaboration paradigm. It deals with the use of contingency tables in the analysis of survey research data.

References

Babbie, Earl R.
1979   *The Practice of Social Research.* 2nd ed. Belmont, Calif.: Wadsworth.

Hyman, Herbert
1955   *Survey Design and Analysis.* Glencoe, Ill.: Free Press.

Kendall, Patricia L., and Paul F. Lazarsfeld
1950   "Problems of Survey Analysis." In *Continuities in Social Research: Studies in the Scope and Method of the American Soldier,* ed. Robert K. Merton and Paul F. Lazarsfeld. Glencoe, Ill.: Free Press.

Rosenberg, Morris
1968   *The Logic of Survey Analysis.* New York: Basic Books.

17 / Multivariate Analysis and Statistical Inference*

CHAPTER OUTLINE

INTRODUCTION
MULTIVARIATE ANALYSIS
Regression Analysis
Path Analysis

STATISTICAL INFERENCE
Tests of Statistical Significance
The Misuse of Tests of Significance
SUMMARY

KEY TERMS
EXERCISES
SUGGESTED READINGS
REFERENCES

Introduction

In the first part of this chapter we deal with one of the most widely used multivariate statistical techniques, REGRESSION ANALYSIS. A comprehensive treatment of the topic is beyond the scope of a first course in research methods, but a brief introduction to regression analysis is essential because it so frequently appears in the quantitative social research literature. The aim of the present discussion is to give the reader a basic overview and some suggestions for learning more. One reason that regression analysis is so often employed is that it lends itself to causal modeling. In recent years one of the most common forms of causal modeling has been *path analysis*. Therefore, we provide an outline of this technique as well.

This chapter also examines the issue of statistical inference. Social researchers use a great variety of TESTS OF SIGNIFICANCE in order to draw conclusions about a population (or universe) of interest on the basis of evidence obtained from a sample selected from that population. Many researchers have high confidence in these tests of significance. Therefore, it is important that they, as well as all consumers of the results of social research, understand what these tests are all about. It is wise to be aware of which questions can be legitimately answered on the basis of such tests and which questions cannot. Finally, it is important to be sensitive to the various ways in which tests of significance are commonly misused.

---

*Parts of this chapter will be difficult for the reader who has not taken a course in basic statistics.

Multivariate Analysis

REGRESSION ANALYSIS

Linear regression is a statistical procedure used to estimate the amount of change in a dependent variable that can be expected for a given change in an independent variable. We shall begin by considering SIMPLE REGRESSION, which involves one dependent variable and one independent variable (or *predictor*). We shall then consider MULTIPLE REGRESSION, which involves one dependent variable and two or more predictors.

Recall from elementary algebra that the equation for a straight line is:

$$Y = a + bX$$

Figure 17.1 is an illustration of the interpretation of the constants a and b in this equation. We find that a is the value Y takes when X is equal to zero. It is referred to as the Y intercept because it is the value of Y at the point where the straight line crosses the Y-axis. The constant b is equal to the *slope* of this line. If we move an arbitrary distance along the line described by this equation, recording the amount that Y has changed (call it ΔY) and the amount X has changed (call it ΔX) and then divide the change in Y by the change in X, the result is the slope of the line (i.e., $b = \Delta Y/\Delta X$).

In this example from elementary algebra, the Y values refer to points along the straight line defined by the equation: $Y = a + bX$. There is no concern with or mention of any Y values that do not fall on this line. For any arbitrary value of X we can find the corresponding Y value that satisfies the equation by locating the Y value on the straight line that falls directly over the specified X value (i.e., we would determine that point at which a line constructed perpendicular to the X-axis from the specified X value intersects the straight line given by the equation: $Y = a + bX$).

Simple regression is a procedure for fitting a straight line to a set of points in a scattergram, as illustrated in Figure 17.2. The regression line is that line through the set of points for which the sum of the squares of the deviations from the line are a minimum. These deviations are shown in Figure 17.2. For any line other

FIGURE 17.1   The Equation for a Straight Line

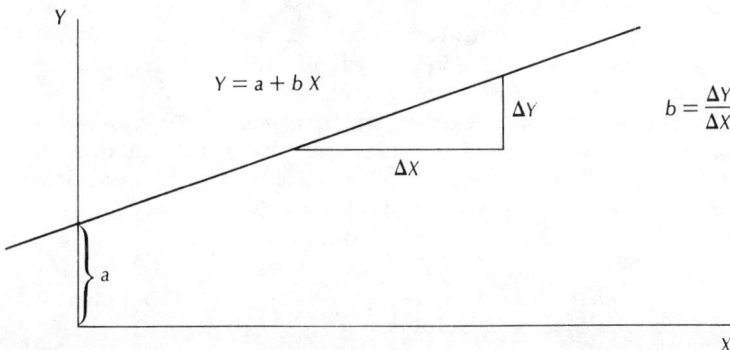

FIGURE 17.2   Fitting a Least Squares Regression Line to a Set of Points in a Scattergram

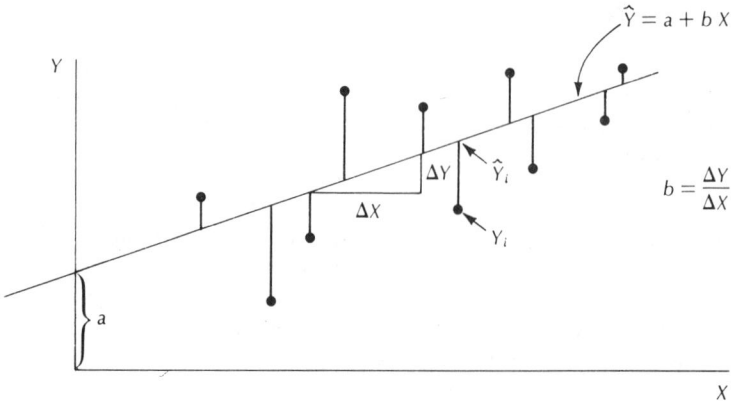

than the regression line through the same set of points, the sum of the squares of the deviations is greater.

The major distinction between the equation for the regression line and the corresponding equation for a straight line from elementary algebra is that the values of Y for regression rarely fall along the actual regression line, but the values of Y for the elementary algebra example always fall along the line. By constructing a vertical line from each observed Y value to the regression line, as illustrated in Figure 17.2, we can locate a set of $\hat{Y}$ (called Y-predicted) values that do fall along the regression line. Thus the equation for the regression line becomes:

$$\hat{Y} = a + bX$$

Suppose that Y is *annual income* and that X is *years of education*. In simple regression the slope (b) is referred to as the REGRESSION COEFFICIENT. If the regression coefficient has a value of 500, we would estimate that for a one-year increase in level of education there will be a $500 increase in annual income. More generally, the regression coefficient gives the number of units of change in Y (in whatever units Y is measured) that can be expected for a one-unit change in X (in whatever units X is measured).

In regression analysis it is important to distinguish between the actual Y values that do not fall on the regression line and the corresponding $\hat{Y}$ values that we would estimate on the basis of knowledge about a given respondent's X value. The discrepancy between the actual Y value and the estimated $\hat{Y}$ value represents prediction error. When the Y values tend to cluster very close to the regression line, Y and $\hat{Y}$ values will be very similar, and the error in prediction will be low. But when the Y values tend to deviate markedly from the regression line, the Y and $\hat{Y}$ values will be quite different, and the error in prediction will be high.

Multiple regression is an extension of simple regression: instead of one predictor we include two or more predictors in a single regression equation. When there are four predictors, the equation is as follows:

$$\hat{Y} = a + b_1X_1 + b_2X_2 + b_3X_3 + b_4X_4$$

The b values in multiple regression are referred to as PARTIAL-REGRESSION COEFFI-CIENTS.[1] These coefficients give the change in the dependent variable (in what-ever units the dependent variable is measured) that we would estimate for a one-unit change in the specified predictor (in whatever units the predictor is measured).

THE MULTIPLE-CORRELATION COEFFICIENT (R) is used to summarize the accuracy of our prediction equation.[2] It is equal to the Pearson correlation between Y and the $\hat{Y}$ values. Recall that the difference between Y and $\hat{Y}$ represents error in our prediction. If we have selected a set of predictors that yield accurate estimates of Y, then the difference between Y and $\hat{Y}$ values will be small, and the multiple correlation will be high. If, on the other hand, we have selected a set of predictors that yield poor estimates of Y, then the difference between Y and $\hat{Y}$ values will tend to be larger, and the multiple correlation will be low. The multiple correlation ranges from .00 (when the independent variables in no way help to predict Y) to 1.00 (when the independent variables predict Y with complete accuracy). The multiple-correlation coefficient squared (R^2) gives the proportion of the variance in the dependent variable that is accounted for by the set of predictors included in the regression equation. If $R = .50$, then $R^2 = .25$, and we would conclude that the predictors being considered account for 25 percent of the variance in the dependent variable.

Let us assume that our goal is to predict the grade-point average for 1,000 seniors who have just graduated from college. Suppose we decide to use the following four predictors: *high school grade-point average* (X_1), *father's educa-tion* (X_2), *verbal SAT (Scholastic Aptitude Test) score* (X_3), and *father's occu-pational status* (X_4). These variables are all measured in different units; con-sequently, we cannot make direct comparisons among these partial-regression coefficients $(b_1, b_2, b_3,$ and $b_4)$ to determine their relative strength as predictors of grade-point average.

Fortunately, there is a way to deal with this problem. It calls for computing STANDARDIZED PARTIAL-REGRESSION COEFFICIENTS (these coefficients are commonly re-ferred to as BETA WEIGHTS) for each of these predictors. The beta weight is a partial-regression coefficient that has been adjusted in such a way that the unit of mea-sure does not influence its value. The way this is done is that all units are changed to standard deviation units. Thus, when a beta weight equals .50, our interpreta-tion is that there will be a .50 standard deviation change in the dependent vari-able (grade-point average) for a one standard deviation change in the specified predictor. Since each of the coefficients is now stated in standard deviation units, it is possible to compare the relative strength of each predictor.

---

[1]The b values are referred to as partial-regression coefficients because they are esti-mates of the change in the dependent variable that is estimated for a one-unit change in a specified predictor after we statistically control for the effects of the other predictors in the equation.

[2]The subscripted version of the multiple-correlation coefficient is designated symboli-cally as "$R_{1.2345}$" where the subscript 1 refers to the dependent variable X_1 and the sub-scripts 2, 3, 4, and 5 refer to the predictors X_2, X_3, X_4, and X_5. There will be as many numbers following the period in the subscript as there are predictors. Note that the notation system has been changed here so that the dependent variable referred to in the text as Y is referred to here as X_1. For the subscripted multiple-correlation coefficient, as for several other multivariate statistics (e.g., the partial-correlation coefficient), the notation is simpler if we refer to our variables as X_1, X_2, X_3 and so on, rather than as Y, X_1 and X_2.

The statistic referred to earlier as the partial-regression coefficient is also called the UNSTANDARDIZED PARTIAL-REGRESSION COEFFICIENT. As we recall, this statistic indicates how many units the dependent variable is estimated to change (in whatever units it is measured) for a one-unit change in the independent variable (in whatever units it is measured). For this reason the units in which the variables are measured make a difference. If income were one of our predictors, we would have a choice of units for measuring it. We might decide on yen, dollars, or lire. Depending on which of these three units we selected, we would get a different unstandardized partial-regression coefficient for income. But the standardized partial-regression co-efficient is not influenced by the unit of measurement and would be the same for each of these three alternatives.

PATH ANALYSIS

Now that we have considered multiple regression, it is appropriate to discuss PATH ANALYSIS, a form of causal modeling based on multiple regression. Path analysis can be viewed as a procedure for presenting the results of a series of multiple regressions, or as a procedure for doing causal modeling with multiple regression. To be more concrete, we will consider a model of socioeconomic achievement.

The model in Figure 17.3 includes four predictors and the respondent's *present occupation,* which is the main dependent variable. The arrows in the model specify a seemingly plausible causal order among these variables—before looking at the data. The selection of predictors and the assumed causal ordering among these predictors is based on prior theory, past research, and common sense. In the present model we are willing to assume that *father's education* (X_5) influences *father's occupation* (X_4), that father's education and father's occupation influence *respondent's education* (X_3), that all three influence *respondent's first job* (X_2), and that all four influence *present occupation* (X_1). This model is then used to set up a series of multiple-regression equations. In this case four separate equations would be called for, one for each variable in the model that is used as a dependent variable. (Any variable that has an arrow coming toward it is being used as a dependent variable.) For equation 1 (see below) respondent's present

FIGURE 17.3   A Model of the Process of Socioeconomic Achievement

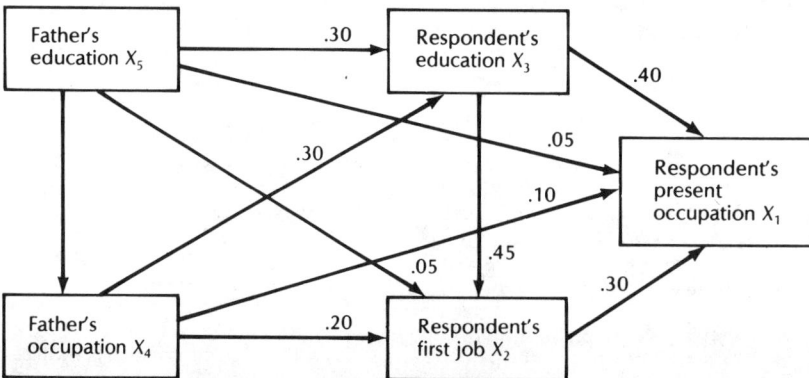

occupation is the dependent variable, and it is predicted by the other four variables. In equation 2 respondent's first job is the dependent variable, and it is predicted by the three variables in the model that are causally prior to it. In equation 3 respondent's education is the dependent variable, and it is predicted by the two variables that are causally prior. Finally, in equation 4 father's occupation is the dependent variable, and it is predicted by the one variable, father's education, that is causally prior to it. These four equations may be summarized as follows:

$$\hat{X}_1 = a_1 + b_2X_2 + b_3X_3 + b_4X_4 + b_5X_5 \qquad \text{(Equation 1)}$$
$$\hat{X}_2 = a_2 + b_3X_3 + b_4X_4 + b_5X_5 \qquad \text{(Equation 2)}$$
$$\hat{X}_3 = a_3 + b_4X_4 + b_5X_5 \qquad \text{(Equation 3)}$$
$$\hat{X}_4 = a_4 + b_5X_5 \qquad \text{(Equation 4)}$$

These equations yield a set of unstandardized partial-regression coefficients that are sometimes used in path analysis, but it is more common to use the corresponding standardized partial-regression coefficients, or beta weights. In path analysis the beta weights are called PATH COEFFICIENTS and are often presented along the corresponding arrows as we have done in Figure 17.3. Thus the path coefficient for the so-called direct effect of respondent's education on respondent's present occupation is .40; that is, for every increase of one standard deviation in respondent's education we would estimate an increase of .40 standard deviation in the score for respondent's present occupation. On the basis of the path coefficients in Figure 17.3 we would conclude that the direct effect of respondent's education on respondent's first job (.45) is much greater than is the direct effect of father's education on respondent's first job (.05). It is also possible to use path analysis to estimate the indirect effect of one variable on another through an intervening variable, by multiplying the appropriate path coefficients.[3]

Because of space limitations the presentation of path analysis has been simplified in many ways. We have made no mention of the so-called *residual paths* or of the decomposition of the total relationship between variables into the so-called *causal* and *noncausal* components, and we have only briefly touched on the decomposition of the causal component into the so-called *direct* and *indirect* components.[4]

Statistical Inference

In quantitative research we are rarely interested in our sample per se. Rather, we want to make generalizations about a larger population on the basis of what we know about the sample drawn from it. When our goal is simply to describe the characteristics of the sample or to describe the relationship between variables for the sample, we engage in descriptive statistical analysis. But when our goal is to

---

[3]In Figure 17.3 we may obtain the indirect effect of respondent's education on respondent's present occupation, which occurs through the intervening variable, *respondent's first job*. To do so, we multiply the direct effect of X_3 on X_2 (which is .45) by the direct effect of X_2 on X_1 (which is .30) and obtain an indirect effect of X_3 on X_1, through the intervening variable X_2, equal to .135, which we might round to .14.

[4]For a good introduction to path analysis, see Nie et al. (1975).

infer certain characteristics of the population on the basis of characteristics of the sample or to make inferences about the relationship between variables in the population on the basis of information about the relationship between these same variables in the sample, we engage in STATISTICAL INFERENCE. Tests of significance are often used as a basis for statistical inference.

TESTS OF STATISTICAL SIGNIFICANCE

TESTS OF SIGNIFICANCE are widely used in both descriptive and explanatory research. One of their most common uses is as an aid in deciding whether to infer, on the basis of the relationship between two variables in a sample, that there is a relationship between these same two variables in the population from which the sample was drawn. Suppose we interview a representative cross section of a local community and find that the sample estimate of the mean income for Republican respondents is $30,000 and that the sample estimate of the mean income for Democratic respondents is $15,000. On the basis of this evidence we know that there is a difference in mean income between Republicans and Democrats for the sample, but we are probably more interested in knowing whether we can infer from this that there is a tendency in the community as a whole for Republicans to have higher incomes than Democrats.

Estimates based on a sample rarely correspond to the exact value for the population. Probability theory assures us that there will be SAMPLING ERROR (the deviation of the mean for our sample from the true population mean) in our estimates of the mean; that is, sample estimates will fluctuate around the true population value. Since some sample estimates will be too high and others will be too low, we do not know whether our estimate of $30,000 is above or below the actual mean income of Republicans in the community. It is even possible that the mean income for Democrats is higher than the mean income for Republicans. This would be the case if, owing to sampling error, the sample estimate for Republican respondents overstates their actual income in the community by $8,000 (so that the actual mean income in the community is $22,000), and the sample estimate for Democratic respondents understates their actual income in the community by $9,000 (so that the actual mean income in the community is $24,000).

Suppose that prior to looking at our data, we have the idea that in the community the mean income for Republicans is higher than the mean income for Democrats. How might we test this RESEARCH HYPOTHESIS? As a first step we might compute the mean incomes for Republicans ($30,000) and Democrats ($15,000) in our sample. But our hypothesis refers to the community, not to our sample. One way to address ourselves to this issue is to determine whether a difference in mean income as great as that found in our sample could be expected as the result of sampling error (chance) alone—if in the community the mean income for Republicans were actually exactly equal to that for Democrats. More generally, whenever we want to test the hypothesis that one group is different from another, the way to go about it is to ask whether the difference found in the sample could be expected on the basis of chance alone. To this end we formulate what is referred to as a NULL HYPOTHESIS. Our null hypothesis in this case is that in the community the mean income of Republicans is equal to the mean income of Democrats.

Tests of significance always call for the formulation of a null hypothesis, which typically states that there is no relationship in the population between the variables of interest. Along with the null hypothesis we always formulate a research hypothesis. In the preceding example we specified a DIRECTIONAL RESEARCH HYPOTHESIS, that is, that the mean income of Republicans is higher than the mean income of Democrats. Sometimes we do not specify a direction in our research hypothesis. A NONDIRECTIONAL RESEARCH HYPOTHESIS appropriate to the example would be that the mean income for Republicans is not equal to that for Democrats. Note that the income for Republicans could be either higher or lower than that for Democrats and still be consistent with this nondirectional research hypothesis. When our research hypothesis is directional, we use what is referred to as a ONE-TAILED TEST OF SIGNIFICANCE. When our research hypothesis is nondirectional, we use a TWO-TAILED TEST OF SIGNIFICANCE.[5]

When carrying out a significance test, we always specify a SIGNIFICANCE LEVEL. It is a common practice to select in advance one of the conventional significance levels, such as .05, .01, or .001. These levels refer to there being a chance of 5 in 100, 1 in 100, and 1 in 1,000, respectively, of getting a relationship as strong as that in our sample due to chance (sampling error) when there is no relationship between the variables in the population. If, for example, we select the .05 level, this says that we are going to classify the difference in means as statistically significant if there are fewer than 5 chances in 100 that the difference is due to sampling error alone. Suppose we carry out a test of significance on the difference between the mean incomes of Republicans and Democrats for our sample. If the difference is significant at the .05 level, we refer to the relationship as being statistically significant; that is, we reject the null hypothesis that the incomes of Republicans and Democrats are equal for the community. But, in so doing, we realize that we are taking a 5 percent chance of being wrong. We realize that there are 5 chances in 100 that a difference as great as that found in our sample could have resulted from sampling error alone. Even though we have decided to classify the difference in income as statistically significant, it is still possible that the incomes for Republicans and Democrats in the community are equal.

What if we had carried out a test of significance and found that we were not able to reject the null hypothesis that the mean incomes for Republicans and Democrats are exactly equal? Does this mean that we accept the null hypothesis and conclude that the incomes are exactly identical? No, we do not. There is a difference between failing to reject the null hypothesis and actually accepting it. It is very unlikely that the mean income for Republicans will be exactly equal to the mean income for Democrats even if we have failed to reject the null hypothesis. There is an important distinction between the conclusion that the difference in means found in our sample could result from chance (sampling error) alone if the population means were exactly equal and the conclusion that the population means are exactly identical.

A test of significance is a procedure for deciding how likely it is that the relationship we have found in the sample (in this case the difference in income between Republicans and Democrats) can be accounted for in terms of sampling

[5]The rationale for the names "one-tailed" and "two-tailed" tests of significance is too technical for the present treatment; a full discussion of the issue may be found in any introductory statistics text.

error when there is actually no relationship between variables in the population. A test of significance cannot be used to prove that there actually *is* a relationship in the population, nor can such a test be used to prove that there actually is *no* relationship in the population; it can be used only to indicate how likely we would be to obtain the relationship we find in the sample if there were no relationship in the population.

The test of significance that we use when we are interested in comparing the means for two samples or two categories of the same sample, as in the case of a comparison of the mean income of Republicans with the mean income for Democrats, is the *t*-test. The null hypothesis for a *t*-test is that the population means are equal, in this case that the means for the Democrats and Republicans are equal. When we want to compare the means for more than two groups in the same test of significance, we use the *F*-test. The null hypothesis for the *F*-test is that the means for all the groups being compared are equal (for example, the means for the Democrats, Independents, and Republicans). The research hypothesis for the *F*-test is that the means are *not* equal; there is no directional (one-tailed) option when more than two groups are being considered.

Tests of significance are often used in contingency table analysis. The test most often used with contingency tables, when at least one of the variables concerned is at the nominal level, is the chi-square. The null hypothesis for the chi-square test is that there is no relationship between the two variables in the table; that is, the respondents are distributed among the table cells as would be expected by chance.

The Pearson correlation coefficient can be tested for statistical significance. The null hypothesis here is that the correlation between the two variables in the population is zero. If we have grounds for predicting the direction of the correlation, we choose an alternative research hypothesis that states that there is a positive correlation between the variables (or states that there is a negative correlation, depending on the direction of the relationship we are predicting), and we use a one-tailed test. If we do not have a prior hypothesis as to the direction of the correlation, the alternative research hypothesis states that in the population the correlation between the two variables is not equal to zero, and we use a two-tailed test. In this case if the correlation proves to be statistically significant, we accept the research hypothesis that the correlation in the population is not zero. Note that the significance test does not say the correlation in the population is equal to the correlation for the sample. In fact, it says nothing about the actual strength of the correlation in the population. More generally, the strength of a correlation and the statistical significance of a correlation are conceptually independent. In general, for a given sample size, correlations that are statistically significant will tend to be larger than correlations that are not. But with a large enough sample, a weak correlation will be statistically significant; and with a small enough sample, a strong correlation will not be statistically significant.

The reason that the same-strength correlation is more likely to be classified as statistically significant if it is based on a larger sample is that there is less sampling error for a large sample. If we were to draw a sample of 5 to estimate the mean income for a community, our estimate would tend to be less accurate than if it were based on a sample of 500. In general, a sample statistic based on a larger sample will more closely approximate the corresponding population parameter than will the same statistic based on a smaller sample. Thus a nonzero correlation based on a large sample is less likely to be due to chance than is the same correlation based on a smaller sample. The same logic applies to all measures of association. For a given strength of association, the larger the sample size, the more likely it is that the association will prove to be statistically significant.

THE MISUSE OF TESTS OF SIGNIFICANCE

There has been a great deal of debate among social scientists over the use of tests of significance. Of particular concern is the evidence that such tests are frequently used in situations for which the requirements underlying the test have not been met. Some argue that the problem has been exacerbated by pressure from journal editors and reviewers who encourage the use of such tests (so that the results will seem more scientific?) despite the violation of the assumptions that underlie them. Others argue that tests of significance do have their use even when these assumptions are not completely satisfied.

All tests of significance assume we have a probability sample, and most assume a simple random sample. But it is not uncommon to find tests that assume that a simple random sample is being used when what is being used is not even a remote approximation to a simple random sample. Most social research is based on cluster, quota, or accidental samples, which are rather poor approximations to a simple random sample. With such samples the error is much greater than in a simple random sample. This can lead to inflated estimates of statistical significance.

A related problem is the use of tests of significance when the researcher is working with the entire population. Suppose we are using state-level data, and we find a correlation of .30 between *median income* and *level of state educational expenditures*. Suppose also that we are working with data for all fifty states. In such a situation our sample (N = 50) is the population, and so it is inappropriate to compute a test of statistical significance. If the correlation between these variables is .30, then .30 is the correlation in the population, and it is meaningless to compute a test of significance to test the null hypothesis that in the population the correlation is zero.[6] In short, if we already have the population, there is no need to make the inferences that tests of significance are designed to help us make.

It is not uncommon for a researcher to use a test of significance to make generalizations beyond the population from which the sample was drawn. Suppose we have a simple random sample of the seniors at a college, and we find that the Jews in the sample are more likely to support gun control than are the Catholics. If this difference turns out to be statistically significant, we can generalize to all the seniors at the college. It might seem plausible that a similar trend would hold for seniors at other colleges, or for all college students, or for the adult population in general, but we have no grounds for making such a generalization on the basis of the data we have.

Statistical significance is often confused with SUBSTANTIVE SIGNIFICANCE. It is fairly common for a researcher to suggest that a finding is important because it is

---

[6]See Winch and Campbell (1969) for an alternative perspective on this issue.

statistically significant. While it is generally reasonable to discount findings that are *not* statistically significant, statistical significance per se does not make a relationship important. We can often find statistically significant relationships between variables that are causally unrelated (for example, the relationship between birth rates and stork counts), variables that are alternative measures of the same thing (for instance, the relationship between age and year of birth), and variables that are sociologically uninteresting (such as the relationship between weight and waist measurement). There can also be relationships based on very large samples that are statistically significant but so weak as to be substantively unimportant. And finally, a correlation can be very close to zero (even .01) and still be statistically significant if the sample size is large enough.

Another misuse of significance tests is illustrated by researchers who compute a very large number of tests and then prepare research reports based only on those relationships that are statistically significant. Such researchers are capitalizing on sampling error and may prepare an entire report around a set of correlations that could not be replicated. Suppose a researcher computes 1,000 correlation coefficients and tests each for statistical significance. Even if all of these correlations in the population are zero, we would expect on the basis of sampling error that 50 (or 5 out of every 100) of these correlations would be significant at the .05 level. Thus if the researcher looks through the 1,000 correlations and bases the report on the 50 or so that are statistically significant, the findings reported run a risk of being highly unreliable. Most of these correlations will have been due to sampling error alone. For this reason it will not be possible to replicate the findings of the study.

There are different tests of significance for different types of data. Some tests are appropriate for nominal-level data, some are appropriate for ordinal-level data, and still others are appropriate for interval- and ratio-level data. A common error is to use a test of significance appropriate for interval-level data when the data are actually only ordinal level. A typical example of this error is the computation of a test of significance for a Pearson correlation between two ordinal-level variables.

Summary

Regression is one of the most commonly used statistical procedures in social research. In simple regression analysis we consider only two variables, one dependent variable and one independent variable (the predictor). The regression line is the line through the set of data points being considered that minimizes the sum of the square of the deviations from the line. For any other line through this same set of points, the sum is greater.

Multiple regression, an extension of simple regression to include two or more predictors, is the most widely used form of regression analysis. The coefficients that result when we do multiple regression are called partial-regression coefficients or unstandardized partial-regression coefficients. These specify the number of units of difference in the dependent variable we would estimate (in whatever units that dependent variable is being measured) for a one-unit difference in the predictor being considered (in whatever units that predictor is being measured) when we statistically control all the other predictors in the equation. For some purposes, such as path analysis, it is useful to obtain a set of standardized partial-regression coefficients, which are called beta weights in the context of multiple-regression analysis, and path coefficients in the context of path analysis. The beta weight gives the number of standard deviations difference in the dependent variable we would estimate for a one standard deviation unit difference in the predictor being considered. When using beta weights, it is possible to directly compare the "effects" of the various predictors because they are all being measured in the same standard deviation units.

Tests of statistical significance are extensively used in explanatory research. A test of significance cannot be used to prove that there actually is a relationship in the population or that there actually is no relationship in the population. Such a test can, however, be used to indicate how likely we are to obtain the relationship we find in the sample if there is no relationship in the population. Tests of significance are used incorrectly by many social researchers. One of the most common errors is the use of such tests when there are flagrant violations of the assumption of a simple random sample. In such situations levels of statistical significance are often greatly inflated. They are also inflated when the researcher uses a test that assumes interval-level data on measures that are clearly ordinal. Another error is explicitly or implicitly to convey the impression that statistically significant relationships are substantively significant when in fact they are not. When the sample is large, a very weak relationship, one that many account for less than 1 percent of the variance, may turn out to be statistically significant.

Key Terms

beta weight	one-tailed test of	simple regression
directional research	significance	standardized partial-
hypothesis	partial-regression	regression coefficient
linear regression	coefficient	statistical inference
multiple-correlation	path analysis	substantive significance
coefficient	path coefficient	test of statistical
multiple regression	regression analysis	significance
nondirectional research	regression coefficient	two-tailed test of
hypothesis	research hypothesis	significance
null hypothesis	sampling error	unstandardized partial-
	significance level	regression coefficient

Exercises

1. If we are considering a simple regression in which the dependent variable is *monthly income measured in yen* and the predictor is *time at work measured in hours,* what would be the units for the regression coefficient? If the numerical value of the regression coefficient were to be 1,000, how much of a difference in income would we expect between two persons who differ by six hours with respect to hours worked?

2. Consider a multiple regression in which X_1 is the dependent variable, with X_2

and X_3 as predictors, where each is defined as follows:

X_1 = monthly income in lire
X_2 = time worked in hours
X_3 = years of education completed

a. Set up the appropriate regression equation for the above example. Be sure to use subscripts for the partial-regression coefficients.

b. If you wanted to compare the relative strength of time worked (X_2) and years of education completed (X_3) as predictors, which would you use—the unstandardized partial-regression coefficients or the standardized partial-regression coefficients? Defend your choice.

c. If we are considering an equation based on unstandardized partial-regression coefficients, how much of a difference in X_1 would we estimate for a one-unit difference in X_3? If we are considering an equation based on standardized partial-regression coefficients, how much of a difference in X_1 values would we estimate for a one-unit difference in X_3? Assume that $b_2 = 1,000$ and $b_3 = 50,000$ and that the corresponding standardized coefficients are .63 and .47.

3. Construct the series of regression equations that would be used to estimate the path coefficients in this model. Would you prefer to use the unstandardized partial-regression coefficients or the standardized partial-regression coefficients to estimate the path coefficients? Defend your choice.

4. In what ways is a standardized partial-regression coefficient similar to a partial-correlation coefficient? In what ways is it different?

5. If for the equation described in exercise 2 it turned out that the multiple-correlation coefficient was .70, what could be said about the proportion of the variance in the dependent variable X_1 accounted for by the two predictors X_2 and X_3?

6. For the path model below compare the direct effect of X_3 on X_1 with the indirect effect of X_3 on X_1 through the intervening variable X_2. Which is larger?

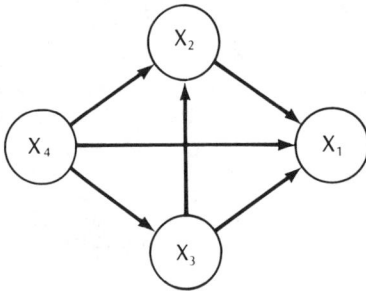

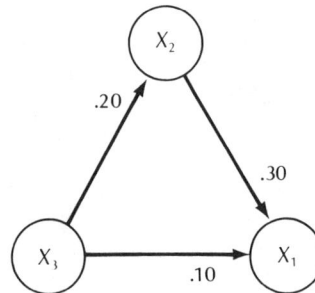

7. Select a recent issue of the *American Sociological Review*. Comb through it for articles in which you believe that tests of statistical significance have been used incorrectly. Where you think that a test of significance was, or may have been, misused, state your reasons for the conclusion.

Suggested Readings

Blalock, Hubert M., Jr.
1979 *Social Statistics*. 2nd rev. ed. New York: McGraw-Hill.

This book contains a useful introduction to multivariate analysis. The treatment of regression analysis is very well done. Among the other multivariate techniques considered are: analysis of variance, partial correlation, and analysis of covariance. This book includes a good discussion of tests of significance.

Hays, William L.
1973 *Statistics for the Social Sciences*. 2nd ed. New York: Holt, Rinehart and Winston.

This book is an alternative to the Blalock text for those who want an overview of various multivariate statistical techniques. It tends to be more thorough than Blalock, particularly on techniques commonly used by psychologists, such as analysis of variance.

Kerlinger, Fred N., and Elazar J. Pedhazur
1973 *Multiple Regression in Behavioral Research*. New York: Holt, Rinehart and Winston.

This is a good place to go after the Blalock text for a more comprehensive treatment of various issues in multiple-regression analysis. The book also considers such multivariate procedures as canonical correlation and discriminant function analysis.

Morrison, Denton E., and Ramon E. Henkel
1969   "Significance Tests Reconsidered." *American Sociologist* 4 (May):131–140.

An easy introduction that argues against the use of tests of statistical significance. It then reviews the most frequent misuses of such tests, especially the use of nonprobability samples and treating the population rather than a sample from a population. One of the most valuable aspects is a content analysis of the major sociological journals over a twenty-year period, citing the proportion of quantitative articles in which tests of statistical significance have been misused.

Nie, Norman H., et al.
1975   *SPSS: Statistical Package for the Social Sciences.* 2nd ed. New York: McGraw-Hill.

This manual describes the various bivariate and multivariate statistical programs in the SPSS system. It is also useful as a statistics text for those working with the SPSS system. Among the multivariate procedures discussed are: partial correlation analysis, multiple regression, analysis of variance, discriminant analysis, multiple classification analysis, canonical correlation analysis, and factor analysis. Chapter 21 provides an excellent introduction to path analysis.

Winch, Robert F., and Donald T. Campbell
1969   "Proof? No. Evidence? Yes. The Significance of Tests of Significance." *American Sociologist* 4 (May):140–143.

A defense of the use of tests of significance, this article can be read as a reply to Morrison and Henkel (1969). One of the important arguments made is that tests of significance often can be used to exclude certain relationships from further consideration. While the violation of various assumptions associated with tests of significance may inflate significance levels and lead to the invalid conclusion that a specified relationship is significant, if the relationship turns out not to be significant we have little ground for attempting to account for it.

References

Nie, Norman, et al.
1975   *SPSS: Statistical Package for the Social Sciences.* 2nd ed. New York: McGraw-Hill.

Winch, Robert F., and Donald T. Campbell
1969   "Proof? No. Evidence? Yes. The Significance of Tests of Significance." *American Sociologist* 4 (May):140–143.

Epilog: The Value and Limits of Social Science Knowledge

By now you have spent many hours reading about the craft of social research. You have encountered a new vocabulary of "key terms" and have become familiar with the general issues that are involved in the use of any data collection technique—issues such as representative sampling, objectivity, reliability, validity, and precision. It is now time to take stock of what you have learned.

This book has been designed to convince you of the importance of social research by demonstrating its many uses—in the formulation of public policy and plans for social change, as the basis for social criticism, and in the testing of theories about human behavior. We have focused on the great variety of methodological techniques that are employed to accomplish these tasks and to achieve the basic goal of satisfying your own intellectual curiosity. The importance of social science, after all, lies primarily in producing knowledge that matters to each of us.

One way to think about the various methods we have described and analyzed is as "inventions." Each technique is designed to collect certain types of data about the world. Each raises one set of research issues more than another, and each has its own strengths and weaknesses. That social scientists have seen the need to invent the number of methods covered in this volume confirms the judgment that social life is an enormously complicated affair. We cannot use the same tools to investigate historical trends as we would use to ascertain contemporary attitudes and beliefs. Our grasp of basic processes of social interaction depends on modes of inquiry different from those we would use to compare social values cross-culturally. Observational techniques do us little good if our research goal is to forecast world population trends.

The methods with which you are now acquainted vary along a number of dimensions. Some are best employed to study people in their "natural" settings; other allow researchers to exert maximum control over variables extraneous to their immediate research interests. If we wish to assess attitudes, we choose certain methods; but if we wish to directly catalogue people's behaviors, we need others. The methods described vary in degree of obtrusiveness. Some, such as survey research, are highly obtrusive; others, such as content analysis, are unobtrusive. One technique lets us systematically study large numbers of people, while another best helps to capture the flavor of behavior in small groups. We choose our procedures according to whether we seek breadth or depth in our investigation. Sometimes we need quantitative renderings of social phenomena, and other times we need more qualitative images. We can test a priori hypotheses with certain methods. Others are better suited to the discovery of theoretical explanations.

The differences mentioned are revealing. They substantiate the idea that we cannot adopt uniform procedures to deal with the quite varied problems that are legitimately part of social, political, and psychological investigation. But it would be a mistake to underscore only how and why social scientific methods differ from one another. While it is certainly true that the method chosen must fit the theoretical questions, the distinctive goals of the research, and the available data sources, it is also true that *all* research methods are employed to realize a common end—providing complete, honest, reliable, valid, objective descriptions or explanations of social phenomena.

Researchers want to say at the conclusion of their investigation: "We have employed every safeguard feasible to ensure that our findings are correct." As bodies of procedural rules, social science methodologies are designed to cause researchers to continually ask themselves: "What might we do to be even more certain of our findings?" Your knowledge of methods, then, should make you critical of the accuracy and validity of research. You should now be equipped to look at any study and quarrel with it, question its possible errors, and ask how the research might have been done more convincingly. Have the researchers employed the method(s) most appropriate to their research problem? Have proper sampling procedures been used? Have necessary steps been taken to reduce bias and error in the findings? To what extent might the researchers' own assumptions, ideologies, or interests have colored the findings offered? Have they taken care to use the most precise measurement procedures feasible? Is there any question about the validity of the presented findings? Might the researchers have shown greater sensitivity to the ethical issues raised by their research? Are statements of cause and effect warranted by the data collected and the methods used? Have investigators remained true to their data in making their interpretations and inferences? You should be able to address each of these questions.

Although this textbook may have increased your sophistication about research methodology, you may not be pursuing a career in the social sciences. Many of you will never carry out your own research outside the context of a college classroom. Does this mean that the knowledge of methods is of no use to you? To the contrary, the same criteria used to evaluate social science research equip you to consider critically the wide range of assertions about social life that all of us read and hear daily. A knowledge of the obstacles to a sure understanding of social phenomena should enable you to evaluate the generalizations offered in the mass media, in literature, and in informal conversation.

Scientists are not happy with explanations of events or situations that rely on guesswork or casual observation. We must acknowledge, however, that methodological scrupulousness will not easily and inevitably yield unquestionable, universal, or unalterable findings about social life. There are limits to knowledge. We must be candid about these limits and consider why it is impossible to discover the absolute truth about social life. Indeed, we can know certain things only partially; knowledge is often a matter of degree. Information that is useful at one moment may be inapplicable at another. Let us amplify this point.

What does it mean when we speak of "knowing" someone? Certainly, it does not suggest that we know absolutely everything there is to know about a person, that there is nothing we do not comprehend. Our knowledge of people may be a function of the type of relationship we have with them. People may show different sides of themselves in different social situations. There may, in other words, be aspects of people that we will never learn. We also realize that people change and that what we previously knew about them is not altogether helpful in explaining their present behaviors. And since people are always changing (getting older, taking new jobs, getting married, and so on), we recognize that there are always new things to be learned about them.

Social scientists who endeavor to know or to explain how a society works face a distinctive task. A society, like an individual, is multifaceted and will look different to us depending on the angle from which we view it. We cannot hope to incorporate into one explanation every aspect of social life (although some have tried). Most important, society is always changing. In some cases the change may be so rapid that our prior knowledge no longer applies. Whether rapid or slow, however, social change ensures that there will always be new things to learn— that we will need to continually amend, specify, or enlarge upon our already acquired knowledge.

Many essays have been written comparing the social sciences with the natural sciences. The conclusions drawn from the comparison nearly always place the social sciences in a negative light, stressing their relative failure to surely explain and predict phenomena. The comparison seems, on the face of it, a legitimate one. Why has natural science apparently been able to produce more certain findings? Why is its knowledge cumulative, while social scientists continue to argue the validity of theoretical propositions produced, in some cases, two centuries ago? Why haven't social scientists discovered laws about society as natural scientists have done for the physical world? How is it that we seem unable to predict events any distance into the future? Natural scientists, it might be pointed out, can predict certain phenomena (for example, eclipses) years in advance.

Invidious comparisons can be made between the nature of physical and social scientific discoveries. The discovery of DNA's molecular structure is a convenient example. After reading Watson and Crick's findings, scientists uniformly agreed that the researchers had found the structure of DNA. There was no question but that one of the mysteries of life itself had been solved. Scientists did not say "perhaps this is the structure of DNA" or that Watson and Crick's description of the DNA molecule "seems plausible" or that their data "generally seem to confirm" their picture of the structure as correct. In comparison, social scientists can rarely establish the incontrovertible truth of their findings or interpretations.

The critics are correct in these assertions. Social scientific knowledge does not have a high cumulativeness to it. It is not easy to make accurate predictions about future social life; many events take us by surprise. How many social scientists accurately forecast the civil rights activity of the early 1960s, the urban riots of the mid-1960s, the antiwar movement of the late 1960s, or the women's rights activity of the 1970s? Indeed, we frequently seem to be in the business of trying to explain why something happened after its occurrence.

It is also true that social scientists disagree about the theories used to explain a body of data to a much greater extent than do natural scientists. A casual search will find frequent debates in the literature about the causes of deviance, poverty, prejudice, and so forth. One can, as well, easily find studies where findings directly contradict cne another or where the same variables are measured in thoroughly different ways.

We must, however, ask whether these criticisms are misplaced. Should social scientists apologetically bow their heads and merely promise to try harder in the future? Certainly, progress can be made in further refining methodological techniques. It is, however, appropriate to point out that the social world and the physical world are really two quite different kinds of subjects. The structure of a DNA molecule remains constant, but that simply is not true of social structures. It may be appropriate for natural scientists to claim that they have discovered absolute truths, but it would be unwise to assert that social truths are absolute. Human beings are continuously rearranging their social worlds. We simply do not respond in completely predictable ways to the situations in which we find ourselves. Unlike atoms, molecules, or stable elements of the physical universe, people think, construct meanings, and interpret the behaviors of others. Individuals possess a certain "plasticity" that allows them to respond creatively to their environments. The meanings of events, people, objects, and institutions can change over time. Values and attitudes change. Behaviors once thought taboo become incorporated into our repertoire of legitimate or conventional activities. We create new social forms if they seem better able to meet our needs. We participate in unpredictable fads of our own making. In short, human activity and hence the social world are continually in a state of process, a state of production. It is human beings' unparalleled capacity for adaptation that makes any generalization produced by social scientists time-specific.

It is for these reasons that social scientists must be prepared to alter their theories as people alter their views and perceptions of the world. The emergence of certain types of leaders, the outbreak of wars, and unpredicted changes in the economic structure transform the face of society. Theories, methods, and explanations must reflect the nature of the objects with which they deal. If the world is continually changing, theoretical constructs must also change. Explanation, in this sense, never ends. We can and must produce good, complete contemporary explanations. We can with a high degree of certainty and accuracy say, on the basis of our carefully collected data, this is the way the world is operating now; these are peoples' attitudes, beliefs, ideologies, and these are the behavioral consequences of their present constructions of the world.

It is important to realize that individuals are, in some measure, limited by the boundaries of their own experience. Their knowledge of social life emerges from the distinctive social positions they occupy and their realities are constrained by their own life situations. Our private understandings of social life are generated from a limited data base. The promise of the social sciences is to let us transcend our own realities so that we might be freed to view the world from unfamiliar perspectives. Therefore, a major goal of social science investigation must be precisely to question, critically examine, and frequently show the faulty character of many commonly held generalizations about social life. Social scientists must be preoccupied with "debunking" the validity of longstanding "truisms." Shorthand characterizations of the social world often do not capture its complexity. The generalizations that all of us make on the basis of our own experience and observation certainly operate to help us make our individual and collective experiences more intelligible. At the same time such generalizations are, by definition, based on only selected aspects of social reality. Therefore, a continuing task of social science investigation is to uncover those features of life that lie hidden beneath the veneer of accepted social knowledge about the world. In some instances our investigations will cause us to thoroughly reject commonly held images or stereotypes. In other cases our research will let us specify those images in important ways.

The methodologies used by social scientists are indispensable in enabling them to discover how assumptions, images, stereotypes, or generalizations may blind people to the way the world is operating. Methodologies serve the function of helping us become strangers to that which is normally familiar to us. They act as safeguards in that they force us to question what we usually do not. Once we commit ourselves to systematic, dispassionate, rigorous investigation, we maximize the likelihood of seeing how and why our individual understandings of the world may be dramatically incorrect. It is when we accomplish this end that research fulfills the promise for which methodologies were invented.

We have been careful to suggest the limits of social science knowledge. We need not, however, be overly modest about the significance of our work. Research can be profoundly liberating by letting us see how social forces shape our identities and life situations and how we are influenced by the institutions with which we live. Close examination of the social world informs us about the delicate balance between social order and personal freedom existing in a society. It serves to raise our consciousness about the constant interplay between individuals and social structures. The knowledge and insight provided by social scientists have direct implications for collective action. Those groups in any society that are oppressed socially or economically will be better able to alter their situations once they correctly perceive how that oppression has been accomplished.

On a more concrete level, social scientists have successfully questioned longstanding beliefs about the poor, demonstrated the faulty character of racial stereotypes, uncovered the "informal" structure of bureaucratic organizations, and caused us to better understand the behaviors and attitudes of segments of the population with whom we might rarely come into contact. When they explain such life constancies as the allocation, distribution, and use of power in a society, modes of social interaction, group formation, and patterns of deviance, researchers are talking about processes that touch us all. The clarity and insight that social scientists gain about such processes can be only as good as the data that are the basis for their explanation. Methodologies ensure that the data from which the understanding of society is inferred are as correct as possible.

Why is all this important? Why must we worry so about the correctness of the data from which we draw our generalizations about social life? All decision making, all policy formulation, must proceed from some knowledge base—not just the decisions that we make privately, but also, and perhaps more importantly, the decisions often made for us. The type of schools we shall have, the character of our cities, the programs developed to eradicate prejudice, rehabilitate criminals, treat the mentally ill, and so on, must be grounded in some conception of how and why people behave as they do. Social scientists proceed with the belief that it is possible to avoid creating social policy with information or knowledge that is intuitive or developed with inadequate data. Is punishment a deterrent to antisocial behavior? Does the physical deterioration of an area lead to family disorganization? To what extent is education related to future occupational success? Does integration raise the academic achievement levels of minority students? Does welfare destroy people's incentive to work? Do persons learn better in classroom type X than in type Y? These are the types of questions to which clear answers can be provided. These are also the kinds of questions that must be answered as we work to develop plans for creating beneficial social change in a society.

The dangers of using intuition, common sense, or what appears to be the obvious to answer questions like those posed above are very great. Time and again enormous amounts of money and energy have been invested in programs that were bound to fail because they were based on faulty knowledge. Planners, for example, have torn up areas of cities because they incorrectly believed there to be an obvious relationship between the physical appearance of an area and social disorganization. Our prison system reflects the faultiness of another "obvious" assumption—that if people are severely punished, they will cease to engage in antisocial behavior. In other words, as long as common sense is frequently shown to be neither common nor necessarily sensible, social scientists will have a crucial task to perform.

We face extraordinary problems in our society and throughout the world. Social scientific knowledge alone will not solve these problems, but we have no hope of forging solutions without a sensitive and deep understanding of how people relate to one another in the social structures and institutions of their own making. In social science we may seem to overstress such issues as objectivity, reliability, and validity, but it is only because these are the yardsticks against which we must judge our knowledge. To be a social scientist, you must reconcile yourself to the apparently obdurate fact that you will never be able to say that you fully and completely know why human beings act as they do, or that your findings have universal applicability. You *can* say, however, that you honestly tried to assess the validity of knowledge at every step in its production. This is, indeed, the ultimate purpose of the research craft.

Name Index

Abert, James, 347
Adelman, Irma, 320, 326
Adorno, T. W., 356, 376
Albrecht, Milton, 266, 282
Allen, Frederick, 265, 282
Allon, Natalie, 26, 34
Allport, Gordon, 251, 258
Almond, Gabriel, 327
Alston, Jon, 161
Amer, Michael, 326
Anderson, Charles, 246, 258
Angell, Robert, 257, 259
Appell, G. N. 101
Aristotle, 307
Armstrong, J. Scott, 302
Arnheim, Rudolf, 266, 282
Ary, D., 33
Asch, Solomon, 322, 326
Asher, J. W., 346
Atkinson, J. Maxwell, 321, 326

Babbie, Earl, 385, 403
Backstrom, Charles, 45, 61, 62, 114, 121, 159
Bales, Robert, 264, 268–269, 282
Banaka, William, 188, 189, 191
Barber, Theodore, 96, 102
Barcus, Francis, 266, 279, 282
Barthel, Diane, 312, 326
Beard, Charles, 245, 258
Becker, Howard, 6, 13, 26, 34, 89. 93, 101, 102, 165, 167–168, 191, 198, 208, 212, 251, 258
Bensman, Joseph, 93–94, 102
Berelson, Bernard, 45, 62, 130, 159, 162, 261–263, 282
Berger, Arthur, 281
Berger, Peter, 16, 31, 34
Berlew, David, 266, 282

Bickman, Leonard, 237
Birdwhistell, Ray, 268, 281, 282
Blackwood, B., 308, 326
Blake, Joseph, 26, 34
Blalock, Hubert, 33, 85, 121, 402, 416
Blau, Peter, 26, 34, 160
Bloom, Benjamin, 18, 19, 35
Blumberg, Nathan, 265, 282
Blumer, Herbert, 207–208, 212, 267, 282
Bogardus, E., 367, 376
Bogdan, Robert, 211, 251, 258
Bonjean, Charles, 81, 86
Bordua, David, 160–161
Borgatta, Edgar, 303
Boskoff, Alvin, 256–257
Bounds, William, 402
Bradburn, Norman, 266, 282
Brislin, Richard, 326
Brisset, Dennis, 281
Brown, Claude, 251, 258
Bruyn, Severyn, 211
Burgess, Ann, 165–166, 181, 191
Bynner, John, 61

Cahnman, Werner, 256–257
Campbell, Angus, 160
Campbell, Donald, 73, 85, 86, 219, 221, 236, 238, 345, 346, 413, 417
Campbell, Stephen, 85, 86, 402
Carney, Thomas, 280
Carr-Saunders, A. M., 248, 258
Cartwright, Dorian, 280
Cassell, Joan, 101
Cavan, Sherri, 212
Child, Irvin, 308–309, 314
Clark, Burton, 26, 35
Cloward, Richard, 23, 33, 35, 253–254, 259, 322
Coch, Lester, 230–231, 238

Cochran, William, 121
Cole, Stephen, 33
Coleman, James, 85, 86, 126, 160, 161, 165, 191, 345, 347
Coles, Jane, 251, 259
Coles, Robert, 251, 258-259
Collins, Mary, 237, 347
Comte, Auguste, 246, 259
Converse, Jean, 159
Cormier, William, 402
Cottle, Thomas, 251
Crandall, Rick, 101
Cressy, Paul, 193, 212
Crick, Francis, 421

Dahrendorf, Ralf, 29, 35
Darwin, Charles, 9
Davis, Fred, 193, 212
Davis, James, 115, 121, 135-137, 150, 161
Davis, Kingsley, 28, 35, 304, 325, 327
DeFleur, Melvin, 265, 282
Denney, Reuel, 259, 283
Denzin, Norman, 33, 94, 101, 102, 121, 165, 191, 233, 238, 257
Deutsch, Morton, 237, 347
Deutscher, Irwin, 85, 86
Dickson, William, 237-238
Diener, Edward, 101
Dogan, Mattei, 303
Dornbusch, Sanford, 266, 282
Douglas, Jack, 85
Duncan, Otis, 160
Dunham, H. Warren, 304
Durkheim, Emile, 9, 155, 242, 248, 259
Durkin, Mary, 85

Eckhardt, Kenneth, 367, 376
Eddy, Elizabeth, 26, 35
Edwards, Allen, 375
Eifler, Deborah, 47, 62
Elmore, Richard, 347
Emerson, Joan, 198, 212
Engerman, Stanley, 258
English, Clifford, 26, 35
Erikson, Kai, 94, 101, 102, 210, 213, 248-250, 257-258, 259
Ermann, M. David, 367, 376
Evan, William, 230, 237, 238

Faber, B. L., 96, 102
Fair, Jerilyn, 339, 348
Fallaci, Oriana, 190
Faris, E. L., 304
Fenno, Richard, 26, 35
Festinger, Leon, 204, 213, 224-225, 238
Filipe, Nancy, 227, 235, 238
Filstead, William, 211
Fine, Gary, 229

Finsterbusch, Kurt, 334-335, 348
Fleming, Jeanne, 320
Fode, K., 224, 238
Fogel, Richard, 258
Forrester, Jay, 304
French, John, 230-231, 238
Freud, Sigmund, 9, 309-310
Friedman, Milton, 225
Friedman, Pearl, 371-372, 375, 376
Friedrichs, Robert, 93, 102

Gallup, George, 116, 122
Galton, Sir Francis, 315
Galtung, John, 299, 300, 305
Gans, Herbert, 14, 35, 193, 213
Gaudet, Hazel, 130, 159, 162
Geer, Blanche, 167-168, 191, 208
Genovese, Eugene, 258
Genovese, Kitty, 235
Glaser, Barney, 26, 35, 211
Glazer, Myron, 52, 62, 199, 213
Glazer, Nathan, 259, 283
Glock, Charles, 159
Goehring, Harvey, 402
Goffman, Erving, 22-23, 24, 35, 174, 191, 193, 210, 213
Gold, Raymond, 198, 213
Goldner, Fred, 96-97, 102
Goleman, Daniel, 51, 62
Goodman, Ellen, 190
Goodwin, Leonard, 347
Gorden, Raymond, 189
Gordon, Gerald, 343, 348
Gottschalk, Louis, 243, 251, 256, 257, 259
Gouldner, Alvin, 28, 33, 35, 89, 99, 101, 102, 193, 213
Gray, Paul, 166, 191, 211, 327-328
Greenwald, Harold, 193, 213
Gregg, James, 267, 282
Grimshaw, Allen, 326
Groves, Robert, 159-160
Gubrium, John, 26, 35
Guttman, Louis, 368, 376

Hall, Edward, 193, 213, 268, 282
Hammond, Philip, 34, 55, 61-62
Handlin, Oscar, 258
Hannan, Michael, 303
Hansen, Edward, 328
Harrington, Michael, 98
Hartman, George, 227, 238
Hays, William, 416
Henchy, Thomas, 237
Henkel, Ramon, 417
Herodotus, 306
Hesse-Biber, Sharlene, 281
Hibbs, Douglas, 320, 326
Hickman, Lauren, 266, 282
Hill, Richard, 81, 86
Hirsch, Paul, 267, 282

Hoffing, Charles, 227–228, 238
Hofstadter, Richard, 257
Holmstrom, Lynda, 165–166, 181, 189, 190, 191
Holsti, Ole, 263, 280, 282
Holt, Robert, 326
Homans, George, 34
Horowitz, Irving, 55, 62, 92, 102
Huck, Schuyler, 402
Hudson, Michael, 319
Huff, Darrell, 402
Hughes, H., 251, 259
Hull, C. Hadlai, 363, 376
Humphreys, Laud, 94, 102, 198, 213
Hursh, Gerald, 45, 61, 62, 114, 121, 159
Hy, Renn, 160
Hyman, Herbert, 76, 86, 156, 160, 161, 393, 403

Inkeles, Alex, 310, 315–316, 326, 328, 375

Jackman, Robert, 304, 311–312, 320, 326
Jackson, David, 303
Jackson, P., 193, 213
Jacobs, Jerry, 26, 35, 55, 62
Jacobs, L. C., 33
Jacobson, Lenore, 85
Jaffe, A. J., 81, 86
Jencks, Christopher, 85, 86
Johnson, John, 338, 348
Jung, John, 224, 236, 238

Kahn, Robert, 159–160, 199, 213
Karp, David, 193, 213, 268, 282
Kassebaum, Gene, 343
Kelman, Herbert, 92, 95, 99, 101, 102, 323, 326
Kendall, Patricia, 393, 403
Kerlinger, Fred, 416
Kershaw, David, 226, 238, 339, 342, 348
Kinsey, Alfred, 5
Kirkpatrick, Jeane, 26, 35
Kish, Leslie, 121
Klein, Malcolm, 346
Kluckhohn, Clyde, 257, 259
Kolodny, Ralph, 341
Krippemdorf, Klaus, 280
Kubler-Ross, Elisabeth, 166, 188, 190, 191
Kuhn, Thomas, 28, 35

Land, Kenneth, 290, 303, 305
Lane, Robert, 166, 191
Langbein, Larua, 303
LaPiere, Richard, 78, 86
Lazarsfeld, Paul, 34, 69, 86, 130, 159, 162, 394, 403
Leites, Nathan, 266

Lejeune, Robert, 193, 213
Lewis, Howard, 265, 282
Lewis, Lionel, 281
Lewis, Oscar, 313
Levin, J., 281
Levinson, D. J., 363, 376
Levy, Gerald, 26, 35
Lichtman, Allan, 303
Liebow, Eliot, 193, 212, 213
Lindesmith, Alfred, 165, 191
Lipset, Seymour, 165, 191, 248, 257, 259, 311
Lizotte, Alan, 160–161
Lockhart, William, 98, 102
Lofland, John, 26, 35, 194, 205, 211, 213
Lofland, Lyn, 210, 213, 247–248, 259
Lonner, Walter, 326
Lundberg, George, 34, 371–372, 375, 376

McCaghy, Charles, 164, 191
McClelland, David, 265, 270, 282, 322
McCollough, Celeste, 403
McDill, Mary, 343, 348
McDill, Edward, 343, 348
McDowell, James, 267, 282
McDowell, Sophia, 337, 348
McGinnis, Joe, 281
McKinney, John, 192, 213
McLemore, S. Dale, 81, 86
Maine, Sir Henry, 242, 259
Malcolm X, 251, 259
Malec, Michael, 403
Malinowski, Bronislaw, 310
Mann, Floyd, 199, 213
Markoff, John, 280
Marsh, Robert, 326
Marshall, Harvey, 304
Marx, Karl, 242, 246–247, 307
Meadows, Donnella, 295–298, 305
Merton, Robert, 16, 35, 69, 86, 96, 102
Milbrath, Lester, 26, 35
Milgram, Stanley, 95, 102, 232–233, 236, 238, 322–323
Miller, Arthur, 42, 62
Miller, Delbert, 85, 160, 375
Miller, Herman, 304
Mills, C. Wright, 30, 31, 35, 241, 256, 257, 259
Mitchell, Robert, 318
Moore, Wilbert, 28, 35
Morris, Cynthia, 320, 326
Morrison, Denton, 417
Morse, Edward, 343, 348
Mosteller, Frederick, 85, 86, 244–245, 259, 276, 282
Motz, Annabelle, 334–335, 348
Moursund, Janet, 346
Moynihan, Daniel, 85, 86
Murdock, George, 307, 313
Myrdal, Gunnar, 328

Nadel, S. F., 311
Nagel, Ernest, 97, 101, 102
Nelson, Ann, 249, 259
Nelson, Hart, 249, 259
Nicolaus, Martin, 91, 102
Nie, Norman, 363, 376, 409, 417
Nisbet, Robert, 241, 259

Oglivie, Daniel, 264, 282
Ohlin, Lloyd, 23, 33, 35
Orlans, Harold, 346
Osgood, Charles, 85, 264, 282
Osherson, Samuel, 307, 327
Osmond, Marie, 85
Otto, Herbert, 266, 282

Paige, Jeffrey, 264, 282
Park, Robert, 192
Parmelee, Pat, 238
Parsons, Talcott, 23, 24, 28, 29, 34, 35, 91
Patton, Michael, 346
Pechman, Joseph, 347–348
Pedhazur, Elazer, 416
Peterson, William, 303
Pfohl, Stephen, 348
Pfuhl, Edwin, 190
Philliber, Susan, 359, 360, 376
Phillips, Derek, 76–77, 86
Pittman, David, 98–99, 102
Piven, Frances, 253–254, 259, 322
Plutchik, Robert, 236–237
Politz, Alfred, 116, 122
Polyani, Karl, 248, 259
Pool, Ithiel de Sola, 280
Pope, Harrison, 193, 213
Priest, T. B., 190
Przeworski, Adam, 326–327

Quinney, Richard, 29, 35

Rainwater, Lee, 98–99, 102
Raser, John, 303
Razavich, A., 33
Redfield, Robert, 242, 259, 313
Reed, John, 161
Richardson, Stephen, 189
Riesman, David, 248, 259, 265–266, 283
Rist, Ray, 348
Robinson, John, 85, 358, 363, 375–376
Robinson, W. S., 34, 303
Rodman, Hyman, 341
Roethlisberger, F. J., 237–238
Rokeach, M., 359, 376
Rokkan, Stein, 303
Rosenberg, Morris, 393, 403
Rosenthal, Robert, 85, 224, 227, 238
Rossi, Peter, 337, 346

Roszak, Theodore, 98, 102
Roth, Julius, 79, 86
Roy, Donald, 26, 35
Rubin, Lillian, 6, 35, 251, 259

Sagarin, Edward, 193, 213
Sanders, William, 16, 34, 35, 189
Sanford, R. N., 363, 376
Schaeffer, Nora, 85
Schatzman, Leonard, 118, 121, 122, 192, 206, 213
Schmid, Calvin, 11, 35
Schneidman, Edwin, 282
Schuman, Howard, 159
Schwartz, Charlotte, 208, 213
Schwartz, Morris, 208, 213
Scriven, Michael, 340, 349
Sears, Robert, 308–309
Sebald, Hans, 266, 283
Seeman, Melvin, 76, 86
Seider, Maynard, 264, 283
Selltiz, Claire, 132, 162, 331, 345
Sennett, Richard, 248, 258, 259
Shaffir, William, 211
Shaver, Philip, 85, 363, 375–376
Shaw, Clifford, 251, 258, 259
Shaw, Marvin, 376
Shils, Edward, 28, 35
Simmons, Willard, 116, 122
Simon, Julian, 356, 376
Sjoberg, Gideon, 101
Skipper, James, 164, 191
Slonim, Morris, 115, 121, 122
Smigel, Edwin, 26, 35
Smith, David, 310, 315–316, 326, 328, 375
Sommer, Robert, 193, 213, 227, 235, 238
Sorokin, Pitirim, 248, 259
Spates, James, 281
Spencer, Herbert, 9, 246, 259, 307
Spilerman, Seymour, 303
Spradley, James, 34, 211
Sprehe, J. Timothy, 343, 348
Stanley, Julian, 85, 219, 221, 236, 238, 345, 346
Stark, Rodney, 26, 35
Stebbins, Robert, 188, 189
Stephens, J., 26, 35
Stern, Paul, 62
Stewart, Charles, 81, 86
Stinchcombe, Arthur, 257, 343, 348
Stone, Philip, 276, 280, 282, 283
Stouffer, Samuel, 126, 161, 162
Strauss, Anselm, 26, 35, 118, 121, 122, 192, 206, 211, 213
Stribley, Keith, 61
Strub, Peter, 190
Suchman, Edward, 333–334, 342, 346–347
Sudnow, David, 118, 122, 193, 204, 213
Sutherland, Edwin, 193, 213, 251, 259, 290, 305

Taeuber, Alma, 287–288, 302, 305
Taeuber, Karl, 287–288, 302, 305
Taylor, Charles, 319
Tellmann, Katherine, 346
Terman, Lewis, 51
Teune, Henry, 326–327
Thernstrom, Stephan, 253, 259
Thomas, W. I., 250, 259
Thorndike, Robert, 326
Thorne, Barrie, 96, 102, 193, 213
Thucydides, 307
Timpane, P. Michael, 347–348
Tocqueville, Alexis de, 9
Tönnies, Ferdinand, 242, 259
Trow, Martin, 165, 191
Turner, John, 326

Vallier, Ivan, 327
van den Berghe, Pierre, 93, 102
Vanecko, James, 348
Verba, Sidney, 327
Vidich, Arthur, 93–94, 102

Walker, Evelyn, 264, 282
Wallace, David, 276, 282
Wallerstein, Immanuel, 29, 35
Ward, David, 343
Warwick, Donald, 307, 327
Watson, James, 13, 35, 421
Wax, Murray, 101
Wayne, Ivor, 265, 283
Webb, Eugene, 211
Weber, Max, 9, 88–90, 101–102, 230, 238, 241, 242, 247, 259
Weinberg, Martin, 198, 213
Weiss, Carol, 338, 341, 343, 347

Weiss, Joseph, 320, 328
Weitzman, Leonore, 47, 62
Wenglinsky, Martin, 237
Werner, Carol, 238
Wertham, Frederick, 267, 283
Westoff, Leslie, 190
White, Garland, 158, 161
Whiting, John, 308–309, 314–315, 327
Whyte, William, 193, 212, 213
Wilcox, Leslie, 303
Wilensky, Harold, 320
Williams, Bill, 121
Williams, Walter, 347
Williamson, Henry, 251, 259
Williamson, John, 161, 320, 328, 348, 360, 376
Wilson, P. A., 248, 258
Winch, Robert, 413, 417
Wingrove, C. R., 161
Winks, Robin, 257
Wise, George, 308–309
Wolf, Bernard, 267, 283
Wolf, Eric, 328
Wolfenstein, Martha, 266, 283
Wolff, Michael, 198, 213
Wright, Jack, 376
Wrong, Dennis, 34
Wuebben, Paul, 46, 62, 237

Yoels, William, 268, 282

Zelditch, Morris, 45, 62
Zetterberg, Hans, 34
Zimbardo, Philip, 46, 62
Znaniecki, Florian, 250, 259
Zuckerman, Harriet, 165, 191

Key Term and Subject Index

Page numbers given in **bold face type** show where the definitions of the *Key Terms* in the text can be found.

Access, 173–174, 197–198
Accidental sampling, **105**
Accuracy, **67**
Address, **147**
Adjusted percentage, **378**
Aggregate data, **285**
Alpha, 363
Anonymity, **93**
Applied social research, **28**, 330
Appraising judgments, **97**
Area studies, 312
Areal groupings, **284**
Atomistic fallacy, **299–300**
Available records, **252**
Axiomatic theory, **23**, 24

Back translation, **317**
Bar graph, **378**
Base period, **355**
Baseline measurement, **355**
Before-and-after study, **335**
Behavioral indicator, **69**
Beta weight, **407**
Bias, **75**
    researcher, 76, 87–88, 96, 157
    respondent, 76, 77, 186, 318
    sampling, 115–117
Biographic research, 241, 250–251
Bivariate analysis, **386**
Bogardus Social Distance Scale, 366–367

Card number, **149**
Case study, **207**
    historical, 248–250

Causal connection, **214**
Causality, 218–219
Cell, **147**
Census block, **286**
Census data, 286–289
Census tract, **286**
Characterizing judgments, **97**
Chi-square, 412
Classification error, **288**
Closed-end question, **137**
Cluster sampling, **111**
Codebook, **148**
Coding, **148**
Coefficient of reproducibility, **370**
Cognitive dissonance, **204**
Cohort study, **51**
Column, 387, **388**
Common sense, **10**, 11–12, 424
Complete observer, **198**
Complete participant, **198**
Composite measure, **353**
Computers, in content analysis, 275–277
    in recoding data, 385
    in social surveys, 147ff.
Concept, **41**
Conceptual equivalence, **316**
Conceptualization, **42–43**
Concurrent validation, **72**
Confidence limits, **114**
Confidentiality, **93–94**
Conflict theory, **28–29**, 91
Construct validity, **72**
Consumer Price Index (CPI), 355–356, 362, 364, 373
Content analysis, **45**, 260–278
Content validity, **71**, 357

Context unit, 276
Contingency, 394
Contingency question, 142
Control group, 216
Control variable, 393
Controlled experiment, 335
Controls, in evaluation research, 336
  in experimentation, 215–217, 233–234
  in statistics, 393ff.
Convergence theory, 320
Co-optation, 98
Correction factor, 111
Correlation, 358–359, 363, 389, 390, 391, 399–400
Correlation coefficient, 389–390
Courtesy bias, 318
Critical perspective, 16–17, 423
Cross validation, 73
Cross-cultural comparison, 287
Cross-sectional design, 128
Cross-tabulation, 386–387
Culture specific analysis, 306
Curvilinear relationship, 309

Data, sources of, 4–5, 44–45
Data analysis, 4
Data banks, 156, 315
Data cleaning, 151
Data collection, 4, 52–53
Data matrix, 147
Data processing, 53
Data reduction, 354
Deduction, 25–26
Demographer, 294
Demographic categories, 12, 134, 287
Demography, 252
Demonstration experiment, 232–233
Dependent variable, 216
Description, 4, 202, 377
  in fieldwork, 201–202
Descriptive model, 21
Descriptive research, 377
Deviant case, 381
Dictionary, 276
Differential scale, 367–368
Directional research hypothesis, 411
Disaggregation, 292
Disconfirmation, 8
Disguised observation, 94
Dispersion, 382
Disproportionate sampling, 111
Distribution, 49
Double-blind experiment, 224
Dramaturgical paradigm, 22–23
Dynamic model, 295

Ecological fallacy, 298–299
Elaboration paradigm, 393, 394–398

explanation in, 394–395
  interpretation in, 395–396
  specification in, 396–397
  suppressor variables in, 397–398
Element, 105
Enumeration, 45
Error, 73ff.
Error of coverage, 288
Ethnography, 194, 312–313
Evaluation research, goals in, 333–334, 339–340
  misuse of, 342–343
  poor quality of, 343
  sources of data in, 338
  sponsorship of, 332–333
Evolutionary theory, 242, 246, 247, 307
Exhaustive categories, 274
Exhaustive measure, 18, 64
Expectancy effect, 223
Experiment mortality, 221
Experimental group, 216
Experimentation, 8–9, 45–46
  causality in, 218–219
  ethics in, 95
  in evaluation research, 335–337
  procedures of, 217–218
  validity problems in, 219–225
Explanation, 4, 394–395
  and description, 24, 40
  in models, 21
Explanatory model, 21
Explanatory research, 377
Exploration, 4
External validation, 363
  in experimentation, 223–225
  in index construction, 363–364
External validity, 73, 220

F-test, 412
Face validity, 71, 75, 356–357
Face-to-face interview, 132–133
Feedback system, 296
Field experimentation, 225–228
Field notes, 201–206
  coding of, 205–206
Fieldwork, 9, 47–48, 52
  conceptual categories in, 204
  in evaluation research, 236–237
  limitations of, 206–208
  problems in comparative studies, 312–315
  recording dialog in, 202
  research roles in, 198–201
  sampling in, 117–119
Final report, 54
Findings, 8
Forecasting, 293–294
Forensic social science, 13
Frequency, 49
Frequency distribution, 378

Freudian theory, 309–310
Fudging effect, **96**

Galton's problem, **315**
Gatekeeper, **197**
Generalization, **104**
Goal-based evaluation, **340**
Goal-free evaluation, **340**
Guttman Scale, 368–370

Harris Political Data Center, Louis, 156
Hawthorne effect, **223**
Hired-hand research, 78–79
Historical case study, **248**
Historical data, 49
   generalizability of, 245
   sources of, 243–245
   uses of, 246
Historical determinism, **242**
Historical specificity, **245**
Homogeneous (population), **109**
Human Relations Area Files (HRAF),
   313–315
Hunch, **7**
Hypothesis, **25**

Identification number, **148**
Independent variable, **216**
In-depth interview, **164**
Index score, **354**
Indicators, **67**
   behavioral, 69
   multiple, 136
   social, 290–293
Induction, **26–27**, 196–197
   in interviewing, 171
Information, in communication, 264–265
   loss of, 64, 292, 385–396
   types of, 48–50
Informed consent, **95–96**
Incipient relationship, **164**
Intellectual craftsmanship, 29, **30**, 31
Intensive interviews, **164**
   characteristics of, 166–171
   reliability of, 171–172
   strengths and limitations of, 182–186
Internal validation, **362–363**
Internal validity, **73**, **219**, 220–222
Interpretation, **53**, 395
Interval measure, **65**, 380–381
Intervening variable, **395**
Interviews, 138, 144ff.
   guidelines for, 178
   in comparative studies, 318
   intensive, 163–188
   preparation for, 145
   rapport in, 145–146
   recording data in, 178–179

Introspection, **14**
Item analysis, **363**
Item-to-item correlation, **363**
Item-to-scale correlation, **363**

KR-20 coefficient, 363
Keypunch, **149**

Latent consequences, **334**
Latent content, **263**
Level of aggregation, **285**
Life history reports, **250**
Likert scaling, **360–361**, 365
Linear regression, **404**
Linguistic relatedness, **315**
Loaded question, **138**
Logical record, **149**
Longitudinal research, **51**
Longitudinal survey design, **129**

Machine-readable data, **147**
Macrolevel variable, **311**
Manifest content, **263**
Marginals, **378**
Mean, **381**
Measure of central tendency, **379**
Measure of variability, **382**
Measurement, **63**
Measurement decay, **221**
Measurement equivalence, **316**
Median, **380**
Methodological notes, **203**
Methodology, **5**
Missing data, 361–362
Mixed type, **369**
Mode, **371**, 380
Modeling effect, **223**
Models, **20–21**, 295–297, 395, 400, 408
Multiple indicators, **353**
Multiple objectives, **334**
Multiple regression, **405**, 407
Multiple-correlation coefficient, **407**
Multistage cluster sampling, **112**
Multivariate analysis, **398–399**
Mutually exclusive categories, **274**
Mutually exclusive measures, **64**

National Opinion Research Center
   (NORC), 156
Negative cases, **195**
Nominal level measures, **64**, 379–380
Nondirectional research hypothesis, **411**
Nonlinear relationship, **391**
Nonprobability sample, **105**
Nonsampling error, **115**
Nonschedule standardized interview, **173**
Nonstandardized interview, **173**

Nonverbal communication, 181–182, 268
Normal curve, **384–385**
Null hypothesis, **410**

Objectivity, 13–14, **88**–90, 92–93, 261–262
Observer-as-participant, **198**
One-dimensional question, **138**
One-shot study, **335**
One-tailed test of significance, **411**
Open-end question, **137**
Opening persons, **174**
Operational definition, 37–38, 67–69
Operationalization, 64, **67**
Ordinal level measure, **65**, 354, 368, 379–380

Pace, **180**
Panel study, **51**, **129–130**
Paradigm, **22**
Parameter, **108**
Partial correlation, **398–399**
Partial regression coefficient, **407**
Participant observation, **45**, 48, **192**–193
Participant-as-observer, **198**
Path analysis, 408–409
Path coefficient, **409**
Pearson's *r*, 390–391, 412
Personal documents, **250**
Pie diagram, **378**
Pilot study, **128**
Population, **104**
Posttest, **218**
Pragmatic validation, **72**
Precision, **15**, **66**, 67, 79
Precoding, **147**
Predictive validity, **72**
Preemptive techniques, **180**
Pretest, **143**, **218**
Primary data, **51**, **243**
Probability sample, **105**
Probability theory, 108–109
Probes, **133**, 146
Project Camelot, 92, 323
Proportionate sampling, **111**
Proxy variable, **322**
Pure research, **27**
Purposive sampling, **106**
Pygmalion effect, **72**

Qualitative research, **117**
Quasi-experiments, 228, **229**, 230–231
Questionnaires, layout and response format
    in, 141, 360, 361
    self-administered, 132, 144
    sequence of questions in, 141–143
    wording in, 137–139
Quota sample, **106**

Random assignment, **217**
Random error, **73–74**
Random numbers, 108
Random sampling, **107**
Random-digit dialing, **133**
Randomization, **335**
Range, **382**
Rapport, 145–146, 164, 166–168, 179–182
Ratio level measures, **65–66**, 380–381
Ratio scaling, **360**
Raw data, **39**
Reciprocity, **166**
Recording unit, **272**
Regression analysis, **404**, 405–408
Regression coefficient, **406**
Reliability, **14**–15, 69, **70**, 71
    in comparative studies, 321
    in interviewing, 171–172
Reliability coefficient, **71**, 363
Replication, **14**
Reported rate, **289**
Representative sample, **103**
Research design, **36**
Research hypothesis, **410**
Research problem, **40**
Respondent, **21**
Roles, in fieldwork, 198–201
Roper Public Opinion Research Center,
    156, 315
Row, **388**

SAT (Scholastic Aptitude Test), 285, 384,
    389–390
SPSS (Statistical Package for the Social Sciences), 385
Sample size, 113–115
Sampling, **50**
    in comparative studies, 314–315, 318
    in content analysis, 270–272
    in fieldwork, 117–119
    in intensive interviewing, 185
    strategies of, 131
Sampling error, **115**, 410
Sampling frame, **105**
Scalability, **370**
Scalogram, **369**
Scattergram, **299**
Scientific method, **6**
Secondary analysis, **155**, 318
Selection interval, **109**
Selective observation, **12**
Self-administered questionnaire, **132**, 144
Self-selected subject, **216–217**
Semi-structured interview, **173**
Sensitivity testing, **296**
Shifting program, **340**
Significance level, **411**
Simple regression, **405–406**
Simulation model, **295**, 296–297
Situational error, **75**

Social distance scale, **366–367**
Social indicator, **290**
Social surveys, **45**, 47, 49–50
   comparative, 315–317
   strengths and limitations of, 156–157
Solomon four-group design, 221–222
Spearman-Brown coefficient, 363
Specification, **311, 396–397**
Split-half correlation, 363
Spurious relationship, **394**
Stability, **363**
Standard deviation, **382**
Standard error, **109**
Standardization of indices, 371–373
Standardized interview, 173
Standardized partial regression coefficient, **407**
Static model, **295**
Statistic, **108**
Statistical inference, **410**
Statistical significance, tests of (*see* Tests of statistical significance)
Stimulus, **218**
Stratified random sampling, **110**
Stratum, **104**
Structural functionalism, **23**, 28, 91
Structured interview, **166**
Structured observation, 267–269
Structured question, **137**
Subtable, **394**
Subject mortality, **221**
Subscale, **363**
Substantive significance, **413–414**
Summated ratings, **359**
Suppressor variable, **397**
System of enumeration, **262**
Systematic error, **75**
Systematic sample, **109**
Systems theory, **23**

t-test, 412
Tag word, **276**
Taxonomy, **18**
Telephone, use of, 133–134, 187
Telephone survey, **133**
Term papers, 36–37
   final reports, 54–55
Test factor, **393**
Test variable, **216**
Test-retest reliability, **70**
Tests of statistical significance, **410**, 411–413
   misuse of, 413–414

Theoretical memo, **203**
Theory, **6**, 7, 17–29, 46–48, 197
   and comparative research, 308–311
   axiomatic, 23–24
   in content analysis, 273
   in fieldwork, 206
   labeling, 6–8
   selection of, 90–91
Theory failure, **334**
Thurstone Scale, 367–368
Time-series data, **290**
Topics for research, **40**, 41ff., 90, 196–197
Topic outline, **178**
Trend study, **51**
Triangulation, **81–82**
True experiment, **228**
True rate, **289**
Two-tailed test of significance, **411**
Two-way table, **393**
Typology, **21**

Validity, **15–16**, 64, **70**, 71–73, 75
   See also External validity; Internal validity
Value judgments, **88**
Value-free social science, **89**
Variables, **21**, 41–42, 79
Variance, **385**
Verification, **7**
Volunteer research subjects, characteristics of, 224

Unbiased sample, **103**
Unidimensionality, **357**
Unit of analysis, **272, 284**
Unitary objectives, **334**
Univariate analysis, **377**
Universe, **271**
Unobtrusive technique, **277**
Unstandardized partial regression coefficient, **408**
Unstructured interview, **173**
Unstructured questions, **137**

Weighting, **361**, 364–366
Whitewash, **342**

Zero-order correlation, **399**, 400